CAPITALISM VERSUS DEMOCRACY?

ALSO BY BORIS FRANKEL

Democracy Versus Sustainability

Fictions of Sustainability:
The Politics of Growth and Post-Capitalist Futures

Zombies, Lilliputians and Sadists:
The Power of the Living Dead and the Future of Australia

When the Boat Comes In:
Transforming Australia in the Age of Globalisation

From the Prophets Deserts Come:
The Struggle to Reshape Australian Political Culture

The Post Industrial Utopians

Beyond the State?
Dominant Theories and Socialist Strategies

Marxian Theories of The State: A Critique of Orthodoxy

CAPITALISM VERSUS DEMOCRACY?

RETHINKING POLITICS IN THE AGE OF ENVIRONMENTAL CRISIS

BORIS FRANKEL

GREENMEADOWS

First published in 2020 by Greenmeadows

P.O. Box 128

Elsternwick,

Melbourne 3185

A catalogue record for this book is available from the National Library of Australia.

Name: Frankel, Boris, author.

Title: Capitalism Versus Democracy?

Rethinking Politics in the Age of Environmental Crises/ Boris Frankel.

Includes Notes and References and Index.

Subjects:

1. Politics of environmental sustainability. 2. Fascism, socialism and democracy.

3. Post-capitalism – post-growth societies. 4. Social reform – alternative policies

ISBN: (pbk) 978-0-6483633-4-7

ISBN: (epub) 978-0-6483633-5-4

Typeset in Hoefler Text.

Cover Design by Emile Frankel.

Once more with love and gratitude

For Julie and Emile

CONTENTS

PREFACE

This book is part of a larger project on capitalism, democracy and sustainability that has preoccupied me in recent years. My previous work *Fictions of Sustainability: The Politics of Growth and Post-Capitalist Futures* published in 2018, analysed the connection between environmental sustainability issues and technological innovation, economic growth, financialisation and changing relations between advanced capitalist countries and low and middle-income societies. The highly problematic responses of mainstream policy makers and radical technological utopians or greens to these major problems has often been determined by what I call 'analytical apartheid'. A majority of both pro-market and anti-capitalist political economists ignore environmental issues or treat them as marginal problems. Conversely, many environmentalists display minimal knowledge or interest in political economy. In *Capitalism Versus Democracy?* I concentrate on political issues and how the dominant paradigm of capitalism in conflict with democracy has changed from the Great Depression and fascism of the 1930s to the Great Financial Crisis and the rise of neo-fascism and Green New Deals in the period from 2008 to the 2020 Pandemic. A variety of Right and Left parties, policy makers and activists continue to share a 'pre-environmental political consciousness'. This perspective is evident in both anti-democratic authoritarian regimes in low and middle-income countries and across the political spectrum in representative democracies.

Apart from eco-socialists or advocates of degrowth, most of the anti-neoliberal Left or mainstream Greens have a circumscribed environmental consciousness. While supporting the urgent task of preventing climate breakdown, there is a tendency to either ignore or be unaware of how the larger complex problems surrounding material footprints and ecological sustainability (not just carbon footprints) affect political agendas for the 'good life'. In fact, the vast majority of public debates on the environment are dominated by endless scientific reports on the merits of renewables versus fossil fuels, economic analyses of the cost of delaying or rapidly implementing decarbonisation. These reports and debates often mirror conventional political divisions between pro-market business and political forces and anti-capitalist parties and movements over how respective national governments are obstructing or supporting the transition to a post-carbon society.

Instead of following this familiar approach to contemporary politics, in Books One and Two I analyse how the dominant paradigm of 'capitalism versus democracy' has evolved and outlived its capacity to explain the multiple crises we currently face. Book Three discusses why a rethink of contemporary politics needs also to focus on the multiple aspects of 'democracy versus sustainability'. If the biophysical carrying capacity of the earth is already so seriously impacted by the current size of per capita and national material footprints of affluent populations in OECD countries, how is global equality to be achieved? This problem also affects all proposals for post-capitalist societies. Without a fundamental reconfiguring of the utopian notions of a high-tech, affluent post-carbon or post-capitalist society, we will continue to see profound domestic and global material and socio-political inequalities continue in the future. For those who do not wish to read the larger thesis presented in this book, I have also written a modified version of Book Three which is published under the title *Democracy Versus Sustainability*.

Completing this project during a global Pandemic has been a mixed experience. Observing the daily casualty rate and scale of unnecessary deaths across the world (more than one million to date and over 34 million reported cases) warrants the International Court of Justice in The Hague to initiate proceedings against a new category of criminals, the Covid-19 criminals. From the US, Brazil and India, to Mexico, the UK and other countries, these Right-wing elected political leaders have wilfully contributed to the enormous death rates and serious ongoing illness of millions of people. They have either failed to act in time, dismissed the seriousness of the disease or deliberately run-down health care and aged-care resources prior to the Pandemic with their pro-market attacks on necessary health and social services. Of course, if there is any justice in the world, then the International Court of Justice would also prepare proceedings against a wider range of leaders who are wilfully ignoring or delaying dealing with the climate emergency – a global policy failure that unless quickly remedied will almost certainly result in untold millions of deaths in coming decades to human and non-human species. In countries with authoritarian governments, the public are severely constrained in their ability to act. However, in so-called democracies, the failure to respond adequately to the twin crises of the Pandemic and climate breakdown are occurring under the watchful or indifferent eyes of polarised electorates and governments that are sleepwalking towards disaster.

On the positive side, like many writers, Covid-19 has been an unexpected blessing in that it has provided the enforced isolation that has enabled me to complete this book. I am grateful to the many authors whose work has enriched my understanding of socio-political and environmental issues. I particularly thank Director Brendan Gleeson and all the engaged colleagues at the Melbourne Sustainable Society Institute (MSSI), University of Melbourne for their support in providing a congenial and stimulating home over the past several years while working on this project. Together with Sam Alexander, I have organised MSSI's Political Economy of Sustainability group over the past few years. I thank Sam and the many other participants for the spirited discussion of topics that have helped shape and clarify aspects of this book.

Finally, once again, my love and deepest appreciation for her indispensable and complete everyday support goes to Julie Stephens. She has improved the final draft by her many socio-cultural insights, including feminist and psychoanalytic interventions. Julie continues to be both a severe critic and a disciplined reader trying to curb my excesses while at the same time she is a true intellectual soulmate and companion providing nourishing care and love. Also, our son Emile has enriched this book through his own creative work in everything from contemporary musical composition to a philosophical critique of the politics of machine learning and virtual Green modding. His discussions about current art and politics have helped to keep me in touch with avant-garde developments. I thank him for not only producing the covers of the various books in this project but also for his book design and typesetting. I dedicate this book to both Julie and Emile.

Boris Frankel
Melbourne
September 2020.

INTRODUCTION – SETTING THE SCENE

Across the world, both opponents and supporters of capitalism continue to speculate about the social and political economic effects of the Covid-19 pandemic. Initially, we saw wild claims about the revival of communism, the collapse of the European Union (EU) and the demise of Chinese Communist Party rule.[1] Fears were also expressed about national economic collapses due to debt defaults in developing countries and the possible end of feasible solutions to prevent climate catastrophe. If optimists were more confident that Green New Deals would be implemented, Marxists such as John Bellamy Foster and Intan Suwandi argued that Covid-19 has seen the emergence of 'catastrophe capitalism' via interlinked ecological, epidemiological and economic crises.[2] Others such as prominent mainstream economist, Dani Rodrik, predicted few if any major changes:

> Covid-19 may well not alter – much less reverse – tendencies evident before the crisis. Neoliberalism will continue its slow death. Populist autocrats will become even more authoritarian. Hyper-globalisation will remain on the defensive as nation-states reclaim policy space. China and the US will continue on their collision course. And the battle within nation-states among oligarchs, authoritarian populists, and liberal internationalists will intensify, while the Left struggles to devise a program that appeals to a majority of voters.[3]

Whether what Rodrik predicts can be interpreted as a modified 'business as usual' or is actually closer to Foster and Suwandi's 'catastrophe capitalism' is up for debate. Like sociologists, philosophers and political economists, business leaders have also made bold forecasts. For example, Australian and New Zealand Bank CEO, Shayne Elliott declared that Australia in the future won't look the same because a whole generation of customers will change the way they think about technology, borrowing, employment, and even "the way they think about frankly the capitalist system and democracy."[4]

Before we get carried away with crystal ball forecasts, it is important to remember how often in earlier times others have been proven wrong about the relationship between 'capitalism and democracy'. Take for example, the prematurely hopeful but mistaken views expressed twenty years earlier by well-known multi-billionaire hedge-fund operator and philanthropist, George Soros. As the world entered the new millennium, Soros expressed an optimistic Western liberal outlook by declaring in June 2000 that democracy was on the march: "Totalitarian and authoritarian regimes have been swept away. Popular resentment against the remaining ones is growing. But it is too early to declare victory. For although capitalism is triumphant, we cannot speak of the triumph of democracy..."[5] In typical liberal social democratic terms, he then went on to argue that businesses were motivated by profit and self-interest, but without institutional safeguards private market capitalism could not be relied upon to assure democracy, freedom and the rule of law. This is certainly true. However, Soros completely misdiagnosed the health of capitalism and the political conjuncture that produced a variety of threats to democracy.

One year after his pronouncement, the 'forward march of democracy' stalled and was put into reverse, especially following the September 11th attacks by Al Qaeda. Capitalist triumphalism was deflated, and democratic civil liberties were curtailed and threatened by subsequent extensive anti-terrorism laws and military invasions, followed by the Great Financial Crisis, the crushing of the 'Arab Spring' and the growth of racist authoritarian movements and new regimes of 'illiberal democracy'. Representative democracies now began to look like an endangered species. Soros was personally attacked and became the principal villain for anti-Semites such as the alt-Right in the US and Right-wing movements in Europe. By September 2018, the Viktor Orbán regime in Hungary passed the 'Soros law' making it a criminal offence to help undocumented immigrants (especially Muslim refugees) who threatened to undermine 'European Christian democracy'. Eighteen months later, under the cover of the Covid-19 crisis, the Orbán government suspended any pretence to democracy and declared rule by dictatorial decree. Within the EU, the failure to expel Hungary is closely related to the varying shades of illiberalism that have long pervaded both EU institutions and the practices of many so-called democratic and liberal countries across the world.

The change from 'democracy on the march' to 'illiberal democracy' and dictatorship is a narrative that fits comfortably within mainstream liberal accounts of the world since the fall of Eastern European Communist regimes in 1989. This narrative which includes the rise of 'populist' movements and their demands for trade protectionism and curbs on immigration has caused endless 'hand-wringing' among media commentators, academics, centre-Left politicians and business analysts. It is noteworthy that apart from the US-led campaign against China, these anguished concerns have not produced widespread calls by liberals to stop doing business with authoritarian regimes such as those led by Orbán, Erdoğan, Putin, or Trump.

While I will discuss some of these issues, it is important to note that this book is *not* another version of the prevailing liberal social democratic narrative that longs for open market globalisation and views Right and Left nationalist 'populist' movements or Donald Trump's erratic policies as a kind of rude interruption. There is already far too much written about 'populism' that is either based on endless and conflicting definitions or is so vague that the concept 'populism' has virtually become an almost meaningless 'catch-all' political label.[6]

Instead, I aim toward a critical analysis of the conventional paradigm of 'capitalism versus democracy' in its liberal, social democratic and Marxist versions. I argue that we need to rethink this complex relationship in the light of contemporary socio-economic developments and especially within the context of massively deteriorating environmental conditions. An alternative politics requires a new political paradigm. Unfortunately, the dominant conceptions of capitalism in opposition to democracy still shape much policy-making and political action on both the Right and the Left as well as among sections of green movements.

Countries in Latin America, Asia, Africa and the Middle East have long experienced violent anti-democratic governments. Yet, it was in Europe, the so-called contemporary bastion of democracy, that the tension between 'capitalism and democracy' became manifest in the exercise of brute financial power behind a 'democratic' facade. During the strained negotiations in 2015 between the EU and the new Greek government, the Greek Finance Minister, Yanis Varoufakis, informed the EU finance ministers that he had a duty to help alleviate the suffering of the Greek people who had recently elected him. In response, the German Finance Minister Wolfgang Schäuble is reported to have asserted: "elections cannot be allowed to determine economic policy!"[7] In other words, democracy is secondary and should never interfere with what is best for the management of capitalism.

It is important to recognise that Schäuble's response in 2015 was not surprising given he was educated within the tradition of German Ordoliberalism (or European neoliberalism) that was taught at Freiburg, best known for the ideas of Walter Eucken, Wilhelm Röpke and others.[8] Like their Anglo-American neoliberal cousins and various authoritarian supporters of capitalist social orders across the world, Ordoliberals have long-held strong fears of democracy viewed as successive waves of 'clamouring demanding masses' (or code for organised militant workers and citizens) threatening to derail the apparently smooth functioning of market economies.[9] Ideally, these defenders of capitalism prefer a strong state based on conservative pro-market fiscal, monetary and social policies to be applied by sympathetic politicians and state administrators. Not for them a government that could potentially be pushed 'off course' by anti-market democratic decision-making, especially one that promised to fulfil the needs and wishes expressed by the democratic majority.

Following the March 2020 release of Varoufakis's secret recordings of the 2015 EU finance ministers' meetings, plus the initial refusal of Germany, The Netherlands and others to provide speedy and adequate medical and financial assistance to Italy, Spain and other member countries devastated by Covid-19, Varoufakis argued that the Eurogroup ministers had not learnt the lessons of 2008. They are 'hardwired', he stated, to defend the interests of 'capital' against the needs of 'democracy'.[10] This claim has much merit. However, Varoufakis along with Wolfgang Streeck and a section of the radical Left are still stuck in the period 1992 to 2019 (from the Maastricht Treaty to the outbreak of Covid-19) and have not yet come to terms with the unfolding new European and global political scene (see Chapters Seven and Eight).

CAPITALISM AND DEMOCRACY: COMPATIBLE OR INCOMPATIBLE?

The divisions within the EU remind us that disputes over the compatibility of 'capitalism and democracy' or whether 'democratic capitalism' is an oxymoron, have been raging since the nineteenth century. What we do know is that there has been no capitalist society where all the major economic, legal, social and political institutions have been democratised, let alone one where the product of workers' labour has been democratically redistributed in an egalitarian manner. Instead, we continue to have varying degrees of power exercised by elected politicians co-existing with public and private institutions that remain secretive, unaccountable and beyond democratic control. Although Marx wrote little about democracy, he pointed out in 1843 that winning civil rights through political emancipation from absolute monarchs was a great step forward, but it was not equivalent to human emancipation.[11] Despotism and absolutism may have been overthrown in some public spheres, such as those emerging capitalist societies with republican constitutions, but absolutism retreated to the private sphere and entrenched itself behind the doors of private businesses and within the patriarchal family sphere (including Marx's own family).

Right up until the present day, only a small minority of families in the world aim to conduct their interpersonal relations as democratically as possible. Even fewer workplaces – whether privately or publicly owned – bother with the veneer of democracy, let alone practice democratic decision-making. Many liberal social democrats have long aimed for a 'democratic capitalism' where markets thrive and also meet the needs of those disadvantaged segments of contemporary societies. Unfortunately, this goal has proven to be a mirage, as the majority of business owners and managers strongly prefer no internal democratic decision-making within their own enterprises and minimal or no accountability to the electorate as a whole.

I use the phrases 'capitalism and democracy' and 'capitalism versus democracy' in quotation marks because both 'democracy' and 'capitalism' are thinly disguised synonyms or codes used by a range of ideologists, policy-makers and political activists who view society and politics in either class or non-class terms. From the nineteenth century onwards, despite an assortment of conservatives fighting liberal reformers, most of the latter were still opposed to granting full political rights to the emerging working-class and other non-propertied segments of society. Liberty for the new industrial and commercial urban bourgeoisie was not to be confused with 'democracy'. Instead, 'liberty' was largely conceived to be perfectly fine for propertied and 'educated' citizens rather than for wage workers, let alone for slaves, colonised peoples and non-propertied women. Leading liberals, such as John Stuart Mill, argued that various social evils would result from universal voting unless extra weighted votes were given to those who were better 'educated', such as lawyers and university graduates. The old anti-democratic attitudes of the nineteenth century, that only the educated or property-owners should be given the vote, remain alive and well as the contemporary advocates of weighted voting demonstrate.[12]

Yet, today, a mixture of contempt, concern and fear of the 'uneducated' is now expressed in different terms by those on the centre-Left rather than by traditional conservatives and liberals. Hilary Clinton's description of Trump supporters as a 'basket of deplorables' sums up widely held views about the 'poorly educated masses'. As a condemnation of a whole class of people it is wrong and foolish, despite the fact that it would be naïve to ignore the many examples of appalling prejudice and ignorance displayed by sections of voters who supported Trump and similar leaders in other countries. Political economists such as Thomas Piketty have also documented that the majority of university educated voters in recent decades have changed from supporting conservative parties to voting for centre/Left and Green parties.[13] The fear of universal voting held by traditional liberals and conservatives has evaporated as significant numbers of workers and other 'uneducated lower classes' have abandoned socialist and social democratic parties and now tend to increasingly support Right-wing parties and authoritarian policies.

As to socialist parties, from the nineteenth century to the early decades of the twentieth century, they were in no doubt that the policies and interests pursued by the respective advocates of 'capitalism' and 'democracy' were in conflict with one another. The main division between Left reform and revolutionary parties from the 1830s to the first four decades of the twentieth century was over whether capitalism could be 'civilised' by bringing it under the democratic control of workers 'as voters', or whether it had to be overthrown by a class-conscious working-class that would end 'bourgeois democracy' by creating a 'proletarian' or revolutionary 'classless democracy'.

With the world divided between 'Western liberal-democratic' powers and Communist dictatorships, the onset of the Cold War in 1946 saw both social democrats and conservatives champion capitalism *not* as the enemy of democracy, but rather as being *impossible* without the continued survival of the capitalist 'Free World'. According to Gareth Dale, "elitist conceptions of democracy à la Mosca, Weber and Schumpeter – democracy as a set of procedural political rules, not a 'type of society' – became hegemonic. Capitalism re-stabilised and entered a period of unprecedented growth, with welfare expansion and steady rises in average incomes. Democracy, it appeared to social democrats, was being deployed to successfully tame capitalism."[14]

DEMOCRATISATION AND THE 'CONTRADICTIONS OF THE STATE'

By the 1960s, a new generation of social critics and political movements began to not only reject the 'impossibility of democracy without capitalism' but to expand the very notion of 'democracy' and social justice well beyond the earlier dominant socialist notions developed during the period from the nineteenth century to the 1950s. Democratic political and social rights for blacks, women, gays and other discriminated against social groups – both within OECD countries and within exploited and colonially repressed developing societies – now exploded the complacency and the illusion that capitalism had been tamed and 'civilised'.

It was increased political conflict and the rise of new social movements in the 1960s and 1970s that produced a re-evaluation of the compatibility of 'capitalism and democracy'. Whereas classical liberals and Marxists from the nineteenth century to the 1940s believed that 'capitalism and democracy' were either incompatible or at the very least in tension with one another, most of the leading capitalist societies of the twentieth century were representative democracies (apart from the brief, devastating fascist interlude). This political reality created divisions within the Left. Orthodox Marxists adhered to Engels' and Lenin's view that a "democratic republic is the best possible political shell for capitalism..."[15] because representative democracy disguised the fact that workers were still 'wage slaves', thus sustaining capitalist class power. Emerging neo-Marxists, in opposition to Leninist positions, argued that the relationship between the political system and the economic productive system was more complex, more fluid and unpredictable than it had been previously portrayed. Claus Offe, James O'Connor, Jürgen Habermas[16] and other neo-Marxists now investigated not just the general 'contradictions of capitalism', but the specific 'contradictions of the capitalist state'. These states had to simultaneously maintain capitalist accumulation and the legitimacy of these policies with voters.

According to neo-Marxists, the tensions between the competitive political party system ('mass democracy') and the diverse public and private institutional component elements of the 'Keynesian welfare state' were far from smooth or predetermined.[17] The 'marketisation of politics' and the 'politicisation of the private economy' were characteristics, Offe argued, of only "a specific version of democracy, political equality and mass participation that is compatible with the capitalist market economy. And, correspondingly, it is a specific type of capitalism that is able to coexist with democracy."[18] In short, the compatibility of 'capitalism and democracy' was not true of all types and levels of democracy. Nor was it true of all forms of capitalism.

Importantly, there was no 'general law' of capitalist societies that determined the point at which the rate of profit and the depth of democracy made 'capitalism and democracy' incompatible. Rather, 'compatibility' was the outcome of interrelated, complex and delicately poised relations between social classes and their political institutions. During major crises, some countries maintained their parliamentary democracies while others suffered from imposed dictatorships. Business and political leaders also continue to be divided over different levels of social welfare that have long been accepted by their counterparts in other capitalist countries but which they bitterly oppose being introduced into their own societies. One central contradiction, Offe concluded, "is that while capitalism cannot coexist *with*, neither can it exist *without*, the welfare state."[19]

Politically, the focus of the New Left on the contradictory role played by state institutions legitimised both revolutionary anti-capitalist action and reformist change through social movement agitation and 'the long march through the institutions'. I too shared neo-Marxist perspectives on the 'contradictions of the capitalist state'. Ironically, our analyses were written in the 1970s and early 1980s, just when harsher neoliberal policies were beginning to replace so-called 'Keynesian welfare state' policies and institutional practices. Our attempts to develop more 'sophisticated' and nuanced accounts of capitalist states tended to downplay secret deals, rampant corruption, endless blatant lies, and the barely disguised attempts by businesses to bully, manipulate and gain policy favours from political leaders and public administrators. All these features of debased 'democracies' have increasingly defined key aspects of political economic relations in recent decades.

The rise of human rights movements after 1945 also took a different turn from the late 1970s with the increasing dominance of neoliberal governments seeking to subordinate human rights to corporate rights. The more that bilateral and multi-lateral free trade treaties were negotiated between governments, the more human rights were eroded by the strong enforcement of pro-market agreements at the expense of both national social rights and universal human rights. Today, there are still few tribunals that can enforce human rights treaties. The highly controversial issue of when it is legitimate or not to use military force to defend populations against genocide (e.g. Rwanda) or other horrific human rights violations cannot be reduced to standard arguments about neoliberalism and imperialism. After all, even anti-imperialist Trotsky advocating sending in the Red Army to stop the Nazis in

1932 (before Hitler crushed the Left) which could possibly have saved tens of millions of lives.

During the 1980s and 1990s, non-government organisations such as Amnesty International and Médecins sans Frontières intentionally and unintentionally became fellow travellers with neoliberals by failing to oppose business violations of human rights or by redefining human rights so that they often excluded social rights such as equality and redistribution.[20] In the conflict between 'capitalism and democracy', human rights were now divorced from the classical notions of the equality of all human beings or the United Nations declaration of the right of all people to essential needs such as food and shelter. Despite the recent 'rediscovery' of inequality and poverty, human rights campaigns remain divided, like liberal and radical notions of 'capitalism versus democracy', between those who mainly emphasise individual and property rights and others who stress the importance of social rights as inseparably related to democracy and citizenship.

Today, those political and business leaders who subscribe to tough neoliberal policies often admire powerful new authoritarian capitalist societies and are envious that these countries do not have to deal with frustrating democratic political institutional processes. Many low and middle-income societies have thus made neo-Marxist theories of the tension between political legitimacy and the private accumulation of capital either increasingly irrelevant in large parts of the world, or less pertinent in representative democracies. It is also the case that the contradiction between 'legitimacy and capital accumulation' ceases to be crucial if mainstream electoral parties endorse dominant market practices and differ only on less fundamental issues.

DISILLUSIONMENT AND DEPOLITICISATION

By the end of the 1980s and early 1990s, it was the consolidation of neoliberal policies and the defeat of labour movements in OECD countries that led analysts to reflect upon 'failed promises' and the widespread public disillusionment with parliamentary democracy, just as Eastern European post-Communist countries were tasting their so-called multi-party freedoms. In OECD countries, many people became disillusioned with 'democracy' and questioned whether citizens could shape their local and national 'sovereign' institutions given that key political and economic decisions were often made beyond their borders.[21] Could a 'political community' only exist within a nation state and if not, how could supranational states such as the EU become democratic? Unsurprisingly, the lack of democratic international institutions has led to 'national sovereignty' being increasingly championed by both Right and Left nationalists. Whether democracy can control capitalism at local and national levels remains a very divisive concern that I will discuss in later chapters.

Unlike either Marx or Lenin, it took a mainstream and far from radical American historian, Edmund Morgan, to show how the ideological fiction of 'people's sovereignty' has replaced the divine right of kings as the new reigning fiction. According to Morgan, governments rest on make believe:

> Make believe that the people have a voice or make believe that the representatives of the people are the people. Make believe that governors are the servants of the people. Make believe that all men are equal or make believe that they are not. The political world of make-believe mingles with the real world in strange ways, for the make-believe world may often mould the real one. In order to be viable, in order to serve its purpose, whatever that purpose may be, a fiction must bear some resemblance to fact. If it strays too far from fact, the willing suspension of disbelief collapses.[22]

In contrast to the eighteenth and nineteenth centuries, the crisis of political 'make-believe' in the era of what is called 'capitalist globalisation' manifests itself as mass citizen disillusionment with politicians and domestic political institutions not living up to democratic ideals or what political analysts commonly call 'the democratic deficit' and the rise of 'anti-politics'. At the same time that Morgan was writing about 'make-believe' in American history, the politics of a 'fake' society was in its final years in the Soviet Union. Alexei Yurchak showed how the 'last Soviet generation' lived through what he called 'hypernormalisation', a condition in which both citizens and politicians lost their belief in the system. For decades everyone had known the Soviet system was failing, but no one could imagine any alternative and pretended that what was 'fake' would be the reality that lasted forever.[23] Television documentary maker, Adam Curtis, argues that a similar crisis of hypernormalisation is pervading Western 'democracies'.[24]

Whether dominant policies are implemented despite the wishes of the vast majority of citizens or with their full cooperation or even the zealous prosecution of these policies by 'the people', depends on conflicting perceptions of citizenship. In highly coercive societies, when it comes to decision-making, most people have *no* say in formulating state policies. In political theory, the lack of power over decision-making has been traditionally conceived as the difference between 'subjects' and 'citizens': *subjects* are ruled by others above them while *citizens* are supposed to have some say in 'who gets what, when and how'. Unfortunately, most citizens in this sense are not treated as citizens by governments and vast numbers of the electorate 'self-restrict' their own rights and abilities by acting more like passive subjects rather than as active citizens.

Using Michel Foucault's ideas, Indian political theorist Partha Chatterjee also argues that under neoliberal governments, 'populations' are distinguished from citizens. Populations have interests which they express through demands and protests whereas citizens have rights and are in theory the sovereign foundation of the state.[25] Governments target 'populations' through a range of policies and security actions while individuals making up populations are 'split' between being a subject of 'interests' and a citizen-subject of 'rights' (depending on whether they live in countries with free elections.) The prevailing neoliberal and social democratic notion of 'the individual' rests on the fiction that only the individual citizen can know her or his interests. It is the use of governmental power to regulate 'populations' and produce disciplined 'normal citizen-subjects' or what is called liberal and neoliberal hegemonic order, which is now in shambles. All the characteristics of colonial and post-colonial practices in developing countries that Chatterjee argues were once seen by liberals "as belonging to the unenlightened zones of the contemporary world" – tribalism, nepotism, cronyism, xenophobia, populism – are "now raising their unseemly heads in the sacred lands of liberal democracy."[26]

If lack of enthusiasm for political engagement benefits the status quo, there is no agreement about why large numbers of people are not politically active and do not even vote. Those who focus on 'passivity' often fall back on public ignorance or generalised social psychological traits such as apathy and acceptance of authority as explanations. It is worth recalling that Freud rejected the notion of an 'individual psychology', as people were not isolated 'Robinson Crusoes' and developed their psyches within the context of family and other relations.[27] He also criticised notions of a 'group instinct' or a shared psychic structure. While still a Freudian, Erich Fromm observed in 1930: "The greater, therefore, the number of subjects of an investigation in social psychology, the narrower the insight into the total psychic structure of any individual within the group being studied."[28] This continues to pose a challenge for radicals and liberals fearing fascism and other anti-democratic tendencies, including those who follow social psychological insights made by

Fromm's former colleagues in the Frankfurt School (such as Theodore Adorno) who developed a profile of the 'authoritarian personality'.[29]

COUNTER-DEMOCRACY

Conversely, critical analysts who stress 'active' reasons for the rejection of conventional 'politics' usually cite non-psychological reasons. These include the public's contempt for existing political institutions because major parties are too similar to bring about fundamental changes or that conservative governments and corporations monopolise political power and prevent genuine democratic decision-making. The 'active' rejection of 'parliamentary democracy' can fuel either neo-fascist movements or radical anti-capitalist demands for direct, participatory democracy. Some dissenters, such as French political theorist, Pierre Rosanvallon, reject the notion that democracy has declined even though voting may have declined. Instead, he sees a 'counter-democracy' or 'other democracy' that occurs between elections in the form of citizen and social movement 'oversight' through vigilance, denunciation and evaluation of politicians and government legislation. There is also 'prevention' of unpopular legislation through resistance and the denial of legitimacy in the form of 'judgement' of governments.[30]

Despite Rosanvallon's praise of 'counter-democracy', the results have so far been ineffective in reversing or altering the main characteristics of political power and social inequality in capitalist systems. He has acknowledged the paradox that: "Democracy is manifesting its vitality as a regime even as it withers as a social form."[31] The growth in inequality driven by capitalist markets now threatens democracy as a political regime.

It is not surprising that the first two decades of the twenty-first century has also seen the rise of notions such as 'post-democracy', 'post-politics', 'de-democratisation' and 'anti-politics', all signifying declines in political activity or the rejection of mainstream establishment parties and politicians. Not only are state institutions widely perceived to be unable to control corporate power, but politics is claimed to be riddled with corruption and run by a self-interested 'political class'.[32] Traditional political conflicts over 'capitalism versus democracy', namely, disputes over inequality and the distribution of wealth and power between classes have not disappeared. But pervasive lying by prominent politicians and 'fake news' has eroded public life by making it very difficult to cut through and effectively counter the dishonesty in public discourse.

Alongside notions of 'post-politics' and anti-politics' is the masquerade of both Right-wing movements and politicians as being the 'true democrats' or 'tribunes of the people' against the 'political class' while doing the very opposite. 'Democracy' has always been used to justify war, racism and intolerance. Little has changed except the devious methods and language deployed. Today, in the light of onshore or offshore concentration camps for refugees in representative democracies such as Australia, the US and Mediterranean countries or mass repression of whole ethnic minorities such as the Muslim Rohingya and Uighur in authoritarian Myanmar and China, many now question whether there is any difference on substantive human rights issues between liberalism, Communism and fascism. When some radicals argue that there is no difference between centre-Left parties and Le Pen or Trump apart from their rhetoric and methods, are we reliving the 1920s when Communists attacked social democrats as a variety of fascism called 'social fascists'?

By contrast, political theorist, John Keane, believes we are living in the era of 'new despotisms' rather than neo-fascist regimes.[33] These regimes in Eastern Europe, Central and South Asia, Latin America and the Middle East have adopted techniques from China and Russia where governments permit a certain degree of grumbling, social dissent and even electoral participation so long as there is no real threat to Putin's, Xi's or other new despots' power. Repression is evident when needed but it is qualitatively and quantitatively different to practices used by Hitler, Stalin and other dictators. These new 'despotic' regimes are highly integrated with capitalist markets and use the latest digital surveillance and communication technologies alongside the promotion of consumerism to keep the majority of their populations simultaneously passive and loyal. While containing valuable insights, Keane tends to minimise the differences between these 'new despotisms', the targets of their repression and the degree of violence applied.

Across the political spectrum, 'political participation' has also been redefined to include a heavy dose of online blogging and social media activity rather than earlier forms of direct face-to-face political action in parties and movements.[34] Social media, as we have seen, can help mobilise mass protests and ideas by serving as an alternative to the conservative mass media. It also has transformed political campaigning by facilitating anti-democratic practices via the use of mass data algorithms. The 'digital party' is also evident in various countries and the Five Star Movement in Italy formed government after a decade of online political activity.[35] So far, 'digital parties' have changed few policies and little of the day-to-day practice of government.

Whether off-line or on-line, since the 1950s, the discourse about 'capitalism versus democracy' has been significantly *decoupled* from the old discourse about the 'working-class versus the capitalist-class'. During the past sixty years, anarchists, feminists, gays, anti-colonialists, greens, First Nations indigenous people and other socio-cultural groups have redefined 'capitalism versus democracy' as something much broader or quite different to class struggle between capitalists and workers. Today, it is not just a question of which social and political agents could advance or oppose further democratisation, but whether 'democracy' itself poses one of the greatest obstacles to environmentally sustainable societies. In other words, environmental issues will affect not only the future success of Right-wing politics and business practices, but also the very character of mainstream centre/Left politics as well as alternative politics, whether eco-socialist, green or other radical notions of post-capitalism.

DEMOCRACY VERSUS SUSTAINABILITY

Stephan Rammler, Director of the Institute for Future Studies and Technology Assessment in Berlin recently proclaimed: "I'd rather die in a democracy than live in a sustainable dictatorship. Climate change is still a better option than losing our civil liberties."[36] Defiant, but foolish words because we currently live in a world where most people do not enjoy the luxury of civil liberties and those living in countries with representative democracy have governments that put their capitalist market economies well above sustainability. There is little point in a mindless truncated 'democracy' if climate breakdown leads to major socio-economic crises including food shortages, devastating natural disasters and hundreds of millions affected by epoch-defining death and social dislocation. Similarly, there is little point in a 'greenwashed' adulterated form of 'sustainability' if this neither achieves sustainability nor overcomes profound levels of global social inequality with only token forms of democracy.

In recent decades, the old conflict over 'capitalism and democracy' has mutated into a new or parallel dispute: 'democracy versus sustainability'. Actually, this new political debate is unintelligible without understanding previous disputes over 'capitalism versus democracy', but it is not reducible to this old conflict. We have seen analyses of 'capitalism versus the climate'[37] but currently the discussion of 'democracy versus sustainability' has been undeveloped. It is also the case that many critics of capitalism do not support traditional or modern versions of socialism but have their own environmental, feminist, post-colonial and other socio-political agendas.

Today, in the midst of major environmental crises, three interrelated issues prevail. Firstly, is democracy the best way of preventing not just climate breakdown but other deeper ecological catastrophes that could lead to the collapse of capitalism; secondly, does the future of capitalist growth depend on curbing or reducing democracy; and thirdly, in what ways do post-capitalist scenarios have to be rethought, particularly given that most past and present socialist schemes have ignored the natural constraints for the sustainable delivery of more equitable standards of living for over nine billion people in coming years?

Currently, strategic geopolitical scenarios devised in Washington, Beijing, Berlin, Tokyo, Paris, Moscow and other capitals are focussed on recovering from the socio-economic crises caused by Covid-19. Democratic rights rank incredibly low as a priority issue compared with military power, industrial capacity or energy, food and natural resources security. Several governments, including those in the US, Brazil, Hungary and other countries have already used the crisis of Covid-19 as a cover to roll back environmental regulations and democratic rights. Major political and socio-economic divisions will also continue to grow over what 'environmental sustainability' means and how to achieve it. One of the major problems confronting both defenders of capitalist markets and advocates of greater democracy is that democratisation is an unknown process with unpredictable consequences. It may well be that the democratic desire to protect environments and the biosphere will threaten the future of capitalism. On the other hand, democratic decision-making in different countries could result in policy decisions that oppose the need for urgent environmental measures if these jeopardise jobs, income and material wellbeing.

However, given the continued failure of governments to take adequate action to prevent catastrophic climate breakdown, it is increasingly likely that emergency action will become unavoidable. Can it be democratic? Most emergency action has invariably been *undemocratic*, as in war-time emergencies. Rammler's empty rhetoric about preserving democracy rather than habitable human life on large areas of the planet is not the only choice facing citizens. This is why the urgent task of preventing major crises of sustainability requires us to rethink earlier democratisation struggles of the past 100 years and their suitability for the new challenges we face.

The goal of environmental sustainability is both inseparably related to democratic struggles as well as significantly different to former and current notions of democracy. In Book Three I will discuss why there is no inbuilt recognition, let alone demand that environmental sustainability ought to be the foundation of any democracy. Just as there is no inherent connection between democracy and anti-capitalism, so too, there is no automatic support by free democratic electorates for either environmental sustainability or social equality. Instead, many countries are still characterised by deep divisions based on increased racism, misogyny and homophobia. They have also seen strong attacks on environmentalist agendas by those sections of the population (including significant sections of the working-class) that were formerly supportive of radical Left or centre-Left mainstream parties.

In my earlier book, *Fictions of Sustainability*, I analysed the contrasting policies and visions of sustainability proposed by both defenders and opponents of capitalism. Defenders of capitalism are divided between those who wish to keep 'business as usual' and others who advocate 'green growth' ecological modernisation, especially in relation to averting dangerous climate breakdown. Decarbonisation is yet to overcome major political roadblocks and industry is still unable to surmount technical difficulties such as readily available mass-produced carbon-free steel, alternatives to cement, many basic chemicals and other key component elements commonly used in goods and infrastructure. However, as I will discuss in Book Three, these pale into insignificance when compared to the enormous task of a radical reduction of material footprints of which carbon emissions merely plays one part.

Most anti-neoliberals, including Keynesian and post-Keynesian liberal social democrats, Marxists and moderate environmentalists favour action to prevent climate breakdown combined with varying degrees of reform or radical restructuring of markets. Yet, as I will argue, they continue to be stuck in the old paradigm of 'capitalism versus democracy' rather than also seeing the deep tension between 'democracy and sustainability', especially the struggle over the size of per capita and national material footprints. Very importantly, they still believe in the necessity of *economic growth*. This is also true of some Green New Deal proposals. Most still have an impoverished understanding of the enormous challenges facing the world, especially high-income OECD countries, in reducing affluent per capita material consumption by what some environmentalists argue is a massive 80 per cent of current levels. Whether this figure proves to be a gross exaggeration in order for global equality or the 'good life' to be achieved without dangerously transgressing biophysical planetary boundaries is a crucial mainstream debate that is yet to occur.[38] Either way, if 80% is too high, then we are still left with the task of persuading the affluent to reduce their material consumption by approximately 25% to 60% in order to preserve biodiversity.[39] This in itself constitutes an unimaginable political obstacle if contemporary voting patterns and anti-radical policy preferences become the measure.

TECHNO-FIXERS VERSUS DEGROWTHERS

In contrast to advocates of degrowth, corporations and governments are banking on future technological innovations that will allow the vital room for high growth and high material consumption to continue expanding by *decoupling* economic growth from negative environmental impacts. Pro-marketeers such as Andrew McAfee (*More from Less*[40]) argue that the 1970s claim of natural limits to growth has been completely disproven by fifty years of incredible capitalist growth. While I agree with McAfee that peak oil, peak copper, peak nickel, and the like have not happened, this is not because of the competitive ingenuity of markets. Rather, finite limits of certain natural resources may never be reached as long as capitalist social systems perpetuate shocking levels of global inequality. Importantly, McAfee's arguments have been attacked by scientists as cherry picking facts and scientifically groundless.[41] He and other believers in the market ignore the already dangerous changes to four out of the nine planetary boundaries identified by earth system scientists.[42] There is far too much change to bio-geochemical boundaries such as excessive use of nitrogen in agricultural production, acidification of oceans and loss of biodiversity, not to mention greenhouse gas emissions. It is not a simple matter of just certain natural resources running out, but rather of limits to the capacity of the biosphere and other planetary boundaries to cope with excessive pollution and alteration of bio-physical capacities due to incessant capitalist production and consumption.

The rose-tinted faith in free markets ignores the reality that three-fifths of the world's population only consume a fraction of American per-capita material consumption. If the rest of the world were to enjoy the wages, material consumption and services of most people in OECD countries, there would be no more 'cheap food', 'cheap energy', 'cheap raw materials' or 'cheap manufacturing goods and services' to fuel so-called 'dematerialised' markets.[43] Far too many champions of capitalism conveniently ignore that the 'digital economy', for instance, is based on digital hardware that is produced in often appalling conditions in Asian and other low and middle-income countries. They also remain silent about the millions of rural labourers working on cash crops in low-income countries or the low-paid, precarious immigrant labour that is imported to work under exploitative circumstances in the agricultural sectors of Australia, the US and Europe.[44]

Contra the technological cheer squad – whether of the Right or the Left – rates of *relative* decoupling or efficiency dividends in various industries due to intensified productivity gains, new technologies and synthetic manufacturing materials are far from adequate to meet present or future global needs based on lifestyles in high-income countries. Relative decoupling in a few industries does not lead to absolute decoupling and is not translatable to whole economies. The notion that absolute decoupling will produce environmentally sustainable capitalist or post-capitalist societies is based on myth making, selective use of one-off productivity gains in some industries and other such claims. In short, no evidence has been produced between 1990 and 2019 that the extremely difficult or highly improbable technologically driven goal of absolutely decoupling growth from nature is attainable.[45] Similarly, claims that poverty has been falling in most countries is not borne out once China is excluded from global poverty figures.[46] Equally untrue is the assertion that markets are now 'treading lightly on the planet'. This claim ignores 'offshoring' carbon-intensive production and shipping waste to non-OECD countries.

Despite the so-called wonders of technology combining with competitive markets, the world is still heading for an increase in temperatures of at least 3.7° Celsius degrees if all countries avoid drastic cuts and merely adhere to the 2015 Paris COP 21 agreement. Not only is it almost certain that the ability to *absolutely* decouple incessant economic growth of manufacturing, mining and construction from the limits of nature will fail, but so too will other key hopes that are invested in innovative technology. Many agricultural scientists, environmentalists and the United Nations Food and Agriculture Organisation have voiced alarm about current forms of grain stock meat production and chemical agribusiness that only have a life expectancy of less than sixty years. McAfee and others would be more convincing if they could show that food, water and other vital natural resources could be sustainably produced and equitably consumed without relying on synthetic food, desalinated water, vitamin supplements and other non-natural resources generated by commercial markets. Artificial food is not the so-called 'better future' that most people desire.

Two simultaneous political economic disputes are likely to become even more divisive and affect the old contest between 'capitalism and democracy'. The first dispute between the advocates of pro- or anti-capitalist policies will continue to be characterised by struggles over the distribution of wealth and power, despite most of the opposing groups continuing to base their policies on environmentally *unsustainable growth-orientated* futures. The second contest that is likely to exacerbate political tensions will be between a growing minority (mainly living in developed capitalist countries) who recognise the need for degrowth, and a large majority of the world's population in low and middle-income countries who either lack essential necessities (electricity, running water) or who aspire to the affluence that is currently enjoyed by only a minority of the world's population.

Whether we live in countries with parliamentary democracies or not, the tension between 'democracy and sustainability' is increasingly becoming a key part of or even separate to the conflict between 'capitalism and democracy'. Currently, the political choice between either sustainability or 'business as usual' is often depicted in caricatured or starkly oppositional ways. That is, one is either an advocate of all the glamour and comforts of market consumerism, or else one wants to take people back to the dark ages of austere, primitive deprivation. Even opponents of capitalism can reproduce the political caricature of environmentalists promoted by advocates of incessant capitalist growth. Take for example, American communist, Jodi Dean, who describes critics of economic growth in deliberately hyperbolic terms. Sounding more like a conservative business leader defending fossil fuels, Dean claims that:

> Degrowth feels a lot like neopeasantisation. Instead of advocating a better and cleaner use of industrial processes and resources, it just cuts them off entirely. I like flying places, I think penicillin and public health are great things, and I don't like to work in a garden. Degrowth wants to redo social relations around a particular relation to the land. This makes sense as a symptom of and reaction against planetary urbanization. But it doesn't combat it for most of the world's people. Combined with movements around the city such as municipalism, this neopeasantisation becomes neo-feudalism.[47]

Just as one can find extremists in a range of political movements, it is also true that there are some advocates of degrowth who do reject all modern technology and comforts. However, Dean's characterisation ignores the majority of supporters of 'degrowth', 'post-growth', 'good growth' or 'wellbeing' (these are often interchangeable labels) who reject a return of all to the land and instead live in cities rather than in rural communes. Like some on the Left and many on the Right, Dean presents a false picture that assumes that most critics of prevailing levels of wasteful and environmentally damaging capitalist production and consumption want to eliminate modern science, reject public health and other social programs and want to turn urban residents into peasants. With anti-capitalists such as Dean espousing a mixture of ill-informed and old-fashioned technocratic views, it is unsurprising that radicals are disunited on this issue.

Regardless of whether alternative political movements grow or not, we are fast approaching a world of escalating environmental crises that will necessitate citizens and policymakers having to make difficult choices. Do they continue existing or slightly modified unsustainable levels of growth and consumption that ignore the destructive structure and level of use of natural resources? Or do they accept the necessity of moving to a major reorganisation of social and individual levels of consumption and production that are incompatible with capitalist accumulation and socio-political inequality.

While Dean and other radicals are free to stay out of the garden, it is common to find amongst many urban dwellers a widespread and deep lack of awareness of how central land and food production are to attaining and sustaining the post-capitalist society that Dean and others so desire; or for that matter, central to any future type of society. As I discussed in *Fictions of Sustainability*, any possible reorganisation of environmentally unsustainable, chemically-based food production and consumption processes will have to include: the need to drastically reduce greenhouse gases from agriculture, preserve biodiversity and yet produce sufficient affordable food for large numbers of low to middle-income people; change the high dependence of urban residents on large-scale agribusiness based on either capital-intensive production or on exploitative rural labour; and provide employment, community services and improved social relations for both rural and urban residents. How to achieve the extremely difficult goals of sustainability within a democracy and avoid past experiences of authoritarian mass slaughter (such as Stalinist forced collectivisation of agriculture) is a challenge that many urban arm-chair Marxists, anarchists and liberal social democrats appear not to have given adequate consideration.

Similarly, as I discuss in *Fictions of Sustainability*, there are the radical technological dreamers who oppose the advocates of degrowth. They elaborate a range of technological fantasies about trillions of sensors providing abundance for all via the internet-of-things, zero marginal cost goods, 3D printing or millions of earthlings colonising other planets and replacing scarce natural minerals or food resources. These imaginaries of a desirable post-capitalist future usually ignore crucial elementary environmental problems and natural limits.

If far too many Marxists, Keynesians and greens have not yet caught up with the digital transformation of capitalist institutions and social practices, the opposite is true of a new generation of digital analysts. Currently there is a profound disconnect between the 'software' creating the images of the future and the major sustainability problems of manufacturing and managing the 'hardware' of cybernetic capitalism or post-capitalism. It is not just the millions of low-paid workers creating high-tech hardware, but the growing crisis of carbon emissions from this so-called 'sustainable' production, the inability to reuse much of the toxic materials and equipment through the so-called 'circular economy' and safely manage mountains of E-waste.

Most people supporting 'green growth' ignore the horrific conditions under which rare metals are produced primarily in China and the Republic of the Congo. There would be no mobile phones, wind turbines, LED screens or dozens of other digital products without the 10,000 mines and the 'cancer villages' in China alone, the high volume of water and energy needed to produce each ton of these indispensable rare earth metals.[48] All this even before the need and ability to safely dispose of the coming predicted avalanche of batteries for the estimated 2.5 billion electric cars by 2050, the hundreds of millions of past-their-use-date solar power panels and other hardware. Additionally, 3D printing currently relies heavily on a multitude of fossil-fuel based chemical polymers that pose a massive threat to global warming and waste management. So too the impact of mass space flights on earth's fragile life support systems is disregarded, not to mention the enormous cost yet negligible impact space colonies may make on resolving natural constraints on earth within the urgent timeframe that is now required. It is quite likely that technological solutions to E-waste and other major environmental problems will be developed. However, technological research and development has never been equivalent to the adoption of innovative technology by capitalists. The chances of private businesses implementing ecological modernisation technologies (so that they are profitable and cost-effective) in the next ten or so years on a scale necessary before the real crunch of green-house gases becomes irreversible, is either very patchy or remote.

It is important to keep in mind that with or without Covid-19, businesses and governments cannot even find a sustainable fuel solution for mass airline travel. Restrictions on flying may well be imposed due to escalating dangers from carbon emissions and the extremely difficult technological obstacles preventing airlines from replacing fossil-fuels.[49] The tension between local needs and global desires are already highly visible in the environmental and social damage caused by escalating air-borne mass tourism, such as lack of affordable housing due to short-stay rental crowding out residents in many cities, and scenic but fragile eco-systems being destroyed by uncontrolled tourism.

Conversely, although I am very sympathetic to many of the goals of degrowth, in Book Three of this book I will discuss the profound contradiction between goals advocated by 'degrowthers' and their failure to resolve political economic feasibility problems associated with these proposals. Many activists supporting degrowth appear to espouse confusing notions of degrowth and political strategy. Democratic societies of the future will need to avoid entropy and decay by promoting cultural and technological innovation. What forms these will take will always remain politically controversial. So far, few advocates of degrowth have specified in detail which technologies they favour and how an urban avant-garde cultural vision can help promote innovative forms of social relations and cultural creativity.

SUSTAINABILITY, INEQUALITY AND VIOLENCE

It is commonplace but nevertheless true that we live in a world with dramatically unequal control of production and resources, as well as unequal incomes and standards of living. Of the almost two hundred separate nation-states, only a minority have free elections while a majority have democratic 'facades' with varying levels of authoritarianism or outright dictatorship. How then, are the interrelated uneven struggles between 'capitalism and democracy', 'democracy and sustainability' and 'affluence and poverty' to be played out in all those capitalist countries where the income of close to five billion people is currently far less than the income of people living at or below the official 'poverty levels' in affluent OECD countries?

Raising seven billion out of nine billion people in the next thirty years to the standard of living currently enjoyed by a majority in affluent countries is environmentally unsustainable. This will entail a dramatic change to the traditional historical narrative of 'capitalism versus democracy'. Creating and sharing a 'larger pie' capable of delivering 'fully automated luxury communism'[50] or some other such affluent scenario for all remains an unsustainable environmental fantasy. Importantly, this is not an issue that merely affects relations between high-income and low and middle-income nations. It is very much a political distributional struggle within *all* nations, whether the US, China, India, the UK, Brazil, South Africa, Indonesia, Italy or Egypt.

One looming consequence of unsustainable growth is the likelihood that business owners, managers and administrators of capitalist societies will increasingly use police and military apparatuses to either stop citizens from protesting and voting or else prevent their newly elected government from moving away from unsustainable forms of production and consumption. Unpalatable choices between incessant market growth and potentially catastrophic environmental pressures face businesses, political parties, social movements and citizens leading to irreconcilable divisions over desirable policies and solutions. Take for example the violence in France in late 2018 and through 2019 between the *gilets jaunes* ('Yellow Vests') and the police. The fact that this was triggered by the Macron Government's increase in diesel fuel taxes can be interpreted in two ways: deep public hostility to environmental measures when they increase the cost of living; or reaction against the Macron government's deliberate use of 'environment' policies to cynically increase fuel taxes in order to fund tax cuts for the wealthy while simultaneously slashing and underfunding the social state. Joshua Clover argues that the *gilets jaunes* represent an early example of 'climate riots' that are bound to increase in other countries in coming years.[51]

If minor taxes on carbon emissions have already produced violent reactions, it is a far greater challenge for the much larger agenda of degrowth in material consumption and production to be accomplished democratically. The contest between 'capitalism and democracy' now includes conflicts over energy, transport and other aspects of the *circulation process* and *social reproduction* system rather than just the production system. These new areas of dispute are the product of social and political realignments in recent decades. They require a reappraisal of traditional capital-labour conflicts as depicted in pre-1945 notions of the conflict between 'capitalism and democracy'. It is true that the New Left from the 1960s revised old 'classical' concepts of class struggle to embrace white collar workers and new social movements. Now even these 'revisions' are dated or inadequate to grasp the environmental implications and interconnections of 'capitalism versus democracy' *and* 'democracy versus sustainability'.

No earlier society with free elections has had to decide whether preserving the 'democratic will' is more important than preventing impending environmental disasters, especially if the majority of voters oppose necessary restrictions on capitalist production and consumption. This is *not* an argument against democracy. I merely wish to puncture the illusions associated with naïve advocates of the 'infallible' power of democracy. It has long been optimistically assumed by many socialists that the exercise of democratic power by 'the people' is either a threat to, or incompatible with capitalist practices. This has certainly not proved to be the case in most parliamentary democracies where 'democracy' is largely confined to the vote and to free speech. Let us not forget that racist and exclusionary policies have already been reinforced by democratic electorates in OECD countries against refugees and immigrants in the name of 'protecting our communities, jobs and way of life'. We should therefore also not assume that existing parliamentary democracies will necessarily endorse urgently needed sustainable environment policies at the expense of existing profits, jobs and consumption.

Despite massive global protests demanding emergency climate action, few socialists or greens have contemplated a possible eventuality where majorities in key national electorates may oppose deep-seated policy adjustments necessary to ensure a safe climate. Now think of the political distance that still needs to be travelled before major governments propose degrowth measures. So far, anti-capitalist movements have produced few alternative planning measures. Instead, various scientists and government agencies are working on geo-engineering and military 'planning scenarios' concerning controlling greenhouse gases or dealing with national and international climate-induced crises. However, none of these military and other 'planning scenarios' have anything to do with democratic participation, reducing inequality or decelerating economic growth. Importantly, the revival of nationalism within the context of 'globalised capitalism' has also created new political realignments across the political spectrum. Much of this new nationalism is hostile to existing civil rights, increased democratisation, equality and environmental sustainability.

COMPETING NARRATIVES AND PARADIGMS

The paradigm of 'capitalism versus democracy' continues to intersect with or compete with other religious and secular paradigms, whether Christian narratives of original sin and redemption or the Enlightenment belief in liberal progress via reason, technology and the overcoming of ignorance and superstition. Since the late nineteenth century, we have also seen nihilistic and pessimistic paradigms such as Nietzsche's rejection of equality and his critique of both Christianity and socialism for defending 'the meek' against the powerful.[52] Similarly, Max Weber's theory of the 'disenchantment of the world' and the development of an 'iron cage' due to the spread of bureaucratic technical rationality was ultimately also a critique of socialist participatory democracy. For behind the revolutionaries on the barricades, he warned, stood the experts ready to take over and wield real power. Some of these arguments have been used once more against green visions of small, communal direct democracy.

The dominant stream engulfing disputes over 'capitalism and democracy' has also produced tributaries sometimes flowing in parallel or different directions. These include feminist narratives of patriarchy which challenge male domination of both liberal capitalist institutional practices and also socialist and green images of post-capitalism. A range of post-colonial movements and writers have also rejected having their own nations and cultures subordinated to the dominant political and intellectual narrative of 'modernity' originating in Europe.

Today, historians are divided between those who interpret social life as either belonging to the grand sweep of large global movements and others who focus on the multiplicity of micro-histories that do not conform to the grand theories of world history. Understanding the micro-histories 'from below' and how they are 'spatially' linked to the macro-political economic and cultural historical processes 'from above' is a challenge that contemporary analysts of the global and the micro are still trying to understand.[53] The more that globalisation processes directly and indirectly link local communities, the more that former relatively isolated micro-activities, beliefs and histories begin to lose part of their identities and differences.

Any possibility of major social change depends on how each individual sees herself or himself connected to the micro (or local) and the global. At the macro-historical level, environmentalist George Monbiot argues that "those who tell the stories run the world" and that in recent decades, the lack of competing narratives from major political parties has led to the dominance of neoliberalism.[54] Monbiot's call for a 'competing narrative' in fact belongs to the larger 'master paradigm' about 'capitalism versus democracy'. It is common to see the origins of contemporary capitalism based on subdividing history into roughly three stages:

- Stage one – the pre-Keynesian era of liberal capitalism from the early nineteenth century to the Great Depression of the 1930s which also included the subordination of Asia, the Middle East,

Africa and Latin America to European, Japanese and American
imperialist power;
- Stage two – the rise of communism and fascism followed by the
Second World War and Cold War which saw the world divided
into 'Three Worlds': the 'First World' based on the 'Keynesian
welfare state' from 1945 to 1975, the 'Second World' of Communist
states from 1917 onwards, and the 'Third World' of ex-colonies and
developing countries;
- Stage three – the transformation of the 'Three Worlds' from the
late 1970s to the present-day by anti-Keynesian neoliberal
governments, the collapse of Eastern European Communism and
the extension of capitalist globalisation to both the 'Second
World' and the 'Third World'.

Also, within this generalised master paradigm of capitalism in opposition
to democracy, there is a widespread tendency on the part of reformers and
radicals to overemphasise certain years that can overshadow other significant
developments or important years. We are all familiar with the weight
attached to years such as 1914, 1917, 1929, 1933 and 1939. In the past fifty
years, much importance has also been attributed to 1968 as the peak of anti-
capitalist protests and to 1989 as marking the triumph of capitalism with the
fall of Eastern European Communist regimes. Both Paris 1968 and the fall of
the Berlin Wall were largely unimportant or irrelevant to most of humanity
living in Asia, Africa, the Middle East and parts of Latin America. While I
am aware of earlier debates about the problematic use of 'narratives' to
explain the connection of the past to the present,[55] one does not have to
subscribe to a historical 'narrative' as having a clear end-goal or being
invested with exclusive rights of interpretation of particular historical
periods.

WAS 1979 AS SIGNIFICANT AS 1989?

An alternative history could be constructed by highlighting notable events
that took place a decade earlier in 1979, events that helped shape the world
we face today. (Of course, like in the other dates mentioned, these events
were the culmination of earlier processes and narratives). Significantly, on
January 1st of 1979, the United States normalised relations with China for the
first time since the People's Republic had been established thirty years earlier

in 1949. Two weeks earlier, the recently appointed pre-eminent leader of China, Deng Xiaoping, stamped his modernising vision on the third plenary meeting of the Central Committee before visiting the United States in January 1979. Deng's US visit confirmed the first of two stages that would inaugurate a spectacular transformation of China that continues to have a major impact on the global economy. Over subsequent decades, China's 'capitalist road' also helped alter the domestic balance of power in many OECD countries as 'offshoring' by Western businesses bolstered those corporations and political forces looking to seriously weaken most national labour movements. Today, the question also needing an answer is whether or not China has become an imperialist power challenging and provoking older imperialist powers, notably the US and allies? There is no doubt that the rise of China has undermined classical pre- and post-1945 Marxist theories of imperialism. It has also caused a rethink of dominant radical notions of the world still perceived in overgeneralised terms as divided into countries of the so-called 'North' and 'South'.

February 1979 also saw the Shah of Iran finally overthrown by the Islamic revolution and the year ended with the Soviet Union invading Afghanistan. Responding with characteristic myopia and even greater military force to the changing situation in the Middle East and Gulf region, the US helped fund the anti-Soviet Mujahideen rebels in Afghanistan who later unleashed a wave of terrorism primarily directed against the US and Europe. Analysts such as Max Blumenthal argue that "if the CIA had not spent over a billion dollars arming Islamist militants in Afghanistan against the Soviet Union during the height of the Cold War, empowering jihadist godfathers like Ayman al-Zawahiri and Osama bin Laden in the process, the 9/11 attacks would have almost certainly not taken place. And if the Twin Towers were still standing today, it is not hard to imagine an alternate political universe in which a demagogue like Trump was still relegated to real estate and reality TV."[56] Instead, almost four decades of utter destruction resulting in the death of hundreds of thousands of soldiers and untold millions of civilian casualties and refugees have plagued the Middle East and Gulf regions through direct invasions and proxy wars. The catastrophe continues unabated with mass refugees and terrorism proliferating.

Historians will not only record the horrendous waste of life, but that every President – from Carter to Trump – has wasted trillions of dollars in shoring up the flow of dangerous fossil fuels at the expense of developing renewable energy to prevent climate breakdown. It should be remembered that in 1979 in Pennsylvania, far from and seemingly unrelated to the Middle

East, the Three Mile Island nuclear plant leaked radiation. The crisis at Three Mile Island should have triggered and encouraged the rapid quest for alternative energy instead of persisting with nuclear, oil, coal and gas. Despite President Carter installing solar panels on the roof of the While House (which were soon removed by his successor Ronald Reagan), four lost decades of relying on fossil fuels makes the present task of securing a safe global climate infinitely harder.

In that same year, Margaret Thatcher's government was elected to office and the Right-wing American think-tank, the Heritage Foundation, decided to draft the first *Mandate for Leadership*.[57] Thatcher did not inaugurate neoliberalism, but she did give neoliberal policies a big push forward. These ideas and policies had been brewing for a number of years. Indeed, eight months before Thatcher came to power, Democrat President Jimmy Carter initiated the first of many subsequent industry deregulation policies, beginning with the aviation industry in October 1978. He also appointed Paul Volcker as chairman of the Federal Reserve. At a secret meeting on October 6, 1979, Volcker and other members of the Federal Reserve agreed to tackle high inflation by limiting the money supply. Within a year, official rates were increased to over 20% and what became known as the 'Volcker shock' helped to knock out high inflation in most OECD countries for the next forty years. From outside of government, the US Heritage Foundation helped consolidate neoliberalism by drafting over 2000 proposals for Ronald Reagan should he win the 1980 presidential election. Two-thirds of these neoliberal proposals were enacted by the Reagan administration and six different *Mandates for Leadership,* or sets of policy proposals, were produced for subsequent Presidents between 1979 and 2005.

On the cultural and social front, two important interventions took place in Paris in 1979. Both moments signified the transition away from the earlier upsurge in radical socialist politics during the 1960s. The first was Michel Foucault's lecture course on liberal 'governmentality' in 1978/79 in which he both analysed and displayed his attraction to neoliberalism. The second moment was the publication in 1979 of Jean-Francis Lyotard's *The Postmodern Condition: A Report on Knowledge*.[58] While Lyotard did not create 'postmodernism' and only used it in relation to schools of art and architecture, he synthesised and developed various post-structuralist critiques of 'grand narratives' such as Enlightenment progress and socialist emancipation. According to Lyotard, a global system based on the rise of the techno-sciences and managers replacing the owners of capital plus profound changes to the old proletariat required a new politics.[59] Others expanded his 'incredulity towards metanarratives' by declaring that the era of emancipatory social change was dead.

Reinterpreting Kant's question: 'what is enlightenment?', Foucault affirmed the anti-radical and anti-grand narrative theme by arguing that instead of the 'empty dream of freedom',

> [we] must turn away from all projects that claim to be global or radical. In fact, we know from experience that the claim to escape from the system of contemporary reality so as to produce the overall programs of another society, of another way of thinking, another culture, another vision of the world, has led only to the return of the most dangerous traditions.[60]

If Foucault held an ambivalent position of being simultaneously anti-Marxist yet vaguely anti-capitalist, other prominent intellectuals on the Left Bank of Paris such as the 'New Philosophes' were in full cry as they echoed the old 1950s Cold War critiques of 'Marxism as totalitarianism'.

It took several years for Thatcher's and Reagan's savage attacks on the public sector, unions and defenders of anti-market cultural values to have a wider impact across the world. Initially, traditional Left political movements were mobilised in opposition to neoliberal decision-makers and business lobbies. Likewise, many intellectuals and educators rejected Lyotard's, Foucault's and other similar critiques of universal 'grand narratives' of emancipation, equality and justice. Foucault was not a postmodernist like Jean Baudrillard, but within a decade, postmodern ideas seeped into everyday cultural life, especially in OECD countries alongside neoliberal practices and policy frameworks which were adopted by many governments and mainstream parties.

The postmodern turn from the late 1970s was particularly manifest in the work of Baudrillard. Summarising the February 2010 issue of the radical French journal *Lignes*, dedicated to Baudrillard after his death in 2007, Adrian May states that he is now seen as a symptomatic figure of a cultural Left that abandoned political economy to then overemphasise the role of linguistic signs and symbols in theories of postmodern play.[61] The postmodernist preoccupation with the symbolic, May points out, became particularly evident in the 1990s when Baudrillard claimed that people were living in an 'age of weightlessness' because "the realm of mobile and speculative capital has achieved so great an autonomy that even its cataclysms leave no traces".[62] In other words, "financial capital (and its satellites, debt and unemployment) had become so virtual that it was now in orbit above the planet, so unreal that its crises would no longer tangibly impact the real world."[63] It is ironic that in 2007, the year of Baudrillard's death, the fashionable post-modern concepts of 'virtual, weightless capital' that supposedly 'no longer tangibly impacted the real world' came crashing down to earth as capitalist countries entered the greatest financial crisis in history. Although derivatives and many other financial instruments (worth multi-trillions of dollars) can take virtual, digital and symbolic forms, it is the absurd divorce of socio-cultural symbols from political economic processes and material institutional relations that is now viewed as a case of superficial postmodernism that is both misleading and politically disabling.

In the aftermath of 'peak postmodernism' we now live in a strange polit-ical and cultural stalemate, like a demilitarised zone where the antagonistic parties on either side maintain hostilities by other means. The old liberal-Left and the old Right continue the 'culture wars' through mainstream media and the old fragmenting public sphere. However, for a new digital generation on social media and numerous on-line sites, there is no 'demilitarised zone' as postmodern 'irony' has mutated into extreme Right-wing forms of hate, misogyny, violence and all forms of attacks on what is called liberal-Left 'political correctness'. Despite her more problematic political and techno-cratic environmental views, Angela Nagle makes a significant point in her ethnographic study of the complex and vicious on-line culture of the 'alt-Right':

> Manuel Castells and numerous commentators in the *Wired* magazine
> milieu told us of the coming of a networked society, in which old hier-
> archical models of business and culture would be replaced by the
> wisdom of crowds, the swarm, the hive mind, citizen journalism and
> user-generated content. They got their wish, but it's not quite the
> utopian vision they were hoping for.[64]

Instead, the old 'polite' gatekeepers of mass culture have been over-shadowed by a reactionary, destructive, internet-assisted subculture, main-streaming hatred. The internet, of course, is infinitely more than just social media and a platform for the 'alt-Right' (that now goes under new names and proliferating groups). Nonetheless, we are guaranteed that the original innocent Enlightenment visions of the internet as a positive medium for global communication in the years before and after 1979 will remain an unrealisable ideal as long as the 'voices of hate' also proliferate *offline* on the streets and in the institutions of contemporary societies.[65] Despite being repeatedly warned, Facebook and other commercial libertarian social media have irresponsibly and unintentionally led to thousands of people being killed and seriously injured in countries such as Myanmar, Philippines and elsewhere in the quest for market share. A commercial model based on winning members via attention-grabbing fake news and extremist hate speech and accompanying visuals is a major corrosive threat to democracy.

Another contemporary political paradox is that neoliberalism (or hybrid combinations of neoliberal and other policies) continues to dominate in many but not all countries, despite millions of people being more aware of the disastrous consequences flowing from decades of these pro-market policies. It is true that the term 'neoliberalism' has been overused[66] and that there are many definitions of 'neoliberalism' and no single form of 'neoliberalism' is practised in capitalist countries.[67] Inequality and greater authoritarianism are not exclusively associated with neoliberalism. Despite all these variations, the short-hand terms 'neoliberal' and 'neoliberalism' remain useful in that they broadly describe and encompass both an ideology and actual policies implemented since the late 1970s (to a lesser or greater extent) depending on the country concerned. These policies and practices include:

- the active restructuring of state institutions including the corporatisation and privatisation of administrative bodies, utilities and public services;
- increased inequality, regressive tax policies and the reformulation of regulations favouring businesses and high-income individuals;
- either aggressive global free trade policies supporting corporations that allows the free movement of capital and labour combined with attacks on domestic working conditions, or free market policies which fuse with specific nationalist and thinly disguised racist preferences (e.g. Boris Johnson's 'global Britain') that purport to advantage national businesses and other constituencies;
- more authoritarian state policing, incarceration and surveillance; and very importantly,
- a profound deepening and extensive marketisation of not just many cultural and social aspects of public and private life that were formerly not subject to price and exchange market mechanisms, but also the erosion of social bonds and commitments and their replacement with calculated strategies of

'choice' and 'non-commitment' to love, personal relationships or joining political and social movements.[68]

Historically, it is necessary to distinguish between the various phases of neoliberalism and the way it has been practised or resisted in different societies with their own specific histories and cultures. Neoliberalism evolved from being a small proselytising ideological movement between the 1930s and the mid-1970s, especially in Anglo-American countries while its German variant, Ordoliberalism, gained a powerful influence over governments in West Germany from the 1950s onwards. Beginning with the years of social conflict and uneven consolidation of its programmatic agenda in OECD countries during the 1980s and 1990s, neoliberalism has become an ad hoc and ineffective crisis-management philosophy during the past two decades.[69] Before the onset of the Great Recession in 2007-8, it took different forms such as the hard line versions pursued by Thatcher and Reagan or the 'neoliberalism with a human face' of Australian Labor governments under Hawke and Keating (1983 to 1996) and New Labour under Blair.[70]

While neoliberalism survived the Great Financial Crisis, as a political philosophy and mode of political economic practice it has lost much of its former élan and vigour. For pragmatic electoral reasons, many decision-makers in OECD countries now adopt hybrid policy frameworks (mixtures of neoliberal market policies and other fiscal and social policies) in order to try to stimulate growth (especially in response to the crisis caused by Covid-19) and prevent probable future financial and social crises. Gone is the former zealous confidence in market solutions except, of course, amongst Right-wing fundamentalists in the US and other countries. Even though some key aspects of neoliberalism are practised by businesses and governments in countries such as China, Iran, Saudi Arabia or Russia, they cannot be characterised as predominantly neoliberal in respect to their other national political and social goals.

As to postmodernism, these exhausted disputes have long been overtaken by paradoxical new realities, such as far greater cultural and social *standardisation* through global market consumption and integration. This market standardisation is often the outcome of what outwardly appears as its opposite, namely, the promotion of cultural diversity and niche consumer markets, fragmented identities, discourses and audiences. In practice, and with minor exceptions, 'cultural diversity' has quickly metamorphosed into homogenised 'market diversity' in many countries – characterised by similar subcultures, fashion, music, media, alternative movements – rapidly spread by online sites and social media. While I do not subscribe to media clichés that 'Left' and 'Right' are meaningless terms, it is nonetheless increasingly necessary to distinguish between the different elements within the broad Left and Right, not just whether they are moderate or radical and where they stand in relation to 'capitalism and democracy', but also their positions concerning a range of cultural, social and environmental questions. I use 'Left' and 'Right' as shorthand terms, but these broad political alignments were never historically homogeneous groups and are even less so today.

There is no doubting the significant political transformation or fragmentation of traditional alignments and social constituencies. All the old familiar signposts of an earlier historical period such as a militant industrial labour movement or a somewhat common bourgeois public sphere of mainstream political discourse have either disappeared, been marginalised or shattered by online social media and new forms of consumption, employment and urban space. Within old nation states, newly revived but old national independence movements such as the Catalans, Scots or Kurds may want national sovereignty. Yet, their desire for political sovereignty is not matched by deep cultural independence and diversity. Instead, these movements want their own flag and government but often the same standardised global market brand names and lifestyles. The crucial difference between national independence movements is whether their struggles take place under conditions of war and deprivation or are asserted within the context of affluent representative democracies such as the UK, France, Spain or Belgium.

Apart from radical environmental degrowth movements, there are *no large* political parties in OECD countries that call for a completely and radically different society despite the availability of countless publications, radical on-line sites and the technical resources to organise simultaneous political action within nations and across the world. Instead, the nearest we get are demands couched in neo-Keynesian 'green growth' reform agendas or amorphous protest movements like the Chilean anti-austerity riots or the French 'Yellow Vests'. Of course, 'radical' is a relative term. American advocates of the Green New Deal are depicted by their opponents as revolutionaries when in fact their policies are closer to a European social democratic 'green growth' agenda.

As to most low and middle-income countries such as Colombia, Mali, Philippines, Sudan, Palestine, Thailand, West Papua or Yemen, the guerrilla/independence movements active in these places are predominantly mixtures of religious, ethnic and regional based rebellions with only a handful driven by Marxist or anti-capitalist agendas. Traditional indigenous movements fighting to preserve their old way of life against intrusive capitalist transformation also rely on their own political cultural arguments rather than on Marxist critiques of capitalism.

The central thesis of this book is to show why long-held ways of thinking about political economy and social change by both the Left and the Right are being rendered inadequate at the explanatory level and obsolete as solutions to enormous contemporary crises. In *Fictions of Sustainability*, I began by paraphrasing German philosopher Max Horkheimer's 1939 warning 'whoever is not willing to talk about capitalism should also keep quiet about sustainability'. In this book I return to Horkheimer's original 1939 statement: 'whoever is not willing to talk about capitalism should also keep quiet about fascism."[71] It is necessary to analyse how the current conflict between 'capitalism and democracy' is qualitatively different to the socio-political conditions that helped produce earlier forms of fascism. Nonetheless, we will not understand 'capitalism versus democracy' unless we broaden our focus well beyond Horkheimer by asserting that: 'whoever is not willing to talk about capitalism *and* democracy should also keep quiet about *sustainability*'.

Importantly, few answers about the environmental sustainability of capitalism will be found from writers who developed their major ideas before 1945. This now vital issue was outside the experience of revolutionaries such as Lenin, Gramsci, Kautsky, Luxemburg or Trotsky as they confronted a vastly different world of empires that were either soon to collapse (Czarist, Habsburg and German) or be permanently weakened (the British and French empires) by the cataclysmic First World War. Similarly, the post-1917 world of socialist revolutionary militancy, the rise of fascism and the Great Depression of the 1930s leading to the war years of the 1940s all heavily influenced Horkheimer, Polanyi, Keynes, Hayek, Kalecki, Schumpeter and a generation of conservatives, liberals and Marxists. The 'capitalism' they analysed and portrayed to students, policy analysts and political activists may appear familiar to contemporary readers but was actually quite different to present-day capitalist societies. If most of the pre-1945 thinkers were preoccupied with issues such as the compatibility/incompatibility of 'capitalism and democracy', they were certainly unconcerned about whether capitalism was environmentally sustainable or not. Adorno, Horkheimer and Polanyi may have followed Marx in opposing the 'domination of nature' by capitalism but this philosophical stance is hardly equivalent to the proliferation of detailed analyses of the multiple threats to environmental sustainability posed by both multi-party capitalist systems and hybrid capitalist production and consumption presided over by one-party, Communist regimes.

During the nineteenth and twentieth centuries there were many spontaneous riots and rebellions. Nevertheless, these political actions were far outweighed by the rise of parties and movements necessary to make social change in societies that had elaborate state institutions, urban spaces and business enterprises. Mobilising workers and citizens in these new organisations required large numbers of people to become *future-orientated* rather than adhere to old ways of doings things. This is increasingly necessary given that several crucial problems currently affecting the world (such as climate breakdown) have no precedents in the history of capitalist societies to guide us.[72] Consequently, we should not see everything through the past and certainly not try to solve contemporary problems as if most of the familiar organisations and their solutions remain relevant and effective for future needs.

Many people quote Marx's famous observation about 'the tradition of the dead generations' that 'weighs like a nightmare on the minds of the living' and why men and women make their own history but 'not under circumstances they themselves have chosen'. However, few ever reference the concluding part of Marx's insightful passage where he observes that it is precisely in a period when people are trying to create a new society by transforming themselves and their material conditions, that "they timidly conjure up the spirits of the past to help them; they borrow their names, slogans and costumes so as to stage the new world-historical scene in this venerable disguise and borrowed language."[73] One can certainly recognise this 'timidity' and the 'weight of dead generations' in the responses of present-day social change activists. They are divided between those who continue to borrow the worn-out slogans, rituals, 'costumes' and strategies of the past, while others confront contemporary issues with innovative solutions and conceptions of the future. It is our 'fictional expectations' or imagined futures that help shape the future.[74] How we imagine the future is crucial in determining whether we are either complacently comfortable in our expectations or paralysed by fear and feelings of helplessness, or else driven by the need for transformative political action.

Social theorist Daniel Innerarity rejects the Foucauldian critique of 'grand narratives' and defends the 'politics of hope' by examining the various 'enemies of the future'. We are dominated, he says, by instantaneous, short-term time frames, whether electoral cycles, media deadlines or 'just-in-time' production. Hence: "designs for the future are scarce. The future has poor advocates in the present, and it suffers from chronic weakness. The problem with our democracies is that our political antagonisms are bound to the present. We live at the expense of the future; our relationship to it is completely irresponsible."[75] As Innerarity goes on to point out: "Anticipatory behaviours seem to favour prevention and precaution rather than planning and preparation...our absence of plans subjugates us to the tyranny of the present."[76]

THEMES AND ISSUES TO BE DISCUSSED

This volume is about shifting political paradigms and how they relate to historical and present-day conflicts and competing goals for the future. The paradigms I discuss are not chronological. Rather, various political, economic and social thinkers and movements continue to adhere to old paradigms or ways of thinking even as others long ago abandoned these socio-political perspectives. In the world of politics, paradigms do not get permanently replaced as some imagine happens with scientific discoveries where so-called 'better explanations' replace earlier scientific methods. The fact that in the world of science there is no singular all-encompassing scientific truth and conflict continues between competing scientific theories is just as true in the realm of politics and social relations. Arguments *cannot* be won at the level of rational theoretical disputes and the defeated parties, classes or theorists then safely consigned to the 'dustbin of history'. What needs to be examined is how some ideas endure and are revived under quite different political economic conditions and others are no longer powerful or have virtually disappeared.

Book One closely scrutinises the political implications of the revival of Karl Polanyi's highly influential but seriously flawed work on the relationship between 'capitalism and democracy'. I analyse Polanyi's work as emblematic of the dominant paradigm about 'capitalism and democracy' in the context of evaluating and comparing a range of other theorists, political movements and historical developments that shaped the twentieth century. Fascism is often depicted as the polar opposite of democracy and as the political form that when market societies suffer from major crises will be embraced by capitalist classes to prevent socialist revolution. With the rise of neo-fascist movements in recent years, what does fascism mean today, and are the earlier forms of Nazi territorial expansionism politically feasible in an age of weapons of mass destruction and the forthcoming demise of the era of fossil fuels? The dominant political paradigm of 'capitalism versus democracy' is based on how the first 'great transformation' or the rise of the 'self-regulated

market' in the nineteenth century supposedly led to the second 'great transformation' of the 1930s in the form of fascism, the American New Deal and
Stalin's Five-Year plans. This paradigm is critically assessed and rejected as
the foundation for understanding the present-day world.

Book Two analyses how and why the dominant Left paradigm has been in
flux for the past few decades. Prominent analysts such as Wolfgang Streeck
and the editors of *New Left Review* have reformulated the old pre-1945 debate
over capitalism's relationship to democracy with specific reference to what
they call the power of the neoliberal 'Hayekian state'. Once again, I use
Streeck and others as convenient examples to illustrate a body of thought
that continues to rely on problematic notions such as 'Fordism', the 'Keynesian welfare state' and their successors like 'post-Fordism'. Despite updating
the pre-1945 conceptions of 'capitalism versus democracy', these contemporary theorists are still very much influenced by the classical theorists from
the 1840s to the 1940s. In focussing on capitalism in its current manifestations, and despite becoming increasingly aware that climate breakdown is
becoming a major crisis, this group of analysts represent the last gasp of the
now old New Left, a global Left that has largely failed to come to terms with
the full implications of environmental sustainability. The ground has literally
been shifting under their feet for decades. They continue to make knee jerk
responses to political and ecological tremors that are no longer merely
delayed 'after shocks' of the extensive shifts to the political tectonic plates
that occurred between 1789 and 1989.

Finally, in Book Three I explore the emerging new political paradigm
required to reconceptualise how environmental factors will affect the relation
between 'capitalism and democracy'. There are no emblematic thinkers or
theories that represent this new emerging political paradigm. All is in flux
and undeveloped. Despite the massively boosted attention paid to ecological
issues, it is remarkable how little this has affected the dominant paradigm of
'capitalism versus democracy' or the discussion of organisational forms, policies and strategies. Conventional political debate over whether the climate
emergency is best resolved by democratic or non-democratic processes will
continue to divide people. Yet, there is also much more to the debate over
'democracy versus sustainability' than only how to deal with the climate
emergency. Whether political movements aim for post-neoliberal reforms
within capitalist countries or the creation of post-capitalist sustainable
democracies, there is a pressing need to discuss the various notions of
democracy and whether they are compatible with sustainable forms of
production and consumption at both the local and the global level. It is

therefore necessary to go beyond the dominant paradigm about 'capitalism and democracy' and explore the complex unfamiliar problems of 'democracy versus sustainability'. I believe that democracy is essential for future sustainability but am critical of the simplistic and problem-ridden accounts of how we can make this goal a feasible reality.

If, as I believe, we will see governments having to increasingly manage and regulate unfolding ecological crises that are beyond the capacity of private capitalist markets to resolve, what does this mean for old debates about planning, democratic sovereignty, social rights versus sustainable resources and the generations-old belief in equality and social justice? How does any resolution of threats to sustainability affect the possibility of providing universal basic services or a universal basic income? If social welfare is currently funded by revenue collected from unsustainable capitalist growth, how is this 'Faustian pact' to be broken in any transition to post-capitalist degrowth? This is a massive problem in developing countries that lack even a rudimentary 'welfare state' but are immersed in a global race of environmentally unsustainable export-orientated industrial development. Can we simply defrost the old conceptions of 'capitalism versus democracy', reheat them and serve this political food as if it is fresh and nutritious? The lessons learnt from how democratic practices have been crushed, thwarted or reduced to a symbolic level are therefore essential preparation for any possible attempt to bring about environmentally sustainable, egalitarian democracies in many if not all countries.

Finally, are the challenges we face simply too large and insurmountable? After surveying radical theory and practice during the past century, anarchists Stevphen Shukaitis and David Graeber quote Eduardo Galeano's observation that: "Utopia is on the horizon: I walk two steps, it takes two steps back. I walk ten steps and it is ten steps further away. What is utopia for? It is for this, for walking." They then ask: "What then is theory for? It is a question that is best answered through walking, through a constant process of circulation and movement that we begin here, following in the footsteps of many who have come before us."[77] While I am not an anarchist and am agnostic when it comes to certain forms of utopian thought, I agree that it is necessary to keep 'walking'. Any construction of a new political, theoretical and activist paradigm demands not only engaging with how 'capitalism versus democracy' has shaped past and present thinking but also how the contradictory elements of 'democracy versus sustainability' need to be recognised as both obstacles and opportunities for new political practices.

BOOK I

THE DOMINANT PARADIGM OF CAPITALISM VERSUS DEMOCRACY

1. FORGET POLANYI! MISREADING THE POLITICAL AND ECONOMIC ORIGINS OF OUR TIME

MORE THAN A CENTURY after the Russian Revolution, it is curious that Hungarian academic Karl Polanyi (1886-1964) is arguably more influential today than either Lenin or Trotsky. Apart from some tiny politically marginalised radical parties, few people turn to Lenin's or Trotsky's analyses of the world or to their model of the vanguard party as either politically relevant or attractive.[1] Yet, why do so many diverse political economic analysts, social movement activists, academics and journalists invoke Polanyi's similarly questionable and historically obsolete analyses? Perhaps his account of early market liberalism bolsters a vague anti-neoliberal sentiment that links those with disparate political perspectives. Given the widely aired view in the media that we are reliving the 1930s, does the return to Polanyi reflect the desire for an explanation of the connection between neoliberal capitalism and the rise of contemporary neo-fascist and other authoritarian movements? One possibility is that Polanyi's popularity is due to his analysis of how the destruction caused by the so-called liberal self-regulated market led to the 'great transformation' of the 1930s which included Roosevelt's New Deal? This political economic transformation of the past is now seen as a precedent for current attempts to replace neoliberalism with a Green New Deal.

Regardless of the likely reasons, Polanyi's work now resonates with many people who are concerned with the troubled state of the world today. While we can admire Polanyi for analysing key issues of his day, I will argue that Polanyi's analytical framework and his answers are highly problematic. Like Lenin's writings directed at specific historical developments, Polanyi work is historically dated and largely inadequate when it comes to trying to understand and change contemporary societies. Nonetheless, his focus on the conflictual relationship between 'capitalism and democracy' remains highly relevant.

Writing about fascism in 1935, Karl Polanyi, like many other socialists of his day, argued that the "mutual incompatibility of Democracy and Capitalism is almost generally accepted today as the background of the social crisis of our time."[2] He went on to assert that there were only two basic solutions to the incompatibility of democracy and capitalism: either democracy must go or capitalism must go. Eighty years later, German sociologist and political economist Wolfgang Streeck repeated Polanyi's two solutions.[3] Whereas Streeck focuses on how capitalism de-democratises societies, particularly those countries within the EU, Polanyi was preoccupied with the violent threat posed by Hitler and other fascists. Hence, he declared:

> Fascism is that solution of the deadlock which leaves Capitalism untouched. The other solution is Socialism. Capitalism goes, Democracy remains. Socialism is the extension of Democracy to the economic sphere.[4]

Although Polanyi preferred socialism, the choice between fascism or socialism hardly exhausted the political options available in capitalist countries before the outbreak of war in 1939 which included Roosevelt's American New Deal, Swedish Social Democracy or British parliamentary democracy. It is important to recognise that in our politically fragmented contemporary world, where even conservative forms of representative democracy endure renewed threats from all kinds of authoritarianism, socialism is once again merely one of several alternative solutions to neo-fascism supported by citizens in different countries.

The revival of fascist and socialist movements in recent years has produced much debate on whether neoliberalism, neo-fascism and socialism are essentially similar or different to pre-1939 'classical' versions of liberalism, fascism and socialism. Within the broad Left that embraces both parliamentary social democrats and radical anti-capitalists, there are a few 'master narratives' which have been knowingly and unknowingly passed down over the years and repeated by numerous political groups and individuals. Polanyi's 'great transformation' is one of these 'master narratives'. His work is not only a useful entry point for evaluating why these narratives need to be questioned, but equally importantly, why we need a much more nuanced and persuasive understanding of the 'origins of our time'. Polanyi's influence in recent years has resulted in a new generation of political analysts and activists repeating many of the political and analytical errors that he and others of his generation made in the 1930s and 1940s, only this time in relation to the character of neoliberalism and its connection to new anti-democratic movements.

While I will discuss a range of publications on Polanyi, I am not interested in Polanyi's work as simply another academic exercise to further Polanyian academic scholarship. Rather, I am interested in Polanyi's thesis about how the 'great transformation' illustrated the conflict between 'capitalism and democracy' and why this very flawed analysis continues to influence contemporary political responses to present day crises. Even though Soviet Communism, fascism and the American New Deal are old defunct regimes, they are not simply historical curiosities. These regimes have had a direct and indirect impact on the re-shaping of the post-1945 world and their influence is still highly visible today. In Book One, I will compare and contrast Polanyi's version of the conflict between 'capitalism and democracy' with other accounts and political theories of capitalism, state institutions and political movements both during his lifetime and right up until the present-day.

THE CURRENT POLANYIAN TURN AND ITS IMPLICATIONS

Thirty years after the outbreak of World War One and in preparation for the post-Second World War era, an agreement on the new international monetary system was shaped at the conference held in the New England village of Bretton Woods in 1944. In the same year, two former members of the defunct Austro-Hungarian Empire both published their most influential books. One was Friedrich Hayek, whose book, *The Road to Serfdom*, helped re-arm a new generation of post-1945 liberals. These were later called neoliberals by their opponents. Hayek's book is still a seminal text for Right-wing defenders of the market. The other was Karl Polanyi (Károly Polányi), who published *The Great Transformation: The Political and Economic Origins of Our Time*.[5] Simultaneously identifying himself as a cosmopolitan and internationalist, Polanyi was also a quasi-Hungarian socialist patriot and supported a form of Christian communitarianism. At different times he adhered to an eclectic mixture of social democratic, Marxist, Christian socialist and other ideas.[6] It is Polanyi's account of 'the political and economic origins' of 'his time' that continues to be widely misconceived by many people as holding a key to the origins of 'our time'.

Although Polanyi lived another twenty years after the publication of *The Great Transformation*, his analytical framework belongs to the dominant paradigm primarily developed by the pre-1939 generation of socialist theorists who analysed why capitalism is either hostile to, or incompatible with democracy. It is claimed that next to Michel Foucault, Polanyi is now one of the most cited theorists in the social sciences and widely discussed by sociologists, political economists and anthropologists.[7] His moral critique of the self-regulating market was one of the first provided by any theorist and is largely responsible for Polanyi's current popularity. Although his moral critique is still relevant, once one delves into more specific details of his overarching analysis, Polanyi's work is revealed as an extremely poor foundation upon which to base an explanation of the profoundly altered socio-political and environmental dynamics of the contemporary world.

Waves of renewed interest in Polanyi's book *The Great Transformation* followed in the decades after his death, first generated by the rise of neoliberalism in the 1970s, then through to the financial crisis of 2008 and the ensuing decade of austerity. It is not just prominent mainstream economists such as Joseph Stiglitz, Mariana Mazzucato and Dani Rodrik who have been influenced by Polanyi.[8] Diverse Left theorists such as Perry Anderson, Colin Crouch, Nancy Fraser, Jürgen Habermas, David Harvey, Thomas Piketty and Wolfgang Streeck also admire Polanyi, although not endorsing all of his ideas.[9] Many European social democrats and liberal-Left American Democrats as well as environmentalists such as Naomi Klein[10], and George Monbiot[11] plus philanthropist George Soros or conservative critics of neoliberalism like John Gray[12] reference Polanyi to advance the case for either a socially regulated 'civilised capitalism' or a post-capitalist socialist or green society. As testimony of his reach, *The Atlantic's* contributing editor, Heather Horn, even argued that Pope Francis' first Apostolic Exhortation in 2013 was very close to Polanyi's critique of the market.[13] Moreover, within the context of post-2008 austerity-driven crises affecting the US and the EU, one critic proclaimed in 2015: 'Why Brussels Needs to Read Karl Polanyi',[14] while analysts in the US associated Polanyi with Bernie Sanders' 2016 presidential campaign.[15]

In recent years, Polanyi's anti-fascist contemporaries, Theodore Adorno and Antonio Gramsci, have been reinterpreted and appropriated by the alt-Right and assorted neo-fascists in order to justify their 'counter-hegemonic' attacks on 'neoliberal elites' and the 'culture industry' which they claim has produced so-called 'effeminate men'.[16] Even though Polanyi originally directed his analysis against the rise of fascism, he has also been utilised by Marine Le Pen, the leader of the French neo-fascist National Front (renamed National Rally), in her campaign against the EU.[17] Equally startling, is that despite Polanyi's long preoccupation with critiquing liberal capitalism, in 2016, Nicolas Colin, French promoter of venture capitalists and co-founder of European investment firm *The Family*, rejected Polanyi's own description of the target of his work. Instead, Colin argued that *The Great Transformation* is "really about the social and economic institutions that are necessary to support the market system and to make economic development more sustainable and inclusive."[18] Influenced by an eclectic range of theorists (including Carlota Perez, Mariana Mazzucato and other analysts of the relationship between technology and 'the Entrepreneurial State'[19]), Colin asserted that "we are currently going through another 'Great Transformation', this time from the Fordist economy to the digital economy."[20] Moreover, in his distorted political analysis, Colin proclaimed that in "this new Polanyi moment, Entrepreneurs form a vanguard" against Jeremy Corbyn and Bernie Sanders on the Left and Nigel Farage on the Right who all wish to return to 'Fordism' and a 'regressive corporatism'.[21]

Given that we live in a world of 'fake news' and political appropriation from antithetical sources, it is not surprising that the ideas of influential figures such Adorno, Gramsci and Polanyi can be made to advance political agendas that they personally detested. Whatever the serious flaws in Polanyi's work, and despite his contemporary use by liberals, social democrats, greens, entrepreneurs and even neo-fascists, it is important to remind ourselves that Polanyi strongly criticised capitalism and that without question, he championed a democratic socialist society.

The first five decades of the twentieth century were certainly very bloody and volatile. It is not surprising that many people changed their political views. Polanyi also switched political positions on several occasions and either supported or opposed Marxism, social democracy, Stalinism and Roosevelt's New Deal. Given that few of his political contemporaries from either the Left or the Right are still read today, is it the fluid state of contemporary politics or Polanyi's actual ideas that prompt so many with opposing political perspectives to continue to find something of value in his work? At best, Polanyi was only on the fringe of the emerging New Left in the late 1950s and early 1960s.[22] Had he lived, it is hard to imagine that Polanyi would have also become an icon of the New Left like his contemporary, Herbert Marcuse. The reason being that Polanyi was culturally conservative, too aligned with or imbued with the strange mixture of Christian socialist, old style interwar social democracy and later Cold War sympathy for the Soviet sphere. These positions were at odds with emerging New Left alternative cultural politics that rejected both capitalism and Soviet Communism, and with a New Left that also later promoted new forms of feminism and environmentalism. If the New Left generation of 1968 (including this author) now confront a different world to that of the late 1960s and early 1970s, Polanyi's pre-New Left views are even more remote to contemporary green and identity politics (even though admired by some environmentalists). They are equally remote to post-Cold War debates about what could or should replace neoliberal globalisation, including ideas about post-work societies, degrowth and other new socio-cultural issues related to the 'digital society'.

When considering Karl Polanyi's most notable work, *The Great Transformation*, it is understandable why many people are seduced by his grand narrative of the rise and decline of the self-regulated market and hence attempt to apply it to the rise of neoliberalism and the various forms of opposition to these dominant policies.[23] Polanyi's *magnum opus* contains illuminating insights concerning the interaction between the early development of liberal capitalist markets and related political, cultural and social practices and ideas. Unfortunately, it also displays a range of dubious historical interpretations and concepts that rest on Polanyi's overly schematic explanation of the rise and subsequent crisis of liberal capitalism. Just as Polanyi announced at the beginning of *The Great Transformation* that 'nineteenth century civilisation has collapsed',[24] so too, much of Polanyi's world and his analytical apparatus has long been either rendered historically redundant or else insufficiently reliable even when it was originally written.

Of course, we do not know what Polanyi would have thought of the massively changed world we confront today, let alone what political agenda, if any, he would have supported had he lived well beyond 1964 to see the rise of neoliberalism, the collapse of Eastern European Communism, the withering of many social democratic parties and the emergence of powerful non-Western capitalist powers. We certainly cannot blame Polanyi for the way he is currently used to justify an entire range of antithetical policies and contradictory social objectives. Take for instance, the fact that EU-sceptics on both the Left and Right calling for the break-up of the European Union similarly invoke Polanyi, while other admirers use his work to champion the opposite goal, namely, the extensive social democratisation of the EU.

All theorists are shaped and limited by their own historical environment and knowledge. Some surmount their origins by offering concepts and analyses that continue to remain insightful. Polanyi asked some especially important questions but his analytical framework and answers are largely of marginal use when applied to the contemporary world.[25] Although in what follows is an extremely critical analysis of his work, very importantly, my critique of Polanyi is *not* a rejection of what impelled and motivated him to write. On the contrary, he *is* to be admired for trying to explain and surmount the highly negative and violently disruptive social impact of capitalist markets and the political forces that constructed and sustained these market societies.

Nonetheless, we must ask: why do various anti-neoliberals continue to use Polanyi as a substitute for developing a more comprehensive understanding and critique of contemporary capitalist societies? Indeed, some opponents of neoliberalism go as far as to claim that 'Karl Polanyi explains it all' and that he is "the 20th century's most prophetic critic of capitalism".[26] As a 'prophet' he apparently not only anticipated modern environmentalism but can also help restore full employment and the welfare state by leading us out of the wilderness created by neoliberalism. By contrast, even fervent admirers, such as Fred Block and Margaret Somers, conclude that Polanyi "was very much a failed prophet."[27] I go further and argue that his failed predictions were not accidental or psychological. Instead, it is crucial to recognise that Polanyi was completely wrong in several of his major assessments and predictions about regimes and political trends because this was a direct outcome of the serious flaws in his analytical framework.

Benedetto Croce famously said that "all history is contemporary history" and, as historian Martin Jay notes, "no past context is manifest without its current reconstruction, which is an active not passive process."[28] Hence, my critique of Polanyi is an active reaction against contemporary reconstructions of his work, especially those who overly inflate his political relevance to our contemporary world. Introducing the 2001 edition of Polanyi's major work, leading Polanyi scholar Fred Block claimed that, "after more than a half a century *The Great Transformation* remains fresh in many ways. Indeed, it is indispensable for understanding the dilemmas facing global society at the beginning of the twenty-first century."[29] I agree with Block that Karl Polanyi is to be respected as a strong critic of earlier capitalist practices. However, it is misleading and a gross exaggeration to claim that Polanyi's book is 'indispensable' for understanding the dilemmas facing global society at the beginning of the twenty-first century. In 2018, English academic, Christopher Holmes, echoed Block and other admirers of Polanyi by arguing that *The Great Transformation* has become a canonical text in international political economy. Holmes claims that it has influenced analysis of the 'big issues' such as neoliberalism, globalisation, financial market practices, the EU, climate change and the role of the state.[30] This is true, but Holmes also admits that apart from Polanyi's analysis and concepts being ambiguous, unclear and lacking precision, he concedes that "most major parts of his conceptual and empirical scheme have been shown to be problematic in one way or another over the years."[31] If so, why do so many contemporary analysts resurrect Polanyi only to conclude that we need a 'post-Polanyian' analysis?

Unfortunately, popularity is not equivalent to insightfulness. On closer examination, despite Polanyi being widely used, he throws very little or no light on contemporary big issues such as the structure and character of global inequality, the rise and changes to neoliberal policies and practices, why contemporary financialisation processes are quite different to the role of finance capital in the interwar years, not to mention major crises such as climate breakdown, the emergence of new powerful rivals to Atlantic geopolitical powers, the ongoing crises within the EU, as well as the emergence of major technological and social problems that Polanyi and his generation could not have even imagined.

BRIDGES AND BREAKS

Today, many advocates of greater social justice and sustainable environments are confused and disturbed by the negative changes in capitalist societies over recent decades. Some keep one foot in the present and the other in the past; their part-immersion in a bygone era that pre-dates our common lived reality sustains both anger and pain. One sign of this failure to adequately confront new global realities is that growing numbers of the broad Left have tried to make sense of present-day life by returning to Polanyi's timeworn analysis of nineteenth and early twentieth century liberal capitalism. Yet, if the aim is to construct future post-carbon sustainable societies that are socially just and democratic, there are abundant reasons why turning to Karl Polanyi is not the answer.

The fact that we live in a new historical conjuncture that is quite different to the world described in *The Great Transformation* is not to deny the presence of many bridges to the past. These simultaneous connections to an earlier era alongside substantial clear breaks with the past are what makes the present-day world so confusing to many people. As history does not repeat itself, the contemporary application of Polanyi's theory is sometimes stretched so far as to be farcical at best and misleading at worst. Contemporary supporters of historical ideas formed generations ago, such as self-regulated liberalism, Marxism and Keynesianism, still remain locked in policy battles and give the appearance that we are reliving the first half of the twentieth century. The key point to remember is that while former ideas may still be active, the socio-economic and political terrain where they strive for dominance is completely different. Economist John Quiggin has observed that:

> Ideas are long lived, often outliving their originators and taking new
> and different forms. Some ideas live on because they are useful.
> Others die and are forgotten. But even when they have proved them-
> selves wrong and dangerous, ideas are very hard to kill. Even after the
> evidence seems to have killed them, they keep on coming back. These
> ideas are neither alive nor dead; rather, as Paul Krugman has said,
> they are undead, or zombie, ideas.[32]

Polanyi's work is relevant to many because of his strong critique of self-regulated capitalism. This is particularly true for those who take the *ideology* of market fundamentalists at face value and believe that liberal capitalism has been somehow *reincarnated* as neoliberalism. Sadly, many who use Polanyi to understand and decode contemporary neoliberalism risk overlooking fundamental methodological and political problems. Comprehending the complexity of societies dominated by neoliberal values and practices may possibly help to partially understand earlier, less complex forms of liberal capitalist societies. Still, we should not project contemporary concepts back onto earlier social and economic relations and misrecognise these as merely less developed present-day forms.[33] Conversely, it is equally flawed to project the specific historical analysis and concepts that Polanyi used to understand early liberal capitalism onto much more complex contemporary capitalist societies. Such a method loses sight of crucial differences and profoundly changed circumstances.

The ideological residues of pre-1945 European socialism, communism or fascism (such as Polanyi's moral critique of liberal capitalism) live on just as do monarchies or old religions like the Church of England. These ideological relics of a bygone age can still resonate and activate the political mobilisation of small groups, but they cannot supply the political solutions needed to solve quite diverse types of socio economic and environmental crises in present-day Europe, the US or globally.

Importantly, one must not confuse the rhetoric of current advocates of self-regulated free markets with the dominant forms of contemporary capitalism. The actual policies and practices pursued by governments and key business policy makers influenced by neoliberal ideas are certainly not laissez-faire. There is no doubting the widespread marketisation and privatisation of many government utilities and agencies over the past few decades. Bernardo Bortolotti and Domenico Siniscalco found that between 1977 and 1999 there were 1,415 full or partial privatisations of state-owned assets in developed capitalist countries alone.[34] The privatisation of public sector assets has often created new private monopolies and oligopolies benefiting private shareholders alongside decreasing public control over important industry sectors. Yet, privatisation of state assets is of itself not equivalent to a full return to earlier forms of self-regulation or liberal capitalism. Contemporary state apparatuses continue to play highly regulatory roles. Notably, these regulatory roles are different to those which existed both before the 1970s and before the 1930s.

One of the reasons it is a mistake to see neoliberalism as a return to pre-1930s laissez-faire is because the period 1945 to 1975 was actually never characterised by the universal institutionalisation of democratic control or full state regulation in the first place. This is not the place for a detailed analysis of which industries and institutions as well as which socio-economic practices were either substantially regulated or left relatively untouched during the past century. Crucially, the actual political economic reality we confront today is that apart from a minority of market fundamentalists, most neoliberal policy makers, while strong opponents of socialism, actually practise what Polanyi could only assert in theory. That is, neoliberal governments fully realise that the goal of a self-regulated market preached by market fundamentalists has always been utopian and in the present world (compared to the nineteenth century) *would be even more impractical, undesirable and highly dangerous for the enduring stability of capitalist societies.*

Contemporary societies are not homogenous and certainly do not constitute a return to an early form of self-regulated liberalism. Rather, present-day societies are the outcome of political struggles and the emergence of new national and supranational policies and institutional practices designed to simultaneously manage both national and international problems – contemporary issues with which Polanyi was largely unfamiliar. Many admirers of Polanyi cite his focus on the role of the state rather than simply on the mode

of production like orthodox Marxists. However, apart from repeating generalities about how the state helped institutionalise liberal capitalism, Polanyi's
work lacks even a rudimentary analysis of the variety of crucial roles played
by state institutions.

The 'master paradigm' of 'capitalism versus democracy' underwent significant changes in the 1970s. Marxists argued that the deep-seated causes of the
1973-75 crisis had been brewing for years. By contrast, mainstream economists and the media attributed the major recession of 1973-75 to stock
market fears following the breakdown of the post-war Bretton Woods monetary system in 1971/2, plus the substantial increase in oil prices (known as the
'oil shock'). While oil prices certainly played a part, more fundamental problems were ignored or played down. International trade and national production systems suffered a decline in profitability caused by overproduction,
militant demands by labour and new social movements all seeking improved
working conditions as well as better public services and more social justice
and social recognition, to name just a few causal factors. To regenerate profitable growth, corporations and business groups reacted by demanding that
governments restrain social demands by cutting taxes and expenditure on
public services as well as implementing pro-market deregulatory and
privatising policies. The new era of neoliberalism had begun.

In broad terms, there is much that is valid about this 'master narrative'.
Nevertheless, it is important not to homogenise political economic disputes
and to overlook significant socio-economic, legal-administrative and political
differences within capitalist societies. Not all businesses eagerly embraced
zealous neoliberal policies. Significant divisions between different sectors of
business in a range of countries were evident. For instance, in those countries
where manufacturing businesses had stable corporatist arrangements with
unions over wage increases and work conditions, business leaders were reluctant to destabilise production compared to those in other sectors such as
finance that sought the liberalisation of state controls on the international
flow of capital. Also, in the years 1973 to the mid-1990s there were a range of
hard Right regimes in various countries. Take for example, Pinochet's
outright brutal dictatorship in Chile or Thatcher's parliament-approved
privatisation of public utilities and industries, plus the militarised smashing
of the miner's strike. Yet, in this emerging neoliberal era, we also had
contrary or less uniform developments such as the move to the centre/Left
after the collapse of dictatorships in Greece, Spain and Portugal, as well as
the extension of some features of the social state in various countries. For
instance, France legislated the 35-hour week and nationalised many private

businesses in 1982 even as the Mitterand government later increased unemployment and inequality by moving Right on other policies. Meanwhile in China, a new hybrid state/capitalist giant was emerging on the global stage that neither conformed to conventional Left notions of neoliberalism nor to communism.

By the beginning of the twenty-first century, most governments in OECD countries were dominated by aggressive market values and practices even though, very importantly, there had been no wholesale reversion to pre-1914 social policies and no restoration of laissez-faire and the minimalist 'nightwatchman state'. Discussing the growth of the social state (such as welfare, education and health) during the twentieth century, Thomas Piketty observed that while not all revenue was spent on the social state:

> Total tax revenues were less than 10 per cent of national income in rich countries until 1900-1910; they represent between 30 per cent and 55 per cent of national income in 2000-2010.[35]

Tony Blair consolidated Thatcher's economic framework as well as increasing expenditure on some social protection policies, as did other governments in Europe and Latin America (such as Brazil) which were then run by Left-of-centre 'pink tide' parties. Instead of restoring the so-called pre-1930s liberal state (although historically there was never a uniform version of the 'liberal state'), Right-wing and centre/Left governments in developed countries implemented a range of complex state institutional restructuring and social disciplining measures to shore up business profitability within the constrained political conditions of different electoral processes and fluctuating balance of power relations. Nonetheless, a familiar variety of symptoms appeared but differed in their scale and intensity. These included varying increases in levels of inequality, government and business corruption, outright criminality and lies dressed up as 'spin' that globally caused untold loss of life, not to mention deceptions with tragic consequences such as the 'weapons of mass destruction'. The lack of enforcement or erosion of regulatory standards across many industries like pharmaceuticals and health provision, food standards, industry pollution, toxicity and carcinogens that depended on both the political profile of national governments and supra-national laws. The latter either pandered to the needs of industry lobbyists or feared monitoring by active social movements.

Additionally, governments of both the centre/Left and centre/Right implemented varying degrees of public sector cuts and market rationalising policies. Most did *not* savagely dismantle social welfare, education and health institutions but instead transformed the latter by introducing more means-tested and targeted welfare rather than universal entitlements, as well as marketizing and outsourcing the delivery of services. Some governments, like those in the US, blatantly increased the misery of the poor under the 'work-fare' policies of presidents from Reagan onwards. Unlike governments in Europe and Australia, the US had never established comparable levels of the social state (such as a universal public health system) in the first place. Consequently, despite the occasional inchoate and unsuccessful protest such as the Occupy movement, there has been a relative absence of massive oppositional protest movements against neoliberalism. By contrast, few protest movements have rivalled the responses of the populace to the savage attacks on living conditions and public services carried out in Greece prior to 2015. Even so, the Greek fate has not been the fate of most other OECD countries although very high unemployment prevails in Spain and other Mediterranean countries and Covid-19 has caused massive unemployment globally.

Leaving aside the brief rise and decline/stagnation of Left movements such as *Syriza* and *Podemos*, it has been Right-wing racist parties (called 'populist') that have risen on the back of failed domestic neoliberal policies and the human cost of regional wars in the form of mass refugees. Not only has the depth of economic crises varied greatly, but so too has the imposition of policies ranging from Great Depression style austerity in Greece or Argentina, to less severe forms of marketisation of public services and job cuts in other countries. These policy variations are part of the reason why the strength of anti-capitalist movements has fluctuated and failed to mobilise majorities of national electorates during the past few decades.

THE GREAT TRANSFORMATION: FROM LIBERAL MARKET TO FASCISM

What was 'the great transformation' and why is this particular 'master narrative' so problematic when it comes to understanding the prevailing debates about 'capitalism versus democracy'? Any understanding of democracy – whether it is liberal democracy (called 'bourgeois democracy' by Marxists) or various alternative socialist, green or other models – must have a conception of the institutional and socio-economic foundations of past and present forms of democracy, how they came into being, what challenges they faced and what are the future prospects for further democratisation. Polanyi's account of the rise of democracy in market societies and their suppression by fascism actually rested on not one, but *two* transformations. First, he devoted a large part of his book to a description of the emergence of liberal capitalist societies and ideas from the eighteenth century to the first half of the nine-teenth century. Focusing on Great Britain, Polanyi argued that the advocates of the new market economy wished to free the market from any social, moral or natural constraints. Instead of established 'organic' social practices shaping economic relations, a disembedded economy now began to subordi-nate 'organic social relations', thereby transforming pre-capitalist society into a 'market society'.[36]

According to Polanyi, the First World War brought about the end of nineteenth century civilisation as the destruction it unleashed eventually culminated in the 'great transformation' of the 1930s. From the opening page of *The Great Transformation*, he presents the reader with four foundations of nineteenth-century civilization: the balance of power system that since 1815 prevented long wars between the European Great Powers; the international gold standard; the self-regulating market; and the liberal state. "Classified in one way, two of these institutions were economic, two political. Classified in another way, two of them were national, two international."[37] Polanyi goes on to make some highly questionable claims:

> ...Of these institutions the gold standard proved crucial; its fall was the proximate cause of the catastrophe. By the time it failed, most of the other institutions had been sacrificed in a vain effort to save it. But the fount and matrix of the system was the self-regulating market. It was this innovation which gave rise to a specific civilization. The gold standard was merely an attempt to extend the domestic market system to the international field; the balance-of-power system was a superstructure erected upon and, partly, worked through the gold standard; the liberal state was itself a creation of the self-regulating market.[38]

First of all, while most historians would agree that the nineteenth century European balance of power system collapsed, they would reject Polanyi's claim that the cause of the catastrophic First World War and the sacrifice of the balance of power system was made in a vain effort to save the gold stan-dard and the self-regulated market. Next, to describe the imperialist political and territorial advances made by the Great Powers (between 1815 and 1914) as 'a superstructure erected upon and, partly, worked through the gold standard' is an example of the crude economism that Polanyi rightly criticised orthodox Marxists for in other parts of his work. Imperial ambitions would have been pursued regardless of the gold standard and the trade it facilitated. Of note, Polanyi had a contradictory relationship to the prevalent 'mechanical Marxism' of his day; he fluctuated between either rejecting economic determinism or accepting the problematic model of the economic 'base' determining the political and cultural 'superstructure'. Not only is the base/superstructure model a crude method to explain socio-economic and political relationships, but it was rejected by some of Polanyi's Marxist contemporaries and later on by most post-1960s Marxists and neo-Marxists. Even the economic determinists of Polanyi's day would have not agreed that the gold standard was a 'base' upon which the balance of power 'superstructure' was erected.

As the post-gold standard world of recent decades has confirmed, gold like money is not indispensable to international trade but rather a symbolic medium that can be replaced with other exchangeable currencies or symbols. Present-day market societies facilitate trade and investment through digital, cashless transactions, financial derivatives or new forms of bitcoin based on political economic agreement as to the intrinsic value that the new exchange currencies represent. Polanyi was correct in showing the important role of central banks and other institutional networks as well as emphasising the widespread political belief, prior to 1931, that the gold standard was indispensable. But he was fundamentally wrong in arguing that without the gold standard, international capitalism would be unable to function. In fact, Polanyi had to qualify his sweeping claim by citing that because of the strength of the US currency and financial market as well as Great Britain's disproportionately large share of world trade, both were not as affected as other countries by the demise of the gold standard.[39]

Further, his claim that 'the liberal state was itself a creation of the self-regulating market' is another example of crude economism and contradicted one of Polanyi's central theses, namely, that the liberal market could not have come into being without the liberal state coercing society by implementing the laws and institutional arrangements necessary for the creation of a 'market society'. Take away Polanyi's emphasis on how the liberal state helped create the liberal market ('laissez-faire was planned'[40]) and it is impossible to understand his most widely quoted pronouncement, namely, that without the state "the idea of a self-adjusting market implied a stark Utopia. Such an institution could not exist for any length of time without annihilating the human and natural substance of society; it would have physically destroyed man and transformed his surroundings into a wilderness."[41] While

I agree with Polanyi on this point, crucially, he never tells us how long a 'self-adjusting' market could survive or even if such a self-regulated market ever actually existed.

Instead, there seem to be two Karl Polanyis writing differing accounts that contradict each other. He constantly and simultaneously attacked self-regulated liberal capitalism for all the problems it had caused, and yet argued that this 'self-regulated market' was *a utopian goal* because the state was indispensable in creating and sustaining market mechanisms. In Chapter Five, I will develop this point by discussing the critical issue of the way the 'liberal state' is depicted in overgeneralised terms by Polanyi and many of his admirers who ignore the complex character and differing roles of a range of actual historical state institutions.

In *The Age of Surveillance Capitalism*, Shoshana Zuboff admires Polanyi as a "great historian".[42] This he certainly was not. Actually, Polanyi proudly claimed that his thesis was "not a historical work".[43] Instead, his four schematic foundations of nineteenth century civilisation were both arbitrary and ahistorical as he tried to squeeze in all those historical socio-economic developments which, on closer inspection, conflicted with his contentious framework. Little wonder that these exaggerated concepts provided such a poor guide to twentieth century history and became untenable as he slid from one explanation to another. Polanyi gives far too much historical weight to the gold standard, for example. This is a mistaken emphasis repeated by admirers of Polanyi's work, such as Wolfgang Streeck, who also inflates the importance of the Euro (as a modern form of gold standard) which he sees as one of the central causes of de-democratisation within the EU, as I will examine in Chapters Seven and Eight.

Part of the reason for Polanyi's lack of clarity is that he wanted to explain two separate phenomena: the rise and fall of nineteenth century self-regulated capitalism and secondly, how fascism emerged from the conflict between 'capitalism and democracy'. The first 'great transformation' of pre-market society into liberal market society was followed by the second 'great transformation'. Polanyi argued that it was during the 1920s and the 1930s that the liberal state and the so-called self-regulated market fought for survival on two fronts: against the immediate post-1917 threat of Communist revolution and concerted reform movements on the one side, and against rising fascist movements on the other. I will leave aside for the moment that Polanyi (and he is not alone in this) thinks of 'the market' and 'the state' as akin to human subjects that act and speak with one voice. During the 1930s, Polanyi claimed that it was Roosevelt's New Deal, the Soviet Five-Year Plans and Hitler's political economic controls that ended the self-regulated market. This thesis was hardly new, as leading German sociologist Karl Mannheim (with whom Polanyi was familiar) had a decade earlier in 1935 already analysed the end of laissez faire and the need for 'planned democracy'.[44] In contrast to many of Polanyi's current admirers who see neoliberalism as a revival of pre-1930s liberalism, Polanyi believed that laissez-faire had come to an end. Moreover, his analytical categories lacked historical and political economic rigour leaving readers unclear about whether laissez-faire and liberal capitalism were identical or separate.

With the outcome of the war still not confirmed in 1943 as he sent off the book for publication in 1944, Polanyi speculated on what the 'great transformation' would produce in the post-war world. He hoped that democratic socialism would succeed rather than either fascism, Soviet one-party Communism or versions of Roosevelt's New Deal regulated capitalism. Two years later in 1945, even before the promise of Roosevelt's New Deal was replaced by Cold War antagonisms, Polanyi was pessimistic about the US ever establishing an adequate social protectionist, embedded economy.[45] In contrast, Ludwig von Mises, one of the key ideologues of the free market, wrote in 1944 that the New Deal was destroying democracy and instituting 'tyrannical bureaucratism'.[46] Similarly, Joseph Schumpeter, another champion of the market who long detested the New Deal, thought in 1949 that the US was becoming socialist![47]

Today, all three regimes that constituted what Polanyi called the 'great transformation' of the 1930s have long collapsed or significantly changed. They each met with different fates. Hitler's regime was the first to be destroyed in 1945. While the Soviet system officially ended in 1991, aspects of its administrative, repressive and cultural legacy lives on in new forms. Similarly, key parts of the New Deal were either curbed or unevenly dismantled between the 1940s and the 1990s, despite President Johnson's mid-1960s attempt to revive social aspects of the New Deal under the name of 'the Great Society'. In fact, the rise and fall of these regimes can be explained without Polanyi's schematic thesis of the 'great transformation'. Moreover, Polanyi's predictions for the post-war world did not eventuate, thus leaving his contemporary admirers with highly unreliable concepts that are ill-equipped as ways to understand the present-day world. I will now try to critically evaluate the three regimes at the heart of Polanyi's 'great transformation' and why we need a much better explanation of the changing relationship between 'capitalism and democracy' than that offered by Polanyi and many of his admirers.

FALSE HOPE AND POLITICAL BLINDNESS

Despite acknowledging that the Soviet regime was a dictatorship and that socialism had yet to be fully developed, Polanyi still strongly adhered – from the 1930s until his death – to the ideological notion that the USSR was a 'socialist society'. His fear of fascism before 1945 and his hostility to American capitalism during the Cold War helped cement his admiration of Stalinism. Once again, he was not alone in mistaking the USSR as 'socialist' or a 'workers' state' simply because major enterprises were state-owned and market practices were curtailed. This gross mistake is repeated today by all those who continue to call China, Vietnam, Laos, Cuba and North Korea 'socialist'.[48]

Like many other socialists, Polanyi had been a strong critic of the new Bolshevik regime because of his dislike of Lenin's and Trotsky's political tactics and their suppression of other parties. However, during the 1930s, Polanyi's fear of fascism led him to invest far too much hope in Stalin's regime. As with many of his generation, he condemned the suffering caused by capitalist markets and longed for a new socialist world. While not a Communist Party member, Polanyi's hope and fear overwhelmed his judgement and he was unable to distance himself from Soviet propaganda. Vivian Gornick captures well the mixture of faith, activism and blindness that Communist parties across the world inspired during the 1930s and 1940s. Writing about American Communists, she observes: "While it is true that the majority joined the Communist Party in those years because they were members of the hard-pressed working class (garment district Jews, West Virginia miners, California fruit-pickers), it was even truer that many more in the educated middle class (teachers, scientists, writers) joined because for them, too, the party was possessed of a moral authority that lent concrete shape to a sense of social injustice made urgent by the Great Depression and World War II."[49]

Paradoxically, the more that Stalin crushed the last vestiges of domestic criticism inside the Soviet Union, the more that Polanyi became a staunch supporter of Stalin's authoritarianism. His gullibility included illusions about the USSR becoming more democratic in the 1930s precisely as the terror was unleashed. He preferred instead to accept the propaganda verdicts of Stalin's 1930s terror-propelled 'show trials', even when his own niece Eva became a victim in 1936.[50] Despite some criticisms of the Soviet system during the 1950s and early 1960s (especially after the crushing of the 1956 Hungarian revolt by Khrushchev), incredibly, Polanyi still remained a supporter of the

USSR as the leader of the 'socialist world'. He naïvely held out hope that Khrushchev would democratise the Soviet Union.[51]

Polanyi was consistent in his misreading of Soviet politics and his misconception of the Russian revolution and its later development. His four foundations of nineteenth century civilisation led him to see two Russian revolutions rather than one. The so-called first Russian Revolution of November 1917 was a purely Russian event that "achieved the destruction of absolutism, feudal land tenure, and racial oppression – a true heir to the ideals of 1789."[52] The second revolution that started with the collectivisation of farms and the Five-Year Plan, would help bring about socialism and "formed part of a simultaneous universal transformation."[53] It is true that the collapse of Czarism and the Bolshevik seizure of power in 1917 led to the destruction of absolutism and feudal land tenure. Racial or ethnic oppression may have been condemned officially, however, the Union of Soviet Socialist Republics varied from granting cultural autonomy to minorities (within the confines of Communist Party control) to fluctuating levels of Russification or 'great Russian chauvinism' right through to the dissolution of the USSR in 1991. It is Polanyi's sweeping abstract thesis about the rise and fall of laissez-faire combined with his flawed political analysis that resulted in his equation of the Russian Revolution with the English Civil War and the French Revolution. What made the Russian revolution so different from the English and French experiences is that historically new forms of party-state institutions or apparatuses were inaugurated based on the Communist Party, the Red Army, planning ministries and internal security forces.

Instead of recognising this new type of state institutional system, Polanyi erroneously asserted that it is "not usually realized that the Bolsheviks, though ardent socialists themselves, stubbornly refused to 'establish socialism in Russia.'"[54] What he both misread and minimised were the internal conflicts between factions within the ruling party/state between 1922 and 1928 over the rate of industrialisation and collectivisation. These party conflicts reflected debates over whether socialist industrialisation and agricultural policies could be implemented under extremely unfavourable conditions without also exacting a massive human price to be paid by peasants and workers. Polanyi overlooked that Stalin's so-called 'building of socialism' in the 1930s would have been impossible without the construction and institutionalisation of the new Soviet state apparatuses between 1917 and the early 1920s. The nationalisation of industry and the reorganisation of all aspects of military, economic, social and cultural life made the new Soviet state fundamentally different to both its Czarist predecessor and the 'liberal state' and self-regulated market into which Polanyi tried to fit both nineteenth century Russian and early Soviet history prior to the 1930s.

Paradoxically,   Polanyi   adopted   the   Comintern's   (Communist International) division of history into three periods: the first from 1917 to approximately 1923 covered War Communism in the USSR and the failed revolutionary outbreaks in Central Europe. It also included the 1921 New Economic Plan (partial re-establishment of market mechanisms) alongside state nationalisation and control of industry, to ensure that sufficient food alleviated mass starvation caused by civil war. The second period 1924 to 1928 covered the decline of revolutionary activity in Europe and the need to consolidate Bolshevik power within the USSR. The notorious third period from 1928 to 1935 was characterised by a disastrous sectarianism in which the Comintern predicted a major economic crisis in world capitalism and instructed Communists to attack the non-Communist Left as 'social fascists'. I say paradoxically here because Polanyi as a non-Communist was undoubtedly labelled a 'social fascist' while in Vienna, even though a few years later he was hailing Stalin as the 'builder of socialism'.

ILLUSIONS ABOUT THE SOVIET STATE

The cause of the so-called 'second Russian revolution' is largely misunderstood by Polanyi because he focused on the 'great transformation' of liberal capitalism rather than the significantly different conditions and policy disputes inside the USSR that did not fit his overall thesis. While the Soviets survived military invasion by the major powers in the early years of the revolution, the inability of the League of Nations to prevent Japanese, Italian and German expansionism and rearmament in the 1930s certainly put pressure on the Bolsheviks to rapidly industrialise. Both Weimar Germany and the USSR were treated as pariahs by the victorious powers in the interwar years. Polanyi, like most of the world, was unaware that the Red Army and Reichswehr signed a secret agreement after 1922 which permitted the German military to test modern equipment inside the USSR in return for German industrial aid to modernise Soviet industry, such as tank production in Leningrad. From 1925 to autumn 1933 (nine months after Hitler came to power), Stalin had allowed thousands of German military pilots to be trained at a secret military air base at Lipetsk. The Soviet leadership's misreading of German politics during the 1920s and 1930s (especially its twists and turns over how it treated the non-Communist Left before 1933) and subsequent domestic purges of Soviet military, engineers and loyal Bolsheviks between 1935 and 1940 would lead to a catastrophic unpreparedness for the Nazi invasion in June 1941.

As to the first Five-Year plan, Polanyi argued that "the inability of the world market to absorb Russia's agricultural produce, forced her reluctantly into the paths of self-sufficiency. Socialism in one country was brought about by the incapacity of market economy to provide a link between all countries; what appeared as Russian autarchy was merely the passing of capitalist internationalism."[55] This assessment was fundamentally wrong on at least two grounds. First, 'socialism in one country' was advocated by Stalin in 1924 while capitalist societies were experiencing not 'the passing of capitalist internationalism' but the boom of the 'roaring twenties' prior to the Depression of the 1930s. Unemployment may have been very high in European countries, but many businesses boomed and traded, especially those in the US.

Additionally, since the early 1920s, there had been major debates inside the Soviet Communist Party over reviving industry after the civil war, preventing the hoarding of grain by richer peasants and the demand by the Left Opposition to replace the NEP with policies that countered new class divisions. It was not, as Polanyi claimed, that the Bolsheviks leaders 'stubbornly refused to establish socialism in Russia', but that Stalin, Bukharin and others constituting the majority initially opposed Left Bolshevik demands and then Stalin swung around to these policies after removing Trotsky and the 'oppositionists' by 1927. Importantly, by 1927, it was not 'the incapacity of the world market to absorb Russia's agricultural produce' but rather the serious shortage of food in the cities (due to hoarding by peasants and other factors) that forced the Soviet government to act on the shortfall of two million tons of grain.

Following the chaos of the initial implementation of collectivisation (from September to December 1929) *Pravda* printed Stalin's famous cautionary article 'Dizzy with Success' on March 2, 1930, warning about the 'excessive zeal' shown by 'Party comrades'. When writing *The Great Transformation,* Polanyi was so enamoured with Stalin's policies that he said nothing about the horrors of collectivisation resulting in 1.8 to 4.5 million 'kulaks' being deported and killed, even though the horrors (but not the scale of the statistics) had been reported in the Western media. He was also unaware of or silent about the approximately eight million people who died or suffered from the ensuing major famine in 1932-33 – a total of 4 to 14 million deaths depending on more recently uncovered sources used and the ideological disposition of the assessor.[56] We will never know the exact figure of the millions who died on 'the slaughter bench of history', to use Hegel's words. But we do know that such was the devastating scale and extent of the destruction wreaked by forced rapid collectivisation (a veritable civil war resulting in farmers killing their own animals and burning crops followed by mass deportations), that livestock numbers did not recover to 1928 levels until the late 1950s.[57]

What Polanyi saw as 'two revolutions' was in fact only one, but with different emphases and stages supported by different factions in the Party. The reverberations of the horrific human and environmental cost of rapid collectivisation and industrialisation and the associated Stalinist terror is something that affected the whole future of the USSR. Globally, Stalin's brutality discredited the reputation of communism to the extent that communism is still shunned by most of the world's population. What was seen by Polanyi and many Western 'fellow travellers' as 'building socialism', in fact became a 'time bomb' eventually undermining the viability of the Soviet Union and East European Communist regimes in the four decades after 1945.

Along with millions of Western supporters of the new 'Soviet civilisation' who rejected the shocking poverty and irrationality of market forces that caused the Great Depression, Polanyi swallowed Soviet propaganda and interpreted Stalin's policies as 'society' seeking protection from the self-regulated market. Nothing could be further from the truth. Instead of 'society' seeking protection, the forced industrialisation of the Five-Year plans instituted slave labour conditions in which Soviet workers experienced shocking labour processes enforced by security police on penalty of incarceration or death if labelled 'saboteurs', 'wreckers', 'hooligans' or other forms of 'traitorous' behaviour for failing to fulfil work targets, absenteeism, or uttering criticism.[58] Certainly, the short-term benefits of the ability of the Soviet Union to combat Hitler was in part due to rapid industrialisation, combined with the mobilisation of nationalist fervour that Stalin labelled 'the Great Patriotic War'. However, the single-minded racism of the Nazis in persecuting the *Untermensch* or 'sub-human Slavs' was also a factor that antagonised potential domestic allies against the Communist regime, many of whom greeted the invading Nazis only to suffer death and repression. In August 1940, shortly before he was assassinated by Stalin's agent, Trotsky penned some deluded unfinished remarks on soldiers in Hitler's army. These working-class and peasant soldiers, Trotsky naïvely proclaimed, "will in the majority of cases have far more sympathy for the vanquished peoples than for their own ruling caste," thus "infecting them with a revolutionary spirit" that would lead to the disintegration of the occupying Nazi armies.[59] Instead, the 'workers and peasants' of the Nazi Wehrmacht massacred many more civilians than were exterminated in the Nazi concentration camps.

With American hegemonic anti-Communism and Soviet vested interest in sustaining its new superpower status, the massive and very costly post-war Soviet military-industrial complex and related investments in the space race simultaneously had two effects: domestically, enormous resources were diverted from improvements in the Soviet population's standard of living while internationally, in the late 1950s, the US was stunned and shocked by Soviet technological achievements. This created the fear and the illusion that 'building socialism' might be effective, especially when Khrushchev stated that the USSR would surpass and 'bury America'. In reality, the Five-Year Plans that Polanyi lauded, merely disguised the negative consequences of undemocratic 'command planning' that eventually resulted in the sclerotic state of Soviet industry and agriculture. This is not to minimise the truly heroic cost of defeating Nazism and reconstructing a war-devastated country – on a scale unimaginable in any other society – that was undertaken in the two decades between 1941 and 1960. With twenty-seven million dead, thousands of cities, towns and villages destroyed, tens of millions homeless, countless enterprises obliterated, and food crops destroyed leading to starvation across the country in 1945 to 1946, it was a combination of patriotism and ruthless coercion that saw the regime survive. However, by the 1960s, the Soviet system was no closer to developing democratic socialism than in the 1930s, a naïve hope that Polanyi held until his death. Leaving democracy aside, the repressive regime in its last decades was not even able to satisfy its population with adequate domestic food supplies or basic goods and services.

We know that Polanyi's ultimate version of socialism, never fully elaborated,[60] differed from the Stalinist dictatorship of his times. Yet, Polanyi's own writings were highly contradictory and exhibited some embarrassingly naïve assessments, such as his belief that Stalin would promote the democratisation of Eastern European countries after the defeat of the Nazis.[61] Polanyi correctly saw Stalin's USSR as having abandoned Lenin and Trotsky's agenda of world revolution. He was so blind to the nature of the Soviet regime that he ignored Trotsky's 1933 analysis of the 'bureaucratic caste' structure of the Soviet bureaucracy exploiting workers[62] and the arguments of James Burnham (1941) who labelled the USSR as part of a new 'managerial class' or 'state capitalist' regime that was developing similar political methods to fascism.[63] In fact, Polanyi so disliked advocates of world revolution like Trotsky, that he warned the US in 1943 not to see the USSR as a 'mad dog' that would 'run amok' and return to the 'rabid years' of 1917-1923.[64] According to Polanyi, the startling novelty of Stalin's policy in building a new post-war regionalism in Eastern Europe is that it will cure "at least three endemic political diseases – intolerant nationalism, petty sovereignties and economic non-co-operation. All three are inevitable by-products of a market-economy in a region of racially mixed settlements."[65] As he put it, this new regionalism was not socialist since the Russians merely wished to safeguard their own security. "For all that", he claimed, "they may achieve a democratic socialist transformation more effectively than anything world-revolutionary socialists ever attempted."[66]

Not only did Stalin crush the attempt to build democracy in Eastern Europe but Polanyi's simplistic assumptions about the connection between the liberal market and the 'three endemic political diseases' was another example of his regular lapse into a crude economism. It was Communist government policies in East European countries rather than the liberal market that continued to perpetrate old anti-Semitic policies or racism against the Roma (ranging from involuntary assimilation and relocation, sterilisation, to forced employment in dangerous jobs in heavy industry), as well as the forced assimilation of Muslims in Bulgaria. Although Polanyi had personal experience of the 'three diseases' before he departed for the UK in 1933, their cause was much more complicated than his simplistic claim that they were due to the liberal market.

More than four decades of 'socialism' had mixed positive and negative socio-cultural affects that ultimately only papered-over deep-seated parochial nationalism and racism. Take the 'petty sovereignty and nationalism' in the 1993 break-up of Czechoslovakia where a return to 1918 was enforced despite the desire of many Czechs and Slovaks to remain one country or at least a confederation. As usual, the main losers were marginalised people like the Roma who were caught between two countries. Tragically, the bloodshed and eventual dissolution of Yugoslavia in the 1990s could not be attributed solely to the adoption of neoliberal policies after Tito's death. Domestically, Tito's government and also Yugoslav citizens and ambassadors abroad had to deal with hundreds of Croatian fascist/nationalist terrorist acts (bombings and killings) between 1946 and 1985. The eruption of Serbian, Croatian and other nationalist intolerance during the late 1980s had long been brewing in the six republics due to political and social inequality which market socialism could not resolve, even though it was significantly different to the liberal market that Polanyi blamed.[67] Right up to the present day, the combination of authoritarian religious and Communist practices, ethnic animosities and market corruption have helped produce racist, illiberal regimes in Poland, Hungary, Bulgaria and other Balkan countries as well as strong support for the far-Right Alternative für Deutchland in the regions of the former Communist East Germany.

HISTORICAL LEGACY

Finally, Polanyi's notion of the 'great transformation' was based on his claim that: "Fascism, like socialism, was rooted in a market society that refused to function."[68] This was only partly true in regard to fascism. His misreading of the Russian revolution was due to his attempt to fit the collapse of non-liberal Czarism and the 1917 revolution into his formulaic thesis about the end of the self-regulated market. Hence, his pro-Stalinist exaggerated claim that the so-called second Russian revolution of Five-Year Plans in the 1930s was not a specific Russian event like the 'first revolution' of 1917, but rather a 'universal transformation' that would change the world. Polanyi's crucial chapter entitled, '*Conservative Twenties, Revolutionary Thirties*', rested on the assumption that "Germany and Russia respectively became the representatives of fascism and socialism in the world at large. The true scope of these social movements can be gauged only if, for good or evil, their transcendent character is recognized and viewed as detached from the national interests enlisted in their service."[69] There is no doubt that globally at the level of ideology, Soviet Communism and German Nazism inspired hope or created fear for Polanyi's generation. It is also true that as a superpower, the Soviet Union helped change the world in its global rivalry with the US. Nonetheless, the Soviet model did not bring about universal socialist change as Polanyi had hoped it would. Even other 'socialist countries' refused to toe the Soviet line as became clear especially with the China/Soviet split before Polanyi's death.

Above all, the 'universal transformation' of the 1930s was nothing of the sort. The Soviet model did not successfully translate to other countries. It eventually failed wherever it was imported, despite extensive Soviet military and civilian aid and domestic coercion. Exactly fifty years after the publication of *The Great Transformation* and with the benefit of hindsight, historian Eric Hobsbawm delivered a more accurate assessment of the Russian revolution than Polanyi. Like most Communists of the Depression and post-war years who vested much hope in the Soviet Union as an alternative to capitalism, Hobsbawm had been an uncritical Stalinist and refused to acknowledge the terror and the many disasters, such as collectivisation perpetrated by the Soviet regime. Yet, reflecting on the USSR after its demise, Hobsbawm observed in 1994 that "the Soviet experiment was designed not as a global alternative to capitalism, but as a specific set of responses to the situation of a vast and spectacularly backward country at a particular and unrepeatable historical conjuncture."[70]

What Polanyi defended as a 'universal transformation' was actually its opposite. Once most of the world became aware of the Gulag[71] and the sheer brutality of Stalin's rapid collectivisation and industrialisation, Soviet Communism was not alone in being discredited in the eyes of mass electorates. All other revolutionary socialist movements and even Left-of-centre parliamentary social democratic parties continue to unjustifiably suffer from the stench emanating from the former USSR despite these movements being staunchly anti-Stalinist. It was too late by the time Gorbachev's *Glasnost* enabled the domestic debate in the 1980s concerning the contemporary implications of Stalin's policies. Whether an alternative method of Soviet planning or a slower rate of industrial transformation could have been adopted in the 1930s was not just an academic debate. It directly and indirectly affected both the future of planning and the USSR.

Polanyi's claim that the USSR was 'still the best hope for mankind' ended disastrously. Ironically, the Soviet chapter of the 'great transformation' culminated not in the revival of pre-1917 laissez-faire but the triumph of Yelstin's and Putin's mixture of illiberalism and the rule of criminal oligarchs. The pro-capitalist faction within the Communist Party of the Soviet Union did not necessarily want the end of the USSR but they helped engineer 'revolution from above' in conjunction with the desire of millions of people in the Soviet Union and Eastern European Communist countries for consumerism but not the lack of social protection evident in American capitalism.[72] Ironically, in Putin's Russia, the Georgian Stalin is admired for his ruthlessness as the nationalist saviour and not as Polanyi would have it as the great 'builder of socialism'.

Many enthusiasts for Polanyi champion his critique of self-regulated markets at the expense of ignoring or minimising his seriously flawed account of the Soviet experience – a discredited and costly experiment which, during the period between 1979 and 2008, helped undermine Left opponents of neoliberalism in the West and consolidate the neoliberal expansion in Eastern Europe after 1989. Polanyi continues to enjoy an inflated status as a 'canonical theorist' of international political economy partly because many contemporary academics ignore his naïve ideological account of the USSR, an account that was heavily infused with a largely uncritical acceptance of Soviet propaganda. For this alone, Polanyi's 'master narrative' of the so-called 'great transformation' and 'the origin of our time' should be rejected as a blinkered analysis by contemporary social change activists and theorists. As the next chapter will illustrate, Polanyi, like so many others was no less myopic when it came to fascism than he was about Stalin, socialism and the liberal market.

2. FATALISM, ECONOMISM AND NATURALISM: MISUNDERSTANDING FASCISM

ONE OF THE central themes of the Left version of the dominant paradigm of 'capitalism versus democracy' is that any major threat to capitalism in the form of potential revolutionary action or sweeping social reform significantly increases the chance of an authoritarian or outright fascist reaction. By contrast, some conservatives and liberals have long argued that fascism is one of the direct outcomes of the 'levelling' effect of democracy, specifically, once traditional class and cultural restraints are weakened or removed and 'well-bred' or 'civilised people' lose power.[1] Hence, 'people power' or the 'popular will' leads to demagogues and other political figures claiming to represent 'the people'. Given the rise of Right-wing movements in recent years as well as looming environmental and economic crises that could lead to social breakdown, many people fear that fascism is once again either a serious threat to democracy or the by-product of 'unlimited democracy' and 'unlimited tolerance', as claimed by the co-founders of the Mont Perelin Society, Friedrich Hayek and Karl Popper.

Although I make no pretence of providing a comprehensive analysis of fascism, my aim in this chapter is to show how particular theories and accounts of fascism still suffer from common flaws of economism, naturalism and fatalism. One can divide the enormous literature on fascism into several categories including those who provide detailed historical studies of the differences between fascist regimes, as opposed to others who focus on whether there are common fascist ideas, policies and goals. A new generation of writers now debate the causes of fascism in the 1920s and 1930s and whether these were similar or different to contemporary Right-wing and neo-fascist movements. There is no consensus about the definition or origins of 'fascism'. Nevertheless, it is often defined negatively in relation to 'democracy' and usually only the Left see it as inseparably related to capitalism when the latter is suffering severe crises. Many on the Left believed that fascism was the direct outcome of the crises caused by the failure of liberal markets in the 1920s and 1930s and now see it as similarly related to the failure of neoliberal markets in the past few decades.

From the 1930s to the 1950s, philosophers debated the meaning and origin of fascist ideas. Karl Popper's crude thesis saw totalitarianism as the consequence of a philosophical tradition stretching from Plato to Hegel and Marx. The 'enemies of the open society' were those who believed in predetermined inexorable 'laws' and sought to transform society through social engineering.[2] Later variations of this thesis have been developed by a range of Right-wing writers such as Austrian Erik von Kuehnelt-Leddihn's 1991 book, *Leftism Revisited: From de Sade and Marx to Hitler and Pol Pot.*[3] In contrast, Hungarian Communist, György Lukács, focused on the 'destruction of reason' that evolved from what he saw as irrationalist philosophies (including Nietzsche's and Heidegger's) that ultimately led to Nazism.[4] Like his contemporaries, Popper and Lukács, Polanyi did not provide a detailed explanation of the causes of fascism, including which social classes supported the rise of the Italian, German and other fascist movements, or why various liberal capitalist countries did not become fascist. Instead, he delivered little more than vague generalities. In fact, Polanyi represents a classic case of how not to analyse or understand fascism. Apart from two philosophical articles on the fascist consequences for freedom and spirituality written in 1934-1935, Polanyi failed to analyse the character and varieties of fascism as political phenomena.[5] This is perplexing, particularly given that his main purpose in writing *The Great Transformation* was to warn the world that fascism was the greatest threat to democracy and that fascism itself was the legacy of the political and socio-economic havoc created by liberal utopians in the pursuit of an unrealisable self-regulated market.

HISTORICAL OR ORGANIC?

As with many of his generation, such as Adorno, Horkheimer, Marcuse and others in the Frankfurt School, Polanyi's social theory was heavily over-determined by the rise of fascism and all that it entailed. In 1934, Herbert Marcuse, another refugee fleeing Hitler, published an analysis of the ideas and philosophical sources of fascism entitled, *'The Struggle Against Liberalism in the Totalitarian View of the State'.*[6] This essay covered the connection between fascism and a range of anti-Enlightenment and anti-rationalist philosophies that the Frankfurt School critiqued, as well as the development of fascist values in certain forms of liberalism, such as those espoused by Ludwig von Mises and others. Polanyi also wrote about some of the same philosophical sources of fascism that Marcuse covered. However, one of the stark differences between Marcuse and Polanyi was their conflicting attitudes to organic naturalism.

Critiquing the Nazi reliance on naturalist/organic theories, Marcuse argued that "[T]he interpretation of the historical and social process as a natural-organic process goes behind the real (economic and social) motive forces of history into the sphere of eternal and immutable nature."[7] In contrast, Polanyi's work was founded on an unchanging and ahistorical concept of human nature even though it was different to the 'blood and soil' naturalism of the Nazis. In *The Great Transformation* he proclaimed:

> For if one conclusion stands out more clearly than another from the recent study of early societies, it is the changelessness of man as a social being. His natural endowments reappear with a remarkable constancy in societies of all times and places; and the necessary preconditions of the survival of human society appear to be immutably the same.[8]

One of the central themes of Polanyi's work was that the natural embeddedness of pre-market societies was overturned by the development of the self-regulated market. Accordingly: "To separate labour from other activities of life and to subject it to the laws of the market was to annihilate all organic forms of existence and to replace them by a different type of organization, an atomistic and individualistic one."[9]

Unsurprisingly, Polanyi's ultimate concept of socialism rested on the establishment of a new 'organic democratic communitarianism' in contrast to liberalism, fascism and Soviet Communism. Consequently, one of the main differences between Polanyi and other Left theorists was that he conceived fascism in almost metaphysical and teleological terms as the culmination of the inbuilt forces propelling the self-regulated market. In 1944, Polanyi wrote:

> The fascist solution of the impasse reached by liberal capitalism can

be described as a reform of market economy achieved at the price of the extirpation of all democratic institutions, both in the industrial and in the political realm. The economic system which was in peril of disruption would thus be revitalised, while the people themselves were subjected to a re-education designed to denaturalise the individual and make him unable to function as the responsible unit of the body politic.[10]

Polanyi's notion of the 'individual' as a 'natural' being was completely ahistorical as the concept of 'individual' was foreign to most historical societies based on kinship, caste, tribe, clan and other social bonds. Fascist regimes savagely crushed democratic institutions and their Left political opponents. However, they could no more 'denaturalise' individuals than other types of political regimes.

PERILS OF THE TRUE RELIGION

Importantly, Polanyi's 'organic naturalism' was inseparably related to his Christian socialism. After moving to England, he became part of the Christian Left alongside people such as R. H. Tawney and debated how to develop a synthesis of theological and secular justifications of socialism.[11] Thus, there was a consistent Christian socialist theme running through Polanyi's discussion of 'capitalism versus democracy' during the 1930s and 1940s. Fascism, he argued, was against the individual and was anti-Christian, while socialism embodied a higher form of individualism and democracy. By the end of *The Great Transformation* he observed that after the Old Testament instructed Western man about the knowledge of death and Jesus in the New Testament revealed the uniqueness of the person, it was living in industrial society that instructed modern Man 'knowledge of society'. The 'discovery of society' meant that civilisation was at the crossroads of either the end of freedom or the rebirth of freedom. "The fascist answer to the recognition of the reality of society" Polanyi asserted, "is the rejection of the postulate of freedom. The Christian discovery of the uniqueness of the individual and of the oneness of mankind is negated by fascism. Here lies the root of its degenerative bent."[12]

Polanyi was not alone in seeing the struggle against fascism as a 'crisis of civilisation'. Nonetheless, once he put forward the notion that fascism was based on anti-individualist, pseudo-Christian ideas, he succumbed to the intractable theological argument, ever-present today, namely, the belief held by radical or tolerant Christians claiming that their interpretation of the bible is more authentic than the intolerant version extolled by fundamentalists and authoritarians. We should not forget that many past and present-day fascists as well as millions of defenders of free market policies also claimed, and continue to claim, that they defend Christianity, the White race, the heterosexual family, the nation and so on as well as all other 'true believers' against the threats coming from socialists, atheists, homosexuals, feminists and 'non-Christian races'. During the 1930s, Latin American and Central American countries were the sites of numerous Right-wing coups brought about by an active alliance between authoritarian fascist movements, the military and the Catholic church.[13] The attempt by Pope Pius X and the hierarchy of national Catholic institutions to combat secularism, liberalism and communism by 're-Christianising society' took the political economic form of corporatism and a strong state.

While Polanyi was correct in recognising authoritarian corporatism as the enemy of democracy and the individual, he ignored the fact that millions of devout Christians believed that corporatism was the answer to both socialism and laissez-faire – a 'third way' between atheistic communistic class struggle and liberal individualism and capitalist greed. Pope Leo XIII's 1891 encyclical, *Rerum Novarum* or Rights and Duties of Capital and Labour, preached 'class harmony' against socialist class conflict. Both fascists and Catholic anti-communists in non-fascist parties used *Rerum Novarum* to justify state involvement in social policies whether fascist corporatism, or non-fascist policies such as the Australian Labor Party's wage and welfare policy, post-1945 Christian Democracy in Europe and Latin America or Catholic inspired non-state co-operatives such as Mondragon that developed within Franco's fascist Spain.

It was problematic enough for socialists in the 1930s and 1940s to conceive the relationship between 'capitalism and democracy' in metaphysical Christian terms, let alone applying Polanyi's Eurocentric, Christian socialist, 'crisis of civilisation' anachronistic framework to the contemporary world. At present we are witnessing Hindu, Buddhist, Islamic and Judaic forms of neo-fascism as well as numerous other anti-democratic governments and religiously based racist movements stretching from Myanmar to Saudi Arabia, India to Nigeria and the US to Brazil. Today, adherents of each of the major religions are divided between those who are culturally tolerant, supportive of refugees, uphold non-violence and democratic values, as opposed to those of the same faiths espousing dogmatic intolerance, racism and nationalist exclusivity regardless of their support for capitalist markets or not.

FASCISM AND THE LIBERAL MARKET

On the broader political cultural front, defenders of Polanyi argue that he was countering the Marxist focus on economic relations by developing a more comprehensive social and political analysis of liberal market society and its connection to fascism. It is true that many socialists and Communists advocated a vulgar economic determinism that Polanyi rightfully rejected. However, Polanyi provided no alternative to economism. This is in contrast to other theories at the time, such as Wilhelm Reich's 'mass psychology of fascism'[14] or the Frankfurt School's large project on how fascism was linked to the structure of authority in the family, the relationship between the culture industry (media, Hollywood) and authoritarianism as well as the socio-psychological formation of the 'authoritarian personality'.[15] Also, Polanyi provided no insights about how fascism was linked to various modernist critiques of European socio-cultural decadence and the need for a 'creative destruction' of old aristocratic and bourgeois values.[16] Instead, he attributed the rise of fascism (as distinct from fascist ideology) to narrower political economic causes, predominantly the crisis in the market and the liberal state.

While this political impasse was important, Polanyi, in stark contrast to the kind of analysis provided by his contemporary, Antonio Gramsci,[17] did not explore it in any systematic manner. Put another way, Polanyi glossed over the changing relationship between state apparatuses and classes in society, how hegemony was constructed at social, political and cultural levels, and why the loss of hegemony by traditional conservative and liberal parties was closely related to the struggle by fascists to gain dominance within a crisis-ridden and unstable anti-socialist Right-wing power bloc. Instead, he argued that:

In order to comprehend German fascism, we must revert to Ricardian England. The nineteenth century, as cannot be over-emphasised, was England's century. The Industrial Revolution was an English event. Market economy, free trade, and the gold standard were English inventions. These institutions broke down in the twenties everywhere

– in Germany, Italy, or Austria the event was merely more political and more dramatic.[18]

Paradoxically, this is a very economistic interpretation, despite Polanyi arguing that in "this final phase of the fall of market economy the conflict of class forces entered decisively."[19] These vague generalities did not explain the politics within capitalist countries or why fascism did not succeed in England, the home of Ricardian free markets. Polanyi said very little about the conflict between classes or their representatives. In fact, he mainly avoided any discussion of how the capitalist class dominated and gave a strong impression, as I will show, that the fall of democracy and the triumph of fascism was an easy and an inevitable part of the break-down of liberal capitalism and the 'great transformation'.

In recent decades, there have been numerous academic studies of fascism with no agreement on how to define it as a political phenomenon.[20] It is therefore important to distinguish between 'fascism' as an academic concept and how anti-fascist political movements defined fascism between the 1920s and the 1940s.[21] To better understand why Polanyi's explanation of fascism was inadequate in his own day, let alone of marginal relevance to those who wish to comprehend contemporary authoritarian governments and neo-fascist movements, it is necessary to return to some of the key divisions amongst the Left prior to 1939. Among the leading opponents of fascism during the 1920s and 1930s, there were major debates and disagreements within the Communist and the non-Communist Left over both the causes and the very nature of fascism. This was partly due to the pre-1918 classical socialists, especially those in the German Social Democratic Party (SPD), theorising that the bourgeois stage of history would inevitably be succeeded by socialism while providing no explanation of fascism or counter-revolution. Rosa Luxemburg's 1915 alternative scenarios of 'socialism or barbarism' were a partial exception here, but still not much use in analysing fascist movements that were still to emerge. Hence, disputes raged over some of the following questions:

- What distinguished fascist parties from conventional liberal and conservative defenders of capitalism?
- Which social classes supported Mussolini, Hitler and other fascist movements?
- Was fascism the open terrorist expression of the new chauvinist and reactionary stage of monopoly finance capitalism?

- What was the nature of social democrats and labour party members – were they the 'Left-wing of the bourgeoisie' (Zinoviev and the Comintern, 1922) that were relabelled 'Left fascists' in 1924 and then 'social fascists' in 1929 simply because they opposed revolution or used the police to repress radicals?
- Should Communists and socialists form informal united fronts 'from below' or officially ('above') in a Popular Front between all Left parties as well as with those liberals and conservatives who were anti-fascist?

Polanyi did not directly address or analyse the strengths and weaknesses in these critical questions that were being debated at the time. Instead, his post-1935 writings displayed a combination of Moscow's Popular Front line and his Christian socialist perspective. Crucially, his over-generalised, abstract analysis of the collapse of laissez-faire leading to fascism expressed a strong historical fatalism – a teleological approach that minimised human agency. Take, for example Polanyi's claim that:

> Nineteenth-century civilization was not destroyed by the external or internal attack of barbarians; its vitality was not sapped by the devastations of World War I nor by the revolt of a socialist proletariat or a fascist lower middle class. Its failure was not the outcome of some alleged laws of economics such as that of the falling rate of profit or of underconsumption or overproduction. It disintegrated as the result of an entirely different set of causes: the measures which society adopted in order not to be, in its turn, annihilated by the action of the self-regulating market.[22]

Polanyi did not question 'the measures' which an abstract 'society' rather than particular agents (parties, business groups, Brown Shirts and others) adopted to prevent annihilation by an equally abstract 'self-regulated market'. In short, he did not discuss whether fascism's triumph was merely a spontaneous protective mechanism adopted by 'society' against the 'self-regulated market', an inevitable, quasi-automatic manifestation of Polanyi's 'double movement' or rather a deliberately planned and engineered Right-wing takeover. Similar confusion reigns today in regard to how the broad Left and greens should interpret and respond to neoliberalism and the rise of so-called 'populist' parties. Complicating matters are the political divisions over the causes and 'measures' needed to prevent particular capitalist industries and governments from causing irreversible environmental disasters.

TRANSFORMATION OR CONTINUITY?

In fact, Polanyi overstated the 'great transformation' and disregarded the context of the continuity of Italian fascism and German Nazism with the power-wielders of 'nineteenth century civilisation'. Mussolini and Hitler were both anxious to ensure that their respective movements did not antagonise the military, large landholders, industrialists, the Catholic or Protestant churches and small business. As respective 'saviours' of their countries from the so-called threat of Bolshevism, they forged new corporatist policies via a nationalist ideology to ensure that the interests of the old order were largely safeguarded, minus various liberal 'centrist' politicians and the 'interference' of parliament, free trade unions and Left political parties. Polanyi's preoccupation with the so-called end of the 'self-regulated market, meant he magnified the end of key aspects of 'nineteenth century civilisation' and minimised the uneven socio-economic and cultural characteristics of countries that were only partly highly industrialised. These countries were also still characterised by the adherence to pre-capitalist and early market social practices.

Rather than a 'great transformation', other historical political sociologists such as Barrington Moore and Michael Mann viewed fascism differently, not as just a political reaction to the failure of the self-regulated market but as a specific response to historical socio-economic legacies that Polanyi ignored. While I do not share a number of the conclusions arrived at by Moore and Mann, they nonetheless illustrate the deep problems and inadequacy of Polanyi's grand theory. Barrington Moore, for example, analysed the historical transformation of agrarian classes (lord and peasant) and the rise of industrial capitalism in Europe, Asia and America. Why was it that fascism developed in Germany, Italy and Japan, that is, in countries that had never had successful peasant revolutions in contrast to France, Russia and China? He also examined the social transformations in Britain, America and India between landed and urban classes that did not result in fascist 'modernisation from above' as in Germany, Italy and Japan.[23]

Similarly, Michael Mann's study of fascism, although focussed solely on Europe, was much more differentiated than the account provided by Polanyi. According to Mann, in interwar Europe there was a geographical division between Northwestern Europe (Britain, Ireland, the Nordic countries and

the Netherlands and Belgium) that remained liberal democracies, and Eastern, Central and Southern Europe that were all despotic (apart from Czechoslovakia). Instead of Polanyi's historical fatalism, Mann argued that Germany
and France were intermediate countries and despite a series of crises and
varying political movements in the 1920s and 1930s, they could either have
become fascist or retained their liberal democracies. In contrast to Polanyi's
lack of analysis of the specific historical socio-economic profiles of these
societies, Mann showed how the political institutions in the various countries in the 'two Europes' dealt quite differently with multiple economic,
political and ideological crises, especially the impact of the First World War
and the Great Depression.[24] Despite having a more complex analysis of
fascism in Europe than Polanyi, Ishay Landa makes valid criticisms of Mann
for exaggerating the strength of the liberal tradition and political institutions
in Britain as being able to resist fascism had it also experienced the scale of
defeat and domestic political violence like Germany.[25]

Nonetheless, Mann and Landa offer much more advanced understandings
of fascism than Polanyi's theory of fascism which was largely asocial and ahistorical. After listing all the different countries, cultures, and industrialised or
only slightly industrialised nations in which fascism appeared, Polanyi
asserted that "there was no type of background – of religious, cultural, or
national tradition – that made a country immune to fascism, once the conditions for its emergence were given."[26] According to this view, it neither
depended on the size of the fascist movement nor the level of resistance to
it. The 'fascist situation' waxed and waned depending on the 'objective situation' of the world economy. Once the traditional self-regulated world market
ceased to function then individual nations succumbed to the 'fascist virus'.[27]
Polanyi's explanation reminds me of those cynical responses to the question
of whether the CIA was involved in Pinochet's 1973 military overthrow of
Chile's democratically elected Allende government, namely, that 'the CIA is
everywhere in Latin America just like the influenza virus, some countries
catch the flu and succumb while others do not.'

Contemporary admirers of Polanyi such as Richard Sandbrook also
subscribe to the notion of fascism as a virus. According to Sandbrook:

> The 'virus' metaphor is apt. Fascism is like influenza. Often, flu takes
> a relatively mild form (right-wing populism). But under certain
> conducive conditions, it assumes the virulent form of National Social-
> ism, which threatens death and war. The mild forms can mutate into
> the more virulent one.[28]

Sandbrook's notion of fascism as a virus may be seductive as a spontaneous tweet or neat media soundbite. However, once we eliminate the role of social and political economic agents and succumb to biological metaphors and explanations (such as milder or more virulent strains), it becomes impossible to understand the historical, social and political economic differences between current illiberal regimes in Poland or Hungary (that were democratically elected to power), and repressive fascist dictatorships appointed by conservatives or seizing power by military coup d'état. Inappropriate metaphors help close down critical thinking. If fascism is a virus, perhaps Sandbrook following Polanyi, believes that a new anti-fascist vaccination for parliamentary democracies would prevent an epidemic? If so, would we need a new vaccine every year as anti-flu vaccines have a limited life given that viruses mutate into new strains?

One of Polanyi's other key arguments about fascism was based on the separation between the liberal state and the industrial economy which led to political paralysis. He claimed this paralysis created the opportunity for fascists to step in and crush democratic institutions. While this a more plausible causal factor, such a scenario was inapplicable in those Central and Eastern European countries that were relatively unindustrialised and were dominated by authoritarian rural landholder and peasant-based agrarian parties that later aligned with Nazi Germany such as Hungary and Romania. Italy was also divided between largely agrarian regions and northern industrial cities. The demoralising impact of war on Italian society contradicted Polanyi's thesis that the vitality of nineteenth century civilisation 'was not sapped by the devastations of World War One'. Polanyi was partly right in arguing that fascism either became a threat or melted away in the 1920s largely due to the state of the world economy. Yet, his focus on the world economy at the expense of specific national political cultures and institutional relations, lost sight of the reasons national political conditions were not replicated and why fascism did not succeed in all countries despite the disastrous impact of the Great Depression.[29]

In *The State and Revolution* (1917), Lenin echoed Friedrich Engels in arguing that universal suffrage still ensured that workers remained wage slaves,[30] hence, a "democratic republic is the best possible political shell for capitalism..."[31] In contrast, Polanyi believed that, fascism was "merely the outcome of the mutual incompatibility of Democracy and Capitalism in our times. If Democracy were really the appropriate political superstructure of Capitalism, Fascism would never have come into existence. But the opposite is the case."[32] Polanyi also espoused a teleological view of the inevitability of socialism. Fascism, he argued, was only a temporary stage that violently prevented socialism by destroying democratic practice. Ultimately, he asserted: "Post-fascist capitalism cannot hold out against democracy and the advance towards socialism."[33] Unfortunately, as all post-fascist capitalist societies since 1945 have confirmed, there is no inherent connection between democratisation and socialism. Therefore, both Lenin's and Polanyi's view of the relationship between 'capitalism and democracy' needs to be reconceptualised.

DISPUTING THE REASONS WHY FASCISM SUCCEEDED OR FAILED

A crucial area to address is why fascism never triumphed in Great Britain and the US if it purportedly is the pathological and protective 'counter-movement' against the havoc caused by the so-called liberal self-regulated market. Both countries were severely hit by the Depression, and places where liberal market practices had either originated or long dominated. Polanyi claimed that fascism in Germany and Italy used nationalist grievances to advance its popularity but in France and Britain, fascism was rejected because it was viewed as 'unpatriotic'.[34] The fact that France did not become fascist after the Right-wing riots of 1934 and instead moved Leftwards to establish a Popular Front government in 1936, is also evidence that counters Polanyi's fatalistic thesis of the 'fascist virus'. After all, fascism in Britain and France adopted political cultural forms that tried to capitalise on either the British Empire or on French patriotism. Rather, it was the relative strength of anti-fascist political forces and the strength of non-fascist conservative forces that ultimately counted. There was no shortage of fascist and other Right-wing anti-democratic supporters in France, but it took the military defeat of France for Hitler to establish Petain's collaborationist mixture of conservative and fascist elements into the puppet government in Vichy.

As to the causes of fascism in the 1920s and 1930s, other explanations at the time included the claim that fascism only grew or came to power in countries that had weak and relatively young parliamentary systems, or as a reaction against strong Communist parties, or was supported by middle-class state employees and an active petit-bourgeois class caught between large business cartels and organised labour, or was the last-ditch intervention of a powerful monopoly sector that financed fascist parties to fight the Left, given the weakness of conventional conservative and liberal parties. Polanyi ignored these varied explanations arguably because his conception of the rise and demise of liberal capitalism was too abstract. It lacked both a developed theory and a historical analysis of changing rural and urban social classes or an account of the emergence and strategic roles of mass political parties. It also failed to grasp the internal divisions within distinct parts of increasingly complex national state institutions. In an era of mobilised urban electorates and fearful bourgeois classes and traditional landed gentry or aristocrats, the exercise of political power in different capitalist countries could not be reduced to formulaic explanations. Additionally, Polanyi had no adequate analysis of why the development of large-scale trusts, monopolies and cartels required significantly different state policies and government structures to advance their specific interests in comparison to earlier state policies that were historically more favourable to family enterprises or small and medium individual businesses.

Polanyi could not tell us the given 'conditions for its emergence', and why 'the objective situation of the world economy' did not affect all societies in the same way. His heavy dose of fatalism implied that no market society could immunise itself from fascism, as the level of resistance to fascism was irrelevant. In short, Polanyi's sweeping analysis of the demise of the self-regulated market combined historical events with ahistorical abstraction that was devoid of a detailed theory of agency. Instead, he argued that the 'fascist situation':

> ...was no other than the typical occasion of easy and complete fascist victories. All at once, the tremendous industrial and political organizations of labour and of other devoted upholders of constitutional freedom would melt away, and minute fascist forces would brush aside what seemed until then the overwhelming strength of democratic governments, parties, trade unions.[35]

This was partially true of Mussolini in 1922 and Hitler in 1933 who were officially handed government by King Victor Emmanuel and German President Hindenburg, respectively, with the strong backing of conservative politicians. The various political and labour movements opposing fascist parties did not melt away but rather were banned and crushed by the new fascist governments unleashing repressive forces such as the 1933 'Enabling Act' (supported by the Catholic-led Centre Party) following the burning down of the Reichstag. Equally importantly, the relatively easy triumph of Hitler and Mussolini could not be projected onto other countries and certainly could not explain the failure of fascism during the 1930s in the heartland of liberal capitalism – Great Britain, the US, France, Canada and Australia – nor the bloody years of resistance against fascism in the Spanish civil war, nor the twenty authoritarian/fascist military coups (between 1930 and 1940) that crushed elected democracies in Argentina, Brazil, Peru and the majority of Latin American countries.

Like other socialists and anti-fascist liberals, Polanyi lumped Japanese imperial militarism into the same boat as various European fascist movements. Recall his claim that Germany and Russia became the 'universal representatives of fascism and socialism'. Mussolini certainly tried to universalise fascism in the early 1930s and gained a number of adherents in Japan. However, the various constituent nationalist myths and traditions that fascist movements tried to mobilise politically in different countries made it hard for fascism to succeed as a single universal movement. Japan, for instance, was hit hard by the Depression thus helping bolster a range of authoritarian movements, including admirers of Italian and German fascism. Yet, during the 1930s, it was the various factions inside the military (rather than predominantly civilian political movements in Europe) that struggled for dominance over an imperial agenda and culture that long pre-dated the emergence of European fascism. The 1878 law giving the Japanese military independence from civilian control was quite unlike liberal constitutions that elevated parliamentary democracy over the military. Also, authoritarianism had been instituted via the 1900 Public Peace Police Law and the 1925 Peace Preservation Law directed against all forms of radicals and dissenters including anti-colonialists and Communists.[36]

The Japanese imperial forces had long-advocated statist control of society and industry rather than civilian pursuit of liberal market policies, especially after the civilian government cut military expenditure in the 1920s. While the military-dominated regime aligned itself with Germany, Italy and other fascist countries via various pacts between 1936 and 1940, its decades-long imperial objectives (domestic purification and external expansion) already included the annexation of Korea in 1910. This was followed by military clashes with Chinese nationalist and Soviet forces between 1918 and 1930, before the full invasion of Manchuria in 1931 and China in 1937. Japan's expansionism did not fit Polanyi's over-generalised thesis about the end of 'nineteenth century civilisation'. On the contrary, Japan's imperialists wanted to strengthen nineteenth-century post-Tokugawa imperial tradition even though their attack on Left domestic movements and liberals shared some of the fascist characteristics evident in European countries.

The establishment of the Japanese war economy with planning boards to organise resources, production and everything necessary for imperial expansion was *not* a protective measure which, according to Polanyi, 'society adopted in order not to be, in its turn, annihilated by the action of the self-regulating market'. His abstract notions of 'society' countering an equally abstract 'self-regulating market' were irrelevant. Rather, after years of terrorism and assassinations in Japan, the dominant military faction took *de facto* power (behind a political façade) and pursued military and colonial expansionism – a throwback to 'Great Power' imperialism rather than Polanyi's 'great transformation'. Under the figurehead emperor, the militarised power structure wanted to replace nineteenth-century British, French, Dutch and Portuguese colonial power in the Asia-Pacific region and challenge rising American interests. The fact that there was no Japanese fascist movement that took power as was the case in Germany and Italy, not only raises the issue of the conditions under which fascism can emerge but also whether fascism can flourish, as various American critics have argued, without removing elected representatives (for further elaboration see Chapter Four).

It is not Polanyi's 'great transformation' that lives on to the present day in the tension between Japan and its North and South East Asian neighbours but rather the legacy of Japanese imperial military and industrial expansionism. Not only did Polanyi misunderstand the differences between Japanese military imperialism and European fascism but he said nothing about the giant *zaibatsu* monopolies or family holding companies (Mitsui, Mitsubishi, Sumitomo, Yasuda and others) that dominated key sectors of the economy from the nineteenth century onwards and had close links with the military and controlled major political parties, such as *Seiyukai*. These *zaibatsu* were only dissolved and reorganised after military defeat in 1945 but continue to play vital roles as multinational corporations to the present-day.[37]

FASCISM: 'ORGANISED CAPITALISM' AND 'DISORGANISED' STATE '?

The role of large trusts, cartels or monopolies raises major questions about Polanyi's whole analysis of fascism as emerging in response to the malfunctioning of the so-called self-regulated market. It should not be forgotten that fifty years before he wrote *The Great Transformation*, and following Marx's death in 1883, a generation of socialists, such as Rudolf Hilferding, Karl Kautsky and Rosa Luxemburg debated the role of cartels and the 'revisionist' theses of Eduard Bernstein. One of the central divisive issues between 1890 and 1914 was whether the contradictions of capitalism would usher in socialist revolution or whether capitalism would be replaced in a smooth transition to socialism via winning electoral majorities and legislating socialism. Both orthodox Marxists and 'revisionists' argued that the development of cartels significantly changed the relationship between large capitalist businesses and governments compared to earlier relations between competitive market capitalists and state institutions. The concentration of capital was seen as either exacerbating the crises of capitalism or facilitating a smoother transition to socialism This was due to the fact that these large monopolies had a 'quasi-socialist' form in that they straddled finance, manufacturing and other sectors and would simply need a change of ownership from private to public control.[38] By 1915, Hilferding eventually called this new phase of capitalism 'organised capitalism'. The greater integration of state support for cartels (via domestic economic policies and imperialist expansion) meant that the notion of a self-regulated market was already being seriously eroded by the end of the nineteenth century.

It is here that we come to identify a significant problem in both Polanyi's notion of the self-regulated market and his account of its demise in the 1930s. On the one hand, he observed that from the 1870s onwards a range of major countries "passed through a period of free trade and laissez-faire, followed by a period of anti-liberal legislation in regard to public health, factory conditions, municipal trading, social insurance, shipping subsidies, public utilities, trade associations, and so on."[39] This demand for protection against market practices and giant cartels was also evident in the breakup of large monopolies like Standard Oil in America. On the other hand, Polanyi argued that this protection was against freedom of contract or laissez-faire rather than against the self-regulated market. He was correct that pre-1914 anti-trust legislation and many other government regulations were not equivalent to state planning in the form of Soviet Five-Year plans or post-1945 Keynesian indicative planning in various European countries. Still, one could not describe the implementation of an increasing range of state regulatory interventions before the 1930s as in any sense a 'self-regulating market'.

Polanyi believed that a self-regulating world market implied "absolute independence of markets from national authorities".[40] "Nations and peoples" he asserted, "were mere puppets in a show utterly beyond their control. They shielded themselves from unemployment and instability with the help of central banks and customs tariffs, supplemented by migration laws."[41] This view predates the widespread contemporary and equally overblown and misleading belief that national governments and citizens are powerless in the face of global capitalist markets. Within national boundaries, Polanyi argued that protectionism helped to transform competitive markets into monopolistic ones, as individuals were replaced by associations of non-competing groups. The self-regulation of markets was gravely hampered, and this 'strain' needed political intervention to restore the economic balance. Nevertheless, Polanyi argued, "the institutional separation of the political from the economic sphere was constitutive to market society and had to be maintained whatever the tension involved."[42]

This panoramic view of the nineteenth century was based on a mixture of keen observation and rhetorical exaggeration. As I have argued, it is as though there are two Polanyis in *The Great Transformation* each one contradicting the other. The first Polanyi overstated the 'absolute independence of markets from national political authorities'. The second Polanyi recognised the growth of indispensable roles played by state institutions even though he tended to adhere to the liberal fiction of the separate spheres of 'the political' and 'the economic'. During the decades prior to 1914, an increasing number of government schemes vital to private capitalist markets and involving varying degrees of planning were implemented by city, regional and national governments in the form of sewage and water supply, urban transport, ports, public education and especially the arms race and imperialist expansion. In Germany alone, production in state factories accounted for 40% of military output at the beginning of the First World War.[43] It was during 1914-1918, that major governments implemented state coordination of the production of munitions, food and other military necessities (albeit with poor to mediocre results). The breakdown of 'absolute independence of markets' had already occurred in the decades well before 1914 and not just in the 'great transformation' of the 1930s.

REGULATION AND DEREGULATION

Like so many contemporary political economists who continue to misconceive state apparatuses as merely 'political-administrative' institutions that 'intervene' in or regulate 'the economy', Polanyi also failed to recognise that the growing roles of state institutions through their mass employment of administrators and workers, provision of civilian infrastructure and services, military expenditure and many other functions crucial to so many aspects of socio-economic life – from health and working conditions through to public safety – were inseparably part of 'the economy' and 'society'.

The bureaucratisation and increasingly integrated roles played by large businesses and state apparatuses was a theme not only developed by socialists but also by Max Weber, Werner Sombart and German liberals, such as industrialist and politician Walter Rathenau between 1900 and 1918. The concept of 'organised capitalism' (Hilferding) as a half-way house between private enterprise and public administration[44], ultimately affected former orthodox Marxists such as Hilferding himself who, in the 1920s, pursued policies closer to Bernstein's 'revisionism'. In 1946, the Social Democratic Party (SPD) rejected its pre-war policies on cartels and adopted a policy of nationalising large private cartels to prevent a repeat of the Nazi destruction of Weimar democracy. This policy of nationalisation was eventually removed by the SPD congress at Bad Godesberg in 1959 and replaced by the need to accept the 'discipline of the market' and 'to reconcile economic performance with social security'. By the end of the 1970s and early 1980s, a new generation of socialists began discussing the end of 'organised capitalism' and the onset of 'disorganised capitalism' or neoliberalism.[45]

In short, Polanyi adhered to the increasingly fictional notion of a self-regulated market despite simultaneously recognising the rise of 'organised capitalism' and greater state involvement between the 1870s and the onset of the Depression in 1929. Crucially, in Germany, which replaced Great Britain as the largest capitalist economy in Europe by the end of the nineteenth century, there was widespread state-ownership (at local, regional and national levels) in banking, metals, steel-making, railways, ship-building and other industries and services between 1871 and 1932. What Polanyi and his current enthusiasts overlook is that it was Hitler's regime that embarked on an extensive privatisation program of state-owned enterprises and welfare services between 1934 and 1938.[46] Those who argue that contemporary neoliberalism is a return to the liberalism of pre-1930, uphold an erroneous and simplistic thesis. In fact, Hitler privatised many state-owned enterprises such as *Deutsche Reichsbahn* (German Railways) the largest public enterprise in the world, giant banks such as Deutsche Bank, Commerz, and Dresdner Bank, as well as *Vereinigte Stahlwerke* or United Steelworks, the second largest joint stock company in Germany after IG Farben. Selling state-owned enterprises enabled the Nazis to achieve their military and domestic objectives. These privatisations helped part-finance military rearmament, rewarded those cartels that had backed Hitler's regime and also disguised his secret rearmament by taking the activities of former state-owned industries off the official government budgetary accounts.

The Nazis increased their control over private businesses even as they sold them important state assets. This was not as systematic or totalitarian as is often presented. Rather, different competing centres of power based on powerful individuals and groups in the Nazi Party, the SS, the military and various state apparatuses (all swearing loyalty to Hitler) often had special relations with cartels and businesses that were not always rationalised or standardised in a so-called monolithic state. Hence, Franz Neumann called the Nazi state a 'behemoth' – a chaotic, multi-shaped and lawless monster – rather than a 'leviathan'.[47] The 'spoils' of Hitler's privatisations benefited different private cartels depending on their relationship with the Führer and other key power-wielders. Nazi privatisations also had different political objectives to the contemporary neoliberal aims of liberalising business from state control.

Therefore, Polanyi's central argument about the 'great transformation' from the privately-owned self-regulated market to state intervention in the 1930s rested on the fiction of 'the separation of the political from the economic' – a fiction that was in conflict with the increasing fusion and interdependent relationship of political and economic spheres from the second half of the nineteenth century onwards. Powerful industrialists in this earlier form of 'organised capitalism' were opposed to more rights for workers, even if later on they were far from united in their support of fascist parties and other authoritarian solutions. These anti-democratic business tendencies continued in less extreme political forms in the post-1945 era of new forms of 'organised capitalism' characterised by an expansion of public sector industries, greater joint state and business involvement in the shaping of labour markets, R & D, social welfare and urban development.

Moreover, the so-called 'disorganised capitalism' that emerged since the early 1980s has certainly not been a return to Polanyi's self-regulated market that he paradoxically depicted as both a 'stark utopia' and as an actually existing pillar of 'nineteenth century civilisation'. While a number of contemporary capitalist countries are characterised by 'crony capitalism' and authoritarian political leaders delivering government contracts and new businesses to their favoured 'oligarchs', neoliberal governments have in most instances presided over a different relationship to corporations that was typical in both pre-fascist liberalism and Hitler's regime. Instead, there has been a much more targeted form of intervention ranging from 'law and order' and 'social reproduction' strategies (designed to minimise costs to business and maximise productivity and efficiency), right through to planning the development of new industries and resources. Targeted intervention has been combined with selective deregulation and indirect forms of control, depending on the conflicting needs and agendas of different industry sectors, social classes and regional problems.

MISUNDERSTANDING FASCISM

The late sociologist, Walter Goldfrank, argued that Polanyi provided an alternative theory of fascism to both liberals and Marxists. Liberals focused on how fascism, like Communism, threatened parliamentary democracy because they were both dictatorships. Conversely, Marxists argued that fascism, like liberalism, defended bourgeois capitalism and threatened working class interests. Goldfrank claimed that Polanyi borrowed arguments from each of the rival theories in order to emphasise that the success of fascism as an independent movement depended on 'the objective situation of the world economy', that is, fascism's temporary success was due to the breakdown of the gold standard and world trade due to tariff protection.[48] I would also agree that we should never lose sight of how the political struggles within individual nations are situated within a context of developments and crises in the larger world. However, Goldfrank admired what was one of Polanyi's major failings, namely, that he developed an ideal type of fascism largely based on the German experience that was extrapolated and applied to other countries in conjunction with the crisis in world markets. Polanyi claimed that fascism "should never have been ascribed to local causes, national mentalities, or historical backgrounds as was so consistently done by contemporaries."[49] This was valid insofar as fascism was not inherently a product of the 'German' culture or 'mentality'. Yet, it is his overgeneralised analysis from lofty heights that lost sight of the 'local causes' and national institutional and political obstacles. Polanyi neither explained why fascism was not adopted globally, nor illuminated how the specific political institutions and struggles in a range of countries (all severely affected by the Great Depression) did not universally end in the defeat of anti-fascist forces.

To sum up, Polanyi's conception of fascism rested on a mixture of metaphysical Christian socialist notions about how fascism was anti-individualistic and anti-Christian, plus a historical fatalism that lacked socio-political clarity as to which constituencies in particular societies supported fascist parties or which political economic forces could have prevented fascism. It is true that interwar fascism promoted a form of corporatism that eliminated individualism. Still, Polanyi did not explain why or how fascist corporatism[50] differed from the corporatism practised during the New Deal and within parliamentary democracies – from Swedish Social Democracy before 1945 to the post-war corporatism practised in post-war Germany, Austria and other countries. His sweeping generalisation about how the so-called self-regulated market ended due to malfunctioning, failed to provide a persuasive analysis of how the Nazi and Italian fascist state apparatuses differed from state institutions in other capitalist countries, including Roosevelt's New Deal. Polanyi wrote *The Great Transformation* before the full horrors of the Nazi extermination camps were revealed. Apart from the destruction of democracy and state repression of political enemies, Polanyi's account of 'capitalism versus democracy' failed to outline the key characteristics that differentiated fascist states, as capitalist states, from other capitalist states in Australia, the UK, Canada, France or Sweden.

While Polanyi occasionally cited class struggle, he avoided any explicit detailed discussion of social classes, especially the historical social agents that facilitated the triumph of fascism in some countries but not in others. Just as an earlier generation heatedly debated the nature of fascism and how to counter it, so for the past few decades the global Left have debated the nature of neoliberalism and how to counter or dismantle these regimes. It is not surprising that some outdated theories of fascism were unable to adequately explain pre-1945 fascism. These same outworn theories of fascism remain inadequate as explanations of the recent rise of contemporary Right-wing 'anti-politics' parties and political figures or the profound changes in contemporary social relations. As I have argued, one will find little in Polanyi's writings to explain why the masses were attracted to fascism in the 1920s and 1930s and why fascist movements had relatively few triumphs in the vast majority of countries in the world. Despite his current popularity, Polanyi's work is even less likely to help us understand the Trumps, Le Pens and a host of other new Right-wing, so-called 'anti-establishment' movements.

In 1936, British Fascist leader, Oswald Mosley, answering the question about the differences between fascism and capitalism when both supported private enterprise, stated: "Capitalism is the system by which capital uses the Nation for its own purposes. Fascism is the system by which the Nation uses capital for its own purposes. Private enterprise is permitted and encouraged so long as it coincides with the national interests."[51] Paradoxically, many anti-neoliberals and anti-globalists, whether Right, Left or green, would today share Mosley's sentiments about 'capital having to serve national interests'. In an era that has witnessed new political realignments such as the rise of authoritarianism and anti-neoliberal movements desiring the reassertion of 'democratic control', it is necessary to question in what way Right, Left and green versions of 'national capitalism' differ from each other as I will discuss in Chapter Nine.

Despite the popularity of the concept of 'globalisation', a seamless globalised economy has never existed. Aside from the deregulation of capital flows and many other aspects of production and trade, the vast majority of multi-national corporations are still based in their home countries. They face a range of national regulations concerning work conditions, tax rates, environmental standards and consumer protection policy which many businesses try to evade or minimise. Nonetheless, the liberalisation of trade, investment and capital flows in recent decades has put an end to the viability of new attempts to revive fascist nationalist autarky. The crisis of supply lines revealed by Covid-19 has produced a chorus in many countries calling for de-globalisation and a return to 'national capitalist production'. It remains to be seen whether this will occur across all industries or in only a few selected sectors such as medical supplies, energy and some essential goods. After all, multi-national corporations depend on global markets, non-white labour and 'foreign' cultures. Short of nuclear war or decades-long protracted occupation of distant countries in the Middle East, the era of expansionary military invasions of adjacent foreign territories to gain *'lebensraum'* (as in the 1930s and 1940s) is over. Occasionally, some authoritarian leaders such as Turkey's Erdoğan may ape Western powers in the Middle East by sending troops to oil rich Libya (a former part of Ottoman Empire). Instead of territorial conquest, corporate leaders and technological utopians now tend to dream of *'lebensraum'* on Mars and other planets in the quest for mineral resources.

3. THE NEW DEAL'S CONTROVERSIAL LEGACY

IN CONTEMPORARY AMERICA, the New Deal remains controversial. Presidential candidate Joe Biden invokes Roosevelt's New Deal and Left Democrats, like the Left in other countries, reject Biden's conservatism and call for an update of the New Deal in the form of a Green New Deal. It is therefore important to understand the key features of the original New Deal and how it helped shape America in the second half of the twentieth century.

No analysis of 'capitalism versus democracy' is adequate without discussing the greatest capitalist power in history. Generations of socialists from the 1840s to the 1940s focussed on the development of European capitalism and imperialist global expansion. Hence, insufficient attention was paid to how the US became the largest capitalist economy by the end of the nineteenth century and how it dominated the twentieth century and still retains its hegemony (despite major challenges) in the twenty-first century. Four decades before the US became the global military superpower after 1940, it had already surpassed Great Britain and its empire (the world's former powerhouse) as a financial, manufacturing and consuming giant between 1890 and 1916. Moreover, by 1914, the US was also double the industrial and financial power of Imperial Germany, the largest capitalist power in Europe.[1] American banks, for example, had to rescue a bankrupt France in 1916 and a very weakened 'Great Britain' that was unable to continue its currency policy without US support in the late 1920s and early 1930s. After World War One, the US became the world creditor and major powers such as Germany, France and Britain depended on loans provided by US financial institutions.

In 1932, Franklin D. Roosevelt had campaigned on the "restoration of democracy" and in 1936 on "the preservation of their [the people's] victory".[2] Was there a 'restoration of democracy' during the New Deal and if so, what did this mean? Like many other socialists, it is striking that Polanyi wrote little about America apart from references to US monetary policy and the gold standard, a few paragraphs about American liberal capitalism, the conflict between Wall Street and the White House and the hope that America would not become fascist.[3] In fact, Polanyi's American 'blind spot' is also one of the reasons why his thesis about the 'great transformation' remains so flawed; a thoroughly inadequate account of the 'origins of our time'. In order to understand why Polanyi's account of the struggle between 'capitalism and democracy' offers at best a rudimentary and distorted guide to contemporary political conflicts, it is necessary to discuss the New Deal in relation to both the 'great transformation' of the 1930s and the subsequent development of American and global capitalism. Communists and 'fellow travellers' like Polanyi were deluded about Stalin increasing 'democratisation' in a Soviet Union stricken by a wave of terror and also in their misguided optimism that fascism would only temporarily crush the inevitable triumph of socialism in post-fascist Europe. If this is the case, were their analyses of the New Deal just as deluded?

AMERICAN EXCEPTIONALISM

Since the nineteenth century there has been a debate over 'American exceptionalism' or why, and to what extent, American socio-cultural and political economic institutions and practices represented either an immature version of Europe or the future of Europe. The question was whether America would become Europeanised or Europe would become Americanised. The French and the Germans were particularly fascinated by America and were simultaneously admiring and critical of this new 'civilisation'. In his influential *Democracy in America* (1835-1840), Alex de Tocqueville saw white America as more egalitarian and democratic, a glimpse of the future of Europe. Yet, he also claimed that America lacked a leisure class and hence democracy would produce no lasting works of art or literature as social equality cultivated practical thinking rather than an aesthetic sensibility. Sixty years later, economist Thorstein Veblen was to make a biting satirical critique of the 'leisure class', especially how business leaders and the wealthy engaged in conspicuous consumption and aped the 'barbaric practices' of tribal and feudal societies.[4]

Despite being preoccupied with a pessimistic analysis of Western rationality, Max Weber was inspired by his visit to America in 1904 and would go on to analyse America as the new industrial capitalist manifestation of the Protestant ethic. He also thought that America might possibly avoid the 'soullessness' of European society – a fate propelled by the rationalisation and bureaucratisation of the modern world.[5] American liberal democracy, he speculated, might take capitalist development in a new direction. Otherwise, Weber believed that each step towards greater equality and democracy would not only result in the dissolution of traditional forms of aristocratic, tribal and patrimonial power, but also lead to an increase in bureaucracy. Friedrich Hayek would later go much further than Weber and warn of the 'road to serfdom' and 'totalitarianism' if socialist bureaucratic planning replaced the competitive market.

However, if 'equality' stood as a defining feature of American democracy, as visiting Europeans claimed, Weber's colleague, Werner Sombart pointedly asked in 1906: 'why is there no socialism in the United States?'[6] Sombart explained this 'American exceptionalism' by claiming that workers 'loved capitalism' and shared the passion of business people for money-making. He also focussed on how the two-party system prevented the development of a large socialist party. Sombart arrived at his conclusions by homogenising the American working class, thus largely ignoring the immigrant workforce, slavery and racial divisions. While the International Workers of the World and the Socialist Party of America tried to unite trade unionists, as well as 'populist' farmers and immigrant workers in the decades prior to the Great Depression, by the early 1930s Roosevelt's New Deal coalition and the growing Communist Party now challenged them. American Communists, however, were not exempted from the debate over 'exceptionalism'. In 1929, Stalin rejected 'American exceptionalism' and used American Communists Earl Browder and Joe Zack to criticise other Communists led by Jay Lovestone for arguing that Marxist laws do not apply to the US due its natural resources, industrial capacity, and absence of rigid class distinctions.[7]

While the debate over 'Americanism' has continued until the present day, it was long ago clear that American domestic and international relations did not fit comfortably into the collapse of Polanyi's four pillars of 'nineteenth century civilisation' thesis primarily concerning Europe. Moreover, to understand contemporary neoliberalism, an appreciation of why the US does not neatly fit important aspects of the broad Left 'master narrative' is also needed. I will later analyse the reasons the US failed to develop comparable levels of the European so-called 'Keynesian welfare state' between 1945 and

1975 that supposedly succeeded the 'great transformation' of the 1930s. Similarly, I will also discuss whether these states were themselves replaced by what is called the 'Hayekian state' from the late 1970s to the present day.

When considering the contest between 'capitalism and democracy', it is vital to analyse whether the New Deal significantly altered the power relations between state institutions and the so-called self-regulated market. Recall that Polanyi argued that the demise of 'nineteenth century civilisation' was not brought about by external or internal barbarians, nor by the revolt of the socialist proletariat or fascist middle class. Moreover, its failure, he argued, "was not the outcome of some alleged laws of economics such as that of the falling rate of profit or of underconsumption or overproduction."[8] Insofar as the social struggles that led to the introduction of the New Deal in 1933, this is partly correct. There certainly was neither a socialist revolution nor a revolt by middle-class fascists. However, overproduction and constraints on consumption did play a particularly important causal role, even if the latter did not unfold as inevitable economic 'laws' predicted by orthodox Marxists.

Polanyi's overemphasis of the role played by the gold standard and his hostility to Marxian political economy meant that he ignored key characteristics of American capitalism. He acknowledged that the US was not as heavily exposed to international trade as other countries, even though it contributed to the collapse of world trade by imposing high protectionist tariffs in 1930. Importantly, adherence to the gold standard and the imposition of tariff protection worsened and spread the Depression globally, but these factors did *not* cause the catastrophe. There remains no agreement among mainstream and radical economists as to the causes of the Great Depression.[9] The various conflicting explanations include the level of money supply, depressed wages and growing inequality, increased productivity and a crisis of profitability due to overproduction (both in manufactured goods and in agriculture), major increases in private debt and adjustment shocks caused by new emerging industries alongside stagnation and decline in old sectors. The immediate causes were attributed to political conservatism and the failure of the Hoover administration and the Federal Reserve to act in a more interventionist manner to curb financial speculation and the Wall Street bubble before the stock market crash of 1929. The deepening Depression was also due to the failure to increase demand and halt deflation after the crash between 1930 and 1932. These failures certainly exacerbated the disastrous aspects of the Depression before Roosevelt was elected in November 1932.

All these explanations continue to remain intricately connected to contemporary ongoing ideologically driven policy debates between monetarists, Marxists, Keynesians and various heterodox economists. The truth is that there was no single cause of the Great Depression. Unsurprisingly, a new generation of scholars and policy analysts now debate the causes of the crises of 2007-08 and the Pandemic crisis of 2020 in terms of how these recent crises are similar or different to the causes of the Great Depression.[10] Related to these debates is the issue of whether alternative policies to neoliberalism could have prevented the rise of Right-wing threats to democracy since 2007. Overall, most mainstream and radical accounts of the Great Depression directly and indirectly reject Polanyi's claim that the self-regulated market's adherence to the gold standard was the main cause of the Depression, or else argue that this was merely one of a number of probable causes

THE EMERGING POLITICAL ECONOMY OF 'AMERICAN CIVILISATION'

In his preoccupation with the rise of fascism and the end of the four pillars of 'nineteenth century European civilisation', Polanyi's myopia and proximity to events meant that he could not see the proverbial forest for the trees. He analysed America through the formulaic framework that he had developed for Europe. This prevented him from seeing the rise of a new 'American civilisation' that would eventually influence and help transform other developed capitalist societies following their post-war recovery and rebuilding in the period 1945 to 1960. By the time of Polanyi's death in 1964, new industries based on consumer production had become well established in many OECD countries. While consumer production had always been present in European countries prior to the 1930s, it was the specific character of new industries geared around automobiles and suburbanisation that had first rapidly developed in the US well before Europe.

The early stage of 'American civilisation' had already emerged in the three to four decades before the New Deal and was heavily based on the growth of consumer production fuelled by credit that would transform social relations, the character of urbanisation and industrial relations, including the rise of the 'mass worker' replacing many craft workers. Together with support from federal and state governments, the American consumer economy would eventually become one of the twin pillars alongside the military-industrial complex. These twin pillars would be based on new domestic budgetary priorities and greater US dominance of international monetary and fiscal policies (especially after 1945) at the expense of alleviating poverty and social inequality both within America and globally. The growth of science and technological research and development were to become critical to the military and civilian sectors and would in turn be closely interrelated with the vital education industry that would both socialise individuals and create the necessary skills and professional administrative foundation of the 'new civilisation'.

From 1870 to 1930, the US underwent a massive transformation of its political economy and social conditions that should not to be confused with Polanyi's 'great transformation'. The steady rise of the urban population and major increases in single dwelling houses, as opposed to tenement housing and rural farms, were closely related to the growth of mass manufacturing. Both housing and durable goods manufacturing (automobiles, whitegoods, furniture and electrical goods) were fuelled by an explosion of credit. By 1890, 29 per cent of homes had a mortgage and government legislation in the 1920s permitting a second and third mortgage led to increased home purchasing. From 1910, a spurt in credit growth over the next two decades resulted in fifty per cent of all consumer products being purchased on credit by 1929. Car registration per household grew from near zero in 1900 to one car for every six Americans in 1929. Over 75% of cars were sold to farmers and to residents of small towns with less than 50,000 people rather than to residents of the largest cities. By contrast, Germany only had 486,001 cars in 1932[11] compared to over 23 million cars in the US. Similarly, it was not until the period between the mid-1950s and the late 1960s that France (another former Great European Power) rapidly modernised its rural post-empire society into an 'Americanised' industrialised consumer economy with affordable cars.[12] In fact, by 1930, a staggering 78 per cent of all the cars in the world were registered in the US. Just as railroads had been one of the key drivers of investment and growth in the nineteenth century, so automobile production and all related industries (gasoline, steel, rubber, plate glass, chrome and nickel) expanded from 1900 to 1929. The growth of the automobile industry necessitated the largest government road-building program in history that reached 387,000 miles of paved road in 1921, and 662,000 miles by 1929 – far in advance of other countries.[13]

Importantly, the developing American car culture of the early twentieth century was associated with contradictory notions of freedom and selfhood. On the one side were the 'mass workers' toiling in giant 'Fordist' factories of car production forced to surrender their notions of freedom and sovereign individuality in order to conform to Taylorist enforced methods of severe discipline and productivity. On the other side, were the customers of automobiles that increasingly associated 'automobility' with emancipation, freedom of movement and the essence of American liberal culture.[14] Marketing of cars was initially directed to affluent women, small town residents and farmers before becoming a central part of American liberal ideology before the Second World War and during the Cold War. Today, similar divisions between 'hardware' and 'software' characterise contemporary digital culture. The 'hardware' of digital culture is mainly produced by low-paid workers in Asian factories while the Internet and digital freedom are divorced from these factories and celebrated as the essence of individual freedom and communicative mobility.

Although suburbanisation was massively expanded in the decades after 1945, the forty-year period before the Depression of the 1930s had already witnessed the emergence of a consumer economy. With the expansion of credit, consumer goods that were unattainable luxuries for an earlier generation of workers and their families, were now accessible. This is not to ignore the extensive poverty among rural workers, black families in both rural and urban areas and approximately a quarter of all white workers and their families. Nonetheless, by 1939, despite the shocking impact of the Great Depression on mass poverty, a majority of urban housing units were connected to electricity, gas, sewage pipes, running water and telephones and radios, including many with refrigeration and other electrical appliances.

Much of this increase in manufacturing, services and housing required federal and state regulation, provision of land and financial funding. The self-regulated market was both part reality and part myth. It was not just the massive road construction programme by governments, for instance, that linked the so-called separate political and economic spheres. From the 1880s to the 1920s, American businesses witnessed a massive growth in the role played by all types of engineers applying scientific research, standardisation and new management practices.[15] President Herbert Hoover presided over the regulation and standardisation of sizes and measurements in everything used by businesses, from nuts and bolts to plumbing supplies and other industrial parts. This standardisation facilitated the mass production of civilian goods on assembly lines and later on, the immense production of weapons after 1940. However, the self-regulated market was also a deadly and costly reality in those industries like the production of food (especially milk, meats and so forth) that were adulterated to such an extent that processed food resulted in the deaths and serious illnesses suffered by countless numbers of people. Some of the worst excesses of self-regulation in food production were eventually brought under some form of government control but the human cost of insufficiently regulated processed food production continues today.

At the opposite extreme, government control over personal alcohol consumption was a significant socio-economic intervention as Prohibition, beginning in 1920, proved to be highly unpopular, led to numerous deaths through illicit unregulated alcohol, and spawned a massive increase in organised crime that has lasted despite Prohibition being overturned in 1933. While processed food was a key industry in the US manufacturing sector and featured as part of the American consumer society, this was not true of many countries in Europe and other parts of the world. The far greater reliance on non-processed food outside the US meant that pre-1940 American levels of industrialised food production and consumption were only developed much later on in the second half of the twentieth century.

The significance of the greater availability of credit manifested itself in a crisis of both overproduction and constrained consumption that came to a head by the late 1920s. Following the cutback in armaments production and the slump in 1920-21, the frenzied growth in consumer goods production and consumption and also housing construction led to an overproduction of producer goods such as steel and other material inputs. However, employer attacks on wages and conditions, plus declining union membership (from 5.1 million members in 1920 to 3.6 million in 1929) led to stagnant or falling real wages. Workers could not afford to sustain consumption levels, as their increased debt and repayment levels combined with massive increases in industrial productivity (innovative technology, harsher work conditions) produced the twin crisis of overproduction and a fall in aggregate demand, especially household consumption. Between 1929 and 1933, the official unemployment rate reached 25 per cent and US gross national product collapsed by 29 per cent, caused by plummeting individual, household and business income. It was the New Deal that boosted government-funded infrastructure projects, job creation and other measures to increase aggregate demand. The collapse on Wall Street in October 1929 was a recognition that stock values had far outpaced company profits and was also partly due to the dangerous speculative bubble conditions, such as the extension of credit enabling investors to buy shares with only 10 per cent deposit. Stock market prices did not recover to pre-crash levels until 1954, almost as slow a rate of recovery as Soviet livestock numbers by the end of the 1950s after the slaughter induced by the introduction of collectivisation in 1929.

When we consider some of the major causes of the Great Depression in the US and the key policy initiatives of the New Deal, there was no 'great transformation' or major departure from liberal capitalist practices – a continuity eventually and belatedly recognised by Polanyi in 1945. Instead, greater government involvement emerged but not to the extent that private capitalist businesses were subordinated to state control (except during the war years 1941 to 1945). Rather, some of the main regulatory measures of the New Deal were related to reducing risk rather than countering inequality or the dominant control of the market by private businesses. Legislation such as the Glass-Steagall Act of 1933 that separated commercial from investment banking, the Federal Deposit Insurance Corporation and the Securities and Exchange Commission were introduced to minimise bank failures, risky and corrupt stock market practices and protect the savings of bank customers. In 1920, there were 30,291 banks due to the boom in agricultural prices generated by the First World War. Agricultural commodity prices declined during the 1920s despite the boom of the roaring twenties in consumer goods and the rise in industrial corporate profits. The Great Depression compounded rural problems with the collapse of world commodities prices and trade. Thousands of banks failed between 1920 and 1932. The new regulations of the New Deal were not a complete success as another 4,000 banks failed throughout the 1930s (a total of 9,000 bank failures) and hundreds of mainly rural banks collapsed in later decades as well as 1,000 savings and loan societies that were declared insolvent during the 1980s. It was the repeal in 1999 (under President Clinton) of the separation of commercial from investment banking, that partly helped fuel dangerous financial practices and contributed to the Great Financial Crisis of 2007-08.

It is important to distinguish between the New Deal of the pre-war years (1933 to 1941) and the war years when more regulations over production, prices and labour conditions were implemented. Most of the pre-war measures were interventions designed to revive the American capitalist economy through employment programs and infrastructure projects such as the Tennessee Valley Authority. They were also partly implemented to meet the needs of the Democratic Party's new working-class base[16] as well as the urban and rural small business constituencies needing minimum protection against a risk-prone market. Compared to his Labor Secretary Frances Perkins (a suffragette and workers' rights advocate), Roosevelt reluctantly supported the Wagner Act which gave protection for unions and the right of workers to organise. American businesses and governments had long violently repressed – through the use of both public and private police forces, industrial spies and strikebreaking thugs – attempts by a growing industrial workforce to unionise. During the 1930s, additional millions of dollars were spent by businesses on machine guns, tear gas and other munitions in response to growing worker militancy. Violent confrontations resulted in the deaths of workers, such as the infamous 1937 Memorial Day massacre in Chicago,[17] regardless of legislation protecting unionisation.

HOW ORGANISED LABOUR HELPED CONSOLIDATE SOCIAL INEQUALITY

There is a nostalgic view that the New Deal promoted 'industrial democracy' for all workers but this view glossed over the significant divisions within the labour movement and within the coalition of diverse political forces backing the Roosevelt administration. Certainly, the rise of the mass production worker (as opposed to craft workers) and the militant activism of the newly united industrial unions known as the Committee of Industrial Organization (CIO) in 1935 (which split from the old conservative American Federation of Labor), marked an important development in the conflict between labour and capital.[18] The wave of mass strikes and sit-ins beginning in the San Francisco Bay Area in 1934 and moving in the following years to the automobile industry, steel and other large production enterprises peaked in 1934, 1937-8 and with returned soldiers in 1946-7. During the late 1960s, and in the wake of militant strikes at Fiat and other large corporations, Italian radical theorists such as Mario Tronti celebrated the rise of the 'mass worker'. "Yesterday's American political situation" he wrote, "is the historical Western-European present."[19] However, the radicalism of the mass workers during the New Deal was far from revolutionary. Although conservatives labelled unionists 'Reds', there was no concerted assault by workers on corporations with the aim of creating a revolution. Instead, John Lewis and other CIO leaders interpreted 'industrial democracy' to mean improved conditions and wages. Unionists also helped form the backbone of political campaigns in many cities and states for the election of supportive mayors and other politicians to achieve improved social conditions.

In 2002, labour historian Nelson Lichtenstein argued that 'rights consciousness' centred on the workplace and radiated out to the wider political sphere during the New Deal. Besides the rise of conservative union leaders during the Cold War, such as George Meany, the labour movement bureaucracy was seen by many new social movement activists in the 1960s and 1970s as a hostile entrenched force, even though many unionists were supportive of civil rights, feminist and anti-war campaigns. The democratising 'rights campaigns' now shifted away from the workplace and became more strongly associated with cultural and social identity politics.[20] I will return to recent debates over class politics versus identity politics in Book Three of this book. It should not be forgotten, however, that the union movement's Operation Dixie was an attempt to unionise white and black workers in the South during the late 1940s but encountered a very strong backlash from Southern racist political, business and landowning elites.[21] The level of Southern conservative backlash against 'industrial democracy' in the 1940s was so severe that union membership declined from its low base in Southern states as major union-busting tactics were consolidated in subsequent decades. According to Lichtenstein, Operation Dixie "would have required a massive, socially disruptive interracial campaign reminiscent of the CIO at its most militant moment in the late 1930s – indeed, a campaign not dissimilar from that which the modem civil rights movement would wage in the 1960s."[22]

As to the legacy of New Deal industrial militancy, Michel Aglietta of the French Regulation School, building on Gramsci's fragmented observations, developed the notion of 'Fordism'.[23] While focusing more on the post-New Deal period from the 1950s to 1970s, Aglietta analysed how 'Fordism' during the 1930s superseded earlier applications of Taylorist 'time and motion' methods and other mechanisation of labour techniques deployed by management – speeding up the assembly line, hiring married workers with a mortgage that were less strike prone – all of which required replacing the craft worker mentality with the construction of a 'collective worker' capable of maximising efficiency and productivity in the new industrial processes.[24] It was the reaction against low wages and Taylorist and other managerial productivity drives that fuelled the rise of industrial unionism. Labour-management struggles now saw government involvement in the resolution of strikes and the New Deal fostered a new stage of management-labour-state relations called 'Fordism'. However, Aglietta's thesis about 'Fordism' ignored or minimised the quite different consequences of 'Fordism' in America compared with Europe. The New Deal may have helped pioneer 'Fordism', as this tripartite stage had similarities to the so-called Keynesian corporatist developments in post-1945 Europe. Yet, despite the limited application of Keynesian policies between the 1940s and 1960s, America never did develop a social democratic Keynesian political and industrial wing, particularly given that the Democratic Party was not a 'labour party' and post-war unions were not united around building a social welfare state. Instead of European and

Australian industry-wide collective bargaining that would affect large and small firms alike and also improve social welfare benefits for all workers and their families, most American unions either voluntarily pursued or were forced into enterprise-centred struggles and agreements, both before but especially after 1947. These negotiated benefits applied only to workers in a particular corporation such as General Motors or the U.S. Steel Corporation. The trend of enterprise bargaining rather than industry-wide collective bargaining produced great disparities between unionised workers and the vast majority of non-unionised workers. It also later affected other countries from the 1980s onwards as neoliberal policies swept the OECD, resulting in various governments supporting businesses in undermining industry-wide collective bargaining negotiations.

By ignoring so many aspects of America's political economy, Polanyi's attempt to link the New Deal to the European 'great transformation' was tenuous at best. America neither fitted the original European 'great transformation' of pre-capitalist society into market society, nor key aspects of the second 'transformation' during the 1930s. The relevance of Polanyi's thesis to contemporary capitalism is therefore marginal for a number of reasons, including his failure to see or analyse the emergence of the 'new worker' and how 'Americanism' was simultaneously linked to, but developed along a different path to 'European civilisation'. Instead, Polanyi focussed on the self-regulated market as an abstract entity and therefore missed the vital roles played by both businesses and state institutions in transforming work processes and consumption patterns, especially the integration of work and consumption in the construction of new forms of everyday life. The Great Depression and the Second World War temporarily interrupted the growth in household consumption but consolidated the transformation of labour processes, without which new production methods and the circulation of goods and services would not have occurred.

It was the surging militancy of industrial workers in large enterprises that particularly frightened corporate leaders and gave the New Deal the exaggerated image of being the first stage on the 'road to socialism'. Instead, the reality was that despite the enormity of the socio-economic crisis confronting the New Dealers, their legislative program was fairly mild and barely caught up with late nineteenth century to pre-1914 protective legislation in Europe (such as Bismarck's limited health and accident insurance or old age pensions) and Australia's pensions and basic wage for male workers. The New Deal also had little of the post-1945 European social democratic agenda that supported the nationalisation of various large privately-owned enterprises and also more comprehensive social welfare programs. It is largely a myth that the far-sighted liberal-corporatist wing rationalised and modernised American capitalism during the New Deal by accommodating democratic demands. While it is true that there were a minority of modernising liberals in the business sector, far too many of the largest corporations fought even the smallest concessions to workers and any extension of government regulations to protect citizens from a range of corporate practices and products. In later decades, many businesses adjusted to global competition by adopting endless new management and public relations techniques as 'good corporate citizens' while at the same time vigorously resisting political and industrial democratisation and social reforms.

The New Deal coalition of political forces temporarily broke the power of the old conservative bloc. Moreover, a decade after the rise of worker militancy in the 1930s, the conservative political and corporate counter-offensive succeeded when the Republicans won control of Congress in 1946 and passed the 1947 Taft-Hartley Act. This legislation, under the cover of rising Cold War hysteria, was aimed at Communist members of unions and legalised other measures to firmly shift the balance of power back to employers. The outlawing of mass picketing, wild cat strikes, and sympathy strikes or secondary boycotts, is a case in point. This meant that no direct and indirect action taken by unions in other enterprises or sectors in support of those workers on strike left workers weaker and more isolated.

Even though strikes were quite prevalent during the 1940s and 1950s, by the end of the 1940s most of the former militant industrial unions had been deradicalised and bureaucratised under the power of single union leaders. Kim Moody observed that we now saw the rise of 'modern business unionism'[25] which later presided over a declining unionised workforce into the second half of the twentieth century. There has been a slight increase in labour militancy and union recruitment in the first two decades of the twenty-first century, mainly in the public sector. Nonetheless, unionisation in the overwhelmingly dominant US private sector continues to languish at approximately a tiny 6.2 per cent of the workforce with key industries in many of the fifty states of the US such as finance, insurance, technical services and food and drink all registering almost no unionisation at an abysmal level of between 1.1% and 1.4% of workers employed. [26]

Overall, the New Deal was not a coherent plan but more a set of emergency measures necessary to revive an America on its knees, a programme to eliminate the fear and hopelessness felt by tens of millions of people. During the 1930s, the New Deal was interpreted in maximalist and minimalist terms depending on a variety of regional and national politicians and administrators. However, Franklin Roosevelt and key members of his administration were 'sound money men' or fiscal conservatives rather than advocates of the 'great transformation' against liberal capitalism. Although millions of unemployed workers were given jobs in public works programmes, these were temporary measures to get private businesses 'moving' again.[27] Roosevelt opposed a permanent expansion of the public sector as 'socialist'. The recession of 1937-38 was partly caused by Roosevelt cutting back government expenditure to balance the federal budget, hardly a Keynesian policy given that unemployment was still over 14% and jumped to 19% in 1938.

Little was done to undermine corporate power, even though Roosevelt's rhetoric moved to the Left in his attack on Republicans and their big business allies. Harvard economist Alvin Hansen's famous December 1938 address warning about the onset of deep-seated 'secular stagnation' was indicative of the failure of the New Deal to transform key aspects of US regional socio-economic disparities and the underlying dynamics of pre-1929 American capitalism.[28] While inequality slightly decreased under the New Deal, Roosevelt's reluctance to abandon liberal capitalist practices was also evident in his opposition to a national health scheme and other social welfare reforms necessary to combat poverty, inequality and neglect. It is often forgotten that when one excludes its post-1940 military apparatus, the US never developed a large federal government or public sector compared with Western European countries. This significant difference continues to the present day. Take the fact that in capitalist Finland, one third of the economy is in the public sector which employs a third of the workforce and almost 90% of private and public sector workers are covered by a union contract. For America to match Finland in similar percentage terms, Matt Bruenig of the People's Policy Project argues that the US government would have to "not only build a social-democratic welfare state, but also socialize $35 trillion of assets, unionize 120 million workers, and move 25 million workers into the public sector."[29]

On the other hand, the New Deal did provide limited funding to federal agencies and the states and cities to build tens of thousands of public housing project homes, plant tens of millions of trees, create public green spaces and electrify large numbers of rural and urban residential areas. Relatively speaking, it was the most concerted involvement of professionals such as engineers, designers or architects working in the public sector in American history, an involvement that would recede and be monopolised by the private market until the present day. These public designs (demolishing old areas and building freeways and the 'projects' or slums of the future) would be later widely criticised by urban movements led by Jane Jacobs and many others for their soulless modernism and destruction of old communities. Tellingly, Polanyi ignored these vital public sector challenges to the market in the construction of public housing, green areas and the harnessing of professional knowledge by the public sector. Leaving aside the New Deal's technocratic modernist designs, a new generation of urban designers now seeks a revived public sector under the Green New Deal to combat America's appalling dilapidated public infrastructure, homelessness and rampant private property development that has ruined city after city.[30]

Apart from his adherence to liberal capitalist policies, Roosevelt was a political tactician who was not prepared to undermine his electoral coalition for the sake of policies and principles. This meant pandering to a range of conservative Democrats, especially the powerful Southern Democrats eager to veto any legislation that threatened highly discriminatory race relations. Therefore, the 1935 Social Security legislation excluded retirement and unemployment benefits for workers in particular sectors such as agriculture and domestic labour. Apart from poor whites in these excluded sectors, Ira Katznelson documents that the Social Security Act was 'policy apartheid' in that nationally, 65% of all African Americans (given the high percentage of black maids and rural labourers) and between 70 and 80 per cent in parts of the South were excluded from receiving retirement income until this racism in social security was partially rectified in 1954.[31] Many non-whites still retired on lower incomes given that they were employed in low-paying jobs. The New Deal legacy on social welfare effectively consigned America to a truncated 'welfare state' unworthy of its name, despite better services in several of the fifty states. Subsequent federal administrations up until the present day have, apart from minor improvements, not only failed to rectify these areas of welfare neglect, but actually cut some of these meagre provisions from the 1980s onwards.

INDUSTRIALISATION AND SECULARISATION

The classic European sociological arguments about how industrialisation, modernisation and mass education led to democratisation and major declines in church attendance plus the loss of power by religions were seen by many as not applicable to America. Those who still subscribe to this view today, usually cite such things as the fact that seven Southern state constitutions still have clauses outlawing atheists from holding public office, despite the US Supreme Court overruling this in 1961. They also cite the public display of religiosity by politicians even though America has been one of the leading industrialising and modernising forces in the world. However, the socio-political situation is much more complicated.

Just as Polanyi ignored the internal transformation of work processes and consumption patterns, those who argue that the secularisation thesis does not apply to contemporary America usually focus on the 'Bible belt' states in the South and Mid-West rather than on large urban centres. They also over-look that US church attendance figures in recent decades have been grossly inflated and religious influence over public policies (excluding abortion) has declined significantly.[32] In contrast to Europeans and Australians who aban-doned church attendance in larger numbers, Americans secularised their interpretations of Christianity, especially on issues such as what constituted 'sinful behaviour'. Churches now have to market their message in a highly competitive social leisure market, a vastly different society to that of the 1930s, one characterised by high divorce rates, changing family structures and sexual practices as well as cultural fragmentation and commercialised social values and lifestyles.[33] Not only have leading religiously affiliated universities become secular,[34] so too, more non-church attending Republi-cans voted for Trump than religiously observant evangelicals. Significantly, the American alt-Right are markedly non-religious and suspicious of Chris-tianity compared to conservative Republicans.[35]

Historian Jefferson Cowie rejects both the Right-wing and New Left critiques of the New Deal and presents an overly benign image of the period from the 1930s to 1978 as the 'great exception' of progressive achievements in American history bookended by the gilded age of 'robber barons' before the Great Depression and their revival as corporate capitalists in the 1970s.[36] In regard to religion and immigration, Cowie argues that the economic crisis of the 1930s and the post-war boom saw religious tensions subside as the greater role of the state and a broader conception of 'the congregation' led to a growing acceptance of non-Protestant religions such as Catholicism and Judaism. This consensus fractured by the 1960s as a militant nativism attacked both new immigrants and black civil rights movements. A revived evangelical Protestantism in the form of the Moral Majority and other Chris-tian movements repoliticised religion around issues such as abortion, prayer in schools, busing of school children, birth control and pornography.[37] This religious division and 'culture war' has extended to the present day with particularly strong Right-wing attacks on Muslims and Hispanic immigrants and their so-called threats to Christianity or economic wellbeing and law-and-order.

Secularisation in the US, as in other societies, has been an uneven process. During the past one hundred years, mass education, industrialisation and Enlightenment 'scientific progress' has co-existed socially and at the individual level with the widespread social adherence to new and old political and cultural myths (practised outside organised religions). An increase in numbers of those with university education coexists with the fact that more than 73% of Americans and Europeans believe in various paranormal phenomena such as ghosts, witches, telepathy or astrology, despite significant differences in church attendance.[38] Similar contradictions are evident in the simultaneous denial of science when it comes to climate change but the worship of science and technology in ideologically 'legitimate' areas such as finding cures for cancer, military R & D or space exploration.

While living in the US through the New Deal, Adorno and Horkheimer focussed on the 'dark side' of Enlightenment 'progress' and why the domination of nature and sadism were linked to technical rationality and the persistence of myths.[39] The 'dialectic of Enlightenment' undermined prevalent notions of 'liberal progress' by highlighting the fact that rationality and magical thinking were not inherently incompatible with one another. However, the Frankfurt School's associate, Franz Neumann, remained an uncritical devotee of Enlightenment rationality as being inherently anti-fascist. Towards the end of *Behemoth*, his classic study of Nazism, Neumann naïvely placed his faith in German engineers (the 'most rational of vocations') being able to counter Nazi myth and fanaticism because German production would founder without rational input from engineers.[40] Just as Trotsky was deluded in thinking that German worker and peasant members of the invading Nazi armies would be infected by their European and Soviet proletarian counterparts and trigger revolution, so too, Neumann's 'rational engineers' overwhelmingly failed to heed 'the call' to counter Nazi irrationality.

Today, rationality and myth once again underpin not a 'reactionary modernism' as in the interwar period (Ernst Jünger, Carl Schmitt, Werner Sombart, Oswald Spengler and Martin Heidegger[41]), but a 'reactionary postmodernism'. New forms of technical rationality embodied in the 'digital economy' requires mass formal educational credentialism or training, as opposed to education. This cognitively based employment, especially in the services sector, appears quite compatible with new and old types of domination, racism, paranoid fear, moral panics and superstitious cultural practices. Political movements and groups have always tapped into 'feelings', 'common sense' and 'folklore'. Also, the claim to advocate 'evidence-based policies' instead of 'ideology', has itself become a technocratic new version of 'common sense' that can be used to justify irrational political economic policies such as environmentally destructive incessant economic growth, even if it is called 'green growth'.

THE NEW DEAL AND THE POST-1945 WORLD

With Hitler facing imminent defeat in 1945, Polanyi restated his main thesis but with an important major revision, namely, he virtually excluded the New Deal from his so-called epochal change. This was two years after he finished writing *The Great Transformation*. Expressing a cautious optimism about the emerging new international order made up of regional powers, Polanyi proclaimed: "The tremendous event of our age is the simultaneous downfall of liberal capitalism, world-revolutionary socialism and racial domination – the three competing forms of universalist societies."[42] He celebrated the triumph of 'regional' socialism, in other words, 'socialism in one country' (or Stalinist terror) over 'world-revolutionary socialism' by which he meant Trotskyism. Furthermore, he argued that liberal capitalism had also been overcome in Europe by the collapse of the gold standard and Hitler's racial model of world domination was in the last stage of being destroyed on the battlefield. From the 'three competing forms of universalist societies', Polanyi predicted the emergence of "new forms of socialism, of capitalism, of planned and semi-planned economies – each of them, by their very nature, *regional*." [43] He saw this new regionalism as "an almost exact replica of the establishment of the European states-system about the end of the fifteenth century. In both cases the change sprang from the collapse of the universal society of the period. In the Middle Ages that society was primarily religious, while in our time it was economic."[44]

The United States, in Polanyi's view, was the one notable exception to this imagined scenario. The threat to new forms of international regional co-existence was American liberal universalism that had been virtually untouched by the New Deal. Whereas before he had argued that America was part of 'nineteenth century civilisation', now Polanyi echoed earlier social theorists such as Werner Sombart in stressing a version of 'American exceptionalism'. Citing its free supply of land, unskilled labour and paper money, Polanyi conceded that the US had been largely unaffected by the damaging effects of the self-regulated market for most of the nineteenth century. This is why he argued that for the vast majority of Americans and American businesses the Great Depression merely dimmed 'the aura of adulation' associated with laissez-faire.[45] As a self-appointed spokesperson for the world's population, Polanyi pronounced that:

> Americans still believe in a way of life no longer supported by the
> common people in the rest of the world, but which nevertheless
> implies a universality which commits those who believe in it to re-
> conquer the globe on its behalf. On the crucial issue of foreign econ-
> omy, America stands for the nineteenth century.[46]

While it is true that many people opposed the inequality and destruction inflicted by liberal capitalism, the allure of the affluence of the American 'way of life' was certainly not rejected by the 'common people' across the world. On the contrary, liberal capitalist consumerism, Hollywood and Coca Cola were all attractive 'soft power' models and lifestyle goals desired and imitated by hundreds of millions of people outside America. Polanyi hoped that the New Deal would have proved a starting point out of the liberal social impasse that destroyed Europe, but he was realistic enough to recognise that 'the time' for this political economic transformation had yet to arrive given the ideological dominance of liberalism. Instead, he asserted that all of Roosevelt's New Deal policies "have affected the position of liberal capitalism as little as similar departures towards interventionism and socialism had done in Europe up to 1914."[47] If so, his grand thesis of the global 'great transformation' stands as a case of Polanyian hyperbole with little historical evidence to support it. Polanyi's summation of the world in 1945 therefore warrants some brief observations, particularly regarding American liberalism, the 'great transformation' and the so-called emerging world of 'regionalism'.

Firstly, given the New Deal did not end liberal capitalism in what was the most powerful country in the world, what remained of Polanyi's claim that there had been a global 'great transformation' in the 1930s. After all, Polanyi had similarly misunderstood the Russian revolution and its relation to his grand thesis. The Soviet Five-Year plans were the outcome of the transformation of non-liberal Czarist autocracy that began in November 1917 through the establishment of a new Soviet state, rather than the so-called transformation of the liberal self-regulated market in the 1930s. Let us not forget that in Polanyi's 'master narrative' the self-regulated market began in Great Britain. It was only on the European continent that the disastrous consequences of liberal capitalism led to fascism. Yet, the liberal economies of North Western Europe, France, the UK, and most other countries in the world had not been significantly transformed before 1940. Therefore, Polanyi's crisis of 'nineteenth century civilisation' would perhaps have been more plausible had he merely tried to explain how liberal capitalism gave rise to fascism in a few countries such as Germany, Austria and Italy. Instead, he erroneously inflated the so-called 'great transformation' into a global transformation.

Despite Polanyi's claim that the New Deal had as insignificant impact on liberal capitalism as had European interventionism before 1914, the conflict between 'capitalism and democracy' did not result in either socialism or fascism in America or in most of the rest of the world. What occurred in Germany and a few other fascist-dominated countries was disastrous. These regimes only temporarily resolved the old conflict between 'capitalism and democracy' in capitalism's favour until fascist dictatorships were defeated in 1945. New modified forms of this old conflict continue to the present day. As for the much longer lasting Soviet dictatorial system, this was a historical development that was not only at odds with Polanyi's thesis about 'capitalism versus democracy', it also confirmed his life-long delusion that these Eastern European regimes would become socialist *and* democratic. In short, there was no 'great transformation' in capitalist countries during the 1930s apart from Nazi Germany and to a lesser extent in fascist Italy, or the beginnings of new forms of state interventionism in Social Democratic Sweden. It is worth noting that Polanyi viewed these latter social democratic developments with 'distaste'[48] because he erroneously did not see the 'Swedish model'[49] as a significant departure from pre-1914 liberalism.

TRAPPED IN THE PAST

Polanyi claimed that America in 1945 stood for the 'nineteenth century' and threatened the new regionalism with its universalist attempt to restore global trade via the Bretton Woods agreement to regulate monetary policy. There is no doubt that the US pursued a global strategy to enhance its economic and military power. However, this was not a return to the nineteenth century trade order but the attempt to build new alliances and a buffer against Communism following the catastrophes of the Great Depression and fascism. In a war-devastated Europe and parts of Asia there were no other non-Communist powers capable of preventing US global dominance on their own. War-torn and occupied Germany and Japan, impoverished Italy, a near bankrupt and severely weakened France, Belgium, Netherlands and 'Great' Britain all clinging to their colonies through costly, last ditch military counter-insurgency wars in Africa and Asia in the late 1940s and through to the early 1960s, were hardly strong enough or interested in forging a new regionalism with the USSR. On the contrary, the imminent onset of the Cold War by 1946 meant not the starry-eyed 'regionalism' of Polanyi's dreams but the new power rivalry between the US and the USSR as they divided up Europe and tried to secure strategic alliances across the world.

In contrast to Habermas, Pierre Rosanvallon and others who mistakenly accredited Polanyi with heralding the post-war 'embedded liberalism'[50] of the Bretton Woods system based on the welfare state, the opposite in fact was true. Polanyi regarded Bretton Woods as a threat to British Labour's attempt to create a socialist society.[51] Besides, there was no attempt to restore the free market of 'nineteenth century civilisation' which Polanyi claimed rested on the old balance of power between the European imperial powers. Bretton Woods had all sorts of inbuilt problems, but it was not a return to the nine-teenth century nor a mere replica of the old gold standard and the liberal international market. Instead, the lessons of the earlier collapse of global trade and competitive devaluations required thoroughly new institutions of global co-ordination. The Bretton Woods system was certainly not designed for a world of socialist planned economies. Rather, it tried to promote trade stability, helped post-war recovery and extended American power and consol-idated other capitalist countries via agencies such as the International Mone-tary Fund and the International Bank for Reconstruction and Development (later part of World Bank Group).

In actual fact, most of the Bretton Woods institutions did not come into full operation until the end of the 1950s and the US-backed gold standard ran into trouble a decade later. Instead of Polanyi's version of a new 'regionalism', by 1947 the Marshall Plan was proposed to help rebuild Europe. Originally, the Marshall Plan also offered aid to the Soviet Union and Eastern European Communist countries knowing that Stalin would reject this aid offer and the implied American intrusion into the Soviet system. When it began in 1948, the Marshall Plan benefited US businesses as European countries were provided funds and loans to buy American equipment and goods. Also, five percent of the Marshall Fund was secretly used to finance anti-communist labour movement activity, journals, newspapers and cultural groups. Strategi-cally, the US formed anti-Communist pacts such as NATO, OAS, CENTO, SEATO and ANZUS[52] – from the North Atlantic and Latin America to the

Middle East, the Gulf, South East Asia and the Pacific – in order to secure the capitalist 'free world' from first the Soviet Union, and later from the Chinese, North Korean and Vietnamese Communist 'totalitarians'. There may have been a fragile and threatening Cold War stand-off in Europe (apart from civil war in Greece), but actual savage wars and civil wars in Asia, Africa, Central America, Latin America and the Middle East raged in different countries from 1945 onwards.

Third, it is noteworthy that Polanyi based his regional hopes on the USSR and Britain plus the British Commonwealth and other countries. Just as he was silent on the pervasive character of institutional and social racism in America and evaluated American liberalism in narrow economistic terms, so too, he said nothing about colonial racism and the need for the UK to abandon its sordid imperial past. Contrast his position with that of George Orwell who argued in 1939 that British democracy was just as bad as German fascism because of the way it treated the overwhelming bulk of the 'British proletariat' who did not live in Britain, but in Africa and Asia.[53] Racist contempt for local populations resulted in over sixty million people dying in the famines in the Indian sub-continent alone under British rule either from deliberately induced policies or inaction to prevent escalating casualties.

Polanyi's simplistic equation of fifteenth century religious universalism with mid-twentieth century economic universalism overlooked all the cultural and racist forms of domination anti-colonial movements were fighting against in their opposition to European imperialist powers. Instead, he pinned his hopes on British Labour promoting socialism and resisting American liberalism. This proved to be a pipe dream despite Labour's domestic social reforms, as the UK under both Labour and the Conservatives became America's closest strategic partner across the world.

Equally noteworthy was Polanyi's glaring failure before his death in 1964 to signal any interest in or support for a new European supranational social democratic or socialist regionalism as a counterweight to American liberalism. Conservatives such as Jean Monnet, Konrad Adenauer, Robert Schuman and others supported the formation of a united Western Europe to prevent another world war and also to develop a buffer against the Soviets by creating a large internal market. In contrast, Socialists and Communists were largely opposed to a capitalist 'common market' and were terribly slow to develop alternative democratic notions of a 'social Europe'. As a result, a new form of supranational regionalism evolved from its earlier American-supported incarnation as a customs union in the period 1951 to 1958, right through to the more elaborate present-day EU. Interestingly, decades later a new generation of 'regionalists' or Left nationalists who oppose neoliberal globalism in the EU and the US are now repeating some of Polanyi's illusions about a possible international order based on democratically sovereign small nation states. In Chapter Eight, I will discuss Wolfgang Streeck's problematic use of Polanyi's concept of 'regionalism' to explain contemporary geopolitical power relations.[54]

WRONG TIMING OR FUNDAMENTAL MISREADING OF NEW WORLD?

Some contemporary analysts argue that Polanyi was ultimately correct about the 'great transformation' but just that his timing was wrong, as it occurred after 1945 rather than in the 1930s.[55] It is true that various liberal and social democratic forms of state interventionism flourished after 1945. Importantly, this was not the 'transformation' that Polanyi had outlined if we analyse in detail his writing on the way Soviet Five-Year plans, Nazi state control and the New Deal would bring an end to the self-regulated market. It should be noted and underlined that his book *The Great Transformation* was written before the crucial post-war settlements in Europe that were much more immediate responses by Western European governments to the devastation caused by fascism and the need to rebuild capitalist economies. These 'settlements' or political compromises included integrating returning soldiers and well-organised working classes with more extensive social welfare programs and other stakes in the system. The sacrifices made by millions of people to defeat fascism meant that voters and Left industrial unions and parties were not going to have their legitimate social needs ignored, especially given the need of pro-market governments to shore up support against what was perceived as the rising real or imagined 'Communist threat' posed by the USSR.

I agree with Polanyi's 1945 revised thesis that the New Deal did not transform American liberal capitalism in the direction of socialism or even towards a coherent state-planned capitalism. But he was delusional about British Labour and the Austrian Social Democrats implementing policies on the road to socialism. He failed to recognise that a divided Western Europe was too weak or too frightened to pursue an independent path against both the US and the USSR. Hence, the *transformation* in Western Europe after 1945 was neither Communist, fascist nor American New Deal but rather a set of specific national strategies that reformed and stabilised capitalism given the political compromises that had to be made within the context of a

Cold War divided world. These national reforms were a mixture of social democracy, corporatism, Keynesian demand management and Ordoliberal 'social market' policies, plus specific national political ingredients ranging from 'Christian democracy' to militant union wage and social demands, as well as bureaucratic technocratic planning models for rebuilding cities, managing economies and resettling millions of displaced people.

Commenting on Polanyi's illusions about Labour and Social Democracy, Gareth Dale concludes that while his "critique of the market system carries an enduring force", Polanyi "failed to come to grips with social democracy's sidelining of its maximum program, and, consequently, *The Great Transformation* can legitimately be read either as an anti-capitalist manifesto or as a social-democratic bedtime story: a provider of sweet dreams that help chastened idealists to rise in the morning, to get to work on the countermovement, more or less ruefully reinterpreted as a mission to improve, upholster, and repair the cogs of the market machine."[56] Dale's book is a valuable and detailed account of Polanyi's life and ideas. However, I strongly disagree with his assessment that Polanyi's "ideas are particularly applicable to the neoliberal phase of capitalism, if less so to its étatiste predecessor."[57] On the contrary, I would argue that Polanyi not only failed to understand the post-1945 period but that his work is even less applicable to the neoliberal era which, at best, only exhibits superficial similarity to pre-1929 capitalism.

Far from being 'the twentieth century's most prophetic critic of capitalism', Polanyi's predictions for the post-1945 world were heavily shaped by past conflicts and old power structures. He did not even consider the possibility that the institutional predecessors of the European Union that were already quite visible while he was still alive in the 1960s could evolve to become the largest regional market of capitalist production in later decades. Like many other analysts of his generation, Polanyi was too focussed on the legacy of the rise and fall of 'nineteenth century civilisation' to see that the post-colonial struggles after 1945 might eventually help reshape global capitalism rather than build socialism. In the last years of his life, Polanyi continued to place his faith in the Soviet Union and hoped that the 'New West' (which would preserve the best of Western culture free of 'Americanism') would join with newly decolonised countries in constructing a peaceful world. There were some grounds for Polanyi's hope in the movement of Non-Aligned countries, even though most developing countries or what was then called the 'Third World' were still too weak and only emerging from the shadow of Western imperialism. Any prediction that the Soviet Union would eventually collapse, and that China would become the second largest capitalist power, was dismissed as pure phantasy by Polanyi's generation.

With hindsight we can now understand why Polanyi's analysis of pre- and post-1945 political economy was so flawed and based on naïve hopes. His polarised view of the conflict between 'capitalism and democracy' never allowed for the possibility that capitalism could be made safe without fascism or that democracy would not inevitably lead to socialism. Hence, Polanyi was confounded by the way capitalist social formations evolved in OECD countries, and he provided even less understanding of the manner in which capitalism spread globally in recent decades. These new forms of production and consumption were quite different compared to those short-lived regimes of the 'great transformation' in the 1930s. Nonetheless, what appeared as the consolidation of capitalism in the second half of the twentieth century was itself problem-ridden and far from stable. The warnings from the 1960s onwards by numerous critics about social, financial and deep systemic crises of environmental sustainability were largely ignored by governments and mainstream parties until the twenty-first century. Apart from greater recognition and improvement in the rights of women, ethnic and racial minorities or LGBTQI people, the way most of these crises were handled by governments did not result in further democratisation. Instead, there is widespread fear in some countries that democracy is once again being threatened by new forms of fascism and 'post-fascism'.

4. FROM WINDRIP TO TRUMP: THE EVOLUTION OF 'AMERICAN FASCISM'

AMERICA HAS EITHER BEEN a beacon of hope for oppressed people or the incarnation of brutal global power that has prevented democratisation by maintaining appalling authoritarian regimes. During the 1930s, it was common for many on the Left to portray Roosevelt and the New Deal as either fascist or very similar in style of government and outlook to Hitler's Nazism and Mussolini's fascism.[1] Before the Comintern adopted the Popular Front strategy in 1935, namely, that Communist Parties should make alliances with non-Communist parties in the struggle against fascism, both socialists and Communists shared a deep suspicion and hostility to the New Deal. In 1933-34, Roosevelt was depicted in Communist and non-Communist Left papers as either a 'social fascist', a dictatorial fascist or a saviour of capitalism who was implementing policies similar to those introduced by Hjalmar Schacht, Hitler's Minister of Economics. Similarly, but from an anti-Left perspective, British Conservative Party Member of Parliament and future Prime Minister, Harold Macmillan, admired fascism and advocated quasi-fascist policies in 1933 which he called 'orderly capitalism'. A few years later, former British Labour politician and leader of the British Union of Fascists, Oswald Mosley, regarded the New Deal as a failure because 'Jewish finance' prevented the creation of a 'new civilisation' that only a fascist movement could build. Hence, in 1936 he declared: "Roosevelt's New Deal is an attempt to plan without the power to plan."[2]

Although most of the Left later warmed to Roosevelt's pro-union policies and his anti-Nazi war effort, by 1944 socialists like Polanyi expressed grave doubts about whether the New Deal had changed liberalism. It should also not be forgotten that during the 1920s and 1930s, Roosevelt was an admirer of Mussolini, as was Winston Churchill and many other conservatives and liberals, as well as Fabians George Bernard Shaw and H. G. Wells.[3] Despite his own lack of principled opposition to fascists or 'fellow travellers' such as Franco, Petain and others, Roosevelt was the target of home-grown pro-fascists. According to the testimony by Marine General Smedley Butler before a US Congressional committee in November 1934, Roosevelt was to have been toppled (or merely kept as a 'puppet') by an attempted fascist coup organised by leaders of prominent corporations such as DuPont, General Motors and J. P. Morgan. One of the reported plotters who supposedly organized the finances for 500,000 ex-soldiers to march on Washington D.C. was Prescott Bush, father of President George H. Bush and grandfather of President George W. Bush. Roosevelt labelled the plotters 'economic royalists' but was never able to prosecute some of them until 1942, when Prescott Bush's pro-Nazi enterprises were seized by the US government.[4] It remains disputed as to whether there was a real attempted coup or just 'cocktail talk' by prominent business leaders. Regardless of the veracity of coup conspiracies, Roosevelt's policies were strongly disliked and opposed by both leading corporations and political conservatives. There were also many fascist sympathisers in the US thus making German refugees from Hitler fear that it was only a matter of time before fascism would come to power in America.

The fact that a possible fascist coup did not go beyond the planning or 'talking' stage was not due to good luck, but rather to a combination of political economic factors such as the conservative federal institutional system of checks and balances that made it very difficult for non-elected fascists to succeed. The constitutional differences between a president such as Hindenburg being able to appoint Hitler and the need for a US president to be elected by the voters and the Electoral College was also a factor. As to a possible military-backed fascist coup, this would have required the coordinated support of a sizeable number of senior military officers and the suppression of all political processes – an unlikely and highly risky scenario given Roosevelt's great popularity. Behind the friendly public persona, Roosevelt was certainly not averse to authoritarian practices. The American presidency also gives the office holder extensive war and emergency powers. This was evident in Roosevelt's internment of 120,000 Japanese in 1942, two thirds of whom were US-born citizens. Later on, Nixon's 'imperial presidency' and, more recently, Presidents George W. Bush, Barack Obama and Donald Trump have continued to employ these war and emergency powers.[5]

DIFFERENCES BETWEEN AMERICAN AND EUROPEAN FASCISM

While the Left largely recognised and feared the presence of fascists in America, they consistently overlooked or paid inadequate attention to the crucial historical differences between national political institutions. Concerning the US, Polanyi and others did not explain why the institutional structures and widespread popularity of policies pursued by New Dealers made it unlikely that fascism was either needed or desired by a majority of small businesses, farmers and working-class voters, in spite of the dangerous views expressed by a number of pro-fascist corporate and political leaders. Nonetheless, at a social level, non-party aligned authoritarian prejudices and practices were omnipresent. Almost a decade after Roosevelt's election in 1932, the Frankfurt School (Institute of Social Research) was commissioned by the American Jewish Committee and the Jewish Labor Committee in 1942 to study the level of anti-Semitism in society, especially amongst workers. The results were so alarming, aside from the fact of America being at war against Nazism, that the Institute decided not to publish its report for fear that it would damage the labour movement.[6] Unsurprisingly, anti-Semitism in the form of the 'Jewish threat' and racism were also deeply entrenched and widespread in the US military's senior ranks.[7] In a vivid example of racism amongst the lower ranks, historian Arno J. Mayer recalled losing his two front teeth in 1944 at a Kentucky military training camp for proclaiming his Jewishness following the reading of a poem by fellow soldiers that declared: "Once we have defeated the Krauts and the Japs overseas, we'll come home to kick the shit out of the Kikes and Niggers."[8]

Deeply ingrained authoritarian personal attitudes and social values sympathetic to neo-fascist solutions were insufficient on their own to bring about fascist or authoritarian regimes. German-style fascism also required more than an economic crisis such as the Depression. The presence of an active fascist party was also inadequate given the institutional structure, that is, government departments and leading non-fascist politicians could not facilitate a relatively smooth fascist takeover of state power as was the case in Germany. In short, the historical conjuncture characterised by the absence of sufficiently well-organised business and political groups meant that despite millions of fascist sympathisers, America in the 1930s was never seriously at risk of becoming fascist. This did not mean that America was not at risk of authoritarian politicians given the very undemocratic processes within the Republican and Democratic parties and Congress. The latter were able to curb free public discourse and 'cleanse' unions and social institutions of

Communists and assorted critics via electoral institutions such as the Senate, as occurred in the late 1940s and 1950s with the rise of McCarthyism.

Apart from General Douglas MacArthur (who was removed from command in Korea by President Truman in 1951), the threat of Bonapartism or a military coup has never been great in the US. Importantly, there has been no need for a military takeover of government considering most Republicans and Democrats have long subscribed to key bi-partisan foreign and domestic agendas. It is worth remembering that in 1956, C. Wright Mills argued that a 'power elite' relegated democratic decision-making to minor or secondary issues as the elite presided over the military-industrial complex.[9] The notion of a military-industrial complex entered mainstream discourse after it was referred to by President Eisenhower in his January 1961 farewell television address, without reference to Mills critique of a 'power elite'. Nonetheless, Mills' estimation of the power of the US military as a separate power base equal to corporate and political power is difficult to assess, despite the circulation of prominent military and business figures holding political appointments.

The military in many other countries have constituted a distinct and highly visible power base from which they have either 'tolerated' or removed elected governments. In contrast, the relation between military chiefs and corporate and political leaders in the US is complex, depending on whether it is domestic socio-economic issues or foreign policy. US civilian politicians have usually voluntarily followed the advice provided by the military and intelligence 'establishment'. Notable exceptions include President Donald Trump, whose maverick and unstable behaviour upset officers and policy makers in the Pentagon, CIA and FBI, despite having had a very high number of ex-generals in his administration.

The significant shift of the Republican Party to hard Right policies over the past forty years (especially under George W. Bush and Donald Trump) has led to much debate as to whether America is in danger of becoming fascist or is already fascist. During the New Deal, Sinclair Lewis published his novel *It Can't Happen Here* in 1935. Lewis based his character Berzelius (Buzz) Windrip (a racist, anti-Semitic demagogue) on Senator Huey Long, the former Democratic Party Governor of Louisiana who planned to run for president against Roosevelt in 1936 but was assassinated just prior to the release of the book in 1935. Long had been attacked by the Right as a 'communist' for his non-socialist 'Share the Wealth' movement (that had over seven million members) and by Communists as the 'Hitler of Louisiana' for his dictatorial politics. Forming an alliance with Father Coughlin, a rabid anti-Semitic and pro-fascist radio talk-show host with over thirty million listeners, Long pushed for more redistributive policies than Roosevelt. He simultaneously attacked both 'big business' and socialists while projecting an 'American' emphasis on the 'little man'.[10] Coming from the 'progressive' or Left-wing of the American Democrats, Long's political shift during the 1930s indicated a somewhat similar trajectory (before he was killed) to Oswald Mosely (who was formerly on the Left of the British Labour Party) and French ex-Communist Jacques Doriot who both became leaders of fascist parties. In Sinclair Lewis' novel, President Windrip was elected in 1936 and proceeded to introduce an Americanised version of fascism. Variations on the concept of an 'American fascism' were repeated by radicals in later decades.

As a case in point, take the Frankfurt School members, Herbert Marcuse, Franz Neumann and Otto Kirchheimer who had fled the Nazi regime and arrived in the US during the New Deal. They later joined the Office of Strategic Services to fight the Nazis and were part of the US government task force to de-Nazify Germany. Instead of the anti-Semitic fake news propagated by the alt Right about the conspiracy of 'cultural Marxism', including Marcuse being an agent of the CIA engaged in mind-altering experiments, the opposite was the truth. Before the CIA was established in September 1947, Marcuse, Neumann and Kirchheimer made some of the most radical anti-capitalist and anti-Nazi recommendations ever produced by advisers in the Office of Strategic Services and the US State Department. These included nationalising key German private cartels and businesses, arresting and incarcerating 220,000 Nazi officials immediately, as well as 1,800 business leaders who were 'active Nazis'. Once the prisons were filled, they advised that the allies should use the emptied Nazi concentration camps to hold Nazi war criminals. De-Nazification policy also involved extensive proposals on how to create a democratic society and avoid a repeat of the destruction of the Weimar republic by business and political forces. Most of these proposals were ignored by the US government, as this project was eventually aborted due to the revised Cold War objective of keeping ex-Nazis as a bulwark against Soviet Communism.[11]

After the OSS was disbanded in 1945, and while still working for the US State Department in a climate of increasing McCarthyism, Marcuse used his experience of both Nazism and working in the US government to write *33 Theses* in 1947 on how fascism had changed both the workers' movements and liberal democracies. In contrast to Polanyi who believed that Stalin would democratise post-war Eastern Europe, Marcuse maintained at the time that two anti-socialist and anti-democratic blocs now threatened the world: one was a neo-fascist capitalist bloc led by the US and the other was the Soviet camp.[12] His position was quite different to Hannah Arendt's analysis of totalitarianism which focused on the Soviet and Nazi regimes rather than critiquing the US. She was seen by many on the Left as a Cold War warrior, despite her admiration of Rosa Luxemburg.[13] In contrast, Marcuse, throughout the 1950s and up until his death in 1979, reiterated his concern about an American 'incipient fascism' coming to power by democratic means. The onset of a consumer-fuelled 'totally administered society' and the imposition of military-backed global imperialism, Marcuse argued, meant that a modern form of American fascism would have quite different characteristics and emerge under new domestic and global conditions compared to German Nazism.[14] However, Marcuse never specified what an 'American fascism' (as opposed to an incipient fascism) would look like and in what way it would take an institutional form that would distinguish it from existing American government structures and capitalist practices.

Roosevelt's New Deal and the extension of military-industrial power during the war years is one of the historical markers that contemporary analysts see as laying the foundation for the development of an actual or potential post-1945 'American fascism'.[15] American moderate and radical Leftists both within the Democratic Party and in small parties and social movements have long been divided between two traditions. The first group celebrate the 'democratic promise' of the written and unwritten American constitution which has seen 'the people' thwarted by ruthless corporations, racists, militarists and assorted opponents of equality and justice. The second group believe that the constitution, American political institutions, dominant corporations and conservative market ideology supported by large sections of the American citizenry have always been inherently opposed to democracy and equality.

Political critics such as socialist Daniel Lazare[16] and radical democrat Sheldon Wolin argued that the American political system was founded by those who were either sceptical about or hostile to democracy. It is a system that was based on slavery, that still denies full rights to blacks, women and trade unions. "Far from being innate, Wolin declared that "democracy in America has gone against the grain, against the very forms by which the political and economic power of the country has been and continues to be ordered."[17] If Wolin was so concerned by the 'totalitarian' threat of George W. Bush, he would have been even more alarmed by Donald Trump, had he lived to see his presidency. Paradoxically, even neo-Conservatives such as

George W. Bush's former speechwriter David Frum (a hawk who coined the infamous phrase 'axis of evil') calls for reform of America's constitution and the undemocratic institutions that permitted an authoritarian such as Trump to be elected.[18] Conservative, Anne Applebaum, also fears the illiberal and neo-fascist policies or 'treason of the clercs' in Europe and America perpetrated by people that include some of her former friends and associates on the Right.[19]

Earlier in 1980, it was former adviser to the Roosevelt New Deal administration, Bertram Gross, who coined the concept 'friendly fascism'.[20] Following others like Marcuse and Mills, Gross warned of the dangerous American-style fascist authoritarianism that was developing due to the concentration of corporate, military and executive power. In contrast to the 'totalitarian' regimes in Germany, Italy and the USSR, Wolin went beyond Gross and argued that America's 'inverted totalitarianism' emerged not as an abrupt regime change but rather evolved out of a "continuing and increasingly unequal struggle between an unrealized democracy and an antidemocracy that dare not speak its name."[21] According to Wolin, what is different about 'fascism' in America is that increased executive power and elite rule are combined with anti-democratic practices that do not take the form of overt attacks upon the idea of government by the people.[22] Instead, Wolin maintained that 'inverted totalitarianism' worked at two levels.

Firstly, at a corporate and state level it manifested itself through corporations shedding their identity as purely 'private enterprises' and becoming globalist co-partners with the American state at the same time as government privatised many of its former domestic roles and functions. The conception of 'globalist co-partners' is somewhat similar to Hannah Arendt's late 1940s thesis that nineteenth century imperialism marked the first stage of the political rule of the bourgeoisie who were formerly content to leave government and the protection of property to others. By the twentieth century, she observed, "businessmen became politicians and were acclaimed as statesmen, while statesmen were taken seriously only if they talked the language of successful businessmen and 'thought in continents,' these private practices and devices were gradually transformed into rules and principles for the conduct of public affairs."[23] In post-1945 America, the big difference between Arendt and theorists of 'American fascism' was that Arendt, despite her criticism of US policy in Vietnam, did not see America as fascist or as moving toward fascism.

Secondly, at the level of the American people, Wolin believed that authoritarianism worked indirectly through job insecurity, the intense pace of work and everyday pressures that combine to act as a formula for political demobilisation, or for the 'privatisation of the citizenry'. As he put it:

> Citizens are encouraged to distrust their government and politicians; to concentrate upon their own interests; to begrudge their taxes; and to exchange active involvement for symbolic gratifications of patriotism, collective self-righteousness, and military prowess. Above all, depoliticization is promoted through society's being enveloped in an atmosphere of collective fear and of individual powerlessness: fear of terrorists, loss of jobs, the uncertainties of pension plans, soaring health costs, and rising educational expenses.[24]

Whereas the Nazis sought the support of the working class through social programs, according to Wolin, American 'inverted totalitarianism' "exploits the poor, reducing or weakening health programs and social services, regimenting mass education for an insecure workforce threatened by the importation of low-wage workers."[25]

CHARACTERISING THE CURRENT THREATS

In recent years, Wolin's and Arendt's critical conception of the relationship between politicians, businessmen and voters (the relationship between 'capitalism and democracy') has been revealed as too 'tame', polite and civil compared to Right-wing advocacy of new and more ambitious action roles for corporate billionaires. Apart from buying votes and candidates, the new roles for the super wealthy include more than funding direct and indirect political intervention by numerous 'front' organisations and the installation of 'sympathetic' political agendas. These well documented plutocratic funding practices – driven by the belief in the ability of electoral processes, legislatures and court appointments to overturn legislation that is 'undermining liberty' such as social security or environmental law – have now taken undemocratic interventions much further. In 2015, Right-wing analyst Charles Murray published his alarming book *By the People: Rebuilding Liberty Without Permission*. Among the many arguments criticising the poor outcomes from democratic electoral processes, Murray claimed that when the Supreme Court upheld Roosevelt's 1935 Social Security Act in 1937, it destroyed limits on the federal government's spending authority. Therefore, Murray called on wealthy donors to contribute hundreds of millions of dollars to fund the rebuilding of the 'American project' of liberty by obstructing, harassing and legally challenging numerous pieces of government legislation.[26] Ian Millhiser, in commenting on Murray's book, pointedly observes that:

> *By the People*...bypasses the law entirely. It abandons even the trappings of a legitimate constitutional process, and instead places government in the hands of billionaires loyal only to an anti-government agenda. It is, in many ways, the perfection of post-Obama conservatism, barely even bothering to pay lip service to the notion that the American people should be governed by the people they elect.[27]

A variation on the theme of plutocrats subverting democracy is also seen in Jacob Hacker and Paul Pierson's analysis of 'plutocratic populism' in *Let Them Eat Tweets: How the Right Rules in an Age of Extreme Inequality*.[28] Trump, they argue, is the end point of a forty-year shift of the Republican Party to the extreme Right. Accordingly, powerful corporate elites have pushed the Republicans to adopt highly unequal tax and social policies while using a range of far-Right racist and nationalist constituencies to distract attention away from 'plutocratic' policies that work to the disadvantage of Trump's popular base. The danger of fascism does not lie in Trump's personal style alone. There is no doubt that the Republicans have moved to the Right for more than four decades. However, what was considered very Right-wing under George W. Bush is 'tame' compared to Trump's Republicans. As ex-Bush neo-conservative Frum warns, if Trump fails to win re-election then he and his supporters will blame voter fraud or the 'deep state'. If he wins then authoritarian tendencies will be vindicated and more norms and institutions will be trashed. If his opponents lose despite winning a large majority of votes (but not the electoral college), then belief in the electoral system will be seriously eroded as conflict moves to the streets.[29] These scenarios affect the possible reactions of Trump's base and the general electorate but do not tell us what the so-called 'plutocratic populists' will do to ensure that their corporate privileges are defended and advanced if Trump loses.

It is not surprising that the behaviour of Trump and members of his administration have sparked an outpouring of articles, books, social media comments and public debates on whether they are fascist or merely the most recent office holders to take deep-seated American systemic authoritarianism to a new and very aggressive level. Philosopher Jason Stanley, for example, also notes that 'fascism' sounds extreme to most people but even before Trump, extreme policies such as racialised mass incarceration, the rounding up of undocumented workers in concentration camps (euphemistically called 'detention centres') and lack of safe gun laws that pave the way for ongoing mass shootings had become normalised in contemporary America.[30] By contrast, other liberals such as Timothy Snyder and Madeleine Albright may view Trump as a precursor to Nazi or Communist totalitarianism,[31] but pay little or no attention to the home-grown American historical traditions of authoritarianism embodied in America's political and economic institutions and violent cultural relations. Tyranny is supposedly 'foreign' to America and Trump is mistakenly seen as merely importing dangerous practices and dressing them up in his own authoritarian style. Crucially, it would be a political mistake to think that if Trump loses in November 2020, then America will return to 'normality'. The 'normality' of American political, economic and social life is one of polarised hate and major divisions that fuel neo-fascism. Trump has merely bolstered these divisions which will fester and erupt regardless of whether or not he is re-elected in 2020, as the underlying causes remain unresolved.

Recently, political radicals such as Carl Boggs,[32] Christian Fuchs,[33] Henry Giroux,[34] David Renton[35] and many others have joined Marcuse, Mills, Gross and Wolin in analysing how America functions as a potential fascist or an actual quasi-authoritarian system. Boggs argues that Michael Mann and many non-radical analysts of fascism misconceive contemporary forms of neo-fascism by depicting them as largely associated with small minorities of extremist admirers of Nazism, thereby overlooking the deep-seated institutional characteristics of a potential future American fascism. While Boggs agrees with Gross and Wolin that American authoritarianism is fully compatible with its traditional liberal political institutions, he thinks that they fall short in providing an adequate theory of contemporary fascism. For example, Boggs regards Gross's concept of 'friendly fascism' as too seamless, that is, unclear about where advanced corporate capitalism or 'state-capitalism' ends and a new fascist regime begins.

Shane Burley and Mathew Lyons go further and argue that 'American fascism' is not the old liberal military-industrial corporate state but a direct assault on the liberal establishment by a reborn white nationalism.[36] They document all the violent racist and misogynist Right-wing movements at 'street level' that have flowed from repackaged 'internet white nationalism' to form Trump's support base. But in contrast to an earlier generation of analysts of 'American fascism', Burley and Lyons are more preoccupied with the immediate task of building anti-fascist movements in the streets. Importantly, they fail to explain the policy divisions within the structure of American businesses and political institutions and why key sectors of the corporate and military-security establishment have little to gain from supporting Trump's divisive and overt dismantling of bi-partisan political conventions and practices. Many support nationalist agendas in the conflict with China, Russia and the EU. Others prefer a restored American hegemony leading a renewed global multilateralism under Joe Biden or another future less polarising leader. Cooling the global temperature both at the level of greenhouse emissions and defusing potential military conflicts is incompatible with inflamed and volatile nationalism, whether internationally or domestically. In other words, reverting to an updated version of pre-Trumpian American 'democratic authoritarianism' is a preferred option so long as 'the basket of deplorables' can be put out of sight and political paralysis overcome. This would require major reform packages to tackle unemployment and inequality, an economically feasible but politically improbable solution in the current politically polarised climate of America as a 'failed state'.

Boggs, Burley and Lyons and many others believe that new forms of fascism in the US and the rest of the world have much more chance of success if they do *not* imitate the Nazis.[37] Enzo Traverso, for instance, also argues that few of the authoritarian Right-wing 'populist' movements and political figures in present-day Europe and the US copy the fascism of the 1930s or neo-fascist movements of previous decades. Instead, an 'anti-politics' or 'post-fascism' emerges from the hollowing out of representative democracy due to the consequences of the broad neoliberal policy consensus implemented by centre-Right and the centre-Left governments.[38] As a result, this 'post-fascism' fuses old elements of anti-Semitism, racism, homophobia and misogyny[39] with weaker forms of nationalist identity politics when compared to the aggressive nationalism of Nazism. At the same time, in contrast to Nazi persecution of Jews and gays, these latter-day Right-wing populist and alt-Right movements have had prominent members or leaders who are gay[40] and lesbian (for example, in the US, Holland and Germany) or have a Jewish son-in-law and key Jewish supporters as in Trump's case. Support for the state of Israel among the evangelical Christian Right and alt-Right coexists alongside virulent anti-Semitism, such as the torchlight procession of the Far Right in Charlottesville in 2017 chanting 'Jews will not replace us'.

Despite emerging gay and lesbian social movements in the late 1960s slowly changing old Left attitudes, it was during the period from the 1920s to the 1990s that homophobia – amply evident in Left literature, newspapers and films[41] – prevailed in Socialist, Communist, Trotskyist and Maoist movements. According to these old Left views, homosexuality equalled bourgeois decadence and therefore fascism, or was a sexual perversion that undermined working-class masculinity by creating effeminate men (the latter fear now articulated by neo-fascists). Today, Right-wing electoral movements have, at best, been very resistant to abandoning homophobic and misogynist practices, while smaller alt-Right groups actively champion homophobia and misogyny – from hate crimes to online abusive trolling of feminists. Importantly, 'post-fascist' movements and politicians have not yet mobilised uniformed mass movements like Hitler or Mussolini to attack opponents. It was frightening enough to see Trump refuse to condemn armed gatherings of the Far Right in Charlottesville or those demanding an end to Covid-19 lockdowns and attacking and killing people protesting police killings of African Americans.

Crucially, the Left is active at street level but demobilised or relatively unorganised at the party and institutional level. In the past, uniformed street militia usually appeared as adjunct wings of large fascist and Communist parties. This party mobilisation has not yet happened although there are unaffiliated neo-fascist armed militia and black armed groups. Unlike during the interwar period, to date there has been no need for fascist street militia (black shirts and brownshirts) to respond to non-existent mass radical Left parties in contemporary OECD countries. Still, a politically and socially polarised America plagued by mass unemployment, more than 200,000 deaths from Coronavirus at the time of writing, and violent street clashes over deep-seated racism could, given an escalation of conflict, lead to the suspension of formal democracy by federal or state authorities. The deployment by Trump of special, secretive federal troops to arrest and quell Black Lives Matter protests signalled a test case on the durability of the right to protest. No such pretence at adhering to democracy was needed by elected Brazilian President Bolsonaro who, incredibly, attended a rally in 2020 calling for a military coup d'état!

At the cultural level, members of 'post-fascist' movements reject old conservative moral codes and indulge in 'consumer hedonism' in the form of libertarian approaches to drug-taking and sexuality. This is a legacy of cultural liberalisation and the breakdown of pre-1960s work processes, religious attendance and the hollowing out of old political institutions. Political theorist, Wendy Brown, draws a link between 'no future for white men' and

Nietzsche's suggestion that Judaic-Christian morality was born as the revenge of the weak, the meek and all those who suffered at the hands of the strong and powerful. Paraphrasing Nietzsche, she observes: "The weak were resentful not of their own weakness, but of the strong, whom they (mistakenly) blamed for their suffering. And so, they invented a new value system in which strength would be reproached as evil and weakness lofted as good."[42] By contrast, authoritarian alt-Right movements are animated by deep and bitter resentment and rage as a reaction to the humiliation and suffering under four decades of neoliberalism. Trump, himself, according to Brown, "identifies revenge as his sole philosophy of life"[43] and his working-class and middle-class supporters seek revenge not against strong and powerful capitalist corporations but against democracy and equality or what they call 'political correctness', meaning multiculturalism, feminism and black culture.

In America, she argues, black males have different responses to decades of neoliberalism compared to white males who fear that they will have 'no future' and rage against their loss of social status, even though they are still dominant. Thus, a new form of Nietzschean nihilism prevails amongst the male alt-Right: "As this type finds itself in a world emptied not only of meaning, but of its own place, far from going gently into the night, it turns toward apocalypse. If white men cannot own democracy, there will be no democracy. If white men cannot rule the planet, there will be no planet."[44]

However, Brown and many other analysts of the 'populist Right' and neo fascism make the mistake of seeing these movements and Right-wing voters as comprising mainly of socially conservative 'angry white males'. While it is true that racism and the rise of 'whiteness' as a political identity is influential in America,[45] recent studies have shown that up to 45% of voters for Right-wing parties in various countries are women and men who are 'sexually-modern nativists'.[46] Whether LGBTQI or heterosexual, in the past decade their sexual preferences have not been an obstacle to supporting anti-immigrant, racist and anti-socialist and anti-green political movements.[47] Also, in contrast to Trump's and the alt-Right's misogyny, there are European Right-wing neo-fascist movements that instrumentalise 'liberated' French or German feminists by claiming women's' rights are threatened by foreign patriarchal Muslim cultural practices.[48] The other significant feature of new 'post-fascist' movements, as maternal feminist Julie Stephens has observed is that alt-Right online culture adopts many of the disruptive strategies of the 1960s counter culture and combines these with postmodern irony.[49] Nonetheless, these cultural strategies cannot disguise their hate-filled and anti-democratic political messages.

Apart from those who cultivate old or new iconic fascist dress or identity codes, many of the 'post-fascists' are often outwardly indistinguishable from ordinary consumers. Historically, Traverso is wrong to argue that fascism was born in the era of 'Fordist capitalism', of assembly-line production and mass culture. Instead, European fascism was a product of 'pre-Fordism' in Italy and Germany. Also, he is only partly correct to argue that "Trump has emerged in the age of neoliberalism, in the age of financialised capitalism, of competitive individualism and endemic precarity. He does not mobilise the masses but attracts a mass of atomised individuals, of impoverished and isolated consumers."[50] That Trump attracted atomised individuals as 'isolated consumers' is valid. But he also appealed to de-industrialised communities and the affluent rather than just impoverished consumers. Whether Trump or various 'post-fascist' leaders and movements are merely transitional and will soon decline and disintegrate, or whether they will harden into political forces that crush limited democracies is not a political outcome that will be fulfilled uniformly across the world. Rather, the answer to this question will in part depend on levels of mass resistance and the ability of political alternatives to 'post-fascism' being able to succeed in solving or alleviating major social problems *without* incorporating 'post-fascist' values and policies.

According to followers of Deleuze, Guattari and Foucault, such as Brad Evans and Julian Reid, we cannot escape fascism because it is inside all of us.[51] Therefore, one cannot conduct politics non-fascistically because all 'politics' is inherently fascist (even revolutionary anti-fascism) and assumes the love and desire for power. While we should certainly be on guard against authoritarian desires and behavioural tendencies, such an indiscriminate definition of the connection of politics to fascism implies that anything beyond combatting private individual 'micro-fascism' is meaningless and ineffective in the public realm. Instead, it is more fruitful to ask, following Aurelien Mondon and Aaron Winter, how did racism and far Right values become mainstream in recent years, that is, how did 'reactionary democracy' emerge as a legitimate redefinition of democracy?[52]

In most OECD countries we are not yet facing the prospect of outright authoritarian rule compared with many low and middle-income developing countries which have long been familiar with a range of military and authoritarian regimes. Nonetheless, the social dislocation and authoritarian emergency measures introduced by governments during the Covid-19 crisis offer new opportunities for regimes to roll back democratic rights and accountability. At the moment, some analysts of 'classical fascism' emphasise the need to be alert to the various 'stages' of fascism that signal the transition from marginalised extremist theorists to the growth of large movements followed by the occupation of state power.[53] Others such as Marilyn Ivy, offer a less predictive or patterned approach. "How much fascism is necessary", she asks, "before one can answer the question in the affirmative? When do we know fascism is fascism? One possible answer is that we know fascism is fascism when it's too late, always after the fact."[54] This answer was given over a decade ago before the recent escalation of polarised street and institutional battles in America. No hindsight is needed to recognise that the agendas of far-Right white nationalists and other extremists are fascist and constitute a major threat.

THE 'NEW FASCISM', FOSSIL FUELS AND EXPANSIONISM

While allowing for definitional problems and differences between old and new fascism or 'post-fascism', major questions about the relationship between 'capitalism and democracy' remain unanswered. Has the growth and exercise of American global military power since the New Deal, for example, been equivalent to the Nazi, Italian and Japanese use of war as extreme nationalist expansionism in the 1930s and 1940s but under new conditions? Some Left analysts such as William I. Robinson subscribe to simplistic analyses of the 'transnational capitalist class'(TCC) that now supposedly dominate nation states and share a common agenda. Robinson claims that due to the global crisis in accumulation, the TCC "has acquired a vested interest in war, conflict, and repression as means of accumulation. The global police state refers to the ever more omnipresent systems of mass social control, repression and warfare promoted by the ruling groups to contain the real and the potential rebellion of the global working class and surplus humanity."[55] Such oversimplification fails to recognise that there is neither a 'global police state' nor unified policies shared by the US, China and other leading capitalist countries. Take the fact that currently G7 and G20 meetings cannot even reach agreement on carefully worded bland joint statements. The global crisis today is therefore characterised by the fact that major governments are too divided to deal with numerous unfolding disasters. Parallel to this rudderless world is the reality that despite various resistance movements, there is also no homogenous and unified 'global working class' eager to make revolution.[56] Instead, there has been a hardening of geopolitical conflict between policy makers in the US and China that is forcing other countries to choose economic or military alliances (or both) with either of the two superpowers.[57]

The other enormous difference between China and other authoritarian regimes is that the Chinese central government moved quickly to contain the Covid-19 crisis once provincial officials covered it up. By contrast, a string of Right-wing governments and movements (including those led by Trump, Bolsonaro, Orban, Lukashenko, Modi, Salvini) have either promoted a fascist, masculinist criminal neglect of containing the virus or continue racist scapegoating of the Chinese, immigrants, Muslims and others.[58] Reducing all capitalist states and their socio-economic and environmental policies to the interests of a coherent 'transnational capitalist class' is thus proven to be highly misleading.

For example, the critique of Western imperialism/liberalism does not just come from the Left. Current geopolitical tensions have also given rise to new forms of fascism such as advocated by leading Russian fascist and former Putin adviser, Alexander Dugin. He supports 'Eurasia' centred on Russian and Chinese 'civilisations' and underpinned by Russia's nuclear weapons and China's economic strength.[59] As the foundation of an anti-Western multi-polar world, this Russian fascism advocates cooperation between Right-wing ethno-nationalists in the East and the West, including white neo-fascist supporters of Trump who advocate a politics of American isolationism. Similarly, Islamic fascist/theocratic 'caliphates' that reject secular democracy are, like Right-wing anti-immigrant and racist movements, part of the contemporary redefinition of earlier forms of political conflict between 'capitalism and democracy'.

Within the US, ongoing historical tensions between American conservative and liberal globalists and isolationists partly account for the inconsistent policies of the Trump administration that simultaneously promotes 'America first' and global 'liberal order' policies that either undermine or enhance strategic military and business alliances. Given that nuclear weapons place unbearable costs and restrictions on previous forms of war and conquest, how can the old fascist objectives of *'lebensraum'* (living space) or extensive military occupation (as opposed to military bases) be sustainable for any future American fascism in a world where American corporate power is under constant challenge economically by rival powers? It is relatively easy to see authoritarian regimes content to be confined to running nation states such as the Philippines, Hungary, Turkey or Brazil. However, any new forms of fascism must be able to generate production and consumption by either capitalist or post-capitalist socio-economic methods given that countries in

Europe or other continents are hardly going to rush into war and territorial expansion as in the 1930s. This said, we cannot entirely dismiss the possible exercise of war plans by megalomaniac authoritarian leaders even if these plans are highly self-destructive to medium or long-term business interests. A case in point is to speculate on how many businesses would have supported Hitler before and after 1933 had they known what devastation would occur several years later.

Yet, the ability of a new authoritarian leader to lead America into a new land war (involving large numbers of occupying troops) with a country such as Iran, North Korea, let alone China, is over. As we have seen, the miscalculations of George W. Bush and company that somehow superior air power would result in quick, decisive victories in Iraq and Afghanistan have resulted in exceedingly long, costly and unwinnable wars. Despite the frequently bellicose inflated words from Trump and others about war, thankfully these have not translated into major troop involvement in Syria or elsewhere. Even authoritarian US presidents realise that massive military superiority has limited ability to attain strategic political economic objectives by old types of military invasion. The new era of protracted 'dirty' campaigns run by much smaller groups of combatants – whether terrorists, cyber warriors, or others disrupting transport, communication, food production and other industries – means that capital accumulation or 'business as usual' will face lengthy periods of disorder if violence is the main chosen strategy of extending American dominance.

Some would argue that the difference between former fascist regimes and Chinese Communist rule is marginal and symbolic given the long history of repression and especially considering that capitalism has thrived in both contemporary China and earlier fascist regimes prior to 1945. The notable difference is that China has explicitly rejected military expansionism. Such a military strategy is neither possible (in terms of China's military weakness) nor consistent with the Chinese government's grand ambitions to expand trade and investment globally through the massive Belt and Road initiative – a policy strategy which is environmentally destructive but not fascist expansionism. Crucially, there is no evidence that large powers such the US and China wish to repeat Nazi or Japanese Imperial plans for military conquest. Given their need to balance military expenditure with larger political economic agendas, when does American military overstretch become far too costly (as it became for the Nazis and the Japanese Imperial forces) not just in military terms, but also fiscally in relation to federal deficits, skewed long-term economic investment compared with other capitalist powers that spend far less on their military? How would any future American fascist regime maintain international alliances and political legitimacy and stability given the guaranteed major domestic instability from social divisions evident in past wars and military occupations in Vietnam and Iraq? Short of outright suppression, could a potential American fascism secure and stabilise its domestic and international economic growth while still allowing free speech and free elections in the public sphere?

FASCISM AND THE ECOLOGICAL CHALLENGE

In Book Two and Three, I will discuss the political implications of all those who currently support Right-wing ethno-nationalist and neo-fascist parties in OECD countries. Many are disillusioned with liberal democracy because they aspire to the cultural desires and material consumption they have been excluded from due to neoliberal policies of low or stagnant economic growth including industry restructuring that has left many communities de-industrialised and depressed. Yet, neo-fascists and ultranationalists are divided on ecological issues. An influential historical strand of the far-Right in Europe has always associated particular landscapes, flora and fauna with national identity and organic harmony (as opposed to global environmental issues). Hence there is no consistency amongst various far-Right movements in different countries as to their support or opposition to issues such as climate change.[60] Others resent all those promoting green agendas that further constrain levels of material consumption and have become useful allies to Right-wing politicians defending fossil-fuelled growth. Tapping into working-class constituencies that blame the failure of liberal democracy to secure their material and cultural desires, they also oppose environmentalists and their agendas which will create even more fossil-fuelled industry jobs casualties. This is an explosive mixture that has already boosted Right-wing and neo-fascist parties and could become a significant threat in the future.

Meanwhile, earlier forms of territorial expansion by military conquest are either rejected by many corporations as too costly or unnecessary for 'friendly fascism' to be durable. If so, what purpose does an overtly authoritarian regime serve if most of the objectives of corporate capitalism are already achievable within existing parliamentary political processes? Moreover, present-day arguments about American 'friendly fascism' particularly overlook the divisions in corporate America that are already evident between the old, and still dominant fossil-fuel energy sector, heavy industry, military contractors, chemical and other related sectors, and those growing new business sectors (both domestically and globally) which see future profitability in knowledge-based, service sector, health and other industries far less constrained by environmental factors. How will the outdated fossil-fuelled industries that were the foundation of previous wars (and still remain centrally involved in all current wars) overcome the major consequences of global warming, even if democracy is crushed? Dangerous carbon emissions never affected protagonists in earlier wars where victory depended on conventional strategies such as ensuring adequate oil and coal supplies and other raw materials necessary for the steady production output from steel furnaces and arms producers.[61]

In 2007, the Centre for Strategic and International Studies and the Centre for New American Security published *'The Age of Consequences: The foreign policy and national security implications of global climate change'.*[62] While marred by a simplistic 'clash of civilisations' perspective, the 30-year global scenario depicting major social and political upheavals likely to result from increased carbon emissions is indicative of why the military are taking an ever-growing interest in environmental issues. Today, the US Pentagon, like other national military planners are becoming increasingly aware that global warming, if not checked, poses all sorts of major threats well beyond the capacity of existing military forces. Everything from rising sea levels in major global cities, extreme weather incidents and food shortages right through to millions of climate refugees are likely to be more frequent and on a larger scale than previous natural disasters. Many critics fearing fascism, as well as those promoters of corporate authoritarianism have not fully factored in the distinct possibility of climate breakdown exacerbating the incidence of extreme natural/social crises. Potentially severe disruptions to the ability of military-industrial systems and the consumer economy to function or expand remains the biggest (and often unrecognised) dilemma facing authoritarian political, corporate and military leaders, many of whom erroneously assume that abolishing or curbing democratic rights will be a solution.[63]

At the moment, there is a fundamental disjunction between the development of increasingly automated military or civilian technologies and the high dependence of these systems and technologies on limited rare minerals and other natural resources. These are resources that are strongly sought by civilian manufacturers. To avoid scarcity of finite natural resources, both representative democracies and authoritarian fascist regimes would have to ensure high degrees of inequality in terms of civilian consumption or increased coercion to ensure political control. Repressive regimes have a limited life expectancy depending on whether the standard of living will improve regardless of the lack of political freedom. Notably, household and individual consumption accounts for approximately 60% of GDP in OECD countries. Rapid expansion of the military-industrial complex at the expense of civilian consumption is actually at odds with the trajectory of capitalist development since 1945. An illustration would be the Vietnam War where military expenditure exposed the inability of the US to simultaneously maintain domestic civilian commitments, competitiveness with other capitalist powers and ultimately the viability of the Bretton Woods system without inflationary pressures and threats to the value of the American dollar. Smaller potentially fascist governments would lack the economic power to survive international market pressures, currency devaluation and other political economic factors if they pursued a military build-up and repressive domestic measures without the support and protection of one of the global great powers.

When one adds the fact that there is virtually no prospect in the coming decades that future technological innovation can absolutely decouple economic growth from the finite limits of natural resources and also safeguard very fragile ecosystems, one is talking about an entirely different global scenario to that which fostered fascism in the 1920s and 1930s. This puts into question the frequent comparisons made between the 1930s and contemporary political changes. Once it is confirmed that even achieving the very difficult goal of *relative* decoupling will only briefly extend available natural resources and the limited room for incessant economic growth, then the old dilemma for authoritarians – whether to suppress or coexist with democracy – will begin to take on a new political complexion. As to the *absolute* decoupling of economic growth from nature, this remains a utopian goal well beyond the reach of science and technology. Incessant capitalist growth, regardless of whether it is pursued in authoritarian or democratic forms will prove to be ecologically unsustainable and will generate a period of profound political instability in the absence of the adoption of peaceful and sustainable alternative socio-economic practices.

The geopolitical reality that countries or sub-regions will be affected to different degrees by environmental constraints is one of the reasons why some can avoid facing the truth about the damaging impact of climate change. Unfortunately, as we are already witnessing, there are political leaders and sections of national populations who may well resist the need to change to a sustainable economy. Authoritarian leaders will continue to hold deluded beliefs about growth in military and civilian production and consumption aside from the increasing negative impact of climate breakdown.

Whatever the future relation of capitalist production to environmental processes, capturing and holding class or elite political power to ensure the unequal and undemocratic organisation of socio-economic life is no longer just a question of political organisation, violence, demagoguery, nationalist myth, propaganda or military power. The 'authoritarian temptation' can affect even ecological fundamentalists and not just neo-fascists. For example, after he left the Greens in 1985, prominent advocate of abolishing industrialism and reverting to a pre-industrial society, Rudolf Bahro, openly embraced the spiritualism of the Nazis and the need for a 'Green Adolf' to save the world.[64] Bahro's rejection of conventional politics is overwhelmingly unrepresentative of contemporary environmental activists even though there are tiny pockets of 'ecological spiritualists' who espouse confused mystical conceptions of the climate crisis.

At the more conventional Right-wing and technocratic end of the political spectrum, it is well known that while Hitler was a vegetarian who loved nature, modern-day authoritarians in the corporate world often adhere to healthy diets, fitness regimes and enjoy secluded retreats in nature. Although controlling and suppressing radical political opponents may have its own major challenges, it is nowhere nearly as difficult as operating an environmentally *unsustainable* military-industrial complex and a credit-fuelled consumer economy. This fundamental environmental constraint on durable political power is yet to fully register with most global political and business leaders because the vast majority are preoccupied with immediate short-term issues and adhere to the old paradigm of 'capitalism versus democracy'. Many policy makers are also locked into the old way of thinking and continue in their misguided belief that technological innovation or the 'techno-fix' (everything from geoengineering to absolute decoupling of economic growth from nature) will miraculously solve future problems without the need for fundamental political and socio-economic change. The question remains: how much social and environmental damage will current or future authoritarians or 'post-fascists' inflict on their own society and the world in the short and medium term before they are stopped by oppositional political movements?

5. FLAWED NOTIONS OF THE 'LIBERAL STATE'

In 1964, the same year that Karl Polanyi died, members of a new generation of young Leftists, Perry Anderson and Tom Nairn, inaugurated a debate on the nature of the British state that has continued in different forms to the present day.[1] Anderson and Nairn argued that the historical absence of a bourgeois revolution or foreign invasion during the twentieth century accounted for the continued presence of antiquated monarchist and aristo-cratic features of the British state and culture in comparison to other capitalist societies in Europe. Yet the UK was not alone in this respect, as other nation states such as US also have their own *ancien régimes* that in part helps explain their conservative constitutions, cultural practices and inability to resolve socio-economic crises.

Remember, this debate on the 'liberal state' took place in a world two decades after the Second World War, a world that had defeated fascism, supposedly consolidated democracy and saw the end of the old imperial empires. Yet, 1964 was notable for several events and developments that were to play out in the decades to come and affect the notion of the 'liberal state'. For instance, Nelson Mandela and others were sentenced to life imprisonment in South Africa, the Brazilian military overthrew a democrati-cally elected government and inaugurated twenty-one years of brutal dicta-torship, the Vietnam war entered a new phase of escalation and the Mozambique Liberation Front (FRELIMO) launched its war of indepen-dence against Portugal, one of many anti-colonial struggles across the world.

Turning to the USSR, despite Polanyi's earlier naïve hope that Khrushchev would democratise the Soviet Union, the latter did preside over the end of Stalinist terror and was himself pensioned off rather than executed. As the USSR entered what would be its last decades of ossified conservative Party rule under Leonid Brezhnev and his successors, China detonated its first nuclear weapon thus signifying its ability to match the great powers. Two years later, China would be in turmoil caused by the explosive years of the Cultural Revolution in which other Communists would be denounced as 'capitalist roaders'. Meanwhile, almost two hundred years after the drafting of the oldest liberal democratic constitution, President Johnson signed the Civil Rights Act that officially abolished racial segregation (even as civil rights activists continued to be murdered) and the student movement clashed with police at the University of California campus in Berkeley over the denial of liberal rights to free speech. Far from being liberal and democratic, social protests were met with state violence. This was the beginning of what would become an even more violent decade of war abroad and unofficial civil war in the US at home.

While I have already noted that Polanyi provided no detailed comparative analysis of state institutions, the Anderson/Nairn critique of British institutions later intersected with international debates on the very nature of the 'capitalist state'. Polanyi may have made a few brief remarks on how different societies had particular taxation systems, social laws and constitutions, but he failed to develop an adequate comparative analysis of diverse historical liberal states. Instead he worked with an ideal type of the 'liberal state' and the 'self-regulating market'. This was a poor foundation for understanding the specific national struggles for democratisation, and the obstacles that social movements confronted. These obstacles would continue to be encountered against state institutions regardless of whether democratic struggles occurred in representative democracies or in authoritarian regimes.

DISPUTING THE 'ECONOMIC' AND THE 'NON-ECONOMIC'

No theory of democracy or the barriers preventing the exercise of democratic power is adequate without a corresponding account of the relations between an 'economic system' and a 'political' and 'socio-cultural system'. Until recently, such as the case of leaders like Silvio Berlusconi or Donald Trump, it was rarer for most members of capitalist classes outside the US to directly occupy senior state administrative offices or jointly hold and exercise military and policing power. Hence, there have always been disputes over the 'the economic' and 'the political'. Are they distinct and separate spheres or arbitrary divisions between what are overlapping and interrelated socio-economic and political relations? These questions continue to cause divisions amongst social theorists and political economists across the political spectrum.

For generations of orthodox Marxists, the emphasis has always largely been on socio-economic relations of production from which the legal-administrative state institutions were derived or emerged rather than an equal emphasis on how state institutions helped shape society and capitalist market relations. From the 1940s, Polanyi rejected the Marxian notion of how class struggle helped shape state institutions and instead developed the concept of 'institutedness'. Human economy, he argued, is always embedded and enmeshed in non-economic institutions, whether religious or governmental.[2] Yet, this undeveloped theory was based on ahistorical and quite fragmented examples from ancient, tribal and industrial societies. It also lacked a detailed analysis of whether state apparatuses in capitalist societies were instituted by social conflict. Importantly, the notion of 'institutedness' particularly ignored how state activities both simultaneously helped *reproduce* and *undermine* capitalist social relations.

Because Polanyi favoured a communitarian 'organic society', he either disregarded or only paid lip service to the reality that pre-capitalist and capitalist societies were not organic but historically class-divided social formations. Consequently, Polanyi's over-generalised notion of 'institutedness' lacked any dynamic *comparative* quality to show how any changes in so-called 'non-economic' socio-political relations might possibly affect both the viability of capitalist production and power, and also why levels of democracy varied in quite different contemporary capitalist countries. These differences are now quite telling, as I will discuss in Book Three of this book where I consider the different paths and obstacles confronting those favouring an environmentally sustainable democracy.

A century before Polanyi, Marx had argued that any concept, whether it be 'labour', 'exchange value' or 'production' would be mere one-sided abstractions unless situated within the context of actual historical communities and social relations. In short, capitalist societies are inconceivable without comprehending the crucial role of what today would be called 'non-economic' social and political relations. The immediate process of capitalist production was, he argued, an interaction between 'constant or fixed capital' (machinery, buildings, etc.) and 'variable capital' better known as labour or labour-power. Marx called labour-power 'variable' because there were two determinants of the length and intensity of the working day.

First, there were physical limits to the number of hours a worker could perform every day before productivity declined or the worker dropped dead. Second, all aspects of workers' physical and mental health were related to the crucial 'historical and moral elements' that he said determined the intensity and character of particular working conditions. In regard to physical limits, where possible, capitalists artificially extended the working day by introducing two or three shifts per day to have their factories, mines or other businesses operating 24 hours non-stop. Under extreme conditions, say during World War Two, Nazi forced labour or Japanese war industries based on Korean slave labour actually worked tens of thousands of people to death, prisoners who were considered sub-human. Consequently, even in far less extreme capitalist countries, workers' social requirements for 'non-work' time depended on the 'general level of civilisation' which was itself a result of prevailing moral and historical conditions.[3]

The social reproduction of labour-power was thus determined by three distinct but ultimately interrelated processes: one was immediately and directly 'economic' and two were indirect or 'non-economic' (the boundaries between 'economic' and 'non-economic' often overlapped). If Polanyi's 'institutedness' was an abstract and ahistorical concept, Marx's theory of social reproduction also lacked an analysis of how state and social institutions helped shape particular modes of production. Hence post-1960s Marxists and socialist feminists extended Marx's work by analysing the following three social and political processes:

- the *direct* character of production affected by the presence or absence of organised labour struggles within particular enterprises and industries; these struggles were often determined directly and indirectly by changing state policies affecting production and trade, levels of unemployment and investment, the degree of strike-breaking by police or the enactment of laws permitting or impeding unionisation. Crucially, the character of many work-place conflicts was partly shaped by whether struggling workers were connected to particular moderate or radical trade unions, political parties or had widespread support within the broader community.
- the *indirect* impact of society-wide state legislation, delivery of public services, the attainment of social and political rights resulting from ongoing social struggles, for example, everything

from prohibition of child labour and the winning of the eight-hour day, to minimum compulsory levels of education, laws against gender, race and other forms of discrimination as well as social legislation in the form of health and recreational services to enhance notions of the 'healthy and productive body' plus what minimal or adequate retirement income should be made universal or market driven.

- the *indirect* impact and consequences of family relations, especially how the daily reproduction of male labour-power continues to depend on unequal gender roles such as unpaid domestic labour performed mainly by women as a cost-free subsidy to employers, plus the amount of public taxation that should subsidise or be invested in child care and other care work, once again, mainly performed by women.

Unlike the lives of slaves and serfs and their progeny which were directly controlled by their lords and masters, capitalists had no direct jurisdiction over the private lives of workers off the job. Hence, up until the present day, labour power and productivity is also directly and indirectly affected by moral and legislative conditions that sanction or disapprove of domestic violence, alcohol and drugs, divorce or gambling or the ideal size of families. The structure and form of educational institutions, as also the absence or presence of state and non-state community and family social care support networks, continue to be crucial in socialising individuals into the occupational structures of capitalist societies and their ability or inability to self-manage their private lives without the direct support from employers.[4] Variable capital has thus always been enmeshed within a range of quite different social and political institutions depending on the capitalist country itself. Marx's 'historical and moral elements' are closely related to the very character of state institutions (especially the degree of democratisation or authoritarianism, legal protection and so forth) that have differed widely between all kinds of developed and developing capitalist nation states.

The key point here is that while neo-Marxists and feminists developed analyses of how the 'economic' related to the 'non-economic' or 'political', most citizens and workers continue to have great difficulty recognising the direct and indirect links between their work conditions, private household social relations and the lack of full democratic decision-making power in public institutions such as state apparatuses.

Feminist theorist Nancy Fraser has argued that many contemporary disputes within capitalist societies are 'boundary' conflicts between the 'economic' and the 'political' and the 'social'. They affect institutional practices and social relations in the production and social reproduction system mediated by class, gender and race relations or between society and nature.[5] While acknowledging her debt to Polanyi, she criticises him for only seeing two options: either more marketisation of the 'economy' or more social protection of an undifferentiated 'society'. However, 'boundary' conflicts since the nineteenth century have always been more diversified than the single 'fault line' between free marketeers and social protectionists. Hence, Fraser argues that "Polanyi overlooks a number of epochal struggles that raged throughout the nineteenth and twentieth centuries: struggles for the abolition of slavery, the emancipation of women, and the overthrow of colonialism and imperialism."[6] Despite these major criticisms, Fraser's work remains closely tied to Polanyian concepts (see Chapter Six) and it is difficult to see where 'boundaries' begin and end and in what way they illuminate the so-called 'internal' relations of 'the state', 'class', 'nature' or 'gender' even before we 'cross' these so-called 'boundaries' and enter another sphere of society or environment.

No better contemporary example of why we don't need a revival of notions of 'boundaries' are the varied responses of governments to the Covid-19 Coronavirus and how these illustrated the interconnectedness between social relations, the organisation of production and consumption, and the crucial role of state institutions in mediating and shaping the latter. The mass disruptions, the differences between inept or efficient action of authorities, the underfunding of vital health services or class inequalities suffered by workers laid off or quarantined, the mass panic evident in the clear-out of supermarket shelves signifying a breakdown of ideological notions of 'community' all amply illustrate the relations between the so-called 'non-economic' and the 'economic'. One doesn't need the threat of social revolution to see the secretive and strong-armed authoritarian emergency action by many governments characterised by the suspension of any pretence of democracy. Despite prioritising government aid to businesses, Covid-19 has illustrated why there is no uniform 'liberal state' and especially the fact that capitalist societies can neither function without state institutions and a certain level of co-operative social relations, nor protect and reproduce capitalist societies before a crisis, during a crisis or after a crisis.

NEOLIBERAL STATES ARE NOT OLD LIBERAL STATES REBORN

When it came to analysing democracy, Marx shared with Polanyi a failure to develop a detailed comparative analysis of capitalist state institutions. Neither wrote a fully elaborated analysis of the connections between social classes and the character of state institutions. Today, contemporary critics of capitalism have long had to construct their own 'maps' of class-divided societies; societies that are far more complex and significantly different to the prototypical analyses provided by the 'classical' Marxists from the 1840s to the 1940s. The working class has profoundly changed in its composition from unskilled and skilled labour to a plethora of occupations in many new industries. New fissures among workers characterised by levels of education, culture, and global geographical location in different production value chains have also opened up. The very character and relative strength of local, national and transnational capitalist classes has equally changed in profound ways. All these dramatic changes in class composition are crucial in understanding the conflict between 'capitalism and democracy' and the indispensable yet quite distinctive socio-economic, policing and cultural roles played by particular state institutions in different capitalist countries.

We know that apart from a few brief references, Marx provided no clear concept of the social organisation or the political and legal institutional structures of a future socialist society that would make it democratic. A century later, Polanyi's famous definition of socialism as "the tendency inherent in an industrial civilisation to transcend the self-regulating market by consciously subordinating it to a democratic society"[7] was equally unsatisfactory. It was a clear indication of his failure to develop an adequate analysis of capitalist states or of any type of modern state. Why was this the case?

Earlier, I discussed why Polanyi's dismissal of the importance of local and national factors resulted in his problem-ridden analysis of fascism, particularly his failure to explain why fascist parties did not succeed in acquiring state power in most capitalist countries. He ignored the need to compare the way that particular capitalist industries or forces of production were 'instituted' (to use his own limited concept) within historically specific non-economic socio-cultural and legal relations in different countries. Just as there was no uniform 'self-regulated market' that failed and supposedly led to fascism, so too, 'socialism' has not, and will not succeed as some overgeneralised tendency to subordinate the fictitious 'self-regulated market' to an equally uniform or unspecified type of 'national democracy' or 'world democracy'.

Between 1919 and 1943, the Comintern, for example, required all Communist parties to subordinate their own quite different national political, economic and cultural conditions to a uniform strategy formulated in Moscow. This strategy was disastrous and an abject failure. Unsurprisingly, political movements in many capitalist countries have tried for decades to devise strategies and conceptions of democratic socialism that are immediately relevant to their own political institutional cultures. Conversely, the notion that 'socialism' and 'democracy' can be 'instituted' at a national level without taking into account opposition from powerful international businesses and governments is just as unreal as the belief that a seamless global market can be subordinated to a 'global working-class' or controlled by a single global democratic movement.

Later, I will discuss why it is highly unlikely that a plausible political strategy of social change towards an environmentally sustainable society could emerge and succeed without a theory of how the complex roles and character of specific state institutions differ within numerous capitalist countries. Of course, no theory on its own can be sufficient without the corresponding practice embodied in particular types of political organisations or significant levels of social mobilisation. We can be sure of one thing though, just as there has never been one historical type of 'liberal state', so too, political movements should avoid basing their action on a theoretical template or an ideal type of the 'capitalist state' as though it is applicable to all capitalist countries.

If we have learned anything from the deficiencies of old Marxist and non-Marxist theories of the 'liberal', 'fascist' or 'capitalist state', it is that actual historical relations, institutional practices and distinct conflicts always ensure that 'the state' and 'the market' are not some fixed or uniform 'things'. Rather, political economic institutions and processes are constantly changing, continually fought over and reshaped by intense competition and political campaigns. No set of state institutions is immune to struggles over social justice, even though coercion may suppress these struggles. No administrator in any state institution can assume that existing dominant values and practices – whether maintaining socio-economic inequality or ecologically unsustainable production and consumption – will forever prevail and not be reformed or overthrown. It should not be forgotten that state institutions are not 'above' social conflict and are also very much affected by intense 'internal' competition, obstruction or conflicting agendas pursued by different departments, groups and individuals within the same government as well as between different tiers of local, regional and national governments.

These intra-state struggles also affect quasi-independent statutory bodies, administrative executives and judicial, policing and legislative wings, not to mention conflicts between national governments and supranational agencies and organisations, including the IMF, World Bank, WTO, EU Commission and United Nations' organisations.

While this is not the place to engage in a detailed discussion of state theories, any analysis of 'capitalism and democracy' must at least provide some account of how state institutions affect democratic practice and how these state institutions are both shaped by and are also the sites of conflicts over the character and extent of democracy in various capitalist societies. Looking back at Polanyi's writing on the rise and demise of the 'liberal state', it is striking how archaic and problematic his analysis is when compared to the valuable insights made by participants in state theory debates since the late 1960s.

Like many socialists of his generation, Polanyi veered between two extremes. On the one hand, he argued that market failure would produce fascists who in turn would use the state to defend capitalism by crushing socialists and democracy. On the other, he posited that once British Labour or other socialist parties such as the Austrian Socialists, won a majority of the vote, then socialism could be legislated and implemented by their respective state institutions. In rejecting class analysis, Polanyi naïvely believed that winning office for socialists was equivalent to gaining power. Hence, 'the state' was either autonomous of capitalists or a mere pliant instrument that could be wielded by liberals, fascists or even socialists. Today, many greens and Left opponents of neoliberalism still hold these conflicting accounts of state institutions.

Due to this simplistic theory of 'the state' and the struggle between 'capitalism and democracy', Polanyi did not anticipate the unofficial 'post-fascist settlement' in Western Europe after 1945 that witnessed key business associations and non-socialist politicians acknowledging the need to make social concessions to labour movements and social reformers. The high rates of taxation levied on businesses and the wealthy in capitalist countries to pay for the war effort included Roosevelt imposing a tax rate of 94% on incomes above $200,000 in 1944 (an unimaginably high rate by current political standards). These high tax rates largely remained in place in Western capitalist countries until the early 1980s where top marginal personal income tax rates never dropped below 70% in the US or 80% to 90% in Europe and Japan. Within most countries of Western Europe and some, but not all OECD countries, the tactical and temporary policies of partial 'class-compromise' or 'social integration' were effectively used – both intentionally and unintentionally by conservatives and reformers – to 'incorporate' and de-radicalise working-class movements, as governments extended the state provision of social welfare benefits, education, health and housing in response to militant, organised demands. Regardless of political motives or objectives, the upshot of post-war reforms was the securing of an extended lease of life for capitalist societies as a majority of voters preferred the 'mixed economy' of private and public sectors to either utopian notions of domestic revolution or 'actually existing socialism' in the form of the austere and repressive Soviet or Chinese alternatives.

Like many other socialists, Polanyi's conception of the role of 'the state' in the struggle between 'capitalism and democracy' disregarded or was unaware of Lenin's critique of socialist illusions about the 'parliamentary road to socialism'. According to Lenin, the state bureaucracy and repressive apparatuses would not stand idly by while a parliamentary majority of socialists nationalised all capitalist businesses. Yet, at another even more fundamental level, Polanyi was stuck in the same time warp as Lenin because he failed to develop an alternative to Lenin's extremely limited and primitive notion of capitalist states as 'bodies of armed men' (see *State and Revolution*). It is not that repressive apparatuses (police, army, courts, prisons) ceased to play a vital role. These were in fact extended in the century after 1917 to include new high-tech apparatuses for intelligence gathering, surveillance of civilian populations and all kinds of paramilitary, rapid response and crisis control units. Crucially, 'the state' is not a mere superstructure that administers capitalist society on behalf of a capitalist class that is constantly threatening to tear itself apart by internal divisions. Rather, as capitalist societies became increasingly complex and faced all kinds of new challenges during the twentieth century, so the need grew for more elaborate and specialised state institutions and agencies to deal with a multitude of conflicting demands. These now include attempts to ensure the smooth functioning of cities and the management of new socio-economic and ecological problems. Instead of seeing state institutions as mere 'political-administrative superstructures', we must always remind ourselves that millions of workers are employed in local and national public institutions and that 'the state' is a vital integral part of 'the economy'.

Despite the claims made by Polanyi's admirers about his 'prophetic' insights and relevance to the contemporary world, there are several reasons why Polanyi's notion of 'the state' is an extremely poor foundation upon which to understand the relationship between democracy and neoliberal capitalist societies. This inadequacy is also found in the work of Marx, Weber, Lenin, Gramsci, Schumpeter, Keynes and other theorists of the period from the 1840s to the 1940s. They also only experienced and wrote about much less developed or less complex capitalist societies and state institutions than we face today, even before the appearance of major environmental threats that now require far greater state involvement in transforming all aspects of local and global production, consumption and social structures. We can certainly draw on these 'classical' theorists, but we need to go well beyond their historically limited ideas for a comprehensive understanding of the complexity of contemporary states. Polanyi may have lived longer than Gramsci, Keynes and other 'classical' thinkers, but he neglected to update his redundant framework or fully understand the systemic critical roles that state institutions play in most aspects of political economic and cultural life. It is therefore necessary to briefly highlight a number of developments that have rendered the old ways of seeing 'the political' and 'the economic' as either historically obsolete or in need of major revision.

THE CHANGING ROLES AND STRUCTURES OF STATE INSTITUTIONS

One of the main reasons 'neoliberal states' are not a return to the old 'liberal state' is that contemporary state institutions cannot be successfully dismantled without also dismantling or at the least, severely undermining key capitalist industries, creating mass unemployment and a major depression. The boundaries between private sector and state or public sector production activities, organisational models, delivery of services, legal obligations, conflicting accountability to shareholders or citizens, methods of political control and social responsibility – to mention several contentious boundary areas and issues – have now become much less distinct and more interrelated. Today, private corporate as opposed to national government objectives often intermesh. Similarly, several newer and parallel political economic practices and organisational models co-exist with older forms of administrative hierarchy and control in private and public enterprises and institutions. These include the following:

- the adoption of the latest but ever-changing organisational and management techniques by state or public sector institutions; the deployment of marketising practices pioneered within private corporations, such as the adoption of management 'cultures' supposedly 'breaking down hierarchies' by having more 'collaboration with stakeholders', flexible hours, open plan offices, hot desks, casual dress, pseudo-collective or 'participatory decision-making' over minor rather than major policy decisions.

- the subordination of social need and care to performance targets aimed at reducing budgetary costs such as the quick 'turnover' of hospital patients and an increase in welfare caseloads under the guise of maximising efficiency and 'democratic access'.

- outsourcing of many public services by state administrators to private contractors while requiring private contractors to conform to publicly legislated social entitlements and 'risk-minimisation' regulations.

- extensive formal 'public-private-partnerships' that include everything from major urban transport and energy infrastructure, prisons, hospitals and education facilities, through to military equipment, communications networks or water supply.

- unofficial 'public-private partnerships' between the police, army and drug cartels and illegal arms traders in nation states stretching from Mexico and Latin American countries to Central Asian countries such as Afghanistan and former Soviet republics through to Guinea-Bissau and other nations in Africa. These illicit state and non-state involvements have also included the CIA and other similar agencies in Russia and North Korea to name just a few prominent partnerships.

Sociologist Max Weber influenced Polanyi and generations of analysts with his famous definition of the modern state as a "...human community that (successfully) claims the monopoly of the legitimate use of physical force within a given territory."[8] However, within both 'successful' and 'failed states' the question of who determines what is 'legitimate' and what constitutes a 'monopoly of force' is not just a contested question regarding the extent and use of state power. Weber's definition of the 'modern state' is inadequate and dated because it fails to deal with a range of vital issues associated with 'legitimacy' and the extent of 'democratic control'. For instance, 'legitimacy' is not given and 'democratic control' is not present when it comes to secretive government activity popularly called the 'deep state' of government agencies and apparatuses practising surveillance, violence or commerce alone or in 'underground' government partnerships with private market forces. Legitimacy and democratic control only become belatedly and marginally relevant if the illegitimate action is possibly discovered well after the relevant state activity has been perpetrated.

Of course, beyond illicit public-private partnerships, it was during the second half of the twentieth century that many old theories of the relationship of 'the state' to 'the market' and 'society' – whether liberal, Weberian, orthodox Marxist or Polanyian – struggled to adequately comprehend the way state institutions, especially those in OECD countries with large service sector industries and employment, became increasingly interlinked with the lifecycle needs and conditions of members of households, from birth to aged care. State agencies and institutions became directly and indirectly involved in all facets of cultural life, social reproduction and the management of households, protection of endangered habitats, the establishment of new industries or the crisis-management of the breakdown of communities due to de-industrialisation.

The overlap of private and public administrative, ideological and socio-economic practices resulted in complex reactions in the decades after 1945. New constituencies and social movements seeking greater social expenditure and civil rights for excluded and discriminated against minorities challenged business groups and conservative parties and institutions. These new social movements demanded the overturning of conservative religious and authoritarian cultural and moral codes enforced by state authorities. It is conventional for many on the Left to see these new movements and demands peaking in the 1970s followed by a 'neoliberal counter-offensive' from the 1980s to the present day. There is some truth in this division of pre-1975 and post-1975 politics. However, it is also clear that there was no cessation of social justice and anti-authoritarian cultural struggles in either developed or developing capitalist countries during the past four decades. Certainly, it is clear for a range of reasons that corporations, political parties and assorted 'social entrepreneurs', technocrats and 'digital' libertarians sought to transform the relation between state institutions and private businesses through all kinds of deregulation, public-private partnerships and the marketisation of public institutional management practices. Importantly, neoliberals also successfully appropriated the language of earlier anti-statist radical cultural and civil rights activists by transforming the demand for recognition of minorities' democratic rights and identity politics into 'consumer choice' and attacks on 'big government'.

Despite decades of liberalisation, privatisation, reduced taxes for businesses and so forth, many of Polanyi's admirers fail to recognise that while free market ideologues call for developed capitalist societies to return to the 'good old days' of massively reduced state expenditure and employment, this would be disastrous for most capitalist businesses. In fact, the reduction of taxation and expenditure to pre-1910 levels when tax revenue was less than 10% of GDP compared to an average of 30% to 50% in present-day OECD countries would almost certainly create another Great Depression and threaten the viability of capitalism in different countries. This is because state institutions play an indispensable role in monetary and fiscal policies, sustaining aggregate household and business demand via income for millions of people and businesses through everything from welfare benefit entitlements to business contracts. Governments also provide an extensive range of material infrastructure, immaterial knowledge, policing and administrative services and social crisis-management without which national and international political economies would descend into depression or even chaotic disorder.

Neither the regular pronouncements by free market political and business ideologues, nor the implementation of neoliberal organisational and marketising practices within state institutions, including joint public-private partnership projects, constitute a revival of the 'liberal state' of more than a century ago as claimed by Polanyians.[9] This is not at all to deny the significant growth in social inequality, the many daily abuses of the unemployed and of those on welfare as well as the deterioration of work conditions. It is also not to ignore the widespread corruption perpetrated by poorly regulated businesses, the continual exercise of violence by the US and other powers in various developing countries or the prevention and overturning of minimal environmental legislation by Trump, Bolsonaro and other Right-wing governments.

If we develop and update Marx's notion of the historical and moral elements of 'variable capital' or even Polanyi's vague concept of 'institutedness' (a concept of capitalism that somehow magically functions without classes), it is clear that there can be no return to early liberal capitalism. The character and dynamics of present-day capitalist production, consumption and the volatile social practices of everyday life at national or international levels remain co-determined and integrated with state institutions. Without regressing to an earlier mode of society, a regression that large numbers of existing businesses would strongly oppose, these practices cannot be dispensed with or replaced by the undeveloped processes of an earlier liberal state. One reason is that business profits and their organisational practices in high-income OECD countries presuppose mass attainment of minimal individual and household income, high levels of formal university and technical education and elevated levels of affluent consumption. Prior to 1929, these conditions were only ever available to small minorities in most countries. This was the case even in the US, which had developed a consumer economy while having a majority of people on low wages and without a college education. It is only superficial and abstract views of 'the state' that can view present-day capitalist relations as a retreat to or a repeat of the past, whether it is the 'liberal state' before 1914 or the 'fascist state' of the 1930s and 1940s.

Crucially, any understanding of how state institutions and agencies 'regulate' societies must have a much broader and more nuanced conception of both 'regulation' and 'self-regulation' than the conventional political economic relationship between 'state' and 'market'. Unfortunately, Polanyi's notion of regulation remained both very limited and economistic. This was a characteristic also evident amongst many radical and mainstream political economists. There are two aspects of this limited notion of regulation versus freedom. Firstly, like Polanyi, far too many economists operate with an essentially dualist framework in which the growth of the 'self-regulated market' conflicts with the needs of 'society' – an abstract 'society' that periodically seeks the 'protection' of the 'liberal state' against the activities of an equally abstract 'market'. As a consequence, 'regulation' and 'self-regulation' continue to be seen as confined to the freedom or constraint placed on businesses and individuals by 'the state' and their social consequences. The fact that millions of workers are employed in local, regional and national state institutions, and moreover, that 'the state' is an integral and vital part of 'the economy' and 'society' is an ongoing reality often denied by pro-market ideologues and even some radicals who only see state institutions as repressive apparatuses threatening the freedom of either the 'individual' or the working class.

Both 'market' and 'state' are therefore misconceived as two homogeneous and separate spheres with opposing or antagonistic logics. On the one hand, as the tendency to increase state political economic control or on the other, as the desire of market forces to be free and autonomous. These two polarised logics remain caricatures of actually existing historical practices in which the many institutions and social practices of private and public spheres are extensively interrelated. It was not just an abstract 'society' that sought government protection in the form of regulation of markets. Different industries and sectors of the 'market' also sought state regulation against a 'free market', especially when it was in the mutual interest of political and business leaders to provide 'stability' and minimise domestic and foreign business competition. Since the nineteenth century, this 'mutual interest' of state administrators and businesses has historically taken various forms: monopoly capitalism, corrupt 'crony capitalism', corporatism in the form of tripartite arrangements between organisations representing capital, labour and government or a variety of public-private enterprises running everything from transport and prisons to hospitals and schools. In other words, there has never been a uniform 'liberal state' and correspondingly, there is no uniform 'neoliberal state'.

THE 'DARK SIDE' OF STATE REGULATION

Like many socialists of his generation, Polanyi's concept of 'regulation' was one-sided. It was characterised by a 'political innocence' that ignored the 'dark side' of socio-economic regulation which developed quite dangerous forms, especially during the twentieth century. Although Polanyi recognised the Nazi support for violent racial policies, he was not fully aware of the extermination camps until after he finished writing *The Great Transformation*. Nonetheless, there was a notable absence in his work, as in the writings of most Marxists and non-Marxists prior to 1945, of an analysis of how nineteenth century race policies, eugenics, population control, surveillance and other forms of state regulation evolved into twentieth century genocide. Following the legacy of the slave trade, colonialism and state violence against indigenous peoples in white settler societies (between the 16th and 20th centuries), state agencies in developed capitalist countries turned their attention to the diverse 'misfits' within their own market societies. All sorts of people classified as 'deviants', social 'outcasts' or 'dysfunctional' blights on productive society, including those suffering from substance abuse and mental illness, were subjected to a mixture of horrific 'treatments' based on eugenics and other 'scientific' and 'civilised' medical and social interventions and 'cleansing' policies.

These earlier forms of state 'regulation' were now increasingly identified and criticised by emerging social movements and a new socio-cultural discourse developing in the 1950s. From Stephen Sondheim's 1957 lyrics *'Gee, Officer Krupke'* (West Side Story) and Erving Goffman's analysis of 'total institutions' (asylums, prisons, the army)[10] to the mass black civil rights movement, anti-censorship campaigns in the media and the arts, or new rights for prisoners and psychiatric patients, many authoritarian and religiously-based state regulations and social controls were challenged and resisted in various countries from the 1950s to the 1980s. This was particularly evident in the feminist second wave where women demanded control over their own bodies and also in the gay and lesbian rights movements fighting for civil liberties. The central role played by state institutions and agencies in so-called 'non-economic' practices geared to the crisis-management of individual, family and other social 'problems' became well recognised in the booming disciplines of sociology, feminist studies, queer theory, criminology, psychology and social reproduction theory. These criticisms of discriminatory practices and laws were directed at governments whether conservatives on the Right or social democrats on the centre-Left. In these analyses, 'Fordism' and the 'Keynesian welfare state' were often equated with a particular form of white male paternalism or authoritarianism that needed to be reformed or replaced.

With hindsight we can see that academic accounts of all forms of social regulation were still stuck in a fast disappearing stage of policy making being eclipsed by neoliberal policies. Take, for instance, Christopher Lasch's *Haven in a Heartless World: The Family Besieged* (1977),[11] Jacques Donzelot's *The Policing of Families* (1979),[12] and the outpouring of Foucauldian studies on 'micro-power' influenced by Michel Foucault.[13] Lasch had blamed the crisis in American family life on a combination of capitalist consumerism and individualism, corporate work values and the social pathologizing of the family by state-employed 'experts'. Notably, his self-described 'populist' defence of the working class against elites has heavily influenced alt-Right figures such as Steve Bannon who has employed Lasch to promote far-Right agendas in ways that would have shocked Lasch.[14] Similarly, in France, Donzelot echoed the theme of state regulation or 'government conducted through the family', a disciplinary process designed to complement what he saw as Keynesian post-war capitalism. The unintended and intended consequences of a joint attack by new social movements and neoliberal policy makers on the 'Keynesian welfare state' produced a new set of state practices. It was only after experiencing decades of neoliberalism that many critics of liberal Keynesianism longed for a return to the pre-1970s 'welfare state', if not the return of the sexist, racist, paternalistic and authoritarian values and practices. The two were, unfortunately, inseparable.

Prior to the 1950s, the main protagonists in the debates over 'capitalism versus democracy' were liberals and conservatives on the one side and various Marxists, anarchists and socialists on the other. Between the 1960s and the 1990s, two variations and refinements of the classical pre-1940s paradigm of capitalism's relationship with democracy emerged. The first was associated with the outpouring of neo-Marxist theories of the 'capitalist state' (Miliband, Poulantzas, Offe, O'Connor and numerous others).[15] The second approach within the dominant paradigm was the prominent anti-Marxist or post-Marxist school of thought, namely, the Foucauldians who gravitated to either a liberal pro-market or an anti-capitalist position. If neo-Marxists have been able to show the complex roles and untidy boundaries of state and private institutions, Foucault and his many followers have shown how various forms of 'discipline and punishment' are not just a matter of direct state control over individuals and socio-economic groups. These 'techniques of rule' have become more varied and more intricate through the historical emergence of 'self-regulation' as a means of state governance.

Neoliberal policies have long been described as 'rolling back the state'. This is a fundamental misunderstanding of contemporary governments as their actions cannot be adequately explained in Polanyian terms. It is true that many public enterprises were privatised. But 'the state' was *not uniformly* rolled back. Instead, the different forms of rationality deployed by neoliberal states are not a return to the 'self-regulated market'. Using the post-1960s' demands for cultural diversity against statist bureaucratisation and standardisation, neoliberal technologies of regulation and self-regulation (instituted alongside cuts to state welfare programs) increasingly took the form of 'government through community' and 'governing the soul' or 'self-rule' by individuals.[16] According to leading Anglo-Foucauldian Nikolas Rose, the old dichotomy of the 'individual confronting state power' or "of a society programmed, colonised or dominated by 'the cold monster' of the State is profoundly limiting as a way of rendering intelligible the way we are governed today." [17] Instead, new forms of state rationality devised by political authorities, managers and experts have relied on pseudo 'participatory democracy' or 'consumer choice', in other words, the successful complicity of individuals and groups in actively sustaining state power via their own 'self-governance'. This may take different forms, such as parents wanting parental training skills, 'social entrepreneurs' substituting for welfare departments, governments outsourcing training and job skills which mostly result in precarious employment and poor welfare, or university departments and community welfare institutions suggesting ways of cutting their own budgets and increasing their own workloads. A pseudo decentralised system of centrally audited 'self-management' and other such techniques of 'self-rule' replaced overt centralised administration.

As old practices of direct bureaucratic state management were diversified, national state fiscal measures and numerous forms of physical, mental and social control were now devolved to face-to-face techniques or to smaller units of 'self-regulation' rather than a return to the pre-1929 'liberal state'.

Similarly, the inbuilt 'paradigm' or 'ways of seeing' in many social sciences, applied sciences and 'human resources' techniques have become increasingly geared to socio-economic and environmental strategies without relying on old classificatory labels such as 'deviant' or 'cripple'. At one level, neoliberal policy strategy is fully compatible with pluralistic identities such as the 'disabled', various forms of 'impairments' (whether, physical or mental), multiple or fluid sexual and gender preferences or the replacement of a pre-environmental language with euphemisms called 'green growth', which actually means environmentally damaging capitalist accumulation policies. At another level, most of this embrace of 'democratic pluralism' paradoxically reduces pluralism by the deliberate failure of neoliberal governments to adequately fund the provision of services or employment and social opportunities for most of the plural 'identity' social groupings.

PRIORITISING TECHNIQUES WITHOUT POLITICAL ALTERNATIVES

The forms may have changed, but multiple techniques of regulation continue to be an inseparable part of everyday socio-economic and political practice in both parliamentary capitalist societies and authoritarian capitalist countries. Any conception of the conflict between 'capitalism and democracy' must first recognise both the more covert, normalising aspects of self-regulation through communities, families or individuals as well as the more traditional violent, coercive and overtly controlling 'dark side' of social regulation. However, it is not enough to identify these new forms of rule. Despite Foucauldians providing many illuminating insights, the critical question is why they, like Foucault, are reluctant to advance few positive alternatives to liberal or neoliberal governmentality? After all, socialists, liberals, greens, anarchists and other political currents may disagree with each other, but they have a vision of the 'good society' no matter how positive, vague or contestable.

There are at least two reasons why Foucauldians remain unable to offer a clear political alternative to neoliberalism. Firstly, many are politically inactive and more preoccupied with focussing on various forms of state and non-state governance. Theoretically, as Habermas and Axel Honneth show, Foucault failed to consider that any one society may have diverse cultural worlds co-existing within it. By focussing on the 'discourse' that determines the 'society as a whole', Foucault was unable to explain how his own theory (like some foreigner looking in) could break from the prevailing 'discourse' and critique the workings of society.[18] Foucault's method was different to Marx's who, in analysing the ruling ideology of the capitalist class nonetheless argued that there were other classes, especially the proletariat and their political organisations, which were divided between those that accepted the dominant 'discourse' and others who opposed it. Unsurprisingly, those Foucauldians who are critical of capitalism obtain their social and moral perspectives from non-Foucauldian sources. Some are socialist, anarchist, liberal or green, and it is from these political philosophies, rather than from their analyses of 'regulation' and 'self-rule' that they derive their opposition to neoliberalism.

It is important to remember that Foucault was active on the Left during the 1960s and 1970s and was a strong critic of the 'liberal state'. Although he engaged with new debates on the capitalist state, he was an anti-statist and like many others on the New Left, opposed bureaucratisation and the rigid orthodoxy and conservative socio-cultural policies of the French Communist Party. Foucault's involvement in Left political discourse and social movements was quite different to most of the Anglo-Foucauldians in the UK, Australia, Canada and New Zealand who had briefly flirted with Althusserian Marxist theory and then became direct and indirect supporters of the neoliberal policies implemented by the Australian Labor Party and British 'New Labour', despite voicing a few minor criticisms. While criticisms were made of Blair's Third Way communitarianism, it was rare to find any public endorsement by Anglo-Foucauldians of any political action or ideas to the Left of Labour. Instead, in private, a number of Anglo-Foucauldians regularly expressed sneering, put-downs of radicals. A heavy diet of the anti-socialist ideas of Nietzsche, Heidegger and Carl Schmitt was most unlikely to result in anti-capitalist analyses. On the contrary, in Australia, Foucauldians strongly supported the neoliberal transformation of universities and other marketising strategies associated with converting education and culture into 'culture industries'.[19]

Similarly, the upsurge of interest in Foucault by American academics and students in the decades before the onset of the Great Financial Crisis in 2007-08, like the popularity of Foucault in other European countries, was essentially liberal rather than radical, and mainly took the form of a politically detached academic discourse. If they did show an interest in politics, their choice of topics such as sexuality, cultural identity rights, prison reform, undocumented immigrants and other issues were rarely connected by Foucauldians to the political economy of capitalism.

Despite a minority of radicals who attempted to combine Foucault's insights with Marx,[20] the impact of Foucauldian 'discourse theory' across the world has been largely to de-radicalise academics, as their analyses posed little threat to the larger political economic agendas pursued by neoliberal governments. In rejecting 'totalizing' analyses of capitalism, Foucauldians preoccupied themselves with the micro 'technologies of rule' and said little or nothing about the larger purpose of these new forms of rationality. Foucault argued that his focus on micro-power was not intended to replace the existence of 'the state'. He not only discussed capitalism but had a good knowledge of the works of major political economists. Sadly, his example has been ignored by his followers who have replaced an analysis of the capitalist state with the notion of 'governance'. Few have asked why these techniques of rule were introduced in the first place. By the 1980s and 1990s many Foucauldians were either reluctant to mention the dreaded term 'capitalism' or acknowledge the existence of a capitalist class. In fact, most deliberately rejected these concepts.

If one examines a range of Foucauldian academic papers and books, they are often characterised by elaborate codes and terminology that skilfully discuss contemporary institutions and policies without reference to the fact that we are still living in class-divided capitalist societies. Euphemisms such as 'advanced liberalism' and a variety of earlier historical forms of economic and social liberalism are discussed without spelling out the fact that liberalism was and remains inseparably connected to capitalism. Given their vocabulary and 'discourse', it remains unclear what the connections are between all the various micro-power 'capillaries' or practices and the larger agendas of maintaining or reforming capitalist societies. In short, most of the discussions of 'governmentality' have been largely divorced from the political reasons for the adoption of new technologies of rule in prisons and social welfare services which have constituted an important part of the larger, neoliberal agenda. Little or no energy has been devoted, for example, to analysing how 'governing through community or individuals' helps resolve state fiscal crises in order to restore business profitability, depoliticise workers and legitimise greater social inequality.[21]

In recent years, there has been much debate amongst Left and Right Foucauldians and former-Foucauldians about whether or not Foucault developed into a strong admirer of neoliberalism.[22] While there is evidence to support his attraction to neoliberalism, I am more interested in the serious limits of the Foucauldian approach to understanding contemporary state institutions and capitalist practices. It was therefore unsurprising that some former loyal Foucauldians experienced a crisis of identity[23] in the first decade of the twenty-first century as neoliberal policies resulted in the largest economic crisis since the Great Depression. The imposition of austerity policies that affected hundreds of millions of people after 2008 made the widespread Foucauldian neglect of political economy (with a few minor recent exceptions[24]) particularly difficult to justify. Claims that there was no ruling class, that state power was decentralised and dispersed were revealed as discredited idealist assertions. The concentrated power wielded by financial and other corporations, central banks and a minority of policy makers in the top G7 to G20 countries continues to make a mockery of those Foucauldians who ignore class power and focus primarily on 'dispersed' micro-power without reference to the crucial centralised exercise of political economic power by corporations and capitalist state institutions.[25]

'Governmentality' or piece-meal, decentred approaches that reject 'totalising' or universal analyses of capitalist societies are also revealed as being incapable of accounting for the world-wide impact of capitalist production on carbon emissions and the earth's life support systems. Hence, alongside the need to understand the techniques of 'government through the family and community' are the 'macro' political economic issues, such as the policy divisions within the most powerful corporations and capitalist states over the rate of national and global decarbonisation and its varying impact on the profitability of different carbon-intensive or non-carbon intensive industries. Without recognising that so much political power is actually centralised, it is difficult to assess the capacity and desire of governments to manage the casualties of climate breakdown or the mitigation and adaptation policies necessitated by climate policy 'transitions'. This does not entail reverting to a simplistic two-class orthodox Marxist model of class struggle which also largely neglected crucial environmental crises. But neither does it mean denying that we live in complex capitalist societies where there is profound inequality in the ownership of wealth and the concentration of power.

Between the nineteenth century and the late 1960s, theories of the capitalist state were dominated by crude orthodox Marxist notions of the state as little more than 'an executive committee of the ruling class'. Non-Marxist theories were just as bad. These included various elite theories that divided society into 'ruling elites' and undifferentiated populations called 'the masses' and American liberal pluralism that effectively denied the existence of class power and a 'class state'. Just as a new generation of neo-Marxists were developing more sophisticated analyses in the 1960s and 1970s of how capitalist state institutions mediated the complex relationships between 'capitalism and democracy', the arrival of anti-Marxist Foucauldian theories of dispersed micro-power and bio-power had the intentional and unintentional effect of removing a focus on the power of centralised state apparatuses. This unfortunate digression lasted until the onset of the Great Financial Crisis of 2007-2008.

HISTORICALLY DATED EUROCENTRISM

Another clear example of the limitations of Foucault's version of the conflict between 'capitalism and democracy' is the historically dated view (shared with other prominent sociologists in the early 1970s) that penal confinement was receding as corporal punishment was being replaced by the new 'normalising' techniques of creating 'docile and productive bodies'. Focussing less on physical punishment and more on new forms of liberal regulation and 'rehabilitation' may be true in a few isolated places such as Norway. However, Foucault's thesis becomes questionable if we turn to the massive increase in prison populations in the US and throughout Latin American countries, Asia, Europe, Africa and Australia. In most countries, the notion that prisons are engaged in 'rehabilitation' is laughable, as Foucault himself knew from personal involvement in prisoner rights' campaigns. Instead, the 'warehousing' of overcrowded prison populations characterised by daily forms of time-passing routine, neglect due to lack of resources, prisoner divisions and hierarchies based on race, religion, physical brutality, or addiction and market exchanges mediated by corrupt guards, all remain common features.

Critiquing Foucault, sociologist Loïc Wacquant pointed out that Bill Clinton, Tony Blair and other 'Third Way' governments in Europe liberalised restraints on private capital and expanded the life chances of the social classes holding most of the economic and cultural capital. When it came to the 'lower classes' who were suffering from the social turbulence generated by deregulation, precarious labour, retrenchment of social welfare and loss of affordable housing due to property investment, the new Leviathan revealed itself "to be fiercely interventionist, bossy, and pricey. The soft touch of libertarian proclivities favouring the upper class gives way to the hard edge of authoritarian oversight, as it endeavours to direct, nay dictate, the behaviour of the lower class." [26]

Wacquant also criticised Foucault's notion that the new carceral disciplining techniques would spread beyond prison throughout the entire social body. On the contrary, prison confinement is ethno-racial and class-based in the US where an urban sub-proletariat lives in a 'punitive society' but middle and upper classes do not. For ethno-racial minorities, targeting has resulted in new carceral disciplining techniques spreading beyond prison. These include:

> a proliferation of laws and an insatiable craving for bureaucratic inno-
> vations and technological gadgets: crime-watch groups and 'guarantors
> of place'; partnerships between the police and other public services
> (schools, hospitals, social workers, the national tax office, etc.); video
> surveillance cameras and computerized mapping of offenses; compul-
> sory drug testing, 'Tazers' and 'flash-ball' guns; fast-track judicial
> processing and the extension of the prerogatives of probation and
> parole officers; criminal profiling satellite-aided electronic monitor-
> ing, and generalized genetic fingerprinting; enlargement and techno-
> logical modernization of carceral facilities; multiplication of
> specialized detention centers (for foreigners waiting to be expelled,
> recidivist minors, women and the sick, convicts serving community
> sentences, etc.).[27]

In the decade since Wacquant wrote his powerful critique, statistics in 2019 showed that the American criminal justice system held almost 2.3 million people in 1,719 state prisons, 109 federal prisons, 1,772 juvenile correctional facilities, 3,163 local jails, and 80 Indian Country jails as well as in military prisons, immigration detention facilities, civil commitment centres, state psychiatric hospitals, and prisons in the US territories.[28] Others on the Left, such as John Clegg and Adaner Usmani focus on the class explanations for the rise of violent crime since the 1960s as more than 40% of prisoners – disproportionately African-American – have committed serious violent crimes rather than the image that most are jailed for drug offences.[29] Opting for punitive prison solutions rather than social welfare policies has been driven by both white and black communities electing local police and judicial officials committed to tough 'law and order' policies. By contrast, the Black Lives Matter movement is a direct response to a violent, racially based punitive system combined with a seriously underfunded 'social state' that has exacerbated the specific political economy of race relations in the US affecting generations of disadvantaged black people.

The explosion in ethno-racial and class-based incarceration is also true of Europe and many other parts of the world where corporate white-collar crime flourishes but low-income, non-white, immigrant and indigenous populations together with poor white social classes are disproportionally imprisoned or monitored in the criminal justice system. This has been due to the importation of US-style slogans and methods of law-enforcement such as zero tolerance policing, mandatory minimum sentencing and boot camps for juveniles. Despite the recent wave of mass social protests, such as the Black Lives Matter movements against the long history of US police officers regularly killing and beating black men, it is far worse in countries such as Brazil, Mexico and the Philippines. Exceeding Wacquant's analysis of US racial violence, organised police and military death squads in these countries continue to actively target and murder many innocent people and those involved with drugs rather than bothering with the formal justice system.

While I would largely agree with Wacquant and others who emphasise the ethno-racial character of the application of carceral disciplining policies and technologies, it is important to also recognise that biometrics and various new digital surveillance technologies as well as the use of algorithms now extend well beyond the racial profiling and monitoring of the sub-proletariat.[30] In recent years, not only China and South Korea but also many other countries have installed surveillance technologies in factories, offices and in public places. Online transactions are also now widely used for both commercial and controlling purposes that undermine both Foucault's thesis and that of his critics such as Wacquant. Highly contested authoritarian intrusions by state institutions maintain 'whole population' surveillance operations (using anti-terrorism and anti-crime as excuses) while corporations deploy it to increase productivity and profitability. These techniques and purposes now far exceed the ethno-racial surveillance that Wacquant highlighted two decades ago. Importantly, the difference between Foucauldian notions of surveillance discipline in prisons (as a so-called more 'humane' advance over physical punishment) and workplace surveillance, is that workers in factories and offices subjected to surveillance technologies are under no illusions. They know that these methods only benefit strongly disliked owners and managers. The same is true of online activity which entails the reluctant provision of personal information for the sake of shopping or access to services.

It is a truism to highlight that these very recent technological developments are in marked contrast to the previous three to four centuries of world history. In fact, when taking a global account of the 'liberal state', Foucault's history of 'discipline and punishment' is a Eurocentric travesty of the historical record that is not applicable to the vast majority of people living in Asian, African and Latin American countries. During the nineteenth century, corporal punishment and public executions began to slowly disappear and were replaced by Benthamite panopticon surveillance of prisoners in Europe, the US and convict settlements such as Port Arthur, Tasmania. However, news of the new coaxing rather than coercive rationality did not seem to reach 'civilised' colonialists such as King Leopold II who personally presided over shocking atrocities in the Congo Free State between 1885 and 1908. Millions died from disease, terrible prison conditions and the notorious cutting off the hand suffered by countless numbers of indigenous workers. Public displays of brutal physical punishment and executions continued through the twentieth century in many colonies and 'independent' countries with the display of severed bodies and heads to warn off other opponents of these regimes.

In Nazi occupied Europe, widespread ferocious beatings, torture, executions and public acts of punishment were displayed for all to see and fear. Rendition and torture have not disappeared in the world today and is practised by both representative democracies and authoritarian regimes. In recent decades, public lashings in Saudi Arabia or public executions of homosexuals in Iran, the numerous rapes of women in police stations in India, and the thousands of political prisoners who were tortured and thrown out of military planes in Argentina and Chile in the 1970s or earlier by French troops in Algeria in the late 1950s – are a few examples of how 'discipline' has not followed Foucault's 'normalising' trajectory. As to state violent repression and the regular exercise of coercion against dissidents by security forces, this continues to be amply evident across the world from Egypt to China, Sri Lanka to Sudan and from Myanmar to Turkey.

As Foucault was developing his histories of the innovative technologies of discipline and forms of punishment in the 1960s and 1970s, an alternative history was unfolding, especially in Asia. In 'democratic' Indonesia, the savage open massacre of between 600,000 and 900,000 Indonesian Communist Party (KPI) members and anybody designated 'Leftist' by the military and assorted individuals and gangs (including the CIA providing the military with over five thousand names of Communists to be liquidated) occurred during 1965-1966. Conversely, the mass public killings and brutalisation of 'capitalist roaders' during the Chinese Cultural Revolution or the atrocities committed by both sides in Vietnam were the very opposite of liberal 'normalising'. Ferocious 'justice' in Cambodia, anti-Red repression by Pinochet in Chile or 'Red terror' by the Mengistu regime in Ethiopia in the 1970s, followed by the 1989 Tiananmen Square massacre of students and mass incarceration camps and prisons continue to be common in countries such as China, Egypt, Iran or Turkey.

One could object to my critique of Foucault's Eurocentrism by arguing that most of these countries were dictatorships or engulfed by war, civil war and military takeovers rather than examples of liberal 'governmentality'. But this is precisely the point, namely, that the history of 'law and order' and 'justice' from the eighteenth century to the twenty-first century did not follow the very limited Eurocentric narrative presented by Foucault and was instead characterised by widespread colonial brutality and post-colonial conflicts. Foucault even deliberately avoided a detailed examination of the Nazi perpetrated holocaust in Europe for fear that it would overshadow his thesis on liberal 'discipline and punishment'.

Ironically, while the above-mentioned atrocities were happening in Asia, Foucault was an active Maoist between 1968 and 1973 and espoused naïve, 'rose-tinted' views that either denied or glossed over the violent irrationality unleashed by Mao's Cultural Revolution. He even called in 1972 for the establishment of 'popular justice' independent of a future 'revolutionary state apparatus', as advocated by other Maoists – a modern version of the violent 'revolutionary people's tribunals' of 1792![31] A few years later, he and other Maoists such as André Glucksmann would abandon Maoism.[32] Foucault spent the remaining decade of his life dwelling in a politically contradictory space in France characterised by the embrace of Cold War 'anti-totalitarianism' and neoliberalism on the one hand and support for 'uprisings' and human rights.[33] Many of these former Leftists justified their naïve support for obnoxious, repressive 'Third world' regimes under the banner of 'anti-imperialism' only to later embrace the neoliberal definition of human rights which divorced socio-economic justice from narrow political rights.[34] By 1983, Paris was, in the words of Perry Anderson, "the capital of European intellectual reaction," just as London had been three decades earlier (when Polanyi was alive).[35] This was confirmed in 1985 by the CIA in a secret report which proclaimed: "There is a new climate of intellectual opinion in France – a spirit of anti-Marxism and anti-Sovietism that will make it difficult for anyone to mobilise significant intellectual opposition to US policies."[36]

UNTENABLE 'NEUTRALITY'

If many orthodox Marxists in the West shared Polanyi's 'political innocence' about the 'liberal state' by either ignoring the 'dark side' of state violence and surveillance or espousing similar 'normalising' regulatory techniques under Communism or capitalism of 'governing through family and community', the

Foucauldians bent the stick too far the other way. Fascinated by 'techniques of rule', most remain reluctant to declare what kind of society they support or desire and the explicit forms of freedom, democracy, social justice, or treatment of patients or levels of ecological sustainability they are 'for' or 'against'. Instead, they mainly espouse a value-free, amoral attitude and merely analyse the differences between how one set of practices in schools, hospitals, prisons or other institutions replaced earlier rationalities. Foucault was adamant about this when he stated: "I'm not a prophet; I'm not a programmer [*programmateur*]; I don't want to tell people what they should do. I'm not going to tell them, 'This is good for you, this is bad for you!' I try to analyse a situation in its various complexities, with its functions, for this task of analysis to permit at the same time refusal, and curiosity, and innovation."[37]

A 'neutral' approach may have been fine for Foucault but in the real world of policy-making and oppositional political activism no such 'detachment' is politically viable. The moment that any such moral and ethical preferences and social and environmental objectives are declared, the central question of who or what is preventing the realisation of these goals quickly emerges and becomes more than a 'technical-administrative' problem; it turns once again to the political issues over the conflict between 'capitalism and democracy'. In the face of the mounting social and political economic crises caused by neoliberal policy makers, some leading Anglo-Foucauldians no longer adhere to the anti-Left and anti-totalizing theoretical position that they held in earlier decades. Although Nikolas Rose rejects the overuse of 'neoliberalism', he does, with qualifications, ultimately accept that poor mental health is linked to neoliberal capitalism across the world. Rose retains many of his Foucauldian concepts, but now talks about 'capitalism' in a manner that would have been unthinkable for him in the 1990s.[38]

We have now come full political circle. Peak Foucauldianism has almost passed. This is largely due to the failure of 'governmentality' analyses to fully come to terms with not just the micro-physics of power but with the macro political economic roles of capitalist states. Forty years ago, in 1978-79, Foucault gave his lectures on 'governmentality' in which he focussed on neoliberalism, including the German Ordoliberals of Freiburg and Geneva who were depicted as advancing a modern form of 'governance' compared to the old and rigid Socialist and Communist parties in France. Four decades later, it is the neoliberals who are old and dogmatic in their inability to resolve major socio-economic and environmental crises.

While I do not believe in political or economic cycles, it is worth noting that forty years before Foucault gave his lectures on 'governmentality' and liberalism, it was German economist Alexander Rüstow who coined the term neoliberalism in 1938. It was also at the 1938 Lippmann Colloquium in Paris that neoliberalism was born as a response to both the Great Depression and the narrow focus of the Austrian liberals (Mises and Hayek) on markets. Quinn Slobodian observes how Rüstow prefigured Polanyi's 1944 critique of the self-regulating market when he argued that "the market had become a domain of atomization" and rejected the belief that the market could operate by itself. Rüstow called this belief in self-regulation a "theologico-rational error."[39] In Slobodian's words, Rüstow asserted that the one-sided focus on efficiency, profit, and productivity "had led to a sociologically damaging isolation and the degeneration of morality as the individual became detached from all community."[40] In short, there was a need, the neoliberals argued, to combat the 'disease called proletariat' by enabling the individual to develop meaningful community and family relations through religion and the land, namely, a 'social market'.

The Ordoliberals in post-war West Germany went on to implement 'social market' policies in contrast to the Chicago School's concept of neoliberalism that was adopted by Thatcher and Reagan. Nonetheless, despite the horrors of the Nazi regime, most of the European and American neoliberals were hardly champions of democracy. Some prominent Ordoliberals like Wilhelm Röpke were high profile racist defenders of apartheid in South Africa. While Hayek was not directly racist, he opposed sanctions on the racist Rhodesian and South African regimes in the name of economic 'freedom', as did Milton Friedman. Hayek also defended Pinochet's dictatorship in Chile while the 'Chicago boys' advised Pinochet on economic policy. It is significant that Foucault in his lectures on these neoliberals said nothing about Röpke's racism or about the Chicago School's support of Pinochet. At a domestic level, the German Ordoliberal policy makers saw the need to protect the liberal market within a conservative social order and also using legal state institutional regulatory mechanisms. This political economic strategy relied on state social policies that were different to the Anglo-American neoliberal emphasis on either privatisation or the marketisation of all institutions and social relations regardless of whether they were state or non-state.

What is notable about the different schools of liberalism/neoliberalism is that Polanyi ignored the Freiburg and Geneva Ordoliberals' concept of the 'liberal state' and assumed that the Austrian and Chicago School liberals were politically dead following the 'Great Transformation' of the 1930s. In contrast, Foucault was not the only one who uncritically succumbed to the Ordoliberal 'social market' as an attractive modern form of 'governmentality'. During the decades between the collapse of Bretton Woods in 1971 and the Great Financial Crisis of 2008, many post-Keynesian social democratic advocates from the Variety of Capitalism school were also seduced by the illusion of the German 'social market' as a progressive alternative to Thatcherism and the 'Washington Consensus'. It took the near collapse of the international financial system in 2008 and the imposition of austerity within the EU to reveal that 'social market' liberalism was so very conservative and far from immune to major crisis. Crucially, as the European Central Bank replaced the Bundesbank (formerly the de facto central bank of Europe), fiscally conservative Ordoliberal policies now officially dominated EU Eurozone countries rather than just Germany.[41] These conservative neoliberal policies have had a terrible record in exacerbating mass unemployment and social crisis within the EU, a crisis that continues to affect millions of people to the present day, as I will elaborate in Book Two.

BEYOND ONE-SIDED STATE THEORIES

Too many Marxists and neo-Marxists have often adopted models of the 'liberal state' or the 'capitalist state' rather than analysing the development of different historical practices and institutional structures of state institutions in each country. While Polanyians and Foucauldians present two influential but different versions of the early 'liberal state' and the later 'neoliberal state', both are inadequate and one-sided. As we have seen, Polanyi focused primarily on the rise and demise of the so-called self-regulated market while ignoring the 'dark side' of how state institutions regulated 'populations' through disciplining and punishing rationalities. If Polanyi remained ever hopeful that a democratic socialism would eventually replace liberal capitalism, most Foucauldians have rejected this political agenda. Instead, they have lost sight of the larger roles and functions of state institutions and continue to be preoccupied with micro 'technologies of regulation' through the use of statistics, classification, auditing of organisational practices and so forth.[42] Paradoxically, in the last years of his life, Foucault intended to research a project that covered the same historical period or narrative as Polanyi's 'great transformation' but with quite different emphases. At Berkeley, he and his students mapped out a study of the rationalities introduced by the American welfare state, Soviet Communism and fascism.[43] These regimes were of interest because they deployed new technologies of administration, production and the management of populations through a range of policies affecting, productivity, health, and other forms of social and economic regulation. In contrast to Polanyi, Foucault rejected the 'grand narrative' of 'capitalism versus democracy'. He was interested in studying how these new states introduced new technologies of conduct rather than how these regimes in the 1920s and 1930s set about destroying or containing democracy within limited parameters.

Very importantly, this over-emphasis on regulation and surveillance, including an explicit and implicit anti-statism and decentred approach to power can mean that Foucauldians on the whole fail to acknowledge how various state policies and practices in different countries have actually helped improve the quality of life for many citizens during the past one hundred years. The provision of public education, health and social services has been a necessary advance to combat poverty and neglect despite bureaucratic and other negative organisational features. Although some Foucauldians may support piece-meal reforms, they are largely silent when it comes to opposing the macro-political economic framework that prevails in leading capitalist countries. Hence, they neither propose new forms of democratic state and social institutions nor offer any alternative socio-political values and agendas in opposition to those dominant 'normalising' practices in neoliberal capitalist societies.

Yet, Foucault also pointed to a serious deficiency that socialists have not yet been able to either clarify or resolve. According to Foucault, socialism lacked an autonomous governmentality as socialists had partially incorporated liberal techniques of rule.[44] In other words, it is not enough for socialists to critique the lack of democracy within capitalist societies and campaign for the distribution of wealth and power. Crucially, they must also outline how a 'socialist governmentality' in a post-capitalist society would organise institutional practices and social relations. Therefore, it was necessary for socialists to spell out how alternative local, national and international institutions engaged in the production and delivery of goods and services, social care and cultural and political interaction could avoid repeating existing forms of capitalist market rationality or bureaucratic state institutional practices. In contrast to defenders of capitalist markets, socialists could not implement models of 'socialist governmentality' from textbooks. They had to invent the new 'socialist governmentality'.[45] On this issue, Foucault and the Foucauldians were of little help, as they deliberately avoided moral questions of why we need equality, why it is right to fight against oppression and what were the elements of social practice that made for a good and caring society. Importantly, Foucault and the Foucauldians did not ask how this 'socialist governmentality' or any future governmentality could be organised in such a manner as to end the environmentally unsustainable values and practices of both private and public institutions in existing capitalist societies. I will return to this fundamental issue in Book Three.

6. ABANDONING SIMPLISTIC CONCEPTS OF SOCIO-POLITICAL CHANGE

DESPITE SOME SIMILARITIES, current struggles over greater democratisation significantly differ from the conflict-ridden histories of earlier political battles between the defenders of capitalism and the advocates of either representative or direct democracy. As I have argued, Polanyi's very influential but deeply flawed misconception of the 'origins of our time' distorts our understanding of the contemporary conflicts between 'capitalism and democracy'. His thesis of the 'great transformation' was based on how 'fictitious commodities' and the interplay of the 'disembedded/embedded' liberal market was part of what he called the 'double movement'. In the century before the 1930s, Polanyi argued that the cyclical expansion of the 'self-regulating liberal market' was periodically checked by a countermovement that sought to restrain, regulate and protect 'society' against the destructive tendencies of capitalist markets. In recent years, the so-called 'double movement' of 'society' that aims to 'embed' or regulate market forces has been revived by contemporary Polanyians seeking to understand and curb neoliberalism.[1] Three preliminary comments are necessary before discussing the political implications and applicability of Polanyi's 'double movement'.

Firstly, it is those influenced by Polanyi rather than Polanyi himself who use the 'double movement' as a quasi-law that supposedly governs a full range of political economic developments in international relations and social movements. This goes well beyond Polanyi's original meaning of the concept.[2] Secondly, the dispute amongst contemporary Polanyians revolves around whether or not Polanyi argued that the double-movement against the liberal market was proto-socialist and would eventually lead to socialism. In my view, in contrast to the so-called 'double-movements' in the nineteenth century, Polanyi tried to show that the crisis in the 'self-regulated market' had become terminal by the 1930s. However, the 'counter-movement' assumed quite different political forms of 'social protection' that resulted in either Soviet Five-Year Plans, fascism or the American New Deal. Thirdly, while Polanyi only used the concept of an 'embedded economy' twice,[3] the academic debates of recent decades as to whether all economies are 'embedded', like the concept of 'double movement' has taken on a life of its own.[4] Rather than engage in a detailed discussion of these academic debates, I will instead emphasise the political consequences of the way Polanyi's concepts are being employed.

In the 1930s, along with a handful of radical theorists such as Herbert Marcuse and Henri Lefebvre, Polanyi belonged to the first small group of socialists who read Marx's recently discovered 1844 manuscripts on alienated labour.[5] Consequently, Polanyi's understanding of Marx was infused with an appreciation of the philosophical and moral critique of how capitalist markets created not just the alienation of workers from the products of their own labour, but also their alienation from their own communities and from the natural world. Yet, he went on to reject Marx's theory of commodity fetishism and the centrality of exploitation to alienated labour. Instead, he regarded the degradation of human relations or cultural degradation as more important than economic exploitation. He therefore misunderstood or precisely ignored the key points in the early Marx, namely, that exploitation was not just narrowly 'economic', but *simultaneously* produced both alienated workers and cultural degradation in the form of alienated citizens, alienation from nature and also alienated communities. In capitalist market societies, social co-operation was devalued, and competitive individualism was elevated. The freedom of market relations, Marx argued, was that 'wage slaves' were not like bonded slaves and therefore individuals were now 'free' to 'collide' with one another in the marketplace.

While Polanyi borrowed elements of Marx's analysis of commodification and alienation, the conflict between 'capitalism and democracy' was based on his own notion of commodification which, in contrast to Marx, he called 'fictitious commodities'. According to Gareth Dale, Polanyi was also heavily influenced by the German sociologist Ferdinand Tönnies who developed two ideal types of the change from *Gemeinschaft* or organic community to *Gesellschaft* or a large society based on inauthentic, abstract, fictitious and artificial contract relations.[6] *The Great Transformation* was thus an analysis of how the artificial contract relations of Gesellschaft (or self-regulated market) destroyed the old organic Gemeinschaft. Both Marx's theory of alienation and Polanyi's adaptation of Marx and Tönnies raise once again the old controversial major question: to what extent will it ever be possible to politically and socially overcome alienation and 'disembeddedness' – either partially or fully – in large industrial societies?

THE POLITICAL DISTRACTION OF AN 'EMBEDDED ECONOMY'

Much has been written about Polanyi's most famous concepts of labour, land and money as 'fictitious commodities', so I will confine my brief discussion to particular aspects. As usual, Polanyi's work was often ambiguous and contradictory. One can find Polanyi arguing that prior to the development of the liberal market, economic relations were embedded within the totality of social relations within communal institutions. It is the rise of the liberal market (in contrast to local and long-distance markets in pre-capitalist societies based on barter and other forms of trade) that produced the 'separation' of 'the economy' from traditional social practices, thus causing massive poverty and destruction. This leads to the oft-quoted statement: "Instead of economy being embedded in social relations, social relations are embedded in the economic system."[7] However, the growth of specialised legal, administrative and socio-economic institutions eventually sees the construction of a 'market society' because, as Polanyi emphasises, the new 'market economy' "can only function in a market society."[8]

As to labour, land and money being 'fictitious commodities', this is because they are not pure commodities for sale on the market but also have an intrinsic role and value as part of life, nature and social exchange. While he critiqued the ideological fiction put forward by defenders of the market that labour, land and money were commodities, he also accepted the reality that this was not just an ideological dispute between liberals and socialists. If left without social protection, the self-regulating market would destroy labour, nature and the medium of social exchange.[9] The opposite interpretation of Polanyi is provided by Fred Block who argues that the existence of 'fictitious commodities' proves that Polanyi thought that a 'disembedded economy' was impossible because market societies need the state to play an active role in managing markets. When state and market policies move in the direction of 'disembedding' or destroying labour, land and money, a 'counter-movement' emerges to protect the 'fictitious commodities' from further incursions and erosion by market forces. The result is the subordination of liberal capitalism to social and political control.[10]

Of course, Block's interpretation conveniently suits his advocacy of a 'civilised capitalism' characterised by social democratic regulation rather than socialist revolution. Yet, Polanyi's thesis of the 'great transformation' was so generalised in pitting 'society' against the 'market' that both the Nazi and Soviet 'counter-movements' were supposedly unleashed to 'protect society' against the liberal self-regulated market. Instead, the 'fictitious commodities of labour and land were subjected to catastrophic abuse during Stalin's forced industrialisation and collectivisation of the 1930s. Similarly, Hitler's 'counter-movement' produced six years of suppression of the German labour movement, Jews and other social minorities before 1939, followed by the unleashing of historically unprecedented militarised barbarism and systematic extermination. If both the Soviet and Nazi 'double movement' were deemed by Polanyi to be forms of 'social protection' against the attack by the liberal market on 'fictitious commodities', then one would shudder to see what *no protection* looked like!

Regardless of whether or not Polanyi believed that the liberal market was originally a 'disembedded economy', he saw the establishment of this market in the late eighteenth and early nineteenth centuries as a social calamity. This emerging economy began to 'annihilate all forms of organic existence' that flourished in pre-capitalist communities and replaced them with an alien, atomistic and competitively geared system – the self-regulated market.[11] Like many critics of capitalist industrialisation, Polanyi laboured under the illusion that one could eventually re-establish an 'embedded' 'organic community', not as a return to pre-capitalist community, but rather as a decentralised form of democratic socialism. Unsurprisingly, many advocates of degrowth also long for the 'embedded society' and cite Polanyi approvingly. In Book Three, I will discuss why the political goals of achieving a future socialist or eco-socialist society does not depend on adhering to 'organic' concepts of socialist or green 'embedded' societies. In fact, the danger of accepting 'organic' theories is evident in Polanyi's simplistic dualism of pre-market and market societies.

One of the fundamental flaws associated with his notion of 'fictitious commodities' is Polanyi's essentialist and binary approach: 'pre-market equals good' but 'market bad'. This ignores how these 'fictitious commodities' were already saturated in prejudice and injustice before the advent of capitalist market societies. As social philosopher Nancy Fraser points out, "long before they were marketised, social constructions of labour, land and money typically encoded relations of domination – witness feudalism, slavery and patriarchy..."[12] Given that Polanyi was single-mindedly focused on critiquing self-regulating markets, I agree with Fraser's observation about *The Great Transformation* that it:

> ...overlooks harms originating elsewhere, in the surrounding 'society'.
> Preoccupied exclusively with the corrosive effects of commodification
> upon communities, it neglects injustices within communities,
> including injustices, such as slavery, serfdom and patriarchy that
> depend on social constructions of labour, land and money precisely as
> non-commodities. Demonising marketisation, the book tends to
> idealise social protection, as it fails to note that protections have
> often served to entrench hierarchies and exclusions.[13]

It is not only that Polanyi romanticised pre-capitalist relations, but he also failed to acknowledge the contradictory oppressive/progressive roles played by the liberal bourgeoisie in simultaneously creating new forms of exploitation but also sweeping away many old forms of domination, superstition and prejudice. One of the significant differences between the socialism of Marx and Polanyi is that Marx did not romanticise pre-capitalist societies as 'organic communities'. Instead, Marx and Engels in the *Communist Manifesto* understood the complexity and progressive quality of the bourgeoisie far better than Polanyi, and far better than many Foucauldians and Marxists who both tend to emphasise only the negative, repressive and disciplining qualities of state administrators and ruling classes. This is evident in their famous appraisal that:

> The bourgeoisie, wherever it has got the upper hand, has put an end
> to all feudal, patriarchal, idyllic relations. It has pitilessly torn asunder
> the motley feudal ties that bound man to his 'natural superiors' and
> has left no other nexus between people than naked self-interest, than
> callous 'cash payment'. It has drowned out the most heavenly
> ecstasies of religious fervour, of chivalrous enthusiasm, of philistine
> sentimentalism, in the icy water of egotistical calculation.[14]

During the twentieth century, the global spread of capitalist relations was similarly characterised by numerous complexities and contradictory outcomes. Government and market forces promoted Western science, education and health that challenged or destroyed both old prejudices and privileged hierarchies as well as valuable pre-market communal relations and forms of knowledge. To see 'bourgeois relations' and forms of knowledge in only negative terms is myopic. Unfortunately, Western rationality still remains largely tied to market practices and rapid forms of social disruption that have triggered fundamentalist religious and secular reactions as billions of people continue to be exposed to the 'icy water of egotistical calculation'.

If all economies are 'embedded' but are only embedded in different ways, what is the rationale behind the debate over whether an economy is 'disembedded' or not? Either 'disembedded' is an irrational or undesirable state of affairs denoting a fundamental disconnect between the logic of the production system and the social needs of workers and communities, or 'embedded' is emptied of any clear political and socio-cultural meaning. However, if we take the boundary between 'the economy' and 'society' to be an arbitrary and artificial distinction, then the debate over what is an 'embedded economy' becomes a purely academic distraction from the wider political objectives to either maintain, reform or overthrow the existing social order.

Today, the definitions and boundaries between 'society' and 'the economy' exist for statisticians, administrators, academics and as short-hand terms in everyday discourse. Otherwise, these 'spheres' have long been intermeshed and increasingly blurred in most countries. Businesses ignore these distinctions as they actively commercialise and commodify the private household and social sphere. There are, of course, small, relatively unincorporated marginalised indigenous communities living in remote local environments or dependent on government funding of services, rather than being fully integrated into market practices. Also, for the past forty years, businesses have largely succeeded in breaking down old religious and other social customs/regulations (such as a day of rest for religious observation) in order to make social life amenable to hyper-market practices on a 24/7 basis. Ironically, these 'traditional' values and practices co-existed with Polanyi's 'liberal market' capitalism during the nineteenth century and up until the 1970s, thus highlighting that Polanyi's notion of 'market society' was far, far less marketised than the diverse forms of market practices that prevail in both private and public sectors of contemporary societies.

We may reject and despise the dominant forms of competitive consumer individualism, or the way that financialisation has affected all aspects of everyday life. Such is the integration and intertwining of capitalist business practices and culture with intimate social relations that most of us regularly or occasionally misconceive commodity fetishism as an almost 'natural' state of affairs. This is evident in the digital tracking of an individual's online preferences or leisure or forms of life-style marketing necessary for the continued profitability of many businesses. In fact, the vast majority of those under the age of forty living in developed capitalist societies, cannot remember a world where their identities and the deepest level of their subjectivities (their dreams and desires) were not interpolated or enmeshed in consumer market relations. A mere thirty years ago, digital profiling of individuals was confined to serial killers and madmen. Today, we are all 'embedded' or profiled through endless consumer websites and government agencies.[15] The very transformation and expansion of the dominant private services sector (over old-style manufacturing that employs a diminishing proportion of the workforce) now depends on its very interpenetration and shaping of social relations. While these service sectors employ a mixture of well-paid professionals and highly exploited, low-paid workers, they are not as isolated or as invisible as former and current workers in factories and mines. On the contrary, the general public (including all service sector workers themselves) are fully enmeshed as they interact with other service sector workers on a daily basis consuming a range of services in retailing, entertainment, hospitality, health, financial services, tourism and other industries.

STUCK IN A BYGONE WORLD

Polanyi's analysis of social relations in early historical capitalist societies is starkly at odds with key social practices in most OECD countries today. Consider the fact that families were much larger in earlier contexts and that most women were not in the paid non-agricultural labour force. Secondary school attendance and higher university and technical education were in most countries the privilege of a tiny minority. New information technologies that linked private and public life did not exist and health and education were not the massive industries that we take for granted today. Certainly, market forces accelerated the commodification of family relations, natural resources and labour. The change in gender relations within the home and public sphere, the shift from first being agricultural labourers and domestic servants to manufacturing workers, and then to various forms of service sector employment was also partly due to businesses demanding lower-paid female workers. These changes within capitalist production intersected at the same time with women and socially underprivileged groups demanding equality, better education and social services and a preference for urban life over rural poverty and suburban isolation.

Feminist debates have changed since the 1970s. First, were the historical debates over how nineteenth and twentieth century capitalism 'disembedded mothering' from womanhood in order to legitimate the nurturing of the new market individual. However, during the past twenty years, feminists have turned this perspective on its head. Now, in response to the informal coalition between neoliberals and various careerist, work-centred feminists, the burning issue is whether feminism has been co-opted into the marketplace and needs to revalue the non-market relations of mothering and the broader care ethic which challenge commodification.[16]

The political crisis confronting contemporary Left movements and environmentalists is not one of recognising or debating 'fictional commodities' but more the difficulty of decommodifying existing consumer capitalist socio-cultural relations. Most women who struggle against patriarchal domination would not be drawn to the old Left's or Polanyi's 'embedded' or 'instituted' patriarchal socialism as a so-called alternative to liberal capitalist society. Social divisions are no longer *solely* defined by who owns the means of production and how wealth is concentrated or distributed. Many workers would join their bosses in rejecting the idea of living in an environmentally sustainable society free of cars and high consumption. The old notion of 'privacy' has also been thoroughly eroded by digital 'big data', face recognition CCT cameras and drone surveillance technologies combined with the increased fusion of social media and individual identities. Yet, despite massive inequality and poverty, it is one thing to identify and oppose the excesses of commodity capitalism, and quite another to unite people in capitalist countries around an alternative cause that, rightly or wrongly, appears as either new anti-consumerist forms of austerity, or full-employment agendas based on consumer-fuelled environmental destruction.

While the endless academic debates on the meaning and merits of 'embeddedness' continue, including the claim that we must also talk of 'cognitive, cultural and political embeddedness',[17] most of these debates minimise or remain blind to our 'embeddedness in nature'. Importantly, the usefulness of Polanyi's concept of 'embeddedness' in helping to create an alternative society is questionable. In high, middle and low-income capitalist countries that are becoming increasingly integrated globally, it does not matter whether disembeddedness or embeddedness came first. In fact, the old concept of uneven and combined development assumes different 'layers' or modes of life co-existing within the same social formation but with one mode of production (for example, the capitalist mode and related socio-political institutions) either dominating or fusing with earlier indigenous, aristocratic, peasant or craft segments and social relations. Any such notion of highly uneven historical and social development is at odds with the Polanyian fiction of homogeneous societies that somehow become 'embedded'. If most societies contain dominant or subordinate segments or layers that are characterised by different social relations – not just for instance, rural village life alongside urban industrial capitalism but also digital capitalist enterprises and professionals occupying a quite different social space to old fossil fuelled factories – then no society can be wholly embedded or disembedded in the same way.

Consequently, all the diverse social elements of complex societies do *not* react simultaneously in a 'counter-movement' against the self-regulated market. Polanyi was silent on the critical issues of race and cultural diversity. Moreover, his pre-1940s world has been replaced by one where more than 80% of the world's population are now living in diverse low and middle-income capitalist countries. These countries are part of a transformed global order characterised by a mixture of emerging capitalist giants (with increasing middle-classes but also mass poverty) and a vast array of societies unable to surmount domestic and global barriers imposed by developed capitalist countries. I have discussed these issues in more detail in *Fictions of Sustainability*.

Neo-Marxists such as Elmar Altvater and Birgit Mahnkopf used Polanyi's concept of 'disembeddedness' to show that global financial, energy and other markets constrain social systems.[18] More than a decade before the Great Financial Crisis, Altvater and Mahnkopf argued that the monetary system had become uncoupled from 'the real economy'. While this view of 'disembedded money' is now fairly familiar, the distinction between Wall Street and High Street (or finance and the 'real economy') belongs to an earlier historical era of what constituted a capitalist 'economy'. I outline these distinctions in Chapter Five of *Fictions of Sustainability*. Leaving aside the character of a socialist society, there is little agreement on the role money could play in a socially and politically controlled post-neoliberal capitalist or socialist society. Some see a so-called 'embedded' socialist or degrowth society as one in which the relationship between production, consumption, credit and trade would be totally transformed, that is, money and credit severely controlled or abolished. Others wish to keep money and credit but only modify or eliminate speculative high risk and high-profit transactions. All those who advocate political controls over capital flows and a range of major reforms to subject finance institutions to social controls – whether social democrats or radical greens and socialists – are politically divided over solutions to financialisation. Many are not even aware of how extensively 'embedded' within societies all forms of derivatives and other financial instruments and commodities have become. This is a degree of 'embeddedness' that would require a social revolution if de-financialisation is the goal to achieve a so-called genuine non-market 'embeddedness'.

Similarly, political economists Bob Jessop and Michael Burawoy argue that 'knowledge' should also be included as a 'fictitious commodity' because it is both an intrinsic part of humanity and yet vital to the 'knowledge economy' of commodity production and battles over intellectual property rights.[19] Shoshana Zuboff goes further and declares that:

> surveillance capitalism annexes human experience to the market
> dynamic so that it is reborn as behaviour: the fourth 'fictional
> commodity.' Polanyi's first three fictional commodities – land, labour,
> and money – were subjected to law. Although these laws have been
> imperfect, the institutions of labour law, environmental law, and
> banking law are regulatory frameworks intended to defend society
> (and nature, life, and exchange) from the worst excesses of raw capitalism's destructive power. Surveillance capitalism's expropriation of
> human experience has faced no such impediments."[20]

But if knowledge and human experience are also 'fictitious commodities', regulatory laws will not decommodify them so long as capitalist markets exist. Regulation will only curb the worst excesses. Even the break-up of Google, Facebook and the other giants would still see 'knowledge' and 'human experience' used as 'exchange value' by smaller high-tech businesses unless the collection of online data on human behaviour were outlawed.[21] It is the notion of 'intellectual property rights' and its legal enforcement that underpins commodification. This is abundantly evident in trade disputes, industrial espionage, the unavailability of critically needed medicines for poor people, the debasement of art and the prioritisation of funded scientific research for potentially profitable civilian or militarily destructive purposes rather than for safeguarding ecological habitats and improving social well being. All forms of knowledge used in business, art and communication can only be fully decommodified in a post-capitalist society that values, cultivates and supports knowledge and intellectual creativity in non-commercial terms.

Rather than updating and adding to Polanyi's list of 'fictitious commodities', it is his concept of 'fictitious commodities' that is simultaneously illuminating and limited as an understanding of commodification. Marx had used the concept of 'fictitious capital' when discussing how state and bank bonds, securities and so forth were different from real capital embodied in such things as machinery and the physical capital of production. Polanyi uses the concept of land, labour and money as 'fictitious commodities' in a different sense because they are both commodities for exchange and because they preceded the arrival of capitalism and have intrinsic value outside market relations.

One of the major problems that besets Marx's *Capital* was the failure to adequately specify the interconnections between national and international state institutions and their involvement in commodity production and political class struggle. If the capitalist mode of production is *not* one giant seamless, global system, how do political and social struggles at the *national* level affect social relations of capitalist production in other nation states or at the level of so-called international class relations? The same problem was evident in Polanyi's work as he conceived of the self-regulating market as both international and national. It was at the *national* level that the political 'counter-movement' against the liberal market took place. Even the attempt to impose state controls was limited because of what he claimed was the "absolute independence of markets from national authorities".[22]

Accordingly, the breakdown of the international market during the Great Depression produced a 'double movement' or the turn to 'social protection' in the form of fascism or the New Deal. While some Polanyians claim that the post-1945 world until the early 1970s was 'embedded liberalism' (the Bretton Woods system combined with national welfare states), Polanyi rejected Bretton Woods as a regressive return to the 'nineteenth century self-regulated market' and also criticised welfare states. Short of an internationally fully regulated global socialist economy, Polanyi pinned his hopes on a limited system of 'regionalism', a secular version of the European states system of the fifteenth century. Contemporary Polanyians are divided over whether the politics of 'fictitious commodities' should be largely conducted at national level or at regional EU level or at a global level. In other words, the expansion of 'disembeddedness' countered by the demand to 'embed' or control national and international markets is contentious because the political goal of an 'embedded national economy' is today regarded as either *the* central political goal or an unrealisable utopia.

AN EMBEDDED SOCIETY IS NOT INHERENTLY DEMOCRATIC OR JUST

Actually, the notion of an 'embedded society' tells us little or nothing about the social norms and morality guiding such a society. Consider that for the past seventy-five years, most citizens and national businesses in affluent OECD countries have cared little about the welfare of strangers in other countries, except when they impacted their profits and jobs or when they dared to arrive in their home countries uninvited. Hence, it is theoretically possible to imagine a nationally 'embedded economy' characterised by full-employment, affluent consumption and overall social contentment that is abhorrent. Importantly, such an economy could be environmentally unsustainable, based on the blatant exploitation and misery of workers in other countries, and characterised by racism, the absence of democracy and an intolerance of cultural practices that do not conform with the conservative values of the so-called embedded 'organic community'. We cannot therefore assume that 'embeddedness' is inherently democratic, egalitarian and environmentally sustainable.

Polanyians make much of 'disembedded' societies where 'economics' rather than 'politics' is in control. One could argue that China is an example of 'embedded capitalism' or 'command capitalism' where the economy is subordinated to the political agenda determined by the Chinese Communist Party. This would horrify Polanyi's supporters who understand 'embedded' to mean a democratic socialist society rather than authoritarian one-party rule. In practice, Chinese society is characterised by a mixture of planned socio-economic development and widespread lightly regulated market practices. These market capitalist small and large enterprises are far from 'embedded' as they exploit and subject hundreds of millions of Chinese workers, consumers and local environments to daily abusive practices. In short, China's socio-economic and political institutions do not fit into the artificial binaries of 'embedded' and 'disembedded'.

Also, the moment that one begins to extend the geographical boundaries of 'embeddedness' or to include all those who are *not* citizens, employed, or without adequate sustenance or social rights, then the notion of 'embeddedness' becomes something quite different to the very limited notion of labour, land and money treated as commodities. One can understand why critics of neoliberalism are attracted to Polanyi in their desire to subordinate contemporary capitalist societies to political control. Nonetheless, the problem today is far more complex. Even gaining full socialist or radical green political control over national or international markets is not equivalent to establishing an 'embedded economy'. This is because medium to large cities, let alone nation states are inherently impersonal and based on distant, abstract relations that are doomed to remain 'disembedded' as daily life experiences.

So much discussion of 'disembeddedness' and 'fictitious commodities' avoids the key question of what would constitute an 'embedded society' in the twenty-first century. For if we are not talking of small, face-to-face, self-sufficient communities, then all nation-states are to varying degrees, remote and 'disembedded', not to mention supra-national entities such as the European Union or global markets. In addition, there is no clear idea or consensus about what level of social and political control will end 'disembeddedness' and commodification. Some small face-to-face, self-sufficient communes could possibly claim to be fully embedded only if the residents had no major dependence on external goods, services or income – an utterly utopian social model for organising billions of people in the world. It is possible that future populations might even regard socialist egalitarian societies that engage in global trade rather than just local, self-sufficient, face-to-face interactions as remote or 'disembedded'. Yet, even this would be hardly a sufficient reason to oppose such societies.

As I will later discuss, it borders on delusionary to believe that 'embedded' self-sufficient, stateless, small-scale communities are politically feasible or viable as the main form of a global alternative to capitalism. If we are mindful of Polanyi's warning that self-regulating markets are utopian and dangerous, the same warning also applies to socialist or green stateless societies based on equally utopian small, self-regulating communities.[23] Despite being characterised by powerful and attractive critiques of bureaucratisation and oppressive hierarchies, there is a high chance that these stateless anarchist and green alternatives to neoliberalism would also degenerate (especially by the second and subsequent generations of communalists) into new authoritarian nightmares or selfish parochial communes that refuse to help other less fortunate communities or 'outsiders'. Rather, we need solutions that will reorganise existing complex national and global institutions to maximise social justice, democratic control and co-operative cultural values. The goal of global 'embeddedness' remains then a utopian distraction from the difficult task of combatting inequality, racial and discriminatory social hatred, or ending and preventing wars and catastrophic ecological breakdown. We need alternative political economic agendas to dominant neoliberal practices even if these do not conform to a Polanyian unspecified ideal type of 'embeddedness'.

CLIMATE BREAKDOWN AND FICTITIOUS COMMODITIES

The current crisis of dangerous climate breakdown best illustrates, like no other issue, the drawbacks in Polanyi's influential concepts of 'fictitious commodities' and the 'double movement'. Remarkably, Polanyi's work continues to be used by some environmentalists in their analyses of threats to sustainability.[24] This is largely due to environmentalists reading into Polanyi a much broader conception of ecology than he ever intended. In his brief but most frequently cited comment, Polanyi warned that if the liberal utopia of a self-regulated market came into being we would see society robbed of "the protective covering of cultural institutions, human beings would perish from the effects of social exposure; they would die as the victims of acute social dislocation through vice, perversion, crime, and starvation. Nature would be reduced to its elements, neighbourhoods and landscapes defiled, rivers polluted, military safety jeopardized, the power to produce food and raw materials destroyed."[25]

Professor of theological ethics, Gregory Baum, argued in 1996 that Polanyi was the prophet of the environment movement and that were he alive today, he would see environmentalism as part of the 'counter-movement'.[26] This may well be true. However, Polanyi was mainly focused on the social and environmental devastation caused by uprooting people from the land as part of early primitive capitalism – a devastating process that has been repeated in many countries outside Europe and is still ongoing today. In recent years, leading environmental scientists who developed the notion of the Anthropocene, such as Will Steffen, directly referred to Polanyi's 'the great transformation' in the early nineteenth century (not the 1930s) as influencing their theory of the 'great acceleration'.[27] Others have argued about whether a carbon market is a 'counter-movement' to neoliberal capitalism. Diana Stuart, Ryan Gunderson and Brian Petersen conclude that the carbon market is not a 'counter-movement' and that the degrowth movement is the real 'counter-movement'.[28] But there is neither a single degrowth movement (despite international links) nor a single carbon market that operates in the world. Hence, the Polanyian 'double movement' supposedly functions in a vague political space without any clearly specified national as opposed to global state institutional policies and business opponents. These are all examples of a Polanyian ill-fitting theoretical framework super-imposed on an important set of environmental issues.

Of course, the enormous growth of capitalist industrialisation in both developed and developing capitalist countries since 1944 has been far greater than anything Polanyi envisaged. Crucially, the depth of environmental destruction in the USSR and former Eastern European and current Asian countries dominated by Communist parties has matched and even exceeded that caused by rapacious market forces. Communist governments, especially the Chinese regime, have presided over a double bureaucratic state-led and capitalist assault on their environments. This devastation, as also the earlier destruction under Soviet command planning, cannot be reduced to Polanyi's analysis of the liberal self-regulated market and the threat of this market to 'fictitious commodities'. Widespread corruption combined with zealous state-planned industrialisation, a wilful neglect of and contempt for preserving the vital intrinsic quality of species biodiversity and habitats has resulted, tragically, in much irreversible environmental damage in former and current one-party Communist countries. Only now, is China addressing these despoiled environments due to negative effects on productivity and public health.

Apart from a few brief mentions, Polanyi was no prophet of environmentalism. Still, he cannot be blamed for lacking an adequate insight into the multiple causes of environmental destruction, as he and his generation could never have imagined or predicted that climate breakdown and incessant economic growth would become the greatest crises confronting the world today. While many on the Left are active in demanding drastic measures to prevent catastrophic climate change, there are also others who are still locked into the old paradigm of 'capitalism versus democracy' and focus exclusively and narrowly on traditional Marxian or post-Keynesian political economy and merely devote a few lines or a paragraph to environmental issues. Radicals like Perry Anderson or Wolfgang Streeck, as well as a majority of socialist and social democratic economists familiar with Polanyi, have invoked his concept of 'land' as one of the 'fictitious commodities' threatened by the market but assumed, unfortunately, that little more needed to be said about ecological issues.[29] Remarkably, Wolfgang Streeck, in an otherwise important analysis of the 'crises of democratic capitalism', did not even mention climate breakdown, until very recently.[30] The very title of Streeck's book, *Buying Time: The Delayed Crisis of Capitalism,* would have been ideal for including a discussion of the inability of policy makers to resolve the relationship between capital accumulation and environmental crisis that has been unfolding for decades. Instead, despite decades of public discussion about environmental destruction and climate change, a myopic minority of radical political economists continue to treat it as a secondary by-product of the 'contradictions of capitalism'.

A close reading of *The Great Transformation* shows that Polanyi was essentially concerned with 'land' or agricultural land as an elemental part of nature just like labour. In his chapter on 'Market and Nature', Polanyi argued that land supported many forms of traditional life before being destroyed by the liberal market.[31] While this is no doubt true, as we know, nature is far more than land. Modern ecological concepts embrace all aspects of the natural world and not just those fertile portions that sustained different forms of agriculture and traditional communal village life transformed by capitalism.[32] Paradoxically, we have gone to the other extreme where in 1989, environmentalists like Bill McKibben pronounced 'the end of nature' due to climate change.[33] It is important to remember that carbon emissions are not to be confused with simple resource depletion and the mindless, 'cowboy capitalist' destruction of nature that admirers of Polanyi highlight. Technically, one can have relatively unpolluted cities and natural habitats – compared with the polluted, pea-soup lack of visibility in smog-filled nineteenth century cities or current cities in China, India and other developing countries – and still have dangerously high greenhouse gas emissions causing global warming. This is not to ignore that outdoor and indoor air pollution shortens the lives of about 9 million people each year especially in China and India and including between 450,000 and 600,000 premature deaths in the EU alone.[34]

BEYOND MARX AND POLANYI

The second aspect of the way radicals use Polanyi's brief discussion of nature is similar to the way Marx's fleeting and fragmented comments on nature have been inflated. Far from ignoring the crucial role of nature like earlier generations of radicals, many now attempt to show that both Polanyi and Marx are highly relevant to modern environmentalism. This is done by overstating or stretching their concept of nature to make it appear that Marx and Polanyi somehow anticipated modern environmental critiques of capitalism. During the 1980s, political economists such as James O'Connor used Polanyi in order to broaden Marx's theory of the contradictions of capitalism. In his

1988 editorial that launched the new journal *Capitalism, Nature, Socialism,*[35] O'Connor argued that Marx's contradiction between the forces and relations of production (the struggle between capital and labour) was inadequate because it needed to be supplemented by the contradictions in the 'conditions of production' of which nature was central. If labour movements were the leading agents of social change in the old orthodox Marxist theory of capitalism, ecological Marxists needed to also focus on the related second contradiction of capitalism, that is, the threat to the 'conditions of production' and the struggles of social movements battling against capitalists and governments. O'Connor, like other neo-Marxists, raised the twin issues of the old internal limits to capitalist growth characterised by a crisis in the falling rate of profit and class conflict, and also the new ecological Marxist concern with the natural limits to growth caused by exhausted resources and environmental destruction. Puzzlingly, O'Connor said little or nothing about climate change.

Marxists and other radicals struggle to preserve the relevance of Marx and Polanyi to key aspects of the contemporary world such as climate breakdown and the need for societies based on post-growth or wellbeing. Large parts of Marx's body of work is much more complex and far more relevant and durable than Polanyi's. However, more than a century of debates by orthodox and neo-Marxists over theories of surplus value, the tendency of the rate of profit to fall and the 'transformation problem' (that is, how the production of surplus value is transformed into the price of commodities and the sum of profit), sadly remain at the level of abstract academic debates and bear little relevance to formulating actual strategies to counter neoliberal policies.[36] I know of no persuasive Marxist account of how to measure the rate of surplus value produced by the 'global proletariat' employed in multinational production processes with very large divergent wage and working conditions, as well as multiple component assembly plants based on such things as complex secret transfer pricing schemes between subsidiaries of corporations. The heavy support of national, regional and city governments through tax, infrastructure and social policies that subsidise the cost of fixed capital infrastructure and human capital (such as education and training policies) to mention just a few of the numerous intertwined relations between private capital and state apparatuses, all influence but also prevent accurate calculations of surplus value and profitability.

Additionally, the fact that Marx's division of capitalist production into Department One (producing the means of production, such as steel) and Department Two (producing goods for individual consumption, such as clothing) makes the calculation of surplus value and profit extremely difficult as gas, electricity, oil, solar and digital symbolic goods such as software are both the means of production and the means of consumption.[37] If this were not enough, we still have the major headache of which Department the massive expenditure on mainly state-purchased military goods adequately fits. Ernest Mandel, for example, tried to rescue Marx's problematic reproduction model by creating Department Three to explain arms production.[38] Such schema risk that we get bogged down in sterile mathematical disputes rather than trying to understand contemporary capitalist societies. Even if one could accurately measure the sum of surplus value in the production and circulation systems, this would not be sufficient to understand how significant levels of profitability in dominant finance sectors are based on all kinds of 'productive' financial instruments and digital transactions that are not directly dependent on the traditional labour/capital relation.

Marx's analysis (like Polanyi's) was not designed to comprehend everything from climate breakdown to the social relations transformed by financialisation. It is true that Marx saw nature as the source of all use values (and hence material wealth) rather than labour.[39] Yet, this was not equivalent to contemporary ecological concerns. To highlight a central limitation of Marx and Polanyi in relation to the biosphere and biodiversity, take the fact that both theorists believed that socialism would utilise the advanced forces of production developed by capitalism but reorganise social relations and redistribute the benefits in a socially just manner. However, it is precisely the character and level of technology and science alongside the threat to biodiversity embodied in capitalist production and consumption that makes the technological continuity between capitalism and socialism dangerously problematic. The inseparable role of science and technology in sustaining profitable capitalist growth necessitates stringent social and scientific evaluation and critique.

Kohei Saito argues that Marx was not a Promethean championing new technology's ability to control nature, but became an eco-socialist as he recognised the negative implications of deforestation and chemicals on food production.[40] While this is true in part, Saito and others engage in the dubious method of projecting the social and scientific meaning of ecological concepts from a developed capitalism of the twenty-first century back onto the far less developed capitalism of the 1860s with its quite different conceptions of the relation between industrial production, science and the environment. Saito's image of Marx as a modern eco-socialist would be more persuasive had Marx mounted a critique of fossil fuel production and consumption and their link to climate breakdown. After all, it was American scientist and feminist, Eunice Newton Foote in 1856 who first established that changing the proportion of carbon dioxide in the atmosphere would change its temperature. However, Foote's discovery did *not* at all mean that she should be hailed as a prophet of contemporary environmentalism.

We do not need to justify post-capitalist societies by constantly seeking the endorsement of 'the master'. What counts is not what Marx, or any other classical theorist said about 'this' or 'that', but rather how others have used their work to justify current policies and political action.[41] In recent decades, numerous critics have pointed to the many technologies – from nuclear to various biotech and nanotechnologies – which are either dangerous or constitute potentially threatening implications for many species including our own. We are at the infant stage of many of these technologies and are still unaware of the social and natural consequences of advanced biotech, robotics, neuromorphology, polymers and other technologies heavily promoted by corporate and military sectors. Various new technologies may prove to be benign and beneficial. Others are driven by profit and by unethical research unconcerned about the seriously negative consequences for society and for non-human species.

It is important to remember that there were two different versions of 'Marx' that tended to contradict one another. There is Marx the positivist who wanted to discover the 'laws of capitalist production' modelled on the natural sciences (hence, his desire to dedicate *Capital* to Charles Darwin) and there is Marx the critical social theorist who stressed the importance of changing historical social relations rather than detecting fixed laws.[42] Marx's failure to fully understand the contradictory implications of science is partly due to the fact that he lived well before this became very apparent by the middle of the twentieth century. The same excuse can also be given to Polanyi in regard to the fact that he lived before many recent technologies. That is why his concept of nature as a 'fictional commodity' fails to understand how various new technologies and forms of knowledge deployed by markets are equally dangerous to humans and the natural world even if deployed as 'non-commodities' by well-meaning socialists.

NATURALISING THE SOCIAL AND SOCIALISING THE NATURAL

So, while Polanyi and his followers emphasise either the *socially* 'disembedded' or 'embedded' character of capitalism, many still treat the *environment* as something 'external' (just like neo-classical economists) and moreover criticise the market for making incursions *into* nature or exploiting nature. Similarly, the endless theoretical disputes over whether all humans are responsible for the geological age called the Anthropocene[43] or whether it should be called the 'Capitalocene'[44] because capitalism is to blame for the unfolding environmental crisis, is an issue that will not be resolved in philosophical disputes. In attributing the Anthropocene to an undifferentiated humanity, one is reminded of the young Marx's critique of Feuerbach's focus on 'man' instead of historically specific social relationships and material conditions.

If many environmentalists regress to the 1840s and have ahistorical notions of the 'Anthropocene', contemporary theorists like Jason Moore bend the stick too far the other way and almost reduces nature to capitalist social relations. He argues that it is more illuminating to speak of the past five centuries as the development of the 'Capitalocene' (specific forms of class divided capitalist production) rather than blaming an abstract and undifferentiated 'humanity'. One can go part of the way with Moore. Yet, the 'Capitalocene' is a limited umbrella concept in that it reduces or subsumes the whole natural world to a 'productivist' logic of the development and practice of capitalist production. In other words, there are no natural processes, no laws of physics, and no evolutionary biology outside capitalism. As Ian Angus wryly observes: "If I wrote a book called *Quantum Theory or Capitalum Theory?*, you would expect me to propose a new explanation for the behaviour of sub-atomic particles. You wouldn't be impressed if I ignored protons and energy levels and explained, 'Capitalum Theory isn't about physics, it's a critique of Max Planck's poetry'."[45]

I believe that one can acknowledge the existence of a new geological era called the Anthropocene without succumbing to an overgeneralised sociological and ahistorical analysis that all humans caused it equally. Specific capitalist forms of production are overwhelmingly and disproportionately responsible for the emergence of the Anthropocene (rather than all humans). If capitalism ended today, however, the danger of climate breakdown would not disappear. Too many people constantly shift from using the 'Anthropocene' as the description of a new geological era, to a concept which mainly applies to specific social formations of the past two hundred years. It is absolutely true that if capitalism collapses without having drastically reduced greenhouse gases then potential climate chaos will make life inhospitable and difficult for whatever social and natural forms continue after capitalism.

The key issue is not how long the 'Anthropocene' lasts, rather whether a safe climate as well as maximum biodiversity can be secured before it is too late. Instead of waiting for social and environmental destruction, the need to prevent climate chaos is immediate and something that has to be done within the context of existing capitalist societies, given that social revolution is currently remote. Identifying the 'Anthropocene' era does not translate into predicting how particular societies will organise their future way of life. This fallacy of attributing a capacity to *determine* the character of *social institutions and social relations* to a generalised concept like the 'Anthropocene' is equivalent to the old Marxist economic determinist belief in the 1920s and 1930s that once capitalism went into crisis then socialism would follow. In its place we saw fascism triumph in various places. Today, who knows how future governments and societies will respond to dangerous climate breakdown if we don't even know what kind of governments will exist in ten to twenty years or the character and power of future political movements.

I do not wish to devote further space to theoretical disputes over the 'Anthropocene' or 'Capitalocene'[46] or related disputes between Moore, John Bellamy Foster and others concerning what Marx meant or did not mean by 'nature', 'metabolic rift' and so forth.[47] All participants in this debate make valid and important points. The problem is that no correct definition of Marx's concept of nature or his other concepts such as surplus value can advance our need to develop specific policies and strategies to deal with carbon emissions or overcome capitalism. Importantly, even though humans are part of nature, as social beings the interactions between the social world and the natural world cannot be completely reduced to one another. Hence, no 'society' or 'economy', even the most environmentally sensitive one has ever been or can ever be fully embedded in a seamless web with nature.

CLIMATE CHANGE AND THE 'DOUBLE MOVEMENT'

As to 'nature' as a 'fictional commodity' related to the 'double movement', this is completely inadequate to an understanding of climate breakdown. To imagine that Polanyi's current followers can conceive global warming as part of the 'double movement' is a dangerous conceit. At what point will the spontaneous 'counter-movement' reverse carbon emissions? Will it be before or after an additional 1, 2, 4 or 6° degrees Celsius of higher global temperatures? Even if governments agree to limit emissions to no more than 1.5° degrees Celsius, the emitted gases remain trapped and continue to affect global temperatures. The 'counter-movement' against the 'disembedding' tendencies of the market cannot restore or provide 'social protection' as with 'labour' or 'money' once an increase in greenhouse emissions triggers climate chaos for centuries.

One could argue that a global 'counter-movement' is already under way to prevent climate chaos. Plainly, this is not Polanyi's 'double movement'. There is no equivalence between Polanyi's 'double movement' at *national* level and the necessity of implementing simultaneous decarbonisation policies within a specific timeframe across the globe, especially within the leading major emitting countries. The powerful resistance of the fossil fuel industries and political allies in key emitting countries such as the US and China, or Saudi Arabia, Canada, Australia, Russia and other key coal, oil and gas producers, each pose quite different political challenges as they are either representative democracies or authoritarian states highly dependent on fossil fuel production, consumption and exports. Coal production is likely to decline rapidly in some countries by 2030, but oil and gas will be much harder to eliminate. Moreover, the Paris 2015 COP21 proposed decarbonisation over a period of at least 30 years compared with 'counter-movements' of much shorter durations in the 1930s. Such a long policy process spread over several decades well beyond 2050 brings with it highly unpredictable political conflicts and a possible series of 'counter, counter-movements' within the original so-called 'counter-movement'. If capitalist countries merely had to deal with decarbonisation as a technical problem centred on the switch to renewable energy, this would in itself entail many political economic difficulties. Nonetheless, simultaneously occurring multiple problems such as near stagnant OECD economies over the past three decades, failed crisis-management policies that merely postpone rather than resolve major inequalities between social classes at domestic levels and globally between high-income and low and middle-income countries – all these major problems are interrelated and cannot be isolated from solutions to climate breakdown.

Not only is decarbonisation not equivalent to a Polanyian 'double movement' but the conventional solutions of 'social protection' based on regulation of markets and social policies are of a different order to what is now needed. Instead of 'embedded' growth, the scale of global threats to numerous habitats now requires *deceleration* or an end to incessant material growth. Such degrowth or wellbeing solutions explode earlier historical notions of socialism as the elevation of the working-class to a 'bourgeois' standard of living by appropriating the wealth and power of the ruling class. Unfortunately, there are segments of the Left who share with the Right a belief in utopian techno-fixes or what is called 'fully automated luxury communism'.[48] Rather than a 'counter-movement' this is a phantasy journey on the well-trodden pathway of environmental destruction. When the brutal Nazi regime triumphed as a so-called 'counter-movement' to the liberal market, the loss of life was horrendous. This monumental human catastrophe, flowing from the so-called 'double movement' in the 1930s and up until 1945, could possibly pale into insignificance if 2 to 6° degrees Celsius global warming is not averted and the incessant march of material capitalist economic growth continues to destroy the planet.

BEWARE 'DOUBLE MOVEMENTS'

If we are to come to terms with both the historical and also the contemporary forms of conflict between 'capitalism and democracy', it is necessary to explain why Polanyi's concept of the 'double movement' needs to be cast-off. There are two dominant contemporary interpretations of the 'double movement'. Firstly, those who believe that Polanyi used it to show how democratic, progressive social change or even socialism would emerge from the process of market expansion followed by the 'counter-movement' seeking social protection. Secondly, there are others who assume that Polanyi was neutral about political outcomes because the protection of 'society' against old liberalism and present-day neoliberalism could take different forms such as neo-fascism, social democracy or socialism. The first group debate who could be the agents of the 'counter-movement' today given the changed conditions of twenty-first century capitalism. The second group are divided between those who nominate no 'progressive' social change agents but favour social democratic forms of social protection, and others who hope for a revival of Left social movements but currently see the rise of Right-wing parties as the dominant version of the 'counter-movement' against neoliberalism.

What is so seductive about the metaphors of waves and cycles that captivate political and economic theorists on both the Left and Right? Take as a case in point the most prominent cyclical theory of the past century, Nikolai Kondratieff's notion of Long Waves of expansion and decline that still supposedly govern capitalism. All kinds of analysts have used these Long Waves including Trotskyist revolutionaries, Schumpeterian theorists of cycles of technological innovation, to World System theorists and even Wall Street stock market analysts.[49] Polanyi's 'double movement' is *different from* Kondratieff's Long Waves. Nonetheless, it has been interpreted as having a spontaneous, mechanical and repetitive quality simply because Polanyi saw the century before the 1930s as governed by regular expansions of the market followed by regular counter-movements. Politically and historically, what makes Polanyi's account of the 'origins of our time' so flawed is that his 'double movement' is founded on the following questionable assumptions.

Firstly, a common and highly pertinent critique of Polanyi is that he had an 'under-socialised' or under-theorised concept of society. In Edward Webster, Rob Lambert and Andries Bezuidenhout's words, Polanyi had "no concept of agency, how a counter social movement is made, no theory of social movements, no theory of power, no theory of scale – from local to global, hence no theory of the contradictions in society, because he operated at the general level of market, society and state."[50] Similarly, Timothy Clark, argues that Polanyi treated 'society' as if it were a Subject that acts against the Market. The 'double movement' is mysterious because 'society' is an unknown 'black box' that reveals no clarity about the dynamic forces and tensions or contradictions that drive social change.[51] Instead, Polanyi gave priority to external or global conditions which produced the 'counter-movement'. As sociologist Michael Burawoy summed up:

> Polanyi suffers from a false optimism on four counts. First, he so
> believed in the power of ideas that he thought the discredited
> ideology of market fundamentalism could not take hold of our planet
> again. Second, he postulated a nebulous and under-theorized notion
> of society, which, in the final analysis, so he claimed, would summon
> up its own defence in the face of a market onslaught. Third, in his
> hostility to orthodox Marxism – especially toward its theories of
> history and the centrality of exploitation – he lost sight of the impera-
> tives of capitalist accumulation that lie behind the resurgence of
> markets. Finally, in focusing on the market and its countermovement
> he too easily reduced state to society, missing their complex
> interplay.[52]

Without a theory of what causes social change, it is no surprise that Polanyi could not explain why local and national conditions prevented fascism from coming to come to power in most countries. As Beverly Silver points out in her study of specific labour movement struggles, Polanyi failed to show how new working-classes are made and old ones unmade.[53] He ignored the geographical and political space in which anti-market forces attempt to organise resistance.

Instead of identifying the specific governments, parties and business groups that attempt to block or defeat anti-market social and political groups, Polanyi was forced to fall back on abstract notions such as the 'double movement'.

Secondly, not only is it important to provide an analysis of the specific social and political economic resources that were needed to form and develop a 'counter-movement' but it is also politically crucial to understand whether these movements erupted spontaneously or were built on existing communal traditions and forms of knowledge as well as international experiences and networks. Without comprehending the origins of a coherent political agenda or a loose coalition of past or present movements, there can be little clarity about whether any so-called 'counter-movement' is compatible with or poses a major threat to a particular existing political system. In contrast, Polanyi operated at such a vague, abstract level of 'market, society and state' that the notion of 'social protection' sought by the 'counter-movement' was never specified. Who was actually 'protected' and was this 'protection' forged 'from below', that is from particular segments or classes in 'society' or was it administratively imposed 'from above' by state policies that originated either from paternalistic action by business and political elites, or in response to a democratic vote or mass agitation? Consequently, the 'double movement' was so unclear that it could be interpreted to mean either the quest for social reform within capitalist societies, the push for a radical authoritarian regime or the replacement of the entire system with democratic socialism.

Thirdly, not only is the 'double movement' a vague and deeply flawed account of how previous social change took place, but this abstract concept is equally unsuitable for explaining who or what constitutes the 'counter-movement' today. While Polanyi did not believe that the 'double movement' could go on endlessly given the fact that the market could never be stabilised, he also seriously under-estimated the ability of business and political leaders to accommodate the regulation of labour and social welfare reforms after 1945. Importantly, the Polanyian 'double movement' is incapable of explaining major changes in recent decades. It would be stretching this 'double movement' beyond recognition to *reverse* the 'double movement' and apply it to former highly regulated 'command planning' Communist regimes in Eastern Europe that have now transitioned to market capitalist systems. Similarly, current one-party Communist state regulated regimes in China, Vietnam, Laos and Cuba are also the *opposite* of Polanyi's 'great transformation' which is based on a self-regulating market being challenged by a 'counter-movement'. In fact, the socio-political configuration of struggles in developing countries – from Islamic militancy through to decades of civil wars in Africa, Asia, Central and Latin America – is a world that finds little or no place on Polanyi's analytical map. Using him as a compass will leave us all stranded.[54] Those who attempt to squeeze the modern world into Polanyi's obsolete categories are perhaps unwittingly abdicating their responsibilities to a new generation of concerned citizens who want to understand the dynamics of present-day societies and how to change them for the better.

Fourthly, even those who admire Polanyi have serious reservations about his 'double movement'. Political economist Mark Blyth argued that the 1970s and 1980s did not conform to Polanyi's model as they were characterised by a 'counter double movement' of businesses wishing to dismantle social protection by freeing themselves from decades of regulation or 'embedded liberalism'.[55] Does this mean that present-day anti-neoliberal movements are 'counter, counter double movements'? Which contemporary social classes or fragments of social classes constitute the anti-free market or protectionist 'double-movement' given that there has never been a homogeneous working-class movement? At present it would appear that so-called 'populist' parties fuelled by racists and people living in depressed communities are more concerned about seeking protection against 'incoming' refugees, Muslims and foreign workers rather than protection against 'outgoing' processes, that is, businesses destroying their jobs by moving work 'offshore' (or both).

Fifthly, if Blyth's notion of the business 'counter double movement' is bad enough for Polanyi's theory, consider the further blow to its credibility when recognising that the former agents of social protection against the market, namely, social democratic and labour parties, were also heavily involved in undermining social protection. Polanyi's periodisation of liberal market developments and its use by the contemporary Left is also highly unsatisfactory. Australia was one of the first countries to implement neoliberal policies. It was the Hawke and Keating Labor governments from 1983 to 1996 that implemented neoliberal policies rather than becoming a Thatcherite anti-union government.[56] Labor dismantled the social protectionist centralised wage system with the co-operation of the majority of leaders of the trade union movement (including prominent Communist union leaders) and also reduced most tariffs thereby laying the foundations for ruthless free trade policies which cost hundreds of thousands of jobs. The Australian situation is highly relevant to European social democratic and labour parties because Blairite New Labour learnt from and later followed key aspects of the Australian model and European centre/Left parties also embraced Blairite 'Third Way' neoliberalism. The German Social Democrats under Schröder, for instance, weakened social protection in the labour market after 1998, more than a decade after Australia. These political developments stand in contradiction to Polanyi's thesis particularly insofar as it was these former 'social protectionist', centre-Left parties rather than the old liberal capitalist marketeers, that were key in implementing pro-market policies. It is the historical transformation of social democratic parties from their socialist historical origins to their post-1970s neoliberal identities that helps confirm Polanyi's political world as historically obsolete.

Revealingly, centre/Left governments tended to implement additional policies of liberalisation than even some centre/Right governments in Europe.[57] Globally, the impact of leading technocrats close to the French Socialist Party, such as Jacques Delors of the European Community, Henri Chavranski of the OECD and Michel Camdessus of the IMF were vital in promoting the liberalisation of capital flows. Notably, this was a global strategy that even the Right-wing 'Washington Consensus' would never have been able to deliver on its own.[58] However, it would be highly inaccurate and misleading to imagine that Polanyi's pre-1929 liberal 'market society' bears any resemblance to contemporary Australian or European socio-economic and political formations, despite the weakening of social protection in recent years.

Finally, the 'double movement' is an inappropriate concept for understanding our much more integrated world. Jürgen Habermas, another admirer of Polanyi, argued that the power of market globalisation cannot be cushioned via 'counter-movement' protectionist policies in a single nation state because the emerging global society cannot be reversed by dividing global processes or re-inserting national segments back into nation states. Hence, the need, Habermas argues, for new post-national institutional structures.[59] Currently, advocates of a more democratised European Union (such as Habermas) oppose anti-EU 'populists' and nationalists. Both sides pursue diametrically opposed forms of 'social protection', not against a self-regulated market, but rather against highly controlling neoliberal central bankers and EU bureaucratic fiscal, monetary and social regulation. These contradictory European developments, alongside other related trends are ample evidence that the 'double movement' should be well and truly abandoned as a useful analytical model for comprehending these conflict-ridden times.

Nonetheless, defenders of Polanyi deploy all sorts of post-Polanyian arguments to salvage or rescue some of his ideas while recognising that the 'double movement' is politically untenable in its original form. Social analyst, Michael Brie, updates the 'double movement' in a series of maps and diagrams outlining different political agents and outcomes.[60] His dizzyingly abstract and elaborate model makes it impossible to believe any such analysis could be meaningful outside the sociology classroom, let alone relevant to social movements engaged in contemporary political struggles. Apart from brief references to such things as Nazi race policies, like many of his generation, Polanyi was silent on deep-seated race issues in America, the treatment of colonised peoples by imperial powers as well as on gender issues and the treatment of minorities.

Social theorist Nancy Fraser recognises that Polanyi's 'double movement' is seriously flawed. She calls for a 'triple movement' that includes movements for emancipation. "There is no going back", she argues, "to hierarchical, exclusionary, communitarian understandings of social protection, whose innocence has been forever shattered, and justly so."[61] The old sexist, racist and exclusionary conservative forms of social relations can never be the basis of a new 'double movement'. In response to the question of why there is no unified 'counter-movement' in the twenty-first century, Fraser points out that "the social movements of the post-war era do not fit either pole of the double movement. Championing neither marketization nor social protection, they espoused a third political project, which I shall call emancipation."[62]

Fraser is rightly sensitive to emancipatory movements and intra-class forms of oppression and domination. However, she still wants to engage in the futile attempt to rescue the 'double movement' even as she converts it to a 'triple movement'. Either the 'triple movement' is now something entirely different to Polanyi's, that is, embracing economic, environmental, social and political processes, or it is still the same old implausible quasi-automatic, spontaneous process as the original 'double movement' but with a modern renovation. Unfortunately, Fraser does not combine her critique with a complementary analysis of complex national and supranational state institutions to give further strength to her focus on emancipatory movements. Moreover, her case is weakened by calling Blair, Schröder and Clinton 'progressive neoliberals' who defeated both the anti-neoliberals and the 'reactionary neoliberals'.[63] While there is a partial truth in Fraser's distinction between 'progressive' and 'reactionary' neoliberals, she cannot have it both ways. Either Polanyi's notion of a 'counter-movement' remains valid (with modifications), or she acknowledges that the so-called 'progressive neoliberals' undermined any semblance of a 'counter-movement' by providing indispensable momentum to the further market liberalisation of society.

CONCLUSION

Not only did Polanyi's analysis of 'the great transformation' ignore many crucial issues of his own time but as I have argued, his work remains largely irrelevant to social relations and conflict in the twenty-first century. The complexity of contemporary societies characterised by profound levels of inequality, transnational corporate power and the rise of digital production and commerce, and the hollowing out of old political parties and labour movements is a world that cannot be understood by reference to Polanyi's framework. In fact, it seems both odd and even ridiculous to revive Polanyi's master paradigm as a theory and narrative that can help explain our fundamentally transformed world characterised by new forms of consumption, new individualist subjectivities, multiple virtual online sub-cultures that link the local to the global yet fragment national public discourses. Add to those factors the phenomena of increasingly de-unionised work places, the splintering of the old large patriarchal family, low birth rates and new gender identities and relations and the rise of smaller, multi-forms of private families and individualised social relations, and we start to get a sense of some of the decentred and fragmented conditions that have enabled neoliberal governments to thrive in many countries. This fragmentation of social relations is in contrast to those pockets in countries and regions of the world such as in Latin America, Asia or Africa where traditional community identity is still relatively strong. It is in these 'traditional pockets' where violence by paramilitary units and thugs employed by businesses and large landowners or authoritarian government brutality meets resistance from poor villagers or urban residents. Most OECD countries, however, are characterised by weakened forms of solidarity, faded or unknown collective memories, and increasingly individualised responses to political economic recessions – social worlds that are light years away from Polanyi's world.

Polanyi is rightly admired for trying to set out a grand theory of the rise and demise of an earlier form of liberal capitalism and for his commitment to a more egalitarian socialist society. Disappointingly, his thesis is over-generalised, full of highly problematic arguments and concepts which ultimately weaken his analysis of the relationship between 'capitalism and democracy'. Reading the large and proliferating literature on Polanyi, one is struck by the number of contemporary analysts who praise Polanyi but then immediately go on to outline why we need a 'post-Polanyian' approach to an entire range of issues. I have tried to show that while his key concepts initially appear to be suggestive and tantalising, we could do far better than adapting or building upon what was a seriously defective analysis of the political and economic 'origins of our time'.

It is a truism that the establishment of nineteenth century liberal markets and late twentieth century neoliberal policies were both political projects. Beyond this starting point, we need new explanations that recognise how infinitely complex local, regional and supra-national state institutions actively crisis-manage populations and social conditions – institutions and practices that bear little resemblance to nineteenth century and early twentieth century social conditions. Think of the range of contemporary political actors such as social movements, NGOs and corporate think tanks, or the pervasive impact of digitalised technologies on social and institutional communication, their use in coercion and surveillance, not to mention the manner in which individual and communal health is now connected to new forms of agribusiness and pharmaceutical biotechnology. Add to the mix all the profound socio-economic and political changes to former colonies as well as the shift in global power relations, and there are far too many aspects of contemporary life that indicate that the Polanyian framework has passed its use-by date.

This is not to deny continuities with Polanyi's world. Despite extensive social change, we still live in capitalist societies based on deep-seated exploitation, growing inequalities and endangered environments. It is the manifestation of these inequalities, forms of exploitation and environmental threats that now take place in profoundly altered political and cultural landscapes. Furthermore, Polanyi's mixture of mechanical and naturalistic binaries is both ahistorical and without a sense of political direction. Importantly, the goal of a democratically controlled 'embedded economy' does not in itself answer pressing questions such as whether economic growth is good or bad, or how a post-neoliberal capitalist or socialist or green sustainable society could prevent a recurrence of the numerous crises plaguing the world today.

As I will later analyse, despite the lack of major unified anti-capitalist political movements, it would be a serious error to imagine that capitalist social orders are secure. We have already witnessed the havoc wreaked by two major global crises (in 2008 and 2020) within little more than a decade. The crises facing present-day capitalist businesses and public institutions are different to those that confronted liberal capitalists in the 1930s. In the highly competitive and unbalanced world of competing economies, future problems of how to sustain national financial and equity markets, how to generate profitable growth through constant technological innovation in the face of natural limits to growth and massive social inequalities, or how to prevent the use of weapons of mass destruction remain on a scale and intensity that makes the challenges of earlier historical periods look relatively tame. Finally, previous decision-makers within capitalist countries and oppositional political movements both did not have to worry about whether they could deliver either continued profits or socialism by decoupling future economic growth from systemic environmental and climatic processes.

BOOK II

SHIFTING PARADIGM: THE LAST GASP OF A PRE-ENVIRONMENTALLY CONSCIOUS POLITICS

7. PERPETUATING MYTHS ABOUT DEMOCRATIC CONTROL

DESPITE THE RISE of urgent environmental issues, a majority of political and business analysts, social movements and governments are still caught up debating policies within the dominant paradigm of 'capitalism versus democracy'. It is not that these disputes over capitalism are irrelevant. Far from it. Rather, many of the participants in these political conflicts have not yet fully understood that the future of capitalism or post-capitalism cannot be resolved by governments, parties or movements that are still largely dominated by views of the world that can be characterised as based on a pre-environmental consciousness. Being aware of climate change or endangered habitats is merely a first step on the road to being environmentally conscious. Far too many people on the Left who consider themselves historical materialists fail to take the next step and put the goal of an equitable per capita and national material footprint (necessary for a globally sustainable environment) at the centre of their politics. They are aware of carbon footprints and the need to reduce or change material consumption if greenhouse emissions are to be drastically cut. Preventing climate breakdown is absolutely urgent and fraught with major obstacles. But this goal is quite realisable and compatible with existing forms of social inequality and lack of democratisation. Not so, the political objective of environmentally sustainable material equality which is much broader than dealing with carbon footprints.

In this chapter, I will examine those critics of capitalism who are still largely frozen within the old paradigm of 'capitalism and democracy' despite the melting of the Arctic and Antarctic ice caps, Greenland and the

Himalayas and all that this entails for the future of capitalism, human habitation and species diversity. In short, much political economic analysis and policy making, even Left notions of Green New Deals or pro-business proposals of 'green growth' lag well behind the scale of the forthcoming challenges and the urgency of rethinking the dominant relations between 'capitalism and democracy'. All may be in flux, but many still desperately cling on to what are familiar *pre-ecological* forms of pro or anti-capitalist politics and solutions. Until very recently, the dominant political discourse has been between defenders and critics of national and global forms of 'neoliberal capitalism'. Now the impact of Covid-19 has raised the issue of whether neoliberal policies have had a serious setback or are on critical life support, and if so, what will replace these policy frameworks. The climate emergency has not gone away, yet most of the debates about class divisions in capitalist societies and their relationship to democratic or authoritarian politics take place with broader ecological issues confined to the periphery.

Within the dominant paradigm, contemporary debates over democratic alternatives to what is called 'neoliberal capitalism' eventually arrive at the dilemma or obstacle of which territorial sphere or political domain is best suited for the implementation of post-neoliberal policies. Contestation continues over whether democratic control over cities, local regions or nation states will be sufficient on their own to subordinate international business activities to various social demands necessary for any transition to a post-capitalist society. If local and national democratic power is not necessarily sufficient to control powerful corporations, how can these corporations be brought under supranational democratic regulatory control in the absence of international institutions capable of or willing to implement such policies? Equally importantly, what is the goal or purpose of such 'democratic control' given that national and local political movements pursue quite diverse goals and often antagonistic social, economic and environmental agendas?

It is not just Left and green movements that are divided over whether to dismantle or reform international agencies such as the World Bank, IMF and WTO or whether to democratise or exit from supranational institutions such as the EU. National sovereignty has long been demanded by conservatives and Right-wing nationalists in OECD developed capitalist countries and also by opponents of Western cultural and economic domination in Asian, Middle Eastern, Latin American and African countries. However, 'national sovereignty' is not to be confused with democratic control. What is perhaps more common today is that what the media call 'populist' Right-wing movements in OECD countries have attracted former supporters of mainstream Left parties. Social democratic, communist and labour parties have already either suffered from decades of attacks on organised labour by businesses and anti-union governments or have colluded in weakening their own movements by implementing neoliberal policies. They are caught in a familiar pincer movement characterised by the defection of voters to Right-wing parties on the one side and environmental and radical movements critical of the conservatism of centre-Left policies on the other.

REALIGNMENTS WITHIN THE RADICAL AND MODERATE LEFT

To understand the belief that social democratic and labour parties can be revived by abandoning existing neoliberal policies requires a comparison of their role in the history of Left-of-centre parties and their current strength and location in the 'political terrain' of each nation state. Looking back over the past 150 years, socialists have long been divided between nationalist and internationalist tendencies despite significant changes to the very notion of nationalism and internationalism. The outbreak of war in 1914 famously led to major splits in the socialist Second International as member parties sided with their own national governments, notwithstanding decades of pronouncing that they would never support the shedding of workers' blood for 'capitalist war profiteers'. The establishment of the Third International or Comintern in 1919 exacerbated tensions between nationalists and internationalists in the interwar years over whether Communist or non-Communist Left parties would become dominant at the national level and what 'internationalism' actually meant. Apart from Germany and France with sizeable but still minority Communist parties, it was not much of a contest in the rest of Western Europe, North America, Latin America, Japan, Australia and New Zealand where Communists gained a presence in trade unions but fared disastrously in all elections prior to 1939.[1] As to genuine democratic internationalism, this proved to be a mirage as the Comintern within a few years after its founding became a vehicle for Stalin's zig-zag policy manoeuvres until he brought the Comintern to an end in 1943.

During the Cold War period 1946 to 1989, formal international links between Communist parties were difficult to sustain due to divisions within and between national Communist parties. The Communist Information Bureau (Cominform, 1947 to 1956) had mainly Eastern European members plus France and Italy, before Stalin expelled Yugoslavia in 1948 for 'deviationism'. Set up to counter 'American imperialism' in Europe or more precisely, the Marshall Plan, prominent Yugoslav Communist Milovan Djilas led the attack in 1947 on the French and Italian Communist leaders for their 'lack of discipline', 'liberalism' and their behaviour like 'little shopkeepers'. Djilas was later imprisoned by Tito between 1956 and 1966 and became a renegade for writing about Communist regimes as a bureaucratic 'New Class'.[2] With the crushing of East German, Polish and Hungarian rebellions between 1953 and 1956, followed a few years later by the Sino-Soviet split, the erection of the Berlin Wall and the later invasion of Czechoslovakia in 1968, a unified Communist international movement that had never got off the ground properly in the 1920s eventually disintegrated by the 1960s in a storm of major recriminations and accusations. Although the USSR and China supported anti-colonial 'national liberation' movements, as did many members of non-Communist parties, it was hoped, but never assumed by many on the Left that these nationalist struggles would become both part of a new internationalism and be democratic. Alas, national independence was won, but in several cases, democracy was either never established or soon lost.

At the same time that the international Communist movement was experiencing its splits, crises and eventual loss of power, a parallel history of decline unfolded within the international non-Communist centre-Left. Following the demise of both the Second International 1889-1916, and the Labour and Socialist International 1919-1940 (set up to rival the Comintern), the Socialist International (SI) was resurrected in 1951 and embraced a variety of social democratic and labour parties across the world. Most had only nominal affiliations including attending conferences and making joint statements. This allowed each member party to attend to their own national affairs. Paradoxically, it was the *nationally* orientated non-Communist Left who, between the 1950s and 1980s, supported the creation of a *supranational* political economic institutional structure that evolved into the European Union. Although establishing a European Parliament and championing the further democratisation of the EU, it is precisely the lack of democratic decision-making in key EU institutions that in the past two decades has re-ignited the old conflict between nationalists and internationalists. While it may be an old conflict, current new conditions mark a significant realignment of political positions vis-a-vis how to best tackle the neoliberal EU. More on this later.

The Socialist International (SI) also intervened in crisis situations like the collapse of authoritarian regimes in Spain, Portugal and Greece during the 1970s or in Easter Europe after 1989 and also in other global trouble spots. This intervention took the form of SI members providing aid and support to like-minded parties to ensure that radical Left parties did not triumph in the political vacuum. Yet, a number of parties disaffiliated from the SI and were even expelled. For example, the leader of the Singapore People's Action Party (PAP), Lee Kuan Yew, had been a socialist who admired Mao Zedong and initially aimed to build a kind of 'social democratic Stockholm' in South East Asia. However, Sweden and Singapore not only stood at opposite poles in terms of taxation and public spending,[3] but also politically as Singapore's government cracked down on all forms of dissent. Following the move by the Netherlands Labour Party (with support from other members such as the Australian Labor and British Labour Parties) to have the People's Action Party expelled for the violation of human rights, Singapore resigned from the Socialist International in 1976. In August 1976, the PAP published *Socialism That Works: The Singapore Way* and attacked "the shrill voices of the radical Left-Wing poseurs" in the SI.[4] Two years later, Lee Kuan Yew's iron rule and combination of state paternalism and market practices became an important influence on Deng Xiaoping and the post-Maoist leadership group in 1978-79 as they moved to open China to market forces while retaining tight political and social control in the Communist Party's hands.

Just as China and the Chinese diaspora in Singapore changed from the pursuit of socialism to the embrace of corporate capitalism, so too, most members of the SI, in contrast to their predecessors in the Second International, fully adjusted their policies by the 1960s to ensure that they constituted no threat to capitalism. Unsurprisingly, the adoption of neoliberal policies by SI member parties from the early 1980s onwards led to the removal of any symbolic association with 'socialism'. In 2012, the German Social Democrats helped set up the Progressive Alliance. Dozens of members of SI joined Progressive Alliance, as well as new members such as the US Democratic Party that had neither been a socialist, social democratic nor a labour party.

In opposition to the SI and Progressive Alliance are a variety of parties and movements. These include the numerous tiny Trotskyist fragments, namely the descendants of the Fourth International set up by Trotsky in 1938, including all the relatively newer parties, tendencies and committees that have emerged over the past eighty years.[5] This proliferation of Trotskyist sects and offshoots makes Monty Python's film *The Life of Brian* look like social realism. Their history has been animated by endless doctrinal splits and serious problems over the lack of internal party democracy. A combination of sharp critique and dogmatic 'revolutionary purity' continues to guarantee their political irrelevancy. In some countries, ex-Trotskyists constitute an even larger 'party' than ex-Communists. Another active force against the centre-Left is the loose alliance of the European Left made up of old Communist parties and newer parties split from mainstream social democratic parties. There also exists a collection of miniscule anarchist activists and over eighty Green parties of the Global Greens network that have both a parliamentary and grass roots presence.

Collectively, the health of both the remaining SI members and Progressive Alliance continues to vary greatly as most member parties have declined significantly compared to the old days when some would poll between 40 and 50 per cent of the vote. Former voters of these centre-Left parties have either switched to Right-wing parties or to increasingly de-radicalised Green opponents as well as to Left parties. Most Left and Green parties poll between 1% and 10% of the total vote in OECD countries with a few Green Parties polling between 10% and 20% at best. At the European Parliament level, between 1979 and 2019, the Group of the European United Left/Nordic Green Left parties share of seats declined from 11.9% to around 4.9% with large parts of Europe such as Eastern Europe barely represented.[6]

There was an earlier time between the 1960s and the 1990s when the Left in OECD countries looked to the Left in Italy or France, the Greens in Germany or to 'Third World' liberation struggles for inspiration. After 2008, despite the rise of Syriza in Greece, Podemos in Spain and La France Insoumise under Mélenchon, these parties were too weak or compromised to serve as international models. The same was true of the German Greens who by the late 1990s had become respectable neoliberal coalition partners after they jettisoned their radical membership. In Latin America, the 'Pink Tide' regimes were better than the military dictatorships that had preceded them or the Right-wing neo-fascists such as Bolsonaro that succeeded them. However, the choice between Lula da Silva's soft neoliberalism and corruption-plagued regime in Brazil or Chavez's authoritarian 'personality cult' in Venezuela was rejected by most other alternative movements in low and middle-income countries. Surprisingly, after 2015, the US and UK became the hope of many on the Left in the form of Bernie Sander's social democratic candidacy and Jeremy Corbyn's revived socialist Labour Party. Within months of their defeat in 2019-2020, Sanders and Corbyn faded from view and the continued growth of the UK and American Left will require different political strategies if they are to retain political significance. The crisis fallout from Covid-19 and the mass protests over police killings and international support for Black Lives Matter may give rise to renewed Left action. But this would require a significant shift in the electorates' political views beyond immediate reactions to mass unemployment, recession and racism.

To understand the divisions within the Left between nationalists and internationalists, it is necessary to recognise the profound fragmentation of politics and social movements between roughly the end of the Vietnam War in 1975 and the Great Financial Crisis of 2007-09. The introduction of neoliberal policies in the late 1970s coincided with the assault on orthodox Marxist and Keynesian policies from both pro-capitalist and anti-capitalist movements and critics alike. Globally, despite the continuation of numerous wars and rebellions, the classical period of colonialism and imperialism was fast ending. By the beginning of the 1990s, the old Cold War proxy battles between the USSR and the US were over and new forms of capitalist development ('emerging markets') had replaced many but not all earlier conflicts. While segments of the Left still adhered to theories of imperialism but adopted the euphemisms of the 'North' dominating the 'South', gone was any conviction (except among dogmatic radicals) that world revolution was either possible or represented a desirable and shared end goal. Certainly, feminists, environmentalists, post-colonial critics of a unilinear path of development from the West to the East, postmodernist cultural disruptors, Foucauldian critics of Marxist theories of power, human rights campaigners against the violation of essential rights in Communist 'gulags' and other social movements campaigning against 'bureaucratic Keynesian welfare states' all shattered the relative coherence of radical and reform movements that were dominant in the pre-1960s.

Apart from NGOs and radicals involved in campaigning against poverty, debt and other deprivations in developing countries, Marxists were divided between those explaining globalisation through the lens of old and updated theories or imperialism, and others who in the light of the rise of China, and North East and South East Asian capitalist countries rejected the classical arguments of Lenin, Luxemburg, Hilferding, Kautsky and others.[7] During the last decades of the twentieth century, radicals fell back on concepts of the 'triad' (US, Europe and Japan) or the 'core' countries of the 'North' exploiting the 'periphery' or the poor countries of the 'South'. Political economic developments and major crises in the first two decades of the twenty-first century gave rise to uncertainty and confusion about the adequacy of both imperialism and globalisation as explanatory tools. Many on the Left also retreated to an even greater preoccupation with national issues in their home countries in Europe or North America.

Earlier struggles against apartheid in South Africa or opposition to wars

in Afghanistan, Iraq, Sudan, Nicaragua and other conflicts distracted attention away from the fact that a disorganised, greatly weakened and often
despairing Left either nostalgically defended the 'good old days' or focussed
narrowly on the 'enemy' at home. This 'enemy' was the seemingly invincible
neoliberal political and business forces, including the social democratic and
Labour parties that had adopted neoliberal policies. The crisis of 2007-09
was a shock to the Left and not just to capitalists. Left parties and green
movements were neither prepared for the economic crisis, nor for the rise of
Right-wing parties and the influx of casualties of international capitalism in
the form of mass refugees. They were certainly not prepared for the fact that
countries in Europe and North America were no longer unrivalled capitalist
powers and that the future of 'Atlantic capitalism' would now be partly determined by undemocratic former victims of imperialism and colonialism in the
Asia-Pacific and Africa. Of particular importance, was the fact that despite
the rise of green movements since the 1970s, including a significant minority
of Marxists and other radicals who took environmental issues very seriously,
the broad Left, like the broad defenders of market capitalism, were either
environmentally illiterate or myopically immersed in a way of thinking and
behaviour that stubbornly refused to deal with dangerous new ecological
threats.

Regardless of their conflicting attitudes to local, national and
international strategies, the present-day health of both the centre-Left and
the radical Left is stagnant at best, despite short-lived occasional upswings,
such as in the British Labour Party between 2015 and 2019 under Corbyn or
in the US with the rise of Democratic Socialists. Outside this upsurge in a
very conservative America, the political malaise of the global Left is the
inability to form political coalitions and attract mass support outside their
own 'political ghettoes'. This lack of unity is driven by fundamental disagreements about the character of capitalism and how to achieve social change.
For all their profoundly dated theories of imperialism, Lenin and the other
classical theorists of imperialism had partially moved away from Eurocentrism to focus on the global impact of capitalism. The opposite is true of the
majority of the contemporary Left in Europe and the US who continue to
dispute the merits of national or international strategies against neoliberalism largely within the narrow geopolitical confines of Europe, or the
Atlantic at best.

While the 'core' states remain immensely powerful, the Left as a whole
has failed to come to terms with the 'down-sized' role of the US, Europe and
Japan in the new world order. For example, old leading Left journal, *Monthly*

Review still adheres to dated theories of imperialism put forward by Paul Baran, Paul Sweezy, Harry Magdoff and others. The late Egyptian theorist of imperialism, Samir Amin (another contributor to *Monthly Review*) was a strong critic of Eurocentrism. Yet, until his death in 2018, he erroneously and exaggeratedly explained the crisis of capitalism as due to the 'core' imperialist countries having five monopolies: technological, financial, access to natural resources, media and communication, and monopoly over weapons of mass destruction.[8] It should be noted that today *none* of these five areas or capacities remain monopolised by the US, Europe and Japan. Covid-19, for instance, showed that the US and EU had to get Chinese and Russian help in the form of medical equipment and supplies. Also, China and other North East Asian countries accounted for the lion share of global economic growth compared to the 'core' or 'triad'. They were also major competitors to the 'imperialist powers' in software, high-tech, machinofacture and communications as well as the largest global users of natural resources. Militarily, the US and Europe remain mighty powers, but they can no longer fight a land war against their new rivals such as China, Iran, Russia and others. Finally, Amin also described the past three decades as the attempt to suppress the state and impose the management of society by the 'market' via "sweeping anti-state ideologies and practices".[9] This confuses the ideology of neoliberals with the reality of state/market relations. Not only were state institutions not suppressed but, as I will now discuss, they were key to both the character and solution of crises in Europe and elsewhere.

FROM 'NATIONAL DEMOCRATIC CAPITALISM' TO SUPRANATIONAL
MARKET POWER

At the centre of numerous Left analyses of neoliberal capitalism is the assumption that Friedrich von Hayek's ideas not only remain highly influential as an ideological defence of markets but have also helped shape the very structure and role of contemporary state institutions. Just as there continue to be widespread over-generalised references to the 'Keynesian welfare state' that supposedly dominated all OECD countries between 1945 and 1975, so too, it is common to read about the 'Hayekian state'. Political economists conceived the 'Keynesian welfare state' as primarily a range of relatively independent *national* state apparatuses operating within the Bretton Woods system, an international framework established by American hegemonic power which, ironically, lacked an adequate welfare state of its own. By contrast, the 'Hayekian state' is depicted as a *supranational* set of apparatuses, namely, the European Union which subordinates national governments to its dictates even though it is not a fully-fledged state with similar powers as those held by national state apparatuses in member countries. The term 'Hayekian state' is also sometimes used to describe neoliberal national governments functioning without some of their former significant state powers due to their *de facto* subservient roles in a globalised capitalist system.

To acknowledge the dominance of neoliberal policies in many countries is by no means equivalent to assuming that there is a parallel set of durable and coherent state institutions called the 'Hayekian state' that replaced the so-called 'Keynesian welfare state'. Importantly, neoliberal policy hegemony does not mean that all national governments have lost most of their former powers to a 'globalised system'. Rather, the question is why is it that some national governments continue to exercise their old powers and others do not? In fact, sixteen of the nineteen largest capitalist countries in the world such as the US, China, India or Japan continue to have powerful national governments while only three of the G20 – Germany, France, Italy – are part of the supranational EU (if we exclude the UK after Brexit and also representatives of the EU who attend G20 summits). While the G7 countries (US, Germany, France, UK, Italy, Canada and Japan) are still extraordinarily strong, they are a hangover from the Cold War when Atlantic powers plus Japan dominated capitalist production and military alliances. The rise of China and other Asian-Pacific national powers has led to the need to re-evaluate past conceptions of the future of capitalism.

Given that authoritarian states pre-dated neoliberalism, why place so much emphasis on the supranational paradigm of the 'Hayekian state' as the key to understanding the relationship between 'capitalism and democracy'? Any political strategy based on alternatives to neoliberalism must have as an essential prerequisite a persuasive account of existing policies, institutional structures and power relations not only in Europe and America but across the world.

Historically, Hayek was influenced by Ludwig von Mises' ideas in respect to his argument in *The Road to Serfdom* (1944) that central planners had insufficient knowledge to plan. Hence, without market exchange prices, not only would their planning be flawed, but the decentralised forms of knowledge in society would have to be controlled by the state, thereby producing totalitarianism.[10] Winston Churchill was so impressed with Hayek's arguments that he tried to print a summary of *The Road to Serfdom* for distribution to the electorate during the 1945 election campaign. However, the continuation of wartime rationing of paper prevented this option. Nonetheless, inspired by Hayek, he warned the public in an infamous BBC speech that British Labour's 'socialist' policies would require "some form of Gestapo" to police their implementation.[11]

Even though Hayek remained in the political wilderness until the 1970s, there continued to exist a section of the British Conservative Party that subscribed to his theory. By 1979, Margaret Thatcher's new government endorsed Hayek as a guiding light and prominent Thatcher ally, Sir Keith Joseph, made it compulsory for his civil servants to read *The Road to Serfdom*. Similarly, President Ronald Reagan feted Hayek in the White House. At the time of his death in 1992, Hayek had lived long enough to see his radical liberal ideas eclipse both Keynesian and socialist policies and become mainstream ideology.

Despite Hayek's direct and indirect impact during the past few decades, his influence peaked some time ago. Nevertheless, he is still accorded significant importance by free marketeers and also by many on the Left. Between the 1920s and the 1970s when the broad Left was much stronger politically, Hayek's critique of socialist planning and state interventionism was widely debated. Today, the earlier historical debates – from Oscar Lange to Alec Nove[12] – over the relationship between knowledge, prices, democracy and the feasibility of either central planning, decentralised planning or market socialism barely exist. Serious discussion of how post-capitalist or post-neoliberal societies could be organised and planned are scarce. Some on the Left, such as Leigh Phillips and Michal Rozworski, [13] discuss how a socialist society could utilise for different purposes the planning lessons adopted by Walmart and other giant corporations via the application of digital technology. In some ways the argument is an updated technological version of the old 1915 arguments of Hilferding and other German socialists about how the giant cartels of 'organised capitalism' made it easier for socialism to be implemented because these monopolies were already based on a complex level of organisation. Others are only now are starting to revive *national* alternative plans rather than *supranational* frameworks (see for instance, the policies developed by the British Labour Party between 2017 and 2019). This is highly ironic given that supranational plans for socialist planning in the EU were being developed in the 1970s when capitalist integration through value chains and financialisation was far less extensive than the much more profound integration of current national economies into *supranational* regional and global markets.

In 1945, Herman Finer proclaimed that: "Friedrich A. Hayek's *The Road to*

Serfdom constitutes the most sinister offensive against democracy to emerge from a democratic country for many decades."[14] Finer's critique proved to be most prescient. Three decades later, Hayek defended Pinochet's Chilean dictatorship in the name of 'liberty'. He also openly declared in 1978 that he preferred 'limited democracy' and admitted that he regarded 'unlimited democracy' as worse than all other forms of unlimited government.[15] The political tables have been reversed since the late 1970s as to who or what threatens democracy. Many critics now depict neoliberalism and the 'Hayekian state' (rather than socialist planning) as the major threat undermining democracy.

MODIFYING THE TRILEMMA OF GLOBALISATION

Debates over the relationship between limited or unlimited democracy and limited or unlimited capitalism have taken two forms: a mainstream debate over what economist Dani Rodrik called 'the trilemma of globalisation', and a Left variation of this debate focussing especially on the political economy of the Eurozone. Rodrik argued that there was a choice between the following: hyper-globalisation; national sovereignty or democracy. One could only have two of the three choices but not all three simultaneously as they were seen to be incompatible. Deeper or hyper-global integration would limit democracy and national sovereignty. Maximising democracy and national sovereignty would limit globalisation and finally a combination of hyper-globalisation and global democracy (unlikely according to Rodrik) would nullify national sovereignty.[16] Rodrik favours a more limited global capitalism that is constrained by national democratic politics. Interestingly, there is a partial overlap of his critique of free market hyper-globalisation with radical Left critiques of supranational processes within the EU. However, critics have either rejected or adapted Rodrik's 'trilemma' as an explanation of the post-2008 crisis within the EU. Italian economist, Gustavo Piga, modifies Rodrik's choices between globalisation, national sovereignty and democracy by positing his own version of the 'trilemma' in Europe:

> If you have austerity and a common currency, you can't have democracy. You have troikas [The ECB, IMF and EU Commission].
> If you have austerity and democracy, you can't have the Euro, you exit it, by majority voting.

If you have democracy and a common currency, you can't have austerity, but fiscal expansion to save employment and cure the recession.[17]

In other words, Rodrik's 'trilemma' is far too stark a set of choices
compared with the interplay of national sovereignty, supranational institutions and levels of democracy. It all depends on actual policies as well as the
presence or absence of intermediate structures (such as those based on
power-sharing federalism or other mediating processes) as to the degrees of
compatibility or incompatibility of globalisation with democracy and
national sovereignty.

Importantly, Rodrik's 'trilemma' also fails to grasp the *internal* political
tensions within nation states between residents, businesses and city or local
governments in growing trade-exposed, multicultural cities and 'mega cities'
on the one hand, and small towns in rural regions characterised by agriculture, stagnant or declining local economies and traditional religious and
cultural values on the other hand. It is the division of nation states into
specific regions with their own predominant local political economies and
cultures that either interact internationally via trade and cultural exchanges
or remain relatively isolated and inward looking. Significantly, rural regions
with smaller populations carry far more weight electorally and politically in
many countries such as Argentina, Australia, Canada, Hungary, Japan,
Malaysia, Turkey and the US.[18] Consequently, it is not just Rodrik's
'trilemma' that determines the level of democracy and sovereignty but the
internal divisions and formal voting systems in most nation states that often
bolsters conservative parties.

In contrast to many conservatives, Hayek was neither a nationalist nor
religious. His project of liberating capitalist markets from the constraints of
national governments, and especially from the constraints of national labour
movements and businesses has produced deep disagreement amongst the
Left over how to respond to Hayek's legacy and other contemporary neoliberal policies. Many on the Left express confusion politically about whether
they are internationalists or nationalists. As there is no shortage of exposi-
tions and critiques of Hayek's ideas,[19] I will focus instead on how these and
other more recent neoliberal policies have affected the Left, especially the
divisions over the future of 'capitalism' or 'democracy'.

Participants in debates over both globalisation and also the neoliberal
'Hayekian state' usually base their respective positions on different notions
of *class power* and *state power*. The concept of a 'global ruling class' and the
'Hayekian state' has taken two forms: a global *class* version and a specific

European *state* version. Despite the rise of the glamorous 'neoliberal billionaires' or 'Davos class',[20] there are many deep-seated geo-political divisions between the major powers. Any close analysis of the multiplicity of different national socio-economic institutions and social relations provides ample reasons why a unified and politically coherent 'global ruling class' does *not* exist. Even in orthodox Marxist theory, a capitalist ruling class requires a capitalist state to defend and reproduce its class power as well as to maintain the overall interests of the capitalist class when different sectors of capital disagree with one another. Despite international organisations such as the IMF, no global capitalist state with complex apparatuses exists, just as there is no single world military industrial complex with a unified 'power elite' or a decentralised 'Empire' (Hardt and Negri[21]) that rules. The exercise of specific international military and other interventions (sometimes under the joint command of NATO or of the United Nations) is not evidence of the existence of a so-called 'global state'.

Much is at stake in how activists and organisations advocating alternative socio-economic and environmental policies understand powerful national or international political forces that are preventing social change. Up until 1991, radicals were not faced with the question: is there a 'global ruling class' and, if so, who belongs to it? Instead, competing theories of imperialism assumed that American and European imperialist powers, as well as Communist powers, sub-divided the world. Today, it is precisely decades of increased global integration and the political economic realignment of former Communist countries and developing capitalist societies that makes the global map much more complex.

Two recent developments have shaken the old American-created post-1945 liberal order, especially since its triumph after the collapse of the USSR in 1991. First, both the rise of anti-EU nationalist Right-wing parties in Europe and President Trump's 'America first' trade and foreign policies have shaken the 'Western alliance'. Second, the old classical pre-1918 theories of imperialism were replaced in the 1950s and 1960s with shorthand euphemisms such as 'First World' and 'Third World' or the global 'North' and 'South'. If once there was validity in designating the 'North' as affluent, comprising technologically advanced capitalist, politically stable, dominant countries as against agrarian, industrially undeveloped and unstable poor countries of the 'South', as others have argued, these political economic conceptual divisions need revision today. International development analyst Robert Wade, for instance, divides the 'North' and 'South' as blocs into two further subdivisions: China and 'transitional economies'. However, he does not say how many 'transitional economies' there are and in what way they are different from other countries in the 'South'. Wade argues that broadly speaking, there has been little change between the 'North' and the 'South' in terms of income distribution and control over trade.[22] This is largely true, but income and trade obscure significant changes to political economic relations, particularly between countries in the so-called 'South'. Currently, quite different socio-economic and military conditions and levels of geopolitical power divide countries within different regions of the 'South' such as Sub-Sahara African countries compared to North and South East Asian societies. Not all in the 'South' are equally weak and powerless and not all countries in the 'North' are equally strong and dominant.

Although the term 'imperialism' is still widely used by the Left, there is no agreement as to whether the old theories of imperialism produced by Lenin, Kautsky, Luxemburg and others are still relevant or in need of drastic revision.[23] Also, a significant modification to the old imperialist dominance over their colonies has occurred. There is no doubt that the current Atlantic members (plus Japan) of the G7 have far more power than more than a hundred small developing countries. However, what has changed is that countries of the so-called 'North' are increasingly integrated economically with those industrialising former colonies that have achieved faster economic growth rates in recent decades. Thus, the impact of supranational institutions and greater global capitalist integration has shaken the old certainties and political divisions between Left radical internationalists and social democratic and Labour nationalists, particularly in regard to how they should proceed politically at both the domestic level and at the supranational and global level.

Pro-nationalist analyst Anatol Lieven recently noted that: "Marriage between the *Economist* and the *New Left Review* may seem like one of Hieronymus Bosch's stranger copulations. Liberal capitalists and Marxists have been drawn passionately together over the past few decades in one area: their common utopian belief in the development of a globalised world without nationalism and national borders, a dream now dying in the West."[24] Clearly, Lieven has not been reading *New Left Review* in recent years! While formerly championing Britain's entry into the EU's predecessor (the European Economic Community) in the 1970s, *New Left Review* editors Susan Watkins, Perry Anderson, Tariq Ali, and also especially contributor Wolfgang Streeck, have strongly opposed the EU in recent years and also supported Lexit (the Left version of Brexit). From being accused for decades by many of the UK Left for ignoring British politics while promoting 'Third

Worldism' and European theory,[25] *New Left Review* formed a *de facto* alliance with 'little Englander' nationalists in not opposing Brexit but naïvely hoping for Lexit. As I will discuss, the notion of the 'Hayekian state' de-democratising member states is a flawed and politically costly theory that has not only helped bring about Brexit and divided the European Left but is associated with a historical political conjuncture that is now passing.

LEFT CONCEPTS OF THE 'HAYEKIAN STATE'

According to the editors of *New Left Review*, the EU Commission, the European Council, the European Central Bank (ECB) and the European Court of Justice constitute the profoundly undemocratic 'Hayekian state' through which the capitalist class rules Europe.[26] Following Anderson and others,[27] Streeck also has argued that Hayek laid the blueprint for today's European Union and the austerity or 'consolidation state' in his important 1939 article, 'The Economic Conditions for Interstate Federalism'.[28] Hayek believed a single European market would eventually lead to economic liberalisation because the entrenched power of national businesses, unions and electorates would be overcome and subordinated to common federal rules governing tariffs, the free movement of capital and labour and, very importantly, that national budgetary policies would conform to the economic needs of the wider federation. Hayek's blueprint, observes Streeck, must have looked absurd to policy makers in the immediate decades after 1945. However, the gradual evolution of the EU and its adoption of neoliberal policies after the late 1970s meant that the Hayekian 'consolidation state' overpowered the old national policies of EU member states.[29]

It is hardly news that the EU is an undemocratic 'common market' that mainly, but not solely, benefits European capitalist classes as well as many non-European corporations with subsidiaries based in one of the member countries; it was so during the era of the so-called 'Keynesian welfare state', well before neoliberal policies triumphed.[30] The fact that large numbers of citizens of EU member countries also benefit from greater and easier work and travel mobility between countries, aid to depressed regions and joint research, cultural and other exchanges and projects, gives the EU a significant but varying degree of legitimacy depending on conditions within member countries. As to the dominance of neoliberal policies, despite the social and political traumas caused by the Great Financial Crisis, Colin Crouch appeared correct when he observed in 2013 the 'strange non-death of neoliberalism' after 2008.[31] However, Crouch's analysis was perhaps premature as seven years later, Covid-19 has significantly undermined some but not all earlier policies based on neoliberal austerity.

Despite momentary impressions, there was never a distinct and durable 'Hayekian state' which would destroy parliamentary democracy in member states of the EU. If the current undemocratic EU institutions are unsustainable, will they either disintegrate or be reformed and replaced with more democratic institutions? German sociologist and political economist Wolfgang Streeck's analysis of 'the delayed crisis of democratic capitalism' is emblematic of an influential strand of Leftist interpretation of capitalism from 1945 to the present day.[32] I will focus on his arguments because they are a distillation of radical anti-capitalist critique and are also based on widely held schematic Left concepts such as 'Fordism' and what he sees as the historical rise of the 'Hayekian state' through several political economic phases or stages. Streeck either depicts these stages in teleological functionalist terms (the final 'delayed' stage signifying the incurable terminal condition of capitalism), or argues in non-teleological terms, that is, each stage only making sense in hindsight. The sequence between these two positions or narrative of succeeding crises that Streeck outlines is crucial, not only because it colours his whole interpretation of post-war capitalism but also as it shapes his controversial response to current political issues.

Importantly, while many on the Left share Streeck's narrative of the 'Hayekian state', they do not share his politics – which fluctuates between despair and romantic national solutions – nor his blatant hostility to immigrants and refugees or his (until very recently) complete lack of focus on crucial environmental issues. Thomas Piketty, for example, concurs with Streeck that the EU is imbued with Hayek's 1939 economic liberal vision. But he also points to non-Hayekian anti-liberal visions of a federal Europe developed between 1938 and 1940 and, in contrast to Streeck, also believes that the EU can abandon its Hayekian qualities if it adopts alternative socio-economic policies.[33]

Just as Polanyi's work constitutes an ideal medium to discuss why he and his admirers have misconceptions about 'the political and economic origins of our time', Streeck's thesis of 'the delayed crisis of democratic capitalism' is important because it throws light on the larger and contentious contemporary interpretations and ramifications of 'capitalism versus democracy', not just in Europe but globally. Streeck's attack on 'cosmopolitanism' and in favour of a *de facto* Left nationalism is emblematic of the current divisions

between Left internationalists and Left nationalists as responses to decades
of neoliberal policies.

The critical issues of immigration and refugees, the rise of Right-wing
racist parties and the larger international debates and conflicts over free
markets or managed trade and protectionism, or how to deal with environmental crises and social inequality are all interrelated aspects that divide Left
and green anti-neoliberals. Take, for instance, Streeck's particularly scathing
denunciation of 'Left cosmopolitans':

> Using Left internationalism for Left disempowerment is a particular
> ironic method to de-democratise a capitalist political economy, espe-
> cially if deployed by the Left itself. It comes with a moral denuncia-
> tion of borders and protectionism...in the name of a misunderstood
> cosmopolitanism, identifying 'globalisation' with liberation, not just of
> capital, but of life in general. ...pipe dreams of a future global or, at a
> minimum, continental democracy are offered as baits for Left ideal-
> ists: promises of a better future in which international democracy will
> have regained control over international capital, if not tomorrow then
> the day after tomorrow.[34]

Apart from unfairly assuming that 'Left cosmopolitans' equate 'globalisation with liberation', it is revealing that the label 'Left idealists' is only
applied by Streeck to those espousing 'cosmopolitanism' but not to Left
advocates of 'national democratic control' in the face of dominant multinational corporations and superpowers such as the US and China.

It is also important to distinguish the critique of 'cosmopolitanism' by
Gramsci and Frantz Fanon from Streeck's abusive use of the term. Gramsci
critiqued Italian bourgeois or traditional intellectuals for being more preoccupied with cosmopolitan ideas than developing an Italian national popular
culture. Similarly, Fanon criticised post-colonial intellectuals in African countries for still being 'colonised intellectuals' and adopting the cosmopolitan
ideas of their former rulers rather than liberating themselves and developing
their own national culture.[35] Gramsci was responding to the political
economic and cultural division of Italy into an industrial north and an undeveloped south while Fanon was engaged in liberation struggles for what he
saw as still mentally and politically 'colonised' African peoples. However, in a
Europe that was almost destroyed by two world wars fought by nationalists,
what do Streeck and other Left and Right nationalists seek to achieve by
their anti-cosmopolitanism? We know that the Right favour a regressive

ethno-nationalism but many of the *de facto* Left nationalists erroneously believe that an anti-EU return to the 'sovereign nation state' can be achieved without mobilising old and new hatreds (see Chapter Nine).

We must also distinguish Streeck's use of 'consolidation' from earlier political analyses of 'consolidation' that were linked to discussions of how to secure democracy, the differences between authoritarianism and democracy and the transition from Communist states to parliamentary democracies.[36] Streeck deploys a different meaning of 'consolidation' which becomes interchangeable with either the neoliberal 'Hayekian state' or the neoliberal 'austerity state'.[37] The cause of the current crisis of the 'austerity state' or 'consolidation state' can be traced back, he argues, to the rise of globalisation in the 1970s which put an end to the post-1945 subordination of capitalism to 'democratic control'. Accordingly:

> For a short period of about three decades, capitalism and democracy coexisted more or less peacefully within a new standard model of a democratic nation-state, instituted by the United States in its sphere of influence after 1945 along the lines of its own New Deal social settlement. Democratic capitalism was state-administered capitalism, different from both liberal and fascist capitalism, as well as from Stalinist communism. It provided for reasonably free elections, governments dependent on parliamentary majorities, broad-based political parties of the centre-left and centre-right, strong trade unions with a right to strike, freely negotiated collective agreements regulating wages and working conditions, a pluralistic mass media, and only moderate repression of opposition, except of course where it came too close to Soviet-communist anti-capitalism.[38]

Elsewhere, Streeck contends that a high price had to be paid by the capitalist class for its 'hunting license to be restored' after the devastation caused by the Great Depression and the war, including all the concessions listed above as well as "a comprehensive welfare state – all negotiated, as it were, with a pistol pointed to the head of liberal capitalism, forcing it into a shotgun marriage with social democracy."[39]

Like Polanyi, Streeck operates at the level of generality and makes sweeping statements about post-1945 capitalist societies that are inaccurate and misleading. As a preliminary comment, the post-fascist 'settlements' in Europe and Japan were not like the New Deal. Even Polanyi recognised the modified liberal capitalism of the New Deal rather than it being the model for a social democratic welfare state. Others argue that it was not the 'shotgun marriage of capitalism to social democracy' but rather, as Mike Davis puts it, the post-war era of American hegemony "was inaugurated by a 'revolution from above' in the 1945–50 period which reconstructed the power of the West European bourgeoisies along a new axis of liberalism and interdependence with US global power, while simultaneously purging and disunifying the European labour movement."[40]

If Streeck overemphasises 'democratic control over capitalism' and minimises American military and economic power in helping to shape postwar Europe, Davis overemphasises American hegemony and minimises the reinvigorated power of labour movements in the UK, Italy, France and other countries. How else to account for the nationalisation of industries (hardly an imitation of the New Deal) and the social gains made, such as the welfare reforms in the UK? Nonetheless, Streeck exaggerates when he claims that a 'comprehensive welfare state' was the price capitalists had to pay. Health care, public housing and social insurance were certainly implemented. Numerous other aspects of welfare including child-care, parental leave, care of the disabled, adequate mental health care and aged care, however, were not delivered and are yet to be adequately delivered along with comprehensive programs to combat poverty.

Streeck also follows the old Frankfurt School political economist, Friedrich Pollock, who named this post-1945 political marriage 'state capitalism' – a 'non-socialist social order' where state bureaucracies had gained such control over the economy that the *primacy of politics* over economics indicated the end of classical Marxian political economy based on laissez-faire markets.[41] It is important to remember that a generation of theorists in the 1930s and 1940s (including Polanyi and the Frankfurt School on the Left and James Burnham on the Right) viewed Nazism, Communism and the New Deal as the end of laissez faire capitalism, but believed these regimes to be either 'state capitalism' or the triumph of the 'managerial revolution' and 'the new class' of bureaucrats.

Furthermore, other misleading generalisations that were inadequate and only applicable to some countries included the belief that the Cold War division of the world into two competing hostile blocs strengthened labour movements in the West and that Keynesian state planning policies were universally adopted by interventionist governments during the *trente glorieuses* or thirty glorious years between 1945-75 of full employment and social protection. As we shall see, Streeck ignores the following inconvenient facts that most women and non-whites did not enjoy full employment and social protection, Keynesian state planning was not present in all leading capitalist countries and not all national trade union movements were strengthened by the Cold War.

The term 'late capitalism' was popular in the late 1960s and 1970s, as was 'Fordism' and later 'post-Fordism'. Adorno, Habermas and many others used 'late capitalism' to signify that 'state-regulated capitalism' had largely eliminated old cyclical market crises of 'boom and bust'. On the other hand, Ernest Mandel, a leading Trotskyist, believed 'late capitalism' would witness new and intense crises.[42] Both proved to be wrong but for quite different reasons. Following the volatility of the protest years in the late 1960s, Streeck is correct to argue that the 'legitimation crisis' analysed by Jürgen Habermas, James O'Connor and Claus Offe proved to be a serious misunderstanding of 'late capitalism'. It was not the loyalty of workers and consumers to capitalism that proved to be in crisis. Rather, he claimed that it was 'Capital' that experienced a legitimation crisis and began to rebel against democratic controls over business activity. According to Streeck, the neo-Marxists of the early 1970s treated 'Capital' as an apparatus rather than as a class capable of strategic action.[43] Instead, he prefers Polish economist Michal Kalecki's theory of why capitalists are active agents capable of investment strikes and strategic responses While Kalecki argued that business leaders opposed full employment because it would make it difficult to discipline and manage workers who no longer feared 'the sack' (dismissal), he treated the thousands of corporations and millions of small businesses as if they spoke with one voice.[44]

Similarly, despite mentioning that there are small and large capitalists, it is Streeck who often homogenises classes by assuming that a particular relation to the mode of production translates into political action. This is a familiar problem for those who focus on 'institutional' analyses at the expense of also examining the ideas and behaviour of actors or participants in these businesses or state institutions. Thus, 'capital' can't rebel any more than the 'proletariat' can express a singular political voice. The capitalist class and the working class have never confronted one another as Subjects or coherent actors. Rather, particular agents – the spokespersons and members of political parties, unions, business groups – speaking and acting directly or indirectly on behalf of 'the capitalist class' or the 'working class' confront one another through advocating and implementing pro-business policies or countering the latter with various reform proposals or radical policies, strikes and dissenting behaviour ranging from voting to revolutionary action.

DE-DEMOCRATISATION

We are now living, Streeck argues, with the consequences of the rebellion of capitalists against interfering state policies and ever-increasing workers' demands that were once made possible under the protective conditions of pre-1970s full employment.[45] It is true that businesses successfully campaigned against regulations that restricted their activities and profits. Even so, initially this was far from a unified rebellion. Rather, deregulation and restructuring were unevenly implemented in different countries over a period stretching from the late 1970s to the end of the century. It is the different rate at which neoliberal policies were adopted in OECD countries in relation to the removal of controls on capital flows, reduction of tariff barriers, labour market deregulation and attacks on social welfare that partially account for the quite diverse levels of resistance to neoliberal policy makers. This opposition ranged from the massive resistance of miners in the UK requiring full-scale militarised enforcement, to the voluntary embrace of neoliberal policies by the majority of Australian trade union leaders.

Given that defenders of capitalism are eager to decouple the economy from democratic control – what Streeck calls the 'de-democratisation of capitalism'[46] – he outlines how the 'tax revolt' and 'fiscal crisis of the state' of the 1970s (a shortage of revenue due to competing demands made by business groups and social movements) were also accompanied by stagflation (stagnation plus high inflation). This led to more businesses supporting political demands for neoliberal state policies. In short, the re-establishment of self-regulation in many industries, the reduction of business taxes and cuts to the welfare state were all matched in the period from the 1980s until 2008 by the parallel growth of financialisation that fuelled massive household and business indebtedness. Wage cuts could not sustain consumer demand. Instead of aggregate demand being fuelled by old-style Keynesian state fiscal policies and deficit budgeting, consumption and production were increasingly tied to an explosion of debt due to credit made available to households and individuals, or what Colin Crouch called 'privatised Keynesianism'.[47]

According to Streeck, the earlier 'fiscal crisis of the state' of the 1970s first morphed into the 'debt state' of the 1990s. Instead of a shortage of tax revenue exacerbating political conflict over state expenditure priorities, the privatisation of public enterprises and assets, reductions of taxes on business and the wealthy, combined with the need to maintain 'social peace', all led to the 'debt state' as governments increased their debt levels. Rescuing the irresponsible and corrupt financial sector after the near collapse of the financial system meant that for neoliberals the 'debt state' could only survive if it morphed into the 'consolidation state' or 'Hayekian state'. This neoliberal strategy required the reduction of state debt, especially cutting what they called 'unnecessary' discretionary public services. One can broadly agree with these developments and the promotion of austerity or 'consolidation' without accepting that these constituted the new 'Hayekian state'.

Crucially, Streeck argues that the 'Hayekian state' is closely associated with the sharp delineation of the respective power of the two constituencies within the 'debt state': the *staatvolk* and the *marktvolk*. For Streeck, the 'de-democratisation of capitalism' is near complete as the *staatvolk* or national citizens who express their voices and votes through elections, public opinions, civil rights and public services, consistently lose out to the *marktvolk* of international investors and creditors who veto democracy by making claims through interest rates, debt servicing and market 'confidence' in pro-business government austerity policies.[48] Apart from these 'two constituencies' being depicted in highly problematic ways (see my critique in Chapter Nine), Streeck fails to recognise that the demands of European and other international bondholders were forecast by Keynesians way back in the 1940s. Analysing the bondholding class in America, Sandy Brian Hager notes:

> In the 1940s, the early Keynesians theorists of the public debt were willing to acknowledge the potentially negative consequences of their policy prescriptions. An expansionary fiscal policy would lead to a growing public debt that in turn would, if large enough, be swallowed up by the rich. Unless kept in check by progressive taxation, the unequal distribution of federal bonds, early Keynesians feared, would redistribute income regressively. Government fiscal policy, originally intended to make capitalist markets more humane and stable, would instead be beholden to the interests of wealthy Americans; a 'top heavy' distribution of the public debt would eventually stifle, rather than stimulate, effective demand.[49]

It is also important to remember the fiscal crisis in New York city in 1974/75 that preceded the so-called 'Hayekian state'. Financial institutions and the teacher's union pension fund refused to buy any more city bonds from a bankrupt city. With President Ford refusing to help, finance capital stepped in to manage the city and replaced local democracy. Social services were cut in subsequent austerity budgets and the future development of the city was reshaped in the interests of the wealthy.

Streeck argues that instead of old struggles between unions and businesses up until the late 1970s, crucial decisions and social outcomes in the twenty-first century are now determined by discussions between ministers and bankers and investors or by negotiation between national governments and supranational institutions such as the EU Commission, the ECB and the IMF. Hence, the "European consolidation state of the early twenty-first century is not a national but an international structure – a supra-state regime that regulates its participating nation states, without a democratically accountable government but with a set of binding rules: through 'governance' rather than government, so that democracy is tamed by markets instead of markets by democracy."[50] The EU usurps the power of sovereign nation-states and binds them in a market straitjacket, thus depoliticising the economy.[51]

PESSIMISM AND SLOW DECAY

Streeck has become much more pessimistic in recent years. To echo Žižek's use of Elisabeth Kübler-Ross's five stages of grief (denial, anger, bargaining, depression and finally, acceptance[52]) one could say that Streeck used to be in the 'bargaining' stage but is now, like many other old Leftists, in the 'acceptance' stage and resigned to the terminal condition of capitalism. In an honest and thoughtful reflection on the past 50 years, Streeck notes that capitalism has always been in crisis but 'we did not take it seriously enough' because of a 'fundamentally optimistic worldview' regarding "the capacity of radical-reformist politics and policies to build an alternative, more communal and solidaristic way of life inside, or with, or around the post-war capitalist economy."[53] Furthermore, Streeck notes that during the 1980s many consoled themselves with the illusion that the 'varieties of capitalism' offered hope that not all countries would follow the Anglo-American neoliberal model. By the 1990s, Streeck believed the Clinton era and Blair's Third Way promoted within Europe the possibility of social democratic 'modernisation' and adjustment to globalisation. It should be noted that Streeck himself indirectly supported the Blairite 'Third Way' by working for Schroder's neoliberal government. Thus, he confesses: "For some of us, certainly for me, it took the 'Great Recession' of 2008 to bring this 'comedy of errors', with its continuously falling level of political aspiration, to an end."[54]

It is clear that Streeck must have ignored the numerous radical critiques of capitalism in the 1960s and 1970s that rejected the notion of the 'general stability of advanced capitalism'. Most of these radicals were unsurprised by the counterattacks on social reform regularly waged by business groups and Right-wing politicians. Belatedly, having left his former social democratic illusions behind, Streeck makes rhetorical gestures (in his less-despairing moments) in favour of national resistance.[55] But he is too honest and critical to believe it will solve the deep-seated crisis. Repeatedly asked about solutions, he replies: "I do not know – I do not see any. I do not see what, today, could allow us to take back control. Marx thought that the alternative would be within the grasp of an International with an organised proletariat. I see nothing like that today – no vast and organised popular movement, capable of that today – no vast and organised popular movement, capable of opposing globalised capital. That is a decisively important difference with the nineteenth century."[56]

Instead, Streeck outlines the impending slow death of capitalism plagued by five disorders for which there is no remedy in sight.[57] First, there is no remedy because these disorders are due to prolonged economic stagnation which will give rise to distributional struggles and political instability. The second factor is the growing insoluble inequality exacerbated by the demise of progressive taxation systems and their replacement by 'oligarchic redistribution' of income from low and middle-income groups to the wealthy. The third disorder is the 'plundering of the public domain', manifested in extensive tax evasion by corporations and the wealthy who reside in luxury in London, Paris or New York while living off the misery of those dependent on underfunded public services and social security. Fourthly, corporate corruption and moral decline, especially in the finance sector, is so extensive that a cynical public has ceased believing that honesty or strong government regulation can be restored. Fifthly, the eclipse of the US as the unrivalled global hegemon has produced 'global anarchy' in the form of international monetary, political and military instability.

As a condensation of views widely held by a section of the radical Left, it is important to grapple with the details of Streeck's narrative of the 'delayed crisis of democratic capitalism' and the development of the 'Hayekian state' for two reasons. First, does the 'Hayekian state' have a structure and purpose beyond securing capitalist markets via the imposition of austerity? Second, if the neoliberal 'Hayekian state' is neither permanent nor the expression of the 'final stage of capitalism', how do we avoid schematic and exaggerated accounts of its origins and current power? Depending on the different answers to these questions, social change activists face the following dilemma in developing a mass democratic political alternative to neoliberalism:

- It is either pointless because anti-neoliberal movements cannot hope for success *within* capitalist societies because these societies are in a state of insoluble, terminal crisis manifested in the form of increasingly ugly and painful socio-economic and environmental breakdown, violence and disorder; or
- Resistance is essential given the causes of current crises. This is because 'capitalism' is not globally homogeneous politically, does not have a predetermined path or clear end game, and the next phase of political economy – whether capitalist or post-capitalist – in different countries is yet to be more fully contested and defined.

However, it would be unjust to adopt a simple for or against position in relation to the thesis presented by Streeck and fellow Leftists. Although exaggerating the inability of governments to deal with some of the disorders, I agree with most of the characteristics of the 'five disorders' that he has outlined. Crucially, there is *the glaring silence about the major crisis of climate breakdown* within his list of crises and, until very recently, a persistent reluctance by prominent Left journals such as *New Left Review* to discuss in detail other major environmental problems.[58] Reading his books, articles and interviews, it is clear that like many on the Left, Streeck waivers on a number of important positions, such as whether anything can or should replace the Euro, or his faint hopes for a democratic counter-offensive against Hayekian policies. Part of the reason for Streeck's pessimism is that as a former social democrat, he did not adopt a radical politics in previous decades. Unlike mainstream social democrats, however, Streeck has become genuinely disillusioned and shocked that former Left social democratic solutions are in his opinion, no longer viable.

More broadly, Streeck displays a totalising mind-set with a long tradition in post-1945 Western intellectual history that has straddled both the Left and the Right. This paradigm, as part of the larger paradigm of 'capitalism and democracy', focused on totalitarianism as the closing of the universe of discourse and the end of ideology. Prominent exponents include George Orwell on totalitarianism, Herbert Marcuse on 'one dimensional society', Theodore Adorno on 'totally administered' capitalism, Michel Foucault on surveillance and discipline, and Daniel Bell through to Francis Fukuyama on the end of ideology and the end of history. It is a tradition that either exaggerates political control and the end of political diversity, or else envisages no exit from prevailing crises and political tendencies. Streeck espouses a Left catastrophism, a pessimistic version of 'post-politics' that revolves around a belief that the 'Hayekian state' will snuff out democracy. Occasionally, he also rages at the so-called 'cosmopolitan Left' and the 'sectarian Left' in Germany who criticise his support for restricted immigration policies.

Previous historical developments have shown that liberal and conservative notions of 'totalitarian' control were exaggerated and that such control was never comprehensive or durable. The populace of the old Soviet Union certainly feared and suffered enormously from horrendous violent state terror while simultaneously showing more awareness of propaganda and the ideological nature of power as evidenced in the numerous political jokes circulating and the private rather than public rejection of the dominant ideology. By contrast, there was less widespread rejection of the dominant ideology by the masses in the 'free world' of the West. One needs to ask, once again, how dominant is any 'dominant ideology'?[59] Little wonder that the hegemony of Communist ideology quickly evaporated with hardly a trace, except amongst a small minority of die-hards. Similarly, the 1950s' 'end of ideology' thesis was rendered absurd or meaningless by the upsurge of protest movements in the 1960s, just as the triumph of liberalism or 'the end of history' (after 1989) proved short-lived when confronted by Islamic opposition and widespread loss of confidence in liberal markets due to the Great Recession and the rise of diverse forms of Right-wing racism. No authority is able to sustain permanent political control, given socio-political resistance and the unpredictable disruptive power of economic, environmental, military and technological developments in contemporary societies.

Like Streeck, we all alternate at various points between subscribing to pessimistic, depoliticising scenarios and more optimistic empowering analyses. It takes enormous emotional and intellectual energy to surmount the impact of years of depressing political developments and to continue to mount challenges against them. Streeck's thesis is therefore very alluring and it is relatively easy to succumb to its pessimism. Intellectually, however, it is difficult to ignore the problems with his narrative of the development and the political consequences of the 'Hayekian state', including its extreme pessimism. Some of the flaws in radical Left analyses that share Streeck's central thesis are outlined in what follows.

POST-1945: A COUNTER NARRATIVE ABOUT 'DEMOCRATIC CONTROL'

If theorists of totalitarianism distorted the actual nature of particular regimes by reducing them to ideal typical models of 'total control', Streeck's problem is the opposite in that he over-emphasises the power of democratic control over capitalism after 1945 and subsequent de-democratisation after 1975. Part of the reason for Streeck's exaggeration in *Buying Time* is that he tends to homogenise 'capitalism' and 'democracy' as separate processes or entities. Instead of analysing the historical variety of parliamentary democracies and the inseparable development of political decision-making and private business sector production and investment decisions, Streeck over-states the changes between 1945-1975 and the following period after 1975. He ignores the contradictions and precarious nature of simultaneously securing state legitimacy and capital accumulation that affects each governing political apparatus and set of business communities in quite diverse ways. Let me illustrate.

There is no doubt that post-Second World War reconstruction and other factors generated a boom leading to higher wages, higher consumption and an improvement in the standard of living in most OECD countries. This does not mean that one should romanticise these years, as up to half the so-called *trente glorieuses* (roughly between 1945 and 1960) were characterised in European countries by lack of housing due to war damaged cities, large scale internal migration and emigration to Australia, Canada and other countries due to high regional unemployment, poverty and the very uneven sharing of the so-called 'affluent society'. Life for many women went backwards as returning male soldiers re-occupied paid jobs and the majority of married women were confined to domestic unpaid labour or quarantined in specific forms of 'women's occupations' such as shop assistants in the retail industry, secretaries or nurses. In most OECD countries, higher university education remained the privilege of relatively small minorities until the end of the 1960s and beyond, except in a few countries such as the US.

It is also true that after the Great Depression and the defeat of fascism that business groups and conservative political parties, especially in some countries in Europe, were forced to make significant concessions to workers in the form of greater social protection. This did not apply to southern Europe where authoritarian regimes were in power in Spain and Portugal until the 1970s, and civil war, political repression and poverty prevailed in Greece until economic growth increased in the mid-1960s only to see the colonels supress democracy from 1967 to 1974. As to other OECD countries, given the post-war boom, most conservative parties prior to the 1970s shared with Left-of-centre parties an acceptance of higher tax rates as economic growth in manufacturing, construction and mining comfortably covered business concerns. The reconstruction and expansionary character of OECD economies also justified the need for state revenue. It is when growth rates slowed, or labour militancy and social movement demands escalated in the 1960s and early 1970s that many businesses began to increasingly object to tax and state social expenditure rates.

However, the dominant narrative is false, namely that between 1945-75 capitalist classes were subordinated to democratic control. Instead, capitalist countries were characterised by a variety of political economic conditions rather than the so-called *trente glorieuses*. For example, the period from 1945 to 1955 was marked by formal and *de facto* military control in Germany, Austria and Japan (officially up to 1952 in Japan but the Korean War extended US power longer). In the US, Cold War tension erupted in McCarthyist witch-hunts, the outright attack on unions and democratic rights via the 1947 Taft-Hartley Act banning Communists and sympathisers, thereby significantly strengthening the power of businesses over most forms of labour activity. Contrary to Streeck's overstatement of the changes in this period, in America, the most powerful capitalist country, the Cold War weakened rather than strengthened the labour movement. These anti-democratic and anti-union powers remain in force today despite the ban on Communists in unions being overruled by the Supreme Court in 1965.[60] Streeck's distinction between so-called Keynesian 'democratic control' prior to 1975, and neoliberal business 'rebellion' is both unconvincing and at odds with the undemocratic concentration of power in American political and business institutions both before and after 1975.

In the other large capitalist country, the Federal Republic of Germany, it was the combination of being a 'front-line' state with American, British and French military bases, plus a conservative clerical anti-Communist Christian Democratic coalition government led by Konrad Adenauer (with a third of his cabinet prominent ex-Nazis), that made West Germany a precarious democracy with illiberal features. Despite the 1951-52 reforms, such as the co-determination laws (a revival and modification of earlier Weimar workplace rights for workers suppressed by the Nazis), Ordoliberalism prevailed. Also, a divided Social Democratic Party abandoned all reference to socialism by 1959 and in 1966 joined a Grand Coalition with the conservatives (led by ex-Nazi Kurt Kiesinger) in order to gain 'respectability' as a *Volkspartei* (people's party) rather than as a former socialist 'class party'. The Cold War climate led to the 1956 ban of the Communist Party (KPD). The German conservative government's attempts from the late 1950s until the early 1960s to legislate 'emergency laws' banning the right to strike and imposing press censorship only failed due to a lack of a two-thirds majority in parliament.[61] The mounting opposition from students, unionists and other movements to conservative policies escalated in the 1960s and 1970s leading to the 1972 *Berufsverbot*, ostensibly to prevent support for Baader-Meinhof terrorism, but framed broadly enough to effectively ban radical Left critics from holding public sector jobs. The affluent lifestyle of a majority of West German male workers by the 1960s is not to be confused with claims about the 'democratic control of capitalism'.

Although the 1945 Attlee Labour government nationalised industries and enacted social welfare reforms in the UK, as did a number of other West European countries and to a lesser extent Canada and Australia, conservative parties took office in these countries throughout the 1950s and into the 1960s and even the 1970s. In Australia, McCarthyism also expressed itself as the Menzies conservative government in 1949 not only tried to ban the Communist Party but also proposed to set up concentration camps to intern people loosely defined as 'communists', proposals that were defeated in the 1951 referendum. Leading capitalist countries from Japan through to Germany, Italy and other European countries were dominated by conservative regimes that were the opposite of 'democratic control over capitalism'. They did not dismantle welfare state reforms and indeed encouraged conservative versions of social welfare as part of the post-fascist social settlement. Nevertheless, they certainly stopped the pace of earlier reforms to ensure that businesses did not feel too burdened by social demands. In earlier writings, Streeck argued that conservative governments in Europe promoted 'cross-class' inclusion via Christian Democratic and other conservative models of social welfare, often relying on non-state bodies such as churches and community associations.[62] This growth in the 'social market' (a term coined in 1947 by Ordoliberal and ex-Nazi Alfred Müller-Armack[63]) is quite different to Streeck's later depiction (in *Buying Time*) of the 'democratic control over capitalism' overthrown by neoliberalism. Rather, Müller-Armack and other Ordoliberals were close to the Adenauer government and key negotiators of the Treaty of Rome (ratified in 1957) that evolved into the EU.[64]

Politically, decolonisation struggles and wars preoccupied France, Belgium, the Netherlands and the UK to varying degrees up until the 1960s, thus affecting the level of domestic democracy tolerated under Cold War conditions, while fascism and dictatorship prevailed in Spain, Portugal and Greece. Some countries, like Japan and Italy, had brief periods of socialist government or coalitions in the immediate post-war years, but essentially had conservative governments right through to the 1990s. While they did enact 'social market' type policies, there was certainly no 'democratic control of capitalism'. Others like France, Australia, the US or Canada had brief or intermittent reform governments. Only Scandinavian countries had long lasting social democratic governments. Moreover, the rose-tinted image of the *trente glorieuses* conveniently obscures the reality that on average within the OECD, it was a bare five or so years between the late 1960s and the early 1970s when either non-conservative governments were elected, or labour and social movements escalated their militant demands for moderate to radical social reform. While it is legitimate to feel nostalgic for what Ken Loach depicted in his 2013 documentary *The Spirit of '45* (the very important creation of mass public housing, health services and education), one should also never forget how conservative and paternalistic social institutions were in most countries prior to the 1970s – the opposite of democratic control and a primary reason for the explosion of protest movements during the 1960s and 1970s.

One of the main objections that Streeck puts forward against Habermas[65] and O'Connor[66] concerns their failure to recognise the legitimation crisis experienced not by workers but by capitalists rebelling against 'democratic control'. This is a valid critique insofar as Habermas and O'Connor wrote their analyses in the early 1970s, at the peak of social movement activism and a few years before the neoliberal counter-offensive by businesses gained so much traction. In my view, this was not the main weakness of their theories of the capitalist state. What characterises their account of legitimation, motivation and accumulation crises is the restricted national dimension of their analyses. Apart from a limited discussion of the domestic rather than global aspects of the American 'warfare-welfare state' (O'Connor) and the danger of world-destruction through nuclear war (Habermas), their 1973 books contained no analyses of how the growing power of multinational corporations and supra-national institutions were shaping or constraining the policies and practices of national state institutions. Forty years later, Streeck is certainly more aware of globalisation but largely ignores the impact of foreign corporate investment (offshoring) and how the growth of low and middle-income countries directly and indirectly affected what he calls the 'Hayekian state' and the 'de-democratisation of capitalism'. Instead, his version of globalisation is a Eurocentric inward-looking one whereby 'national redistributive social democratic' policies are not viable at supranational level yet are being destroyed at national level by a 'borderless Europe'. As I will discuss in Chapter Nine, Streeck represents the views of the nationalist Left who see the 'welfare state' undermined and made impossible by neoliberal support for a flood of immigrants and refugees that erode wages and social conditions.[67]

If 'democratic control over capitalism' had existed in most OECD countries prior to the mid-1970s, the scale of subsequent offshoring would have been stalled or prevented. Neoliberalism did not sweep across the world in a uniform pattern or timeframe. A case in point is that in an earlier work, Streeck notes that inequality actually declined in Germany from 1980 to the mid-1990s and its corporatist model was greatly admired by those suffering from increased inequality in Anglo-American neoliberal countries.[68] Importantly, within OECD countries, the domination of neoliberalism did not occur, as Streeck contends, principally or solely through changes in domestic political economic policies. Instead, a combination of increased outsourcing of production – especially to low-wage developing countries – plus the especially important deregulation of capital investment flows and tariff cuts, all began to seriously hurt Western labour movements.

Crucially, the gradual opening of China to market forces by Deng Xiaoping after 1979, combined with the development of free trade zones in other developing countries, added tens of millions of workers to the global labour pool during the 1980s and 1990s. All OECD governments and societies were affected by this sea change which left both domestic workers and many small-to-medium businesses on the defensive, often unable to sustain former work conditions and rates of profitability. Without this massive assistance first to multi-national corporations and then to small-to-medium importers and producers, the successful 'rebellion' of capitalists would have been much harder. Governments facing deindustrialisation, tax flight and increased unemployment were increasingly forced by the combination of new global capitalist conditions and more aggressive corporate and small business domestic political pressures to liberalise national markets, reduce trade tariffs and scale back public sectors via privatisation. The increasing shift from the production of goods in nationally-located factories to the development of cross-national value chains ultimately affected not just the level of local employment and strength of unions, but also the ability of centre-Left parties to defend their labour base in the face of many consumers/voters wanting lower-priced goods rather than locally-made but higher priced cars, white goods, clothing and electronics. The rise of Ikea,

'Wal-Mart nation', Amazon and other corporate giants, and the decline of the local shopping strip would not have been possible without the transformation of old local and national production processes.

It is the profound material changes in the production and assembly of both producer and consumer goods, as also the ability of consumers to purchase goods and services online across a range of international markets, that affects the whole debate over national 'sovereignty' and democracy. Streeck's inflated narrative of the evolution from 'democratic control' to the 'Hayekian state' is both far too schematic and idealist in romanticising the period between 1945 and 1975. He is also historically blind to some of the major changes within both developing countries and within OECD countries – developments that would have made life difficult for EU workers and citizens, with or without the existence of the Euro. It should be remembered that the 'race to the bottom' in the form of competitive low national corporate tax rates and the erosion of wages and working conditions was a global phenomenon and not something driven solely by the EU 'Hayekian state'.

8. SUPRANATIONAL CAPITALISM VERSUS NATIONAL SOCIAL DEMOCRACY

IN THE PREVIOUS chapter I discussed how the notion of the 'Hayekian state' emerged as a direct contrast to the romanticised account of 'democratic control over capitalism' in the post-1945 period. In this chapter, I will discuss whether de-democratisation has occurred and whether national sovereignty is possible or desirable. Whereas previously many Marxists rejected the possibility of 'socialism in one country', today, sufficient numbers have forgotten the critiques of Stalinism and now also champion the highly problematic notion of small state national sovereignty. It is no surprise that there are still many social democrats and liberals who believe that national democracies control capitalists. Streeck used to share this belief but now mourns the loss of 'democratic control' since the dominance of neoliberalism. Of course, one does not have to be a radical in order to critique the notion of the 'Hayekian state' held by *New Left Review* editors and writers as well as by other critics of the EU. Social democrats Torben Iversen and David Soskice also criticise Streeck and others on the Left for their claim that the 'Hayekian state' has de-democratised national control over capitalism since the late 1970s. They also reject Marxist and other Left assumptions about the power of corporations and the weakness of national governments in the face of globalised capitalism.[1] In doing so, they redefine 'democracy' and national control.

According to Iversen and Soskice because corporations in the advanced sector of capitalism are embedded into national spaces and rely on skilled workforces and their own national government for multiple forms of assistance, they are less able to exit for another country and have less power than democratically elected governments. This is a simplistic explanation of the relative strength of corporations vis-à-vis elected governments. The United Nations Conference on Trade and Development estimates that 80 per cent of international trade is linked to global production networks that are regionally based, such as US corporations relying on Mexican, Canadian and Asian supply and assembly lines. With the supply chains of a mere 50 corporations accounting for 60 per cent of world trade in goods, there is little need for multi-national corporations to exit particular nation states, as only a tiny 6 per cent of the workforces of these fifty giants are directly employed while tens of millions of workers are elsewhere, located in outsourced companies in other countries.[2] The removal of tariffs and inspectors enforcing protective work conditions in OECD countries has enabled businesses to evade democratic control by locating many of their supply chains in undemocratic or poorly regulated nations.

Responding to numerous critics of capitalism who point to an increase in inequality and poverty in recent decades, Iversen and Soskice also argue that the advanced sector of capitalism and the 'decisive' middle-class part of democratic electorates have a mutual interest in advancing capitalism by ensuring that elected governments cater for their urban social needs and continued prosperity. They claim that these middle-class 'democrats' have no inherent interest in redistribution or equality but want to ensure that their children also benefit from their location in the 'knowledge economy'. Notably, they say little or nothing about the constraints placed by undemocratic EU institutions on the power of elected governments to follow the wishes of their electorates.

If Streeck romanticises the 'democratic control' period between 1945 and 1975, Iversen and Soskice under-emphasise the external and internal market pressures on national governments to liberalise capital controls, reduce tariffs and undermine working conditions in both the advanced sectors of capital and what they call the old 'Fordist' industries. While showing the new political and cultural cleavages between higher-educated workers in the urban 'knowledge economy' and the de-industrialised 'Fordist' sector of regional towns, Iversen and Soskice fail to explain or answer the elementary question, namely, why did capitalist enterprises in OECD countries cease employing so many workers making everything from clothing, steel, cars, white goods to electronic equipment and yet continue to make the same products in their offshore factories? Was this due to greater productivity via cheaper wages in Asian and other developing countries and the ability to reimport manufactured goods without former high tariffs or what? Equally importantly, they fail to explain the actions of the former 'Fordist' workers, families and communities who constituted the 'democratic electorates' before the rise and current dominance of the so-called 'knowledge economy'. Did they commit political suicide? Why did the 'Fordist' democratic electorates that were supposedly 'more powerful than capitalists' in getting national governments to deliver their needs, why did this so-called powerful electorate agree to market forces pressuring national governments to dismantle and undermine their own employment, social conditions and future wellbeing?

Iversen and Soskice concentrate on showing how technological changes affected old and new businesses or how national policies determined why mass higher education and vocational education differed in various OECD countries and affected voting patterns. However, they lose sight of the bigger picture of international and domestic market competition and the need for national governments to implement neoliberal trade, tax, labour market, investment and social policies. Despite opposition from workers and others in electorates, these pro-business policies were sold to voters by the major parties as the only 'economically rational' way to keep their nations internationally 'competitive'. Before the 1970s, there was little 'democratic control of capitalism' despite more choice between political parties of the Left and Right. From the 1980s until the recent loss of electoral support for centre/Left and centre/Right parties, 'democratic control' over capitalism has been a farce, an empty façade where both major parties offered voters little choice other than slight variations in the degree of support for neoliberal market policies.

In common scenarios repeated in many countries during the 1980s, 1990s and 2000s, capitalist businesses, associations, think-tanks, media and lobby groups, even a section of the trade union movement, loudly proclaimed their opposition to any party promoting what they saw as 'anti-market' policies; hence, parties eventually dropped any 'controversial' agendas, were dutifully elected and could thus be seen as implementing 'democratic power'. It would be absurd, on the other hand to deny that national governments have the power to set a wide range of regulations, tax rates, working conditions, welfare payments and environmental protection policies. The political question is why these policies have not been implemented? Tellingly, Iversen and Soskice evade the reason why most governments and parties have been most reluctant to support 'market controlling' policies that would shift national conditions away from decades-long pro-market demands for deregulation and 'competitive', profit-enhancing policies.

Importantly, Iversen and Soskice's redefinition of democracy is revealing.

"We suggest" they declared, "that the essence of democracy is not redistribution or equality, as so commonly assumed, but the advancement of middle-class interests, and we capture this idea as the 'fundamental equality of democracy' (to distinguish it clearly from Piketty's (2014) 'fundamental inequality of capitalism'."[3] Too bad for all the others outside the 'middle-class' in developed capitalist countries who miss out on the spoils of 'democracy'. As for the vast multitude of humanity living in low and middle-income developing countries, Iversen and Soskice do not analyse why their lack of democracy and inability to join the 'high-income club' is constrained by the trade, military, financial and development policies pursued by major capitalist countries.[4] Politically located between market fundamentalists and radical critics, Iversen and Soskice write within the framework of the social democratic or centre-Left Variety of Capitalism school. Their controversial redefinition of 'democracy' complacently accepts inequality and poverty, and their misguided optimism about future capitalist growth delivering for the 'democratic' middle-class is an illusion based on their flagrant neglect of crucial environmental issues.

FROM 'FORDIST' DEMOCRACY TO 'POST-FORDIST' DE-DEMOCRACY?

Iversen and Soskice reduce the content and meaning of 'democracy' to anything that essentially benefits so-called middle-class employees of the advanced sector of capitalism compared with the 'losers' associated with the old 'Fordist' industries. By contrast, Streeck offers a narrative that is equally unconvincing because he tends to homogenise capitalist classes. In earlier decades, Streeck was engaged in detailed studies of various industries but in recent years has opted for sweeping accounts of capitalism. Like Karl Polanyi and many critics of capitalism given to overgeneralisation, Streeck now pays little more than lip service to the differences between the scale and location of capitalists from small business to multinational corporations. He also neglects sectoral or fractional divisions between capitalists such as industrial, financial and other fractions. Political economist, Kees van der Pijl, argues that by ignoring the fractions of capital, Streeck fails to see that the dominant fraction after 1945 was industrial or productive capital which saw its sectional interests vested in maintaining reasonable relations with workers through their unions. By the early 1970s, finance corporations (with all their think-tanks, economists and political allies) were challenging industrial capitalists for policy dominance. The ascent of neoliberalism was not a 'general rebellion' of capitalists, but rather a series of widespread divisions within capitalist countries between different fractions of capital trying to either maintain good relations with workers to maximise productivity or seeking to crush unions; these divisions also involved domestic and international struggles over national currency values, capital flows and tariff protection. If worker militancy in the late 1960s was a challenge for industrial capital, the rise of the 'debt state' and the crisis of 2008 now centred on the role of finance capital as the dominant fraction.[5]

While insightful, I would qualify van der Pijl's critique by emphasising the significant changes in many large capitalist firms in recent decades. There are still numerous businesses operating in just one sector, but it is also evident that many diversified corporations have subsidiaries and divisions that straddle more than one or two sectors of industrial, financial, commercial, mining and agrarian capital. In most OECD countries, even small to medium manufacturing businesses have combined production with service provision in what is now called 'servitised' companies. Business-government relations may still be characterised by the presence of old business associations and forms of industry lobbying. There have always been large corporations that simultaneously operated in more than one sector. However, new globally diversified corporations (such as Amazon, Apple, Sony) that pursue multiple political strategies depending on their cross-national interests in manufacturing, retailing, media production or finance have emerged alongside these earlier forms. Business relations with governments and politics in general are more complicated now than previously when the old distinct sectoral divisions of capitalist enterprises known as 'fractions of capital' prevailed.

The thesis of 'democratic control' between 1945 and 1975 is a distortion of political economic reality because it assumes that the post-war boom was based on the direct and indirect power of the electorate via the 'Keynesian state' which exercised its power through the model of 'Fordism'. The theory of 'Fordism' was itself based on the leading role played by corporatist agreements between capital and labour that were endorsed by the interventionist 'Keynesian state'. I do not dispute that corporatist practices existed in a number of capitalist countries as did Keynesian policies. It is the scale and prevalence of these practices and policies, as well as how particular forms of industrial relations management translated into state policies such as welfare provision that I would dispute. Remember, corporatism did not entirely disappear after 1975 in the era of so-called neoliberalism and the 'Hayekian state'.

Thus, even if we ignore Streeck's homogenisation of capitalists, we cannot overlook his elevation of corporatism as the dominant form of labour-capital arrangement prior to the era of the 'Hayekian state'. As previously mentioned, Gramsci discussed 'Americanism and Fordism' as based on the new 'mass worker' and new mass production processes. He greatly admired 'Fordism' as a form of modernism that could not be fully realised under liberal capitalism or fascism because it either required coercion of workers in both America and under Italian fascism, or clashed with old European family-based capitalism and the sexual promiscuity of the upper class 'bohemian layabouts'.[6] Only the disciplined proletariat committed to sexual monogamy could realise 'Fordism' as a technologically advanced mode of production if combined with socialist planning. Gramsci's puritanism, like Lenin's admiration of Taylorism ('scientific management' of a labourer's time and motion) was common in socialist and Communist movements. British political economist Simon Clarke observes that:

> The hedonism of Bohemian layabouts proved to have a greater influence over the working class than Gramsci had anticipated, so that workers were not reconciled to their labour by sobriety, savings, safe sex and an early night, but demanded rising wages, shorter hours, welfare benefits and secure employment to give them access to a wider range of pleasures. In the end the corrosive influence of petit-bourgeois libertinism even undermined the attempt to create the New Man as the psycho-physical foundation of socialism in the Soviet bloc. Despite its best efforts to provide hard work and a frugal life, supported by edifying art, music and literature, with extensive facilities for healthy Fordist sports, the state was unable to protect the working class from blue jeans, rock music, Coca Cola, alcohol, modern art, fornication, homosexuality...[7]

No wonder that Wilhelm Reich attracted mass interest from young activists interested in discussing the 'sexual question' in the early 1930s before the Sex-Pol movement was banned by the hierarchy of the German Communist Party. Elements of this 'puritanism' have survived amongst sections of the contemporary Left.

There are, of course, quite different notions of 'Fordism'. Some conceived of it narrowly as a form of industrial organisation and mass production. Others, such as Marxist Kees van der Pijl deployed 'Fordism' as an ideal type based on three elements: a) the dominance within the labour process of the assembly line and mass production; b) the recognition that wages were not just payment for labour but also the basis of consumer demand for mass produced goods such as cars and other household items; and c) the extension of industrial management into social reproduction, that is, the attempt to manage workers' private lives and social behaviour.[8] Michel Aglietta and others of the French Regulation School saw it in broader terms as both a mode of capitalist production and a form of political regulation that reached its peak in the 1950s and 1960s.[9] As a mode of political regulation based on mass production, 'Fordism' was supposed to have stabilised capitalism via corporatist agreements over productivity, wages, the provision of mass consumer goods and state regulation of markets and welfare services through the application of Keynesian policies. Cruder versions assumed that most capitalist businesses before the 1980s were either characterised by assembly lines or were involved in corporatist relations between management, labour and the state.

However, millions of small to medium companies in numerous capitalist countries did not conform to this ahistorical, simplistic paradigm. The false assumption that capitalism in all industrialised countries was based on a homogeneous 'stage' or 'regime of accumulation' and a 'regime of social control' ('Fordism' linked to the 'Keynesian welfare state') is a gross overgeneralisation. At best, 'Fordism' dominated key industrial sectors while large swathes of small and medium businesses operated outside 'corporatist' agreements. Like 'Fordism', many see 'financialisation' as the dominant form of capitalism, a finance-led capitalism closely tied to neoliberal state policies.[10] In contrast to 'Fordism', financialisation does not depend on one form of mass production, as all spheres of production (whether in manufacturing or services), private consumption, household lifecycles and everyday life are affected by debt, credit and other financial processes.[11]

REVISING 'FORDISM'

In 1998, Aglietta revised his original 1976 thesis in the light of neoliberal policies, the rise of financialisation and what he saw as the breakdown of 'Fordism' in the 1970s. Conceding that there were several wages systems and modes of political regulation compatible with 'Fordism' (Anglo-American, German, French, Swedish), Aglietta also argued that uncertainty for large corporations "was relegated to the margins of capitalist accumulation, to small subcontracting businesses, agriculture, small traders, Third World countries, and so forth."[12] How 'marginal' small businesses, sub-contractors and 'offshore' producers were or are, depends on whether or not one acknowledges the political and economic significance of the non-corporate sector in capitalist countries. These small businesses constitute the vast majority of capitalists compared to large corporations that constitute only between 1% and 5% of total enterprises in various countries. Nonetheless, large enterprises remain the engine of capital accumulation through their domestic and international market dominance over investment, trade, R & D, capital flows, and especially their power as 'price makers' compared to the majority of small and medium businesses who are 'price takers'. Yet very importantly, politically, mainstream parties cannot afford to consistently ignore the various small business associations and lobby groups in their quest for re-election. 'Fordism' also assumed that large corporations reached corporatist 'agreements' with their workers and ignored the determined efforts of those businesses (especially in the US) that either prevented unionisation or waged protracted battles to severely limit the power of unions in their enterprises.

By the 1970s, industrial employment in developing countries (without Keynesian 'Fordism') had already reached half of total global industrial employment. In 2018, a report on 100 countries showed that China, India, Brazil and Indonesia that ranked 1st, 5th, 9th and 11th respectively, as having the largest manufacturing sectors in the world,[13] but still belonged to the classification of lower-middle income countries. The garment, textile and footwear industry in twelve developing Asian countries employs over 43 million workers (75% being women, except in India and Pakistan[14]), more than *three times* the size of the total US workforce employed in *all* manufacturing sector industries. Equally telling, the Chinese province of Guangdong employs over 40 million workers in manufacturing, or significantly more than the total number of manufacturing workers in *all* EU countries.

During the past three decades, the capital accumulation and general growth rates of developing countries have far outpaced the old Atlantic capitalist powers and Japan, with China now accounting for more than 40% of world annual GDP growth or significantly more than the combined contribution of the US, Europe and Japan.[15] Importantly, despite extensive mass production in China, South Korea, Indonesia, Vietnam and other Asian countries, these do not accord with the model of 'Fordism' as there is no 'Keynesian welfare state'. Leaving aside developing countries, the issue is not whether there were different types of state regulation and wages systems, but rather whether 'Fordism' remained useful as a general theory of a 'stage' of capitalism if the political conditions and legal systems in capitalist countries between the 1930s and the 1970s were so different. A case in point is that the political and industrial strength of the Swedish labour movement went from 67% in 1970 to 85% unionisation in 1988 at the so-called end of 'Fordism' and the arrival of neoliberalism, while in the US the opposite trend occurred, namely, approximately 65% to 70% of workers were *unorganised* during the peak of 'Fordism' in the 1950s and 1960s, with union membership declining from 29% to 16.8% between 1970 and 1988.[16]

Another example of overgeneralised notions of 'Atlantic Fordism' is state theorist Bob Jessop's explanation of Brexit as a consequence of the crisis within the British ruling class and its inability to secure prosperity and stability in the decades following the demise of 'Fordism'.[17] If 'Fordism' was an Atlantic phenomenon, how is it that Germany, Netherlands, France and other EU member states did not experience the same levels of British instability within the EU? Either 'Fordism' was the 'regime of accumulation' that kept the social and political peace across the Atlantic, or it never overwhelmingly determined the character and functioning of capitalism but rather depended on the specific historical preconditions and socio-political relations in the UK, France, Germany and other countries. How else to explain the period since the 1970s called 'post-Fordism' and why 'little Englander' tensions with the EU could not be replicated by other countries making the transition between so-called 'Fordism' and 'post-Fordism'.

In short, 'Fordism' was an economistic theory which attempted to explain state institutions and 'political regulation' by deriving these from the 'regime of capital accumulation'. The major problem was that the mode of industrial relations (or the 'Fordist' mode of production based on organised agreements between capital and labour) did not translate directly into the 'welfare state' as claimed by theorists of 'Fordism'. Welfare legislation required political agreements in legislatures made by political parties and representatives who were often *not involved* in dispute resolution agreements struck at enterprise level. Importantly, from the New Deal until the present-day, powerful unions in manufacturing, mining and transport deliberately *avoided* negotiations about social welfare for *all* American workers and their families and instead only sought the improvement of the welfare of their immediate members (such as health cover, company pensions and the like) through strikes and contract negotiations. This was hardly the basis of universal entitlements for all citizens. One major consequence is that despite extensive industrial conflict in the 1930s, Roosevelt kept the racist Southern Democrats onside thus ensuring that welfare entitlements and other rights were not extended

to Black Americans. Clearly, this type of 'Fordism' was different to the political and industrial negotiations in other capitalist countries. In fact, Robert
Boyer, another prominent member of the French Regulation School, argued
in 1997, that for the period 1945 to 1973, only the US and France had fully
developed 'Fordism' (but with France having a comprehensive welfare state
and the US having minimal provision of state welfare) while Germany, Japan,
the UK and Italy as the other dominant economic powers had either a
mixture of 'neo-Fordism' or other systems.[18] In short, 'Fordism' was hardly
the prevailing 'regulation model' in the post-war period before the onset of
so-called 'post-Fordism' in the late 1970s.

Moreover, the analysis and prevailing narratives about 'Fordism' ignored
the massive military-industrial complex in the US compared to other capitalist countries and the corresponding lack of an adequate welfare state. Aglietta subscribed to Marx's problematic division of capitalist extended
reproduction into Department One (producer goods) and Department Two
(consumer goods). Capitalist crises supposedly occurred when there was an
imbalance or disproportionate relationship between the two. An example
would be the overproduction of steel in Department One, but insufficient
cars and whitegoods sold in Department Two. As previously discussed, the
question of in which Department did the massive military-industrial
complex fit has bedevilled Marxist political economists particularly given
that military contracts were state allocated, not subject to the usual forms of
market competition, and constituted vital political economic relations in the
US and globally well beyond the size of military production and
employment.[19]

Aglietta argued that despite variations of 'Fordism' to reflect specific
national circumstances, such variations "cannot cast doubt on the fundamental fact that all Western countries benefited from a common growth
regime."[20] While it is true that the US drove the post-war recovery that
benefitted other OECD countries up until the 1970s, 'Fordism' was not a
'common growth regime' and could not explain the quite different domestic
politics in the US compared with other capitalist countries. In brief, Aglietta
developed a theoretical model of 'Fordism' that was far too economistic.
Numerous Marxists have accepted this model even though there was little
historical and political analysis, especially of quite different state institutional
structures and government policies, and how capital-labour agreements at
the site of production did not translate into a broad range of government
domestic and foreign policies.

CORPORATISM AND DIFFERENCES IN NATIONAL LABOUR MOVEMENTS

Crucially, the character of the various state institutions and policies in OECD countries did *not* originate or derive from the 'Fordist' mode of mass production. Rather, the growth of capitalist accumulation based on mass production was either determined by or had to adjust and interact with quite diverse national state institutions, political parties, domestic political cultures and levels of labour-capitalist conflict in countries as different as Australia and Japan or Belgium and Italy. Trade unions in different OECD countries, for instance, were characterised by either large industry-wide unions or several competing craft unions within the same industry or enterprise; there were also company unions confined to one corporation, or Communist, Catholic and other types of unions with political affiliations to Social Democratic, Labour, Communist or Christian Democratic parties compared with other unions that were unaffiliated. All of these quite variable organisational and political characteristics as well as industrial relations legal frameworks affected the possibility of reaching corporatist agreements with businesses rather than the continuation of volatile and conflictual relations.

Without recognising the significant political differences between and within national labour movements and their relations with business in different countries, not to mention the degree of unionisation of the total workforce and the relative strength or weakness of employer organisations, we can easily succumb to caricatures or ahistorical notions of a 'Keynesian Fordism' that supposedly equalled 'democratic control of capitalism' and the delivery of the 'welfare state'.

Hardly surprising then that there was little agreement on what constituted 'post-Fordism' given this also presupposed the quest for a common 'stage' or new 'regime of capital accumulation' to succeed the historical stage of 'Fordism'. From the late 1970s to the 1990s, radical and mainstream debates centred on whether or not mass production had been replaced by such models as flexible accumulation and specialization based on mixtures of custom-made and standardised products, Japanese 'quality circles' and other production methods, or post-industrial 'knowledge economy' developments that integrated cognitive, digital and other technological innovations – all seen as transforming earlier capital-labour relations and traditional notions of social democracy and Communism.

In the UK, the Communist magazine *Marxism Today* adapted Gramsci's 'Fordism' and then promoted a 'post-Fordist' critique of traditional Marxist class politics. Through a wide-ranging exploration of the rise of new social groupings, identity politics and technology, the former orthodox Communist publication metamorphosed into a mixture of anti-Thatcherism and 'Third Way' politics. From the Greater London Council strategy of developing a new 'local socialism' as well as Tony Blair's 'New Labour' neoliberalism 'with a human face', the 'hundred flowers bloom' of 'post-Fordism' varied greatly and included either fanciful notions of technologically-driven pop sociology to serious attempts to mobilise new social movements. For two decades, the varying interpretations of 'post-Fordism' helped shape Left-of-centre UK politics until the turn of the century. It was the parallel critiques of neoliberalism (also alive during the 1980s and 1990s) that were ultimately vindicated by 2007-08 in showing the deep-seated problems of what had passed for 'post-Fordism' or 'varieties of capitalism'. Even so, critiques of neoliberalism left unclear, not just in the UK, but also across the OECD, why there was no well-defined path forward and also why no return was possible to the so-called age of 'Fordism'.

What is interesting about the various Left interpretations and responses to 'Fordism' is that they were informed by quite different national politics. Streeck's narrative of 'Fordism' is centred on corporatism which, importantly, was unrepresentative of most capitalist countries between 1945 and 1975. It is certainly true that corporatism or tripartite negotiations (unions-business-state) was evident in Germany, Austria, Belgium, Sweden and some other countries. Notably, Germany, never adopted Keynesian policies, as Streeck himself acknowledges.[21] Instead, post-1949 West German governments pursued the distinct German policy framework known as 'Ordoliberalism'. Unlike Keynesian policies, Ordoliberalism rejected the use of expansionary fiscal and monetary policies to help economic recovery in a recession. Recently, Streeck contradicted his own thesis of Keynesian 'democratic control' in *Buying Time* by arguing that Hayek (when he was working at Freiburg University, the home of Ordoliberals) became the bridge between the authoritarian fascism of Carl Schmitt of the 1930s and the anti-Keynesian Ordoliberals who dominated policies at the German Ministry of Economics during the 1950s and 1960s.[22]

While the profile of OECD societies has profoundly changed since the 1950s, especially the financial and industrial interlocking of EU countries, contemporary neoliberal austerity policies in a German-dominated EU are not that dramatically different to earlier anti-Keynesian Ordoliberal policies.[23] Prior to the European Central Bank (ECB), the German Bundesbank – which was Europe's *de facto* central bank – always opposed any expansionary social expenditure and job creation policies that threatened an increase in inflation and 'loose' fiscal management. In contrast to Streeck, Thomas Biebricher shows the influence of prominent Ordoliberal Walter Eucken on Jürgen Stark, who was the Chief Economist of the ECB during the financial crisis of 2008. Biebricher also believes that the Ordoliberalisation of the EU is still a work in progress.[24] It has certainly stalled or regressed in the face of new anti-Covid-19 stimulus policies.

As to corporatism in other G20 capitalist countries such as the UK, Japan, the US, France and Australia, these were either characterised by fractious labour-capital relations or weak union movements. Militant labour union activity by no means translated into social reform-orientated state apparatuses, due to resistance by conservative governments. By the 1960s, Japan had a strong economy but a declining labour movement (including thousands of relatively tame enterprise unions). Not 'democratic control' but rather the 'undemocratic bureaucracy' at the Ministry of International Trade and Industry (MITI) with the cooperation of large corporations dominated industry policy and investment until the early 1980s. Even in recent decades, Japanese conservative governments have either been uninterested or unable to 'free' economic policy from powerful bureaucratic departments. In contrast, the UK had a weak economy but strong, strike-prone unions that resisted both Conservative and Labour governments in their attempts to impose 'incomes policies' and wage freezes during the 1950s, 1960s and 1970s right up to the 'winter of discontent' that led to Thatcher's election victory in 1979.

Turning to Australia, when a quasi-corporatist accommodation was formalised in 1983 after decades of industrial conflict, a trade union/government delegation visited Sweden and Austria in 1986 seeking a suitable corporatist model for Australia. The delegation explicitly avoided the British and US union movements because of a history of bitter non-corporatist industrial conflict culminating in Thatcher and Reagan crushing important strikes. By 1986, however, it was far too late to import Austrian or Swedish corporatism into Australia as the Australian Labor government had already implemented neoliberal policies.[25]

In the largest capitalist power, James O'Connor showed that the US socio-economic order was divided into three parts: the 'monopoly sector' of large capital-intensive enterprises which set prices and had higher levels of unionisation; the federal and local 'state sector' whose many unionised employees often had comparable wages to those workers in the 'monopoly sector'; and finally, the extensive 'competitive sector' made up of millions of small to medium labour-intensive businesses and characterised by low-paid workers, especially women, minorities, students and all other non-unionised people. Only a third of the total American workforce was unionised at its peak in the decade between 1945-1955. In Australia, by contrast, federal and state wages and industrial tribunals from 1904 onwards (well before 'Fordism') presided over numerous state-sanctioned awards that flowed onto most workers including non-unionised workers. The great gap in wages, work conditions and standards of living between those employed in the American 'monopoly sector' as opposed to those in the non-unionised 'competitive sector' was nowhere near as great in Australia, especially in the decades after 1945.

By the time O'Connor published *The Fiscal Crisis of the State* in 1973, unionisation had slipped to between 25% and 29% of all workers. It is the extension of the exploitative and precarious conditions within the 'competitive sector' to significant parts of the 'monopoly' and 'state' sectors, combined with heavy deindustrialisation and offshoring that has characterised the further entrenchment of business power since the 1970s. Union density plummeted in recent decades. In 2019, only a very tiny 6.2% of workers in the dominant private sector (five times lower than public sector workers at 33.6%) and a mere 10.3% of *all* private and public sector employed workers were unionised. Just seven US states out of fifty are home to over half of all unionists in a sea of non-unionised workplaces.[26] Little wonder that de-unionisation has exacerbated social inequality.

What Streeck and some Left analysts of 'Fordism' under-emphasise or gloss over is that corporatism was heavily skewed by gender because of the dual labour market. Unions in manufacturing, construction and mining were, and remain overwhelmingly male dominated. Like many other political economists, Streeck's work largely ignores gender and race issues. Unsurprisingly, he supports Kalecki's thesis on full employment but fails to mention that this was only half true in the 1950s and 1960s when white Western males enjoyed full employment. Far from 'democratic control', discrimination and conservative gender roles kept women's participation rates low in most capitalist economies. The transformation of employment in OECD countries by the end of the 1970s was strongly associated with the rise of services, including the rise of non-unionised female employment in private service industries. Forty years later, trade union membership has dropped to an average of 16% in OECD countries in 2019 compared to 30% in 1985, even though Scandinavian countries such as Sweden still had a remarkably high 66% of unionised workers in 2019.[27]

Neoliberal ascendancy by the 1980s coincided with the transformation of

workplaces, a process that exposed union movements to the historical obsolescence of their old male-dominated agendas and organisational structures.
Rather than blame key unions for their sexism and failure to organise
women, Streeck tended for many years to see women as the new allies of
neoliberal employers. When pressed, he acknowledged that women's entry
into the labour market could also be seen as the history of women's emancipation.[28] In contrast to Streeck, many unions have learnt these painful
lessons of sexism and sought to modernise and recruit women and non-
whites, even though certain industries such as construction or nursing
continue to be predominantly male or female. In a number of OECD countries, more women are now unionised than male manual workers, reflecting
the dominance of service sector employment over manufacturing. However,
in low and middle-income countries there are large numbers of women
employed in manufacturing despite lower percentages in India and Pakistan
due to cultural constraints on women's freedom.

WHY HAYEK OPPOSED ASPECTS OF THE 'HAYEKIAN STATE'

The conflict between 'capitalism and democracy' is a global phenomenon and
has produced continual political battles. Yet nowhere else in the world
except in Europe has the division amongst Left parties, social movements
and theorists over a national or international strategy against neoliberalism
featured so prominently in the first decades of the twenty-first century. I
noted in the previous chapter that Anderson, Streeck and others cite Hayek's
1939 article on federalism as anticipating the model of the EU 'Hayekian
state'. There is no doubt that the EU Commission, Council of Ministers, the
ECB and European Court of Justice increased restrictions on the freedom of
member countries to act as sovereign economic powers, even though Ministers from member countries can obstruct and veto those proposals that
require unanimous support. In this broad sense, some important aspects of
the EU appear to conform to what is called 'Hayekian state'.

Yet, in his analysis of contemporary sovereignty, former judge on the
German Constitutional Court, Dieter Grimm, argues that the EU as a non-
state entity does not possess constituent power or sovereignty. The EU
cannot constitute itself, as the member states remain masters of the treaties.
He also asserts that in a confederation "there is no shift of sovereignty. Nor
is there an independent popular sovereignty belonging to citizens of the
Union as a whole, but only European representation by individual nations at

the level of community bodies, below the level of sovereignty."[29] If formal power is still vested in the member nation states while economic power is both formally and informally increasingly aggregated by the EU Council, ECB, EU Commission and Court, to what extent is de-democratisation of member states actually happening? Is this true only when there is no major crisis in the EU? Brexit and national responses to Covid-19 have shown that nation states have not lost as much power as Streeck and others claim. Shortly, I will discuss whether most nation states, including current EU member countries, ever had full sovereignty or only nominal 'sovereignty' regardless of whether they were inside the Eurozone or outside. As to the original model builder of the 'Hayekian state', it is important to recognise that Hayek's views in 1939 – decades before the European Monetary Union (EMU) became a serious policy option – were significantly different to his views in the 1970s.

In 1976, Hayek outlined why he was strongly opposed to national governments having a monopoly on making money and even more so to the EEC having a single currency.[30] While he supported the economic unification of Europe, he strongly opposed an international European currency that he claimed would be worse than national currencies. In his own words, the "advantage of an international authority should be mainly to protect a member state from the harmful measures of others, not to force it to join in their follies."[31] Ironically, Streeck and Hayek are at one in their critique of the Euro! The difference is that Hayek advocated a crazy scheme for the full privatisation of money. Accordingly, governments would no longer issue money and any bank or institution could issue multiple currencies and let the competitive market set the true value of particular monies, regardless of the numerous casualties of such a scheme. It was a belief in the market taken to dangerous extremes.

Hayek's advocacy of multiple private currencies is different to the *de facto* bypassing of paper currencies in the form of bank credit to consumers and businesses – an explosion of debt that contributed to the Great Financial Crisis in 2007-08 and remains a source of instability and potential economic meltdown. Today, the growth of 'fin tech' digital algorithms (unknown by Hayek) also enables increased privatisation of money through unregulated developments such as Bitcoin and shadow banking that endangers financial stability.[32] A growing number of contemporary Right-wing libertarians as well as young digital activists go beyond Hayek and are seduced by blockchain technology in the belief that it will facilitate all kinds of decentralised socio-economic activities free of state control.[33] Democratic accountability is low on their priority list as this would require some form of transparent social regulation subject to public debate to ensure that people were not cheated by fraudsters. How social inequality could be overcome by these new decentralised technologies is also either ignored or an issue not considered a priority by these new entrepreneurs.

Paradoxically, Hayek's privatisation of money proposal undermines one of the key foundations of what Streeck calls the 'Hayekian state'. In Streeck's and other Left analysts' terms, the 'Hayekian state' could not exist without the European Monetary Union – the key fiscal disciplining mechanism in association with the EU Stability and Growth Pact limiting the size of national deficits and expenditure – thereby de-democratising member countries via the requirement that they 'consolidate' national budgets. According to Streeck, without the Euro straitjacket, national governments could evade strict EU fiscal controls by devaluing their currencies and adopting stimulus budgets instead of austerity. In reality, it is more the EU Stability and Growth Pact that is used to enforce national expenditure restrictions rather than the Euro. After all, austerity policies did not depend on membership of the Eurozone, as non-members like the UK and Sweden confirmed. Actually, Streeck argues that Sweden has transformed from the model Social Democratic state into the most advanced 'consolidation state' with a firmly established austerity regime based upon spending cuts to reduce debt as well as tax cuts to reduce pressure by the electorate for more public services.[34]

Streeck and other anti-EU critics cannot have it both ways. Either the Hayekian 'consolidation state' is a *supranational state* with specific de-democratising structures dominating national governments, or it can also exist as a *national state* with free elections outside the Eurozone. If so, the assumption that the 'consolidation state' has now been institutionalised on more permanent lines needs substantial qualification. Beginning in 2016, the Centre/Left Swedish Budget Bill adopted a cautious hybrid approach driven by union and citizen demands for better social welfare, more jobs and tackling climate change while trying not to frighten markets and the EU. Significantly, tax cuts were rejected as short-sighted and replaced by tax increases.[35] The initial reactions of bond and currency markets to the 2016 budget were negative with claims that Sweden risked 'budget credibility',[36] thus confirming that financial markets were worried about the abandonment of the 'consolidation state'. While only a modest change from the austerity measures that Sweden continued to impose up until 2020, what the Swedish example showed is that in most countries permanent austerity is not a viable policy option if free elections are still in place, regardless of whether countries are in the Eurozone or not. The fall in support for the Swedish Social Democrats in the 2018 elections was not due to their budget policy in 2016 but rather to the rise of anti-immigrant political forces, a common feature in other EU countries. Since 2016, no centre-Left party has won an electoral majority (on its own) in member countries of the EU or has been either strong enough or committed to challenging the Stability and Growth Pact. Instead, it has taken the economic crisis caused by Covid-19 to suspend the neoliberal enforcement of SGP rules.

If the Euro is not vital to the existence of the 'consolidation state', this casts serious doubt on the foundations and structural preconditions of the 'Hayekian state'. After all, one can agree with critics of financialisation about the growth of 'central bank-led capitalism' without assuming that the role of central banks is equivalent to a fully developed 'Hayekian state'. National governments, especially large powers such as leading members of the G20, still have the capacity to change vital fiscal policies even though central banks influence monetary policy such as interest rates. One should remember that while unelected central bank officials can threaten democracy,[37] most decision-makers in departments and statutory bodies of capitalist states have hardly been democratically controlled for almost two hundred years despite free elections and so-called parliamentary scrutiny. Some unpopular decisions can be reversed after new elections, but major decisions such as going to war or allocating trillions of dollars or Euros to rescue banks, are usually irreversible as we have witnessed in contemporary and historical contexts.

As one of the leading critics of the EU 'Hayekian state', Streeck challenges defenders of the European Union by proclaiming that:

> Europeanisation today is by and large identical with a systematic emptying of national democracies of political-economic content, cutting off the remnants of potentially redistributive 'social' democracy, housed in nation-states, from an economy that has long grown beyond national borders into a, politically constructed and contracted, 'Single Market'. Where there are still democratic institutions in Europe, there is no economic governance anymore, lest the management of the economy is invaded by market-correcting non-capitalist interests. And where there is economic governance, democracy is elsewhere.[38]

There is no doubt that neoliberal policies have affected the structure and practices of state apparatuses in recent decades. Yet, Streeck's powerful and seductive critique requires even greater scrutiny.

WEAKNESSES IN THE THEORY OF THE 'HAYEKIAN STATE'

Firstly, to qualify as a new form of durable capitalist state, the 'Hayekian state' must at a minimum exhibit a range of administrative structures and roles in multiple domestic and foreign policy departments – well beyond former undemocratic historical practices. Given the restricted power of the European Parliament (which has to this date been unable to overrule the austerity initiatives of the Council and Commission), it is easy to show the undemocratic character of EU institutions. The ECB is both a relatively new undemocratic institution in Europe as well as a particularly remote central bank compared to other central banks. Most OECD central banks have long become 'officially' independent of democratically elected governments. Secondly, the EU may look like it is systematically 'emptying national democracies of political-economic content' because the EU's administrative and judicial bodies have indeed sought to acquire more decision-making power at the expense of national parties, unions, businesses and parliaments.

Yet, the degree to which the Hayekian supranational state has de-democratised member countries compared to the earlier so-called 'Keynesian state' is disputable. Democracy at national level has been idealised by many anti-EU critics of both the Right and the Left. After all, the IMF, World Bank, the US Federal Reserve, the GATT predecessor of the WTO as well as the High Authority and EEC predecessors of the EU Commission were all unelected bodies established by Keynesians and non-Keynesians well before the neoliberal 'Hayekian state'. National governments may have had 'formal' sovereignty across the world but their power to shape domestic policies has often been constrained by their interdependence and hence only relative 'independence' to defy external trade, military, investment and currency pressures and sanctions.

Since it began operating in 1999 and strengthened in 2012, the restrictive EU Growth and Stability Pact (SGP) requires member countries to have a budget deficit no greater than 3 per cent of GDP and debt levels no greater than 60% of national GDP. This neoliberal straight jacket aimed to maintain the international value of the Euro by ensuring that the budget and debt levels of member countries did not fluctuate widely if some member states implemented 'loose' fiscal policies. It was also designed to curb inflationary tendencies and social demands for greater government expenditure that could affect labour markets and wage levels if policies designed to alleviate unemployment and reduce inequality spilled over to other EU member countries. Despite modifications, the SGP has not met its own guidelines with the median national debt of the eleven original countries in 1999 rising to 70% of GDP in 2019. In the words of a leading pro-market economist, Jean Pisani-Ferry, the SGP is 'hopelessly complex' and ineffective as both a mechanism to prevent crises or resolve dangerous debt levels and enhance risk management.[39]

After two decades of life, both the Euro and the SGP are fragile institutional mechanisms that satisfy neither the goals of dominant neoliberals seeking greater control over national socio-economic policies nor the dreams of advocates of a 'democratised social Europe'. A group of prominent French and German mainstream neoliberal economists with long experience working within key EU institutions and advising French and German governments, had warned in 2018 that the next Euro crisis may be worse than the previous one (which still affects member countries) and that it was necessary to implement new risk prevention and mitigation measures.[40] What is evident from the 2018 report by these economists is that the messy and ineffective financial architecture of the EU, plus the failure to develop proper financial integration cannot be left in its current state of ill-preparedness. Hence, they advocated more room for national decision-making, and new measures to replace the SGP (based on old deficit and debt levels) by introducing new 'shared risk' funds. One such Euro fund financed by national contributions, would help participating member countries absorb large economic disruptions. They recommended that payouts "would be triggered if employment falls below (or unemployment rises above) a pre-set threshold.".[41]

Prior to the outbreak of Covid-19 in early 2020, there was already a fierce debate within EU circles of loosening the tight SGP guidelines and reverting to Keynesian stimulus and debt reduction strategies. Now the massive 2020 global crisis caused by Covid-19 has driven trucks through the so-called 'Hayekian state' regulatory rules (supposedly enforced by the Growth and Stability Pact) as they implement stimulus packages to prevent the total collapse of their economies. So far, the EU has failed to offer comprehensive co-ordination and adequate fiscal support. Only time will tell whether anti-austerity measures and emergency measures triumph over 'market discipline'. It is abundantly clear that the lack of trust between national electorates and the EU as well as the lack of trust between national governments and complex EU institutions micro-managing national budgets and policies will bring matters to a head.

Nonetheless, there has been a notable change in direction among key German policy makers. A continuation of the bitter political legacy of EU and ECB austerity restraints in the decade after 2008 is now recognised by both German and various other governments to be highly dangerous in the face of potential socio-economic meltdown.[42] What lasting new post-austerity policies will emerge are unknown just as it is also unclear whether the Euro will survive if larger countries such as Italy and Spain reel from the crisis. There is now much talk of a 'Hamiltonian moment' to give the EU Commission and ECB greater federal fiscal powers including EU-wide banking and debt raising capacities, a standard minimum tax rate to raise revenue from foreign internet giants and also an EU-wide insurance fund. This notion of fiscal union is quite premature. Neoliberal policy frameworks are battered but are far from dead. Conversely, whether incessant growth is capitalist or socialist or conducted democratically at national level or within a so-called de-democratised EU at supranational level, these all remain backward looking political agendas in so far as they reflect a pre-environmental consciousness and literally an unsustainable politics. I will return to this later.

If even neoliberals favour increased national decision-making and anti-unemployment measures in the future to prevent the collapse of the EU, it raises serious issues about both the durability and the status of the so-called 'Hayekian state'. The 'single market' will most likely still exist in coming years and possibly become more financially integrated and socially conscious if the EU heeds the need to placate or defuse the threat posed by anti-EU political movements. Such a move would prevent the EU from being able to fully de-democratise national member countries as it would require new hybrid simultaneous developments: increased EU integration but also greater involvement on the part of national constituencies to determine the character of any new EU fiscal and social integration. Just as Hayek's 1939 blueprint for the 'single market' seemed absurd before the 1970s, so there is no guarantee that the Stability and Growth Pact and other institutional mechanisms will survive being transformed in coming years by both ex-neoliberals and anti-neoliberals.[43] In fact, the EU suspended the Stability and Growth Pact in March 2020, an indication that the old austerity measures after 2008 are politically too dangerous to be repeated in the 2020s. The socio-economic fall-out from Covid-19 or looming environmental crises may well force the EU to take even more urgent fiscal measures to alleviate or prevent further ecological degradation and social dislocation.

Fiscal conservatives will undoubtedly fight for more post-Covid-19 austerity measures to reign in rising debt levels. But this conservatism is expressed more by national governments (the 'frugal four' of Netherlands, Austria, Sweden and Denmark) rather than just fiscal conservatives within EU institutions. Given the volatility and increasing divisiveness of most national political scenes, de-democratisation has either not yet occurred or was never as deep as Streeck and anti-EU critics claimed. Instead, it is the polarised condition of domestic national politics that still spells political danger for the EU should Right nationalists in member countries reject the restrictive policies of the EU, especially following the social dislocation and impact of Covid-19.

NATIONAL INTEREST VERSUS THE 'HAYEKIAN STATE'

Actually, there are two parallel themes or contradictory narratives that run through the work of anti-EU critics such as Streeck. The first theme is how the political project of freeing capitalism from 'democratic control' produced the supranational EU 'Hayekian state'. The second theme is a detailed examination of the political economies of northern and southern member states of the Eurozone in order to show why Germany, especially, is benefiting from the Euro and the application of 'consolidation' policies.[44] One theme is supranational de-democratisation while the other parallel theme reflects a major contradiction in the thesis of the 'Hayekian state', as it is actually anti-Hayekian, namely, that particular strong national governments, especially Germany, are using the EU institutions to pursue national interests.

Previously, there was overwhelming support amongst the major political parties in Germany for the harsh austerity measures dealt to Greece and other peripheral countries. Why was this the case? Following the fall of the Berlin Wall and the unification of Germany, the tax and debt burden of trying to bring East Germany up to West German living standards (which after thirty years has not been achieved) began to be strongly resented by electorates in West German Länder or states. In the 2005 election, Angela Merkel outlined her strong pro-market personal vision of the need for austerity. Historian Adam Tooze points out that Merkel's vision rested on the figures 7, 25 and 50:

Europe has 7 percent of the world's population and 25 percent of global GDP. But it is responsible for 50 percent of global social spending. This, as Merkel sees it, is not sustainable. Germany's growth is steady, but slow at best. Germany's population, along with that of much of Europe, is aging. What has to give is government spending. Fiscal consolidation is the deep continuity of Merkel's administrations.[45]

If most West Germans were tired of paying for their Eastern cousins while having their own welfare entitlements reduced, they were certainly not going to rescue the Greeks, Portuguese, Spaniards and others. Also, Streeck argues that German manufacturing businesses and unions in the dominant export sector fear countries leaving the Euro and undercutting Germany through competitive devaluations of their restored national currencies.[46] So, while Streeck emphasises Hayekian supranational control over 'democratic national sovereignty', he paradoxically shows why it is primarily German national interest (using EU institutional mechanisms) rather than supranational de-democratisation that counted in previous decades. Accordingly: "Just as the United States sees the world as an extended playing field for its domestic political economy, Germany has come to consider the European Union as an extension of itself, where what is right for Germany is by definition right for all others."[47] A similar theme is articulated by Marxist, Costas Lapavitsas:

> In a nutshell, what we see in Europe is actually hierarchy and divergence among states. At the top sits Germany. Berlin is the centre of power. Berlin takes the real decisions. France has actually lost out in that struggle, no matter what Emmanuel Macron thinks. That's the reality of Europe. At the bottom sit a number of peripheral countries, weak countries, and they are dominated by the core. We have relations of domination, new ways in which imperialism manifests itself. That's the reality of Europe, not the fairy stories of an alliance of nations, overcoming national borders, becoming one big, happy family.[48]

The description of German 'imperialist' power within Europe is inappropriate and a half-truth. Whereas national liberation movements in former colonies struggled to liberate themselves from European imperialist powers, the demand for 'national sovereignty' or 'national liberation' from the EU (aka 'German imperialism') cannot be equated with an imperial/colonised relation for member countries, especially given that these countries were themselves real imperialists (such as Britain, France, Netherlands, Portugal, Spain and Belgium). If what Lapavitsas and Streeck both call German imperialism hiding behind France,[49] why are anti-EU movements not more anti-German rather than anti-EU? Also, if the EU collapses but Germany remains the dominant European political economic power, will nationalist rivalry re-emerge with all its dangers as in the era before 1939?

The distinction between a 'Hayekian state' and nationally driven EU Council policies, plus a German dominated ECB is not a matter of simply splitting hairs. Either the new 'Hayekian state' is de-democratising EU member countries, or German and French electoral domestic politics have been supportive of the neoliberal policies that have been inflicted on the rest of Europe. Streeck therefore contradicts his own narrative about the de-democratisation of nations when he acknowledges that it was France and other EU members, fearing a united Germany, that proposed the establishment of the Euro to Helmut Kohl's government in order to end the Bundesbank's role as the *de facto* central bank of Europe. He observes that by "replacing the Bundesbank with a European central bank, they expected to recapture some of the monetary sovereignty they felt they had lost to Germany."[50] However, the Bundesbank and the overwhelmingly 'Ordoliberal' and anti-Keynesian German economics profession were squarely against monetary union, afraid that it would jeopardise German "stability culture".[51] As it turned out, until early 2020 the other member states got the ECB which largely adopted Bundesbank policies rather than a completely new supranational policy framework.

It was the bombshell ruling of the German Federal Constitutional Court on 5th May 2020 that exposed as untenable both the theory of the 'Hayekian state' and the naïve belief of the centre-Left that the EU treaties could lead to a fully democratised 'social state'.[52] The conservative Court ruled that the German Bundesbank may no longer participate in the European Central Bank's Public Sector Purchase Program at even the austere rates of previous years. In the midst of the greatest downturn in Europe's economies since the Great Depression, this Court ruling threatened to stop the multi-trillion economic stimulus packages, the possibility of any future issuing of Eurobonds and the involvement by Germany's central bank from participating in funding social welfare in poorer EU member states. Without Germany being able to legally help fund either Eurobonds or the EU's socio-economic packages, there will be no major transformation of EU social programs unless new ways are found to bypass conventional methods.[53]

One way around this German legal roadblock and the pathway to greater political and fiscal federation is the Macron-Merkel or Franco-German agreement (following the German court ruling) to get the EU to issue bonds directly and guarantee these bonds from its own revenue rather than relying on the German and other central banks to cover EU bonds.[54] If this does not work, then it will *not* be the supranational 'Hayekian state' de-democratising national governments, but rather the national German legal process and other national governments preventing supranational EU reform.[55] As Adam Tooze observes: "The eurozone bond crisis was not preordained by tensions between democracy and capitalism, citizens and markets, national taxpayers and footloose financial cosmopolitans. The euro area made its own, very peculiar, sovereign-debt crisis. It now has the power not only to unmake the conditions of that earlier crisis but to found a new financial and monetary order – not just with regard to fiscal policy and the constitution of the European Central Bank but the structure of the bond market itself."[56]

Thus, the crisis in Europe conforms to neither the theories advanced by supporters of national solutions (whether Left opposition to the Hayekian state' or Right nationalists) nor to the optimistic theories proposed by supporters of a democratised EU. Instead, a combination of EU regulations, national juridical rulings and conservative national governments thwart an easy path to major social reform and anti-austerity measures such as an extensive Green New Deal. Anderson, Streeck and others on the Left have misread the power of the so-called 'Hayekian state' and the present political conjuncture. Paradoxically, rather than the 'Hayekian state' de-democratising member countries, it is various national governments that are constantly vetoing EU-wide policies. The EU institutions, it could be argued, lack sufficient power to implement more equitable reforms or even to provide adequate solutions to the current economic crisis, witness the national divisions and pared down rescue package in July 2020 of the original Macron-Merkel proposal (which itself was grossly inadequate to counter austerity).

Importantly, like their neoliberal opponents, many Keynesians and Marxists are in danger of becoming political economic dinosaurs in coming years, as the debate has moved on. In September 2018, for example, various groups within the European Parliament sponsored a conference to discuss how the Stability and Growth Pact could be replaced by a 'stability and wellbeing pact' after decades of incessant economic growth that is damaging not just Europe's environment but the safe operating space for humanity on earth.

The issue of how the SGP could be revised so that member states "meet the basic needs of their citizens, while reducing resource use and waste emissions to a sustainable level",[57] is no longer a traditional dispute between neoliberals and socialists. Although still largely lacking detailed EU-wide alternative degrowth or wellbeing proposals, the failure of both national governments and EU institutions to urgently deal with unsustainable growth agendas undoubtedly spells future major political and environmental trouble.

UNCERTAIN FUTURES: DIVISIONS OVER POST-NEOLIBERAL PATHWAYS

As we have seen, contemporary Left nationalists and internationalists continue to be divided over how to respond to neoliberal ideas and policies. Streeck and Thomas Piketty, for example, have both analysed the larger relationship between labour and capital while ignoring gender inequality.[58] Piketty later rectified his inattention to gender inequality and intra-class inequalities, especially those experienced by working-class women and non-whites.[59] Streeck has not to date written anything substantial on these crucial issues. Although I agree with Streeck's critique of Piketty's proposal for a global wealth tax as currently unrealistic,[60] he proposes an even more utopian goal of 'de-globalising capitalism' and in Polanyian terms calls for restoring 'embedded democracy' in order to 're-embed capitalism'.[61] It is a perspective that is more backward looking to the period 1945-1975, even though Streeck himself admits there can be no return to this era.[62] This ambivalence is partly because like other admirers of Polanyi, he veers between almost mistaking neoliberalism as a re-run of pre-1929 liberalism (but under conditions of global capitalism and the EU 'Hayekian state') while simultaneously recognising that present-day conditions are quite different to pre-1930s capitalism. Like other advocates of nationally embedded socialism, Streeck can appear confused, contradictory and inconsistent. He favours de-globalised national 'embedded democracies' while recognising that ending the Euro straitjacket will at best be "a subversive temporary expedient, a means for achieving a stay of execution, and that the nation state as a form of political organization will obviously not be able to support the post-capitalist political economy we need and must somehow build."[63] If so, does he long for utopian local post-nation-state democracies or something else?

Streeck describes himself as a "practising Polanyian".[64] However, like many other anti-capitalists influenced by Polanyi, Streeck fails to identify any contemporary social change agents capable of performing Polanyi's 'double movement' (see Chapter Six) to end his five 'disorders of capitalism'. In his optimistic moments he wants to go 'back to the future'. Therefore, he favours propelling the contemporary global capitalist world forward to an earlier phase of pre-globalised capitalist nations, a future utopian goal where 'embedded national democracies' control capitalist nations, free of mobile workers/migrants and mobile capital. It is a nostalgic yearning for the comfortable but parochial, homogeneous social world of his youth, a world that can no more be restored than his youthfulness. Putting up the fortress walls is no solution to a world of profound inequalities, a world where multi-culturalism will not, and should not disappear. Given that societies are increasingly integrated with one another, multiculturalism based on tolerance and shared struggles for a better life is the goal to be achieved, rather than a threat to be feared.

When Streeck's pessimism takes over, he envisages the slow breakdown and end of capitalism as being like the decay of the Roman Empire.[65] Unfortunately, the metaphor of ageing or the analogy of the collapse of the Western Roman Empire is unconvincing as a representation of the end of capitalism. Capitalist countries are not organic systems like the body that eventually dies through multiple malfunctions and wear and tear. Also, it is questionable to speak of the end of capitalism as a process that will take hundreds of years; a period that is longer than the modern history of capitalism itself. Streeck argues that many regions and communities within the Roman Empire experienced no regular violence and were unaware that the Empire was eventually falling apart. By contrast, the global capitalist system is highly integrated through trade, networked telecommunications, equity and currency markets, military bases and numerous other interconnections. In this respect, serious malfunctions will be quickly noticed. Just look at the current global Pandemic!

Interestingly, Piketty also sees capital in the twenty-first century returning to its 'normal' state of inequality after the 'aberrant' years of reduced inequality between 1930 and 1980. I reject Piketty's notion of 'normal' capitalism, because capitalist societies are ever changing social formations based on fluid social relations and political economic struggles. Despite Piketty's neo-classical misleading conflation of capital and wealth,[66] he nevertheless draws our attention to one of the reasons why 'consolidation' policies were strongly supported by neoliberal governments after 1980. Austerity is not driven primarily by the 'debt state', as Streeck claims, although debt is now a large problem in many countries caused by rescuing the finance sector after the catastrophic binge of financialisation and the necessary stimulus measures to revive Covid-affected economies. Rather, Piketty argues that well before the crisis of 2008, if there had been no curbing of the growth of the 'social state', the rate of tax as a percentage of GDP before 1980 would have seen social expenditure and tax collection increase to between 70 to 80 per cent of national income by 2050-2060 in European countries.[67] Therefore, between 1980 and 2010, neoliberal EU governments stabilised the tax collected, to between 40 and 50 per cent of GDP.[68]

Short of 90 to 100 per cent of GDP, nobody knows what the limits of tax, as a percentage of national income would have to be in capitalist countries before major political conflict erupts. On 2018 OECD figures alone, average tax of member countries was 34.2% as a percentage of GDP.[69] However, the ability of governments in the US, Australia, Ireland, Korea, Japan or the UK, for example, to raise their low levels of tax as a percentage of GDP by another 50% so that they matched higher French or Scandinavian levels, would be impossible without major political change. Conversely, if Belgium, France, Denmark, Sweden or Finland cut their tax revenue as a percentage of GDP to the dismal levels of the US, Ireland, Korea, Turkey or Australia, this would also trigger major political conflict.

Still, one must not confuse tax collected with the size and character of particular public sectors. Most tax collected already takes the form of transfer payments, such as pensions, or is spent on private businesses contracted to deliver civilian infrastructure or military weapons and numerous other material goods and services, not to mention interest payments paid to private bond holders. By contrast, it remains unclear what is the actual optimal size of the public sector before capitalist economies could possibly enter irredeemable crisis or profitable capitalist businesses lose in the shift to public sector production of goods and services. The ongoing struggles to prevent either an increase in revenue collected as a percentage of GDP or the size of the public sector from growing, will not solely take the form of traditional struggles between labour and capital. If low-growth, stagnation or deflation become the 'new normal', divisions will likely intensify among business groups on whether, in the absence of the ability of markets to stimulate investment and consumer demand, it will be necessary to increase demand via more public sector jobs and services.

POLITICAL MYOPIA: TREATING ALL DEBT AS THE SAME

The possibility of the 'consolidation state' becoming permanent is finished following the large but still inadequate stimulus packages in 2020 and the political dangers of reinstituting austerity measures in the next few years while national economies are still so weak. Those on the Left who based their whole analysis of the EU on the continued existence of the 'Hayekian state' are now rudderless. Before the 2020 increases in national state deficits, Streeck's notion of the 'consolidation state' had already homogenised or glossed over the qualitative differences between various forms of debt. Witness the fact that Japan's debt to GDP ratio had risen to 251.9% between 2008 and 2019-2020 and was much higher than Greece's 200.8% in the same period.[70] The significant difference is that Japan's debt is still mainly owed to its own state institutions, businesses and citizens, while Greece's debt is mainly owed to foreign governments and the IMF. Similarly, Danish household debt to income ratio reached 269% at its peak in 2007 compared with only 125% in the US, but Denmark did not suffer massive default rates due to the absence of large numbers of sub-prime mortgages that put a quarter of all US household mortgages in the red.[71]

While debt remains a major problem, it is crucial not to lump the cause and management of all debt into the same boat. Instead, it is important to differentiate between various forms of corporate, household and state debt caused by financialisation as opposed to other forms of sovereign state debt that are non-marketable and not subject to the same risks as profit-induced financialised debt.[72] The crisis of 2020 showed that prior claims by fiscal conservatives that maintaining debt levels was essential if states were not to become incapacitated or insolvent was ideological nonsense. Suddenly, and miraculously, trillions of additional funds were found by governments to cushion the crisis. Even Germany has shifted from its role as the enforcer of EU-wide austerity to one which recognises and supports that higher deficits and a more interventionist stimulus role for the ECB will be necessary to rescue the Eurozone from major economic instability. This does not mean it has suddenly become egalitarian and co-operative, but it does mean that Germany's crisis-management strategy may not be able to rescue the EU if the 'frugal four' and other countries exert their conservative power.

Politically, the 'consolidation state' will be recognised as merely another temporary policy phase that will be looked back on as a disastrous political economic strategy. Neoliberalism did not collapse in the aftermath of the crisis of 2008. Yet, it is also rash to draw the opposite conclusion that the 'Hayekian state' de-democratised nation states. The exhaustion of neoliberal monetary policy before Covid-19 emerged had already witnessed business leaders and policy advisors urging increased fiscal expenditure (especially public infrastructure) as well as wage increases and other forms of post-austerity policy, all in the name of generating growth. Now a double crisis confronts capitalist governments everywhere. The urgency and complex political economic ramifications of preventing climate breakdown means that the viability of the 'consolidation state' is untenable in coming years. Conservatives will undoubtedly clamour for the reimposition of consolidation austerity policies in the next few years. Hayekian policies will linger on or be partially smuggled in under other names. Nonetheless, they are political poison to many voters and are now also both ineffective or incompatible with the needs of business groups and governments to deal with climate breakdown, not to mention combatting stagnation and deflation.

The final nail in the coffin of the EU 'consolidation state' was hammered in during 2020. Now the world confronts an entirely new set of pressures in the coming decade. In conventional pre-environmentally conscious political economic terms, the dilemma facing governments is how to find the fiscal resources and organise the socio-economic capacities to recharge growth after the nightmare of Covid-19? Will the shock of near economic collapse lead to a different form of politics? How will electorates respond to the fact that conventional economic growth (once renewed) may well exacerbate future climate breakdown. This major threat has not gone away just because of a new Coronavirus.

What we do know is that Streeck's focus on the Euro and a return to national sovereignty is no recipe for a successful anti-neoliberal strategy. On the contrary, Streeck and others who attack the Euro could be seen to be mimicking neoliberal policies in placing an over-emphasis on monetary policies at the expense of a broad-based set of fiscal stimulus strategies. From a heterodox post-Keynesian perspective, Geoff Dow had already made a blistering attack in 2016 on Streeck's work and condemned his political pessimism and surrender to orthodox liberal economics.[73] Dow did not argue that Streeck had become a liberal. Rather, he argued that Streeck accepted the neoliberal strictures on the impossibility of raising taxation and debt and therefore succumbed by default to the ideological falsehood that contemporary states have exhausted their capacity to resolve deep-seated crises caused by Hayekians. This so-called lack of state capacity has already been disproved by governments suddenly finding additional fiscal resources to combat Covid-19. Hence, I partly agree with Dow's critique of Streeck's acceptance of neoliberalism's chorus of TINA (there is no alternative) within the EU. Where I partly side with Streeck, is in his recognition that the scale and extent of these alternative policies will remain purely academic while the actual size and strength of Left political movements remains too weak to capture government power at EU and national levels. Also, like Streeck, Dow is largely silent on climate breakdown and hence is not persuasive in his advocacy of anti-austerity policies that could be seen as an updated replay of old pre-1970s social democratic growth policies.

At a policy level, many on the Left who share Streeck's views on the Hayekian 'consolidation state' offer no genuine solution to the size of the 'debt state'. Despite the serious limits of Piketty's social democratic growth politics to take into account the deeper aspects of the environmental crisis, at least he has proposed a solution to the large debt restricting some countries. Just as 60% of Germany's post 1945 debt was wiped out or restructured in 1953, so also in 2015, Piketty and other political economists called for a European conference to wipe out significantly the debts of several EU member countries.[74] Let me be clear, the end of capitalism is a very desirable goal. However, Streeck and many other Left nationalists misunderstand that the choice is *not just* between 'capitalism without democracy' or 'democracy without capitalism'. They underestimate the ability of pro-market governments to restructure debt obligations or to devalorise capital in a crisis by partially writing off debt (for example, giving bond holders a 'major haircut'). This would be a costly and politically difficult solution but one that pro-capitalist policymakers could adopt if needed to save economies and regenerate growth.

Those seduced by the theory of the 'Hayekian state' also ignore the possibility that desperate pro-market governments might also combat austerity by adopting alternative policies to increase the size of EU-wide funds to generate an investment-led jobs recovery.[75] This in fact what they are partially doing at the moment in the form of a Green New Deal lite. Globally, governments and the private sector could possibly increase growth as more than US$90 trillion will be needed for environmental infrastructure by 2030, plus a bare minimum of US$1 trillion per annum on renewable energy.[76] All these possibilities will be highly contested politically and indicate that capitalist countries, contrary to Streeck, do not face inevitable collapse and, at the very least, can still 'buy time' to avoid the deepening of existing crises.

IS DEMOCRATIC NATIONAL SOVEREIGNTY VIABLE?

Some post-Keynesians such as William Mitchell and Thomas Fazi support

Streeck in seeking national solutions. They promote post-neoliberal nationally sovereign socio-economic policies.[77] Yet, contrary to Streeck and other
advocates of the 'Hayekian supranational state', Mitchell and Fazi argue that
neoliberals are just as reliant on the nation-state as Keynesians were before
the 1970s. Like Streeck, Mitchell and Fazi inflate the strength and capacity
of small nation states to surmount corporate cross border production value
chains, financial blackmail and other market reactions that could debilitate
these small economies through unemployment and lack of capital resources.
The EU has the supranational muscle to impose controls on private corporations but will not pursue anti-neoliberal policies while neoliberal governments dominate in Germany, France, Netherlands, Italy and other countries.
As Bishop and Payne point out: "our enemy is not globalisation, it is neoliberalism. The well-intended, but nonetheless troubling, dalliance of some on
the left with forms of nationalism that seek a retreat from the global stage is
a dead end. Worse, they threaten to give succour to a regressive, right-wing
project that paradoxically seeks to entrench yet more pathological forms of
neoliberalism."[78]

Left advocates of national sovereignty have to surmount the reality of
varying degrees of Right-wing nationalism. Paradoxically, these advocates
often locate the main problem as being in supranational institutions rather
than much closer to home in their beloved but conservative national
constituencies. Mitchell and Fazi are typical of other post-Keynesian, Blue
Labour and Marxist supporters of Lexit. These Left nationalists aired their
views on websites such as *The Full Brexit* that was itself a site attracting those
who lobbied on behalf of Nigel Farage's Brexit Party.[79] The Left put forward
a range of policy proposals aimed at 'rebalancing' the UK away from services
and the finance sector and towards re-industrialisation and an export-led
recovery based on a high-wage, high-value British growth economy. Some of
their proposals were valuable contributions aimed at reducing poverty,
replenishing neglected regions and providing better public services. Apart
from now being politically irrelevant – given the Right-wing electoral
triumph of Boris Johnson – the Left nationalists based their whole strategy
on problematic foundations.

As with Streeck and other advocates of a retreat to the nation state, the
grand anti-neoliberal reform and restructuring plans of the Lexiteers rested
on the ability of the Left to win a clear parliamentary majority in the UK, a
prospect that is now little more than a forlorn and distant hope after being
crushed in the 2019 British election. Unless the crisis caused by Covid-19
produces a changed political climate, the prospects for the nationalist Left in

other EU member countries is equally bleak. These anti-EU Left restruc-
turers tend to minimise the international and domestic obstacles to be overcome, whether in areas of currency, trade and capital resources as well as
underestimating the ongoing mobilisation of hostile political opposition.

More importantly, the reform advocates on the website *Full Brexit* and
other media overwhelmingly ignored the fact that their 'rebalancing' growth
models are incompatible with environmental sustainability. While they are
fully aware of the need for cuts to carbon emissions and shifting to renewable energy, even this limited response can only be solved at supranational
level rather than within single nation states. In other words, they are the
mirror image of neoliberal policies in that for all their differences with
neoliberals over how the pie is distributed, they still endorse most forms of
existing consumption and therefore operate within the largely 'environment-
free' growth paradigm of 'capitalism versus democracy'. This outdated
paradigm is still dominant and provides no framework for sustainable solutions to present and future problems. One only has to look at the dilemma
facing a range of governments in Norway, Scotland, Venezuela, Mexico,
Brazil, East Timor and elsewhere that beat the 'national sovereignty' drum
while remaining heavily dependent on keeping fossil fuel industries going.
These governments either make half-hearted noises about transitioning to
renewables or remain silent about how to replace these unsustainable
economic policies.

Across the world, debates over the benefits or negative consequences of
capitalist globalisation have raged for decades. Initially, Left criticisms of
multi-national corporations, the gross inequalities between the developed
metropolitan countries and the poverty suffered by developing countries
gave rise to a range of anti-imperialist political strategies and calls to cancel
poor countries' debts, combat poverty through various types of aid,
favourable trade and investment programs and end military solutions and
cultural imperialism by Western powers. Today, anti-globalisation critiques
are instead fuelled by Right-wing nationalist parties within OECD countries
and by conservative nationalist and religious movements in low and middle-
income countries. Sometimes the arguments and targets identified by both
the Left and the Right overlap. Yet, in most instances they do not, insofar as
political cultural positions on democracy, tolerance and support or opposition to market solutions differ significantly.

During the 1920s and 1930s, socialists, anarchists, Communists, fascists
and agrarian rural movements all had tendencies that supported national self-
sufficiency or autarky. In recent decades, the idea of self-sufficiency has been

associated with green movements and various exponents of nationalism. The obstacles to attaining full or semi-autarky are rarely discussed and often underestimated because the dominant discourse is either about extending global integration or maintaining market societies while exiting from supranational institutions such as the EU. Today, only the US and China have a greater national capacity to reorganise their economies and achieve a large degree of semi-autarky rather than full autarky. Yet, even they would have to rely on the importation of natural resources and various goods despite having large internal markets. No other nation state in the world has the resources, technological development, financial capacity or political strength to withdraw from international markets and become self-reliant, unless, of course, national populations in OECD countries are prepared to accept a massive drop in their standard of living. Self-sufficiency would also mean that low-income countries forgo any hope of reaching middle-income levels, while middle-income countries not only abandon any hope of becoming high-income societies but also struggle to prevent their likelihood of slipping backwards to low-income social conditions.

What is the relevance of whether or not nations can achieve self-sufficiency? In the US, apart from issues such as 'America first' trade tariffs, few on the Left or Right debate the viability of national as opposed to international strategies because of the prevailing insular attitude to social change. These insular and parochial views usually only consider relations with other countries when opposing or supporting American military and economic imperialism. By contrast, within Europe, Latin America, Australia, India and many other countries there has long been division over what degree of domestic social change is possible given the dependency on exports and imports, foreign investment, military alliances and internal national socio-political divisions. It is in Europe that the debate over nations either leaving or democratising the EU revolves around a mixture of contradictory economic, political and cultural positions that illuminate the conflict between 'capitalism and democracy'. Even if a majority of particular national electorates decided to exit the EU, this would only mark the beginning of years of drawn out political conflict over what kind of 'sovereignty' could be achieved. This has been the case with tortured Brexit negotiations even though the UK is not in the Eurozone. Only deluded ideologues believe that an 'independent' UK (if it manages to stay intact in the coming decade) will not need some form of trade pact with the EU.

Brexit and the rise of neo-fascist movements in various countries throws the spotlight on the 'Hayekian state' and its serious conceptual deficiencies.

If this supranational neoliberal state is de-democratising national democracies, why were so many neoliberals led by Boris Johnson opposed to this EU
state? After all, they supported free trade, attacks on workers' conditions and
austerity budgets. The same is true of many business supporters of Trump
who want 'free trade' so long as it benefits 'America first'. Are we now seeing
neoliberalism in its nationalist versions rather than the neoliberalism of
supranational socio-economic, cultural, fiscal and political integration? And
what of neoliberals who simultaneously support market globalisation and
nationalist Right-wing anti-EU movements? One type of response typified
by the Editor of the Marxist *Monthly Review*, John Bellamy Foster,
proclaimed that:

> A popular front with neoliberalism against the rise of neo-fascism
> would not work, given the close relation of these two reactionary
> capitalist political movements. Rather, we are facing today the
> prospect of what David Harvey has referred to as a neoliberal-neofas-
> cist alliance. Nor is there a basis for any compromise on the issue of
> fossil capital, as demanded by the system. The only answer then is to
> turn to the popular bases of revolutionary action...[80]

Leaving aside Foster's delusion about the 'popular bases of revolutionary
action' actually becoming revolutionary in the very near future, it is politically dangerous to conflate all neoliberals as supportive of neo-fascism and to
ignore the potentially disastrous consequences that could arise if extreme
Right-wing governments came to power. A *de facto* alliance of the Left with
neoliberals was evident in Europe in recent years with the support given to
Macron over Le Pen in France and the campaign against neo-fascism in the
elections for the European Parliament. This is not equivalent to a 'popular
front' with neoliberals, but it is preferable to fascists coming to power in the
absence of 'revolutionary' movements.

While it would be foolish to uncritically defend a deeply undemocratic
EU, the onus is very much on those advocating a return to 'national democratic control' to show how this strategy could succeed at several political,
economic, cultural and environmental levels without succumbing to intolerant Right-wing, racist agendas or creating even worse conditions for
workers and their families, exacerbating poverty in depressed regions and
instigating a state fiscal crisis that prevents maintaining even existing inadequate social services. Peripheral EU member countries in the Mediterranean,
Eastern Europe and the Balkans already suffer harsh conditions and are over-

burdened by debt and weak industries. They are dependent on domestic consumption driven by households, domestic non-export-sector businesses and public expenditure. Consequently, leaving aside environmental ramifications, these countries are most unlikely to swing to high growth should they leave the Euro.

Any belief that exiting the EU will enhance both democracy and national capitalist economies for all member countries remains wishful thinking unless accompanied by strong Left electoral majorities that can be sustained for a minimum of a decade. Importantly, the ability to achieve social gains for the unemployed or low-income and precariously employed sections of national populations depends very much on the strength and militancy of trade union movements. When anti-EU critics point to national de-democratisation, they nostalgically refer to the pre-1970s era when labour movements were able to win better conditions through strikes and pressure placed on social democratic and Labour governments. In most OECD countries, working days lost to strikes have plummeted as have unionised workers. It is illusory to believe that all is due to the 'Hayekian state' when countries outside the EU such as Australia, Canada, Japan, the US and others have all experienced dramatic falls in labour militancy. Conversely, all those who dream of a 'democratised EU' are yet to show how labour movements can help achieve this when a number of important West European national trade union movements refuse to support decent EU-wide minimum wages, let alone the equalisation of wages and working conditions for fellow workers in Mediterranean, East European and Balkan member countries.

With a new phase of political economic crises now engulfing major capitalist countries, Streeck and *New Left Review's* theory of the 'Hayekian state' is being overtaken by different political realities. This theory is ill-equipped to explain the multiple socio-economic and environmental crises confronting governments. The legacy of the theory of the 'Hayekian state' has proved to be disastrous as it contributed to major divisions within the European Left and indirectly aided the victory of the Brexiteers by diverting a proportion of the labour movement from supporting the Remain case. Those on the Left who share the narrow nationalist view with Boris Johnson and others on the Right that the EU is only about building an integrated capitalist market overlook the fact that a substantial number of policy makers and voters still believe in Europe as a political cultural project to ensure peace, social justice and co-operation well beyond the narrow needs of the market. Tellingly, prominent Lexiteer, Tariq Ali, praised the European Court of Human Rights in 2020 for overruling the Macron government's ban on groups calling for a boycott of Israel. While the jurisdiction of the Court of Human Rights covers forty-seven member countries and is separate to EU institutions, the European Court of Justice tries to maintain consistency of case law between the two Courts and the EU Treaty of Nice binds the EU to respecting human rights.

In contrast to the proponents of the 'Hayekian state', extensive de-democratisation of national governments by the EU has not occurred; rather, democratic rights have been abused by national governments with limited protection offered by European courts. Yet, it is also clear that the EU has put the violation of rights by illiberal members such as Hungary and Poland low down on its priority list in the attempt to regenerate national economies hit by the Pandemic. Germany has opposed strong action against these illiberal regimes because they are economically important to the German economy. The ability of individual national governments to veto collective action has ensured that social, financial and environmental reforms across the EU are stalled or abandoned. In light of the scale of the economic crisis caused by Covid-19, it remains to be seen whether German, French and other powerful leaders will voluntarily jettison neoliberal policies or be forced to abandon these policies as they battle to save the European Union from stagnation or collapse.

9. COSMOPOLITANS AND NATIONALISTS: A DIVIDED POLITICAL CULTURE

DISPUTES OVER ECONOMIC, political and cultural policies and values continue to divide nationalists and internationalists. Caught in the old paradigm of 'capitalism versus democracy', minimal attention, however, is paid by both nationalists and cosmopolitans as to how their respective political agendas can be made environmentally sustainable. Shortly, I will discuss the cultural dimensions of these debates. In the meantime, several political economic obstacles have to be kept in mind for any nation state desiring to adopt some type of version of a Keynesian or post-Keynesian capitalist 'mixed economy' (with a large public sector), let alone a socialist system.

In the previous chapter, I discussed some of the issues surrounding the notion of 'national sovereignty'. Each country confronts different obstacles. Take, for example, the issues raised by post-Keynesian economist Philip Whyman, who was a supporter of a Left Brexit.[1] Remember that in 2020, the UK was the fifth or sixth largest economy in the world (depending on different measurements) but still faced enormous obstacles compared to the vast majority of much smaller national economies across the world. Among the obstacles that the UK will have to surmount in order to achieve 'national sovereignty' include: its long history of trade deficits that requires either generating new export markets or cutting domestic consumption through import restrictions; significantly improving its poor productivity level by retraining many more workers currently confined to low-paid and low-skilled jobs, and re-equipping and re-organising industries and services that currently underpin major regional inequalities. Other obstacles concern raising sufficient capital from new sources of investment or capital formation and refurbishing neglected infrastructure so that the UK could complete with other leaders in R & D and the new digital economies. Most of the latter would depend on what kind of restrictive or flexible trade agreements the UK could negotiate with the EU and other countries.

Paul Mason comments that "the mantra – 'take back control of our money, our borders and our laws' – has been drilled into Tory politicians. Yet 'sovereignty' no longer resides in money, borders or even laws. It exists in a reality constructed out of standards – in technology, trade, finance, agriculture, intellectual property and consumer goods – which in the EU are shared."[2] This shared reality is also only partly grasped by many on the nationalist Left. Whyman, like others who favoured 'taking back control', placed emphasis on innovation in the manufacturing sector. This is a traditional Left approach which either neglects serious environmental issues or is a sector too small to provide enough good jobs in an economy geared to services and consumption. It especially does little to combat the disproportionately large size of the City of London and the heavy reliance of the UK on all kinds of financialised services. With the defeat of Corbyn's socialist Manifesto in the 2019 election, especially the victory of the Conservatives in many traditional deindustrialised working-class seats, the 'national' socialist agenda of the anti-EU Left has, in the absence of major economic crisis, become largely academic for at least most of the coming decade.

Either major economic stimulus programs help countries recover over the next four or five years or due to continued depressed socio-economic conditions (following the lockdown/depression) export-led solutions become very difficult to achieve. Even before Covid-19, the option of increasing export growth for 'sovereign nations' was difficult enough for countries lacking workers with high skill levels, industries based on innovative technologies or the capital investment needed to enter highly competitive international markets already dominated by a minority of corporations.

Moreover, lack of investment outlets, stagnant wages and high household debt already hamper private domestic growth and employment in many depressed countries. Regenerated public sectors could certainly fund jobs, infrastructure and public services through increased borrowing and more progressive tax systems. One should never rule out the possibility of alternative policies succeeding. However, even bitterly divided national electorates in the most depressed southern European countries have failed to elect strong anti-austerity governments. Radical Left parties in Spain, France and other countries have struggled to get more than between 10% and 20% of the vote. Without Left governments and the continued dominance of various kinds of Right-wing policies, national 'sovereignty' would be worse than belonging to the EU with none of the benefits. Also, in countries such as Spain, most of the radical Left remain committed to the EU rather than face increased poverty under the banner of 'national sovereignty'.

Returning to the debates within the EU between sceptics and advocates of greater democratisation, it is possible to agree with many critics about the inequality and unnecessary divisions caused by the introduction of the Euro.[3] Contrary to earlier impressions, Streeck is ambivalent on whether to abandon the Euro. Rather he and colleague Fritz Scharpf favour some inter-mediate form or looser arrangement involving a 'southern Euro' and a 'northern Euro'.[4] How this monetary arrangement counters the so-called 'Hayekian state' is not entirely clear given the dominance of Germany and northern EU member states. Also, Streeck's colleague, political economist, Martin Höpner, already undermined the theory of the 'Hayekian state' by showing that long before the arrival of the Euro, an 'undervaluation bloc' (consisting of German governments, businesses, unions and others) adopted a strategy of undervaluing the Deutsch mark in the 1950s, 60s and 70s, in order to boost German export income within Europe and globally.[5] This strategy continued to inflict pain on other EU countries regardless of the denomination of the currency (D-Mark or Euro).

Another reason why Streeck is unconvincing about the positive affect of leaving or loosening the Euro is that he follows Karl Polanyi's mistaken belief that the Gold standard was the cause of the Great Depression and the end of laissez faire.[6] However, even if this dubious argument were true, the Euro does not play the equivalent role to the old global Gold standard in the pre-1930s. Instead, EU countries have to swim or sink within the context of the US dollar as the global reserve currency (as well as the relative strength of the Euro against the Renminbi, Yen and other currencies). Thus, multiple capitalist investment and trade pressures emanating from non-European developed and developing countries affect all Eurozone countries.

Let us momentarily assume that under the 'national democratic control' scenario countries have left the European Monetary Union and reverted to their own national currencies as well as implemented extensive anti-austerity measures. Without a growth in exports to fund their trade deficits and weak-ening currencies the 'adjustment' process could be dire, especially for their most vulnerable citizens. The ability of each nation-state in the world to 'delay' international demands that its government implement domestic 'adjustments' (expenditure cuts and austerity) to get its 'domestic house in order' – either made directly by other governments or through agencies such as the IMF – is a sign of a nation's relative strength in the international market order. Most small to medium sized nation states lack sufficient strength. Conversely, some countries have the power to 'deflect' monetary and financial crises onto other countries and thereby avoid painful domestic adjustments. The US is a notable example where despite large current account deficits it has been able to get the world to continue depositing capital (in such things as US Treasury bonds) and selling goods to it because it is the 'consumer of last resort', especially for North East Asian countries.

Thus, the ability of each democratically elected government to implement social reforms, anti-austerity expenditure strategies and other anti-neoliberal measures depends vitally on its capacity to 'delay' or 'deflect' international demands while sustaining strong domestic support from its electoral base. One should never under-estimate how difficult this is to accomplish in the current world without belonging to a geopolitical power and trading bloc. The fact many national governments have introduced emergency stimulus packages to fight Covid-19 is not a sign of 'national sovereignty' but rather a desperate, necessary measure endorsed by major central banks, international agencies and policy makers.

Despite lacking any deep recognition of environmental factors, back in 1997, Colin Crouch and Wolfgang Streeck argued against political nationalism and supported supranational European-level political intervention as the most promising means of preserving national and subnational institutional diversity.[7] As they concluded:

> Domestic democratic sovereignty over the economy, the one sovereignty that really counts, can be restored only if it is internationally shared, that is, if the reach of what used to be 'domestic' political intervention is expanded to match an expanding market. National social institutions and national democratic politics can support internationally viable, egalitarian high-wage economies only in a conducive international context, and it is only within such a context that they can continue to generate and maintain capitalist diversity and its beneficial consequences for economic performance. Existing national institutions, ...can today be no more than the building blocks of a new, larger institutional structure that must supersede them in order

to preserve their contribution to the task of civilizing a, by now, globally integrated capitalist market economy.[8]

Twenty years later, and especially since the introduction of the Euro and the financial crisis of 2008, Streeck is now a champion of small-state national solutions to neoliberal capitalism while Crouch continues to favour a 'larger international structure' to counter xenophobia and neoliberalism.[9] Nonetheless, Streeck confirmed his questionable expectations for renewed national sovereignty by declaring that with or without the 'Hayekian state', the EU and European nations cannot withstand the external neoliberalising pressures of global capitalism.[10]

Reviving Karl Polanyi's 1945 theory of 'regionalism', Streeck now succumbs to similar delusions as those put forward by Polanyi.[11] The difference is that Polanyi's illusions about the Soviet Union forming regional pacts with Britain and other nations against US globalising market imperialism no longer exists even as political fiction. Streeck legitimately asks how the EU, pinned in between the US, China and Russia, can surmount military and political economic pressures without succumbing to building an EU 'power state' based on a European defence force as advocated by Macron, Habermas and other social democrats and neoliberals.[12]

Although mentioning climate change, Streeck and others like Perry Anderson have not yet fully considered the impact of environmental factors. Perry Anderson, for example, provides a sharp historical survey of former American foreign policy debates but does not even mention the fact that US Pentagon analysts are now trying to devise strategies to either prevent or cope with catastrophic climate breakdown.[13] If EU 'carbon capitalism' currently depends on the Russian gas pipeline on one side, and supporting US military interventions in the Middle East and other oil-rich regions on the other side, what happens in ten to twenty years' time when decarbonisation and the phasing out of petrol and diesel cars begins to undermine the present strategic importance of fossil-fuel based military and political economic policies?

Just as Polanyi completely misread how the UK became America's strongest global ally instead of his hoped-for socialist society under Attlee's Labour, so too, Streeck completely misconceives the capacity of Left 'national communitarian' movements to create a new world of 'regionalism' consisting of sovereign nations. If Streeck considers that the large European Union cannot overcome and survive global pressures from the US and China, then there is little hope for most small countries with so-called renewed 'democratic control' to successfully resist global capitalist investment, trade and currency pressures once they leave the Euro. Even *New Left Review* editorial board member and a leading anti-EU Lexiteer, Tariq Ali, acknowledged that the creation of regional entities of small states was utopian and that a *kleine staat* on its own wouldn't work in a German dominated European Union.[14]

Following the Brexit vote in June 2016, Streeck and other radical opponents of the EU fantasised about the dissolution of the existing EU into small national sovereign states and the eventual recreation of a new form of European anti-capitalist solidarity.[15] Given the reality of anti-socialist electorates that are also characterised by significant levels of racism, these small groups of the anti-EU radical Left live in a political bubble of illusory hope while hostile national electorates either cling to the existing undemocratic EU via mainstream parties or support Right-wing definitions of 'national sovereignty'.

After a decade of neoliberal austerity, no Left party has won a national election on its own, the closest being mild centre/Left coalitions in Portugal, Spain, Sweden, Denmark and the capitulating, now ex-Syriza government in Greece. Advocates of Lexit and other such Left anti-EU unrealistic scenarios of creating socialism forget that in order to have even a small chance of building 'socialism in one country' in a sea of global capitalist hostility, one must first have a powerful socialist movement rather than attempt to build it after a country has exited the Euro or the EU. Even Jeremy Corbyn's mass Momentum movement promoted an ecologically modernised, social democratic Labour agenda that was not that different to old pre-1980s versions of capitalism with a 'mixed economy'. This policy agenda is preferable to conservative austerity, but it is neither socialism nor secure on its own.[16]

In contrast to many over-optimistic radicals, Streeck is torn between wishing to "preserve the possibility of converting the remains of post-war social democracy into barricades against technocratic encroachment"[17] and knowing that this is mere 'tilting against the windmills' of the EU. It is a forlorn hope in a Europe where the Left is so weak, especially in the major northern EU countries. His pessimism shines through when he asks:

> Can a democratic renewal – a re-establishment of the primacy of democratic politics over the inherent dynamics of capitalist development – really be expected from a public no longer used to taking politics seriously…Under the spell of post-Fordist consumerism and post-

democratic politainment, how many people still believe that there can be collective goods worth fighting for?[18]

The notion of the de-democratisation of EU member states depends on the assumption that 'consolidation' policies are non-negotiable and that the state structures of the EU 'Hayekian state' are here for decades to come. Yet, after a mere decade of EU-wide austerity and the rise of anti-EU parties, the EU has exhausted much of its political capital. Given the rescue packages to avoid meltdown in 2020, it is most doubtful that the EU Council, Commission and ECB can afford the massive political cost of once again imposing harsh austerity in a future post-Covid-19 situation, especially after the political trauma and divisiveness caused by the 'medicine' dished out to Greece. As Che Guevara argued in the 1960s, US imperialism would not be able to cope with simultaneously combatting three or many Vietnams. The EU 'consolidation state' was already at death's door in 2020 even without two or three other EU countries engaged in a major conflict over debt.

DEMOCRATISING THE EU: IMPOSSIBLE DREAM OR WAY FORWARD?

I would now like to turn to contemporary political cultural debates concerning the conflict between 'capitalism and democracy'. Member countries of the EU collectively account for a considerable proportion of those countries in the world which still have representative democracies. The debate over whether the EU should be democratised or dissolved because it is de-democratising the national sovereignty of member states has global implications for the conflict between 'capitalism and democracy'. Many of the issues that divide the broad Left concerning the future policy trajectory of one of the largest capitalist regions in the world are addressed in the 2013 Habermas-Streeck exchange of views over the EU.[19] While the African Continental Free Trade Area (ACFTA) consists of 44 nations, a population of 1.2 billion and a collective GDP of around US$2.5 trillion that represents more nations and almost triple the population of the EU, it lacks the global political economic power and the elaborate supranational institutional arrangements of the EU. Conversely, India and China have populations that are larger than the 44 African countries but are nation states that, like the US and Japan, do not have to conform to multi-member treaties and regulations (such as the Stability and Growth Pact) that have restricted nation states within the EU.

As leading exponents of divisions over the EU, it is striking that Habermas and Streeck say virtually nothing about the climate emergency or other environmental issues and couch their respective arguments in the pre-environmentalist language of traditional political economy and critique. Although more of the Left now make references to the Green New Deal, this is hardly equivalent to a searching self-reflection on the continued relevance of mainstream and radical political economy. Despite being overtaken by recent events, at the heart of the Habermas/Streeck debate is not only a question of the future of Europe but competing visions of cosmopolitanism versus national control. The debate raises the following concerns: the practicality or utopianism of Habermas and other advocates of EU democratisation given the EU is extremely difficult to reform; the 'Hayekian state' as a new form of administrative fascism without the Nazi paraphernalia and terror; and whether Streeck's and other Left anti-EU political economic agendas are not only impractical but potentially dangerous in that they unintentionally bolster Right-wing nationalists and fascists.

Both Habermas and Streeck oppose neoliberalism and a single super-state based on a federal hierarchy. Both theorists favour giving a voice to national and local citizens. The difference is that Habermas and a range of Left democratising movements favour combinations of the local, national and a democratised EU in the form of shared power. These goals include ending the undemocratic EU institutions by giving greater decision-making power to the European Parliament and making the EU Commission directly accountable to the democratically elected Parliament. In contrast, Streeck and other Left radicals pursue a strategy of national democratising movements in opposition to the EU. Like many Eurosceptics of the Left and the Right, Streeck has long been an opponent of the EU Commission and ECB. Habermas, on the other hand, has argued for decades that Europe's protracted inequality, discrimination and the excesses of neoliberal policies cannot be resolved at a purely national level and necessitates a democratised post-national constellation in conjunction with local and national processes.[20] However, in his fear of rising nationalism, the halt to further EU integration prior to 2020 and an open split between northern and southern member states and western and eastern members, Habermas has in recent years aligned with a mixture of social democrats and neoliberals in order to rescue the EU project (including the need for a united EU defence force) against threats from Trump's America, Putin's Russia and China's growing power.[21] This is a significant departure from his former hopes for the EU of twenty years ago.

While Habermas has a long-term vision of a future democratic 'social Europe', Streeck shows that progress towards a 'social Europe' has not only failed to materialise but has regressed.[22] He also argues that Habermas's version of the feasible democratisation of the EU under the existing Community Method is utopian.[23] Mobilising Fritz Scharpf's analysis[24] that the current legal, institutional and political obstacles make the democratising project utterly impractical, Streeck also makes a valid critique of Habermas for thinking that the problem with the EU is one of combatting technocracy rather than capitalism. He also sees Habermas's project as dangerous, and elaborates by saying, "I am afraid that Habermas and his opportunistic friends in Brussels and Berlin will to the very end and beyond refuse to understand that their brand of Europeanism was, and is, a potent cause of the hostile parochialism that is so frighteningly proliferating even in the most liberal and internationalized countries of Europe."[25]

Crucially, Streeck is unable to provide any convincing answers to Habermas as to how a retreat to the nation can be a viable political economic strategy within the context of global capitalist pressures. Importantly, he is also unable to counter Habermas's valid insight that, nation states "already rest on the highly artificial form of solidarity among strangers that is generated by the legal status of citizen. Even in ethnically and linguistically homogeneous societies, national consciousness is not a natural phenomenon but an administratively promoted product of historiography, the media, universal conscription, and so forth."[26] Unfortunately, Streeck's post-2013 views have moved closer to the very 'organic' nationalist views that Habermas correctly drew attention to in their initial exchange.[27]

From an outsider's perspective, the problem with Habermas, Streeck, Scharpf and many other participants in the EU-wide debate over the European Union is that they all debated the future of Europe within the context of relatively 'normal' political conditions. Both sides in this debate acknowledge climate change but generally ignore the much wider and deeper implications of the ecological unsustainability of the EU's political economy of incessant growth. Like many within the broad Left, all their arguments and plans for further democratisation or a retreat to the nation state in order to solve debt problems, disparities among member states in terms of standard of living, growth rates, social welfare and so forth, ultimately rest on very shaky environmental foundations. This will be discussed in detail in Book Three of this book.

Leaving aside the impact of future environmental factors for now, we know from past history that major institutional reform is not a smooth process. It usually occurs as a consequence of severe political economic crises that make the old order untenable and obsolete. Although early days, as a result of the shock waves caused by Covid-19 we are already seeing a loosening of formerly rigid and hostile attitudes to EU reform. Across Europe there have been many previous discussions and manifestos over the past two decades demanding the democratisation of the EU.[28] These range from calls for a new unitary European republic, a new European Assembly with taxing powers, to variations of federalism, joint power-sharing at local, regional and supra-national level and other such democratic reforms.[29] Most of these proposals not only call for a radical transformation of existing EU institutions, but also for an overhaul of the secrecy and undemocratic forms of rule at national and local levels. Ultimately, all proposals for democratising the EU in recent years have failed not because of many fine ideals, but because they continue to lack the active support of major mainstream parties in key EU member countries.

By contrast, most anti-EU Leftists fail to outline how a post-EU could enhance democracy and equality in a Europe that is based on fragmented nation states that lack the capacity to be independent of Germany or the other global powers. While they direct most of their criticisms against the 'Hayekian state', they inexplicably leave the many undemocratic constitutions, electoral processes and decrepit institutional practices *at national level* relatively uncriticised. In focusing mainly on the EU, they largely de-emphasise the leading role of nationally elected governments in helping the EU to impose and sustain class-based austerity policies.

WHY THE EU IS NOT FASCIST

Like Karl Polanyi, Streeck is preoccupied with the threat of authoritarianism, whether from the 'Hayekian state' or from anti-EU neo-fascist nationalists. He rightly warns about the widespread attraction of business leaders to authoritarian regimes in Asia and why the institutional structure of the EU was deliberately designed to immunise political decisions from democratic control. Nonetheless, in an eagerness to paint the EU as unremittingly bad, Streeck enters dangerous territory with his claims about the new form of 'fascism'. Why, Streeck asks,

> is it so difficult, in spite of a veritable plethora of alarming symptoms, for people to understand the crisis of contemporary democracy and

take it as seriously as it deserves? Too many, I believe, still cling to the traditional, putsch-like view of democracy being abolished: elections cancelled, opposition leaders and dissenters in prison or forced into exile or murdered, TV stations taken over by storm troopers – the Argentinian or Chilean model. There are also the strong voluntaristic illusions associated with democratic institutions, as imprinted on people in civics lessons: that as long as "we" can speak up and throw out the rascals at the ballot box, "we the people" are responsible for the condition of our community.[30]

In order to understand the shifting paradigm of 'capitalism versus democracy' in its contemporary form, a few brief responses are necessary. First, Streeck has good reason to be concerned with the trend of relinquishing democratic control to unelected EU officials but his wider argument tends to be exaggerated and misleading. Either the use of the ballot box and the political contestation of EU policies by social movements and parties are repressed by outright fascist rule, or else democratic action and rights persist. The European Parliament may be largely toothless, but EU institutions are not completely immunised from the democratic political conflicts within member states. It is easy to show that the ballot box is a poor substitute for the lack of widespread democratisation of civic institutions and workplaces in member countries. Conspicuously, like so many on the Left who hold ambivalent attitudes towards parliamentary democracy, Streeck is inconsistent here. He either attacks democracy as entertainment ('politainment') or praises national elections as the means of resistance against the 'Hayekian state'.

While Europeans should actively struggle against the erosion of democratic decision-making, 'politainment' is prevalent precisely because de-democratisation by the EU is not seen to be any greater than the anti-democratic domestic practices of many national governments. As to the differentiation between 'politainment' and taking politics 'seriously', one never knows the boundaries between these two public and private concepts, attitudes and practices. Take for example, the massive protests in Hong Kong in 2019-2020 where tens of thousands of people who were formerly preoccupied with their private lives, popular culture and subscribed to so-called 'politainment', mobilised into daily battles with police and the government when the real threat of de-democratisation called for urgent action. It is notable that the centre-Right politicians and business leaders across the world who praised the Hong Kong protestors for months of city-wide disruption were the same people who condemned the much smaller and briefer actions of Extinction Rebellion groups or the 'Black Lives Matter' protests in the US.

Secondly, during the 2016 Brexit referendum campaign, future Prime Minister, Boris Johnson, compared the EU to Hitler's desire to create a European super-state.[31] Streeck also articulates a analogous view and virtually declares that the EU 'Hayekian state' is a quasi-fascist or potential fascist state without storm troopers.[32] It is instructive to return briefly to Polanyi. In 1934, he argued that fascism "arises out of the mutual incompatibility of Democracy and Capitalism in a fully developed industrial society."[33] Polanyi confronted the real violent fascists but Streeck trivialises fascism and the brutal power of authoritarian regimes by equating the latter with EU institutions. Asian authoritarian governments also use the same style of argument by trivialising democracy. Universal democratic values are dismissed as 'Western' and hence 'not suitable' for the Asian authoritarian notions of 'democracy'. Streeck also dismisses universal values. In contrast to many Left critics of neoliberalism, his anti-capitalist alternative is strictly a democratically controlled economy within national borders. Not for him a socialist internationalism or a socialist Europe that involves shared supranational democratic decision-making within multicultural societies.

Thirdly, Joseph Schumpeter, another theorist admired by Streeck, had two attitudes to democracy. The first attitude was contempt for the masses which the undemocratic EU Commission incessantly replicates on a daily basis. The other attitude was Schumpeter's belief that unlike fascists and Communists, the bourgeoisie could not discipline intellectuals because this would entail the suppression of freedom and critical practices – values that the bourgeoisie admired.[34] Either the 'Hayekian state' is a fascist state in new clothes that suppresses democratic freedoms, or else it will tolerate democracy as a necessary condition to prevent the disintegration of the EU. Given the close interaction between the EU and the domestic politics of member countries, it is highly unlikely that the EU would be able to persistently defy and continually over-rule democratic decisions made at national level (like the treatment of the Greek electorate in 2015), without major political crises in the EU as a whole.

The distinction between 'liberal democracy' and 'illiberal democracy' in countries such as Poland and Hungary, let alone the full suspension of democratic politics, continues to cause significant tension within the EU. So too, does the EU's tolerance and financial support of authoritarian repression in Turkey in order to stem the flow of refugees into Europe. There is a long history of Western parliamentary democracies supporting authoritarian regimes in developing countries in the name of stopping Communism, terrorism or national liberation movements. Yet, in his cavalier equation of the EU with authoritarian regimes, Streeck is repeating a new version of the disastrous policy of 'social fascism' (1928-1935) when Communists were instructed to attack social democrats as a 'soft version' of fascism; the main beneficiary of the theory of 'social fascism' were the real fascists led by Hitler.

While there is some truth in Streeck's characterisation of contemporary democracy as 'politainment', he nevertheless fails to address the deeper connection of the relationship of democracy to contemporary capitalism. In the 1960s, during the Cold War, political sociologist, Seymour Lipset and other modernisation theorists waived the American flag and argued that there was a direct relationship between economic development and democracy, especially how the acquisition of material goods (cars, phones, appliances) helped foster parliamentary democracy.[35] The opposite is the case today. Capitalists are deeply divided between those who are attracted to more authoritarianism and others seeing economic benefits from greater democracy. From the point of view of many influential business leaders and political commentators, capitalist economic development within OECD countries is now driven by democracy. According to this view, innovation, creativity and productive engagement are best achieved in tolerant cities, attracting the so-called 'creative class'[36]and in societies where there is full democracy and civil rights. Hence the familiar argument that China and Russia, for example, have managed middle-income status through authoritarian measures but will never become high income societies unless they democratise.[37]

Moreover, a number of pro-market policy analysts argue that democratising societies also increase their growth rates.[38] If this pro-capitalist argument holds, why would policymakers in the EU jeopardise growth rates and international competitiveness, especially in new high-tech sectors, by de-democratising their member states? After all, in strictly Hayekian terms, the critique of central planning rests on a rejection of the state's need to control all information, knowledge and social activity. The desire of the EU or 'Hayekian state' to control national economies at supranational level is perhaps only the desire to suppress anti-capitalist activity. If this is the case, how can this selective goal be achieved without also suppressing all democratic activity? Many business leaders in new innovative digital technology areas argue that a critical education rather than an authoritarian education is needed to foster adventurous minds and workforces capable of independent thinking. Such a critical education system cannot be introduced or sustained without mass social and democratic freedoms.

In other words, a certain proportion of business and political leaders argue that without democratic institutions, European capitalism will not be able to avoid a future of economic stagnation, alongside simmering social tensions and the likelihood of explosive political eruptions. Whether democratic or authoritarian rule will save capitalist growth is both dubious and myopic. For both of these perspectives and related policies will still inevitably confront the per capita, national and EU-wide material footprints created by incessant affluent growth – material footprints that will far exceed the finite natural resources of the planet and will therefore prove to be unsustainable. This ecological constraint has still not been adequately grasped by many Keynesians and Marxists who oppose neoliberal policies while ignoring how these environmental limitations will affect their own alternative policies.

LEFT NATIONALISM AND NEO-FASCISM: SIMILAR OR DIFFERENT?

Analysing responses to the crisis in Europe since 2008, sociologist Claus Offe characterises the policy disputes over the push toward more capitalism or more democracy as:

- more austerity *versus* tax increases for high income earners and on wealth assets;
- more deregulation and flexible labour markets *versus* public support for the unemployed, poverty relief and social assistance;
- more reduction of debt via public sector cuts and savings *versus* EU-wide tax harmonisations and tighter bank regulation;
- more privatisation of public assets *versus* massive public sector growth stimulation;
- more undemocratic legislation via the ECB, the European Council and the Troika *versus* the latter being placed under the control of the European Parliament.[39]

Offe then divides political attitudes towards the EU into two pro- and two anti-EU blocs. Those supporting further European integration through EU institutions desire this for opposing reasons. Neoliberals favour integration for 'market-making' reasons, that is breaking down national economic rigidities and social protection negatively affecting companies in the Euro-wide market. On the other hand, Left-of-centre reformers advocate 'market constraining' goals such creating a genuine 'social Europe' and democratising institutions in order to roll-back and control the destructive power of market forces.

As for the anti-EU political bloc, this is also divided on the Right and Left between 'anti-integrationist populists' defending identity and socio-economic interests behind national borders, and the 'anti-European hard Right' which is disunited because its economic liberalism is in tension with its ethno-nationalism.[40] Offe also sees a 'renationalisation of class conflict' on the Left and points to Streeck as a prominent exponent of a 'non-nationalist' strategy to resist the imposition of neoliberal policies on member countries.[41] Seven years later, Offe's differentiation of Streeck's and other 'non-nationalist' views on immigration and cosmopolitanism from the views articulated by the ethno-nationalist Right looks both premature and far less clear cut.

Obviously, Streeck's advocacy of national sovereignty, like that of Mélenchon and British Lexiteers is not Right-wing nationalism.[42] He warns that "politicization is migrating to the right side of the political spectrum where anti-establishment parties are getting better and better at organizing discontented citizens dependent upon public services and insisting on political protection from international markets."[43] Yet, on the other hand, anti-neoliberal 'non-nationalism' now risks becoming *de facto* racism. The defence of the 'social state' within national borders has witnessed Streeck's increasingly strident language and concepts of anti-multiculturalism and anti-cosmopolitanism make him and other so-called Left 'non-nationalists' attractive to explicit neo-fascist ethno-nationalists. (see later discussion).

Take, for example, the 'non-nationalist' critique of neoliberalism. Streeck is not a class analyst and instead invokes an old and an updated version of *volk*. The new distinction, as we saw earlier, is between a *staatvolk* of citizens losing out to a *marktvolk* of international bankers and bondholders. There is no doubt that financialisation has given more power to bankers than to ordinary citizens under neoliberal governments. However, these homogenous concepts ignore the fact that citizens or *staatvolk* have always been fragmented socially along class, race, gender and other political divisions. Similarly, *marktvolk* eliminates major political economic differences between national and international businesses and reduces the latter to a *volk* that all supposedly pursue the same policies to 'wayward' Greek, Spanish or other *staatvolk*.

At one level, it is true that major French, Italian, Dutch or German based businesses tend to adopt European perspectives rather than parochial local or old national interests. However, what appears simplistically as a conflict between *staatvolk* and *marktvolk* is in fact much more entangled and complicated. After the EU and the IMF bailed out French and German bank loans to Greece between 2011 and 2012, about 85% of Greek debt was owed not to the *marktvolk* of private bankers and bondholders but to other European governments and the IMF. Also, many European banks were engaged in reckless behaviour worse than even the scandalous practices of American financial institutions.[44] The fear of a Greek default on loans was seen as a potential cause of a major European depression if the contagion of bank defaults spread to larger countries such as France, Italy, Spain and other countries.[45] Importantly, not all the so-called Greek, Spanish, Italian or other *staatvolk* were punished in order to help foreign banks. A proportion of the middle-class could minimise their suffering (by sending money abroad, etc.) compared with workers and their families (the main part of the *staatvolk*) who bore the full brunt of savage cuts.

Also, Streeck's *staatvolk* are not always diametrically opposed to *marktvolk*. These concepts obscure the fact that pension funds and sovereign wealth funds exercise significant power in equity markets and as bondholders of both government and private corporate debt. An OECD report in 2019 showed that the total world GDP was US$85.9 trillion and pension assets in OECD countries alone held US$42.5 trillion in assets of which equities and bonds were the largest holdings.[46] The de facto *part-privatisation* of welfare in many countries in recent decades has meant that the boundaries between the direct and indirect interests of the so-called *staatvolk* and *marktvolk* are blurred. As major players in financial markets, the managers of pension funds represent the savings of tens of millions of pensioners and workers (the so-called *staatvolk*). They often pursue similar policies and strategies to the managers of private banks, hedge funds and insurance companies (*marktvolk*), that is, maximising capital and income returns on equities, bonds, property and other asset classes. Financialisation has been remarkably effective in changing the political culture and material interests of millions of employees so that they too are also now worried about equity markets and potential government bond defaults, a preoccupation that once belonged to a minority of high income and wealthy investors.

Paradoxically, Streeck's fear of Hayekian authoritarianism can be seen to mirror the panic generated by far-Right parties. These racist politicians and sections of the media constantly beat the drums of fear about foreigners invading 'our land' and taking jobs. Streeck also beats the same drums, but for different reasons. At one level, he argues against ethno-nationalists who want to create separate ethnically homogenous states because they create divisions and violence. Instead, he favours 'national nationalism' in which smaller states establish institutional independence from larger entities, for example, the Catalans vis-à-vis Spain.[47] However, these lines are very blurry as many of the demands of ethno-nationalists overlap with non-ethno 'national nationalists'. Streeck argues for 'cultural homogeneity' but this is often virtually indistinguishable from ethno-nationalism. What does 'cultural homogeneity' mean for significant minorities, such as Russians in Latvia, Chinese in Indonesia, English in Scotland or Palestinians in Israel? Also, using the Nordic countries as models, he claims that small states are supposedly more supportive of democratic and egalitarian values, less threatening to their neighbours and strong supporters of international peaceful relations. Of course, one cannot compare affluent Sweden with Lebanon or Rwanda.

It is not population size that counts but levels of material wealth, location within regions of conflict and access to either financial and product markets or having natural and intellectual resources for greater self-sufficiency. On all these scores, Streeck presents a highly misleading picture. Although claiming to be uninterested in an ideal concept of size, Streeck develops all his political arguments around the virtues of small states and calculates the median population size of 193 UN member countries as 8.4 million. Yet, this figure fails to show the much more complex picture of the relation between large and small nation states. On population alone, the top sixty countries range from giants such as China on 1,433 million followed by dozens of countries ranging from between 40 million to over 200 million, including another group with 20 to 30 million people such as Burkina Faso. The next 30 countries range from Mali on 19 million to Sweden with 10 million. It is only when we get to the smallest third of countries with populations ranging from 9 million to numerous island states with thousands of people that we get a sense of the differences between tiny, exceedingly small, small, medium large and gigantic states.

Political scale therefore has quite different consequences today when compared to earlier historical periods. One does not have to go back to imperial city states of Athens and Rome to make this point. Take, for example, the history of imperial domination by 'small states' such as The Netherlands, Belgium and Portugal that lasted through the twentieth century until the 1970s. To divide the virtues of nation-states according to their size is to romanticise 'small' and ignore the violence and resistance to political attempts to break-up larger entities. For instance, the Federal Republic of Nigeria is the largest country in Africa with a population over 202 million. Like other former colonies, its boundaries and institutions were artificially created by British imperialists and since independence in 1960 has continued to suffer civil war between some of its 250 ethnic groups. To give autonomy or full independence to some or all tribal, religious or territorially based secular sections of the population may sound theoretically reasonable to advocates of small states. Under prevailing political economic and cultural conditions any such break away or granting of relative autonomy could possibly constitute a green light to major violence.

ANTI-COSMOPOLITANISM AND NATIONAL SOCIAL DEMOCRACY

Like many other Left nationalists, Streeck also displays an obsessive dislike of cosmopolitanism which he crudely and erroneously equates with neoliberal globalism.[48] Globalisation and multiculturalism, he argues, are incompatible with national social democracy. Far too many Left critics of the 'Hayekian state' fail to see that neoliberalism does not simply take the form of anti-nationalist globalisation. There are also many different champions of national conservative politics across the world that combine neoliberal policies and nationalism, either in its racist or non-racist versions. Left nationalists like Streeck focus on the EU but says little about the racism and the anti-democratic character of many small to medium businesses as well as significant sections of blue-collar and unskilled workers who also support anti-immigrant nationalist parties.

Apart from blaming neoliberalism for the upsurge in Right-wing parties, Streeck appears oblivious to the fact that his anti-cosmopolitanism has a strong and *unintentional* affinity with Nazi-era conservative authoritarian, Carl Schmitt and current liberal critics of immigration and globalisation such as David Goodhart who divides people into those who identify with 'somewhere' as opposed to others who can live 'anywhere'.[49] Remember that it was Hitler who originally articulated this theme in a speech on November 10th, 1933. Without using the word 'Jews', Hitler denounced a small rootless international 'clique' of people "who are at home both nowhere and everywhere, who do not have anywhere a soil on which they have grown up, but who live in Berlin today, in Brussels tomorrow, Paris the day after that, and then again in Prague or Vienna or London."[50] Despite fleeing the Nazi regime, Alexander Rüstow – who coined the term 'neoliberalism' – also succumbed to overgeneralised stereotypes of 'domineering rootless nomads' subjugating settled agrarian communities.[51] Similarly, pro-Nazi Carl Schmitt contrasted mobile sea-faring peoples with those tied to the land. Political theorist, Wendy Brown, observes that: "Schmitt's wariness of seafaring people but also of denationalisation is palpable: loss of ground entails loss of boundary and horizon, loss of ties to the local across time, loss of the primacy of family, tradition, religion. Blood and soil indeed."[52]

According to Brown, however incompletely and problematically, Schmitt "anticipates the experience of globalisation by Goodhart's 'somewheres' for whom attachments to nation, family, property, and whiteness are mobilized as a politically reactionary formation."[53] The 'somewheres' rage against secular cosmopolitanism, open borders, godlessness and rootlessness. They espouse a toxic mix of resentment against neoliberal assaults on their social life and also a nihilist fatalism. In short:

> The somewheres cling to the soil, even if it is planted in suburban lawn devastated by droughts and floods from global warming, littered with the paraphernalia of addictive painkillers, and adjacent to crumbling schools, abandoned factories, terminal futures. Families become shells, ownership and savings vanish, marriages teeter and break, depression, anxiety, and other forms of mental illness are ubiquitous, religion is commercialized and weaponized, and patriotism is reduced to xenophobic support for troops in aimless, endless wars and useless, but spectacular border barricades. Nation, family, property, and the traditions reproducing racial and gender privilege, mortally wounded by deindustrialization, neoliberal reason, globalization, digital technologies, and nihilism, are reduced to affective remains. To date, these remains have been activated mostly by the Right. What kinds of Left political critique and vision might reach and transform them?[54]

It is certainly not the political critique mounted by Streeck and other Left-of-centre perspectives in OECD countries such as 'Blue Labour' or those policies promoted by some conservative trade unions. These traditional defences of national working-class interests do tap into a genuine concern about the negative impact of neoliberal globalisation on communities, wage conditions, underfunded welfare services and local employment. Jonathan Rutherford, co-founder of Britain's Blue labour, articulates this Left nationalism well. Citing Streeck approvingly, Rutherford observes:

What the peripheral spaces, ex-industrial areas and provincial regions share are strong local bonds of community at risk from the loss of old ways of life. People fear the destruction of meaning and purpose in their lives. Their reaction is giving shape to a politics that is radical in standing for economic justice and redistribution, and conservative in yearning for a common culture and more, not less, national democratic sovereignty. The left has lost its connection to them and a radical right takes advantage with its stories of ethnic loss and white identity.[55]

However, it is the conservative defence of essentially white communities – whether dressed up in Left or Right concepts – that is incompatible with multicultural societies. At the political-cultural level, Streeck's preference for the old concept of 'national people' over classes or other social distinctions is quite disturbing as it is difficult to distinguish 'national social democracy' from fascist notions of ethno-nationalism or mono-culturalism. While it is abundantly clear that Streeck prefers a more culturally homogenous society and is extremely critical of multicultural societies,[56] a world based on homogenous nations either never existed in former culturally mixed empires or was a rarity within capitalist countries. It is impossible to create such a world of small nation states short of imposing cultural political exclusivity or violent mass ethnic cleansing. Given that Streeck is strongly opposed to fascist ethno-nationalism, it is unclear how a 'culturally homogenous society' either differs from ethno-nationalism or could possibly come into being. If it is not language, race or religion, how is 'cultural homogeneity' constructed that is different to Right-wing definitions? Take for example, the neo-fascist anti-multiculturalist Stephen Pax Leonard writing about Sweden:

Sweden has gone from being a country that had a eugenics programme to ensure that the State would not have to give financial support to the 'unfit', to a country that has actively promoted immigration from the least developed countries in the world. It represents a 180-degree swing from the radical right to the radical left...Multiculturalism might be perceived as a reversal of an historic event. The Nazis promoted racial superiority where Arabs were at the bottom of the ladder. Sweden's current policy is the diametrical opposite of this, and thus one might call it anti-Nazist.[57]

Now compare Streeck (without the fascist language) who has long openly opposed not just open borders but immigration as a threat to 'stable democracy'. In 1992, he argued that cultural diversity and open borders would undermine an associative democracy and lead to the market rather than the state determining policies.[58] As an intellectual argument against open borders, many share Streeck's concern about the stability of democracy. However, Streeck is opposed to immigration even without open borders. Canada and Australia as the 10th and 13th largest capitalist economies respectively invalidate his parochialism. Although not having open borders, these countries have shown, contra Streeck, that explicitly state-driven multicultural policies can function as stable democratic societies. A majority of Australia's population was either born abroad or has at least one parent born abroad, and Canada also has approximately 40% of people with similar backgrounds. In Australia's case, there is political division over the shameful incarceration and abuse of boat refugees rather than any majority support or desire to abandon multiculturalism and create Streeck's 'homogenous culture'.

Like many ethno-nationalists, but without their overt racism, Streeck argues that "the more heterogeneous a national population is, the bloodier is the history of (successful or failed) attempts to unify it".[59] Hence, he supports small nationalist movements such as the Catalans, Scots and Corsicans that he sees as alternatives to the EU superstate as well as to large nation-states such as France or Spain.[60] However, contrary to Streeck and other similar Left national dreamers, sovereignty movements in Catalonia, Scotland, Flanders and elsewhere have long pre-dated the Euro. Most of these national independence movements do not share Streeck's anti-EU position and see their future as members of the so-called EU 'Hayekian state' rather than as parochial nationalist enclaves.

Whether inside the EU or not, it is utopian to think that a plethora of small nations will foster greater socio-economic cooperation and socialist agendas when most of these nationalist movements are led by non-radicals or conservative nationalists. Importantly, none of these small nations are ethnically homogenous societies and are fully integrated into the global capitalist culture industries which have long fused with or subordinated local 'national cultures' to trends, fashions and celebrity consumption. Local non-American English and non-English film, literature, theatre and other cultural processes struggle to survive in most countries against Hollywood and Netflix.

More alarmingly, and unlike other Left anti-neoliberals, Streeck fluctuates between seeing nations as complex historically manufactured societies that are based on citizenship rather than descent, and yet subscribing to the mythology of an organic 'national consciousness'. Hence, he proclaims:

> Nations are communities of understanding, of shared deep-seated convictions as to what is 'natural', 'reasonable', 'ethical', 'self-evident' and the like. In Europe this includes people's views of what 'Europe' is and what it is good for and what it should and should not be. Each country sees this differently. If this is not recognized there can be no peace in Europe, and I mean this very seriously.[61]

Streeck's 'national peoples' are difficult to distinguish from national stereotypes of what the 'French', 'Germans', 'Italians' or other 'national people' think or believe. Tell that to the English, for example, who have torn each other apart over Brexit. Even more damning is a 2015 interview in which he stated: "The monstrous currency union must be unravelled, so that Europe is not transformed into *a swamp of multinational mutual recrimination, with open borders and in danger of being flooded at any time from outside.*"[62] Consequently, Streeck defended the harsh treatment of refugees by countries such as Hungary which, he claimed, were 'scapegoated' because they were only implementing Schengen border rules and protecting their national sovereignty![63] Tellingly, Streeck does not directly attack any specific immigrant group. In his emphasis on protecting workers' wages and conditions, he displays strong hostility to both refugees and immigration (often lumping these together), thereby reproducing an old-fashioned social-democratic nationalist position. Streeck is partially correct to note that many German business leaders and the government saw letting in refugees as a 'backdoor' immigration policy dressed up as 'cosmopolitan humanitarianism'. Yet, his analysis is notable for the absence of even a single sentence expressing any sympathy for the plight of refugees, the most helpless and powerless people fleeing war and deprivation.

According to Streeck, 'collectivism' "can exist only as particularism, today predominantly invested in nation-states and national politics."[64] Hence the Left has abandoned 'collectivism' to the Right in favour of anti-racism and anti-nationalism. Adhering to a nationalist concept of 'collectivism' led Streeck to argue that 'socialism' must be distinguished from so-called 'liberal cosmopolitanism'. In 2018, he supported the attempt by what he called the 'realist' faction in *Die Linke Party* that advocated curbs on immigration and refugees in order to win back workers turning to the Right-wing *Alternative für Deutschland*. The majority of *Die Linke* (labelled 'sectarian' by Streeck) refused to support this tactic that would have legitimised racism. In response, he declared that:

> Devising a socially just immigration policy would also require
> breaking out of a mode of discussion that in the name of being 'open
> to the world' declares fellow citizens, with whom we had previously
> lived together peacefully, to be Nazis and racists simply because, while
> they may be prepared to share the collective goods they have strug-
> gled for and that they finance with their taxes, they do not want those
> goods to be declared morally liable to being expropriated.[65]

However, the notion that one or two million, or even possibly five million refugees in the future, comprising less than one per cent of the 508 million people in the EU (prior to Brexit), could 'flood' the whole of the EU and 'expropriate' working class 'collective goods' is testimony to the fact that Streeck's ideas can be seen to tap into racist ethno-nationalist sentiments. Compare the whole of the EU with tiny Lebanon (population approximately 6 million) which has taken 1.5 million Syrian refugees alone, or equal to 25% of its citizens. The fact that small EU countries were overwhelmed with refugees is not evidence of cultural 'flooding from outside', but rather the deliberate obstruction by EU member countries to prevent an orderly and proportionate settlement of refugees for barely disguised Islamophobic racist reasons. The choice is not between unregulated 'open borders' or 'walls' against refugees in the name of 'worker solidarity' against the Right.[66] Streeck appears to forget how *Gastarbeiter* ('guest workers') from southern Europe were treated in the 1960s and 1970s. It is important to remember that they were Europeans rather than the 'dreaded' Middle Eastern and African 'other' yet were ghettoised in Germany and other northern countries and treated as inferiors by racist, economistic decision-makers and many local citizens.

DANGEROUS BEDFELLOWS

Although Streeck is hostile to conventional patriotic and nationalist ideolo-gies, it is his unremitting criticisms of cosmopolitanism and multiculturalism that have made him attractive to fascists. Analysing the triumph of Donald Trump, Streeck falls back on conservative clichés about cities being the preserve of pro-immigrant, multicultural cosmopolitans who advance the interests of the neoliberal cosmopolitan elites while deindustrialised rural areas fall victim to ruthless market forces. Even the white middle class, he observes in 'shock and horror', can no longer afford ever-rising urban rents and have to live in areas with growing communities of immigrants.[67] In increasingly hyperbolic tones, Streeck argues that globalisation erodes traditional class solidarity and replaces it with neoliberal cosmopolitan 're-education dictatorships' that deem national protection as culturally reactionary.[68]

It is true that Trump won a clear majority in rural and small regional towns. This in itself is not sufficient reason to homogenise the cultures of cities and rural areas. Very importantly, Streeck rejects the old Marxian recognition that capitalism was also a progressive cosmopolitan force against prejudice, parochialism and old hierarchies. Instead, he argues that "the urban middle classes, economically dependent on a rich supply of cheap service labour, favour open borders for immigration."[69] This is an insult to the millions of non-middle-class workers who did not vote for Trump's racist attacks on immigrants and is also based on a very narrow concept of class interest. It is at odds with the long tradition of generations of Marxists who argued that class-consciousness was not nationalist but rather promoted altruistic values for all humanity instead of narrow self-interest that pitted local workers against foreign workers.

There is no doubt that the divisions amongst wage workers over immigration will grow in many countries if socio-economic hardship caused by neoliberal policies exacerbates existing inequalities and millions of refugees continue to flee countries due to war, poverty and the impact of climate breakdown. Streeck's narrow concept of class interest reduces the conflict between 'democracy and capitalism' to 'national interest'. He is completely at odds with millions of people in the US, Europe, Australia and many other countries, especially young people, who are not part of the 'global elite' but who live in both cities and rural areas and continue to value tolerance, multiculturalism and global connections.

Despite being criticised in the past for ignoring gender, race and multicultural identities, Streeck continually reverts to form and fails to recognise that women, blacks, LGBTI groups not only have identities of their own, but are also all part of the contemporary working class predominantly employed in the service sector. Take away all these private and public service sector workers and we are left with just a small minority of the total workforce who belong to the old, largely white male industrial working class.[70] He mocks Left internationalists who supposedly 'de-democratise capitalism' by advocating cosmopolitan values.[71] At the same time he denies the reality that most European, North American, Latin American and Asian-Pacific countries are not culturally homogenous. Those old social democrats who desire a post-neoliberal future based on preserving countries as culturally homogenous national social democracies dream of a future that is both unattainable and a backward-looking, long-gone world. In their critique of Streeck and other leaders of *aufstehen* ('stand up') or what they call 'pop-up populism', Quinn Slobodian and William Callison observe that "he has also missed one of the New Left's central lessons: capitalism-in-action creates new victims as it creates new agents. Giving up on the young and urban, the educated but underemployed, the paperless and the stateless means falling back to the same problems that sank the old left: seeking salvation only from the factory floor when the material base for that kind of politics no longer exists."[72]

Left nationalist movements such as Jean-Luc Mélenchon's *La France Insoumise*, Streeck's *aufstehen* or Blue Labour and Lexit failed. Similar future movements are unlikely to succeed by directly or indirectly attacking 'cosmopolitanism' and immigrants, even if they deny they are anti-immigrants.[73] Better to campaign for the removal of restrictions on trade unions and for more regulations and inspectors to outlaw and prosecute the low-wage and quasi-slave labour exploitation of both immigrant and locally born labour by businesses, than attack the victims of this widespread abuse across the world. Any future possibility of subordinating capitalism to democratic control has far more chance of being successful if Left parties defend multiculturalism rather than retreating to narrow, unviable and undemocratic fortresses or fictitious monocultural nations. Critiquing 'socialism in one country' and other such Left anti-globalisation and anti-EU positions, Matthew Bishop and Anthony Payne argue that: "socially, a supposedly progressive nationalism as expressed through Lexit is potentially just as regressive as its right-wing variant, particularly when it comes to questions of migration and free movement, the negative consequences of which threaten to fall in painfully racialised ways on the non-white working classes."[74]

In 2015, and a few years before Streeck's increasingly strident attacks on 'cosmopolitanism', the avowed fascist white supremacist, Donald Thoresen, in a glowing review of *Buying Time,* highly recommended Streeck's book to his fascist readers as a work that could help the White supremacist nationalist cause.[75] One cannot always blame an author for the way others use their work. We have all had the experience of being surprised by various interpretations of our writing. However, given current social tensions and hostility to immigrants and refugees in Europe, America and many other regions, it is all the more important not to use concepts or values that are associated with racist and Right-wing nationalist movements. When Streeck concluded in 2013 that the greatest threat to Europe was not nationalism but Hayekian market liberalism,[76] how wrong he was in minimising the nationalist threat.

Streeck may have been correct to point out how the Euro straitjacket exacerbated national divisions inside the EU. However, it is not the Euro alone that is driving dangerous nationalist and racist policies across Europe, as the reactionary politics outside the Eurozone in Denmark, Sweden, the UK, the US, Japan, Australia and many other countries attest. In such a climate, one cannot consistently attack identity politics or 'cosmopolitanism' in the name of national 'working classes' and not be aware that the historical roots of anti-cosmopolitanism go back to the anti-Semitism of the Nazis and Stalinists. These days, many Trump supporters and neo-fascists in Europe expand the notion of 'cosmopolitans' beyond Jews to include Muslims, feminists, blacks and LGBTI people. Indeed, the neo-fascist publisher *Arktos* has a growing list of books denouncing cosmopolitanism in a manner similar to Streeck's critique despite not sharing his socio-economic analysis.[77]

While Streeck's critique of the 'Hayekian state' has been valued by the Left, by contrast, his support for restrictions on immigration has been widely criticised. This anti-multiculturalism and championing of national solutions is a regressive position that should be challenged and disowned. Unfortunately, the editors of *New Left Review* have continued to endorse Streeck's views and by their silence are in danger of becoming *de facto* supporters of a regressive nationalism masquerading as a 'progressive Lexit'. Crucially, it is extremely difficult if not impossible for Left nationalists to compete with the nationalist Right on the latter's chosen terrain. Streeck and other Left anti-EU advocates of national sovereignty inadvertently or deliberately borrow the language of 'national rights' at the expense of more universal values. The end result is to unintentionally bolster parochialism and racist divisiveness. Left supporters of a democratic EU must not only battle Left and Right anti-EU nationalists, but they must also battle Right-wing post-national European federalists such as the neo-fascist Alain de Benoist who calls for a federal union of minority national 'European peoples' against foreign populations.[78] While the Covid-19 Pandemic has encouraged Left supporters of a democratised EU to push for major reforms such as a Green New Deal and EU-wide socio-economic rescue packages and greater co-operation,[79] opponents and sceptics such as Streeck still see the new crisis as leading to the collapse of the Euro and the old 'technocratic EU' project.[80] Should the collapse of the EU occur, a disunited Left within Europe will be ill-prepared to offer constructive alternatives.

CONCLUSION

In recent years, much fear has been expressed within the broad Left over whether neoliberal parties and governments have made informal pacts with neofascist movements in OECD countries and with authoritarian regimes in low and middle-income countries. We have already seen that beyond the current crises within the EU and other parts of the world, debt repudiation and low-carbon infrastructure will not resolve the monumental truth that environmentally destructive consumption and growth is dangerously histori-cally obsolete. This remains the case regardless of whether growth is gener-ated by 'democratically controlled' nations or by global neoliberals.

In 1909, the American philosopher, John Dewey, reflected on how diffi-cult it is to abandon old ways of thinking due to deeply engrained habits, aversions and preferences. Intellectual progress, he observed "usually occurs through sheer abandonment of questions together with both the alternatives they assume – an abandonment that results from their decreasing vitality and a change of urgent interest. We do not solve them: we get over them. Old questions are solved by disappearing, evaporating, while new questions corre-sponding to the changed attitude of endeavour and preference take their place."[81] From the 1970s onwards, 'new questions' were asked by neo-Marx-ists, anarchists and feminists such as Murray Bookchin, Beatrix Campbell, Elmar Altvater, Andre Gorz, Hilary Wainwright, Alain Lipietz, James O'Connor and many others. They all challenged the dominant paradigm and tried to integrate ecological issues into political economy. However, despite these valuable contributions, far too many philosophers, policy makers and political activists continue to pay lip service to environmental issues and are still locked into the old pre-environmentalist paradigm.

On the 200th anniversary of Karl Marx's birth in 2018, conferences were held globally, and many articles, books and media stories discussed his contri-bution and relevance to the twenty-first century. One such conference was held in Hamburg and presentations were made by prominent European and American social scientists such as Jens Beckert, Marion Fourcade, Axel Honneth, Greta Krippner, Thomas Piketty and Wolfgang Streeck.[82] Despite representing a range of diverse liberal social democratic and radical anti-capi-talist views, they shared one thing in common, namely, a *complete silence* on current environmental crises. None discussed whether Marx's analysis of capitalism was adequate to grasp the global dimensions and implications of these environmental crises on the future of capitalist market societies and whatever might possibly replace these unsustainable modes of production and consumption.[83] The attendees were aware of climate breakdown and supportive of measures to reduce carbon emissions. However, their theoretical frameworks disclosed a pre-environmental consciousness or, at best, a 'light green' conception of the relationship between eco-systems and social orders. Hence, issues of environmental sustainability were either ignored or relegated to the periphery of their central political economic, sociological and philosophical concerns.

On the other hand, there are Marxists who write detailed illuminating books on why Marx is relevant to contemporary environmentalists.[84] This is certainly much better than the embarrassing work of Leftists such as Roberto Unger who can write books entitled *The Left Alternative* without a single word on the environment crisis![85] Sadly, when it comes to alternative policy strategies, Marxists who wish to establish Marx's credentials as an environmentalist say little to advance the development of sustainable political economic policies despite their detailed studies of Marx's writings on nature. In short, we have to move well beyond the old textual disputes over Marx's writings on nature if we are going to develop the policies and political strategies necessary to achieve environmentally sustainable societies.

There are some neo-Marxists such as Joel Wainwright and Geoff Mann who attempt to grapple with environmental politics but are still trapped in the logic of old paradigms. They note that "no ecological Marxists have elaborated a theory of the likely political consequences of climate change. Indeed, in some works, the thorny question of the political is almost entirely evaded, except to say that capitalism must be transcended. But what if it isn't?"[86] This pertinent observation on the pre-environmental politics of many on the Left is unfortunately not remedied by their own work. Instead, they squeeze the politics of climate change into four inappropriate stereotypes: climate Leviathan, Behemoth, Mao and Climate X that are based on the theories of Hobbes, Hegel, Marx and Schmitt. Not only is this old theoretical framework too schematic and artificial, but Mann and Wainwright are barely able to recognise that ecological issues extend well beyond climate politics.

The vast majority of academics, policy makers, think tank specialists, and business and political leaders continue to work within the increasingly flawed and limited 'environment-free' paradigm of 'capitalism versus democracy'. Nonetheless, like millions of citizens, these policy analysts and business and political leaders are being forced to modify their conventional political economic perspectives and frameworks by integrating ecological factors. Most are yet to do so in a manner that is more than a cursory or token acknowledgement of the 'ecological'. It is highly paradoxical that Streeck and others who defend the 'historical institutionalist' approach and base their politics on the comparative study of national capitalist societies should borrow their concepts from evolutionary biology.[87] They may stress 'adaptation' and 'interaction', that is, the way particular capitalist societies evolve their own specific institutions and social relations in relation to international and national developments. Yet, they have a blind spot when it comes to crucial environmental issues relating to the biosphere and therefore ignore how these ecological factors will affect the future survival of existing socio-political practices, whether representative democracies or authoritarian systems.

I have attempted to show that the debates between defenders of market capitalism and anti-neoliberals (whether they are international 'cosmopolitans' or Left nationalists) are now in their last historical phase, as their respective positions are being rendered obsolete to a lesser or greater extent by unfolding environmental crises of unsustainability. It matters little whether one examines the policies of business organisations, mainstream political parties, trade unions or the platforms of radical Left parties. All largely ignore broader environment issues other than the immediately obvious issue of the climate emergency.[88] For business groups and their political allies, much uncertainty and fear govern their responses to the need for action to resolve ecological issues. It is clear that a proportion of businesses will not survive the necessary government regulations, increased taxes and social demands for a reorganisation of socio-economic practices. Those countries and industries highly dependent on fossil fuels or lacking the ability to innovate technologically will suffer from international competitors at the forefront of ecological modernisation. Unsurprisingly, businesses and governments are split on the issue of how much democratic intrusion or enterprise innovation is tolerable.

Very significantly, the division within the broad Left over an internationalist or nationalist strategy has been driven by what was perceived to be neoliberal global marketisation. This macro-political economic approach based on open borders and unregulated capital flows was already being seriously challenged before and after the crisis of 2008. Trump's 2016 election victory and the rise of Right-wing parties only added to the loss of confidence in free market solutions by many politicians and businesses. With the shutdown of economies in 2020, the closure of national borders and the recognition that vital goods are no longer made in many countries, it is highly likely that the old pre-Covid-19 'market globalisation' will be difficult to revive. Whether policy makers return to neo-Keynesian national-based policies, new forms of international trade and investment strategies or develop new hybrid solutions is unclear. What is clear, however, is that many of the arguments about the 'Hayekian state' and other related issues articulated by a pre-environmentally conscious Leftism has run its course.

Paradoxically, the widespread popularity of different versions of a Green New Deal both consolidates a pre-environmentalist notion of 'capitalism versus democracy' as well as helping to undermine this old political economic approach. Currently, we are witnessing the pursuit of Green New Deal programs that are conceived in either minimalist or maximalist programmatic terms. The 'minimalist' versions essentially promote ecological modernisation or 'green growth' within the larger paradigm of 'capitalism and democracy'. These are usually characterised by proposals that aim to sustain most of the existing socio-economic and political institutions by creating jobs, renewable energy, 'greening cities' and so forth. While these are preferable to prevailing fossil-fuel energy and production, ecological modernisation is a short-term band aid that is unsustainable without fundamental changes to consumption and production.

The 'maximalist' versions of Green New Deal signal major shifts to the dominant paradigm. How complex societies will produce their food, make and consume their goods and services, raise sufficient tax revenue, employ all who seek work so that policies combatting inequality and poverty are not short-term options but are durable and sustainable, all these and many other issues are still in their initial stages of development. Even within the 'maximalist' conception of a Green New Deal there is still a technological optimism combined with an inadequate political analysis. This tendency assumes that social justice goals and economic transformation may be easier to achieve despite the scale of environmental constraints and the obstacles posed by defenders of existing political economic institutions. What the 'maximalist' versions of Green New Deal signify is that the dominant paradigm is beginning to shift but is as yet not a fully developed project.

Importantly, significant numbers of people on the Left as well as in green movements continue to pay insufficient attention to an updated version of the old dilemma concerning the role of 'the people'. In earlier historical periods, conservative voting patterns were explained by radicals as 'false consciousness', the 'dominant ideology' and other reasons as to why there was mass opposition to socialist policies. Today, 'democracy versus socialism' has mutated into 'democracy versus sustainability', one of the central issues that I will discuss in Book Three. 'Capitalism versus democracy' was largely based directly and indirectly on notions of class conflict and how inequality of income, resources and political power shaped the character of capitalist societies. By contrast, the conflict between 'democracy and sustainability' is less clear-cut and more cross-class in its political economic and socio-cultural ramifications. It is precisely the way issues of environmental sustainability force us to rethink conventional politics that I will discuss in Book Three.

BOOK III

EMERGING NEW PARADIGM: DEMOCRACY VERSUS SUSTAINABILITY

INTRODUCTION TO BOOK THREE

THE DANISH PHILOSOPHER Søren Kierkegaard famously observed in 1843 that 'life can only be understood backwards; but it must be lived forwards.' This is particularly true of life in contemporary capitalist societies where the sheer pace of change makes it difficult to grasp the true impact of endlessly shifting local and international socio-political developments. A stark exception is that when it comes to deteriorating environments and escalating carbon emissions, no hindsight is needed to comprehend its disastrous consequences. We continue to live our lives 'forward' without altering our present-day forms of consumption and production, despite decades of repeated warnings.

BREAKING WITH CONVENTIONAL POLITICAL ANALYSIS

How do we free ourselves from the prison of the concepts and discourses that have helped shape our perceptions of the world? Any new political paradigm must initially use the language of the dominant paradigm before subverting it by asking new questions and moving toward different answers and conclusions. The issues of environmental sustainability force us to rethink conventional politics. While the conflict between 'capitalism and democracy' requires rethinking, as I have argued in the previous two parts of this book, it is being reshaped with new characteristics and inflections by the emergence of a more recent, related and urgent struggle between 'democracy and sustainability'. This final third part of the book proceeds to advance an 'internal' critique of conventional liberal and radical Left and green thinking about transitions to post-carbon democracy and post-capitalist societies. Without considering these new challenges, it will be exceedingly difficult for alternative movements to realise some or most of their political proposals.

The different conceptions of the compatibility or incompatibility of 'democracy and sustainability' are closely related to the historical level of capitalist development in particular countries. For instance, in South Korea, rapid industrialisation in the late twentieth century (under both repressive authoritarian and democratically elected governments) produced a debate from the 1980s onwards about different models of 'anti-ecological democracy' such as 'ecological authoritarianism' based on state-led ecological modernisation. Advocates of neoliberal 'ecological managerialism' rejected this strategy and instead favoured greater non-state or free market-based policies. Within the Korean context, 'anti-ecological democracy' was opposed by supporters of alternative pathways or forms of 'ecological democracy'. First, there was the 'welfare state ecologism' of those committed to making Korea similar to Sweden and other northern EU countries. The 'anti-ecological democrats' were also opposed by those who believed in 'ecological communitarianism and associationism'.[1] The latter position was conceived as agrarian self-sufficient communes or associations that would simultaneously reject capitalism, industrialism and welfare statism.

In some respects, Korean ecological agrarian communitarianism was a modern version of nineteenth century Slavophilism in which the Russian movement rejected both Western capitalism and modernist values. According to Gyu-seok Cheon, state welfare made self-sufficiency impossible and converted people into dependent beggars and slaves while 'community welfare' enabled self-management and self-reliance.[2] The affinity with some later Western ideas of degrowth self-sufficiency is notable. While these Korean debates also echoed similar debates in other OECD countries between authoritarian and democratic pathways to ecological sustainability, they were different to political divisions between 'green growth' and 'degrowth' movements. One reason is that until very recently, farm labour constituted more than 8% of the total labour force in South Korea compared to only 2% or less in Western capitalist countries. This kept alive the illusion of a possible transformation of capitalism into rural self-managed associations which are different to European and Australian urban-based degrowth movements. It is quite clear that like the Korean debates, other specific national debates will determine the future relationship between 'democracy and sustainability'.

If we are to move beyond the form and character of existing discussions of environmental issues, we must first identify the limits of much of the current analyses of ecological crises. For the past forty years, two key aspects have dominated: a) disputes over the socio-economic causes of these crises, especially analyses of the role of capitalist production and consumption; and b) disputes over how to solve these crises (especially the climate emergency) through a variety of technological innovations, fiscal measures such as carbon taxes, urban restructuring and/or transition to a different mode of production based on decarbonisation, as well as limited or radical reorganisation of lifestyle behaviour.

Both these latter discourses are often quite distinct from disputes over the politics of transition, namely, forms of democratic or undemocratic organisations, parliamentary or non-legislative strategies and which classes or groups will be the agents of social change (apart from individual or household-initiated lifestyle change). At the explicitly conventional political level we have ample examples from the past and present where parties or candidates won democratic majorities explicitly aiming not to overthrow or constrain capitalism but rather to limit or suspend democracy. Similarly, it is time to rethink what type of democratic politics is enhancing or undermining the goal of maximising environmental sustainability.

In the following chapters, I will therefore explore and analyse how past and present theories and movements of social change – whether anti-capitalist or post-capitalist in their green or other forms – understand and attempt to deal with major problems in the present-day world. These chapters will include discussion of the following:

- the differences between how capitalist societies came into being and why post-carbon or post-capitalist societies will not follow a similar trajectory;
- whether the social classes and political organisations that transformed societies in the past will also bring about future change or are historically obsolete and ill-suited to create a new politics and a new society;
- whether the old divisions between reformers and revolutionaries are relevant or inappropriate, and why questions of sustainability no longer conform to earlier conceptions of the difference between bourgeois and working-class 'interests';
- why many key ideas and policies about alternatives to environmentally unsustainable capitalism are themselves based on

shaky notions of the compatibility of 'democracy and
sustainability';
- why many well-intentioned notions of how to achieve
  sustainability are based on naïve and benign conceptions of a
  deeply violent and unequal world; and
- which policies and political directions are more likely to deliver
  socio-economic alternatives to capitalist markets while
  simultaneously reducing inequality and maximising environmental
  sustainability.

Past conflicts between representatives of 'capitalism and democracy' were
never troubled by the constraints of finite natural limits. In stark contrast
today, it depends on where one is located on the political spectrum as to
whether environmental constraints are seen to affect policies and attitudes
towards capitalism, equality and democracy. Clearly, those elements on the
political Right who have never believed in democracy and social equality
would be untroubled by ecological limits constraining the attainment of
these political and social goals. Yet, governments and business leaders have
rarely spoken with one voice. They continue to be divided over whether or
how to prolong the transition to zero carbon emissions or else successfully
manage this transformation with minimal impact on socio-economic stability
and their respective power bases. What an assortment of conservatives,
neoliberals, coercive authoritarians and pragmatic technocrats fear and
cannot control is how the contradictory and separate struggles for greater
equality and democracy will be exacerbated in different countries and regions
by environmentally driven material scarcity.

Consequently, those on the political Right who are quite comfortable
with taking precautionary decarbonisation policies will be driven by risk-
minimisation strategies (neutralising the problem) rather than abandoning
their opposition to greater social equality. Nevertheless, no party, government or business enterprise is adequately prepared for escalating environmental and social crises. Indeed, it is impossible to be fully prepared
politically, economically, technologically or militarily. This is partly due to the
unpredictable nature of volatile environmental events. It is also due to deep-
seated political divisions amongst decision-makers across the world over how
to respond to the climate crisis which has the consequence of effectively
preventing or delaying coordinated action.

As to liberals, social democrats and others who fear social conflict and
polarisation while still tolerating major disparities in wealth and power, it is

the prospect of increased social dislocation caused by climatic and other environmental crises affecting food production, economic growth and employment that takes priority over resolving inequality. This fear has already produced conflicting political responses concerning the desirable as opposed to necessary rate of decarbonisation required to prevent catastrophic conditions and political instability. Similar divisions extend beyond centrist and centre-Left parties and are evident in unions and civic organisations over how much social justice is necessary in any 'just transition' to a post-carbon society. Instead, faith in rational social policy adjustments and technological innovation mixed with ad hoc policy responses continue to drive policy agendas. Whether domestically in OECD countries through the emphasis on education and incremental social reform, or in developing countries via support for 2030 Sustainable Development Goals, liberal social democrats have still not come to terms with the scale and depth of social and environmental crises which their incremental policies will do little to resolve.

Paradoxically, it is amongst the politically weakest groups on the political spectrum that the greatest impact of environmental factors on social equality will be felt and become more evident. I am not just referring here to the large numbers of low-income people who currently lack political power to prevent climate breakdown from compounding their already immiserated state of existence. Rather, and ironically, a considerable proportion of those on the radical Left or in green movements who are the most committed to the goal of social equality are yet to adequately confront what environmental *unsustainability* actually means.

It has long been clear that the commitment to social and political equality is hollow and insincere if it is only applicable to the minority of the world's population living in OECD countries but fails to specify how this fundamental political goal can be made environmentally compatible for the entire world. While advocates of degrowth are committed to global equality, they admit that there is a massive gap between the tiny degrowth movement in the 'North' which is urban and middle class with no popular base, and the huge environmental justice movements in the countries of the 'South' that have local activist profiles amongst poor rural and indigenous populations.[3] In response, Brazilian environmentalist Roldan Muradian argues that degrowth is destined to be a Eurocentric movement as 'frugality by choice' is not an option favoured by impoverished masses in low and middle-income countries.[4]

Given the highly fragile state of the biosphere (or the sum total of all world-wide ecosystems), the question remains of whether environmentally sustainable equality is possible for a future population of more than 9 billion people. I am referring here to material equality in the form of adequate housing, health, diet, income and general basic services and not just political and cultural equality in terms of the exercise of institutional and social power. Of course, political and cultural equality remains an absolutely vital and attainable pre-condition for achieving material equality. While I remain committed to this possibility, 'equality' will be far from the 'fully automated luxury communism' and other techno-fixes currently fantasised by radical socialist utopians. We have known for at least sixty years that if we do not wish to abandon *material equality for all the people of the world*, this fundamental social goal cannot be based on the unsustainable standard of living currently enjoyed by majorities in OECD countries. For decades, non-orthodox radicals have also argued that environmental constraints and loss of the biosphere cannot be understood in traditional class terms. Class analysis is powerful and illuminating but insufficient on its own as a theory capable of explaining the political choices we face in contemporary societies.

Future political agendas and social goals will no longer be able to rest on a naïve post-scarcity belief in abundance. We are located at the end of a historical period that despite its setbacks and uneven distribution of material goods and services was driven by the political belief that each new generation would be better off materially than the last. Whether achieved incrementally or through revolution, the belief in material progress of the past two hundred years has not disappeared. Instead, a fundamental reassessment of both the rate and character of environmentally sustainable economic growth will test all shades of politics across the spectrum. Advocates of equality, however, will face the dilemma of how much material redistribution is politically possible in particular societies if it becomes either too ecologically dangerous to keep on growing an unsustainable 'economic pie' or social conflict escalates because there is less to redistribute *without* material growth.

Scarcity and deprivation have been constants throughout history. The so-called cycles of 'fat years' and 'lean years' were often accepted fatalistically as determined by the Gods. We also know that many communities and some civilisations were forced to migrate or collapsed due to inhospitable ecological habitats or depleted resources. From the nineteenth century onwards, 'scarcity' has been used by conservatives such as Thomas Malthus to justify harsh policies towards the poor based on the dubious notion that breeding from lack of constraint on sexual behaviour would see population outgrow food supply. In recent decades, the 'limits to growth' and other environment theories have either fused with a quasi-Malthusian notion of scarcity (Paul Erlich and the 'population bomb', for example[5]) or produced a non-Malthusian conception of enlarged material footprints (due to incessant capitalist growth rather than population growth) overshooting the carrying capacity of the earth.

Analysts such as Lyla Mehta, Ian Scoones and others see a division across the political spectrum between those who adhere to notions of 'absolute scarcity' where scarcity is real, physical and inescapable. They also identify 'relative scarcity' as something that depends on demand that can be allayed by science, technology and economic policies such as solving underproduction of food or goods. Both absolute and relative scarcity are to be distinguished from 'political scarcity' or the deliberate manufacture of 'scarcity' by those who do not wish to solve inequality of power and access to resources.[6] While these distinctions are helpful, the authors fudge the boundaries between those artificial narratives of scarcity that can be remedied by reforms or radical political action, and the non-artificial finite limits of resources that even a socialist revolution cannot overcome. It is the interplay of different real and politically created forms of scarcity that shape this conflict between 'democracy and sustainability'.

Fifty years ago, the notion of post-scarcity prevailed in various anarchist and Leftist circles. In the winter of 1972/73, while staying with radicals Sylvia Federici and Michael Kosok in New York, I remember witnessing the very heated arguments between them over anarchist Murray Bookchin's anti-Leninist collection of late 1960s essays, *Post-Scarcity Anarchism,* published in 1971.[7] However, their disagreements were over political organisation rather than whether scarcity could be overcome. A similar disregard for scarcity is held by both utopian capitalists and technological utopian socialists such as Leigh Phillips who continue to believe in affluence and abundance while rejecting degrowth as austerity-ecology.[8] Displaying either minimal environmental awareness or disregard for what is required to raise about seven billion people by 2050 to a condition of affluence, both corporate capitalists and socialist utopians are in for a rude and painful shock. The harsh reality of scarcity will force a rethink of many policies once the hope of absolutely decoupling economic growth from negative environmental impacts is revealed as a technocratic mirage.[9] Unfortunately, demystifying utopian notions of decoupling economic growth is only a starting point and will not in itself lead to any clear-cut politics, whether democratic or authoritarian, as this will depend on the particular socio-political terrain in each different country. I will return to these issues in later chapters.

10. CONFLICTING PATHWAYS TO POST-CARBON DEMOCRACY

PREVIOUS GENERATIONS LIVING through major historical events such as the French Revolution of 1789, the Russian Revolution of 1917 or the Chinese Revolution from the 1920s to 1949 witnessed enormous social transformations due to the toppling of former ruling classes. However, their hopes or fears were based on either the abolition or reorganisation of institutions and also the redistribution of familiar material resources that underpinned the old forms of inequality of economic wealth and socio-political power. These massive socio-political changes did not include agendas requiring the need to fundamentally alter relations with the natural world. Despite the fall of monarchies and the rise and fall of one-party states, people still produced or relied on essentially similar energy sources and consumed familiar everyday items (before and after the revolution) even if these were unequally redistributed or allocated in varied ways by diverse types of political regimes.

No such continuity between the present material basis of everyday life and the future awaits us in coming years. This does not mean that all will be utterly new and unfamiliar. Rather, we are moving into an era where numerous recognisable objects of household consumption, industrial goods production, transport, food production and other material processes will no longer be possible using many of the old methods and resources. What is significantly different between previous upheavals and the current very early stages of socio-economic transformation is that much of the latter will most likely not be carried out by revolutionary parties. Nearly all former revolutionary parties in non-Communist countries are merely museum relics and new mass formation radical parties currently do not exist. This does not mean that impending far-reaching transformation will be peaceful or driven by technocrats simply implementing innovative technology. It does mean though that any new emerging political movements will need to confront painful choices about material growth and redistribution hitherto not experienced by existing parties and movements.

For the past five decades, the critiques of unsustainable capitalist societies have come from a variety of ecologists and a diverse constituency of counter-cultural groups, animal rights activists and others. Most base their critique of capitalism not on class analysis but on concern for the natural world. They reject the prevailing culture of everyday life driven by material consumption, bureaucracy and wage-enslavement in the pursuit of not 'the good life' but one which is simultaneously alienated from nature, fellow human beings and other species. Disengaged from conventional politics, their philosophies and social agendas of alternative lifestyles begin with nature and energy (especially the destructive power of fossil fuels) rather than class conflict as their central analytical categories. They are anti-corporate capital or anti-big business without holding an analysis of how business is an essential element of a class-based capitalist society. Importantly, these diverse groups have long upheld an alternative vision that has either been ridiculed or rejected by mainstream centre-Left and radical Left parties. The latter have largely accepted the need to either reform society or remove capitalist classes rather than reject the benefits of industrial, high-tech capitalist civilisation.

During the past thirty-five years, the broad Left have slowly become more aware of the centrality of ecological issues even though they have tried to subsume these to class issues and critiques of neoliberalism. Nature and energy now take a larger role in their political analyses than ever before. But most of the Left have neither accepted the necessity of large reductions in material footprints nor fully integrated the political economic implications of such ecologically driven change on their traditional agendas framed within the paradigm of 'capitalism versus democracy'. Meanwhile, a growing number of advocates of degrowth have absorbed the arguments of class critiques of capitalism from eco-socialists and political economists and have tried to integrate these ideas into new degrowth agendas. Nonetheless, it would be myopic to ignore the great gulf that still exists between social and political agendas based on overcoming class divisions as opposed to those that prioritise a new set of lifestyle relations driven by the goal of achieving a sustainable world.

We now face a new unprecedented political situation where a significant proportion of industrial and service sector workers may reject ecological sustainability policies that seriously impinge on their freedom to consume what they please or to keep their jobs in fossil-fuelled industries. Gone are the days when these same working-class 'democrats' supported Left parties and unions because they were told that there was sufficient wealth held by the bourgeoisie that would be redistributed in favour of workers and their families. Making everyone in the world 'bourgeois' in terms of living standards proved politically unattainable in the past. It remains environmentally impossible in the future.

Consequently, environmental sustainability appears to sections of low and middle-income workers as little more than austerity and a diminished material culture, especially when agitators incite racist fearmongering that workers and those on welfare benefits will have to share their meagre social services and threatened jobs with refugees. Evidence shows that even those who have had enough of neoliberal austerity will still vote for mainstream neoliberal centre/Right or centre/Left parties when they are not supporting Right-wing racist and nationalist movements. It remains to be seen whether escalating environmental crises will help remove hostility to greens as the increasing floods, droughts, fires and violent storms of climate breakdown finally registers with conservative populations. Previous socio-economic crises did not, however, change political consciousness in a revolutionary direction as the Left had hoped it would. So, the threat of climate breakdown to production and jobs may prove either a catalyst for change or help consolidate a deeper 'fortress mentality' amongst those who already hate greens and the Left.

Whatever the coming political conflicts, it is also clear that environmentally driven social transformation will not happen simultaneously in all sectors of society or in all countries. The switch to renewable energy is merely one aspect of the forthcoming transition and could be relatively easy technologically despite the bitter resistance of fossil-fuel industries. On current rates of decarbonisation, unfortunately, the chances of limiting global warming to just another 1.5° Celsius or 2° Celsius were calculated in 2017 to be an impossible 1% and 5% at best.[1] In 2020, climate models based on cloud sensitivity data ruled out the ability to limit global warming to a 1.5° Celsius increase, with 2° Celsius being the best possible *minimal* additional temperature outcome, and 5° Celsius warming highly likely.[2] However, these absolutely frightening existential prospects are mathematical projections based on there being no substantial change to emissions reduction policies. They do not factor in potential mass mobilisation to put pressure on governments to force reluctant businesses to adopt more rapid decarbonisation measures. In authoritarian countries, governments will either delay or choose to implement ecological modernisation under international pressure to share the burden; fear of failing to become technologically competitive with decarbonising trade rivals will also drive modernisation. Whether the climate emergency will be solved 'satisfactorily' depends on the degree of political mobilisation rather than on the wisdom of policy makers. Hence, decarbonisation will be implemented in a very uneven manner and at a very uneven rate across the world.

TWO PARALLEL POLITICAL STRUGGLES

We should also recognise that other institutional, production and cultural changes that are necessary to reduce material footprints will be more complex and may take decades longer to achieve. Few supporters of climate emergency action seem aware of the additional challenges, way beyond curbing greenhouse gases. Currently, we are witnessing two parallel political economic struggles that will spark far greater socio-political change in coming years. The first struggle is a familiar conflict that has been ongoing for at least three decades but will reach its most intense stage during the next five to ten years. I refer here to the conflict at national and international levels between the 'rear-guard' political parties, business groups, media outlets and think-tanks desperately trying to both delay and prevent the abandonment of fossil-fuels. Tied to this 'last stand' politics is a defence of multi-trillion-dollar investments and the desperate need to avoid or delay the restructure of carbon-intensive industries in manufacturing, transport, agriculture, chemicals and so forth. This is a fight that the 'rear-guard' cannot win but, unfortunately, will still have the capacity to inflict enormous damage on the biosphere.

The old cliché about generals fighting the previous war applies to numerous business and political leaders as well as to many social change activists. Altered socio-economic and environmental conditions have rendered old strategies and solutions either historically obsolete or only partially effective at best. Many socialists and greens hold onto the belief that capitalist societies will not be able to deal with climate change and that this global crisis will usher in the end of capitalism. Perhaps the failure to act decisively to prevent the havoc resulting from climate breakdown will indeed cause irreparable major political economic crises. However, it would be foolish to think that voters, governments and businesses will sit idly by and allow fossil-fuel industries to create environmental chaos just because these dinosaurs are still powerful in G20 countries. Capitalist businesses and governments have the technical capacity to deal with greenhouse emissions. It is quite another matter when it comes to their ability to adapt to and survive the need to abandon or decelerate incessant material growth.

Hence, the second concurrent and less visible struggle is a more fundamental and far-reaching conflict between ascending pro-market political economic forces promoting ecological modernisation and a range of radical environmentalists and eco-socialists who reject 'green growth' as environmentally unsustainable. Ecological modernisers tend to be optimists and assume we can have it all. This naïveté is widespread and is aptly expressed by people such as economics editor for the *Sydney Morning Herald*, Ross Gittins who believes: "We can have unending growth in GDP *and* sustainable use of natural resources (which is what the environmentalists care about) by changing the way economic activity is organised – including by getting all our energy from renewable sources."[3] Similarly Pollyannish views in the sustainability of 'green growth' are regularly voiced by a mixture of leading international agencies such as the IMF, UN, OECD and pro-business technological innovators and centre-Left parties. I will not devote space to critiquing 'green growth', as there are many detailed analyses of the serious shortcomings and flaws in this approach to environmental problems.[4] Ecological modernisers are nearly all committed to renewable energy *without* a radical renewal or overhaul of existing social institutions and practices.

In opposition to the dominant versions of capitalist ecological modernisation are degrowth movements based on a diverse set of counter-cultural environmentalists, eco-socialists and post-colonial groups who share an anti-capitalist perspective but are presently too unwieldly in terms of their individual specific political agendas to constitute a coherent political coalition in favour of degrowth. On current levels of political strength, the advocates of pro-market 'green growth' will almost certainly win over much weaker degrowth movements. However, their success will be a pyrrhic victory. This is because 'green growth' can only temporarily postpone the need to resolve far deeper ecological problems generated by the unsustainable size of material footprints associated with capitalist production and consumption of biomass, minerals and metal ores. Whether it be water scarcity, deforestation and desertification, the ravages caused by numerous mining ventures, chemical agribusiness, multiple threats to oceans from pollution, deep sea mining and destruction of coastal habitats, not to mention the still unresolved and escalating problem of global waste disposal,[5] all these unfolding crises driven by material consumption are not soluble by simply switching to renewable energy and illusory panaceas such as electric cars.[6]

If 'green growth' is doomed to be an unsustainable 'stop gap' policy option, the question troubling many on the Left or in environmental groups is whether it is better to first achieve 'ecological modernisation' or to oppose it and fight for degrowth. We are not talking here about the classic Marxist theory about first the 'bourgeois revolution' before the final 'socialist revolution'. Remember, that the social justice elements within various Green New Deals are important to fight for but these are not to be confused with the old distinction between 'bourgeois' or 'socialist' revolution; they are simply necessary social reforms. Hence, the dilemma facing us in the form of the climate emergency makes old style Left tactical discussions about 'correct line' strategy both a luxury and counterproductive. The political task is to first prevent complete climate breakdown and co-operate with social and political forces across the spectrum that are committed to this urgent objective. This does not mean rejecting one's belief in degrowth, socialism or whatever, but merely to recognise urgent priorities and the relative political strength or weakness of diverse social forces in the political field.

Instead of the conventional distinction between revolutionaries and reformists, the environmental crisis is witnessing quite different political approaches and strategies. For instance, European analysts Simone D'Alessandro, André Cieplinski, Tiziano Distefano and Kristofer Dittmer have compared green growth, Green New Deal and degrowth proposals to develop a policy-mix model called EUROGREEN that identifies how the three strategies differ, which parts of their policies overlap and what are the likely consequences of each set of policy positions.[7] Environmentalist Daniel O'Neill argues that while D'Alessandro and co-authors leave out key degrowth policies, they nevertheless show that:

> Both green growth and a Green New Deal come close to reaching the European Union's Climate Action target. Degrowth achieves it. However, there are important trade-offs in each of the scenarios. Green growth reduces greenhouse gas emissions, but inequality and unemployment both rise. The Green New Deal dramatically lowers unemployment and reduces inequality, but at the expense of an increase in the government deficit-to-GDP ratio. Degrowth reduces emissions and inequality further than the other two scenarios, but it

leads to a higher increase in the deficit-to-GDP ratio (because GDP decreases). In short, there is no win–win scenario.[8]

Of course, all figures relating to the projected size of budget deficits and levels of inequality have been blown out of the water since the Pandemic of 2020. Whether pursuing 'green growth' or degrowth, theoretical political ecology and model building has its limits, as will become clear later on.

Assuming that leading capitalist countries substantially decarbonise in the next one to three decades, it is almost certain that well before zero emissions are achieved, governments and citizens in emerging post-carbon, but still capitalist societies, will discover that in order to maximise environmental sustainability it will be necessary to transition away from the dominant growth-orientated forms of capitalist production and consumption. Yet, in order to accomplish this massive political economic change, social change activists and policy makers will simultaneously need to plan on how to implement this transition and learn from earlier historical experiences and debates concerning social transformation.

CONFLICTING ORIGINS: CAPITALISM AND POST-CARBON DEMOCRACIES

It is patently obvious that the social change processes and the character of future societies will be quite different to both the original conditions and social agents that brought about the emergence of capitalist societies. What is surprising, nonetheless, is how little comparative analysis of these differences currently exists. Moreover, it is common for people to conceive of 'capitalism' or the 'industrial revolution' as some homogeneous stage of history that replaced 'feudal' society. While appearing to be a truism, it is important to restate that there was no uniform 'capitalism' that developed simultaneously in various countries or originated under the same conditions. The voluminous literature on the origins of capitalism reveals no agreement between historians as to whether, for example, capitalism primarily developed in towns or first required the transformation of agricultural production into commercial capitalist agriculture, thus driving surplus populations into expanding urban centres. These and other developmental paths depended on the specific conditions in individual countries.

A range of mainstream analysts have, for instance, argued that capitalism is essentially a more developed form of commercial market relations that existed in rudimentary form in medieval and ancient societies. The flowering of capitalist commercial life could only proceed after the numerous political, religious, geopolitical and social constraints on commerce and industry or mobile free labour and other obstacles were weakened or removed. Marxists either reject all or various key parts of this perspective. Some view capitalism as a new mode of production with corresponding social relations that was from the very beginning quite different to earlier forms of pre-capitalist commercial activity. Recently, there has been a revival of debates on how 'capitalist' were the 'bourgeois revolutions' from the eighteenth to the twentieth centuries.[9] In other words, there is no agreement between historians on what 'feudalism' was and also how 'bourgeois' was the overthrow of 'feudalism' in France 1789 or in Ethiopia in 1974.

Capitalist socio-political relations and industrial modes of production became dominant in diverse countries and co-existed with either subordinate groups or alongside the residues of earlier social classes and political orders, whether agrarian, aristocratic, merchant traders or First Nations people.[10] I would agree with all those who reject the notion of self-contained homogeneous capitalist societies. It follows that if emerging capitalist societies were hybrid forms that either fused with earlier practices or co-existed with mixtures of pre-existing and new social relations and institutions, then future 'post-carbon' or post-capitalist social orders will also most likely be hybrid social formations.

However, the likely emergence of either 'post-carbon' capitalist or environmentally sustainable post-capitalist societies will not follow the paths that gave rise to the origins of diverse forms of capitalism. Max Weber famously claimed that the development of capitalism required specific Western social conditions such as scientific rationality, Protestant religion and new European urban social classes. Some would argue that Weber displayed a form of Orientalism that depicted the East as dominated by mysticism, magic and spirituality while the West was progressively disenchanting the world through secular technical rationality.[11] Leaving these important historical disputes aside, it is clear that the acquisition and application of particular levels of knowledge, as also the emergence of new social classes and political cultural conditions required for post-carbon societies will definitely not be associated solely with the West. China, for instance, has more scientists, engineers and researchers than the US and Europe combined. Unfortunately, most of them, as in the EU and US are not working on environmentally sustainable technology or new social practices.

Regardless of geographical location, and in the absence of revolution, it is most likely that new environmentally sustainable societies will also emerge from within 'the womb' of existing capitalist societies, just like some early capitalist social relations emerged from within pre-capitalist societies. Nonetheless, it is unlikely that 'revolution from below' will be the catalyst for social transformation as contemporary capitalist societies do not conform to simple two class models of a ruling class and a subordinate working-class or peasantry. Instead, various forms of post-carbon society will be driven by growing protest movements from below but the latter (in the absence of political upheaval) will depend on expanded government legislation and regulations needed to prevent deepening ecosystem crises. It remains to be seen whether currently dominant forms of corporate capitalist power and social relations will be subordinated to emerging post-carbon, post-capitalist democracies or whether capitalist businesses and authoritarian emergency regimes will try to suspend and destroy representative democracies.

Rather than adhere to a variation of neatly packaged 'stages' of history that succeed one another in linear fashion, I wish to emphasise the 'messiness' of historical change, its highly conflictual, chaotic and uneven character, and why any possible transition to environmentally sustainable societies will also be fundamentally different to earlier historical transformations. Momentous social change invariably brings into being new social classes. As usual, it is much easier to see the past than to envisage the future. For instance, historians such as E. P. Thompson outlined the complex rural and urban origins and processes that led to 'the making of the English working class' from the late eighteenth to early decades of the nineteenth century.[12] Yet, Thompson's account was controversial because it involved certain preconceived notions about what it means to 'make a class'. Tom Nairn and Perry Anderson challenged Thompson's assertion that "the working class made itself as much as it was made"[13] and that it developed a class consciousness through struggles and common lived experiences of shared antagonisms to employers, landlords and so forth. The question that Nairn and later Anderson asked: is what did it mean for a class 'to be made', and what constituted 'class consciousness' if the militant English working class before 1832 became so politically docile twenty years later and continued to be non-revolutionary for the next 150 years?[14]

I would add that just as 'capitalism' is never 'completed' or 'made', so too, the making of a class, whether it be capitalist or working class is never finished. Rather, there is constant transformation of either occupations, new industries, living conditions, or larger socio-cultural and political power relations. This is one of the reasons why 'class consciousness' in the 1820s, 1890s, 1930s, 1960s or 2020s is so different in each period, not only in England but comparatively in other countries across the world. We can also never be quite sure when capitalist classes have exhausted their capacity to innovate new forms of production and modes of maintaining socio-political power. As we have seen, capitalist classes are themselves in constant flux in terms of the sources of their capital, their preferred investments, their commitment to defending old production processes or innovating technologies and products, such as the current divisions over opposing or supporting ecological modernisation. Contemporary international communication networks may instantaneously spread particular radical ideas and help shape core topical issues. Nonetheless, the reception of these ideas and the formation of 'consciousness' is never identical in its impact and consequences, as ideas need to be adopted and practised by political organisations operating under quite different national and local conditions with quite specific socio-political histories.

Those who believe that we are in the 'cancer stage' of capitalism or 'catastrophe capitalism', 'end times' and other epithets, must differentiate between the so-called political inability of ruling classes to innovate or reform and whether any potential future 'modernisation' such as 'green growth' will save capitalism or only exacerbate deep-seated social and economic crises. In other words, we may possibly be in a comparable situation to Gorbachev's 'perestroika' where once the political will to 'reconstruct' was finally found by the mid-1980s, it was far too late and only speeded up the disintegration of the old system.

After several decades of dissolution of simple notions of two homogeneous classes (capitalists and workers) and the recognition of a plurality of social groupings and identities, we now find ourselves in a strange fragmented world; still capitalist but without the neat, clear-cut actors of capitalists and workers confronting one another with so-called unambiguous agendas for the future. Not that this simplified image was ever the case historically. Instead, we are living through a period of rapid and as yet unpredictable socio-economic change. It is not just the working class that is being transformed well beyond former familiar divisions of blue and white collar, male and female dominated industries, unskilled, skilled and professional occupations. Sections of other old classes are being dissolved or re-made and it is probable that a new class based on a recombination or offshoot of elements and layers from other classes is also 'being made' at this very moment. However, we are unable to predict its future characteristics and how it will help or hinder transforming the structure of power in coming decades. This is because both older and newer forms of capitalist production, institutional administration and social practice still prevail or appear largely recognisable.

For a new 'post-carbon social class' to emerge, it would require not just a change in occupations but a fundamental alteration in the proportion of people in the paid workforce dependent on wages and salaries as compared to those unemployed, on various state benefits or studying and in retirement. Without this social transformation in the quantity and quality of paid work, there would be little political economic space for the possibility of a new class to survive and function. In other words, a new social class must embody socio-economic relations that are quite distinct from simply being part of a reconstituted wage-dependent class. Since the 1940s, we have seen regular discussion of a 'new class' of professionals and managers standing between capitalists and workers. There is no doubt that this category has grown but most are not self-employed and are in dependent positions subordinate to private or public employers. Others constitute part of a reconstituted middle class that embrace not just lawyers, doctors or shop keepers of the old petite bourgeoisie but also new consultants, self-employed contractors and so on. Most of these are in a fragile position dependent on businesses or governments for their services and are unable to become the dominant class of a new post-carbon society.

While 'professionals' do not constitute a new class, they carry out key administrative and technical roles and help shape cultural practices but lack the economic and political power to create any new social formation on their own without either the support of large capital or unions and other social movements. Many professionals came from working-class families just as former peasants became urban wage workers and developed new socio-cultural relations as part of earlier forms of industrial transformation. The emergence of any sizeable 'post-carbon class' would require existing classes to be dramatically reduced or undermined so that the latter no longer remain central or dominant. Some argue that this is already happening with the unleashing of roboticization and AI. Wage and salaried workers are certainly being made redundant, but AI is unlikely to produce a new social class separate from workers and employers. The related question that needs to be asked of any fundamental change to existing classes is: what kind of political organisations would represent this new class or strata and in what way would state institutions reflect such a significant transition to a post-carbon or post-capitalist society?

Most current discussions of threats to democracy or how to resolve the climate emergency largely and understandably focus on the familiar rather than the unknown. We are in the midst of the rapid implementation of digital technologies and communications systems to produce civilian consumer goods and military weapons or state surveillance. A proliferation of global and regional interlocking corporate supply chains, pervasive cultural marketing techniques and restructured labour markets have already disorganised and undermined the former social and political power of working-class organisations. Capitalist classes for all their internal divisions still remain in the saddle but it is unclear how secure and durable is their power.

Importantly, just as historically there was no sudden, ready-formed capitalist class that clashed with various feudal ruling classes or other holders of pre-capitalist power, similarly, there is currently no already formed new social class that is the standard bearer of post-carbon political economic power and alternative social relations. In fact, there is *no* single class that represents the political economic interests of all who wish to wage political conflict with old social classes in existing 'carbon capitalist' societies. Instead, we have fragments or elements of existing socio-economic classes such as particular non-fossil fuel businesses and self-employed consultants in renewable energy, organic farming and other industry sectors, plus higher educated professionals, urban environment groups and clusters of communities in eco-villages who all favour the establishment of post-carbon democracies. Some of these heterogeneous groups overlap with traditional wage workers and *petite bourgeois* classes but other strata do not.

In contrast to those socialists believing in the crisis-collapse of capitalism which would give rise to a socialist society, currently, there are many 'catastrophists' or 'collapsologists' who believe there will be no post-capitalist society because 'civilisation' itself will perish from climate breakdown. It is difficult to argue against 'catastrophists' because climate breakdown could possibly engulf all types of political regimes rather than just advanced capitalist societies. Even those who do not subscribe to this view of climate catastrophe continue to express fears that the social breakdown of capitalism – whether slow or rapid – will be characterised by the failure of new post-neoliberal institutions and social relations to triumph while the old order falls apart.

In this Gramscian 'interregnum' where 'the new cannot be born', individuals are depicted as increasingly unprotected and exposed to a multitude of socio-economic and political crises as societies become ungovernable.[15] One version of this stalemate is ultra-pessimistic and without a clear politics as it is devoid of any concept of social agency, that is, a notion of social movements or parties struggling to prevent possible chaos. It is a homogeneous conception of 'decaying capitalism' as a *global* phenomenon because it assumes that all capitalist societies will *simultaneously* become *ungovernable* and that all people in these diverse capitalist countries will be left unprotected and helpless as doomsday scenarios of economic collapse and ecocide destroys civilisation. This is an erroneous view of the world that sees history moving in *uniform* stages.

Fortunately, people will act, and they will intervene. This does not mean they will create socialism or a sustainable society, as we don't yet know which ideas and visions of the future will prevail in one country as opposed to another. In short, it is not enough to know the processes of how post-carbon societies will emerge if we don't yet know the key aims and character of the protagonists who will make the future happen.

'STEADY STATE' POLITICS AND ENERGY-FOCUSSED SOLUTIONS

Just as there have been major political economic debates over 'accumulation regimes' or what drives capitalist growth (for example, export-led, consumption-led, investment-led or other business and government 'drivers of growth') so too, there is no agreement as to how post-carbon democracies or post-growth societies will *reproduce* themselves. If class theorists argue that 'environmentally sustainable capitalism' is an oxymoron, they must be able to show which class(es) – whether old or new – will be the bearer of alternative social relations that will be grounded in an emerging environmentally sustainable post-carbon capitalism or in a post-capitalist alternative production system.

To repeat, combatting climate breakdown and identifying which industries are compatible with renewable energy is not equivalent to a sustainable capitalist economy, that is, an economy that is profitable and accumulates capital by incessant growth. Neither is it an explanation of how new post-capitalist environmentally sustainable socio-economic relations and political institutions can survive and thrive.

Actually, there will not be too many choices facing creators of new societies if they wish to promote equality, democratisation and sustainability. Seductive though it might seem, there will not be an infinite range of options. Social change advocates may be forced to rely on a mixture of market mechanisms and government allocation of resources or implement non-market planning and other organisational processes. Planning will be necessary but not necessarily the type of authoritarian planning by state planning ministries, architects, capitalist industrialists and others during the history of the twentieth century or currently in China. Analysing the repeated and all too-frequent large gap between various plans and their failed outcomes, James Scott in his panoramic study, *Seeing Like a State* concludes:

> If our inquiry has taught us anything, it is that the first map, taken
> alone, is misrepresentative and indeed nonsustainable. A same-age,
> monocropped forest with all the debris cleared is in the long run an
> ecological disaster. No Taylorist factory can sustain production
> without the unplanned improvisations of an experienced workforce.
> Planned Brasilia is, in a thousand ways, underwritten by unplanned
> Brasilia...Human resistance to the more severe forms of social strait-
> jacketing prevents monotonic schemes of centralised rationality from
> ever being realised. Had they been realised in their austere forms they
> would have represented a very bleak human prospect.[16]

Yet, Scott's anarchist ideal of stateless self-sufficient communities is utopian because this goal will be impossible to realise for the vast majority of people in a world of profound scarcity and political divisions. Love it or hate it, state planning has been extremely effective in China compared to the shambles and chaotic poverty of India. Since the birth of modern India in 1947 and China in 1949, analysts have continued to compare their development, socio-political systems and quality of life. Both have poisoned their soil, water and air but with quite different outcomes. Richard Smith is scathing about both countries when it comes to environmental sustainability. He notes that:

> India's dysfunctional ruling class can't even provide toilets for its citi-
> zens, or pick up the trash, let alone provide electricity, modern
> container ports, high-speed trains, or a skilled industrial work force.
> In the twenty-first century, hundreds of millions of Indians remain
> unconnected to an electrical grid. Unmanaged refuse accumulates into
> "mountains" that collapse killing people and cause tuberculosis,
> dengue fever, and poisoned ground water. India's air pollution is now
> as bad as if not worse than China's despite having far less industry.
> Minister Narendra Modi wants to compete with China?[17]

In other words, we have to confront 40% of the world's population living in two countries characterised by either planned or minimally planned systems. It is from this far from ideal starting point that we have to think of possible feasible transitions to a post-carbon democracy.

Whether market mechanisms or state planning are adopted as the principal macro-economic processes does not tell us what degree of room there will be for other institutional interactions. Importantly, both Marxists and non-Marxist greens and others must be able to show how a so-called classless society can make the ecologically sustainable transition through either new types of non-capitalist markets (based, for example, on decentralised barter, co-operatives and sharing of the 'commons') or via local, national and supra-national forms of state planning combined with informal transactions. Currently, mainstream and radical political economists agree that capitalist societies are subject to a range of moderate to severe crisis tendencies but disagree as to whether these crises will eventually prove to be fatal.

There is, however, virtually no equivalent assessment of how potential crisis-tendencies could be eliminated in post-carbon or *post-capitalist* environmentally sustainable societies. The nearest we get are the ideas put forward by systems ecologists and ecological economists such as Howard T. Okum and Hermann Daly. Okum was one of the pioneers of energy-focussed analysis of world ecology who argued that we needed 'energy descent' or a transformation of what he called 'emergy' if the world was to become sustainable. This perspective has influenced generations of environmentalists, permaculture devotees and advocates of degrowth. Sadly, Okum's work in conjunction with Elisabeth Okum was a hotchpotch of innovative ideas and contradictory wish-lists of pro and anti-capitalist proposals that essentially revealed a poor and eclectic understanding of capitalist political economy.[18] It is a classic case of the limits of energy-focussed analysis.

Similarly, Daly also saw much through the lens of energy and believed in a 'steady-state' sustainable society where governments essentially regulate and balance material resource utilisation so that natural resources are not depleted. The problem is that Daly relies on cap and trade and other neoclassical market-orientated economic concepts.[19] His vision is based on a mixture of Malthusian population theory, conservative cybernetics ecosystems theory and mainstream economics. Daly relies on the systems ecology put forward by Jay Forrester and others.[20] Their conception of nature and society is governed by a model of interconnecting sub-systems and feed-back loops that with care and the right policies such as 'energy descent', can be restored to a balanced state. These are all well-intentioned goals but rest on what other ecologists regard as highly contentious notions of the internal processes and biodiversity of nature, let alone of human societies. There has never been equilibrium in industrialised human societies characterised by multiple forms of inequality and conflict. It will be revolutionary for us just to aim to achieve post-capitalist societies based on very minimal levels of inequality and conflict, even though these potential future societies will not be fully balanced steady states.

In Daly's case, the 'steady state' is a pseudo solution as his alternative society will have many of the same characteristics of capitalist countries such as those in Scandinavia. Hence, Daly's model is almost the equivalent of the mythical 'balanced' markets long promoted by mainstream economists who believe in the 'equilibrium' of either unplanned capitalist markets attaining stability of supply and demand or reaching this goal through Keynesian state intervention and regulation. None of these methods of the 'invisible hand' of the market or deliberate state intervention were ever able to prevent, control or eliminate major crises in capitalist systems during the past one hundred years.

Daly believes that Japan is half-way on the road to a 'steady state' because of its low growth/stagnation of recent decades. This is a fundamental misunderstanding of Japan's high carbon emissions capitalist economy. Also, like Sweden and Switzerland, Daly's 'steady-state' is not an egalitarian society. Instead of drastically reduced initial income ratios of no more than two or three to one, Daly favours inequality of no more than 100 to 1, which is still enormous and immoral despite being less than the current obscene levels of inequality where multi-billionaires have thousands of times more income and wealth than the poorest in society. This new society will also be based on the usual myth of a small business capitalist utopia without private monopolies.[21] While he sees the 'steady-state' as still largely capitalist, like other Left de facto nationalists such as Wolfgang Streeck, Daly is opposed to 'cosmopolitan globalism' and wants to 'renationalise capital' and impose environmental controls and other regulations over capital and immigration flows.[22] It is a largely inward looking model of future socio-economic relations that aims to minimise external interaction so that national 'steady-state' economies can be regulated. Whether this type of society is introduced in the US or in other countries, governments will nonetheless find it impossible to avoid financial, trade, currency, accumulation and investment crises. As Daly's 'steady-state' is not self-sufficient, it would invariably import external problems because it will still be integrated into international capitalist markets.

It is important to distinguish Daly's conception of the 'steady state' from the many ecological economists and 'degrowthers' who have put forward more radical anti-capitalist ideas of the 'steady state' based on far greater equality, more international cooperation and the development of new socio-economic relations at local and national levels.[23] Nonetheless, there is still a fundamental vagueness about how resources and economic equilibrium will be achieved at national and global levels given that this presupposes a far more cooperative world based on nations with like-minded political economic commitments to post-growth. Such universal commitment is light years away as the polarised politics over climate change testify, let alone more extensive moves towards a post-growth world.

Part of the political and economic impossibility of reaching a 'steady state' is that Daly and many other environmentalists have a benign and therefore unrealistic view of capitalist societies. They ignore the conflict and violence that pervades the world and assume that if only the correct state levers were pulled and a more balanced or 'steady-state' economy was formed then the world could be made just and sustainable. This completely over-looks or minimises the inseparable relationship between economic growth (especially technological innovation) and military power. It is against the background of a profoundly uneven and unequal world, a world characterised by a mere 19 countries out of 195 accounting for approximately 80% of world GDP, a world where almost two-thirds of the global population earn either far less than or little more than US$5 a day. It is also a world where on 2020 figures, the US military budget of $732 billion was 38.2% of the estimated global total of US$1,917 billion of military expenditure in 2019 and equalled the combined expenditure of the ten next largest spenders by dwarfing China's $261 billion, India's $71.1 billion, Russia's $65.1 billion, Saudi Arabia's $61.9 billion and France's $50.1 billion as the next five largest spenders.[24] Sobering figures revealed that only fifteen countries accounted for 81% of total global military expenditure and 32 countries had military conflicts in 2019.

In such a divisive and hostile geopolitical world where the top nineteen countries (by GDP) also have about 61% of the global population, including a large proportion of the world's poorest people alongside incredible personal wealth for a tiny minority, one can have either a very pessimistic or an optimistic view of the chances for future democratisation. Either way, any political analysis that ignores the interconnection between vested government and business interests in developing and maintaining competitive industrial strength in metallurgy, electronics, chemicals, digital technology and other key industries necessary for military superiority will seriously underestimate the obstacles that degrowth and 'steady state' advocates face.

Similarly, ecological economists such as Ann Pettifor use Daly's notion of a 'steady state' to underpin her case for a Green New Deal based on 'localism'.[25] The notion that one could transform national fiscal policy, social and military expenditure and resources use in a 'steady state' locally-based Green New Deal is daring but highly politically unrealistic as both a limited strategy within interlocking capitalist societies and as a feasible post-capitalist system with multiple links beyond local economies. In Chapter Thirteen, I will discuss the possibility of different interrelated local and national economic zones which are not self-sufficient or self-financing. Like Pettifor, Tim Jackson, Peter Victor and Ali Naqvi also ignore military-industrial production and have tried to go beyond Daly by developing a model of the British economy as a series of stock flows between different sectors.[26] Once again, it is entirely unclear how such a theoretical model of local economies within a national economy can avoid importing major economic problems or prevent domestic economic depression if it disengages from or restricts exchanges with international markets. For instance, it is very difficult for domestic industry to disengage from incessant growth as imports and exports constitute over 60% of the UK's GDP. One could possibly transition away from such a heavy reliance on imports and exports over time, but any significant switch to degrowth could see the stock market crash, private investment dry up or go offshore, and employment and income plummet dramatically as many UK businesses, like businesses in most advanced capitalist countries, are highly integrated into international value chains and financial markets. In fact, multinational corporations account for the overwhelming level and scale of international trade in material goods and financial services.

Degrowth policies would not succeed without first identifying and establishing alternative forms of production and political power that were able to counter or control the value chains driven by powerful corporations. Yet, even with government helping stem the fall in income or generating new public employment and services, post-growth scenarios would have trouble surviving in isolated nation states without the strong support of similar post-growth transitions implemented in other leading capitalist countries. Supranational entities such as the EU would possibly have a greater chance of a successful transition to sustainability – both in terms of resources and political power – providing that cross-national co-operation expanded, and domestic political divisions could be minimised. Brexit has effectively instituted or consolidated UK 'weakness' in international capitalist markets while Left nationalists have made the transition to post-capitalism infinitely harder due to adhering to the myth of national sovereignty.

From the sixteenth century to the twentieth century, 'primitive capitalism' was violent and ferocious in different continents regardless of whether it
was backed by monarchies or republics, whether it took the form of
domestic upheaval or imperialist 'development' abroad. The slaughter and
dispossession of First Peoples and their lands, the forced proletarianisation
of millions of people from early nineteenth century rural labourers in
England to late twentieth century China is a process that won't be repeated
with the formation of post-carbon societies. Marx called primitive capitalism
'accumulation by dispossession'. In recent years, Ramachandra Guha, Joan
Martinez-Alier and Shulan Zhang have described ecological struggles in
India as 'environmentalism of the dispossessed' or 'environmentalism of the
poor' in that it is a struggle over inequality and access to natural resources
appropriated by businesses, landowners and developers.[27] It is quite different
to the political ideas of sustainability driving environmentalism in affluent
OECD countries.

Despite inflicting shocking death tolls and suffering on uprooted rural
populations and urban workers, early capitalist entrepreneurs were able to
grow within various empires, kingdoms, nation states and city states without
being destroyed by local and international pre-capitalist ruling classes. No
such luxury of 'peaceful development' is available to 'steady state', degrowth
or other models of post-capitalism in a world of highly integrated capitalist
businesses and their political and military allies. This does not mean that
advocates of post-capitalist green societies will be repressed and killed en
masse. But it does mean that they will encounter very strong political opposition while lacking the military, economic, legal and ideological forms of state
power that helped capitalists rise to become the dominant class power.
Unlike early Christians who were protected by Emperor Constantine, the
fate of radical ecological sustainability will depend on mass mobilisation of
people rather than on just the blessings of benign governments.

Conversely, if we look historically at the Leninist theory of the vanguard
party as a classic opponent of absolutist monarchy and capitalist power this
was closely related to the concept of 'dual power'. If the state was to be overthrown by the proletariat, then a parallel state of 'workers and soldiers councils' (or soviets) had to be established alongside the capitalist state and
effectively undermine the latter's power and authority. This model is politically obsolete in complex OECD countries and is only vaguely applicable in
low-income countries with either 'failed states' or suffering years of civil war
resulting in the possibility of establishing a countervailing system of 'dual
power'. Despite residents of eco-model communities aiming to undermine

the growth-orientated state and capitalist economy, eco-villages and transition towns are too weak and disconnected from the everyday work and life practices of large populations. Hence, they are incapable of establishing 'dual power' as parallel alternative centres of an environmentally sustainable society alongside the dominant capitalist system. Instead, most live harmoniously in a political and social bubble largely or partially disengaged from everyday political struggles.

Rather than maturing within 'the womb' of capitalist society, the ability of 'eco-villages' to expand significantly within the suburbs and cities is virtually impossible given the structural barriers/dynamics of everyday urban life controlled by businesses and governments. It is certainly possible for people to minimise conventional consumerism and adopt a limited range of alternative practices. However, few if any eco-villages or 'transition towns' can provide sufficient paid employment or finance their own infrastructure and services should their populations grow. Most are not fully self-sufficient in either food, natural resources or income and the provision of health and other social services. They co-exist with dominant capitalist institutions but are politically irrelevant as a threat to the future of capitalism.

Ted Trainer, a leading advocate of alternative 'eco-villages', argues that: "The Simpler Way is death for capitalism, but the way we will defeat it is by ignoring it to death, by turning away from it and building those many bits of the alternative that we could easily build right now."[28] This anti-statist strategy is the mirror image of the neoliberal 'trickle down' effect. Both would take between 120 and 200 years to either deliver benefits to the poor (at current rates of 'trickle down') or undermine capitalism if exceedingly small numbers of people opted out of the system. Currently we need urgent decarbonisation to prevent unprecedented threats to society and the environment. Yet, 'degrowthers' such as Vincent Liegey and Anitra Nelson adopt the politically perplexing and counterproductive position of championing the 'snail's pace' of degrowth as guaranteeing that social change will be truly radical if it resists the temptation of quick conventional political tactics.[29] Permaculture co-founder, David Holmgren, had earlier proposed small, 'slow and steady solutions win's the race' as one of the twelve principle of permaculture.[30] This is logical for transforming household and small community cultures but quite limited and ineffective for dealing with major environmental and political economic crises.

Earlier in 2006, Trainer had hoped that an oil crisis in the coming decade would stop people getting to the shops and thereby transform their attitudes to capitalist consumption. Importantly, the popular environmentalist misconception of 'peak oil' resulting in a supply crisis will almost certainly never happen. Instead, there is a glut of oil, with production outstripping demand since 2017, leading to a collapse in prices and profits, mass layoffs of hundreds of thousands of oil workers and price wars between the petro-states compounded by the crisis of Covid-19. 'Peak oil' has now been rede-fined to mean not oil running out but rather 'peak price' which probably will never again reach former price heights.[31] There would have to be an extraordinary increase in the demand for oil over the next 15 or so years before major capitalist countries implement their already legislated manda-tory cessation of production of petrol and diesel fuelled vehicles by 2040. The old theory of 'peak oil' fails to adequately consider the political pres-sures in coming years to reduce dependence on fossil fuels and is also based on a misunderstanding of the fluctuating relationship of the price and avail-ability of oil supplies to levels of capitalist consumption and production. For example, if easy access to oil supplies peters out, major conservative govern-ments will increase subsidies to oil and gas corporations to maintain prof-itability (rather than rapidly switch to renewables). Oil is already heavily subsidised by petrostate governments, such as by the Trump administration, to the tune of more than five trillion dollars as over-production was encour-aged to sustain falling profits. Even within Trainer's and other 'degrowthers' own frameworks, waiting for the 'oil crisis' is hardly the basis for building self-sufficient communities with their own resources, currencies and lifestyles (see Chapter Thirteen). Also, when the shops closed under Covid-19 restrictions, this did not quell the desire of many to consume once the shops reopened. Rather, it was mass unemployment and decline in income and credit that restricted former levels of consumption.

My colleagues Sam Alexander and Brendan Gleeson assume that I not only dismiss 'lifestyle' changes at the household level as trivial (for instance, simplifying consumption, adopting permaculture and implementing energy saving measures), but that I also ignore the fact that major structural changes within capitalism must first be based on cultural changes in behaviour at the micro level.[32] Not at all. Our ultimate positions are closer than they think. We agree that degrowth is not an either/or strategy to be pursued at only the macro or the micro level; both are necessary. The difference is that I do not invest so heavily in alternative household/community practices as a primary form of political practice because these have not really worked for the past fifty years at a pace or at a penetration level amongst the mass of the popula-tion capable of changing capitalism. This is also a strategy that is designed for relatively affluent people with suburban sized residential land and excludes most people in the world who are either poor, live in apartments or in constrained and blighted urban conditions. For those who are affluent, it is possible to have solar panels on the roofs of most homes, greater production of food in backyards and converted community plots and still have the key political institutions and most forms of production, control of digital communication and military apparatuses of capitalism barely touched.

To link all the suburban and urban houses based on degrowth simplicity principles requires political organisations to legislate or demand specific taxation, social welfare, education, trade, employment and many other key policies. Without broad based political movements there will be no transition to a society that reduces material footprints. The scale and complexity of 'planned degrowth' cannot be left to decentralised and fragmented households, as it needs the support of the majority of people who will probably not first adopt frugal lifestyles and instead wait for governments to reduce material throughput at industry levels. Hence, 'degrowthers' in each country, region and locality will need to outline how 'planned degrowth' and the delivery of crucial services and employment will be designed for not hundreds of people or thousands of people, but for millions and billions of people currently dependent on income from capitalist growth orientated enterprises and public sector institutions. Without these concrete proposals they will fail to attract the mass support that degrowth urgently needs.

Ever since the 1960s, minorities of people have adopted alternative forms of self-sufficiency, trying to change the world by educating their children and other forms of 'the personal is political' strategies. Collectively, they are admirable but politically have overwhelmingly failed to change dominant practices. Like Serge Latouche[33] and many other 'degrowthers', Alexander and Gleeson recognise that government policies will be necessary on a full range of fiscal and urban planning policies to make the structure and function of cities more sustainable. They are also correct to argue that it is in the large urban centres that degrowth movements need to show their transformative relevance. Ultimately, various forms and levels of degrowth will largely be driven in the future by a mixture of changed lifestyles, emergency unplanned responses to growing ecological crises and by concerted planned political action to transform existing capitalist political economies.

DIFFERENTIATING 'POST-INDUSTRIAL' FROM POST-CARBON SOCIETIES

To avoid any misunderstanding, it is necessary to restate that any transition to post-carbon capitalist or post-capitalist societies will be unlike the transitions outlined in mainstream theories of post-industrial society that were popular from the 1960s until the 1990s. In these theories, history moved through a variation of essentially three stages: a) the transition from clans and tribes to hierarchical agrarian societies ruled by the sword; b) the transformation of land-based orders into urban industrial society (whether liberal capitalist, fascist or Soviet) where power shifted from the aristocracy and religious orders to goods-producing capitalist industrialists or one-party state bureaucrats; and c) the rise of knowledge and information-based post-industrial social orders where most people worked in services rather than in factories. Post-industrialist theory was an extension or update of nineteenth century classical sociology that conceived human history as going through sweeping 'stages' except that the 'end stage' in post-industrial theory was not 'modernity' in the form of capitalist or socialist industrialisation, but rather an advanced technologically based society.

Not only were post-industrial societies conceived as driven by technological change, but the impression created was that post-industrial societies were no longer class divided, as capitalists were being replaced by managers and professionals who now ruled through their ability to control information and utilise scientific-technical knowledge.[34] Post-industrial theories were either a mixture of simplistic, class-free scenarios about the 'information economy' or more elaborate sociological scenarios. In 1973, sociologist Daniel Bell, the 'father' of post-industrial theory published his book *The Coming of Post-Industrial Society: A Venture in Social Forecasting*, in which he outlined his vision for the next fifty years.[35] Given the passage of five decades, it is now possible to evaluate his prognoses in relation to the contemporary world and the current ecological crisis. Bell saw pre-industrial, industrial and post-industrial societies as based on three axial structures and principals that governed the action and character of each type of society: a) the 'social structure' comprising the economy, technology and occupations; b) the 'polity' concerned with distribution, adjudication and enforcement of power; and c) the sphere of 'culture' which was the realm of expressive symbolism and meaning whether religious or secular, high or popular culture.

According to Bell, industrial societies were characterised by diverse types of political regimes and witnessed the rise of particular occupations in the service sector and the decline of manual workers. In his 1976 book, *The Cultural Contradictions of Capitalism*, Bell argued that three contradictory axial principles governed the economy (efficiency), the polity (equality) and the culture (self-realisation or self-gratification).[36] He was alarmed by the 1960s counter-culture and generation of students and dissidents who threatened social order, capitalist corporations and the traditional values of educational institutions (that is, the culture of 'Western imperialist, white dead males'), even though students benefited materially from market capitalism. It is noteworthy that Bell did not forecast what would happen in the sphere of culture or politics but only in the economy or 'social structure'. He discussed environmental pollution, but like many Weberians, liberals and Marxists working within the paradigm of 'capitalism versus democracy', Bell largely ignored ecological factors as decisive in any future social transformation.

Instead, as an ex-Trotskyist, Bell transposed to capitalist societies the old dilemma of the class nature of the Soviet Union that had troubled anti-Stalinists. Could one have classes in a society where private property had been abolished, and were the managers and bureaucrats a 'new class' or a 'new caste'? Bell partly projected this dilemma onto America as the world's most advanced society heading for post-industrialism. Hence, the new managers, scientists, system planners and technicians of post-industrial society that were clustered around universities, bureaucracies and businesses were, he argued, not a 'new class' but a benign caste or elite. He worried that an upsurge of 'populism' from the lower educated population would lead to resentment against the coming power exercised by new 'knowledge elites' and threaten democracy. This scenario has certainly transpired in conjunction with a combination of racist and economic factors that Bell did not anticipate, particularly the rise of nationalism as a reaction to the socioeconomic pain caused by market globalisation.

As a leading defender of liberal/conservative values, it seems odd that given Bell was a Harvard professor, he ignored the indispensable role played by universities, researchers, technicians and other specialists in the military-industrial complex and the conduct of numerous wars as well as their promotion of market cultural values. Fifty years later, his separation of 'the economy' from politics and culture looks distinctly naïve. Given the increased dominance of capitalist corporations globally since 1973, together with the decline of radical anti-capitalist cultural forces and the political defeats suffered by labour movements, the 'cultural contradictions of capitalism' that Bell feared have been significantly diminished, and barely visible except in one crucial area: anti-materialism. Whereas Bell was alarmed by the 'hedonism' and 'nihilism' of the 1960s counter-culture eroding traditional religious values and the work ethic while also fundamentally weakening the legitimacy of existing political institutions, what he attributed to the destructive role of 'modernism' was made redundant by the subsequent rise of post-modernism which made modernist values positively conservative. Importantly, he largely ignored or like others, failed to predict how the anti-materialist and pro-environmental values of the 'back to nature' 'hippie' and other 1960s movements would evolve into large anti-capitalist green movements in the following five decades.

Bell's emphasis on how a post-industrial knowledge elite would replace capitalist corporations completely misread the fusion of capitalism and technology that would give rise to Google, Apple, Microsoft, Amazon, Facebook and other corporate monoliths. The latter have helped shape not only business and occupational spheres, but also the conduct of politics and key aspects of popular culture and social relations. The fusing of digital culture, financialisation and private sector services into deeply integrated forms of capitalist social orders contradicts most of the 'forecasting' by Bell and others. Even his analysis of professions and related occupational change, which superficially looks closer to the mark, could be disputed if we count the tens of millions of dirty, polluting manufacturing and mining manual jobs in offshore low and middle-income countries that provide the material goods consumed in 'post-industrial' OECD countries.

Hence, the concept of post-industrial capitalism in OECD countries is both a reality and an illusion, that is, a geographical displacement rather than the disappearance of industrial capitalism. If an industrial society was defined as 'goods-producing', then this ignored the vast numbers of service sector workers which were always indispensable to securing the circulation, protection and numerous administrative services necessary to sustain and reproduce capitalist production. Likewise, if the 'post-industrial' society is characterised by 'knowledge and information', then the post-industrial theorists failed to adequately distinguish between the forms of knowledge practice that were dominant. Take for example, technical and scientific knowledge necessary for sophisticated electronics, metallurgy, chemical and synthetic materials or digital software essential to advanced military sectors, space industries and civilian goods production. These are not equivalent to theories and knowledge required in humanities education, health, social care and cultural activity. This distinction is also often ignored by Left technological utopian concepts of post-capitalism.

Little was said by post-industrial theorists about looming ecological crises driven by incessant growth, even though the Club of Rome's *Limits to Growth* had been published in 1972. What is clear today is that the old notion of 'post-industrial society' has certain overlaps but is not equivalent to various conceptions of 'post-carbon society' or 'sustainable society' put forward by technological utopians such as Jeremy Rifkin or Aaron Bastani. In fact, it is difficult to actually find contemporary theorists articulating a model of the power wielders in a 'post-carbon society' that would be equivalent to the aristocracy or capitalist industrialists in earlier types of feudal or capitalist society. Apart from notions of classless, post-work or post-capitalist futures where all seem to have equal power (after the removal of corporations), little analysis is provided today by radicals or liberal technocrats about how we get from 'carbon capitalism' to post-carbon or post-capitalist futures.

Unless there is unforeseen radical change, it is clear that capitalist classes will continue to exist and probably remain dominant during the decades-long transition from fossil fuels to a society based on renewables. If, however, there is a successful push to seriously reduce material footprints, it is doubtful that capitalists will be able to retain their hegemony. Corporations will continue to be run by managers and technocrats committed to profitability and efficiency but a 'transitional society' will require power sharing if socio-political institutions are to be re-geared towards environmental sustainability. This begs the question of whether state institutions will be administered by parties and administrators who will subordinate market values to social and environmental objectives such as biodiversity and equality, or whether governments will continue to prioritise inequality by satisfying the needs of corporate capital and small and medium business lobbies?

Finally, if the axial principle of culture within capitalist societies was, according to Bell, 'self-realisation' or 'self-gratification', will the 'cultural contradictions' of the 'transition period' witness a clash between these axial principles of individualism and the emerging axial principle of co-operation. Although I am critical of Bell's conservative propositions, it is still particularly important to consider whether post-carbon capitalism or post-capitalist eco-socialism or some other type of social formation will be threatened or undermined by new 'cultural contradictions'. If this is the case, what will characterise these socio-economic and political 'axial principles' and to what degree will they differ from those currently dominant in capitalist societies? Sociologist Ingolfur Blühdorn, for instance, argues that in the post-truth age, democratic legitimacy is both hollowed out and based on an ambivalent and contradictory value system. There is now a clash he argues, between the notion of citizens' inalienable right to 'self-realisation' and the incompatibility of this individualist agenda with finite resources and a collapsing biophysical system.[37] In short, individual self-realisation of the affluent 'good life' (promoted by Right-wing and centre-Left parties, as well as by some Left technological utopians) is incompatible with a sustainable biosphere.

Blühdorn's analysis alerts us to the new complexities of 'democracy versus sustainability' but it also espouses a pessimistic theory of 'decline' similar to Christopher Lasch, Richard Sennett and other earlier critics of 'modernity'. At the same time that Bell was bemoaning the 'cultural contradictions of capitalism', Lasch attacked the 'culture of narcissism' while Sennett focused on the 'tyranny of intimacy' and the search for 'authenticity'.[38] Both lamented how the development of capitalism and the corresponding rise of bureaucracy and professional experts led many to retreat to the private self in the quest for meaning; these trends have combined to debase and transform public life. Whereas Lasch longed for a mythical populist bygone era to restore democratic communities in America, Sennett sought refuge in the ideal of the 'craftsman' as an antidote to the specialised division of labour produced by bureaucratic capitalism. Both were pre-feminist analyses of essentially male dominated public life that simultaneously longed for the *gemeinschaft* of small face-to-face associative life while recognising that we lived in the *gesellschaft* of large urban and impersonal relations.[39]

Two decades later, Ulrich Beck, Elisabeth Beck-Gernsheim and Anthony Giddens analysed how 'individualisation' and feminism affected family life, personal relations and the broader public life of democracy, work and culture.[40] The relationship between sexuality, intimacy and democracy changed the possibility for men and women to develop the right to free and equal self-development. The sexual passion of private life and the sexualisation of public life were distinct and yet related. If intimacy and democracy were to be made compatible, then societies would need substantive rather than mere formal democratic rights in public and private life.[41] In recent decades, the notion of 'individualisation' has extended to same-sex and transgender relations. Zygmunt Bauman's notion of 'liquid modernity'[42] and Beck's concept of cosmopolitanism and the 'risk society'[43] highlighted both the fragility of traditional social relations and institutions and the new threats to all facets of political economic, environmental and social life. The positive dimension of greater opportunities and access to global cultures was countered by increasing health and safety risks from toxic products, military and environmental threats, to name just some of the fear-inducing aspects of daily life. Consumption and production were now inextricably associated with both self-realisation and self-gratification on the one side and the unleashing of global and local dangers, fear of catastrophes and loss of meaning and community traditions.

While the notion of a 'risk society' contains many suggestive insights, it is also both dated and politically insufficiently differentiated. One needs a hierarchy of 'risks' that are more dangerous than others, rather than a description of endless 'risks'. For instance, if 'democracy and sustainability' are to become compatible, close attention must be paid to the organising principles of any future sustainable democracy. We know that lack of democratic scrutiny has fuelled an organisational logic in Communist countries based on corruption whereby managers and local party officials risked causing workers' deaths and environmental destruction due to fear of disobeying or critiquing irrational orders. The failure to use safety measures, such as shutting down production in particular factories to save lives or prevent pollution was linked to fear of not fulfilling commands 'from above' such as the central plan. Similarly, hiding serious local problems (such as Covid-19) is also related to a closed system whereby officials fear losing their privileged positions.

By contrast, 'risks' in so-called open competitive market capitalist systems based on 'shareholder value' and quarterly bonuses for managers tends to prioritise and incentivise highly exploitative and destructive practices affecting countless communities, jobs, habitats and lives. A proportion of the public may increasingly calculate the 'risks' from particular industries, chemical products, environments or diets. This social fear of 'risk' is related, yet quite different to the notion of 'risk' held by managers and entrepreneurs. The latter weigh their potential profits and bonuses against the cost of either preventing or causing toxic spills, producing carcinogenic goods or hundreds of thousands of preventable industrial deaths and serious injuries. The wilful abuse of hundreds of millions of workers and consumers continues unabated and is part of a destructive organisational logic that long preceded the 'risk society'.

It is also necessary to note the more pronounced recent cultural changes that Beck and other analysts of 'risk society' did not adequately factor in when developing their theories of post-modern or post-industrial capitalism. Today, there is a sizeable minority of the population in many countries that exhibit contradictory attitudes and responses to a variety of 'risks'. On the one hand, in the era of 'fake news' and conspiracies many people accept the 'truth' of all sorts of *non-risks*. On social media, there are endless claims about everything from 5G networks as the cause of Covid-19 to government and business conspiracies seeking to 'stage' scenes of mass shootings in schools simply to 'take away' the freedom of citizens to own guns. The other side of this cultural syndrome of hyper-market individualism is the rejection or denial of scientifically established risks. Take for instance, the defiant protests against Covid-19 quarantines, opposition to wearing masks and other such ideological manifestations of risk-prone behaviour or especially the widespread Right-wing denial of the largest risk facing the world (climate breakdown) overwhelmingly documented by climate scientists.

The polarisation of social attitudes over the existence, character or extent of particular 'risks' spells acute political dangers for any social movement trying to simultaneously advance democratic rights and post-carbon sustainability. It is the notion of democratic rights which legitimises intolerant and anti-democratic Right-wing groups and movements. Yet, without these democratic rights, any post-carbon society would be doomed to become an authoritarian state. We need to recognise the inbuilt incentives and unintended consequences of existing formal private and public organisational structures which encourage psychotic and other pathological sadistic managerial traits. The onus is on advocates of local, national or international forms of democratic sustainable institutions to ensure that social forces advancing both 'democracy' and 'sustainability' do not contradict one another or replicate existing highly negative practices.

Looking back on the discourse of the 'culture of narcissism', 'liquid modernity', the 'risk society' and 'individualisation/cosmopolitanism' in the decades between the 1970s and the first decade of the new century, one is struck by the mixture of important cultural themes and exaggerated accounts of how much of the old world had been transformed. While Lasch, Bauman and Beck have died, their diagnoses of the 'liquid' world did not lead to their adoption of a radical politics. Instead, Sennett along with Giddens endorsed a mainstream social democratic/Third Way politics[44] but opposed radical green movements. Bauman was sympathetic to the post-growth ideas of Tim Jackson, and Lasch simultaneously supported conservative 'lower-middle class' American industrial culture and Rudolf Bahro's warning that extending Western affluence to the rest of the world would result in ecological catastrophe.[45]

For all the problems with their individual positions, what the writings of Lasch, Sennett, Giddens, Bauman, Beck, Beck-Gernsheim and Blühdorn (in their different ways) alert us to is the need to be aware of the dangers associated with the quest for 'authenticity', 'self-realisation' and small-scale communities or *gemeinschafts*. We can't all revert to becoming 'craftsmen', most women across the world are still heavily dominated by patriarchal relations and lack the opportunity to exercise their 'individualisation'. In those countries where women can exercise their 'individualisation', many are torn between career market competitiveness and maternal feelings. Currently, only a minority of feminists are 'maternal feminists' caught between conservatives on the one side and quasi-neoliberals on the other. An alternative society based on care and equality would need to simultaneously reject both conservative notions of gender and neoliberal notions of the mythical 'autonomous individual' that is not dependent on somebody else for care at some point in their life.[46] If cosmopolitan values continue to be overshadowed by nationalism and racism, the desire for self-sufficient individuals and communities also comes packaged with highly negative narcissistic characteristics. It is common for social change movements to decline and fall apart because of the inability to work with other individuals due to 'personality' clashes despite supposedly sharing common values. Hence, future local communities can easily become a destructive or unhappy *gemeinschaft* just like an open planned tyrannical office based on false intimacy.

The transition to a post-carbon democracy is made more difficult by the erosion of social bonds and personal relationships and the emergence of a new subjectivity in the form of 'non-commitment'. Marx described how in early capitalism 'all that is solid melts into air' and Bauman, Beck, Giddens, Sennett and company analysed the modernist and postmodernist dissolution of earlier relationships in late twentieth century capitalist societies. Lasch focussed on the development of a survivalist 'minimal self' that required people to manage how to cope in a world of constant economic, social and environmentalist crises. "A stable identity" he observed, "stands among other things as a reminder of the limits of one's adaptability. Limits imply vulnerability, whereas the survivalist seeks to become invulnerable, to protect oneself against pain and loss. Emotional disengagement serves as still another survival mechanism."[47]

Building on these theories, Eva Illouz goes one step further in the early decades of the twenty-first century. Analysing the impact of forty years of neoliberal practices, whether in derivatives, outsourcing of labour, multiple sexual relations on Tinder or 'unfriending' people on Facebook with a click of programmed software, Illouz observes that the "moral injunctions that constitute the imaginary core of the capitalist subjectivity, such as the injunction to be free and autonomous; to change, optimise the self and realise one's hidden potential; to maximise pleasure, health, and productivity"[48] now all combine to elevate 'non-commitment'. Rather than a survivalist 'minimal self', Illouz sees 'optimising the self' as also resulting in non-commitment. Choice, she observes, "which was the early motto of 'solid capitalism', then has morphed into non-choice, the practice of perpetually adjusting one's preferences 'on the go', not to engage in, pursue, or commit to relationships in general, whether economic or romantic. These practices of non-choice are somehow combined with intensive calculative strategies of risk assessment."[49]

If Lasch's and Illouz's analyses are plausible and extend to a substantial proportion of the population, advocates of democratisation and sustainability now face the widespread 'non-commitment' of people to either joining or remaining members of parties and movements. Psychoanalyst and sociologist, Ian Craib, qualifies this by noting that if the failure to commit to an organisation is narcissistic because it is based on seeing the world in terms of what can be gained for oneself rather than what can be given, this overlooks the important point of being able to negotiate commitment. A mindless commitment, he argues, "is as narcissistic as an inability to commit oneself."[50]

Transitioning to a new post-carbon society requires not just political commitment and activism but also building a new social subjectivity that counters the hyper-individualism of 'optimising the self' at the expense of others. It is possible that escalating economic and environmental crises and major events will lead to the development of a new co-operative subjectivity. This new 'self' has so far not emerged with existing responses to conventional political, economic and social activity. It would be unrealistic to believe that in a transitional phase between the existing old society and a new emerging social order that individuals would be able to fully jettison their old selves and become 'born again' non-narcissistic altruistic beings.

As decarbonisation will have to take place under quite different parliamentary or authoritarian regimes, there will certainly be multiple political economic and cultural tensions between religious and secular beliefs, between concepts of private and public life, between traditional notions of education and a work ethic versus co-operative values in a 'post-work' society. These tensions and conflicts will change not only our relations with the natural world but also the purpose and goal of knowledge and economic activity. We are only at the doorstep of profound changes to all aspects of familiar socio-economic and cultural practices. It is highly likely that automation and machine learning will transform the structure and content of not just vocational and general education but also other institutional practices in ways that today are yet to be recognised.

The accumulation of capital and the development of military power have been the twin interrelated driving motors of many countries in the past 200 years. How are they to be replaced in a post-carbon or post-capitalist society? Short of revolution and demands to end militarisation, defund the police and abolish capitalism, these goals remain slogans or consigned to the 'too hard basket' of most radical activists and theorists. Much about future post-carbon societies remains unexplored. We do know, however, that unlike benign theories of 'post-industrial' society, any possibility of constructing post-capitalist societies will not be smooth transitions based on new 'green growth' industries, employment and knowledge. A post-carbon society is not to be confused with the creation of a post-capitalist society which will almost certainly involve major political conflict, social convulsion and protracted struggles.

11. THE POSSIBLE EMERGENCE OF NEW SOCIAL CHANGE AGENTS

TO BETTER UNDERSTAND the lack of clarity among theorists and activists about the character of possible emerging new industries, institutions and societies during the next ten to forty years, it is sobering to reflect on the failed prophecies that were made in similar but earlier debates from the 1830s to the 1870s. During this period when agrarian societies were being transformed into varying levels of industrial capitalism, most predictions about the character of future societies either failed to materialise or took quite different directions. These debates centred on identifying which social class or classes would be pivotal in countering existing ruling classes and, equally importantly, recognising which social classes were in decline, as their historical moment had passed. The participants in these earlier debates argued that if the emerging social agents of change were not identified, then it would be difficult to develop appropriate political organisational forms capable or realising the goals necessary for any future alternative society.

It is important to remember that the currently dominant Left paradigm of 'capitalism versus democracy' could dramatically change or become historically obsolete just as struggles between the Third Estate (commoners) and the First and Second Estates (clergy and nobility) within *ancien regimes* in France and other countries before 1789 became increasingly politically irrelevant decades later. It is not that the aristocracy and clergy disappeared during the nineteenth century, but rather that new classes of capitalists and workers as well as other social strata emerged from the dissolution of the Third Estate. One hundred and thirty-years later, is it misguided to ask what could emerge from the dissolution of both the capitalist class and the working class? After all, the Third Estate embraced a more diverse set of classes (including the early bourgeoisie and craft workers) rather than just workers or capitalists. Yet contemporary capitalist and working classes are far from homogeneous and also have no political unity at both national and global levels.

In the early twenty-first century, it is evident that the dominant mode of capitalist production will continue to undergo substantial changes driven by intense global and regional market competition, technological innovation and diverse political responses to unavoidable environmental pressures, not just those driven by the need to reduce greenhouse gases. What is less clear is how private or public ownership and control, levels of full-time or precarious employment, social welfare coverage or austerity and impoverishment, equitable or unfair tax collection will change in coming years. New political organisations, coalitions of movements or other political forms will possibly emerge, but these are currently not visible. Nonetheless, it is important to have some prior rudimentary understanding of what will either not work or struggle to survive, and what type of organisations and policies could possibly succeed in mobilising future majorities in those countries that could be more receptive to changing incessant capitalist material growth. For example, trade unions are defensive organisations that can sometimes promote new social ideas, but they are ill-equipped to lead their members in a full-scale challenge to the social system as opposed to specific campaigns about wages, work conditions and other issues.

It is therefore necessary not to confuse two aspects of class: how classes are constantly changing both in their composition and in their relation to other classes; and why a social 'map' of classes is not equivalent to the way organisations, movements and institutions express or claim to advance particular class policies, especially future political and environmental objectives. In Volume One of *Capital*, for example, Marx cited the 1861 census in England and Wales to show that the largest category of workers were predominantly female domestic servants, an occupation double the size of coal and metal miners, three times larger than metal manufacturing workers and double the size of all the workers in cotton and other textile factories.[1] Yet, it was not domestic servants who led the formation of new trade unions and political parties. One hundred and fifty years later, we superficially appear to have come full circle in developed capitalist countries. While not primarily employed in domestic service, the overwhelming majority of workers are nonetheless once again employed in all kinds of services. What is significant is not their numerical size. Rather, most contemporary service sector workers, like the old domestic servants, are isolated and fragmented, especially in small and medium business workplaces such as shops, offices, leisure and personal care centres, that are once again largely non-unionised. In some countries, however, levels of unionisation are substantial, particularly among public sector service workers and in occupations with a heavy presence of female workers such as nursing and teaching. Will these unorganised and organised workers play a minor or major role in shaping post-carbon societies?

DECLINING AND RISING SOCIAL CLASSES

To illustrate the dilemma facing those who are currently trying to conceptualise future socio-political trends, it is worth reflecting on the conflict over theory and practice between Karl Marx and Mikhail Bakunin (and their followers) in the International Working Men's Association during the 1860s and early 1870s. Both shared many views about the need for socialism but differed on substantive issues including who would make the revolution and whether a state would exist under socialism. Bakunin, the anarchist, was heavily orientated to the past and present size of the peasantry in agrarian Europe rather than to the rapidly industrialising and urbanising capitalist social structures. He therefore argued that peasants would play a leading revolutionary role, as they were closer to nature. Bakunin also championed what he described as the 'riff-raff' or 'rabble' of society (thieves, prostitutes and others *not* employed as wage labour in factories and other workplaces). While Marx called these sub-proletariat the 'lumpen-proletariat', Bakunin saw them playing a vital role because they were 'uncontaminated' by stuffy, property-orientated, law-and-order bourgeois social practices. He liked the 'riff-raff' because too many 'respectable' workers were conservative and aped the manners and values of the bourgeoisie. Bakunin also opposed Marx's argument for the 'dictatorship of the proletariat', a temporary socialist state that would protect the working-class from any attempt by the capitalist class to reimpose capitalism. Marx saw the state as withering away only in the advanced stage of communism whereas Bakunin objected to a worker's state dictating to the peasantry and especially to the 'rabble' of society.

Although their debate may appear archaic, it remains instructive when considering who will bring about an ecologically sustainable democracy and what will be its main characteristics. Both Bakunin and Marx were fundamentally wrong insofar as no complex society can function without new coordinating state institutions, especially those concerned with social justice, legal protection of human rights and redistribution of material wealth, whether one calls these societies capitalist, socialist, communist or post-carbon democracies. Some argue that Bakunin was more prescient in that the major revolutions of the twentieth century occurred in peasant-based societies of Russia, China, Vietnam and so forth. However, in developed industrial capitalist countries most peasants and agricultural labourers were consigned to the 'historical dustbin', as their numerical size rapidly declined during the following four decades until 1914. They were ultimately drastically reduced to fewer than 3 per cent of the workforce within less than 50 years after the First World War.

As for the 'lumpenproletariat', only handfuls of radicals in the 1960s and 1970s romanticised criminals, prostitutes and schizophrenics as the 'true revolutionaries'. These groups were seen to violate the norms of private property, bourgeois ideology and cultural taboos. If Freud had attended to the neuroses and psychoses of the bourgeois individual that developed within the bourgeois family, Deleuze and Guattari, among many others, romanticised the power of desire, and promoted 'schizoanalysis' (the power of 'schizoid' desire as the basis of revolutionary action) in opposition to what they saw as conservative psychoanalysis.[2] Today, no major radical social movement believes that substance addicted individuals, criminals and the mentally ill are the vanguard of the new society even though they condemn the 'war on drugs' and the over-emphasis on treating the mentally ill individual rather than the 'sick society', as well as the incarceration and appalling treatment of prisoners in many criminal justice systems.

If Bakunin's peasants largely disappeared by the mid-20th century in OECD countries, the industrial proletariat also began succumbing to the same fate after reaching their high-water mark in these same countries during the 1950s and 1960s. Despite still retaining strength in some industries and engaging in occasional spasmodic militancy, it has been abundantly clear for over fifty years that the leading role Marx attributed to the blue-collar industrial proletariat is, with a few exceptions, well and truly over in OECD countries. Alas, far too many of the old Left are still too wedded to a deep-seated belief in the leading role of the industrial working class as the vanguard of social change. Militant but unsuccessful defensive actions, such those in France in late 2019 and early 2020 over Macron's pension reforms, only perpetuates the illusion that the proletariat are still the vanguard of the revolution.

Very significantly, at the moment it is already technologically possible to produce all the manufactured goods in the world with between five and ten per cent of the total global workforce. Some countries have larger percentages involved in manufacturing, but it highly likely that the percentage of workers employed in factories will experience the same fate of agrarian workers and fall to between 2% and 5% of workforces in coming years. It will not be automation alone that determines the rate of the demise of the blue-collar proletariat. Rather, the size and power of manufacturing sectors will depend on national employment and industry policies, political struggles over job cuts, levels of private investment and the viability of particular enterprises and industries in the face of regional and global market competition.

Even if we update the debates between Marx and Bakunin and ask which classes or segments of contemporary society will be indispensable to the creation of environmentally sustainable post-capitalist social formations, there is no simple answer. In low and middle-income capitalist societies, especially China, India, Indonesia and various Asian countries with substantial industrial working classes and large peasant or agrarian populations, any fundamental social change will likely involve a mixture of the new urban and old rural social forces either in some form of possible political coalition or in strong opposition to one another. These social classes will either champion reform orientated ideas or pursue higher material standards of living within conservative authoritarian market systems. If global competition and climate breakdown and general eco-system deterioration severely constrain economic growth, the consequences will be explosive domestic and international distributional struggles.

It is not just that service sector workers now constitute the over-whelming majority of contemporary wageworkers in developed capitalist societies. Importantly, the low-employment and highly capital-intensive character of solar farms and wind turbine grids combined with the dispersal of renewables on domestic rooftops and in small communities means that the former strategic leverage of powerful miners' unions and oil workers will *not* be crucial to the emergence and operation of post-carbon societies. Driverless vehicles will also undermine road transport unions, while the move to cashless transactions will decimate bank employees. Some workers in strategically important areas such as passenger and air freight transport, warehouse distribution of supplies and consumer goods, digital equipment maintenance, hospitals and pathology laboratories, police forces, extraction and mining of natural resources and food production could cause serious immediate or delayed disruptions if they went on strike. Given the centrality of property development to financialisation, it is not surprising that governments and businesses will continue to ensure that unions in the construction and infrastructure sectors do not undermine the 'property-industrial complex'.

Yet, with the shift to higher levels of cognitive and care work, or the automation of 20% to 70% of many *job tasks* (rather than full automation of jobs), it is difficult to predict which new clusters of specialised workers will acquire indispensable roles in a range of vital industries. What we do know is that the transition to post-carbon societies will require greater reliance on a minority of highly skilled technical and co-ordinating workers, while a majority of low-skilled and single-skilled middle-wage level workers will face uncertain futures as jobs become automated. Organising these fragmented workers around clear sets of unified political demands in order to defend work and living conditions will require quite different organising techniques and political strategies compared with the earlier historical mobilisation of factory workers and miners who were densely concentrated in close proximity to one another.

As we know, the Marxist dream of a revolutionary proletariat has never been realised and is not likely in the near future. Marx was correct in seeing the working-class as the rising class in emerging capitalist countries in comparison to Bakunin's declining peasant and agrarian class. Yet, the industrial proletariat nowhere constituted a revolutionary majority of wage workers: certainly not in North America, Europe, Japan or Australia. Similarly, the revolutions in Russia, China, Vietnam, Cuba and North Korea were not based primarily on the urban proletariat. In Weimar Germany with its politicised working class mobilised into bitterly divided parties and unions (Social Democratic, Communist, Christian and Nazi), the gap between the symbolic representation of the proletariat in newspapers, films, books, art, theatre and public mobilisation far outweighed the numerical and political strength of the actual revolutionary proletariat.[3] Over the past sixty years, it has become common to read historians, Left theorists and activists acknowledging that most industrial workers were never revolutionary in developed capitalist countries and that in recent years have even, with few exceptions, significantly reduced their support for centre-Left social democratic parties.

The brief upsurge of militant strike action in several countries during the 1960s and 1970s, followed by greatly reduced strike activity in the subsequent forty to fifty years, has merely highlighted how weak and passive the majority of industrial labour movements have become in many countries. Across the world, major disruptions and political clashes by striking workers are in a distinct minority except for 'wildcat' eruptions in China and other places without supportive free unions. Instead, public protests incurring violent police crackdowns have in many instances not been instigated by militant organised workers but by various social movements, disaffected and desperate social strata such as the Yellow Vests in France, anti-corruption activists in Lebanon and Iraq, Extinction Rebellion climate protestors, cross-class anti-austerity Chilean protestors or Hong Kong militants opposed to authoritarianism. In France, union activists have even adopted some of the tactics used by the Yellow Vests, as traditional industrial militancy is less effective today.

A century earlier, the original populists, the Russian *Narodnik* intelli-gentsia, regarded the peasantry as a revolutionary force against Czarism and capitalism. However, the impoverished rural masses rejected the urban middle-class intelligentsia who during the 1870s had come to villages to help 'liberate' these largely illiterate and conservative masses. So too, the earnest attempts of middle-class students in tiny Trotskyist and Maoist parties to 'enter' the proletarian workplaces (between the 1960s and 1980s) and help agitate for militant action failed abysmally, as the vast majority of workers rejected radical politics. Similar hostile reactions from miners and other fossil-fuel workers have greeted greens protesting in their mining regions.

Today, Marxist/Leninists who hold onto the belief in the vanguard party and the politics of industrial class struggle are the latter-day Bakunins. They are blind to the character and evolving structure of present-day societies and cling to a politics based on both a declining and transformed working class just like Bakunin who could not see the disappearing power of peasants. Marxist politics continues to rest on the hope that workers in OECD coun-tries will once again become militant. In their wildest hopes, they tentatively cling to the belief that the mass proletariat in China and other industrialising countries will become the vanguard of revolution. Also, there are a minority of radicals who still dream, like the 'mechanical Marxists' of the Second Socialist International prior to 1914, of the crisis-collapse of capitalism. This 'final crisis' never depended, and still does not depend on the organised power of workers. Instead, the notion of 'crisis-collapse' is the inevitable end product of inbuilt 'economic laws' – such as the so-called law of the 'falling rate of profit' and the inevitable immiseration of the working-class – rather than the politically driven 'contradictions of capitalism'.

In recent years, the concept of 'crisis collapse' has migrated to sections of the environment movement and is now visible in crude, apolitical environ-mental theories that see an inevitable collapse of not just capitalism, but of 'global civilisation' due to ecological overshoot.[4] Prominent Extinction

Rebellion member, Rupert Read, believes that 'this civilisation is finished' and that capitalism will collapse.[5] While there are definite ecological limits to incessant material growth, these 'limits' will *not* be felt evenly across the world and must not be confused with some kind of automatic and inevitable system-like process based on natural laws that lead to either doomsday or to a politics that favours environmental care and sustainable social goals. On the contrary, well before any obvious signs of global catastrophe were to occur, 'politics' will almost certainly intervene in the form of increasingly militant mobilisations of citizens via different parties and protest movements. A good example is that in response to the disastrous bush fires, the centre-Left Australia Institute commissioned a poll in January 2020 which found that 63% of voters wanted the Australian government to mobilise all Australians in emergency action to combat climate change.[6] Whether the 22% who opposed such action would grow or decline depends on the specific detailed policies of any such 'war-time' emergency action (which the Morrison government stubbornly refuses to implement).

While the scenes of bush fire devastation prompted overwhelming support for government action, the alarming claims by some in Extinction Rebellion (XR) that *six billion* people will die this century[7] is either too frightening or too far in the future for many in the media and mainstream parties to discuss. Leading climate scientists such as Johan Rockström, Joachim Schellnhuber and Kevin Anderson have argued that a world 4° Celsius warmer in 2100 would be difficult to adapt to and probably would only be capable of accommodating about one billion people due to large areas of the earth being inhospitable for food production and water supplies.[8] This scenario is different to the impression created by XR that six billion would be killed in coming decades but it is ultimately no less true if emergency decarbonisation action is not taken as soon as possible.

POLITICAL STRUGGLE AFTER THE DECLINE OF LABOUR MOVEMENTS

Let us now compare societies at the beginning of capitalist industrialisation with the significant social transformation of production and consumption during the past seventy-five years. In 1825, Britain accounted for about 80 per cent of global CO_2 emissions from fossil fuel combustion due to its advanced level of industrial production and the fact that the rest of the world was largely pre-industrial.[9] By 2019, the UK was responsible for only a tiny 1.2% of global CO_2 emissions compared with China at over 27 per cent, but was still either the fifteenth or seventeenth largest emitter of greenhouse gases in the world (depending on different methodologies) and had per capita emissions at approximately 7.5 tonnes per annum. Notably, these emissions were much higher than per capita emissions in low-income countries such as India and Indonesia (approximately 2.2 and 2.5 tons) but much lower than Qatar (49.2), Kuwait (25.2), Australia (22.9) Saudi Arabia (21) or US (20.3) and even China at 9.23 tons per capita.[10] Most of these national figures are misleading or inaccurate as they don't count such things as emissions from off-shore production of manufactured or agricultural goods consumed by each individual country.

Aside from growing survey data from 13,000 cities, there is scant detailed comparative data that enables us to gain an accurate assessment of carbon footprints. For example, Daniel Moran and co-researchers argue that: "While many of the cities with the highest footprints are in countries with high carbon footprints, nearly one quarter of the top cities (41 of the top 200) are in countries with relatively low emissions. In these cities, population and affluence combine to drive footprints at a scale similar to those of cities in high-income countries."[11] Thus, measuring per capita emissions functions as a crude averaging process. Despite looking at postcodes or differences between low or high-income countries, urban and rural populations, this form of measurement largely ignores class factors. Postcodes can throw some light on income levels and the presence or absence of particular industries, but they are poor indicators of the inter-class divisions in the same postcode of large cities and of whether industries and businesses rather than individuals and households are disproportionately accountable for emissions.[12]

Importantly, we should not confuse country and per capita greenhouse gases emission levels with the much more significant resources elements comprising per capita and national *material* and water footprints. Take, for example, water usage. We know that in developed capitalist countries such as Australia, agricultural businesses use approximately 70 per cent of annual water consumption while millions of urban residents account for between only seven and ten per cent of water usage and the remaining twenty-plus per cent is consumed by private businesses and public authorities. Importantly, we should not confuse high per capita emissions due to small populations with the strategic role played by fossil fuel exports from Australia, Qatar, Saudi Arabia and other countries that are crucial for carbon intensive industries in China and North East Asia, Europe and North America. As I will later elaborate, the political and social challenge of reducing consumed natural resources in material footprints in order to achieve greater sustainability is infinitely harder than decarbonising societies.

As to fossil fuels, Margaret Thatcher's destruction of the power of the coal miners and the coal industry helped reduce UK emissions compared to countries such as Poland and Germany. The latter have opposed the rapid movement away from coal because of domestic political pressures, such as the Social Democrats propping up their industrial voter base or business groups alternating between opposing or supporting renewables according to their market needs.[13] Given current levels of urbanisation and industrialisation, there is no comparison between the global historical conditions within which coal and oil were adopted and the vastly different political economic and environmental circumstances confronting the development of post-carbon societies.

Two well-known studies by Andreas Malm[14] and Timothy Mitchell[15] inadvertently highlight why the likely transition to post-carbon societies will be quite different from the emergence of earlier carbon-based social relations. Malm's *Fossil Capital* is a detailed study of the socio-economic reasons why factory owners in the English cotton industry abandoned power generated by workers operating water wheels in favour of coal-fired steam engines in the period beginning in the 1830s. The ability to locate factories away from rivers and other sources of water gave coal a clear advantage and led to its adoption as an energy fuel across the world. However, when it comes to post-carbon technology and non-fossil fuels, Malm falls back on Kondratieff's highly problematic Long Wave theory and its interpretation by Trotskyist Ernest Mandel (even though Trotsky critiqued Long Wave theory).[16]

I will not repeat all the reasons why Long Wave theory is seriously flawed in terms of its political economic periodisation and explanation of varied forms of capitalist development.[17] Malm is not a technological determinist but unintentionally highlights another reason why innovative technologies do not correlate with periodic upswings of economic growth, whether fossil-based or future renewables. In trying to tie class struggle to Long Waves of capitalist growth, Malm argues that neoliberalism of the fifth Long Wave (1992 to 2008) "can only be understood as a way out of the impasses of the fourth, the Keynesianism of the fourth as a response to the imbalances and catastrophes of the third, and so on..."[18] He therefore erroneously assumes homogeneous or unilinear political economic 'stages' of capitalism, such as Keynesianism, that was *not* universally practised in capitalist countries prior to the 'universal stage' of neoliberalism, that will also not be succeeded by another uniform stage such as 'climate Keynesianism' or some other global-wide system.

We already know that major capitalist powers such as China and the US may be economically interconnected and that they are driven by quite different domestic and international political goals as well as having dissimilar regimes. Hence, the so-called hypothetical 'sixth Long Wave' will not solve problems of a non-uniform neoliberalism as it attempts to implement new technologies. We also do not know which innovative technologies and sources of energy or what kind of economies and social relations are likely to emerge nationally and globally from present-day antagonistic socio-political forces. What we do know is that Long Wave theory, like neo-classical economics, is based on theories of the supposed cycles or upswings and downswings of capitalist growth. What happens to these theories though when capitalist political economies encounter ecological limits to growth? If not prevented, will these so-called periodic downswings become permanent environmental crises that are relatively autonomous and separate to levels of class struggle? In other words, Long Wave theory presupposes infinite economic growth that is periodically interrupted by dysfunctional markets and class struggle rather than by deep-seated and irreversible environmental constraints.

Politically and culturally, there has been no equivalent historical precedent to the social and environmental debates that are currently waged over which energy source is preferable to sustain biodiversity and human wellbeing. In fact, there is a fundamental de-synchronisation between the reproduction of natural cycles of renewal, that is, the rate at which the biosphere can replenish itself by renewing fragile or irreversibly damaged habitats, and the speed at which natural resources are extracted and consumed. This means that the conflicting demands by market forces and pluralist democratic movements require *deceleration* rather than acceleration if social needs and policies are to be debated carefully and democratically.[19]

Technologically, future post-carbon societies could be based on far less geographically concentrated energy sources such as coal, gas and oil. Yet, just because renewable energy can be more easily dispersed and decentralised does *not* automatically tell us whether it will actually become decentralised or crucially, whether political power will also be dispersed, decentralised and re-distributed. Two contradictory patterns of implementation of renewable energy are currently visible. One process is the widely dispersed installation of solar panels and wind turbines by communities and households. The other trend is the investment by private corporations to capture the renewable energy market via the installation of extensive energy grids to harness renewable solar, wind, hydropower and hydrogen, geothermal and other technologies. Should this latter trend succeed, then energy will likely continue to remain heavily owned by capitalist classes or mixtures of public-private enterprises, but not necessarily controlled in the same way or to a similar degree by the same fossil-fuel corporate giants. Either way, technology and energy do not alone pre-determine how they will be utilised, let alone future social classes or the structure and complexity of prospective political institutions and social relations.

It would therefore be highly misleading to approach 'transition' strategies to a post-carbon world as if this is primarily technologically driven and involves little more than governments and businesses setting favourable frameworks for the technological switchover from fossil fuels to zero emitting production and consumption based on renewables. This may well happen because post-carbon societies are commonly envisaged in mainstream media and public discourse as little more than ecologically modernised capitalist systems operating on renewable energy. Conversely, it is possible that demands for climate justice will necessitate major socio-economic policy change to alleviate escalating poverty, unemployment and inequality.

Remember, that in order to meet international emissions targets, most scientific and policy reports calculate that the most difficult forms of mitigation of greenhouse gases have to take place in the ten to twenty years between now and 2040 to reach net zero emissions by 2050. This is precisely the same period when projected levels of automation will escalate alongside mainstream forecasts of a range of developing countries supposedly surpassing existing leading Atlantic capitalist powers. The full socio-political implications of the obstacles to a smooth post-carbon future are either dimly perceived or unrecognised. This is because decarbonisation will initially occur within familiar modes of capitalist production and familiar social institutions before disruption and erosion of existing practices begin to be felt.

Most of the reports on climate change and decarbonisation have tended to focus heavily on the technical mitigation and adaptation costs of transition while largely ignoring or minimising the multiple political economic problems plaguing capitalist countries. It will therefore come as an unpleasant shock to many people to be told that the political struggles associated with economic growth, debt and inequality cannot be divorced from the equally difficult goals of decarbonisation and reduction of material footprints. So far, most Green New Deal proposals either underestimate the almost inevitable scale of change needed even though conservatives view them as far too radical. Nonetheless, it could well be that political conflicts over simultaneously occurring socio-economic and environmental crises will turn out to be very turbulent, perhaps even as volatile as the massive political economic upheavals witnessed during the industrial transformation of nineteenth and early twentieth century societies. It is not just developed capitalist countries that will have to go through this transition. Even without decarbonisation strategies, low and middle-income developing societies have long encountered massive social problems that require a fundamental alteration to existing domestic policies. To think that successful decarbonisation strategies can proceed smoothly without significant modification or abandonment of disastrous, short-sighted international financial, trade, military and aid policies is to put one's head in the sand.

CARBON CAPITALISM AND FOSSILISED DEMOCRATIC STRUGGLES

Although the full political economic ramifications of decarbonisation are either unknown or barely explored territory, Timothy Mitchell's book *Carbon Democracy* reminds us of the power of fossil fuels in the twentieth and twenty-first centuries and importantly, their connection to various wars, imperialist struggles and the development of Western parliamentary democracies. Mitchell rejects a reductionist explanation of how political outcomes (what is 'above ground') can be directly traced back to the coalface and the oil well ('below ground'). That is, he implicitly rejects the orthodox Marxist 'base' determining the socio-political and legal 'superstructure'. Mitchell argues that the growing reliance on carbon was not a one-sided history of the rise of democracy produced by social movements in the newly industrialising cities. Rather, it was also the history of the suppression of democratising movements in regions such as Europe and the Middle East, especially the inseparable relation between the exercise of violence and political repression in the quest for control over fossil fuels.

Mitchell's observations on the role of organised workers' movements such as coal miners, oil workers and railway workers are worth noting. It is the concentrated location of coal and later oil that gave workers in these industries strategic leverage which is also true of rail workers and dockworkers engaged in the distribution of coal and oil. Most coal miners, rail workers and dockers across the world tended to be organised in Communist, social democratic and other Left unions affiliated to major Left parties. They could paralyse production and consumption through their strategically disruptive actions. According to Mitchell, they were the 'shock troops' of democracy and social reform because of their ability to advance society-wide causes on behalf of workers in weaker sectors, particularly unorganised or disadvantaged people.

However, Mitchell's account unintentionally undermines popular Left notions of 'Fordism' – from Gramsci to the Paris Regulation School – that supposedly dominated capitalism prior to the 1970s (see Chapter Eight). It is not mass production on assembly lines and the corporatist agreements between capital and labour sanctioned by governments that shapes capitalism up until the 1970s. Rather, it is the political struggles over the production and availability of cheap fossil fuels that are the necessary material *preconditions* for the emergence and sustainability of mass 'Fordism'.

If coal miners, railway workers and dockers helped advance the 'welfare state' and democracy in the first half of the twentieth century, it was the switch from coal to oil, Mitchell argues, that was used by businesses and governments (both violently and for narrow economic reasons) to weaken powerful miners' unions and thereby also halt or reverse gains made by workers. Thatcher's crushing of the miners in the 1980s would be a particularly strong example. Mitchell's book was published well before the concluding chapter in the long tradition of British mining and industrial workers' communities was written in December 2019. After decades of deindustrialisation and neglect by successive Conservative and Labour governments, various 'Red Wall' Labour electorates with weak local Labour Party community organising switched in large numbers to neoliberals led by Boris Johnson. They eroded more than a century of proud working-class solidarity that in many instances also barely disguised deep-seated racism and nationalism.

Despite Mitchell's insights, his narrow focus on fossil fuels fails to advance a satisfactory explanation of the political and social development of capitalist societies. He says much about carbon but far less about democracy, namely, how particular historical state apparatuses developed and why their origins, character and level of democratic control differ from one capitalist country to another. *Carbon Democracy* is a thesis that claims too much, both indirectly and directly, on behalf of fossil fuels. It overlooks the way the mobilisation of different classes and segments of society helped shape quite diverse political cultures, levels of social welfare and either more individualist or more communitarian traditions and institutional values, despite the fact that they *all relied* on fossil fuels. We need to differentiate the origins and evolution of many of these political institutional forms and cultural values from their direct or indirect connections to coal and oil. This is not to doubt past and current dependence of production and consumption on fossil fuels. Rather, it is to recognise that socio-economic dependence on coal, gas and oil is not equivalent to an inflexible political commitment to fossil fuels (and all that this entails) if alternative energy is possible and readily available.

Mitchell, like the analysts of 'Fordism', ignores the fact that despite giant multinational corporations, most businesses have never been just large mass-producing entities. Similarly, significant numbers of unionists were not in mining, oil, railways or giant factories. Instead, depending on the country, many workers were members of numerous small and medium craft and post-craft unions or in public sector unions away from factories, mines and oil wells. This is not to deny Mitchell's important highlighting of the significant role played by miners, oil workers, rail workers and dockers or the wider influence of struggles by unionised workers in large manufacturing plants. Rather, it is to also recognise that the pre-existing historical institutional and cultural contexts within which 'carbon democracy' and 'Fordism' emerged (for example, nineteenth and early twentieth century nationalist struggles or secular conflicts against the power of organised religion) were also highly influential in shaping contemporary institutions and political cultures, especially legal statutes, levels of socio-political tolerance and civil rights.

It is important not to reduce struggles for social recognition and political representation by women, non-property owners, people of colour, First Nations peoples and other minorities to simply the 'economy'. Moreover, we should not overlook the contradictory and complex conservative or progressive roles of those employed in services, or small business owners, rural movements and the professions in either strongly opposing democratisation or else advancing social improvements for workers and other disadvantaged people in areas of health, education, housing and political representation. Without the multifaceted forms of all these socio-political struggles, it is not possible to understand why the characteristics of national voting systems, levels of taxation and public services, social welfare or legal-administrative institutions, to name just a few areas, vary so considerably in all fossil-fuel based capitalist countries.

Mitchell's over-emphasis on carbon at the expense of democratic struggles concerning the policies and practices of diverse state apparatuses is a lesson in why there will be *no simple correlation* between emerging post-carbon energy systems and the complex component structures and policies of future political regimes. One only has to look at the stimulus packages in response to Covid-19 to see the difference between low-level expenditure on ecological modernisation in Europe as opposed to the almost complete lack of such investment in the US, Australia and other countries.

If fossil-fuels laid the preconditions for the growth in manufacturing and thereby the growth of workers' solidarity unions and parties, the dawn of the post-carbon era coincides in affluent countries with widespread de-unionisation, precarity and exploitation. Today, coal miners, rail workers and dockers in OECD countries are a shadow of their former strength due to mine closures, road transport, containerisation and automation of docks and so forth.[20] The transformation of rail-freight and shipping by containers began in the US in the 1960s before it moved to other countries. Although the teamsters became a powerful road-based union, they were not supportive of radical social reforms as earlier Left-wing rail and dock-worker unions across the world. In recent years, miners can no longer be described as solidly Left-wing and are often opposed to environmentalists or even support Right-wing nationalist movements and politicians like Trump. In low and middle-income societies, the repression of workers attempting to form unions, the annual deaths of more than 15,000 miners in China, India, South Africa, Bolivia and the Congo or the tens of thousands of children working in the mines of Columbia and other countries are all testimony to the vast disparity in social conditions and political rights across the world. Yet, it is these widely divergent conditions and global imbalances that will shape the pace, the character and the extent to which post-carbon societies emerge via democratic processes or arise without even minimal social rights.

In highlighting the role of labour struggles in the development of carbon society, Malm and Mitchell inadvertently alert us to the absence of significant sections of contemporary labour movements in promoting post-carbon sustainable democracies. It is true that the International Labour Organisation and a considerable number of trade unions (in EU member states, Australia and other countries) have campaigned alongside environmentalists for policies to decarbonise capitalist economies. Yet, it is also true that the positive commitments of trade union peak bodies to combat climate breakdown have been hampered in various countries by the reluctance and even opposition of some mining and manufacturing unions to accept environmental crises as urgent issues. Clearly, there are significant disparities between unions in carbon-intensive and non-fossil fuel industries as to their level of support for climate emergency action. Many weakened union movements are either not strong enough or committed enough to fight for a post-carbon future and reclaim the progressive leading roles that they once played in bringing about 'carbon democracy' in capitalist societies.

WHAT REPLACES CARBON DEMOCRACY?

Will the repression, killings and persistent violence waged by police, armed forces and private police forces to defend capitalist businesses against industrial workers fighting for social justice be repeated in the struggle to bring about post-carbon democracy? It is not enough for environmental economists, theorists of the 'environment state', advocates of degrowth and others to devise ideas about the new sustainable society. They also need to specify which social agents will likely carry out this transformation, what level of obstruction they will encounter and whether the transition will be peaceful or violent.

Strategically and politically, the debates during the past five decades over how to define who belongs to the proletariat have been eclipsed by new social change issues. Orthodox Marxists incorrectly assume that all those who perform so-called 'unproductive labour' (that is, do not produce surplus value) in sales, administration, finance, transport and the circulation of goods, or in nursing, teaching and many other services, that the vast majority of these workers in service sectors ultimately depend on those working in 'productive' jobs and their degree of exploitation. In other words, if the rate of surplus value extraction falls and thereby also profitability, then all those in 'unproductive' jobs in both private and public sectors who help circulate commodities and realise their value through sales and administration – not to forget all the tax revenue derived from production and consumption processes needed to fund social welfare dependents and public services – that all of these 'unproductive' jobs will become unviable and welfare dependents will lose their income as tax revenue declines. If this is true about 'productive labour', then it would be impossible for a post-carbon capitalist society that sheds 'productive' jobs to become economically viable if implementing ecologically modernisation.

Moreover, for those who see post-capitalist societies as simultaneously post-carbon and post-growth, where will the tax revenue come from once those workers producing surplus value (currently a minority of the total workforce) are liberated from their exploitative conditions? If post-capitalist societies are not be based on barter or other moneyless forms of sustenance, then notions of how capitalist exploitation of labour can be replaced and new complex production and consumption relations made environmentally sustainable need urgent answers.

Any development of post-carbon democracies will need to consider how recent changes in labour markets and production processes affect transition strategies. In both the most technologically advanced sectors of the 'digital economy' and the least developed 'informal' sectors of low and middle-income countries, exploitation and self-exploitation now take on countless variations. Workers are often not sure who employs them given outsourcing of production and services, shelf-companies and other business devices such as digital platforms designed to undermine traditional employer-worker relations.

Current political debates concern the classification of people working in precarious 'informal' sectors. In low and middle-income countries, the boundaries between villagers, transitory urban workers, street vendors and numerous other categories of work and income do not conform to employment and work conditions formalised by national state regulations or enterprise agreements. Precarious labour has always existed in capitalist societies. Moreover, the 'informal sector' and 'precarity' are very loose concepts that often encompass diverse social groups, from peasants and street vendors right through to university-educated workers in casual 'gig economy' jobs. These workers have little social, cultural and class relations in common apart from their precarious status as they do not even share similar work descriptions and conditions.

Depending on national labour market legislation and levels of unemployment, approximately 20 to 30 per cent of workers are employed in either 'informal' markets or casual, precarious jobs in OECD countries with much higher percentages in low and middle-income countries, including new forms of slavery and about 152 million child labourers.[21] However, there is a difference between part-time employment and 'gig economy' jobs such as those working for Uber and other platform companies. In many OECD countries 'permanent' employees have remained stable at approximately 79% for the period between 1996 to 2016,[22] whereas in other countries casual and part-time insecure jobs have accounted for almost half of all new positions in the past decade.

We are yet to see whether the 'gig economy' will increase or whether official statistics tell us little about the insecurity felt by most workers even though they are classified as 'permanent employees'. Certainly, the shutdown by Covid-19 witnessed millions of precarious workers left unemployed and unsupported by governments. Also, such is the impact of 'innovative labour processes' that we cannot ignore the real pressures coming from business groups within member countries of the EU and OECD. One such political pressure by employers is to prevent official labour laws from defining what 'standard employment' is or is not.[23] In the US, some business lobbies are going much further and seek to abolish the category of 'employer'. This would legitimise hyper-exploitation based on so-called 'non-existent' employers free from any legal constraints or moral responsibility thus enabling them to adopt ruthless work practices.

Yet, what is the relevance of these socio-economic and legal changes to the growing obsolescence of the paradigm 'capitalism versus democracy'? At one level, the move to informal, highly exploitative labour markets merely confirms the power of private capital when even minimal forms of democratic protection are either substantially weakened or abolished. Remember, that many of the 'precarious' jobs are 'unproductive labour' in the orthodox Marxist sense because they are often found in low-wage service sectors such as retailing and hospitality. At another level, the disintegration of earlier historical notions of the 'working class' combined with the threat of unprecedented challenges to environmental sustainability have the makings of a perfect storm characterised by major political conflict.

Forty years ago, Andre Gorz and others were already arguing that the conflict between workers and capitalists centred on 'the factory' had long been surpassed as the central conflict in society. The 'working class' in Marx's terms could no longer liberate society by liberating themselves from exploitative alienated labour in the mode of production. Instead, Gorz argued that: "It is not through identification with their work and their work role that modem wage-earners feel themselves justified in making demands for power which have the potential to change society. It is as citizens, residents, parents, teachers, students or as unemployed; it is their experience outside work that leads them to call capitalism into question."[24]

Gorz was prescient in focussing on the relation between capitalism and ecology, forecasting how new technology would favour only a minority of skilled/professional workers, and how new work processes such as 'flexi time' and casualisation would undermine the power of unions. Yet, he was wrong in believing that work time would continue to be reduced and hence lose its central meaning in the life of workers. Some countries such as Sweden and Germany have seen a few industries offer four-day weeks in return for higher productivity. But this is atypical of most countries and most industry sectors that have witnessed longer working weeks in the form of involuntary overtime combined with substantial amounts of underemployment.

Old Marxist notions of social change depended on differentiating between two levels of consciousness – a limited 'trade union consciousness' that is mainly preoccupied with improved wage and work conditions, and its opposite, namely, a unifying 'revolutionary class-consciousness'. Both now lose a significant degree of their former political raison d'être. Without a readily identifiable and coherent working class (class-in-itself) let alone a radical proletariat (class-for-itself), there is a question about which social change agents are able to simultaneously represent 'democracy' in its conflict with 'capitalism'. It is little wonder then, that 'democracy' ceases to represent a clear alternative to 'capitalism' or embody a shared political program apart from the belief in the right of all to vote or to make political decisions. This restructuring of the old working class has serious implications for the transition to a post-carbon society.

It has taken the Covid-19 global crisis to reveal why both mainstream social scientists and post-work radicals are promoting superficial theories about automation. There have been many economists and sociologists over the years who have argued that 'capital does not need labour' and that business can happily grow while dispensing with most workers. This may be true for individual employers and enterprises but is profoundly untrue for the total private sector in any single country. One only has to see the disastrous economic impact of the lack of working-class consumers on whole industries and economies due to weeks and months of quarantine measures. Now imagine the dire consequences for capitalist businesses from the permanent retrenchment of 30% to 60% of employees due to escalating automation in coming decades without sufficient well-paid employment replacing these former jobs. Capitalism cannot survive once it abolishes most forms of labour. Can it survive in its current forms if key business sectors and voters pressure governments to engage in mass subsidisation of wages or the creation of government guaranteed jobs?

There is, I argue, also a major difference between traditional forms of class conflict and the forthcoming politics of transitional innovation in an era of environmental crises. Take, for instance, the issue of unemployment. Under the old paradigm of 'capitalism versus democracy', Polish political economist, Michal Kalecki, famously argued that business and political leaders preferred lower profits than the potentially higher profits coming from increased aggregate demand driven by full employment. This is because full employment caused discipline to break down as workers no longer feared losing their jobs and would demand much better conditions.[25] Capitalists also feared democratic state intervention, he observed, as this enabled governments to make crucial public investment decisions that had formerly been largely in the hands of private market forces.

Importantly, Kalecki's thesis ultimately depended on the strength of organised labour movements that were able to take advantage of low unemployment or full employment. Trade unions are, however, shadows of their former strength in many countries. Does this mean that capitalist classes have little to fear? Possibly. Strong organised labour movements remain vital if workers' conditions and rights are to be defended or improved. However, trade unions have historically performed contradictory roles. Apart from defending their members' rights and conditions, they have provided stability for businesses by channelling demands and dissent through recognised processes. Their militancy has also signalled to businesses what technological and organisational innovations are necessary to remain competitive and one step ahead of workers. Take away union strength and all looks rosy for capitalists for a brief period of time. The looming danger for businesses and conservative governments is that the current interregnum of defeated labour movements may not last. The significant difference today is that the union movement may never be revived nationally even though it may continue to be strong in some sectors or industries.

What replaces old labour-capital struggles may be far worse for business than the former 'orderly' channelled character of industrial disputes. Both employers and unions have always feared 'wild cat' strikes because these signalled grass roots rebellion against conservative union leaders and unpredictable danger for employers. Without former historical levels of unionisation being restored, the character of present-day and future environmental challenges means that governments, especially in countries with free elections, will come under mounting pressure from electorates, sections of business and a range of social groups to act to prevent catastrophic environmental events occurring on a frequent basis. Combine this with major socio-economic malaise and we are likely to see eruptions that are far more difficult to control by conventional centre-Left parties or Right-wing governments. The 'Yellow Vests' are possibly a small taste of things to come. Such protests are not like most forms of strike action and confined to a single enterprise or industry. Whole city centres, retailing, tourism, communication and so forth are disrupted and dislocated in ways that are not predictable. Of course, if governments combine rapid intervention to prevent climate chaos with significant social reform agendas, then new forms of 'guerrilla' protests will become less effective. Such pro-active government action presupposes the formation of new political alliances which are unlikely at the moment.

Just as businesses prefer lower profits to full employment, *many companies prefer to live with the risk of global warming* rather than face the consequences of unpredictable and precedent-setting government action on decarbonisation. However, such a choice is not likely to be left to businesses alone. Instead, it is the conflict of 'democracy versus sustainability' that begins to impact or replace old forms of 'capitalism versus democracy'. *Financial Times* columnist, Simon Kuper, declares that: "No electorate will vote to decimate its own lifestyle. We can't blame bad politicians or corporates. It's us: we will always choose growth over climate."[26] Certainly, this is currently true of electorates that haven't yet experienced climate havoc. Questions such as 'how 'urgent is government preventative action' will begin to take on a quite different meaning in the midst of a rapidly unfolding crisis. Even the widespread hostility of a conservative electorate to climate action can be transformed into support for urgent decarbonisation action following major floods, fires and droughts.

Classical Marxist notions of capitalism always assumed divisions among sections or fractions of capitalists (finance, industrial, merchant, mining or agricultural capital) with the dominant fraction(s) of capital determining state policies and ideology. Environmental crises are now splintering the responses of both capitalists and workers as well as creating divisions within various professional, technocratic and other groups at national level and between nation-states internationally. The residues of traditional Right or Left *pre-environmental* consciousness and political aspirations − either capitalism wins, and democracy goes, or democracy (that is, the working class) wins and capitalism goes − still remain clearly visible at the rhetorical and theoretical level. However, in terms of political practice and policy making, these polarised perspectives need rethinking.

Both pro-market and anti-capitalist policy analysts are struggling to keep up with the massive changes afoot. A mere thirty years ago there was much talk about how the 'knowledge economy' based on a new highly educated and highly productive workforce would replace the old industrial 'Fordism' of mass production and create a socially just society. Governments of all kinds, but especially of the 'Third Way', rhapsodised about the dawn of the new era which has now been replaced by the dread of automation wiping out many of these still-born 'knowledge economy' jobs.[27]

Where does it leave those who neither support the old working class nor the illusions about the 'knowledge economy? It is clear to all those desiring an environmentally sustainable society that the traditional organised class politics and working-class culture (still partly visible) remains too rigid and hostile to degrowth values such as reduced forms of material consumption and production. Conversely, many environmentalists and feminists reject working-class and mainstream middle-class forms of masculinist violence and aggression within the family or in public, whether violence at football, motor sports, horse racing or hunting animals. Over the past thirty years, binge drinking, excessive credit-fuelled consumer debt and public incivility has become widespread amongst both women and men. What may be too easily dismissed as old puritanical or conservative censorship is in fact a crucial issue for the construction of any future caring alternative society. For if the future will be more of the same libertarian commercial 'anything goes' culture, respect for nature and biodiversity will be much more difficult to achieve without also concurrently developing a culture of care and civility towards fellow human beings.

THE COUNTRY AND THE CITY

Most discussion of 'social change agents' focuses on urban classes and social strata. Relatively little attention is paid to rural and regional social classes and how these affect the future possibility of any transition to post-carbon societies. Instead, there is no shortage of books and articles by development scholars and radicals on all facets of village life, various struggles conducted by rural movements in developing countries against dispossession of land or polluting industries, harsh living conditions and how populations are forced to migrate to cities in search of work in informal labour markets. What alliances or mutually beneficial socio-economic strategies can be formed between rural and urban social classes are either inadequately discussed or ignored, especially in urbanised OECD countries. This was not always the case. Three decades before Gramsci developed his concept of hegemony and 'organic intellectuals', the German socialist, Karl Kautsky, published his two-volume analysis of *The Agrarian Question* in 1899.[28] Ranked by Lenin and other revolutionaries as the most important work next to Marx's three volumes on *Capital*, Kautsky's largely forgotten classic reminds us of the dearth of work on the political economic relationship between contemporary capitalism, agriculture and environmental sustainability.

While Kautsky's analysis is highly dated, his discussion of the need for a 'cultural state' (education, culture and social welfare) to meet the needs of peasants, rural and urban workers, as well as a political strategy necessary for radical social change stands in stark contrast to the neglect by many contemporary radicals of the relationship between the country and the city in both developed capitalist countries and low and middle-income societies. Much valuable work continues to be done by environmentalists on the need to 'rewild' rural and urban landscapes debased by deforestation. Detailed critiques of the negative impact of agribusiness, chemical agriculture and unsustainable urban development on biodiversity is also readily available. However, most of this work on sustainable food production and consumption is either divorced from or poorly connected to larger political organisational struggles.

It is widely known that earlier Communist agricultural plans based on collective farms and other methods proved to be grossly inadequate at best or disastrous at worst. Capitalist agricultural processes are also now well on the path towards catastrophe. In 2015, the United Nations Food and Agriculture Organisation estimated that chemically-based, industrial agriculture causes over US$3 trillion worth of natural damage each year, a calamitous price that is clearly unsustainable.[29] Such is the loss of soil nutrients, increased desertification and mass extermination of insects through pesticides that current agribusiness and levels of production may only last for approximately another sixty years, and all this despite hundreds of millions going hungry each day. The most recent August 2019 Intergovernmental Panel on Climate Change report on land, food security, desertification[30] also spelt out the very alarming consequences of existing market practices despite being a very conservative report underestimating the true extent of unsustainable agricultural practices.[31]

Switching to alternative food production and consumption systems and practices is absolutely essential but exceedingly difficult to implement in less than a minimum of ten to twenty years. Organic food production is not a solution on its own as yields for some crops are much lower, requires more land-use thereby increasing greenhouse emissions, is labour intensive, unaffordable for low-income people, and for many countries does not reduce their dependence on foreign food imports.[32] Restoring and replenishing chemically polluted or degraded land, changing dietary preferences, transforming cities into food baskets, providing incentives for urban labour to relocate to rural areas while changing trade and industrial food production are all feasible but currently politically enormously difficult to achieve. Rewilding lost forests and natural habitats are also necessary but take decades even as deforestation proceeds at an alarming pace and both large and small landholders actively promote it.

One of the major criticisms made of advocates of 'green growth' who favour ecological modernisation or techno-fixes to the climate emergency is that these approaches fail to pay adequate attention to the twin related problems of unsustainable cities/unsustainable food production once fossils fuels are scaled back. According to analysts such as Graeme Lang and Jason Bradford, there is no realistic way of any major city replacing all the fossil fuel energy that keeps cities functioning. 'Energy descent' will make cities based around fossil-fuel transport, production and consumption very difficult to remain viable.[33] In 2019, there were 1000 urban areas with over 500,000 people, 38 with over ten million and 87 with over 5 million people. Bradford presents several reasons why he thinks that 'the future is rural'. These include the giant circulatory systems of these large cities (roads, sewage, networks of concrete pipes, tracks and waste disposal systems) that largely depend on fossil fuels for which there are currently inadequate substitutes. Once fossil fuels are replaced, cheap fertilizers from natural gas will be unavailable and the importance of natural soil fertility will become more evident. In order to maintain soil regeneration in a significant aspect of an economy (food production) based on renewable energy, there will need to be a much closer relationship of the population to the land as food production will need to be more labour-intensive and current long distances between food baskets and urban consumers drastically reduced. Intermittent energy supply from renewables also constitutes a major problem for industrial agriculture given that battery technology is still insufficiently developed to efficiently run mechanised farm machinery.

The problems identified by Lang and Bradford are already being tackled by natural and artificial substitutes for fossil fuels and other technological innovations. If these fail to materialise in time, then the crisis of unsustainable large urban centres in coming decades is a frightening scenario. Others such as Sam Alexander and Brendan Gleeson utilise the ideas of Ted Trainer and David Holmgren[34] by emphasising the need to convert cities into food producing centres so that the household is not just the site of consumption but also helps produce the food and other cooperative practices needed for sustainable cities instead of the need for a population exodus to rural areas. They cite the possibility of converting large tracts of urban land currently occupied by cars, roads and parking spaces, as well as reducing meat consumption and other strategies.[35] These are all necessary and excellent ideas that could generate new forms of urban interaction and cultural transformation. The problem is that the new urban imaginary can only be achieved by political reform or even radical action at state level that requires instituting legislative changes to convert private property and publicly owned land into green commons. This would require reversing the privatisation of public roads, utilities and other assets acquired by corporations in recent decades. To make a large city sustainable would involve challenging the sacred notion of the ownership and control of private property which is the foundation of capitalism.

Any alternative sustainable food system will thus come up against deep-seated concepts of land ownership and major business, cultural, political and socio-economic obstacles that cannot be reduced to Right, Left or green slogans or quick-fix solutions. We should not shy away from these difficulties. Rather, we must recognize that merely changing what kind of food, and how it is produced, distributed and consumed, is a small part of how the conflict between 'capitalism and democracy' has evolved into the more complex relationship between 'democracy versus sustainability' in the twenty-first century. Currently, the *democratic* choice of what people prefer to eat is clearly quite *incompatible* with ecological *sustainability*. How this tension and incompatibility can be resolved is a political and social problem that needs urgent attention.

Crucially, agro-ecology and sustainable food consumption require an active presence of radical environmentalists in both urban and rural areas but they still have a minimal presence among villagers and rural workers across the world.[36] It is true that organisations like *La Via Campesina* campaigns on important issues related to the negative impact of global marketisation on farmers. Yet, its claim to be a global peasant movement[37] is a misnomer, as there is little in common between the cultural traditions of Latin American, African or Asian villagers. It is also questionable to rename or conceive the social conditions, cultures and conservative political affiliations of small business farmers in Australia, Europe, Japan, North America and New Zealand as equivalent to those experienced by 'peasants', even though they are often in a dependent position vis-a-vis large agribusiness corporations.

Constructing a 'historic bloc' between workers and peasants in China, India, South East Asia or Latin American and African countries is equally remote politically. During Kautsky's and Gramsci's day it was difficult to forge alliances between German workers and peasants or between northern Italian industrial workers and southern peasants. Building a global alliance between contemporary villagers, service sector and manufacturing workers and other social groups in one country is extremely challenging, but globally it is almost utopian. Cash crops and export markets are vital to many farmers in agribusiness-dominated countries like Australia, Argentina, the US and Canada, but they constitute a threat to hundreds of millions of villagers surviving on small plots in low and middle-income societies. Importantly, urban workers and other consumers reliant on low-cost manufacturing and cheap food imports (because of low or stagnant wages) makes any alliance with other rural and urban sections seeking protectionist trade policies highly improbable. How so-called environmentalist 'organic intellectuals' could represent and overcome such antagonistic interests is a question I will discuss in the following chapter. No formation of a new political 'bloc' is possible without the thorough airing and possible resolution of the conflicting interests of social groupings that benefit from either free trade or protectionism, disparities in rural and urban wage levels, as well as other major socio-cultural divisions amongst important segments of contemporary societies.

IS THE SEARCH FOR NEW SOCIAL CHANGE AGENTS FUTILE?

The quest for new social change agents must be differentiated from the mutual cultural and political hostility of racist, misogynist and anti-green conservative workers and their communities on the one side and feminists, non-white social movements, greens and LGBTQI groups on the other. All these cultural conflicts undoubtedly undermine and constrain the possible emergence of a united opposition to capitalist regimes. However, sociologically, none of these constituencies form the basis of a new social class as was the case with the emergence of the working class in the early nineteenth century. Instead, their cultural differences are overshadowed by their lack of political power compared to dominant forms of corporate and state control. Over the decades, hope was invested in new social change agents emerging from 'the outcasts', the 'precariat' or from the new 'professional-managerial knowledge class' or greens and other 'new social movements'. The latter did not live up to the political promise held by optimistic theorists on their behalf. They did help change social agendas but not in the radical manner that anti-capitalists had hoped they would.

While new social change agents continue to emerge, they will most likely come from segments of existing classes rather than constituting a new social class. Whether they will promote the transition to an environmentally sustainable society or emerge as a direct outcome of this transition remains to be seen. These new activist groups may champion greater democratisation, but this goal is not synonymous with awareness of or commitment to sustainability. One of the paradoxes of contemporary capitalist societies that I will explore in the next chapter is that old forms of political opposition have been undermined by profound socio-economic change and yet, new organisational forms are difficult to either create or become effective.

The quest for new agents of social change is a by-product of the exhaustion of political organisational forms. It is also possible that the former agents of social change now part of the established political landscape will transform themselves in the face of extraordinary new crises. After all, if what scientists are telling us about looming convulsions caused by greenhouse gases, there is little chance that conventional politics will remain the same. Will these centre-Left parties disintegrate, or will external events force them to change political direction? Many non-OECD countries are already divided between faith-based parties and authoritarian governments on the one side, and assorted secular and democratic movements desiring capitalist modernisation or social reform on the other. The coming impact of either climate breakdown or decarbonisation is bound to transform existing political conflicts in unpredictable ways.

For over seventy years we have lived with the threat of nuclear annihilation. The threat today is even greater than in previous decades but is widely ignored because most people falsely assume that after the Cold War, we are all relatively safe. Even so, de-escalating the threat of nuclear war does not require a sweeping change to the political economy of capitalist societies. Not so, the task of preventing climate chaos. Wolfgang Streeck argued that 'politainment' (politics as entertainment) prevails because there are 'few collective goods worth fighting for'. This is a profoundly short-sighted view in that it ignores and underestimates how volatile and dangerous a political era we find ourselves in. A combination of escalating environmental and socio-economic factors has the potential to shake and transform segments and groupings of existing social classes and the way that they have previously disengaged from politics. Socio-economic differences of income, occupation, wealth, education, race and gender that currently divide societies and forms of political participation could well be reconstituted into new organisations, new alliances and new cross-class movements and parties.

The search for new social change agents was usually undertaken with the aim of bringing about a socialist society. Such a macro view of history becomes a luxury in crisis-ridden societies. Instead, it will be the immediate threat of socio-economic and environmental problems that will produce new actors and fuel struggles for viable solutions. Socialist Ian Angus put it well while discussing global movements trying to prevent climate breakdown:

There are far more people from non-socialist backgrounds than there are of us. We won't always agree with specific actions or slogans or demands, but that's just how it's going to be. Standing on the sidelines criticizing will get us precisely nowhere: socialists must be in the movement, building it to the best of our ability...we must give priority to fighting fossil fuels because that's where such a movement can actually have a substantial impact, even if we can't change the entire system yet. If we can't shut down a pipeline or prevent fracking someplace or get a university to divest itself of investments in the oil industry, how can we imagine that we're actually going to overthrow capitalism? A socialist movement that doesn't take defending human survival as a central goal isn't worthy of the name.[38]

The quest by governments and mainstream parties to control political agendas and policies by either delaying action or providing inadequate solutions, will ultimately give rise to new political organisations and an increasing eruption of unpredictable action on the 'street'. Currently, too few existing organisations – whether committed to radical change or defenders of the old order – are prepared either organisationally, theoretically or strategically for this rapidly unfolding and unpredictable era.

12.POLITICAL ORGANISATIONAL CHALLENGES

IN THIS CHAPTER, I will attempt to go beyond the familiar debates on organisational politics that have especially grown over the past sixty years. A whole literature exists in mainstream political science on changes in party systems, the relationship between all aspects of electoral politics and internal changes in political organisations. On the Left there is also an extensive literature on the dramatic restructuring of both institutions and production processes in capitalist societies that have helped transform the working class and rendered traditional political forms of class struggle obsolete. While these earlier and current debates remain focussed on how to change or overthrow capitalism, what is missing is any detailed analysis of the conflictual relationship between models of democracy and varying notions of degrees of sustainability. Without considering these vital issues and how they will affect the policies and practices of organisations, the risk is misunderstanding and being ill-prepared for future political struggles.

For over a century, the conception of the role and structure of political organisations have been essentially divided into two differing orientations or end goals: first, the political party as the mode of representing particular groups or classes for the purpose of winning certain immediate goals or influencing the shape of key features of existing society; and second, the construction of a political organisation as the vehicle of an alternative society. Hence, new questions and issues require an answer as to whether existing mainstream and oppositional parties are capable of leading the transition to a post-carbon or post-capitalist society. As to non-parties, especially so-called 'new social movements' from the 1960s and 1970s and their more recent successors, these movements have had mixed successes and mixed goals. They have either sought limited change within existing societies or conceived of themselves as the agents of an alternative society.

Social movements have largely succeeded in raising awareness of the issues and needs of their respective constituencies, but they have failed to replace mainstream parties or alter the centralisation of political power within state institutions. Nonetheless, mainstream political parties have absorbed the rhetoric if not the policies and practices promoted by social movements and most Left parties have also been forced to broaden their agendas. Tellingly, many of the former 'new social movements' replicated a range of organisational problems plaguing political parties even though they professed their commitment to participatory democracy and anti-bureau-cratisation. These problems included: splits due to ideological factions; divisions between leaders and grass roots membership over bureaucratic decision-making and concentration of power; loss of vitality as protest activism was scaled down and replaced by greater emphasis on parliamentary electoral lobbying or fielding candidates; and divisions between older members steeped in an earlier political culture and younger members who were either more conservative or more radical.

In the debates over organisational politics, it is also standard for many Left theorists and activists to draw attention to the fragmentation of political activism into a plethora of racial and sexual identity and environment politics, such as various shades of green (neoliberal, eco-socialist or degrowth), forms of feminism and post-feminism, or a range of First Nations and post-colonial movements. Little is said, however, about how fragmentation affects the broader issue of the conflict between 'democracy and sustainability'.

I have argued throughout this book that the old paradigm of 'capitalism versus democracy' needs to be updated or replaced. In order to rethink political models, it is necessary to evaluate the deficiencies and flaws in the dominant ways of thinking about how to bring about social change either through conventional institutional channels or via radical political action. Given social and political fragmentation, I will therefore analyse the following questions:

- whether the concept of 'organic intellectual' has any practical political meaning in the struggle for an environmentally sustainable and socially just society;
- whether a post-carbon or post-capitalist 'counter public sphere'

based on achieving environmental sustainability can be
established;

- whether the quest for the most democratic and representative
organisation is incomplete without a shared political economic
vision of how to transition to greater sustainability;
- whether the 'social bloc' or populist coalition of movements is the
way forward or the last phase of an exhausted politics?

We live in an era when the residues of old political organisations and
modes of action are still visible or unduly influential. A new politics remains
undeveloped or currently too weak to surmount these old models. The question is: does a post-carbon society require new organisational forms of politics or is this only true for those who wish to create a post-capitalist society?
Max Weber's famous description of politics as the 'strong and slow boring
of hard boards' that takes both passion and perspective[1] is pertinent given
that new political expressions often have the passion but not the patience for
long-term perspectives. Instead, an 'anti-politics' of rejecting both mainstream and radical political parties in favour of decentralised, small group
prefigurative living (eco-villages and so forth) or anti-party mobilisation are
now quite common. The larger public manifestation of 'anti-politics' has
often taken the recent form of flash upsurges of mass energy – such as the
Yellow Vests, Black Lives Matter, Me Too, Extinction Rebellion and student
climate activism marches. We have witnessed a fading of the energy and
commitment to some of these movements over time. In 2019, a quarter of all
countries, from Lebanon and Nigeria to Sudan and Venezuela saw a massive
upsurge in civil unrest. For instance, the riots, looting and violence that were
triggered by the increase in subway fares in Santiago Chile in October 2019,
spread like an epidemic to other cities and led to hundreds of incidents and
billions of dollars' worth of damage to public and private buildings and
infrastructure.[2] A great deal of the spontaneous and co-ordinated political
energy of these electrical energy protest surges or 'flash' events can remain
unchannelled, either forgotten or go underground to perhaps erupt at a later
date.

Significantly, this new national and global political mobilisation fostered
and promoted on social media soon loses its initial threat and element of
surprise and usually is well contained by authorities or leads to conservatives
demanding tough law-and-order responses. On the other hand, we must
differentiate between the political form these protest movements take and
their immediate as opposed to medium-term cumulative impact on existing

regimes of power. It remains unclear whether these unconventional eruptions undermine and erode the legitimacy and effectiveness of governments
or ways of thinking amongst the wider population. Street protests and
battles can only last for a limited period before either a political breakthrough is achieved or tough repression is enforced, as in Paris or Mexico
City 1968 or Hong Kong during 2020.

One of the main reasons why the dominant paradigm of 'capitalism
versus democracy' is historically dated rests on the role of mythical saviours
that are championed by socialist opponents of capitalism and liberal
defenders of capitalist markets: the 'universal proletariat' and the free and
sovereign 'individual', respectively. Marxists still believe that the united
working class through its political and industrial organisations could democratise society by either civilising or overthrowing undemocratic capitalism.
Liberals still imagine that individual citizens can safeguard freedom and
democracy against authoritarian states or persuade governments and businesses of the need for a post-carbon society. Short of revolution or slow
evolution, how do both the 'proletariat' or 'individual' citizens overcome the
repressive apparatuses of the state used by threatened governments and businesses to crush or contain dissidents and opponents demanding action on
the climate emergency? Moreover, how do they get hostile pro-market
governments to implement decarbonisation and reduce material footprints
without state institutional power or free elections?

In reality, despite the rhetoric and significant differences between Marxists, liberals, greens and others in terms of how they explain and account for
who runs and dominates capitalist societies, there is actually not too much
that separates them when it comes to political action. Despite mass demonstrations calling for government action on the climate emergency or other
burning issues, there is to date, no distinct 'Left' or 'green' action or strategy
promoting a post-capitalist society apart from traditional forms of political
action such as changing governments and policies through electoral
processes, street protests, consciousness raising, strikes and online media
agitation. The vast majority of radical activists are non-violent and pursue
their political agendas within the dominant legal-institutional framework,
even when their political goal is the end of capitalism.

WHY ORGANIC INTELLECTUALS ARE POLITICALLY OBSOLETE

Most of the dominant models of socio-political change that prevailed during the twentieth century are now exhausted. These politically drained or disappearing models include the Marxist-Leninist revolutionary vanguard party, the Socialist, Social Democratic, Labour and Green parties which, like the confessional-based Christian Democratic parties may still retain their names but not their largely working class, environmentalist or religious social base. Instead, political analysts have pointed out that most of these parties moved from their traditional social bases to become 'catch all' mainstream parties (to use Otto Kirchheimer's concept[3]) engaged in market electoral competitiveness. This is also true of earlier conservative Right-wing business orientated or liberal middle-class centrist parties that have either been transformed into 'catch all' parties or in the case of conservative business parties have shifted to the Right in their courtship of far-Right nationalists from various class backgrounds.

From being 'catch all' parties, most mainstream parties in OECD countries have evolved into 'cartel parties' which like business cartels, attempt to control the political arena as well as the voting public.[4] These 'cartel parties' recognised the constraints of having to function in competitive global markets where free trade and lack of capital controls restricted the ability of national parties to be able to impose new taxes to pay for new electoral promises. Hence, in recent decades many parties have lowered voter expectations and adopted organisational practices to free the parliamentary representatives of these parties from being controlled or dependent on sectional interests within their respective political bases.

Since the Great Financial Crisis of 2008, the future viability of 'cartel party' systems is in doubt. This is due to the rise of Right-wing parties, austerity policies and the internal divisions within centre-Left parties. Syriza in Greece and the British Labour Party under Corbyn were examples of breaking the pattern of neoliberal 'lowering of expectations' and were initially successful in attracting large numbers of new members hoping for radical change. This phase has ended, and it remains to be seen what will happen in countries reeling from major crises induced by Covid-19. Centre-Left 'cartel parties' are on life support after experiencing either collapse or decline in various OECD countries due to the desertion of voters to mainly Right-wing parties and a few Left parties. In the US, the polarisation of the support bases of Republican and Democratic parties makes the continuation of 'cartel' policies highly problematic in coming years.

Yet, it is not only electoral parties that face ongoing crises and loss of support. Since the 1960s, and despite decades of experiments concerning the formation of non-hierarchical, non-vanguard democratic social change parties and movements, most have failed. As mentioned earlier, the belief in 'new social movements' replacing old Left parties has to a large extent collapsed. Many of the members of these movements formed the basis of Green parties in the 1980s before these parties lost their radicalism and became 'catch-all' and even 'cartel' electoral parties in subsequent decades. It only remains for the last gasp of this model – the 'Left populism' of recent years – to meekly exit the stage. Similarly, the activist environmentalist organisations such as Greenpeace, Friends of the Earth and various conservation and animal protection movements continue to monitor, lobby and protest against corporate and government threats to all facets of the global environment. However, they are incapable of constituting the vehicles for the transition to a new society or reorganising parts of existing societies, even if they desired to take on these roles. Compared to their high profiles in earlier decades, today, these environmental NGOs devote a great deal of energy to fund-raising to keep their organisations afloat. Most young environmental activists have barely heard of them and prefer to join other forms of climate emergency action.

If many of the former activist social movements and environmentalist organisations have lost much of their former vitality or have disappeared, we need to refocus on the larger macro political scene in order to answer questions about organisational challenges concerning any possible move to a post-carbon society. Most previous discussion has focussed on how to create the most internally democratic and broadly representative party, movement or hybrid party/movement. What lessons can we take from these models and are there any other organisational options?

Firstly, there is no secret as to why so many political models live on as zombie parties clinging to diminishing voter support with most (apart from a few exceptions) more dead than alive. Sociologically, there has been a restructuring of class structures and the organisations and means of communication upon which 'counter' public spheres were formerly built. This has destabilised conventional political support bases. Institutionally, a mixture of undemocratic electoral systems, voluntary voting and absence of political choice has kept old parties operating, but only as shadows of their former selves. In most OECD countries with voluntary voting, between one third and one half of eligible voters fail to vote. Culturally, too much has been revealed about the undemocratic, corrupt and narrow pursuit of power. Instead of principled politics promoting social justice and ecological sustainability, voters have been turned off by 'spin'. The 'public' in its fragmented constituencies no longer trusts or retains the same degree of enthusiasm for conventional mass party politics. By default, this 'anti-politics' has also seriously affected support for alternative challengers whether parliamentary or extra-parliamentary opposition.

Historically, the rise of the 'bourgeois public sphere' was dominated by monarchists, the church, republican nationalists, industrial and commercial bourgeoisie, agrarian gentry, urban liberal intelligentsia and bohemian cultural circles. The social manifestations of these old and new social classes varied in strength from country to country. In theory, the 'public sphere' mediated relations between state institutions, the capitalist market and civil society via the new print media and other forums and salons.[5] In reality, these 'boundaries' were artificial, as the 'economic', 'political' and 'social' were directly or indirectly interconnected and affected all social classes. By the late nineteenth century, religious and other civic organisations, as well as conservative and liberal parties and the 'bourgeois media' were challenged by a 'counter' or 'proletarian public sphere' which functioned in developed or less developed forms, depending on the strength of socialist and labour parties, trade unions and national independence forces in particular countries.[6]

The ability of organisations within the 'counter sphere' to delineate a distinct 'working class culture' in opposition to the dominant public sphere depended on the role and activity of working-class militants or 'organic intellectuals'. Whether there were ever clearly defined dominant public spheres and 'counter spheres' is disputed, but their transformation and demise by the second half of the twentieth century has helped shape our current notions of 'public' and 'private'. Shortly, I will discuss the relevance or irrelevance of 'organic intellectuals' to establishing a post-capitalist 'counter sphere' based on environmental sustainability.

Returning to the original central conception of working-class militants, Marxist revolutionaries believed that any political movement or activist committed to radical social change must have a conception of the role of political consciousness, an idea of which social agents can carry out the relevant level of social change needed, and the type of organisation(s) best suited to mobilise and develop class-consciousness and realise the needs of the working class. This strategic legacy lives on even among all those social movements that reject class analysis. The big difference is that when an environmentalist, feminist or other cultural movement rejects the working-class party as a vehicle of change, it has often been either unclear or divided over whether the object of its activism is to change state policy directly by seeking electoral power or indirectly by lobbying, civil disobedience, mass protests, infiltration of mainstream parties, social media mobilisation and other such actions designed to transform 'public consciousness' and policy. In other words, does the movement want to create its own self-contained social network within the larger social order, a totally new society or only a change of those parts of existing society that oppress, exclude or threaten the survival of cultures or natural species?

To understand why political strategies based on organic intellectuals are obsolete and why particular notions of class, party and consciousness must be rethought, it is worth briefly focussing on two classical maxims of Marx-ist-Leninist vanguard theory. These maxims were either challenged or indi-rectly absorbed and modified by many non-Leninist parties and movements. Firstly, it was claimed that constructing counter-hegemonic power could only succeed when the working-class developed its own culture and 'organic intel-lectuals' challenged the 'common sense' elements of bourgeois hegemony. In 1923, Hungarian revolutionary György Lukács argued that 'organisation is the form of mediation between theory and practice',[7] hence radical social change could only be brought about by an *extraordinary* political organisation. Like-wise, Italian revolutionary Antonio Gramsci (who was claimed as one of their own by both Leninists and anti-Leninists), also argued that Machiavelli's 'prince' was historically obsolete because no single person could capture and hold state power. Consequently, the Communist party had to become the 'modern prince' and succeed in the battle of manoeuvre with liberal, fascist and conservative bourgeois parties, state apparatuses and capitalist businesses.[8]

Ninety years later, Gramsci's concept of the 'modern prince' and what constitutes an 'organic intellectual' stands as historically obsolete. It will be recalled that Gramsci challenged the traditional notion of an 'intellectual' associated with literature, philosophy and science, that is, those highly educated aristocratic or bourgeois individuals rather than workers and peas-ants because the latter had minimal formal education or were illiterate. Each type of society had its own 'organic intellectuals', whether the clergy in feudal societies or technicians, ideologues and economists in capitalist soci-ety. The role of working-class 'organic intellectuals' was to facilitate and translate the ideas of the advanced sector of the class (read the Communist Party) to fellow workers in communities and workplaces. In theory, the Party was to educate and simultaneously learn from the daily life experiences of its own class thereby developing a counter-hegemonic culture. This 'counter-culture' would link custom, folk and 'common sense' with grievances against the ruling class and simultaneously develop this suffering and grievance into a higher and more elaborate political consciousness necessary for revolutionary action. Preparation for revolution would entail years of strategic tactics in a 'war of position' in which the 'organic intellectuals' simultaneously combatted capitalist ideological hegemony in both the public sphere and amongst working class social institutions, thus helping develop working-class consciousness and political action.

Why is this conception of 'organic intellectuals' obsolete? To begin with, the notion of 'organic' is highly problematic and assumes there is a 'working class' that is 'naturally', self-evidently and homogeneously distinct from the bourgeois class and 'bourgeois culture' as well as being distinct from other classes and cultures. Before entering factories, mines and the building construction industry, peasant culture had been the background of many workers in the past one hundred and fifty years. Disentangling 'working class' culture from religiously influenced, *petite* bourgeois culture and commercial 'popular culture' has never been easy. Constructing a revolutionary 'national-popular culture' belongs to an earlier historical era and is today fraught with dangerous overtones. Geopolitical power and location in the national 'pecking order' makes all the difference. Nationalist movement intellectuals in Catalonia or Scotland are significant locally but not internationally when compared to the global and regional implications of nationalist ideologues calling to 'make America great again' or for India to cease being secular and become an anti-Muslim Hindu national culture.

Leaving aside the dangerous issue of nationalism and former goals of a working-class 'national popular culture', in present day countries we do not even have the 'constructed' alternative 'working class culture' developed by early twentieth century Left parties through their sports, theatre, music, children's clubs, pubs, housing, community welfare and numerous other social activities. Residues of tradition and memory are still preserved by some unions, social history museums or via ritual commemorative days such as May Day. In practice, Labour, social democratic and radical Left parties, either through their integration into dominant cultural practices, the privatisation of leisure and care, or severe lack of members, now offer flimsy alternatives to commercial popular celebrity culture which dominates the lives of large segments of *all* social classes – from the monarchy and billionaires to the so-called lumpenproletariat.

At best, Left parties believe in non-profit public cultural institutions rather than media entertainment corporations. Most present-day alternative counter-hegemonic cultural forms come from anti-consumerist greens living lives of simplicity, or from students and avant-garde artists (such as those working in new digital or audio-visual mediums) largely unconnected to working-class organisations. By contrast, in low and middle-income countries, the absence of large socialist revolutionary parties means that alternative cultures often take the form of either traditional First Nations practices or various post-colonial movements, including oppressive fundamentalist, patriarchal religious movements mobilised through mosques, temples and other institutions. The latter are able to effectively sustain an anti-Western and anti-secular 'counter-culture' by making mixtures of exaggerated and credible critiques of what they see as alcohol-fuelled, vulgar commercial, pornographic capitalist culture.

Four decades of postmodern culture and the assault on universal political and cultural values and identities has destroyed the former privileged place that socialists allocated to the working class in anti-capitalist political action. Equally importantly, the fragmentation of labour markets and socio-cultural divisions amongst wage workers renders the former role of 'organic intellectuals' almost meaningless or ineffective, as followers of contemporary identity politics refuse to subordinate or submerge their interests under the umbrella of 'working class consciousness', a concept that socialists still mistakenly assume to be 'universal' and all embracing. Such claims on the part of traditional socialists will be resisted as it marginalises those who see themselves as equally important and not reducible to the interests of the working class. In short, the more that capitalist societies evolved into complex social formations, the more that vanguard parties and hierarchical Left parties gradually lost their capacity as organisations to represent diverse social groups that either did not identify as proletarians or rejected the undemocratic political mode of operation of traditional Left parties.

Today, there is neither a 'modern prince' that strategically acts on behalf of the proletariat, nor a unified working-class that is able to surmount the multiple nationalist, racial, gender, ecological and other political interests and identities. In Chapter Fourteen I will discuss whether one can have an 'ecological Leninism' or a non-Communist 'modern prince' that is able to manoeuvre and advance a post-carbon sustainable society without all the undemocratic baggage of earlier Left parties. Crucially, the vast majority of Left intellectuals (mainly academics) are isolated and have no 'organic' connection to the working class regardless of whether the latter work in manufacturing, mining, construction or services. They may be far better read and informed than earlier generations but often they mainly communicate with fellow academics or students. The nearest we have to 'organic intellectuals' are particularist rather than universalist 'community organisers' who mobilise ethnic and racial minorities on behalf of candidates or parties. They are unable to surmount wider socio-economic and cultural divisions but hope that being part of the electoral machine campaigning for individual candidates or for a national party will 'deliver' better policies favouring specific 'community' constituencies. Such electoral politics are fragile and fluctuate given the rise and decline of support by multicultural voters for different candidates and parties.

THE POLITICAL CHARACTER OF 'ENVIRONMENTAL CONSCIOUSNESS'

As to an 'environmental consciousness', how is this to be defined and acquired, and who are the 'organic intellectuals' capable of waging a 'war of position' against capitalist *unsustainable* production and consumption? Globally, a post-carbon 'counter-culture' is still in a rudimentary and fragmented form. It is possible to piece together various strands of degrowth practices, such as slow food movements, or those creating green sustainable cities, living simplicity lifestyles and promoting social values based on care and co-operation. Despite annual 'sustainability festivals' and visual and online networks, this post-carbon 'counter-culture' is less organisationally integrated and more politically fragile in that it has so far failed to overcome the tensions between green entrepreneurs, supporters of alternative lifestyles and anti-capitalist 'degrowthers' and eco-socialists.

These expressions of an environmentally sustainable 'counter-culture' or post-carbon society do not yet constitute a coherent political culture in the same way as some of the Communist and Socialist communities of the pre-1940s which were based on more tightly knitted working-class cultural and political organisations that linked workers across all aspects of their communities. The 'little Moscows' in Scotland and Wales[9], or Socialist 'Red Vienna' (1919 to 1934) before it was crushed by the conservative/fascist Austrian federal government are a case in point. Yet, these Left working-class communities were atypical of working-class social life in the larger society in that the 'little Moscows' were one industry union towns that created a clear delineation of workers against owners in both workplace, household and the local public sphere. Vienna was also different because it was a much larger than other Austrian towns that were often politically conservative. The nearest contemporary 'green' equivalents to these proletarian historical examples are eco-villages or 'transition towns'. Just as 'Little Moscows' were not typical of working-class experiences in big cities, so too, eco-villages are not typical of the experiences of greens in larger capitalist urban centres.

Also, in contemporary capitalist societies there are no green political organisations that hold the equivalent political and economic power as that held by earlier socialists and Communists through their unions and parties. In short, green movements consist of cross-class membership but are poorly represented in workplaces, thus limiting their ability to build alternative forms of environmental consciousness amongst wage employees who will be most affected by any transition to a post-carbon society.

A giant chasm now exists between the anti-hierarchical ideals of alternative movements (espousing environmentalist, feminist and anti-discriminatory values) and the practical politics of any parliamentary or extra-parliamentary transition to a post-capitalist or post-carbon democracy. Old-style class-based politics have largely been replaced by 'non-class' or 'cross-class' social change models. It is therefore much harder to develop an 'organisational model' that maximises diverse social movements co-existing within a Green party or a 'Left populist' party. Constructing new political economic institutions and practices of material sustainability currently lack either clearly identifiable social agents or political organisations large enough and strong enough to carry out these ambitious goals. Many social movements and small political parties exist but none have the organisational capacity or political support base on their own that is necessary to implement society-wide political strategies that climate emergency activists call 'just transitions', let alone implement demands for more comprehensive goals of planned degrowth.[10] So far, only some large mainstream parties have this capacity, but all are either openly opposed to or else too timid when it comes to key aspects of such necessary alternative policies.

In 1990, the German Social Democrats (SPD) had close to a million members which has since more than halved. Even the largest Left party in Europe, the British Labour Party (580,000 registered rather than active members in January 2020) that grew under former leader Jeremy Corbyn, supported major reforms which were mainly 'green growth' policies based on a revived manufacturing sector geared to renewable energy. Despite admirable policies such as ending austerity and reviving dilapidated public services, there was no conscious goal by Corbyn Labour to tackle excessive material footprints amongst sections of the population via policies aimed at reducing consumerism. Hence, the contradictory policies simultaneously designed to cut carbon emissions from fossil fuels could have actually increased non-energy sector carbon emissions (the 'rebound effect') by fostering higher employment but no alternative to commercial consumerist culture.

This brings us to the issue of 'environmental-consciousness' and how it differs from 'class-consciousness'. Within the old Left paradigm of 'capitalism versus democracy' revolutionaries always assumed that the proletariat did not spontaneously or automatically become class-conscious. Rather, this 'political consciousness' had to come about through education, political struggle and the lived experiences of a shared culture and social relations. Whatever the diverse paths to class-consciousness, it was assumed that once developed, the working class would eventually acquire a coherent and class-wide, largely homogeneous or 'unified' class-consciousness in its struggle against the capitalist class. The assumption of a unified national or international class-consciousness has always been an 'aspirational goal' or a fiction that has never been realised and cannot be realised, especially in present-day socially fragmented and environmentally challenged societies. For how can the contemporary restructured working-class in its multiple and diverse forms fulfil its former allocated role as the 'locomotive of history' in the conflict between 'capitalism and democracy'? The political divisions within and between classes in different countries are not defined just by class location in the mode of production, that is, whether one owns or works for the owners of businesses. Heterodox radicals have long argued that since the 1960s crucial issues of ecological sustainability, race, gender and cultural tolerance within the private and public sphere cannot be resolved by reducing these vital issues to any potential overthrow of capitalist ownership and the establishment of workers' power.

In an era characterised by fragmented national and international working classes, it is necessary to ask: what does 'class-consciousness' mean when it is no longer clear what are the global common politicised goals and shared interests of all those who *do not* own or control the means of production? Those who propose that achieving environmental sustainability requires revolutionary action may have a valid point. Yet, it would be utopian to assume that such a revolution is likely to happen in the next decade or so, leaving aside what such a revolution would actually entail. Green New Deals may be viewed as radical proposals by neoliberals and many mainstream social democrats. Even so, most are certainly not revolutionary nor based on a class-conscious working class. Instead, they hope to attract support from broad cross-class constituencies, from at least one or more mainstream parties and are heavily orientated to being national government agendas. There are exceptions, such as the EU Commission's quasi-Green New Deal and DiEM 25's Blueprint for Europe's Just Transition which was devised by a coalition of European organisations advocating greater international co-operation on alternative fiscal, environmental and social justice issues.[11]

Crucial issues of inequality and material footprints continue to be related to 'ownership' and 'control'. Still, it is the very mode of environmentally unsustainable production and consumption that requires far more than the 'change of control' or the triumph of 'democracy over capitalism'. Green parties have a strong awareness of the international or global nature of ecological issues. From being originally social movements with a parliamentary wing, they are now mostly parliamentary parties with a subordinate and subdued social movement wing. Their members are divided between those who either have a good knowledge of political economy or else lack a developed understanding of the class nature of international capitalist markets that propel both social inequality and environmental unsustainability. Those Greens and eco-socialists who are aware of class divisions, nevertheless, are themselves divided over support for degrowth. They also confront great hostility from many workers who oppose green notions of degrowth which the latter see as threats to their concept of the 'good life', namely, access to market-influenced notions of material consumption, affluence and life goals. The old slogan, 'the working class have nothing to lose but their chains' is hard to sell these days in a world where most workers in low and middle-income countries are heavily 'enchained' but aspire to the relatively luxurious 'chains' of a majority of affluent workers in OECD countries. Moreover, Covid-19 is likely to throw about a billion people back to former poverty levels and reverse the less than adequate poverty reduction achievements made over the past thirty years.

As to counter-hegemonic culture, it is difficult to think of a single major extra-parliamentary social issue that earlier Left parties took the lead on during the past sixty years whether it be feminism, anti-racism and First Nation rights, environmental conservation issues, LGBTQI rights, disabled people's rights or climate change. Instead, the record shows that apart from notable exceptions, these parties were slow to recognise new social issues and usually tailed or shadowed other movements that first campaigned and raised awareness of various forms of socio-political discrimination or environmental crises. Looking to so-called Left 'working class parties' to play a prominent role in any future transition to post-carbon societies would be to ignore past inadequacies, especially the conservatism of many unions and 'workerist' socialists. It would be blinkered though to deny the historical success of Left revolutionary parties in disseminating the language and concepts of hegemony and counter-hegemony or extra-parliamentary tactics amongst many individuals and groups with no connection to revolutionary parties. All contemporary social movements and political organisations now recognise that consciousness-raising is a vital part of achieving social change even if they reject class politics and only have limited reforms in mind.

Earlier I noted the distinction made by Marxists between a limited 'trade union consciousness' which had elements of reform but was essentially defensive (protecting workers' conditions and wages) and a transformative or 'revolutionary class-consciousness'. Perhaps there is an equivalent distinction between levels of 'environmental consciousness'. Some would argue that combatting climate breakdown and favouring 'green growth' is a less developed 'environmental consciousness' in comparison to degrowth and ecologically sustainable consumption and production. The problem is that 'green growth' like degrowth is not derived from a single class position similar to working class support for trade unions. Rather, 'green growth' is heavily promoted by businesses and governments (as well as by many citizens and movements) who often disconnect it from greater social equality, let alone anti-capitalism. Importantly, 'green growth' and degrowth are not 'organically' linked to a single class and therefore cannot be advanced by just one type of 'organic intellectual' aiming to build a counter-hegemonic political consciousness. Such an anti-capitalist consciousness is now only possible by building cross-class opposition. This is why alliance building is difficult but nowhere near as difficult as sustaining diverse group political interests once it comes to the actual policies needed to achieve larger society-wide and global goals such as preventing climate breakdown.

A more radical 'environmental consciousness' nonetheless requires much more than an awareness of preventing global warming by switching to renewable energy. It also requires an awareness of not just carbon footprints but also of the cross-class environmental impact of material footprints. Despite the top 10% of income earners accounting for between 25% and 43% of global environmental impact, many advocates of degrowth appear blind to the question of which social classes or social strata constitute the base for an alternative politics. Instead, they often side-step issues of class emphasised by eco-socialists and instead focus on lifestyle changes and mixed actions embracing everything from local self-sufficiency, Green New Deal policies on tax, citizen assemblies and new forms of business favouring cooperatives.[12]

Currently, there is a disproportionately higher percentage of people broadly called the 'middle-class' – professionals, higher educated retirees, students and former members of Left parties and trade unions – who support degrowth and other radical environmental movements. However, their capacity to act as 'organic intellectuals' amongst the restructured working class is constrained or impossible, especially amongst those employed by small and medium businesses in service sector jobs such as retailing, financial services, tourism, personal leisure services, digital communications and marketing. They also have a negligible presence among the very large 'informal sectors' of low and middle-income countries in Asia, Africa, the Middle East and Latin America, and virtually no access to the substantial industrial workforces in countries forbidding free trade unions and free assembly.

A majority of the environmentalists who espouse non-class theories of society tend to see the negative side of 'capitalism' as something associated with unacceptable 'big business' but rarely criticise small and medium entrepreneurs. While some owners of small family businesses, the self-employed and entrepreneurs may be sympathetic to forms of post-carbon democratic innovation, many of the millions of small businesses play very conservative roles in opposing social and environmental reforms. For instance, the idea that degrowth 'organic intellectuals' promoting an advanced 'environmental consciousness' of smaller material footprints can establish political relations with millions of small retailers and other businesses across the world is politically unfeasible and bordering on political fantasy. This is because the income, use of material resources and survival of retailers and many small businesses depend on the continuation of unsustainable high consumption and high per capita material footprints.

Similarly, it is questionable whether marketing software engineers, biotech researchers, fintech analysts and other so-called 'knowledge economy' technoscience 'intellectuals' would abandon their crucial roles in contemporary capitalist industries and become alternative 'organic intellectuals' advancing environmental sustainability. But what alternative non-capitalist vision of science, technology, the human body, the role of finance and personal services could they promote among their fellow workers and business associates without suffering personal identity crises about their current roles or losing their jobs and contracts? It was bad enough in the old Stalinist days of 'proletarian science' when scientists were constantly trying to justify their scientific work which was not reducible to 'bourgeois' or 'proletarian' categories.

Egalitarianism and ecological sustainability cannot be assumed to be clear-cut or shared values within green movements, let alone perceived as compatible by a range of centre-Right movements who also claim to be defenders of democracy. One could add to this pervasive tension between 'democracy and sustainability' the highly contradictory attitudes to science and technology prevalent amongst the Right, Left and alternative degrowth and other social movements. Currently we see alt-Right conspiracy theories about climate scientists or anti-vaxxers and alternative medicine consumers suspicious of conventional medicine (until they rely on scientists and doctors to save them from Covid-19). There are also Left-wing critics of the techno-sciences (such as the Melbourne Arena group[13]) and various green groups that are still reluctant or unable to specify which sciences and technologies (especially in the biosciences) they oppose or support. Opposition to the commercially driven reconstruction of human nature, cloning and genetically modified crops are valid concerns. But is the use of the technosciences for hip replacements, bionic hearing aids, IVF treatment for infertility, manufac-tured skin for burn victims, organ transplants and other such developments politically acceptable, or are they part of the road to the 'post-human' that is to be condemned or welcomed?

All these diverse political positions become debatable and contestable when considering that any future chance of environmental sustainability (not just unsustainable 'green growth') will need to depend on a high input of scientific knowledge if we are to have reliable information and alternative technologies. Democratic freedom and participation are vital to fuel critique and public scrutiny of all science and technology. We should not elevate the rule of experts above the power of ordinary citizens and non-specialists. However, the democratic process can become counterproductive and irra-tional when it opts for a 'pseudo equality' that accords all voices equal weight regardless of the issue. The marketplace of ideas on social media and tradi-tional media is currently indiscriminate and promotes any crackpot opinion whatever the source.

To develop a political consciousness for a post-capitalist society on topics and moral issues such as non-binary genders, electric cars, vegan diets, surro-gacy and numerous other scientific, technical and cultural topics, social change activists will need to go well beyond the historically obsolete choice between rigid or arbitrarily imposed concepts of 'bourgeois' or 'proletarian' values. This will require a much more reflective and open approach to socio-cultural and scientific issues that discusses and recognises what are the valu-able advances made up until the present point and which social and institu-tional practices, technologies and conceptions of nature need to be modified or abandoned in the construction of new societies.

Contemporary working classes are remarkably diverse and have little in common culturally, politically and economically other than that they are dependent on their employers in the private and public sectors as well as on those in not for profit organisations. It is not possible for so-called 'organic intellectuals' to emerge from within the ranks of such socially and institutionally different layers of society and still articulate a shared and coherent consciousness. Workers continue to make the goods, mine the resources and provide services that grow capitalist businesses. Yet, their role until recent decades has never been to largely provide the organisational, technical, scientific and ideological foundations of capitalism. Software engineers, marketing personnel or researchers for 'big pharma' corporations could possibly apply their expertise to creating a post-capitalist society. Yet, in Gramsci's theory, working class 'organic intellectuals' could develop class consciousness amongst their fellow workers precisely because they did not help manage and sustain capitalist institutions and were an integral part of the working class in which they lived and for which they struggled. No such political consistency is open to contemporary service sector and professional employees who provide the indispensable administrative, technical and ideological roles used to exploit other fellow workers or prevent the latter from taking control of capitalist institutions. Few have the opportunity to redefine their job specifications so that they cease enhancing capitalist socio-cultural, political economic and technical control.

ACTION OVER POLICIES

Given the dramatic 'restructuring' of both capitalist production and the workers employed within new private and public service sectors, it is now clear that the concept of 'organic intellectual' has lost all practical political meaning in the struggle for an environmentally sustainable and socially just society. Consciousness raising will only go so far, whether practised by traditional working-class activists or contemporary advocates of degrowth. Very importantly, 'consciousness raising' is also a limited and elementary form of political activism. Beyond creating a common political culture and identification of obstacles to be surmounted, the so-called 'advanced' or militant individuals and groups promoting environmental sustainability need detailed political economic policies to take their political struggle to the next level of struggle and implementation should they gain mass support. Recognition of a climate emergency will not in itself provide the solutions to this crisis. This conclusion and perspective are rejected by activists who in the long tradition of voluntarism believe in mobilising the will of the people as an end in itself.

Nineteenth century revolutionary, Louis Augustin Blanqui, was the classical proponent of seizing the moment. "A revolution improvises more ideas in one day than the previous thirty years were able to wrest from the brains of a thousand thinkers."[14] This is undoubtedly true. But the problem is not one of a shortage of ideas. Rather, the crucial issue concerns which idea or set of ideas is likely to gain the upper hand and resolve major socio-economic and environmental problems once the so-called masses have rebelled and captured state power. Blanqui influenced many revolutionaries including Lenin. However, this model of social change can easily produce unintended disastrous consequences. Even when revolutionaries such as Lenin, Gramsci, Trotsky, Mao and their generation built political organisations and combined an element of voluntarism with concerted plans of how to develop the organisation (Party), their endless strategic manoeuvres overshadowed any substantial allocation of political energy to devising alternative policies. The disastrous consequences of an almost 'empty policy cupboard' soon revealed itself after 1917 and 1949.

No such leap in faith of supporting a 'post-carbon' or 'post-capitalist' revolution will wash anymore if present-day radicals continue to be a largely policy-free zone. Far too many environmentalist and other social movement activists also devote a disproportionate amount of energy to building the organisation or raising consciousness. Many are anti-Communist or anti-political parties without even knowing that they are repeating some of the same mistakes and tactics pursued by earlier revolutionaries. Importantly, the political crisis today partly consists in the difficulty of first mobilising all those disparate people concerned in differing ways about the particular terrible state of affairs, whether unemployment, climate, racism or inequality. Once attracted to joining protests or particular organisations, the equally challenging task is to sustain their new political awareness without simultaneously depressing and depoliticising them by outlining some of the practical obstacles that need to be surmounted. Action is always more attractive than either theory or developing detailed policies about how to create an environmentally sustainable economy and society.

We have known for decades that any new political and environmental consciousness in the contemporary world will usually not be connected to just one social class (as with socialist claims to represent the working class). Neither does such a consciousness lead to a unified set of policy solutions to the climate emergency or the need for a reduction and transformation of material footprints. Today, we find numerous liberal Keynesian 'green growth' advocates of an ecologically modernised capitalism at odds with both eco-socialists who want a post-capitalist sustainable society and separatist green movements who reject both liberalism and socialism and strive towards their own largely self-sufficient eco-communal solutions. If the old belief in one single, undifferentiated social class (the proletariat) having the will and capacity to transform contemporary capitalist societies is a bygone relic, are the political prospects for a 'social bloc' or cross-class coalition for social and environmental change any better?

THE 'SOCIAL BLOC': A TEMPORARY OR SUSTAINABLE STRATEGY?

A 'social bloc' or historical 'political bloc' is a concept that has been used to describe either informal or formal political alliances made by parties and movements of the Right or the Left. In recent years we have witnessed mainstream centre-Right parties in the UK, Australia, the US, Austria, Sweden, Denmark and other countries either court far Right movements and voters or embrace authoritarian policies on refugees, law and order and other social issues. Conversely, centre-Left mainstream parties and policy makers have made rhetorical gestures signalling their concern about inequality and climate change but, apart from minor tinkering, have continued to adhere to many neoliberal policies. Moreover, they have rejected radical change and refused to form electoral coalitions or 'social blocs' with Left parties or what they call 'Left populism' (apart from exceptions such as the Socialists (PSOE) and Unidas Podemos government in Spain since 2019). Various earlier and current coalition governments in other countries have included moderate Green parties. Perhaps the partial abandonment of austerity measures by centre-Right and centre-Left governments in response to mass unemployment caused by Covid-19 will lead to a sharp Leftward shift on the part of social democratic and Labour parties. On current indications this looks unlikely.

Instead, prominent social democrats and liberals such as Dani Rodrik, Branko Milanovic, and many others writing for journals such as *Social Europe* have advocated a range of reform policies which aim to reduce inequality without major restructuring of key parts of the environmentally destructive character of capitalist systems. These proposals include the extension of up to 50% of worker representation on corporate management boards; variations of the discontinued Swedish Rhen-Meidner model of 'wage workers funds' where shares are allocated to all workers in businesses over a certain size; the provision of fixed sums of money or 'lifetime accounts' for education to each child or adult as 'seed money' for better 'life chances'; wealth taxes and various revenue schemes to counter offshore tax evasion and other such proposals designed to redistribute proportions of capital to non-capitalists and also help regulate and outlaw bad corporate behaviour.[15] Most of these proposals either aim to remedy past and present excesses of neoliberal capitalism or institute defensive labour and social laws to protect workers and consumers. It is hoped that changes to the law defining 'the firm' as well as shareholder and management rights will help democratise capitalism and give workers a personal stake in the businesses that employ them.

Thomas Piketty also advocates similar policies. He is representative of those Left social democrats who stand between radical Marxists and neo-Keynesian reformers. In Piketty's view, capitalism and private property can be superseded and replaced by 'participatory socialism', an ambitious quasi-market socialism based on competing enterprises (rather than state planning) and characterised by the redistribution of wealth, education and other social resources via steep wealth taxes and other measures.[16] He revises Marx's and Engels' proclamation about the history of class struggles in the Communist Manifesto by shifting from 'class' to 'ideology':

> The history of all hitherto existing societies is the history of the struggle of ideologies and the quest for justice. In other words, ideas and ideologies count in history. Social position, as important as it is, is not enough to forge a theory of the just society, a theory of property, a theory of borders, a theory of taxes, of education, wages, or democracy. Without precise answers to these complex questions, without a clear strategy of political experimentation and social learning, struggle does not know where to turn politically. Once power is seized, this lacuna may well be filled by political-ideological constructs more oppressive than those that were overthrown.[17]

For all Piketty's unfamiliarity with Marx's analysis of capital and decades long debates on ideology and class,[18] his observations are nonetheless particularly relevant to fragile 'social blocs' divided over key socio-economic policies and unclear about future direction. Yet, when it comes to political change, Piketty, like both liberals and Left social democrats, proposes reforms that are top-down proposals largely disconnected from struggles by social movements. There is insufficient recognition of the need to change not just the redistribution of 'the pie' but its very ingredients. Most centre-Left reforms assume the continuation of regulated market capitalism that will be driven by economic growth (despite decarbonisation). For example, Piketty advocates using different socio-economic and environmental indicators tied to Gross National Income (GNI) instead of GDP to measure and deduct the use of natural resources from national income.[19] This is fine at the level of indicators but is not equivalent to developing a sustainable economy unless governments actually act on the new indicators and order a decrease in the utilisation of resources or a decrease in both carbon emissions and material footprints.

As to environmental sustainability, even radical versions of pension and other worker funds — that it is hoped will eventually gain majority shareholder control over businesses — largely ignore the environmental limits to incessant market growth. Critics of existing pension funds such as Robin Blackburn, provide ample evidence of the inequality and appalling consequences resulting from finance capital's management of pension funds.[20] However, such alternative proposals are framed within an environmental vacuum as to the long-term sustainability of investments needed to provide adequate pensions.

As we have seen, the old paradigm of 'capitalism versus democracy' was based on a struggle between capitalists and workers over redistribution and control of decision-making. However, greater worker representation on boards or the ownership of shares by workers will be ineffective and meaningless if the latter changes to decision-making and ownership result in workers largely endorsing unsustainable growth trajectories adopted by existing managements. How many workers will be prepared to cut their own jobs or share dividends if their own enterprise or whole industries need to be drastically scaled back? The old socialist disputes over how to reconcile the potentially antagonistic interests between the direct producers with the needs of consumers takes on new complexity in the coming period of environmental threats.

Counter arguments that either a substantial or majority shareholding owned by workers will change society are highly questionable if considered only at the enterprise level while leaving the macro-political economic decisions beyond the individual enterprise unchanged. These arguments only appear credible if a change in worker ownership is directly linked to larger political and social movements that explicitly advocate environmentally sustainable social justice policies and institutional practices. For alternative political demands to be effective, they have to go well beyond the current very truncated notions of 'inclusive sharing' of the unsustainable, toxic pie. So far, most centre-Left parties refuse to either adopt such policies or oppose forming a new political 'social bloc'. Given the fragmentation of contemporary societies and political movements, I will therefore discuss the different methods and discourse deployed to sustain a potential 'social bloc' and then discuss the larger socio-economic and environmental issues that need to be surmounted by these potential socio-political 'blocs'.

DISCOURSE AND ORGANISATIONAL METHODS

Over the past one hundred years, we have witnessed many of the Marxist Left abandon the dogmatic belief that revolution could only be made by activists adhering to the Party's 'correct line', a political strategy that was supposedly formulated by the most efficient and all-knowing political organisation, namely, the vanguard party. As Bertolt Brecht's chorus sung 'In Praise of the Party' in *The Measures Taken* (1930):

An individual has only two eyes
The Party has a thousand eyes
The Party can see seven lands
The individual a single city
The individual has only his hour
The Party has many hours
The individual can be annihilated
But the party cannot be annihilated
For it is the vanguard of the masses
And it lays out its battles
According to the methods of our classics, which are derived
from
The recognition of reality.[21]

When Brecht wrote these words in sympathy for revolutionaries struggling for social change in many countries, the Soviet Party had already applied the necessary 'measures' against loyal Bolsheviks and countless numbers of peasant 'Kulaks'. The idea that the Party can take 'exceptional measures' (such as in Brecht's play which concerned the killing of a comrade when a radical mission becomes endangered) has been likened by Oliver Simons to conservative/Nazi theorist Carl Schmitt's idea of the 'state of exception'.[22] (Simons notes that Brecht even had a character in his play called 'Karl Schmitt from Berlin'.) According to Schmitt, political sovereignty is evident in a political crisis when the state can make exceptions to the rule of law and impose its power. This power is either currently held by Presidents Xi, Putin, Erdogan, etc., or aspired to by Trump, Bolsonaro and others. It is, however, no model or ideal for movements and parties seeking to create not deeply entrenched authoritarian orders, but alternative democratic capitalist or post-capitalist societies.

Six decades after the discrediting of the vanguard party as a radical social change model (despite the continued belief by small radical sects), many on the Left have long accepted the necessity of its very opposite. In the words of radicals Nick Srnicek and Alex Williams, every successful movement "has been the result, not of a single organisational type, but of a broad ecology of organisations. These have operated, in a more or less coordinated way, to carry out the division of labour necessary for political change."[23] However, Srnicek and Williams are still reluctant to fully embrace pluralism and prefer a reworked 'Left populism'. Critiquing what they call 'folk politics', or an obsession with constructing the most 'democratic' and pluralist alternative to the vanguard party, they go on to pronounce that:

> There is ultimately no privileged organisational form. Not all organisations need to aim for participation, openness and horizontality as their regulative ideals. The divisions between spontaneous uprisings and organisational longevity, short-term desires and long-term strategy, have split what should be a broadly consistent project for building a post-work world. Organisational diversity should be combined with broad populist unity.[24]

Combining 'organisational diversity and populist unity' is easier said than done, especially if there is a fundamental disagreement between different social movements over the socio-economic and environmental objectives to be pursued. It is not surprising that the stalemate or interregnum between mainstream politics and alternative social change experiments has seen no stable or effective political forms of organisation emerge. Instead, party/social movement experiments are a sign of the dissolution of old class politics and the decline of belief in the power of new social movements that emerged from the 1960s onwards. The residues of this earlier phase of politics is still partly visible in the mobilisation of social movements that have come together under national party/movements such as

Podemos in Spain or supranational organisations such DiEM 25 (Democracy in Europe 2025).

If the 'universal proletariat' remains a dream or political fiction, can the struggle between 'democracy and sustainability' be resolved or reconciled by creating 'political' or 'social blocs' pursuing social justice and environmental sustainability? Moreover, how does a 'social bloc' not become synonymous with vague 'populist' movements that promote old-style class politics under the guise of 'the people' or 'the masses'? Any 'social bloc' to be effective must at least consider the following factors.

Firstly, given that no single party is likely to be electorally strong enough or inclusive enough, a 'social bloc' must be based on a political alliance of parties and movements that share a common understanding of what they need to prioritise and which parts of their own political agendas they need to temporarily suspend or compromise on. If a common enemy such as the extreme Right is to be successfully contained or defeated, then the 'political bloc' can either be based on equal weighting of the participating member parties and movements or built around a recognition that the largest member party or movement will have more influence over policy direction. However, if the largest member of the coalition uses its political weight to harm the interests of other smaller players then the 'bloc' is certain to collapse.

Secondly, such a 'bloc' can either be predominantly electoral or a mixture of parliament and 'the street' in its campaigning and social mobilisation. This is where 'social blocs' have often been found wanting due to lack of internal democracy, accusations of sexism and racism, too much decision-making concentrated in the centralised negotiations between representatives of the constituent parties and factions, or conversely, the desire of a certain propor-tion of the 'bloc' to pursue more radical activist campaigns at odds with the conventional parliamentary politics of others. Political theorists, Andrew Arato and Jean Cohen also argue that socialism and 'Left populism' have a difficult relationship and that socialism generally loses out to the inherent authoritarian tendency in 'populism'.[25] According to Cohen:

> The authoritarian risk increases when social movements morph into movement-parties, or when populist leaders capture an existing (most likely hollowed-out) party and turn it into a virtual movement-party that then gains power. The danger is the importation of populist movement strategy and logic into the commanding heights of govern-ment – thus perverting the functioning of liberal pluralistic democ-

racy, of political parties and of social movements in civil society. Fundamentalism and absolutism in populist movement-parties in civil society pose a special danger to democracy insofar as they aim not simply to influence but to acquire and exercise political power, preferably on their own.[26]

As an anti-radical, liberal social democrat, Cohen is particularly thinking of Hugo Chavez in Venezuela. She is unable to cite evidence that Syriza and Podemos adopted explicit authoritarian practices that are less democratic than those already practised by bureaucratic mainstream parliamentary centre-Left parties. Nonetheless, Cohen's warning needs to be heeded by those attempting to form a durable and broad centre-Left, green and radical 'social bloc' engaged in a 'just transition' to a post-carbon society.

Thirdly, we should dispense with the notion that there are infinite combinations and modes of political operation in contemporary societies. Instead, there is only limited 'empty space' in the 'political field' of each country, as political mobilisation, the occupation of state offices and electoral support is already given to existing parties and organisational allies across the spectrum. For a new 'social bloc' to emerge there has to be a socio-political crisis driven by economic, environmental or military convulsions that leads to new movements from below in combination with loss of electoral support for the dominant mainstream parties. A 'social bloc' could emerge from the coalition of various social movements and organisations that have in common their rejection of class analysis and party organisation. Such a 'political bloc' may become politically influential on environmental and social issues but is unlikely to be strongly anti-capitalist. Conversely, if the 'social bloc' is formed by movements and groups which are post-Leninist but still believe in working class organisations having a lead role in any 'Left populist' project, then this 'bloc' may be vigorously anti-capitalist but not very strong judging by the existing performance of Left movements.

Actually, in OECD countries, it does not matter whether 'social blocs' are formed by explicitly non-traditional movements or by 'Left populist' party/movements. All social change 'blocs' are likely to consist of environmentalists, feminists, anti-racists, post-colonial and LGBTQI activists and representatives from union movements and social welfare organisations. There will also be few industrial workers and wage workers from other sectors, and plenty of middle-class professionals such as teachers, students, retirees, academics and officials from unions, environment and social welfare organisations or First Nations movements. Only the weighting of each

constituent element will differ as will the emphasis on either broad environmental and social issues or the promotion of anti-capitalist positions
amongst 'Left populists'. Both will have a proportion of current or ex-Trotskyist and other small Marxist party activists as open or covert members in
the hope of reviving a moribund Left or transforming the new 'social bloc'
into an anti-capitalist mass formation. The non-class orientated 'social bloc'
will tend to put a premium on maximising equality of voice, horizontal rather
than hierarchical organisational forms, and 'deliberation' and consensual
decision-making over confrontation and hard-headed debate.

With the collapse of traditional working-class political parties, political
theorists have both debated and become engaged in singing the virtues of
either deliberative democracy or agonistic politics. I do not wish to repeat all
these political disputes except to state the following points. Firstly, practical
examples of deliberate democracy work very well in small group settings
where people can discuss the merits and disadvantages of particular
proposals in depth, an option that is either impossible or unwieldly in
national political forums involving potentially thousands and millions of
people. [27] Political struggle is not conducted in rational terms where orderly,
detailed policy explanations are presented to the participants for their deliberation. Instead, distortions, fake news, exclusion of radical proposals by
conservative media outlets, unequal financial resources to fund campaigns
and other obstacles are the norm. Secondly, deliberative democracy remains
powerless to tackle class power in the form of unequal corporate control of
the economy unless combined with radical mass mobilisation that challenges
private wealth and power. As with all proposals of direct democracy or deliberation in complex capitalist systems, the failure to replace day-to-day
bureaucratic and corporate power leaves deliberation nominally in the hands
of 'the people' while the administration and implementation of policies (or
real power) stay in the hands of corporate boards and bureaucratic and technocratic minorities.

In opposition to deliberative democracy, political theorists Ernesto
Laclau and Chantal Mouffe have influenced activists in Podemos and Syriza
by advocating radical reformism or 'agonistic pluralism' based not on a deliberative rational consensus (Habermas, Rawls, et. al) but on the conflictual
pluralism of emotional politics.[28] In short, deliberative democracy is seen as
essentially a soft Left/liberal operating principle underpinned by rational
discussion rather than confronting a class-divided world. However, unlike
orthodox Marxist notions of class interests, Laclau and Mouffe have argued
that the political terrain is a blank map without inherent social interests,

where identities and loyalties are in a constant state of flux and that the participants within 'Left populist' parties must construct policies through debate and not be afraid of disagreements and conflict.

While I agree that politics in capitalist societies cannot be conducted like a university seminar, their own notion of 'agonistic pluralism' is fraught with different problems. Only philosophers with minimal experience of the day-to-day realities of organisations and activists protecting not 'blank' maps, but what they regard as 'their' real material and cultural interests, could come up with a politics based on abstract linguistic theories. Each 'linguistic construction' unavoidably comforts or threatens activists and voters with preconceived interests and identities. And all this before they even get to debate divisive tax, environment, law-and-order, housing and other policies that affect real material interests, let alone how to proceed with the transition to post-carbon democracy!

Ironically, the 'old politics' is still alive and well in the writings of Srnicek, Williams and numerous other advocates of a 'Left populism', such as Chantal Mouffe,[29] even as they critique old proletarian class politics models or reject Keynesian solutions and instead promote models of 'post-work'. Mouffe and many other advocates of 'agonistic populism' are stuck at the level of organisational relations whereby unity through diversity is acquired by baldly stating one's policies rather than searching for a false consensus. All this is fine at the level of political rhetoric. It falls apart once intractable divisions over what environmentally sustainable political economic policies should replace existing 'drivers of growth'. No level of emotional politics or continual negotiation of differences and particularisms can secure a common language and programme in the 'populist party' or 'social bloc' if the members are either uninformed about narrowing future environmental options or continue to support policies that are bound to be unsustainable. Whether 'deliberative' or 'agonistic', both of these approaches are extremely limited. No discourse method or organisational structure can sustain unity and overcome major obstacles without the development of an environmentally sustainable political economy and durable strategy.

ECONOMIC 'DRIVERS OF GROWTH' VERSUS ORGANISATIONAL HARMONY

The survival of any new 'bloc' pursuing environmental sustainability is not possible if it has no clear political economy that underpins its political strategy. This is a neglected issue that has profound consequences. Previously, neo-Keynesians and neo-Marxists argued that the 'social bloc' must have a clear notion of the primary driver(s) of economic growth and how this benefits the movements and parties constituting the 'social bloc'. What is overlooked is that the notion of 'drivers of growth' is no longer appropriate or acceptable in an era where degrowth and environmental sustainability is a key goal for an increasing number of social movements.

Any strategy concerning how the 'social bloc' will capture and hold power either through electoral means or a combination of electoral and extra-parliamentary social mobilisation is no longer sufficient. Call it what you will, 'Left populism', 'beyond the fragments', 'the 99%' or other names, political manifestos and the outline of democratic organisational principles will not get very far by simply listing what the 'social bloc' opposes, whether neoliberal policies, incessant capitalist growth, inequality and injustice.[30] Without a minimally shared agreement over political economic policies and priorities, all is reduced to a mixture of hope, good intentions and temporarily papered over differences.

In the pre-1945 period, the dominant paradigm of 'capitalism versus democracy' was expressed through various forms of economic self-sufficiency. The goal of autarky was embraced in theory by Communists, anarcho-syndicalists, fascists and others even though in practice some of these movements engaged in international trade. By contrast, capitalist 'mixed economies' in the past seventy-five years have rejected self-sufficiency and have been characterised by Keynesian and neoliberal policies that sought economic growth by boosting export-led and investment-led growth as well as consumption-led growth. Critics of neoliberal austerity argue that up until the late 1970s, the Keynesian growth model was driven by productivity growth which drove wages growth. It was wages growth which then fuelled consumption or demand growth. After 1980, the neoliberal growth model was based on increased financialisation as debt. As stagnant wages failed to drive growth, demand or consumption was driven by higher household debt while business debt was used to fund investment and expansion or mere survival. Increased credit helped fuel asset price inflation such as increased property prices and share values which partly boosted confidence and drove increased consumption and investment.

When export-led growth policies are adopted by governments, this often means restrictions on wages and domestic consumption in order to make local industry lean and internationally competitive. Conversely, consumption-led growth is used by Right and centre-Left governments to boost domestic consumption in an economic downturn and is heavily reliant on private households borrowing in order to fund their consumption.[31] This 'disguised pain' is often politically effective in the short-run until trade deficits from higher levels of imported goods and accumulated private household and individual debt lead to constraints on retail spending, forced currency devaluation, cuts to imports, stagnant wages and/or higher prices for households – all characteristics evident in recent decades. Most mainstream parties are reluctant to upset consumers and voters by restricting consumption-led growth. On the contrary, governments are currently preoccupied with Covid-19 stimulus packages to generate and sustain consumption and jobs. Low and middle-income countries also still lack adequate domestic sources of capital formation necessary for essential infrastructure and new economic investments. They are either unattractive to foreign business investment or heavily dependent on foreign capital for any economic growth. These countries are also severely constrained in international markets because of the need to import elaborately manufactured goods and large capital goods due to the absence of industries such as heavy engineering and sophisticated electronics as well as being short of adequately skilled workforces.

Crucially, when it comes to developing a political coalition or 'social bloc' committed to environmental sustainability, earlier and current economic strategy options such as export-led or consumption-led growth are unacceptable to supporters of degrowth for reasons related to carbon emissions or the need to curb the negative ecological consequences of incessant growth in material footprints. The question therefore becomes: how is a future 'social bloc' to be formed or kept together if the 'drivers' of economic growth are replaced by new forms of degrowth objectives? New forms of public investment (such as an expanded 'social state' and increased community infrastructures) may become politically popular and sustainable despite not having anywhere near the same negative impact of large material footprints like existing capitalist production and consumption.

If 'prosperity without growth' (Tim Jackson[32]) is to become economically feasible, it will need to be able to sustain those component members of the 'political bloc' that may oppose neoliberal austerity policies but want more conventional policies geared to industrial growth and wages growth. This difficult policy choice faces those political representatives of workers and communities dependent on either export-led production or imports driving consumption-led private sector jobs in retailing, IT communication devices, clothing, home renovation, private furnishings, whitegoods and cars. For low and middle-income countries characterised by up to five billion people lacking adequate income, essential services, food and housing, the choices are far starker. Any future 'social bloc' committed to environmental sustainability must be able to attract sufficient support and survive politically by simultaneously curbing export-led industrialisation and replacing this with regenerative domestic growth geared to investment-led national infrastructure, social services and other 'drivers' of greater equality. These necessary social investments may sound fine in theory, but without external aid are often beyond the financial, natural resources and technological and skilled workforce capacities of individual low and middle-income countries. Until we actually begin to see proposals for alternatives to unsustainable export-orientated industrialisation in countries with quite different political, economic and cultural profiles, it will be difficult to assess the prospects for a successful 'social bloc'.

CHANGING CONVENTIONAL PATTERNS OF CONSUMPTION

Currently, the world is characterised by entirely different forms of personal and household consumption. In high-income developed capitalist countries, personal and household consumption accounts for between 50% and 70% of GDP. This consumption is subdivided into durable goods such as cars and appliances and non-durable goods like food, fuel, clothing and services. Over the past fifty years, durable goods (which accounted for 40% of US GDP in 1968) has declined as part of total consumption while personal and household consumption of services has risen dramatically and now accounts for up to 60% of personal consumption and approximately 46% of total GDP.[33] Apart from their affluent minorities, this pattern of consumption has not been replicated in developing countries where most low and middle-income people have limited capacity to buy either durable goods or non-durable services. Also, even mainstream economists such as Adair Turner recognise that greenhouse gas emissions from production processes may have declined over the past two decades, but emissions from consumption are significantly higher than before, and continue to rise.[34] This requires not only reduced consumption in developed capitalist countries, but also international border taxes on carbon-intensive goods.

Strategically, a 'social bloc' committed to environmental sustainability in OECD countries would possibly cause divisions between 'green growthers' and 'degrowthers'. If the aim is to make 'durable consumer' items such as appliances genuinely durable and repairable, this might be endorsed.

However, electric cars would be rejected by many 'degrowthers' (who prefer public transport) especially as the *construction* of two to three billion electric cars by 2050 (as opposed to the servicing of these vehicles) would still require a similar use of material resources as those needed to produce petrol and diesel cars. Changing both the mix and quality of non-durables, including more public cooperative services and less private financial, insurance services might be a shared position depending on whether 'green growthers' preferred private businesses to social co-operatives. Similarly, and depending on the low and middle-income country, the 'social bloc' could aim for higher expenditure on public housing, enhancing and redistributing local food production and consumption while boosting household consumption of essential public services such as health and education. Once again, there is no automatic agreement here as it depends on whether advocates of green growth or degrowth are committed to particular social welfare policies, pro-market practices or self-sufficiency goals.

Alternative environment strategies have either been rejected outright or not yet fully considered by mainstream Left parties. To give an example of the difficulty of forging a 'social bloc' either as a coalition or under the umbrella of a 'catch-all' party, one only has to think of Corbyn's Labour Party and the election disaster of 2019. No other Left-wing party in the world has come close to winning office in recent years as British Labour. Although presenting the most Left-wing policies since Atlee's government in 1945, Labour failed on at least two important grounds. Firstly, it failed to form a 'political bloc' with Remain parties and movements (Scottish National Party, Liberal Social Democrats, Greens, etc) because the Labour Party was torn over Brexit and also many in the Party arrogantly and mistakenly believed they could win a majority on their own. No leader and no policy, whether Brexit or Remain, could have prevented a *de facto* split within the Party and the electorate. Secondly, Corbyn partly developed the 'drivers of growth' in policies such as reviving manufacturing by switching to the mass production of renewable technology and also hoping for a revival of industrial exports through mission-oriented innovation. This 'green growth' strategy was a short-term policy fix. Neo-Keynesian growth solutions are not ecologically sustainable beyond the short-term and are not beneficial globally despite being viable at national level.

In other words, export-led manufacturing as the primary 'driver' benefits particular countries for a brief period of time but at the expense of increased global emissions and natural resources depletion. Instead of currency devaluations and protectionism used by nations during the Great Depression in the mistaken belief that these policies would advantage their own businesses and populations, today, jeopardising a safe climate and threatening fragile habitats is the new form of 'beggar thy neighbour'. Decarbonisation and relative decoupling of economic growth from nature appear better than they are simply because national calculations do not count carbon-embodied material imports from other countries. Just as protectionism and currency devaluations exacerbated the Great Depression, so too, key 'green growth' export-led policies will most likely contribute to overall global environmental degradation even though they might curb carbon emissions at a national level. Without a fundamental reappraisal of consumption-led growth (a necessary policy still consigned to the 'too hard basket') any strategy orientated to public industrial regeneration and re-nationalisation of rail and other services is too one-sided and environmentally ineffective. Corbyn's Labour Party, like other centre-Left parties, was too geared to various notions of the 'entrepreneurial state' and mission-orientated industrial strategy.[35] Mission-orientated innovation and industrial strategy should not be dismissed. It is quite valuable in areas such as health, medicine, social investment and innovation as well as supporting curbs on financialisation and re-organising taxation policies. Unfortunately, it is also sold to businesses and governments as a means of harnessing the 'entrepreneurial state' to boost national market competitiveness and other conventional export-led market growth targets. As such, it tends to be a reinvention of the old wheel of unsustainable growth.

All parties and movements have historically had maximum and minimalist programs or goals. They have also been divided by what are called 'fundamentalists' and 'realists'. Alternative 'social blocs' are unlikely to accommodate too many 'fundamentalists' who wish to promote their 'maximum' socialist or environmentalist agenda via electoral coalitions. The nature of contemporary fractured political life unfortunately favours minimalist programs precisely at a time when fundamental change is desperately needed. Sadly, 'social blocs' will have a short life expectancy if the member parties and movements fall out over both the pace and the character of environmentally sustainable socio-economic policies.

Therefore, what appears to be progressive public policies designed to redistribute domestic resources to benefit the poor and disadvantaged in individual countries (via state-generated industrial projects) can have a negative global impact by increasing both economic material growth and global warming. Unless offset by falling material footprints in affluent OECD countries and carefully targeted policies to minimise such negative global outcomes, a high environmental price may be paid later on. Nonetheless, mass poverty in dozens of countries such as Haiti, Ethiopia, Bolivia or Pakistan demands urgent reduction strategies and cannot wait decades for high-income countries to eventually reduce their material footprints. Also, if 'state-led growth' pursued a heavy component of non-material growth in knowledge and care services, government consumption could challenge the heavy reliance on private material consumerism. However, electoral defeat would be guaranteed unless the 'social bloc' parties first prepared voters with mass cultural and educative campaigns to explain why this new form of social consumption was essential to both community wellbeing and environmental sustainability. No country today, not even China, is driven by 'state-led growth'. Instead, China has had a combination of private and public invest-ment-led, export-led and consumption-led growth which is now slowing down.

Herein lies some of the difficult choices facing both reformers and radical social change activists. More importantly, the connection between the possible political success of a 'social bloc' and its endorsement or rejection of particular economic 'drivers of growth' confirms why both mainstream neoliberal policies as well as oppositional Keynesian and Marxist policies need to be radically overhauled. The vast majority of policy makers have failed to register, let alone integrate into their models, the ways in which environment crises will affect the viability of all future growth strategies. Eventually, environmental damage caused by implementing updated versions of Keynesian increased aggregate demand (consumption) to combat austerity will begin to register with policy makers, businesses, unions and households. The high probability that ecological modernisation goals such as decoupling growth from nature will only be achieved in relative terms, rather than abso-lutely is denied or carelessly deferred as a problem to be left for future deci-sion-makers and technology innovators. Little surprise that the 'drivers of growth' debate in its current 'pre-environmentally conscious' form is so myopic, neglectful and backward looking.

WHO SPEAKS FOR 'THE PEOPLE' OR THE 'WORKING CLASS'?

As I have discussed, the viability of a 'social bloc' depends on reconciling constituencies with conflicting political interests. No environmentalist or worker has a singular identity as they may be simultaneously workers and environmentalists as well as be divided by such things as occupations and wages, homeowners or renters, reliance on public or private essential services or other social and cultural signifiers. A durable 'social bloc' is much harder to sustain beyond the first few years of enthusiastic political action. Vanguard parties never had to mobilise workers divided by such complex historical forms of working-class life as do contemporary proponents of a 'social bloc'. Also, we are more aware these days that political alliances at electoral level are either made easier or difficult depending on the formal voting system. For example, proportional and preferential systems are more favourable to potential 'political blocs' compared to old undemocratic voting systems in the UK and US where small parties get virtually little or no representation despite receiving millions of votes.

Within developed capitalist countries with an average of 70% to 80% of workers employed in the private and public service sectors, a 'social bloc' that tries to advance a post-carbon society while simultaneously combatting inequality and austerity, high indebtedness and the negative impact of financialisation is only possible if the parties to the 'bloc' share a macro-economic alternative strategy. In order for such a strategy to have wide democratic appeal, it would have to ensure that tolerant cosmopolitan and ecological values prevailed over narrow authoritarian and nationalist policies that appease mono-cultural or racist protectionist sections of society. Given the current higher propensity of those with lower formal education to hold nationalist, racist and anti-ecological values, a new 'bloc' would most likely require an alliance of working-class and middle-class professional segments. Despite modern working classes being multicultural, it would be an illusion to think that a majority in favour of a cosmopolitan post-carbon democracy could come from those sections of the working class and middle class subscribing to nationalist/racist values, regardless of whether they were employed in services, manufacturing or other sectors.

The precariousness of a 'social bloc' based on working-class and middle-class organisations, communities and activists is vividly illustrated by the post-mortem accounts of the 2019 UK election, even though the Labour Party was not a 'social bloc' but unofficially embraced a wide range of political views. Labour Party member, John-Baptiste Odour, is typical of those who cling to an essentialist, 'workerist' notion of 'class interest' that he claims was betrayed by an equally essentialist conception of 'middle-class' activists inside Labour who refused to accept Brexit.[36] If the Labour Party had to be first democratised before it could democratise society and let the 'hundred flowers' of diverse social movements bloom (Tony Benn), Odour argued that this was subverted by 'middle-class' members who benefited from democracy in the Party thus preventing the northern and other Labour strongholds from having their desire for Brexit respected. This is an expression of the old myth that democratisation inevitably leads to socialism. It is also the old dilemma of what constitutes 'the voice of the people', how is it articulated and under what conditions can coalitions of manual workers and professionals co-exist in mass parties or movements.

The British Labour Party has a one member, one vote constitution, so, there was nothing formally undemocratic about the call for a second referendum on Brexit if the majority of the Party members (who are now overwhelmingly from service sector and non-manual backgrounds) voted for this policy. It will be recalled that Trotsky had famously predicted in 1904 (during his anti-Bolshevik phase) that Lenin's methods would lead to the party replacing the working class, followed by the organisation substituting for the party, then the central committee substituting for the party organisation, and finally a dictator substituting for the central committee. While the Labour party is not a Leninist vanguard party, substitutionalism is alive and well. Those Labour Party members who supported Brexit were no more the 'authentic' voice of the working class (given most manual working-class people do not go to meetings) any more than 'middle-class' members opposing Brexit claimed to represent the so-called voice of 'the people'.

Unless parties take a poll of the population rather than just their membership, the degree of democratisation in any movement or party can only be ascertained if all members are able to submit and vote on proposals. Once organisations become mass parties of more than a few hundred people, they invariably succumb to various degrees of Leninist 'substitutionalism'. Whether one wishes to call it the inherent tendency of the 'iron law of oligarchy' (Robert Michels[37]) is debatable. The solution to 'oligarchies' accumulating power in organisations is not to be found in the ideal model of the party. Only a radical democratisation of decision-making *beyond* the party system can counter the tendency to concentrate power in the hands of officials and influential leadership groups. If most institutions and workplaces outside political parties are not run democratically, it is more likely that party members unfamiliar with democratic decision-making are more likely to tolerate oligarchy (the rule of the few) within their own parties. 'Democracy' means little if there is not a genuine contestation of ideas. Yet, 'democracy' or for that matter, 'working-class interest' does not guarantee social justice or rational policies if a majority of the population vote for nationalist/racist policies or vote to keep mining coal or other regressive policies. A party or a 'social bloc' should also not succumb to democratic or working-class prejudice and irrationality as has been the case for over a century. Witness the classic example of how social democratic and labour parties endorsed their respective governments going to war in 1914, a war that led to millions of workers being needlessly slaughtered.

Little wonder then, that 'capitalism versus democracy' functions as such a limited paradigm when it comes to mobilising 'social blocs' that need to articulate policies that challenge familiar ways of life, communal prejudices and old-style class politics. The political communicative formula for doing this without patronising, offending and alienating those suffering and neglected communities is yet to be discovered. In polarised situations where traditional former militant working-class clubs, such as in Durham, invited Right-wing Nigel Farage to be a guest speaker, meant that there was little a divided Left-wing Labour party could do if it opposed Brexit in such nationalist strongholds. Clinging to dominant forms of production and consumption, distrust of foreigners and parochial and highly prejudiced views of the world may give 'workerists' the comfort of being amongst the 'authentic' but narrow-minded sections of the working class. It will not, however, prevent the necessary fundamental changes required to avoid environmental and social disasters.

In an age when political loyalties are fleeting compared with the 'rusted on' support of earlier generations of voters, 'social blocs' appear less resilient to external shocks. Their future depends on sustaining the unity of diverse internal segments and in particular on how effectively they respond to the reactions of mainstream centre/Right opponents in the political field. Whether called 'Left populist' parties or a 'social bloc, they are 'intermediate' defensive political responses to major market failures rather than clear, well established alternative visions of a potential post-capitalist or post-carbon democracy. In this respect, they reflect a defence of the old forms of employment, social welfare and political representation currently in the process of dissolution while lacking the alternative policies necessary to break with the old capitalist order's destruction of the biosphere.

If we look forward to the next ten to twenty years, it is quite likely that any existing political parties that manage to survive will have to negotiate significantly new forms of employment and social security, new digitalised industries that impact trade and imports as well as threats to existing taxation revenue. Familiar social welfare, education and health institutions or cultural/leisure activities could well struggle to survive in their current forms. The reshaping of industries, employment and public services offer many opportunities for new political demands and new forms of mobilisation around alternative ways to deliver and strengthen public services while combatting inequality.

However, unfamiliar social problems and the emergence of new political and socio-economic constituencies will test the survival capacities of present-day mainstream political parties and any oppositional 'social bloc' or form of 'Left populism'. New political movements will need to be more geared to future issues and problems rather than still mainly fighting the old battles of 'capitalism versus democracy'. International links are important but few substantial connections between Left and social movements other than occasional conferences and joint rallies have materialised. Hybrid supra-national movements such as DiEM25 is currently little more than a loose umbrella organisation with about 128,000 members across dozens of countries inside and outside the EU. Because of its very uneven presence in various EU member countries, it would need to boost DiEM's activist base significantly just to be a counterweight to the more than 30,000 corporate lobbyists in Brussels, let alone becoming a substantial political force in key EU countries.[38] Left parties in Latin America and the Caribbean have *supranational* affiliations but these have also failed to develop any significant grass roots presence beyond a single country.

Not surprisingly, simply replacing the rigidities of the 'old politics' with infinitely malleable identities and policies will be a recipe for political instability and decline. While old affiliations and identification with mainstream parties may have been substantially eroded in recent years, the fact that millions of voters still adhere to these old political machines is a marked sign that people are far less malleable and fluid than our 'agonistic' philosophers make out. The search for new social change agents or the tactical combination of plural identities into an active new 'people's party' continues to place the emphasis on the old political project, namely, how to construct a successful pluralist organisation. A successful organisation is inseparable from its capacity to sustain unity around appealing policies. Unidas Podemos, for example, has already split over its policies and electoral tactics and is in a compromised and weakened position as part of the Socialist Party-led coalition government in Spain with only two out of twenty-two ministries. If an approach is too cautious, it risks stagnation. If it confronts the unavoidable necessity of articulating bold alternative policies, the short-term political costs may be high if former elements leave because the party/movement is conceived as either too 'radical' or too 'conservative'.

Like all political organisations that claim to represent the 'real people', 'the many not the few', 'popular will against the political class' and so forth, the politics of deliberate coalitions of parties around a 'social bloc' are currently too unstable and fragile to survive. In many countries, there is still much education and campaigning to be done before mass constituencies are minimally informed about the necessity of degrowth, the need to build new sources of revenue and the reason why adopting neo-Keynesian and Marxian 'drivers of growth' will only work temporarily rather than prevent future major environmental crises. Like deliberative democracy that prepares information and topics for people to deliberate upon, 'agonistic pluralism' is also pre-shaped by the leadership group despite all the rhetoric about popular democracy. It lends itself to perhaps more democracy than mainstream parties but can also give rise to authoritarian tendencies when in a position of power and encountering internal or external opposition. That is why the term 'the people' has always been a dangerous empty symbol waiting for others to invest it with opportunistic meaning and language. Debates about hegemony and the need to move beyond the 'central role of the working class' are all still locked within the old paradigm of 'capitalism versus democracy'. Laclau and Mouffe and their followers want 'radical democratisation' to replace class struggle but have an uncritical view of the role of democratisation. They naïvely assume (alongside advocates of 'deliberative democracy' that it is not in conflict with environmental sustainability.

The ability of new political movements to emerge and flourish depends on going beyond the agendas of existing social movements and developing an alternative macro political economic strategy that is neither neoliberal nor neo-Keynesian 'green growth'. Such a new party or movement configuration is urgently needed but its political time has yet to come. A majority of Left and Green activists as well as electorates in most countries are not yet either prepared for or sufficiently receptive to such fundamental changes in production, consumption and redistribution necessary for environmentally sustainable futures. Although large numbers of people are receptive to the need for emergency climate action, this is not to be confused with the need to ground greater equality, social justice and non-discriminatory socio-political institutions and practices within environmentally sustainable political economies. I will attempt to analyse and move beyond some of these undeveloped policies in the following chapters.

13.'OUR DREAMS DON'T FIT INTO YOUR BALLOT BOX'

THE TITLE of this chapter comes from one of the slogans used by the Spanish Indignados or 'Real Democracy Now' movement which erupted across Spain in 2011. Reacting to mass unemployment and austerity following the crisis of 2008, they initially challenged the narrow solutions offered by the Spanish mainstream parties through the ballot box. Like many other movements across the world, the Indignados sought a mixture of practical immediate policies and utopian solutions to poverty, inequality and ecological destruction. Globally, there is no shortage of utopian imaginaries. Regardless of whether green or socialist, many politically and social inventive images of the future, and the desires and hopes underpinning them are conceived in a geopolitical vacuum. Most reformers and radicals are of course aware of how existing powerful governments and business groups mobilise and utilise economic, military and other administrative resources. Yet, paradoxically, countless visions of an alternative society are still presented as if they are ready-finished social orders or functioning realities. Hence, key goals and visions are often *disconnected* from the extremely difficult political, economic and environmental obstacles that first need to be surmounted.

In this chapter, I will therefore analyse some of the many admirable values and objectives advocated by various alternative movements and why their socio-political organisational, fiscal and other important goals are often undeveloped or self-defeating. I believe that the task of critical supporters of post-capitalist societies is simultaneously twofold: first of all to defend and campaign on behalf of those alternative ideas and proposals that are vitally needed for future sustainable wellbeing and social justice; and secondly, to vigorously criticise a variety of institutional and policy proposals by radical movements that are counter-productive to necessary social change because they are ill-conceived and politically unrealisable. A good place to start is with the mixture of especially important but also highly problematic alternative ideas that go under the broad umbrella called 'degrowth' – a collection of radical ideas advocated by various environmental movements, anarchists, eco-socialists and other critics of unsustainable and destructive capitalist growth.

INTENDED AND UNINTENDED CONSEQUENCES OF DEGROWTH

To outsiders, degrowth continues to be a both a current of thought and action, as well as an assortment of academic publications and conferences that critique unsustainable capitalist growth. Some 'degrowthers' are linked to a number of small experimental communes and a network of like-minded activities and movements that overlap with such things as climate emergency action and various organisations promoting sustainable living. To date, no distinct degrowth party or movement has emerged (except an earlier failed attempt in France) and there is no clear politics currently manifested in actual political organisations like socialist parties. Degrowth activists are divided between those who are closer to eco-socialists and support state-orientated anti-capitalist policies on a range of socio-economic policies and the majority who oppose any move to make degrowth movements adopt nation-wide organisational forms. Recently, strong supporter of degrowth, Timothée Parrique, completed perhaps the most comprehensive study of this diverse political movement that is alternatively called degrowth, post-growth, wellbeing and other names.[1] Surveying the growing literature on the central policies, aims and strategies of 'degrowthers', Parrique summarised these visions and arguments as the desire for a society where the economy and its way of thinking are no longer at the centre of everything. In what he calls 'degrowthopia', where exploitation of people and nature has ended, the new society rests on three principles: autonomy, sufficiency, and care. These include:

- Promoting care and solidarity towards humans and non-humans. Resource extraction is to be decided by the communities most directly impacted by these decisions who are not just stewards of nature, but also knowledgeable about local ecosystems.

- The production and circulation of goods is to be organised in small artisan circles and cooperatives using convivial tools that are democratically manageable, easily intelligible and geared to circularity, or waste not, want not.
- Self-sufficient bioregional commons of different sizes will have their own community currencies. Most of the financial system is to consist of credit cooperatives governed by strong ethical rules preventing the accumulation of wealth at the expense of others.
- All are guaranteed free access to essential necessities and services, whether food, housing, education, healthcare, transportation, information, water and energy. Any surplus should be shared as there should be sufficiency for all and excess for none.
- Voluntary simplicity is to be based on outwardly simple, but inwardly rich lives which emphasise less stuff and more relationships. People will be less concerned about their career and material possessions and alternate between paid and unpaid self-determined activities. They will do less travelling and live frugal lifestyles but nurture reciprocal networks of care and gift.
- Political life is to be organised around direct democracy at the town or neighbourhood level and representative democracy at the bioregional and national level.
- The ultimate purpose of a post-work economy is to liberate workers' time for joyous non-economic social and cultural purposes, that is, work less and play more.[2]

Like many other defenders of degrowth, Parrique is fully aware that the term 'degrowth' is a confusing and unsatisfactory name that even many supporters of degrowth offer contradictory explanations of the meaning and character of this concept. I will not dwell on these disputes except to say that I share a number of common criticisms that 'degrowthers' are unclear about what they wish to *grow* and which forms and levels of material production and consumption they wish to *degrow*. Some environmentalists argue that we should talk about 'good growth' or 'selective growth' rather than the confusing term called 'degrowth'. It is doubtful that a name change will resolve key strategic problems, such as which parts of economic activity should grow or not. The vast majority of 'degrowthers' advocate frugality but they do not celebrate poverty and do not equate degrowth with an economic recession or depression. Also, while 'degrowthers' do not ignore the plight of billions of people in low-income countries and the poor in OECD countries, they propose few practical degrowth policies that would remedy their mass poverty.[3] As a socio-economic theory, degrowth is so far unable to persuade millions of potential supporters because it still lacks a developed, coherent and plausible conception of how to implement and measure degrowth.

WHAT SHOULD DEGROW?

An unplanned recession such as that currently caused by Covid-19, has witnessed GDP decline by 5 to 20% or more in various countries. Even if 'planned contraction' were less chaotic and damaging to tens of millions of workers and their families, as well as to low-income people in cities and villages, would the necessary level of 'planned contraction' be smaller or greater than the decline caused by unplanned capitalist recessions? Would it be 2%, 5% or 10% of GDP per annum and would it be in the private sector mainly focused on consumption, or military expenditure and other parts of the public sector, or imported goods and natural resources, all of the latter or not? Importantly, how would 'frugality' differ from the enforced and involuntary poverty of recessions or the unintended hardships caused by 'planned contraction'? Remember, these questions are relevant to the transition phase when there is not yet a fully developed degrowth society and we are still in a stage of 'planned contraction' of capitalist societies. A decade ago, Jeroen van den Bergh criticised degrowth movements for favouring a decline in GDP without identifying which good or bad parts of GDP were to degrow.[4] To date, this vague notion of degrowth has not been satisfactorily answered.[5]

Supporters of degrowth reject GDP and prefer other indices and measuring tools such as the Genuine Progress Indicator. Yet, there is also no agreement between 'degrowthers' over which production and extraction processes, or which consumer goods and technologies should be either reduced, banned or exempted. If banned or phased out, how quickly should this happen in countries with large material footprints (and major levels of inequality) and what should be done about those countries, communities and others that lack material and technological substitutes or the capacity to implement these multiple timetables covering numerous individual items? Although versions of degrowth have been around for at least forty years, there is still no specific national analysis that outlines what proportion of degrowth in per capita material footprints would be necessary once industries with large material footprints such national military apparatuses and contractors or the combined production, sales and servicing divisions of the automobile sector and the advertising industry that drives consumption were closed down or scaled back. There is no agreement as to whether we should abolish universities as they currently exist (because of their central role in maintaining key economic, military and administrative practices), whether we still need advanced scientific and medical research centres and what the role of organised knowledge will be in the transition to a new society. All remains too vague and without clear degrowth targets. It is often forgotten that the inventory of materials, products and technologies used in contemporary economies is enormous and produced under quite diverse production conditions across the world.

The task of evaluating which 'bad' or undesirable goods and services are to go, and which 'good growth' goods and services are to remain or expand, can therefore not be left *only* to local community decision-making. Rather, decisions about the safety, sustainability and diverse needs of the majority of people living outside particular localities should be a joint process made by national or supranational environmental and social departments and agencies in combination with the full involvement of local communities and institutions. If left solely to diverse local communities, these vital decisions will almost certainly introduce numerous inconsistencies and fuel disharmony and serious political conflict.

No unplanned market system or planned economy ever works as intended by market ideologues or government planners. There are numerous itemised suggestions across diverse industries and sectors of national economies – everything from agriculture, energy, finance and education to trade, work and waste disposal – that could constitute the basis of an alternative degrowth economy.[6] Yet, some of these proposals are too problematic, like the conservative and dangerous notion of the 'steady state'. Others appear to be mere wish-lists rather than an overall integrated macro-political economy of degrowth that would enable us to make any conclusive judgements.

Once a government signalled that capitalist growth would need to be curtailed and reduced in planned stages, it is unclear what institutional mechanisms 'degrowthers' would utilise to prevent a Great Depression unfolding from falling stock markets, loss of business confidence or even collapse of private investment and ensuing mass unemployment, possible currency collapse and hyper-inflation. Unless governments dramatically increased the size of public sector employment, production and services vacated by or closed down by private businesses, degrowth based on 'planned contraction' would suffer a still birth. It is doubtful that local communities could implement the expansion of public sector production and employment on their own as they would seriously lack the fiscal, material and other resources that only national governments could mobilise in a national depression. Local non-market solutions might emerge in the form of barter, co-ordinating food and other services. It is important to note that these would be grossly inadequate to keep a new transitional economy afloat. Unless 'degrowthers' prepared for a combination of national, regional and local measures to counter the fall in private business activity, failure is virtually guaranteed. Planning requires preparation and I know of no detailed contingency macro-economic plans conceptualised by radical greens or ecological economists other than the limited stock flow models by Tim Jackson, Peter Victor and Ali Naqvi (see Chapter Ten).

If publicly owned enterprises and the democratic control of social institutions or shared commons and cooperatives are to function smoothly, greater clarification will be needed rather than simply being listed as desirable items in radical social change manifestos. Specific policy proposals will be necessary to outline not just the organisational, financial and geographical scale of these new institutions and production processes, but also to formulate some potential strategies to counter potentially powerful foreign and domestic corporate and political opposition. It is not that 'degrowthers' are unaware of the power of military establishments. But little is said, for example, about the vital connection between existing production systems and military and security apparatuses or how to overcome such military-industrial complexes that are closely tied to the incessant logic of capitalist growth. The main focus remains on civilian production, as if calls for degrowth merely affects civilian consumption. There is a naïve notion that military establishments somehow get scaled back or that a new civilian degrowth economy can either emerge or coexist with military industrial complexes. In short, 'degrowthers' say little about the central role of military research and development in civilian technological and product development, the need for massive military budgets and personnel to secure fossil fuels and maintain conservative authoritarian regimes, plus other domestic and international roles carried out by military and civilian apparatuses. These are all effectively detached from their vital roles in the capitalist market economies of the leading G20 powers.

Between the simple dichotomy of the choice between economic growth based on more military weapons or more schools and health care are an infinitely vast range of everyday products and services that are far less clear-cut in terms of the environmental and social damage they possibly cause compared to other readily available options. 'Degrowthers' are divided between those who essentially believe in stateless societies built around local communities and others who are orientated to the local but recognise the need for some national state institutions and roles. The problem is that the latter group are yet to clearly spell out a range of non-local institutional structures. In other words, if national state institutions are necessary, it is imperative to specify how they will support or interact with local democratic communities and facilitate democratic decision-making at national and regional levels. If local power prevails over national government then it is guaranteed that the larger society will flounder in a series of socio-economic crises caused by inadequate coordination of planned contraction. Conversely, if clear power-sharing and decision-making is not specified, representative democracy at national level will likely subordinate the political will of local communities or contradict and negate local direct democracy. One only has to look at existing and previous conflicts in federal and other systems over financial and resource sharing between diverse levels of administration. This old dilemma of the conflict between direct democracy and state planning faced by earlier generations of socialists has now metamorphized into the new paradigm of 'democracy versus sustainability'.

It is not just that 'degrowthers' have produced few alternative socio-economic plans or detailed lists of what goods and services are to be rejected, scaled back, or increased and further developed. Very importantly, after forty years there is still a fundamental lack of clarity about whether there should be a *standard rate of degrowth* for all resources, goods and services or a *differentiated* rate of degrowth per annum or per decade based on varied global reserves of vital commodities and the need to achieve specific local, national or international ecological and social goals. Crucially, the visions of 'degrowthers' are divided between those who desire to live in ecologically and socially transformed existing cities and others who prefer life to be primarily organised in small non-urban local communities.[7] Either way, we need to ask: who would collate and measure the rate of degrowth? Would it be a national bureau of statistics, supranational, national or regional planning bodies, or just tens of thousands of informal local communities and neighbourhoods collating statistics or 'guesstimating' their annual consumption of resources? Trusting fellow local communards and strangers in tens of thousands of other 'commons' to not excessively indulge in consumption at the expense of those adhering to shared objectives of frugality is a naïve politics and a recipe for conflict and highly uneven degrowth.

THE LIMITS OF LOCAL DEMOCRACY

Any transition from market individualism to communal sharing will require the capacity to democratically enforce planned contraction of material resources or what is called 'just transitions'. Without such enforcement of appropriate state rules and regulations, how would those enterprises providing resources, goods and services not available at local neighbourhood or community level actually be required to conform to democratically agreed rates of degrowth? To believe that crime, corruption, irresponsible behaviour, incompetence and preferential treatment will all suddenly disappear or not re-emerge is to believe in fairy tales. It is to be hoped that the vast majority of people will be imbued with a new cooperative spirit and ethic of care, but no society can afford significant social and environmental damage by naïvely assuming that all people will share these values and behave accordingly, especially within the context of scarcity of resources.

Many supporters of radical alternatives recognise but play down the fact that we live in a world of regimes with violent, anti-democratic repressive state apparatuses, numerous neo-fascist and other authoritarian and violent movements, deep-seated fundamentalist religious movements intolerant of secular cultural practices and so forth. Even if a post-capitalist society were to emerge without civil war and violence, one can be certain that a number of countries will continue to repress any attempt to transition to sustainable, democratic societies. At best, a significant minority within potential future degrowth countries will not share the ecological and social values adopted by the majority and also continue to vigorously oppose and attempt to undermine these new social relations. After all, we are not talking about degrowth societies as 'intentional communities' whose members have chosen to join and share a set of values and practices. Hence, if post-growth societies do emerge, they will almost certainly develop from within situations of political polarisation and conflict where a clear majority will, for a range of reasons, voluntarily choose to adopt degrowth policies strongly disliked by minorities.

One should definitely aim to transform the worst aspects of existing criminal justice systems and severely reduce and constrain military, police and other repressive apparatuses. However, a naïve politics based on the assumption that values of harmony and co-operation are shared, could be a recipe for destructive minorities to undermine and attempt to revert back to all the ugly, uncaring individualism and accumulation of wealth that advocates of post-capitalist societies currently oppose. A socially sustainable political system cannot avoid the unpleasant topic of how the new society will protect its members and prevent opponents from weakening and destroying its new institutions and social relations. Education is a necessary long-term solution but may be inadequate and ineffective in the short-term. Pacifism is also an essential long-term goal that unfortunately might well be readily abused in the short-term by violent external and domestic opponents. Regardless of criminal justice reform proposals and conflict resolution methods, such as restorative justice, the limits of social democracy may be tested by questions of how to reduce or eliminate military forces, what forms of surveillance or domestic policing would be acceptable and what kinds of prisons for murderers and other violent offenders would be essential. A small taste of these divisive issues is already evident in the demand of the Black Lives Matter movement to defund the police.

Even without the numerous co-ordinating institutions necessary to prevent society from collapsing, how can social justice be combined with sustainability if left to a largely decentralised society. Think of how the global pandemic of Covid-19 crisis has revealed the glaring problems and shortcomings inherent in anti-statist utopias, whether advocated by free marketeers, anarchists or eco-village 'degrowthers'. It is bad enough that high death rates have occurred with state institutions imposing either draconian measures or inept and confusing guidelines. Imagine the sky-rocketing death rates if tens of thousands of decentralised local communities ignored or lacked the national laws and mass coordination of medical supplies and financial help to rapidly react to major heath, environmental and other crises. One should certainly sharply criticise the current mixture of authoritarian measures that suspended democracy. The neglect by governments of millions of workers, villagers, the poor and disadvantaged while a disproportionate amount of Covid-19 economic aid flowed to businesses is unquestionably related to the class divisions in particular countries and the preferential aid given to those within the dominant class or religious-ethnic grouping. It is the class character of recent stimulus packages that points to the reasons why we need to reject pro-market socio-economic policy. However, the experience to date of this pandemic justifies an alternative set of state policies rather than a stateless society.

Far too many 'degrowthers' pay lip service to the need for comprehensive public institutions and services and instead focus heavily on the direct democracy aspect of the local commons. Hence, admirable principles such as 'sufficiency rather than excess' do not in themselves tell us much about the ability of small local co-operatives to satisfy specific large urban infrastructure needs. This is also the case with food production, vitally

needed medicines and health care, the availability or scarcity of non-carcino-
genic natural or renewable building materials, household goods, machinery
and communications technology or a multitude of other financial and technological resources beyond 'the local'. Often an uncritical assumption that
small is better than large scale comes into play. We are reminded of the
dangers of this assumption by an example from China. The policy of every
rural commune having its own backyard furnace during Mao's Great Leap
Forward between 1958 and 1962, proved to be a human, ecological and
economic disaster as peasants were diverted from agriculture to produce
inferior quality steel. Mass hunger ensued, industrial production went backwards, and everyday life was made extremely difficult.

While 'degrowthers' are certainly not advocating Maoist dictatorial policies, valuable lessons can be learnt about the counterproductive consequences when any political movement pursues either too much
decentralisation or too much centralisation. In a world where a minority of
giant enterprises employ tens and hundreds of thousands of workers while
millions of businesses are small and medium enterprises, there is no clarity
over what 'degrowthers' mean by 'small local artisan co-operatives'. Do they
mean co-operative enterprises of 10 to 100 workers, 500 to 2000 workers, or
larger or smaller enterprises? Will there be upper limits on the size of enterprises and what will be the approximate or maximum size of a local
community?

The widespread assumption about the superior benefits of direct face-to-
face democracy is also only partly valid as this mode of decision making is far
from suitable for all aspects of socio-economic life. For example, urban planning could definitely benefit from the enormous input of local democratic
participation that could help plan neighbourhood needs and overcome the
inequality and neglect of existing urban infrastructure policies. However, the
delivery of city-wide transport, housing, health, energy and cultural facilities
(especially in cities with over fifty thousand people) needs coordination to
ensure accessibility based on equal rights to resources and services. Large
population centres need to also minimise waste of environmental and fiscal
resources by eliminating duplication, better manage scarce resources and
maximise reach to those sections and areas of cities currently neglected.
Participatory budgeting and other such engagement of local citizens is
merely a vitally needed first step. However, this form of increased democratisation and consultation requires vital financial and material resources, as well
as experts and citizens with knowledge beyond the local.

Evaluating the broader political philosophical issues such as whether we need governments, the possibility of ending all political alienation and why a totally self-transparent organisation of society is either utopian or potentially dangerous, social theorist, Slavoj Žižek, cuts through a range of illusions and false hopes when he pointedly observes:

> It is no wonder that today's practices of 'direct democracy', from favelas to the 'postindustrial' digital culture ...all have to rely on a state apparatus – i.e., their survival relies on a thick texture of 'alien-ated' institutional mechanisms: where do electricity and water come from? Who guarantees the rule of law? To whom do we turn for healthcare? Etc., etc. The more a community is self-ruling, the more this network has to function smoothly and invisibly. Maybe we should change the goal of emancipatory struggles from overcoming alien-ation to enforcing the right kind of alienation: how to achieve a smooth functioning of 'alienated' (invisible) social mechanisms that sustain the space of 'non-alienated' communities?[8]

Žižek also reveals the superficiality of the liberal notion of the 'social contract', namely, that the citizens transfer part of their power to the state (in return for security and essential services), a state that can always take this power back or change it just like any other contract with providers of private services. If only that were true. In short, all advocates of either direct democ-racy or representative democracy cannot afford to base their political strate-gies on the illusions of a future totally unalienated politics or the myth of the sovereign power of 'the people' in present or future post-capitalist societies.

CRAFT-BASED CO-OPERATIVES AND URBAN REALITIES

There is no doubting that local communities are best able to voice their needs compared to the imposition of policies by distant and impersonal government agencies. However, the ability of local communities to raise and coordinate scarce material and human inputs in order to realise locally expressed desires is both extremely uneven and limited without national or supranational revenue raising, adequate research funding and the develop-ment of alternative technologies beyond the very small-scale 'convivial tools' (Ivan Illich) idealised by 'degrowthers'. Sustainability should not be automati-cally equated with either small or big enterprises. Rather the complex objec-tive of how to maximise diverse habitats should be considered on the basis of what most effectively makes possible the values of care, democracy and the universal satisfaction of essential needs.

Advocates of radical decentralisation in either its stateless or minimal state forms need to come to terms with the reality of urban life in the twenty-first century where a majority of the world's population live. While many 'degrowthers' wish to harness the creative ideas and energy of neighbourhoods in large cities so that social decisions are not made by remote policy makers, other advocates of direct local democracy make a fetish of the decision-making process and often ignore the ability of communities to be self-sufficient. Any contemporary city with a population larger than a few thousand people, let alone countless cities with populations ranging from fifty thousand to those with twenty to thirty million residents are not capable of having face-to-face direct democracy unless one puts tens of thousands of people into a football stadium to have pseudo-democratic mass gatherings or one conducts decision-making via elaborate digital communication channels. A degrowth society will therefore still need a high level of communications technology which at this point of time, like a range of other non-luxury goods cannot be made in small artisan co-operatives lacking the scale and capacity of substantial R & D, sophisticated metals, rare minerals and so forth.

There is also little agreement over the rate and scale of reducing individual and national material footprints in high-income countries. Tim Jackson and Peter Victor modelled the Canadian economy from 2017 to 2067 by simulating three trajectories of business as usual, reduced carbon and a low growth Sustainable Prosperity Scenario to see what impact these would have on social prosperity while taking into account the need to stay within the earth's 'life support systems' or planetary boundaries.[9] They concluded that the low growth scenario would lead to net zero greenhouse gas emissions by 2040, shorter working hours but higher public debt which could be comfortably managed. Jackson and Victor offer an optimistic scenario of low growth in Canada but did not consider two important factors: the integrated policies and impact on Canada of its major partners (the US and Mexico) in the North American Free Trade Agreement (NAFTA); and also whether the low growth scenario would still be sustainable if many low and middle-income countries also reached Canada's high-income economy by 2040 and thereby threatened the earth's life support system.

Globally, reducing per capita material consumption to an average of 6–8 tons by 2050 would require a lifestyle based on an 80% reduction or an incredible one-fifth of the current level of material consumption in OECD countries in less than 30 years.[10] To be able to politically and economically achieve such a frugal existence poses mind-boggling challenges in the current global political climate. Similarly, convincing upwards of nine billion largely urban residents by 2050 to rely on small local co-operatives for their needs and supplies without regional, national or city-wide production and distribution is ridiculously counterproductive and utopian. Instead, we need to urgently develop new combinations of local, regional and supranational supply chains, restructure the current economies of urban mega cities and small, mid-size towns so that billions of people have a realistic chance of enjoying and satisfying sufficient essential needs. This is especially but not only true for people living in the numerous geographical areas characterised by desertification, mass urban slums, no running water or electricity.

Billions of people in low and middle-income countries will only benefit from the greater equalisation of material per capita consumption if their often corrupt and dictatorial governments are overthrown and global resources are not diverted into the wealthy pockets of prevailing oligarchs and the military. In OECD countries, the voluntary commitment of voters to supporting the reduction of per capita consumption over the next thirty years would require significant trade-offs. If individuals and families could not see a gradual increase in universal basic services (see discussion in Chapter Fifteen) in exchange for periodic decreases in consumption of private goods and services, any such political commitment would soon evaporate. Until governments began funding national and local institutions and communities to provide more universal basic services, no transition presided over by democratic communities is possible.

Neo-Marxists and many feminists in previous decades had re-focussed on the household and family as not something separate from 'the economy' but vitally integrated into its function and form. Wally Seccombe, for example, had analysed how capitalist industrialisation changed the reliance of families on multiple breadwinners so that by the time of the First World War the male breadwinner had become the norm and new gender roles were consolidated. Intricately linked to this were the effects on the family of increasingly centralised manufacture, the introduction of compulsory schooling, the separation of workplaces from the home neighbourhood, the introduction of mass transit and changes in domestic labour brought about by urban housing.[11]

The past sixty years have witnessed the restructuring and reshaping of family life due to feminist struggles and large numbers of women in paid employment, new battles over birth control and child-rearing, access to higher levels of mass education and so forth. What has not changed to the same degree is the separation of workplaces from home neighbourhoods. Modes of mass transit, administration and communication may have changed but the family is not the site of production (apart from home offices and service work during Covid-19) even though it is integrated into financialisation of services and consumption. 'Degrowthers' aim to change this by making the household a site of production and not just consumption. As mentioned earlier, Sam Alexander and Brendan Gleeson wish to bring 'degrowth to the suburbs' by developing several new social practices ranging from food production, energy conservation and changing the car-centred form and function of the city. These are all very good ideas, but they lack at least one central feature – work and income.[12] Until alternative forms of employment and income generating production of goods and services are outlined, the separation of households and local neighbourhoods from 'the economy' will remain the norm. Suburbs can be turned into green cities and food producing centres, but this is only the tip of the urban iceberg and the multiple production and consumption roles that will be needed in the future.

Most advocates of degrowth support a significant role to be played by both small co-operatives and large co-operative enterprises working according to scale. Outlawing large enterprises is illogical if most people in big cities or neglected rural regions go without simply because of the very limited output capacity of small co-ops. Scarce non-luxury goods will inevitably foster a roaring black market, corruption and political disaffection. Hence, degrowth must be based on the specific size, scale and character of diverse populations and political constituencies so that the concept of direct participatory democracy enhances social wellbeing for large populations rather than clinging to fanciful notions of small self-sufficient communities.

To reiterate, self-sufficiency is an impossible goal for the majority of the world's population given the vastly unequal nature of geographical and social resources. It is true that there are many creative and necessary forms of decentralised production and delivery of services compared to existing multi-national and small and medium businesses alike. The degrowth movement would be more convincing if it moved beyond holding rigid, ideologically pure conceptions of an economy based primarily on small artisan co-operatives. It is the almost religious belief in the virtues of horizontal, small-scale enterprises that is so troubling. There is an anti-bureaucratic ideological blindness to the deficiencies and uneven effective capacity of voluntary small organisations to deliver much needed services and wellbeing for the vast majority of humanity.

THE DANGERS OF 'FUNNY MONEY'

If we take alternative concepts of money as an example of social exchange and decision making, it can be seen that local needs and criteria must be balanced against degrees of exclusivity or openness and accessibility. Many advocates of self-sufficient communities and local control favour various forms of alternative 'money' ranging from barter/exchange schemes such as Local Exchange Trading Scheme (LETS) to local currencies based on non-commodified time-sharing and other criteria that treat labour input as equal.[13] One can understand the desire to develop socially just alternatives to existing financial institutional practices and to end the commodification of labour and essential products and services. However, good intentions can have unintended negative consequences if inadequate consideration is given to the expansion of local 'currencies' to embrace whole societies. Kristofer Dittmer has already shown the failure of local currencies and barter in Venezuela and Argentina to achieve their objectives and also enhance degrowth policies even with the support of the Chavez government.[14] Several other complications and barriers arise from schemes that attempt to demonetise and 're-localise' money.

Firstly, it becomes extremely difficult to obtain goods and services from non-local sources if the 'currency' is unacceptable nationally and internationally. Convertible local currencies are currently only feasible if they are pegged to existing currencies such as the Euro.

Secondly, local exchange schemes are very limited in that they can facilitate the exchange of simple services such as body massage, bicycle repair, cleaning, child-minding and so forth, but fail to substitute for the main forms of income and payment of goods by national currencies or the provision of credit. The needs of people living outside the 'local currency' area will be denied if they are not eligible to participate in the local network.

Thirdly, alternative 'currencies' can actually be a barrier to the transition to a post-capitalist society because they force people to make a choice of either accepting the rules and labour value of the 'local currency' or continue adhering to their legal national currency or supranational currency (Euro). Currently, international trade is facilitated by reserve currencies (the American dollar) and directly or indirectly pegged to this national but globally used currency. Local currencies are incapable of replacing national currencies in a world where many countries may either not be governed by degrowth principles or where the exchange of goods and services is impossible if there is no way for a local community to purchase vitally needed resources from a country that refuses to accept 'funny money'.

Fourthly, millions of people are paid pensions and state benefits and will be extremely reluctant to abandon these for insecure local alternatives. The same is true of the larger population geared to existing forms of central government legal tender or fiat money. If two parallel currencies co-exist (for example, LETS and existing national currencies) then the national currency will always be dominant. Regardless of one's position in regard to a universal basic income, this would be impossible without a national uniform currency and the monetised taxation revenue necessary to fund this basic income. Degrowth proponents such as Parrique take the straightforward way out by envisioning alternative currencies operating at community level while national state taxation, monetary and financial institutions remain in place in 'phase one' of any transition to degrowth. The question is: how can future transitional stages to degrowth function *after* 'phase one' if the same problems arise without national currencies or national and supranational fiscal institutions? 'Degrowthers' unrealistically assume that in 'phase two', national pensions, state benefit payments and welfare services will be drastically reduced as local communities will either provide these directly to those in need via actual material forms (housing, food, care services) or via vouchers, tokens or other local currency.

While local provision can certainly be increased, it would be an illusion to think that all communities will be sufficiently well endowed to not need substantial assistance from national or other institutional sources. Some 'degrowthers' dismiss the notion of 'scarcity' as a myth and argue that in a society (rather than a world) of equals, there is sufficient for all. This is a nonsense and contradicts the fundamental reason why degrowth is needed in the first place. Scarcity is either the outcome of involuntary political policies based on institutionalised inequality, or global scarcity is real and hence affluent people in OECD countries will need to reduce their material footprints by between 25% and 80% – as 'degrowthers' themselves argue – if the earth's carrying capacity is not to be exhausted. Hence, either scarcity cannot be overcome politically and there is a need for degrowth, or we can aim to raise all the world's population to 'fully automated luxury communism' as the technological utopians proclaim.

Fifthly, it was Friedrich Hayek who proposed ending fiat money and permitting any institution to issue their own currency (see Chapter Eight). Market competition would determine the value of each currency. This is an extreme form of marketisation (also evident in various bitcoin schemes) and as such, the opposite of social solidarity. Recently, we have seen the rise of utopian blockchain theories that put forward anti-statist notions of 'fully automated blockchain communism' or 'cryptocommunism' and other such fanciful ideas.[15] Implicitly and explicitly the benefit of decentralised currencies that bypass banks and government-issued money is far outweighed by their negative function that monetises all social relations based on contracts. Bitcoin currencies function as exchange value by either being tied to the established value of national government currencies such as the American dollar or calculating all social purchases and contracts according to the particular price or value of labour. This leads to the commodification of every social relation, a process that does not worry libertarian or Right-wing anti-statist free marketeers but should definitely worry all advocates of a decommodified, caring, egalitarian society.

Most supporters of degrowth oppose Hayekian market competition and the commodification of labour. However, they fail to consider the dangers of using multiple currencies that operate as de facto local market currencies (legal tender used by local co-operatives and other production units). What sounds like an attractive alternative at face level, actually undermines solidarity and connectiveness at regional, national and international levels. If the local currency is like a voucher issued by the commons and cannot be traded outside a self-sufficient tight-knit community then without a national government currency people must face either a bleak or happy future depending on their scarce or adequate local resources. If the local currency assumes the de facto role of existing money and can be traded externally, then without non-local government regulation and assistance, most of the problems of inequality will creep back in just like previous and current market-based currency systems.

Sixthly, many of the proposals for alternative demonetised 'currencies' are utopian schemes for the so-called ready-finished, future decentralised society. Yet, they are entirely inappropriate and counterproductive when trying to implement degrowth transitional strategies within the context of existing capitalist societies. The notion of 'local' currency depends on having a geopolitical conception of the 'boundaries' and size of the 'local'. Will it be a few thousand individuals or one to ten million residents of a local city? These parameters are crucial as there are many cities larger than small countries such as Denmark, Lebanon or El Salvador. No viable alternative society will emerge if new local currencies are unable to show how a transitional strategy is possible that enables these 'local' demonetised 'currencies' to replace existing national and supranational government-backed currencies. Planned degrowth requires the voluntary and co-operative action of the majority of the population. However, this co-operation may either not be forthcoming or would quickly collapse if the implementation of 'funny money' leads to major shortages, chaos and disorder due to the poorly thought-through consequences of a monetary system that fails to meet the national needs of millions of people.

As we are not living in the era of city states or medieval barter, it is imperative that any alternative monetary system is able to function in both domestic and international settings. To think that all trade and international exchanges will cease is to regress to an autarkic and isolated future. A degrowth society will still require national and supranational tax structures, fiscal policies and the allocation of resources beyond the local level. These fiscal and monetary systems will hopefully be designed in quite a different manner to existing capitalist practices of financialisation in order to help minimise environmental damage and maximise social justice.

The tension of 'democracy versus sustainability' also manifests itself at the level of symbolic monetary and regulatory processes. Without a more systemic conception of how an alternative degrowth political economy will not only definancialise the worst aspects of capitalism but also create viable monetary and fiscal processes, it is almost guaranteed that many of the half-baked, alternative 'mickey mouse' currency proposals will be social and political disasters and lead to widespread democratic opposition. Far too many radical proposals are situated in a political vacuum. They create wish lists or devise attractive flow charts and diagrams of how each part is connected to the other without considering that these idealised models can be undermined in a flash by the actual political economic struggles that shape transitional strategies. Monetary systems, like so many other aspects of production and administration are often 'path dependent' in that historical and existing processes significantly shape what can be reformed or substantially changed. Even previous revolutions that overthrew most existing institutional arrangements could not entirely free themselves from old practices despite trying to start afresh.

IMAGES OF POST-WORK

Leaving aside the controversial issues of how to fund and create a post-work society, the goal of more play and less alienated work is highly desirable and attractive. Any attempt to create a vibrant and joyous society also involves being on guard against possible new forms of 'community *joie de vivre*' that might legitimise something entirely different. After all, the Nazi regime's vast leisure organization, *Kraft durch Freude* (Strength through Joy) was also based on the principles of non-materialistic 'community' relations rather than market individualism.[16] Fascism, Communism and anarchism were all highly critical of individualism and material consumerism. They all valued 'community' above decadent bourgeois individualism.[17] While each movement had its own artistic *avant-garde,* they also had a pronounced element of Puritanism (less so among anarchists) manifested in suspicion of those who did not perform manual labour or were 'unproductive'. Like some earlier Protestant religions that regarded dancing and non-religious music as sexually arousing and sinful, a Puritan streak ran through earlier Communist movements in the denunciation of jazz, rock and roll and 'bohemian' tendencies.

Some leading advocates of degrowth such as my colleague, Sam Alexander, recognise the importance of the aesthetic dimension.[18] While influenced by Marcuse and other radical critics, Alexander's call for artistic creativity to help the degrowth movement is very important but could possibly be interpreted as still containing residues of the old Communist functionalist conception of art as agitprop. The boundary between a new aesthetics of simplicity and collectively imposed austerity is a difficult cultural set of relations and values to negotiate. These can either liberate people to enjoy a rich set of non-material pleasures or else be used by others to increase domestic and community drudgery based on the ideologically driven rejection of technological labour-saving innovation.

It is worth recalling that Marcuse critiqued the early twentieth century orthodox Marxist conception of art as tied to a rising class (the proletariat) and a declining class (the bourgeoisie) with its so-called nihilistic, decadent individualism. Today, it is now unclear which class is declining and which class is rising, given six decades of falling levels of industrial manual labour in OECD countries. Regardless of the fortunes of different classes, Marcuse believed that a subversive counterculture must contradict the prevailing art industry. He also argued that art must not be judged solely in terms of its proletarian or bourgeois qualities. "The work of art can attain political relevance only as autonomous work. The aesthetic form is essential to its social function. The qualities of the form negate those of the repressive society – the qualities of its life, labor, and love."[19] Alexander agrees with Marcuse, but at the same time also implies that art can be directly or indirectly evaluated in terms of whether it enhances the political possibilities of degrowth.

This is not the place for a detailed analysis of the theorists who advocate a range of visions about the post-work society. Clearly, there is a world of difference between notions of post-work based on simplicity and small artisan co-operatives and the promise of so-called 'fully automated luxury communism'. Both polarised images are unviable. The life of local communities without significant national and international interaction will also constrain education, science, the arts and cultural expression if the resources necessary to communicate and exchange ideas and creative works (whether high-tech communications systems, film distribution and so forth) are absent due to lack of funding or parochialism. Conversely, notions of 'fully automated luxury communism' are environmentally impossible in a world which already far exceeds the earth's carrying capacity, let alone one in which nine billion people have equal access to 'fully automated luxury'.

Importantly, post-work 'liberation' must try to ensure that significantly reduced working weeks in the future are based on cosmopolitan, pluralist cultural conceptions of joy and pleasure rather than narrow 'politically correct' parochialism. Even if we do not have a repeat of earlier repressive 'reconstructions' of people's personal desires and modes of action (such as the construction of 'Soviet man' or adhering to the prescriptions of particular religious sects), any new alternative social system will need to take into account the diverse attitudes of people to the meaning and attraction of 'community'. Currently, the prevailing modes of cultural interaction in capitalist societies are heavily weighted against co-operative interaction. Hence, it would be foolish to believe that all would relinquish their individualism and be happy communitarians actively participating in collective activities. It is worth remembering that Marcuse also warned radicals about the 'psychic Thermidor' (named after the Thermidorian Reaction of 1794 that toppled Robespierre and the radicals of the French Revolution). This was a psycho-cultural condition in which part of the population were still committed to old conservative values and tried to turn back the clock of radical change.[20] 'Degrowthers' tend to have a benign view of their fellow humanity and underestimate the potential violent defence of material interests when threatened by degrowth.

Supporters of degrowth advance varied notions of 'community'. Most are democratic, caring and inclusive and should be strongly supported. However, within broad degrowth movements there are also those elements that promote a type of 'zealous naturalism'. These can potentially become tyrannical and restrictive forms of eco-fascism if permitted to be dominated by ideals of organic, 'natural' social relations that metamorphize into nationalist racism or parochial discrimination and exclusivity. The 'commons' like 'the people' is always open to pressure and manipulation. Increased direct democracy in combination with other national and international institutional practices is a desirable goal. Participatory democracy facilitates the discussion of a range of socio-political views but is itself no guarantee that narrow prejudices rather than broader and more tolerant social values prevail. Hence, the need to strongly critique 'organic' claims of being 'at one with nature'. We must foster the care, protection and respect of the biosphere but also recognise that diverse socio-cultural relations and 'strangers' are usually at risk when ideologues begin reducing 'community' and society to natural 'organic' processes.

Cultural creativity should not be judged according to whether it best serves or supposedly undermines the needs of prevailing social and political institutions. A future co-operative society will not thrive if it does not recognise that collectives are hardly ideal arrangements to produce diverse, exciting or great art, literature and many other forms of cultural creativity. The interaction between the individual imagination and personal space on the one side and the collective needs of the community on the other will require ongoing sensitivity and negotiation. Above all, it will require mutual recognition that present and past forms of both individualism and collectivism – whether in cultural creativity, work practices or social participation – are contradictory and can be counterproductive to flourishing and tolerant societies.

In capitalist societies, the ideology of individualism has fuelled many wonderful as well as far from wonderful creations. The problem is that thousands of artistic creations never see the light of day because they are neither marketable nor receive public funding. Communist countries, on the other hand, gave infinitely more support to most branches of the arts than governments in capitalist countries. As we know, they also prevented and suppressed all creativity deemed unacceptable by these regimes. How to avoid repeating these two unacceptable models remains a major challenge. This immediately raises the issue of how to avoid the unequal allocation of resources by markets without encouraging undemocratic planning.

POLITICAL DILEMMAS OF STATE PLANNING

If advocates of degrowth favour 'planned contraction' of capitalist production and consumption, they are yet to specify what kind of institutional 'planning' they support. Some believe in the continued vital role played by state institutions. Others dream, like many other radicals, of a society without giant bureaucracies (of the government or corporate kind) subjecting powerless citizens to endless rules and perpetuating social inequalities through the accumulation of private wealth and power. Yet, champions of utopian forms of stateless, self-managed societies, anarchist communities or self-sufficient green collectives usually provide few details about how they will organise and solve multiple political economic problems without state planning or nation-wide political and judicial institutions.

Scale is only one of the many problems that plague all conceptions of stateless societies. Many 'degrowthers', anarchists and eco-socialists seem to ignore that democracy can undermine sustainability. Both versions of local or national democracy in its current representative democratic or potential future direct democratic forms provide no guarantee that the non-local and non-national issue of a sustainable global biosphere will be adequately addressed or considered a priority over more pressing local and national matters. It should not be forgotten that representative democracies were compatible with exploitative forms of colonialism and either disguised or made palatable this exploitation to various nationalist democratic electorates. It is only when the death toll and financial cost of fighting national liberation movements in Asia, Africa, the Middle East or Latin America registered with the domestic electorates in imperialist countries, that democratic debates in Europe or America became more aware of action in colonised countries. So too, there can be no automatic assumption in a future world that diverse aspects of production and consumption across the globe will be of equal relevance and concern to local democracies and national electorates.

Importantly, democratic planning is impossible without safeguarding the rights of all people within a particular territorial space. Local communities have a limited ability to ensure the enduring protection of human rights without state institutions. Whatever the long-term objectives, any new post-carbon socio-political institutions will need at the very minimum to advance beyond the rights and freedoms already won under liberal regimes but also to ensure that there is no regression to a historical time (such as we are witnessing today) characterised by the widespread violation of rights. Diverse social constituencies and individuals must be guaranteed civic freedoms and rights through constitutions and national or supranational judicial institutions that also remove privileges and inequality based on wealth, clan, racial group or other hierarchies.

Of course, we know that formal constitutional guarantees are insufficient on their own, as numerous previous violations of rights have shown. However, stateless notions of self-management or worker control are unable to guarantee against the violation of the rights of individuals and minorities, especially if based on unwritten laws or parochial prejudice and discrimination. The moment that one begins codifying human rights and civil liberties applicable beyond a local community is the moment that we immediately begin talking about the necessity of state institutions which can protect these rights.

A range of judicial institutions, including higher courts of appeal, must safeguard against romantic illusions about the benign wisdom of 'worker's courts' or local community tribunals. These dispensers of 'proletarian' or 'citizen' justice have in the past often dealt out much harsher sentences similar to those judgements supported by contemporary conservative law-and-order zealots. A stateless system without checks and balances is dangerous both to the delivery of social justice and to the protection of human rights. We need to reconsider these long held utopian ideals if profound inequality and the concentration of political power are not to reappear in post-carbon societies after existing ruling classes have been fought against for such a long time.

No local self-sufficient community or self-managed workplace can guarantee the rights of citizens and workers unless there is also access to local and national public institutions and all forms of media and cultural institutions are free from potential abuse by local power-wielders. Without institutional checks and balances, initial community enthusiasm may soon dissipate and evolve into the special privileges enjoyed by the members of powerful families or clans in local face-to-face communities. This is why political structures of democratic public discourse and representation must be institutionalised as protective mechanisms against abuses perpetrated in the name of 'the people'. Just as there is a need to remove the inbuilt injustice of liberal procedures of property law that privilege and protect businesses, so too, we must not assume inherent values of social justice or democracy in the fluctuating 'collective wisdom' of self-managed communities. There is no shortage of examples of party organisations, local celebrities and careerists making power grabs via networking, preferencing family members and friends while at the same time espousing 'democratic' rhetoric.

Maximising direct democracy is an admirable goal as so long as complex social orders can actually be managed without multiple conflicting agendas at local and national levels. It is political gridlock and socio-economic paralysis that jeopardises fair and efficient social distribution of public goods and services. Any alternative movement that is critical of capitalist institutions must at least offer ideas and policies about how a post-carbon democracy could be organised in the future, especially new macro political economic coordinating mechanisms or what is called 'planning'. Most discussions of alternative political economic frameworks focus on the ideal model of direct democracy, state planning or other modes of running post-capitalist society. However, all political economic models will be affected by actual everyday political struggles, the availability of resources and the political experiences or capacities of the people who are supposed to implement any such models.

Given the dangers to social justice and human rights posed by stateless models that rely on fragile qualities of trust and goodwill, can a post-carbon democracy implement different forms of state planning without repeating all the disasters of the old Soviet command planning models? No self-proclaimed 'socialist' regime in the past succeeded in developing co-ordinating mechanisms that did not resulted in mass hardship for the general populace characterised by shortages of food and other necessities. Part of the blame can be attributed to civil war and the obstructionist responses of businesses and conservative social classes upset at their loss of power. It would, however, be utterly naïve to think that the deep-seated weaknesses and irrationalities of central command planning could be solely or largely attributed to dictatorial political power. Today, there are ample reasons why Soviet command planning is widely rejected by the radical Left and alternative green movements. The question is: what should replace capitalist market mechanisms and how to reconcile democracy with effective planning? Perhaps is it possible through high-performance super-computers, as many radicals believe, to avoid the pitfalls and incapacities of old hierarchical central planning and have new decentralised planning models that are immediately responsive to grass roots community-decision-making. It would be prudent, however, not to attribute potential problems to just 'technical capacity' issues.

Importantly, advocates of alternative societies need to distinguish two key aspects of any future democratic centralised or decentralised planning system: technical capacity and the character and dimensions of political decision-making. Technically, it has been argued that hierarchical central planning with transparent democratic accountability and sensitivity to local needs is extremely difficult to achieve given the enormous number of calculations and the limited time-frame of publicly debating and then processing and integrating local needs with regional, national as well as supranational planning targets and objectives. Having an annual plan is time-constrained and very difficult. Moreover, in the light of unexpected crises or faulty planning decisions, democratic central planning is too cumbersome, time-consuming and politically contentious to be able to rapidly correct or adjust the allocation of resources while satisfying diverse social constituencies. Several areas remain to be addressed and answered. These include:

- How to facilitate the technical and social possibility of national and supra-national planning by maximising direct democratic input at every workplace and local community?
- If planners must first collate all the local inputs and then ascertain what local and national resources are available before reporting back to each local community, will there be sufficient time for local citizens to modify their wish lists in the light of scarce national or regional resources?
- Will people be involved in endless community planning meetings if the plans are devised annually? If the plans are tri-annual or five-yearly, how much democracy will exist *between* each new plan and how to prevent citizens becoming virtually powerless just as they currently are in-between elections in capitalist societies?
- How are conflicting needs decided, and by whom? Will there be political parties with agendas or just individuals and groups devising plans? Will state planners be professional experts or the very same people who are part of local community bodies?
- In the high probability that there is a deadlock over competing demands, it is unclear whether local self-managed communities or nationally elected bodies will decide, and whether or not independent planners or adjudicating tribunals will make the final decisions.
- How to maintain the effectiveness and legitimacy of democratic central or decentralised plans? Historically, we know that ignoring local inputs is the first step on the slippery road to undemocratic command planning as bureaucrats usurp the power originally held by inexperienced citizens. Conversely, if particular locally organised groups set out to obstruct jointly agreed upon local and national planning decisions, how to resolve contentious issues without the whole planning and political process being delegitimised?

The political emphasis of social change movements in recent decades has been on reversing or depowering existing forms of strong central government and elevating the power of local government. Would a hybrid set of weaker *nationally* based administrative public institutions co-existing with more powerful self-managed *local* communities remain viable? In other words, would decentralised planning with minimal power vested in vertical government administrative bodies be feasible? Technically, the millions and trillions of computations needed to link tens of thousands of organisations and communities have hitherto made *horizontal* decision-making for a whole society technologically impossible. Whether new information and communication technology with enormously enhanced computing power will be able to overcome the need for hierarchical decision-making is not a purely technological question. Imagine groups of people in tens of thousands of local communities and workplaces having to digest incredible volumes of external information in order to make decisions on how local resources and social needs could be planned in relation to the parallel needs of thousands of other communities in the same city or region let alone in a nation-state.

Unless there were regional or national co-ordinating nodal points where the enormous data was collated, sorted and presented to local communities in reasonably condensed form as to choices between items in fiscal budgets, for example, then it would be impossible for *horizontal* communication processes to have the time or energy to prioritise and make local and national needs and resources compatible. Conflicts would invariably have to be sorted out between the different interests of producers and consumers. Moreover, the complexity of decentralised planning would escalate if local planning were linked not just to regional and national planning but also to supranational planning such as in a democratised Europe. It is no surprise that conceptions of world socialism have historically always lacked any clear institutional co-ordinating mechanisms just as do contemporary images of global networks of environmentally sustainable communities.

Networks sound fine in theory, but like various planning systems they can become dysfunctional and overloaded if far too many areas of production and social life have to be decided upon. Of course, citizens could decide that national planners would only plan a limited number of industries, resources, fiscal and social policies and that the vast majority of decisions would be left to local decision-making bodies. If that were the case, then it would still be imperative to ensure that significant inequalities did not emerge between localities and regions.

On the positive side, advocates of decentralised planning are absolutely correct to cite the potential mass infusion of millions of people if just a mere five to ten per cent of the public (let alone a majority of people) were regularly involved in making decisions compared to the current exclusion of the electorate from vital decision-making. The notion that everyone would have to attend endless meetings is a nonsense promoted by opponents of greater democratisation. Nonetheless, extreme forms of Participatory Economics (Parecon) as developed by Michael Albert and Robin Hahnel involve all households (not just workers) in participatory planning.[21] Under this model, households would have to submit their consumption plans to neighbourhood consumer councils which would then forward these to other local planning councils. This is a recipe for local tyranny where extreme levels of public accountability could become intrusive and a perversion of democracy. Parecon makes a fetish out of participation. Despite a number of good ideas about local democratic controls, it bends the stick too far away from capitalist private market relations as to be little more than a modernised version of 'primitive communism' rather than a viable popular model of social planning.

CORPORATIONS AND MARKET SOCIALISM

Some socialists argue that all large corporations such as Amazon, Walmart and thousands of other businesses engage in extensive forward planning across different subsidiaries in their production, marketing and other departments.[22] Hence, these planning models could be adopted and modified for use in post-capitalist societies. Similarly, earlier market socialists such as Alec Nove[23] believed that socialist societies did not need to plan all facets of society. Instead, only the 'commanding heights' of an economy in key strategic industries would be under state control thereby significantly reducing the task of designing forward estimates of which materials, resources and producer goods could facilitate the production and distribution of household consumer goods and services. Under this model, labour markets, product markets and other markets could have more democratic inputs from enterprises, local communities and co-operatives while national governments planned the development and output of strategic industries such as steel, heavy engineering, national transport or energy.

   While sounding persuasive, these market socialist models are also far from problem-free. The notion of utilising planning models borrowed from private multinational corporations overlooks the vastly different profit-making logic built into corporate plans. Once democratic governments try to avoid duplicating narrow corporate objectives based on exploitative labour conditions, tax avoidance and numerous other strategies to enhance 'shareholder value', the tricky problems begin. If workers demand self-management rights, or planners curb environmentally polluting products and exploitative wages or enforce other such socially responsible objectives, it is doubtful whether corporate planning could be easily transposed.

Market socialists must also reconcile leaving key parts of the economy in the hands of small and medium private enterprises or cooperatives while the 'commanding heights' or large enterprises were state planned. If market growth determined demand in both publicly and privately controlled sectors it is likely that non-market values such as degrowth, social need and equality would cease being the operative principles guiding key industries. Similarly, without national wages, incomes and prices policies, in other words, politically legislated 'ceilings' limiting private wealth and income as well as 'floors' preventing poverty, it is almost certain that major forms of inequality would remain. However, if the ratio of income and wealth inequality were legislated, any future plan would have to specify how this could be democratically imposed on small and medium sized businesses (employing one or two people or as many as 100 workers) and not just on co-operatives and other communal forms of collective ownership. Furthermore, if market socialist systems were integrated into global trade, how could a 'socialist market' avoid the crises of capital accumulation such as serious recessions generated by the normal fluctuations in external global and national capitalist markets?

It is quite possible that most of these 'market socialist' theoretical problems could be resolved or minimised. The trouble is that there is currently a dearth of discussion and analysis to determine which industries in the 'commanding heights' of the economy are compatible with sustainable natural resources and a safe climate. Similarly, some market socialists such as David Schweickart propose models of 'economic democracy' for the US which retain key aspects of capitalist markets except that the labour market is controlled to eliminate unemployment in the interest of workers, and capital investment markets are also controlled in the interest of public goods and services to negate the worst aspects of neoliberal financialisation.[24] Earlier market socialist proposals such as the long-discontinued Swedish Rehn-Meidner model of wage-earner funds, sought to gain control over capitalist firms within a few decades by purchasing and issuing strategic parcels of shares to worker's funds.[25] This strategy met with strong business opposition and was abandoned by the 1980s. Any revival of a similar scheme via pension funds would have to be prepared for very hostile reactions from businesses and conservative governments.

Likewise, policies for pension funds in some countries to gain controlling interests over key corporations are compelling but also contain problems. While these strategies can certainly increase the leverage and general power of unions and worker-controlled pension funds, they ultimately depend on the health of capitalist market accumulation (until they gained dominant control after four or five decades). Such a long timeframe would pit the need of pension funds to demand social justice and environmentally sustainable corporate policies against the contradictory need to pursue profitable investment in order to sustain income for their members' retirement. If, however, these pension funds could somehow be largely immunised from market booms and recessions (a big 'if'), they could shape future investment patterns and alter neoliberal policies that deliberately under-invest in, or marketise social welfare, health, housing and other essential public goods and services. Democratically controlled pension funds could certainly promote dis-investment from ecologically dangerous production and help implement the transition to post-carbon democracy.

Nonetheless, state-owned or worker-controlled enterprises and pension funds operating under market conditions are highly constrained as alternatives to capitalist markets. If they could change the regulation and operating conditions required of participants in markets, then this might be a partial advance. Take for example, thousands of state-owned enterprises in China, many of which are unprofitable 'zombie' companies. These enterprises have huge debts but are kept functioning by the government for fear of causing mass unemployment in particular provinces or losing control of important economic sectors. It is true that there would be many more social casualties if the government closed down these enterprises to appease market ideologists. On the other hand, 'zombie' state enterprises are only of short-term benefit so long as they do not divert desperately required resources away from the collective needs of Chinese workers and families who want more and better social services, pollution reduction and income support.

State-owned enterprises constantly face survival problems if the dominant economy is driven by cost-cutting market values and practices at the expense of social needs. Reconciling a market system and a state planning system within the same society is thus an extremely difficult objective unless the private sector is controlled and market values and practices are subordinated to non-capitalist social and environmental priorities. So far, most of the reforms in China have been state-controlled but market-oriented, rather than a much stricter and more comprehensive subordination of private businesses to society-wide social and environmental objectives.

What is also missing from recent discussions of planning is a fuller recognition of the possible benefits or dangers from emerging technologies. The 'internet of things', for example, has the potential to enhance innovative forms of direct democracy by connecting millions of households to production processes and social care services. These innovations could have a positive side (like 3-D printing) in transforming local capacities and freeing the latter from heavy reliance on national and international resources and imported goods.[26] Conversely, new technologies could just as readily undermine democratic processes, civil liberties and cultural freedoms by facilitating new forms of surveillance and control. As I discussed earlier, various innovative technologies such as 3-D printing currently use polymers based on fossil fuels and are unsustainable unless their material inputs can be made sustainable.

Even mainstream reformers of the digital economy are calling for a new Bretton Woods. The difference is that the old Bretton Woods was designed to regulate trade in a world of national borders with tangible manufactured goods. Of course, tangible goods will continue to be important in the future. However, the digital world is the opposite with intangible data production and collection crossing a borderless world (except where censored and controlled by national and regional regimes).[27] Currently, national governments are years away from subordinating tax avoiding giants that undermine vital revenue needed for domestic social programs and other national expenditure. Short of banning or reducing digital platforms and the way modern production and communication functions, the ability to plan digital economies raises new dilemmas not yet given adequate consideration. It is not just a matter of creating a new international architecture to facilitate the democratic control of the growing digital economy. A full and careful reappraisal is needed of how centralised or decentralised planning models designed for tangible goods could be redesigned to make digital production compatible with national and local democratic planning.

Importantly, most discussion of future co-ordinating and decision-making processes assumes post-revolutionary conditions rather than the hostile and confined structures of existing state institutions and capitalist ownership and control. Therefore, instead of just thinking about ready-finished processes such as local community control, centralised planning or market socialism, it is equally useful to think about intermediate objectives, that is, how the construction of post-carbon democracies could go hand-in-hand with the development of new forms of planning in societies that are still predominantly capitalist. It is not an either/or situation of planning in post-capitalist society but no planning within capitalist countries. Let us not forget that planning is indispensable even in key areas of contemporary neoliberal societies such as rail transport, military R & D, energy systems, water and sewage and corporate investment strategies.

The great deficiencies of current government and corporate planning activities is that they are not subject to democratic decision-making, with the public having little or no say about priorities and expenditure allocations other than occasionally at elections. Instead of just thinking about how whole countries could be planned or converted into self-managed communities, social change activists could also identify wide areas of existing political economic activity – from health systems and housing, right through to revenue collection or natural resources use – and develop alternative more equitable and sustainable policy models and practices.

As mentioned before, democracy is an unknown double-edged sword. On the one hand, the internet has facilitated greater democracy of choice and access ranging from numerous online communities to a torrent of anti-democratic Right-wing misogynistic and racist trolls threatening and undermining social tolerance. On the other hand, it has unleashed the capacities of citizens to formulate and contribute to numerous areas of urban planning, the delivery of care services, food production and other activities in liberating and intoxicating ways. Governments and businesses fear real public involvement (instead of token consultation) because increased democratic participation would most likely quickly reject many existing priorities for the production, consumption and distribution of resources. The medium-term goal of extending democratic rights and public planning into more areas of society will be bitterly contested. However, the forthcoming need to increase rates of decarbonisation while simultaneously dealing with numerous fiscal and social problems makes it easier to promote the arguments for extending planning and other non-market solutions.

Whether various forms of planning, or hybrid combinations of larger public sectors, local co-operatives and new conceptions of a democratic 'commons' could replace capitalist societies is not merely a theoretical issue. The big drawback, both politically and organisationally, is that most social change movements have only partially developed these alternative policy interventions. Until alternative post-carbon socio-economic policies and planning options are developed, dominant decision-makers (including neoliberals and social democrats) will encounter little opposition. It should not be forgotten that the evolution of conflict over 'capitalism versus democracy' during the past century is closely tied to the emergence of 'the economy' and its corresponding measuring tool, Gross Domestic Product (GDP) as having both a separate life from 'society' and also defining 'good health' or malaise for both democratic and authoritarian countries. In recent decades, it has become almost compulsory for feminists, environmentalists and others to advocate alternatives to 'GDP'. It is relatively easy to devise diagrams such as new 'doughnut economies' where wellbeing and other desirable goals are neatly included.[28] How these translate into actual alternative planning mechanisms and institutional processes is an entirely different matter.

The other major political obstacle is the widespread acceptance of market solutions by many people who reject socialist and green politics. This is where the contest between 'democracy and sustainability' is closely related to planning issues. Currently, there are a range of alternative scenarios based on untested promises of new technology, block chain economies and so forth put forward by people who imagine that capitalist systems can be transformed into caring and sharing societies by digital high-tech alternatives challenging corporate power. Unfortunately, most of these social change models are devoid of a transitional political strategy and divorced from mass politics. They in turn mirror the logic of high-tech entrepreneurs, except that instead of creating personal wealth, some activists are under the delusion that they can use online market techniques to bring down capitalism.[29]

Crucially, if market exchange mechanisms rather than the planned allocation of resources are not to be controlled by capitalist enterprises, then much greater thought will have to be given to ensuring that there is no return to capitalist markets. People can certainly meet some of their individual needs via informal exchanges so long as these do not begin to shape the whole society into another version of unequal capitalism. The degree to which egalitarian social needs and maximising biodiversity become guiding and regulating priorities, the less that market exchange mechanisms are free to operate as they currently do. Conversely, if state democratic planning is to become more than an abstract technical process, then a democratic society must never lose sight of the human dimension or the original social and environmental goals that planning aims to serve and achieve.

DEBATING THE 'ENVIRONMENT STATE': A POLITICS-FREE ZONE

It is difficult to imagine how an environmentally sustainable world can come into being without a significant implementation of planning by national state institutions and international organisations. Yet, many advocates of degrowth avoid discussing actual political struggles and what kind of state policies and planning mechanisms are necessary to achieve their goals. The same is true of a group of academic environmental political theorists who have, ironically, focussed on whether a 'green state' or an 'environment state' is emerging that will be somewhat similar to the development of the 'welfare state'.[30]

One would have hoped that debates about the 'environment state' would have filled the vacuum concerning the political economy of any future set of state institutions. Sadly, little or nothing is said about whether a future 'environment state' will : a) be based on a particular form of planning; b) be highly decentralised, centralised or a mixture of market and non-market institutional mechanisms; c) will evolve out of existing state apparatuses or constitute a complete break with the administrative logic currently deployed by capitalist state institutions; and d) be shaped by political conflict in contemporary capitalist societies rather than by policy-makers unconnected to political parties and social movements.

Instead, most of the participants in this debate fail to go beyond the abstract discussion of capitalism with minimal discussion of a political strategy to implement green policies. Despite invoking a range of 'critical theories' and concepts of democracy, often little more than an apolitical or depoliticised account of the prospect for an 'environment state' is provided. There is no outline given of which new or existing institutions would make up the 'environment state' and in what way they would differ from current institutions. It is unclear whether the so-called 'environment state' would implement environment policies through departments of finance, transport, industry, education, agriculture and so forth or only through specifically designated 'environment' departments.

Most 'environment state' theorists begin with the false premise that the 'welfare state' is distinct from the larger institutions of the capitalist state and hence debate how an equally so-called separate 'environment state' could emerge by breaking the 'glass ceiling' imposed by neoliberal governments and their business and political allies.[31] At one level, the debates over the character of the present and future 'environment state' mirror earlier historical disputes between reformers who believed (and still believe) in a 'civilised capitalism' and radicals who argue that 'capitalism and democracy' remain incompatible. In short, there is a division between those who hope that the future development of environmentally sustainable policies (known collectively as the 'environment state') can become large and powerful enough to change existing capitalist practices in the direction of sustainability – like the so-called 'welfare state' ameliorating poverty rather than abolishing it. Others hope that the 'environment state' will become sufficiently strong enough to replace unsustainable capitalist modes of production.

We have already seen the clash between advocates of 'deliberate democracy' versus 'agonistic politics'. Similarly, those who believe that deliberative democracy is an essential precondition for the development of the 'environment state' are opposed by Left 'populist' advocates of 'agonistic' politics who favour open disagreement rather than deliberated consensus as the way forward.[32] Will future environmental policies be 'path dependent', that is, shaped by deep historical and cultural traditions and hence unable to transcend the various constrained political economic conditions and institutional relations within existing countries? Those supportive of deliberative democracy believe that 'transformability' (rather than 'path dependence') is at the heart of sustainability as an open-ended, unpredictable and ever-changing democratic process.[33] Others such as Ingolfur Blühdorn posit the view that representative democracy in its current 'anti-politics' form (manifested in Right-wing racist parties) is itself a 'glass ceiling' that prevents sustainability.[34]

Either way, theorists of the 'environment state' cannot afford to use the 'welfare state' as a model for future development and ignore all the negative organisational features of social welfare delivery. If current welfare services are severely limited by all-of-government directives and budgetary outlays that are geared to sustaining profitable business practices, it is also possible that a future so-called 'environment state' could be equally compatible with capitalism. It may break through the glass ceiling of capitalist constraints in particular countries, but neither be democratic nor fiscally or environmentally sustainable.

While a mixture of optimism and pessimism colours much of the theoretical debate about the so-called future of the 'environmental state', it is important to recognise that there can be no separate 'environment state' that has a life of its own and is distinct from capitalist state apparatuses in their various national forms. There has never been an autonomous 'welfare state' that functions according to independent criteria separate from the larger specific national fiscal and administrative regulations of capitalist state institutional systems and capitalist production processes. So too, there will never be an autonomous 'environment state' whose growth and development is unconstrained by existing specific political economic policies and practices, whether capitalist or a possible socialist or green society.

Finally, and perhaps most disappointingly is that theorists of the 'environment state' tend to a Eurocentric focus and have little to say about the vast majority of non-OECD nation states which lack representative democracy and have neither a 'welfare state' nor an 'environment state'. Instead, they cling to the Atlantic region and closely follow the geopolitics of the 'varieties of capitalism' school that compares Anglo-American liberal market economies, with social democratic and socially conservative co-ordinated market models.[35] In assuming that the 'environment state' has a better chance of emerging in Europe, they hitch their hopes to a region that will almost certainly decline over the next thirty years in terms of relative economic, military and technological power as political economic development shifts to the Asian-Pacific region.

With or without 'environment states' or democracy, low and middle-income countries could indirectly and directly determine the future of sustainability policies in Europe, North America and Australia. For example, if the current arms race in North and South Asia continues and the US refuses to de-escalate its desire to contain China while simultaneously demanding that the EU, Japan and Australia become responsible for their own defence, the budgetary cost of increased military expenditure will narrow the possibilities for distinct 'environment states' to emerge. On the other hand, the unfolding climate emergency will force governments across the world to implement mitigation and adaptation measures that change international and domestic political economic practices, not just the switch to renewables, but towards greater controls on emissions from transport, manufacturing and food production. These new measures will not be part of a separate sphere of state institutions called the 'environment state' but could be fully integrated into conventional departments dealing with industry, transport, agriculture and urban infrastructure.

Of course, it is also possible that post-Covid-19 or some other major socio-economic crisis could eventually lead to either Green New Deals or authoritarian climate emergency measures in a number of G20 countries. Achieving 'sustainability' does not presuppose establishing democracy in those countries with tightly controlled authoritarian institutional structures over economic development and social relations. By contrast, the failure to deal with the protracted socio-economic crisis of Covid-19 could either see the EU unravel or become more integrated through the development of an extensive European Green New Deal compared with the current poorly funded scheme for the 2020s. Such measures would look entirely different and have far more impact on other areas of society and production if developed EU-wide as opposed to just within some member nation states or ex-EU member states. A deeper and more extensive EU-wide Green New deal would require the fundamental transformation of the Growth and Stability Pact, far greater fiscal integration through a federal financial system and a phased reduction of the deep divisions between Northern and Southern EU member countries. On the other hand, a non-EU Green New Deal would be largely dependent on the political level of environmental concerns in different nation states, Sweden compared to Australia for instance, as well as the level of political economic capacity of each large and small country to make such a transition. This would be the case whether in the US, Europe, Africa or the Asia-Pacific region.

CONCLUDING COMMENTS

The principle of 'form follows function' has long been debated in discourses about architecture, design and engineering. Whether the *function* or purpose of a building, a machine, a piece of clothing, a web page or a community space limits the *form* it can take or whether a new aesthetic form can both create new functions as well as serve its original purpose is an ongoing part of the creative process. So too, with 'democracy versus sustainability'. The difference is that both are simultaneously functional processes with inbuilt end goals that take many different forms. Organisationally, the political function of the historical socialist party was to capture state power and bring about the emancipation of the working class through the peaceful or revolutionary overthrow of capitalism. As we have seen, the form of particular Communist, Socialist, Labour or other Left parties followed the purpose spelt out by various theoreticians of social change. Today, mainstream centre-Left parties have less lofty aims and now mirror the functions of capitalist states to the best of their abilities and resources. In other words, opposition parties like the party or parties that occupy government office have a division of labour that is determined by the structure and function of contemporary states. Shadow ministers for education, finance, defence, transport, environment and other departments interact with party members and outside lobbies in their attempt to design the 'form' which their government will take should they win the next election.

By contrast, the crisis of social movements, radical parties, the 'social bloc' and the degrowth movement in particular is partly related to the confusion over function and form. Is their 'form' exhausted or limited given that they are divided over whether they are anti-statist or simultaneously desiring to shape state policies? Many social movements have no desire to mirror, shape or replace existing states. Others hope that their actions will ultimately lead to the disintegration of existing institutions without any need for direct confrontation with governments or capitalist corporations.

In this chapter, I have tried to show that degrowth advocates want the 'local community' to be simultaneously the primary 'function' and 'form' of a sustainable society. Diverging from mainstream parties, most advocates of degrowth begin at the opposite end of the state-society spectrum and contradict the existing function and structure of power and social organisation in contemporary societies. In contrast to political parties, they tend to have little or no engagement with state institutions and policies other than to oppose them or ignore them. Hence, they avoid developing any systematic analysis or conception of the role of contemporary state institutions even though planned degrowth will be impossible to achieve without state institutions. Consequently, they share with many socialists a naïve faith that increased   democratisation   will   inevitably   lead   to   environmental sustainability.

Advocates of degrowth are too reliant on the so-called power of face-to-face community relations and have an undeveloped notion of politics beyond the local combined with a benign and unrealistic concept of the local. There is little conceptualisation of what to do in the case of any potential democratic opposition to some or all of their objectives and social arrangements. Because most 'degrowthers' are preoccupied with developing a decentralised or even quasi-stateless form of transformed local communities, larger state institutions and their functions only intrude peripherally as appendages or as back-up reserves to local democratic power. Hence, there is no interest in, let alone detailed conception of state planning and certainly no clear notion of judicial, regulatory or cultural institutions beyond the local. In fact, they are entirely unclear about how both democracy and sustainability will be achieved beyond the local, except by the multiplication of many 'local sustainable communities'.

It is a paradoxical state of affairs in that most advocates of degrowth would acknowledge the need for state institutions yet accord so little of their alternative visions outlining what will be the functions and forms of these new state institutions. Whether it is Australia or India, Poland or Costa Rica, any positive and appealing vision of 'planned degrowth' must be able to specify which parts of existing production processes, the circulation system of goods and services, energy, water and sewage reticulation, delivery of health and social services or research and development are to continue or be scaled back, removed or reshaped. Will state institutions be distinct from communal organisations and units of production or will they fuse with the latter in new hybrid local, regional and national structures that do not stand 'above' or 'against social institutional practices? Consequently, 'degrowthers' offer few conceptions of how to make the degrowth transition. In former Communist countries, there was an emphasis on developing heavy production and infrastructure at the expense of consumer production. Advocates of degrowth face the opposite dilemma. They need to transform and reduce consumption (which constitutes between 55 and 65 per cent of the GDP of advanced capitalist countries) without causing a depression and politically alienating electorates. Unfortunately, after decades of calls for degrowth, we remain unclear about how 'degrowthers' will reduce or transform dominant forms of capitalist production, which technologies will be adopted or abandoned, how they will finance the necessary income and employment or provide the social services, educational institutions and infrastructure that many local communities will be unable to afford.

Finally, if many 'degrowthers' have extraordinarily little notion of the 'form' their political organisations should take, which parts of existing state apparatuses will survive or be transformed, this is also largely true of those academics who devote themselves to studying the 'environment state'. The latter are bereft of any political strategy or even how the so-called 'environment state' relates to or differs from the capitalist state. Little wonder then that the relation between forms of democracy and functions of sustainability remain undeveloped or rest on largely benign notions of compatibility. For we cannot assume that the development of structures and roles of the so-called 'environmental state' will be inherently democratic (whether adopting deliberative or agonistic methods) or that the 'democratic state' will pursue an uncompromised or singular notion of sustainability. It is bad enough to have a naïve notion of the capitalist state and dominant forms of corporate power without also having no conception of how a non-capitalist state can be brought into being. One thing is certain, there will be no post-carbon society or degrowth society without the heavy involvement of state institutions. The sooner these are discussed and outlined, the sooner some flesh will be put on the bare-bone notions of both 'democracy' and 'sustainability'.

14. NATIONAL AND LOCAL DEMOCRACY VERSUS GLOBAL SUSTAINABILITY

THERE HAS BEEN much debate over whether capitalist globalisation is in retreat and whether de-globalisation in the form of regional blocs and nationalist politics will shape the coming decades, particularly since the Great Financial Crisis of 2007-8, the increasing political tensions between the US and China and the rise of Right-wing nationalist parties. Opinions are divided over whether democracy is being threatened or will be the beneficiary of these new anti-globalisation tendencies, as discussed in Book Two. Others argue that environmental sustainability will be the main casualty in the absence of concerted global action. While there are a range of national state institutions and statutory bodies such as environmental protection agencies tasked with managing ecological modernisation in different countries, many of these are either undeveloped and underfunded or lack the socio-political institutional power at national level. Globally, apart from the UN Conference of Parties (COP) and a few other bodies, there are effectively no environmental regulatory or co-ordinating bodies capable of dealing with looming ecological crises that are equivalent to the former Bretton Woods system for managing monetary policy.

The large G20 countries that account for over 80% of global production and trade are far too divided to act decisively on environmental issues. This is a sign that within capitalist classes there is as yet no 'fraction of capital' or combination of sectors or 'bloc' of business and their political allies within the major emitter nation states – China, US, India, Japan, Russia, Saudi Arabia, plus member countries of the EU – either strong enough or sufficiently politically committed to rapidly replacing the powerful fossil-fuel sector that is responsible for almost two thirds of global emissions. It is important to also recognise that rapid decarbonisation entails dealing with related fiscal and socio-economic problems that would be exacerbated by this emergency climate action.

The failure to enact deep-seated major reform of financial practices following the Great Financial Crisis of 2007-08 has now further weakened the financial system's capacity to deal with the dramatic deterioration of economic conditions due to the Coronavirus pandemic in 2020. Without adequate financial funding there can be no rapid response to decarbonisation. And without coordinated action by governments to ensure that financial institutions are properly regulated, there is the danger that the combined financial resources needed to prevent climate breakdown and combat a possible economic depression will be too little, too late. It is the pace and degree of decarbonisation or policies to resolve inequality and poverty that becomes decisive. Too slow, and environmental crises and socio-political problems are dramatically compounded further down the track. Too fast, and conservative political and business interests opposed to interventionist government policies fear that state action to solve socio-economic crises could easily outweigh the short-term impact of the climate crisis.

Leading mainstream policy makers already recognise that earlier crisis-managing techniques (austerity, quantitative easing) will be far less effective and also not be supported by electorates. Looking at the next ten to twenty years, when we factor in the continual restructuring and innovation of capitalist production, the news is not good for millions of workers caught in the crossfire of market 're-adjustments' and declining or stagnant world trade. According to the IMF, world GDP growth in the past few decades has been in the 'danger zone' of 2.5% to 3.5% per annum and must be higher to avoid recession.[1] Tellingly, the IMF does not consider that these rates of growth already constitute a danger zone for environmental sustainability and would be much more dangerous if world GDP growth had been higher. Instead, business leaders and governments fear economic downturns will lead to more radical solutions such as nationalisation of failed financial, manufacturing and other businesses that would seriously threaten the power of corporations. Increasingly, political organisational and strategic questions will therefore revolve around whether the current broad adherence to a mixture of lobbying, electoral participation, street marches and 'consciousness raising' (of both Left and Right) will be jettisoned in favour of much more radical forms of political action. Far Right movements have already increased their use of violence.

On the positive side, it is within the context of escalating social and environmental dysfunction combined with the inability of businesses and governments to regenerate earlier forms of capitalist growth that we could possibly see new hybrid forms of community or public ownership emerge alongside familiar corporations and private enterprises. These hybrid forms will not immediately displace capitalist production and power. However, these new types of publicly controlled local and national institutions and services could constitute an expanded 'mixed economy' that is both qualitatively different to earlier Keynesian public sectors and yet not completely subordinate to the dominant private capitalist sector as are existing public sectors in most countries. I will return to this in the next chapter.

While it is difficult to currently imagine how these new developments or hybrid socio-economic orders and practices could possibly function, expand and survive without a significant change in the balance of political economic power relations, we should not *a priori* rule them out. In any future scenario of weakened private sectors unable to cope with mounting ecological and social dysfunction and malaise, these publicly funded local and national communal enterprises, care services and enterprises geared to the restoration and protection of endangered habitats or degraded urban facilities could turn out to be necessary welcome alternatives to unsustainable forms of capitalism. The degree to which they are introduced or blocked in different countries will be determined by factors such as the varying levels of political struggle, available fiscal resources and the balance of organised socio-political forces in particular nation states.

NATIONAL SOVEREIGNTY AND THE GEOPOLITICS OF SUSTAINABILITY

Previous debates over the feasibility of either centralised or decentralised planning have largely taken place within the framework of nation-states or federations such as the former USSR or a possible future EU federation in mind. Regardless, the tensions of 'democracy versus sustainability' go beyond these national and supranational borders and affect the entire world. The perennial problem facing radical advocates of greater democratisation within either capitalist or post-capitalist societies is how to reconcile the desire for anti-bureaucratic socio-political alternatives with the many local, national and international challenges concerning the organisation of production and provision of social needs.

Unfortunately, the conflict between 'democracy and sustainability' results from the fact that these two processes and end goals are *not* inherently compatible. In other words, not all forms of democracy are well-suited to or maximise all local or global degrees and scales of sustainability. Making them compatible will therefore first require recognition of the tension between organisational or institutional models and secondly, how to compromise or modify proposals and objectives in order for future sustainable democracies to become feasible. Recall in Chapter Seven the discussion of Dani Rodrik's trilemma of globalisation, national sovereignty and democracy. One could only have two of these three choices. To have all three simultaneously was impossible due to their fundamental incompatibility. Deeper or hyper-global integration would limit democracy and national sovereignty whereas maximising democracy and national sovereignty would limit globalisation. Finally, a combination of hyper-globalisation and global democracy would nullify national sovereignty.

Rodrik's trilemma is actually more complicated than it may appear. In my view it is more like a 'quadrilemma' as so many countries are now also characterised by additional major socio-economic divisions. We have multicultural 'global cities' that are integrated into supranational markets, cultural exchanges and attract labour from many countries and on the other hand, in the same country we have regional and rural communities that suffer from deindustrialisation, cultural isolation, stagnation and neglect. The other important factor was whether the political/administrative system of countries were centralised or were federal systems with power sharing between federal and sub-national state governments. Covid-19 has exacerbated pre-existing weaknesses of federal systems. In the US, Mexico, Brazil, Australia, and the quasi-federal system of the EU and other federations, disputes over how to handle the crisis and what aid should be given to weaker or poorer regions undermined effective policies. These disputes were partly related to conflicts over democracy, which branch of government had constitutional authority and the ideological differences between federal and state leaders.

Another type of trilemma has been theorised by environmentalist, Umberto Sconfienza. Once again only a maximum of two out of three options are feasible. The first he calls 'techno-business-as-usual' which combines economic growth and political participation but without environmental protection. This is the dominant model of 'green growth'. The second version of the trilemma is championed by advocates of post-growth or degrowth and combines political freedom plus environmental protection but without economic growth. Finally, the third combination of 'environmental authoritarianism' is based on undemocratic central authority in countries such as China that pursue economic growth and environmental protection but exclude democratic participation.[2]

Sconfienza highlights the current political divisions over environmental sustainability but does not discuss the trilemma or quadrilemma that applies to the conflict of 'democracy versus sustainability'. Briefly, we could well see future geopolitical conflicts and incompatible policies based on:

- the need to protect global sustainability (or the biosphere) against greater local and national democracy;
- the demand to defend greater local democracy against the exercise of both national and global power;
- the safeguarding of national sovereignty against both greater globalisation and local democracy and
- the use global or supranational democratic planning power to override national and local sovereignty.

Given the unknown consequences of democratic decision-making, it is possible that greater local democracy may be fully compatible with national democratic decisions. On the other hand, a proportion of local communities might reject national policies. As with existing federal systems, would the new constitutions grant co-sharing power to national and sub-national governments or would national or local democracy prevail? Also, nationally determined sustainability goals may not concur with global sustainability goals such as serious disputes over time frames (for example, protecting marine habitats from over-fishing) and mutual sharing of burdens and resources (such as controlling water resources affecting several countries in the upper and lower Mekong basin). These incompatible policies could be a direct outcome of the desire by some governments to try to prevent other governments from pursuing their own domestic economic agendas, such as the unequal use of limited global resources in order to rapidly overcome socio-economic inequalities. Global democracy and global sustainability may look quite feasible on paper, but as we know a single world government would be an undesirable nightmare which would itself be incompatible with greater local and national democracy.

Remember, the point here is not to invoke a utopia of all societies simultaneously becoming socialist or green. Rather, it is to consider the feasibility or not of a future world in which various capitalist countries co-exist with socialist, green degrowth or other new hybrid alternatives. Furthermore, *global* sustainability could only be achieved if tens of thousands of local democracies and almost 195 potential national democracies voluntarily agreed to develop a shared set of political economic objectives. One would not need this degree of unanimity of all units of government to develop much more sustainable policies. Nonetheless, any such shared global political economic objectives presuppose tortuous international multilateral trade, development, mutual aid, biodiversity and other agreements that end existing forms of unequal exchange between high-income and low or middle-income countries. Just a few of the controversial areas that are bound to cause major divisions would include bans on the export of military weapons, open or limited access to national markets or non-market economies, abandonment of intellectual property treaties protecting monopoly digital corporations and cultural monoliths such as Hollywood, tariff penalties on carbon-embodied goods and the cessation of mass deforestation and the phasing out or reduction of chemically-based agriculture.

Previous World Trade Organisation negotiations on global treaties have either failed or stalled, and this was with the participation of capitalist countries, let alone in a future world of mixed socio-political systems. Greater environmental sustainability based on maximising biodiversity presuppose regulation, constraint and protection against business enterprises, individuals and communities long used to having their needs satisfied regardless of the environmental costs. With declines in global trade and the Trump administration opposing or ignoring multilateral agreements, Covid-19 has merely added to the near defunct status of the WTO. Before the Pandemic, pro-market analyst Anu Bradford had argued that the EU 'Brussel's effect' determined production standards and many other standards across the world.[3] Given the large affluent consumer market in the EU (which is the second largest economic area after the US), Bradford showed how global corporations adopt EU product and safety standards across a wide range of industries and technologies rather than producing separate and more costly product standards for different countries.

In a future transitional world where a sizeable minority of multinational corporations might lose part of or a great deal of their current power, the EU market would not set global standards. Rising powers such as China or new market societies such as those aiming for limited trade could also adopt local and regional standards rather than international regulations. It is unclear whether these new local and regional standards would be higher and more sustainable and socially beneficial than current inadequate regulations. One would hope that people were imbued with universal altruistic values of care for the needs of strangers that extended beyond love of immediate family,

kinship structures and community. The assumption, however, that democratically made decisions are inherently more enlightened and caring simply
because they are made by a majority of people or some other deliberating
process is not a given.

While it is possible to have international ecological treaties on greenhouse gas emissions or the prohibition of the use of various toxic chemicals
and other such environmental measures, it is most unlikely that we will ever
see a socialist global economy or global green alternatives *simultaneously*
replacing all existing forms of representative democracies and authoritarian
capitalist societies. Moreover, being nominally 'socialist' did not stop the 'red
brotherhood at war', in the form of earlier conflicts between the USSR and
China, Vietnam and China or Vietnam and Cambodia. As the largest global
power, the US has always pursued its own agenda and interests whether they
coincided with or were at odds with international treaties. The same is true
of other G20 countries but without the capacity to impose their preferences
as is the case with the US.

We are currently in the early but crucial stages of decarbonisation with
the necessary future large cuts to greenhouse gas emissions only to take
effect by the end of the 2020s and in the 2030s. This is when we will see
intense pressure on both authoritarian and formally democratic governments
to either comply with international treaties, or rebel. Decarbonisation is
urgent, but carbon footprints are merely one small part of the equalisation of
per capita and national metallic and non-metallic resources footprints,
biomass footprints, water footprints and other marine, land and atmospheric
footprints that need reduction to make a future world environmentally
sustainable.

Although the transition to a post-neoliberal or post-capitalist society will
involve enormous national and international obstacles to be overcome, these
transitional struggles will be completely different to the challenges facing
political movements and communities in a future world no longer completely
constrained by pro-market governments. Just as capitalism is incompatible
with greater democratisation, so too, but for quite different reasons, greater
democratisation can nullify or contradict the goal of greater sustainability. In
an unequal political world, we are likely to see a mixture of the following
societies and governments:

- those that are highly committed to environmentally sustainable
  socio-economic practices;
- others that adopt the rhetoric of sustainability but selfishly place

local/national needs and priorities above international
sustainability commitments and objectives (even though the
former may be democratically determined); and
- those that pragmatically try to maintain *domestic* political peace
regardless of whether their decisions contribute to or undermine
global sustainability.

If global sustainability objectives are to be effectively delivered rather than become mere voluntary 'guidelines' that local and national governments can implement or ignore, there will need to be international agencies to adjudicate and enforce agreements or impose penalties. In a world consisting of mixed types of political regimes during what could be a lengthy period of transition to democratisation and sustainability, common enforceable goals may not always be agreed upon or capable of being enforced. For instance, what will replace the EU Commission, the World Trade Organisation, the International Court of Justice, the United Nations agencies and peace keeping forces and numerous other tribunals and institutions? Often the good intentions of radicals and reformers overshadow the lack of a 'plan B' in the likely event of non-co-operation due to local domestic democratic opposition or the refusal of particular authoritarian national governments to support new social justice and sustainability goals and policies.

It is therefore possible to envisage clashes over the decisions and choices made by local direct democracies jealously defending their democratic rights against national representative governments or vice versa. We may also see a range of divisions over specific sustainability policies and frameworks endorsed by international organisations and the rejection of some or all of these policies and target goals by local and national democratic constituencies. This could be a two-way process. For example, local democratically empowered communities might refuse to allow access to vitally needed natural resources in the quantities desired by other national governments. Conversely, local communities may extract local marine and land based resources or produce goods at a rate much faster and greater than agreed to by international treaties.

CLOSED OR OPEN BORDERS

We have already seen Right-wing free marketeers/libertarians either support or object to 'open borders' in racist terms. In their eyes, America and Europe do not have 'free immigration' policies but rather 'forced integration' whereby local communities, cities and regions have no power to reject 'unsavoury multicultural' immigrants.[4] Hence, they advocate two options: either decentralise decision-making to local communities as to what kind and how many new 'resident aliens' they accept; or else maintain centralised immigration policy but deny immigrants full entitlement rights to welfare. In Chapter Nine, I discussed why people on the Left such as Wolfgang Streeck are also anti-multicultural and support anti-immigration policies in order to protect 'national social democracy' against the free market of open borders for both capital and labour. Actually, pro-market governments rarely give non-citizens welfare entitlements.

While racist and other cultural forms of discrimination could be gradually eliminated as the basic principles of an alternative democracy, issues of community and national population size will remain controversial issues of environmental sustainability. Despite their pre-environmental consciousness, both free marketeers and Left nationalists unintentionally force us to consider difficult aspects of 'democracy versus sustainability'. Future post-capitalist sustainable democracies may have open or closed borders depending on whether local or national bodies prevent people immigrating from other countries or localities in the name of either 'sustainability' or 'democratic control'. The greater the political orientation to self-sufficiency, the greater the likelihood of local or national restrictions on free population movement.

World population movements continue to be from rural to urban areas. Over recent decades, only 3.3 per cent of the world's population have been international migrants. They are not, contrary to Right-wing anti-immigrant parties, flowing mainly from low and middle-income countries to high-income countries.[5] Rather, a higher percentage of international refugees from war-torn countries and also contract workers from low-income nations (domestic servants, construction workers, farm workers and so forth) are continuing to either move to other geographically adjacent low and middle-income countries in the same region or to high-income countries such as the Gulf states and OECD countries. Human movement *between* countries in Asia, Latin America, the Middle East and Africa is far greater than the restricted movement to Europe, the US, Canada, Japan and Australia. In 2020, there were 70.8 million people forcibly displaced by natural disasters, war and conflict and political persecution. Of these, 41.3 million were internally displaced from their homes within their own countries, 25.9 million were refugees and 3.5 million were asylum-seekers. Over 80 per cent of refugees were living in states neighbouring their home countries. Most were *not* to be found in high income countries but located in low and middle-income countries such as Uganda, Pakistan, Turkey and Ethiopia.[6]

According to the United Nations International Migration Report, between 2000 and 2017, there were 258 million migrants in the world.[7] It has long been argued that professionals such as doctors, whose education has been paid for in low and middle-income countries, should not be allowed to migrate to high-income countries (unless fleeing persecution) thus exacerbating the brain drain in their own countries. Many 'degrowthers' envisage a world where immigration is minimal or outdated because local communities will produce most of what they consume and also become vibrant inclusive centres thus removing the need for people to flee to large cities for work and cultural stimulation. This belief, largely driven by the goal of sustainability, is a distant ideal that bears no relation whatsoever to the condition of billions of people in countries with mass poverty and inadequate local resources. Conversely, cosmopolitans who aim for a future borderless world and also advocate so-called *sufficiency*, believe that mobility is an important cultural and human right. In a democratic society, people should not be trapped in small towns or villages waiting for the 'good life' to arrive and denied the possibility to live in other countries or cities.

Thus, conflicting notions of sustainability, mobility and democratic rights will undoubtedly persist. If mobility is democratically approved of by local or national political institutions, would two, three, five, or more per cent of the population in any nation state or local region be permitted to move to another location per annum or over a defined period of time? Would there be optimal population sizes for cities beyond which no new residents would be accepted? 'Internal passport' systems were long a feature of former Communist countries and still pose a major problem in China (see later discussion). It is therefore naïve to believe that immigration and population policy will disappear as controversial issues in future post-capitalist societies, regardless of whether there is greater or lesser local, national or global decision-making. Issues of immigration and mobility are closely related to the provision of social welfare, scarcity of jobs, housing and health care and also the demand and stress placed on local and national urban and natural resources.

Whether an alternative sustainable democracy will opt for relatively closed, familiar communities or open and diverse cultural relations and experiences are decisions that will involve political struggles over the criteria governing eligibility to both residency and social rights as well as struggles over the allocation of natural and social resources in particular local, national or supranational jurisdictions. I do not believe that general principles of open or closed borders for each locality or nation state can be determined *a priori* or absolutely without consideration of the specific needs of those seeking refuge and the very diverse social and environmental capacities of each host community to peacefully and successfully offer new homes to whoever wants to come. Insofar as different forms of democracy are adopted as the principal method of resolving these geopolitical socio-cultural and ecological disputes, there will likely be no final or permanent resolution just because capitalism has been replaced in some or in all countries.

No resolution to the divisive issues of immigration, refugees and mobility is possible in future years without transforming living conditions and achieving a cessation to violent conflict in developing low-income societies. The well-intentioned campaigners for the 2030 Sustainable Development Goals (agreed to by 193 countries in 2015) have formulated 169 different indices (in health, education, biodiversity, etc.) but have made very limited progress in a number of countries. Yet, both the target goals and the support for these goals from developed capitalist countries is more rhetorical than real when it comes to large funding contributions and changing the global political economic structural relations of trade, military and other markets that perpetuate poverty. Such is the distance from achieving many of the Sustainable Development Goals, that there is neither any clear available data nor the capacity in many countries to collect and measure whether any progress has actually been made![8] Moreover, the very issues and areas to be 'measured' are themselves skewed against resolving deep-seated structural poverty and discrimination.[9] There is also a glaring inconsistency between the aims of sustainability and the hoped for economic growth rates that will exceed the material carrying capacity of key bio-physical indicators.[10]

SUSTAINABLE DEVELOPMENT VERSUS CAPITALIST ROADBLOCKS

Countries in Africa and other low-income regions developing strong capitalist economies with the ability to fund EU welfare type regimes remain in the realm of dreams. A 2015 IMF report examined how 167 low and middle-income countries in 1970 had fared in subsequent decades. Only nine countries reached high-income status by 2010 (or the equivalent of 46% of US GDP per capita income) and of these, only Taiwan and South Korea were not small European countries: Cyprus, Czech Republic, Greece, Ireland, Malta, Portugal and Slovenia.[11] Even these nine countries fell well below the social welfare provided in northern EU member countries. One researcher estimated that it would take between 123 and 209 years for trickle-down global growth to deliver a very austere $5 per day to the world's population.[12] International researchers also reported that money in the form of illicit money transfers to tax havens, interest payments or falsely priced invoices used by subsidiaries of multinationals to disguise capital flight, avoid tax, and conceal flows out of developing societies is far greater than the combined total of foreign aid, investment and other income received by these societies from developed capitalist countries.[13] In other words, the ability of most low and middle-income countries to develop comparable social welfare systems such as those in Scandinavia or France under the current conditions of highly unequal and exploitative capitalist markets, is near zero.

Radical critics of 'sustainable development goals' such as Gustavo Esteva, Salvatore Babones and Philipp Babcicky point to the 'three Sachs' conceptions of development operating in the world today. Referring to the dominant 'Goldman Sachs' position, they point out that:

> While academics struggle to define 'development' in theory, Goldman Sachs and its peers in the banking, mining, engineering and oil industries, define development in practice through their commodities trading desks, their infrastructure projects, and their exploration units. These companies staff government offices on a rotating basis, endow the think tanks that promote their interests and employ more lobbyists to work on development-related issues than there are academics working in development studies departments. These companies are 'strategic partners' (that is, major funders) of the World Economic Forum. The press interviews them and their hired representatives whenever their interests are at stake. The Goldman Sachs approach is absolutely hegemonic outside academia at the top of the society.[14]

In reaction to the 'Goldman Sachs' corporate notion of development is the 'Jeffrey Sachs' approach named after its most prominent exponent. This band of well-meaning academics, activists, and celebrities such as Bob Geldof and Bill Gates, includes the major US and European development NGOs and the more progressive wing of the economics establishment. Esteva, Babones and Babcicky describe its adherents as focussing mainly "on the alleviation of obvious suffering – they stand for a chicken in every pot, a mosquito net over every bed, and a condom on every penis."[15] Finally, there is the 'Wolfgang Sachs' approach named after the German critic of Western development policies. This conception of development or post-development is now entrenched in academic departments studying both the structural consequences and neglect of the 'Goldman Sachs' and 'Jeffrey Sachs' policy approaches. It is also popular among global social movements championing the right of billions of people to determine their own priorities and notions of development rather than have these imposed upon them from outside.[16]

While Esteva, Babones and Babcicky highlight the conflicting notions of development, they tend to homogenise a number of other actors and approaches. For example, it could be argued that the Chinese government is also part of the Davos crowd and pursues similar corporate attitudes in other countries. China's 'going global' strategy, especially its 'Belt and Road' project and other commercial initiatives closely tie 'aid' to foreign policy strategy. However, it has also become one of the largest donors of 'humanitarian aid' in the form of medical and other assistance, and also promotes 'soft power' goodwill aid to low-income countries. Nonetheless, the Chinese government is opposed to promoting a post-capitalist sustainability agenda in developing countries, just as it is opposed to such an agenda for its own population. Still, the Chinese also provide aid to low-income countries that are not immediately tied to loan repayments or just business development like the 'Goldman Sachs' approach. Similarly, Cuba provided doctors and aid to African and Latin American countries in the decades from the 1970s onwards that was not entirely altruistic nor a commercial investment. In recent years, however, this 'aid' has changed as 50,000 Cuban doctors working in 67 countries earn Cuba about $USD 11 billion per year, or more than its tourist industry. In other words, there are development models pursued by non-OECD countries that are not strictly reducible to the 'three Sachs' paradigms.

During the Cold War period, advocates of socialist change in the 'Third World' could point to assistance from the USSR and Eastern European Communist bloc, China or Cuba given their rivalry with the US and its allies. Even radical anti-Stalinists could formerly take shelter in 'Third world' countries' under the cover of Communist opposition to imperialism. However, advocates of degrowth and eco-socialism now operate in a totally changed geopolitical environment without any direct or indirect support from a powerful state such as the Soviet Union. Without external support, relatively weak social movements in low and middle-income countries are unlikely to succeed in socially and politically transforming their societies. This vital support will not be forthcoming so long as the G20 countries continue to follow their existing political economic trajectories.

Meanwhile, the US, as the greatest global power, has been a social welfare laggard for the past 100 years as outlined in Chapter Three). Since the 1940s, the US 'warfare-welfare state' continues to be heavily skewed to 'warfare' rather than 'welfare'. On conservative estimates, US governments have *underspent* approximately $1.6 trillion per annum on domestic social welfare, not counting emergency Covid-19 temporary income support measures. No other country or bloc, including China, Russia or the EU can imitate the level of military expenditure and global dominance played by America. Given its massive militarised presence globally and domestically though its military-industrial allocation of resources and drain on public revenue, no fundamental restructuring of US domestic social and environmental priorities is conceivable in the future without progress in the following areas:

- ending the highly discriminatory and unequal taxation system favouring the top 5% of individual and business beneficiaries;
- dramatically shifting global foreign policy away from a mixture of targeted military containment of rival powers, and the use of financial, foreign aid, and trade policies or sanctions to further US corporate and political interests;
- seriously tackling racial discrimination at all levels of society; and
- reforming the gerrymandered electoral system and highly uneven political power in a federal system that favours small rural based states at the expense of populations in large urban centres.

Both Republican and Democratic administrations have presided over the US being the leading obstacle blocking environmental sustainability, social welfare, peaceful development and global co-operation across the globe. Unable to reform those aspects of its archaic constitution that encourages political paralysis, the decades-long unresolved major problems in the US make the inadequate social welfare systems in other OECD countries look positively utopian by comparison with the obscene levels of inequality in America. Given its disproportionate influence over many countries, the US functions as a failed state that threatens the future safety, sustainability and wellbeing of the rest of the world. Although one can cite various former positive contributions made by particular US governments (such as funding United Nations bodies, delivering aid to countries reeling from natural disasters), most of these occurred when American rivalry with the USSR or China prompted altruism to coincide with strategic interests of appearing to be a 'good global citizen'. Most of the features of a benign multilateral American foreign policy that occasionally co-existed alongside its imperial power have long disappeared.

In recent years the US has displayed great hostility to international co-operation. America's negative roles now far outweigh its capacity to do good. Hence, many governments and parties in other countries fear American market coercion combined with diplomatic/military coercion. If domestic political movements cannot reform the excesses of American capitalism, one can only hope that US global power declines over coming decades. This shift in the balance of power will itself be extremely dangerous if US governments opt for military solutions to defend a status quo that ultimately cannot be preserved. Millions of Americans recognise the malaise and violence of American empire both domestically and globally. Whether they can grow strong enough to curb the excesses of imperial power remains to be seen.

In this chapter, I have tried to show that there are two parallel debates or political discourses that barely connect with one another and revolve around quite different objectives. The dominant discourse is conducted by governments, business lobbyists, policy makers and strategic military, technology and socio-economic analysts within the leading G20 countries. In a world of declining and rising powers, the challenges facing the globe are usually presented from the perspective of the US, the EU, China, Russia, Japan, India and other powerful countries. A case in point is that analysts are preoccupied with how Europe can enhance its trade, new technology capacities, military security and yet safeguard its cultural values and social institutions in the face of multiple challenges from other regional powers.[17] China's leaders also debate what kind of unilateral or multilateral roles it should adopt that does not replicate the failed military and colonial strategies of the US and old European and Japanese imperial powers. What appeared to be a broad 'Eurasian' strategy of connecting Asian countries to Europe via Central and South Asia and the Middle East (using the massive Belt and Road infrastructure program) may be modified or abandoned given the hostility of various EU countries to China's rising power. If so, China could pursue a consolidation of its existing regional power that leads to a genuine fragmentation of the world into separate political economic blocs.

Given this potential move towards deep regionalism as a result of the US and its allies trying to contain China, every other region or set of individual countries from within Latin America and Africa to South and North East Asia and the Middle East will be forced to weigh up which regional bloc it will formally or informally join. The marginal or significant decline in America's pre-eminent economic and military power will be closely related to how

US governments facilitate or oppose the decline of fossil fuels in the coming decade or two, plus the outcome of struggles over dominance in digital and other recent technologies. It is not just that OECD countries are facing unprecedented domestic crises in regard to sustaining employment, social welfare and the need to prevent climate breakdown. Soon they will be forced to act to remedy the multiple crises flowing from the almost certain failure of the 2030 Sustainable Development Goals to fulfil key objectives in African, South Asian and other regions. While the military arms race and fleeing mass refugees in the Asia-Pacific, Middle East and Africa continue unabated, most low and middle-income countries are either trapped or caught in the crossfire of great power struggles.

In America and Europe, the advocates of eco-socialism and degrowth are either largely unknown or irrelevant to most decision-makers in the massively powerful state repressive apparatuses and corporations. Yet, it is precisely because eco-socialists and 'degrowthers' see the present world in its fully unequal, destructive and irrational forms that they champion a more rational and caring alternative future. The problem is that their discourse on how to achieve a saner more just world does not in any way match or adequately engage with the enormity of the hostile global forces that they face. Little wonder that their messages remain as faint and obscure to the vast majority of people as if their good news were coming from a far-off planet that is light years away.

THE GLOBAL IMPLICATIONS OF 'DEMOCRACY VERSUS SUSTAINABILITY'

The old paradigm of 'capitalism versus democracy' assumed an inbuilt political finality: either capitalism wins and ends democracy, fascism in other words, or else democracy wins and ends capitalism. The new paradigm of 'democracy versus sustainability' has no such end point unless in the highly unlikely event, citizens across the world, especially in the G20 powerful nation states, permit their governments to pursue global ecocide through mindless unconstrained production and consumption. It is clear, nonetheless, that the conflict of 'capitalism versus democracy' will shape both present and future relations between 'democracy and sustainability'. This is because the reality of violent, massively unequal societies intrudes into every aspect of global political economic life and guarantees that existing political, business and military power will not be surrendered easily, if at all, across the world. As Sharon Burrow, head of the International Trade Union Congress observed in June 2020, "A staggering 85 per cent of countries have violated the right to strike. Strikes and demonstrations have been banned in Belarus, Guinea, Senegal and Togo and met extreme brutality in Bolivia, Chile and Ecuador. In Iran and Iraq, mass arrests have been made at protests."[18] The ten worst violators of workers' rights in 2020 were Bangladesh, Brazil, Colombia, Egypt, Honduras, India, Kazakhstan, the Philippines, Turkey and Zimbabwe. Without the freedom to organise and strike, citizens will not be able to freely campaign on most other social and environmental issues.

Hence, the obscene levels of inequality and exclusion of billions of people from decision-making will not end simultaneously or within a short period of time. If, and when it ever does, politics will not end as any genuine new democracy will embody debate, disagreement and the articulation of either minority or majority interests. As I have argued, there is a reasonable likelihood that in any transitional world a certain number of local or national populations and governments will democratically or undemocratically decide to produce and consume more than other communities. They may possibly decide to continue to exclude strangers, prioritise their own needs and not reduce their material footprint in line with what they may claim are unacceptable global guidelines for sustainability. In other words, even if capitalism is replaced in many countries, 'democracy versus sustainability' assumes never-ending negotiation and dispute over what 'sustainability' means and how local and national social and natural resources are to be democratically shared. It will not be some nirvana of perfect harmony with nature. Consensus will not always be possible and perhaps only be reached in a minority of cases. A shared need to solve problems non-violently will only prevail if the larger conceptions of the mutual benefits flowing from protecting biodiversity and social equality help inform decision making and give new meaning to what socially just and sustainable democratic societies should aim for. Unsurprisingly, this is easier said than done.

Imaginative anti-bureaucratic proposals to allocate greater resources and decision-making to all kinds of local and regional community organisations have been circulating for decades. Nonetheless, most of these alternative proposals inevitably confront viability problems once they have to expand eligibility criteria either to all residents and not just citizens within a particular nation state or to all people beyond national borders. Also, regardless of whether the nation state is a democracy or an authoritarian regime, it is extremely difficult to reorganise existing national boundaries so that nation states are either broken up and reborn as smaller local and regional entities or merged into supranational states. Overturning prevailing discriminatory citizenship and residency rights that treat foreigners as second-class citizens and exclude them from social welfare rights and social entitlements would require much deeper democratisation of large federations and nation states such as the US, China, India, Nigeria, Indonesia or Russia. Debates over identity and citizenship concerning future open borders or the extent and power of local democracy raises the issue of environmentally sustainable alternatives to existing national welfare states.

If 'democracy' and 'sustainability' can be interpreted as either compatible or incompatible, it is expected to find people adopting a familiar political position that is located somewhere on the spectrum between two polar opposites:

- either calling for the implementation of various measures to reduce national and world population size to ease what is claimed to be strains on finite natural and social resources; or
- conversely, calling for the reduction of global inequality by aiming to limit each person and each country in the world to the same level of consumption and use of resources, that is, aiming for the same per capita material footprint.

Revised population projections based on fertility rates now assume peak global population of 9.73 billion in 2064 which will then decline to 8.79 billion in 2100.[19] Within this total figure in 2100 there will be dramatic changes such as China's population halving to 732 million and Nigeria's exceeding China's at 791 million. Capitalists fear a shortage of labour and higher taxes to pay for ageing populations unless there is rapid automation to cover the shortfall. However, the environmental justice movement would welcome the new figures as they could possibly mean greater hope of achieving more equality in most areas of the world other than sub-Saharan African countries which have high population growth. Raw aggregate population figures, however, tell us little about the politics of distribution or whether the unequal use of resources will increase or diminish.

PROBLEMS WITH MATERIAL FOOTPRINTS

Between 1970 and 2010, annual global extraction of materials more than tripled from 22 million tonnes to 70 million tonnes. Growth in per capita income and consumption was the main driver of material use and exceeded population growth as the cause of the unsustainable and unequal growth in material footprints.[20] However, between 1980 and 2008, per capita material consumption in Europe and North America either declined or was stagnant,[21] an unintended form of partial 'degrowth' driven by inequality and economic crisis as well as by the shift to consumption of services and away from durable consumer goods. One of the political problems of assessing the level of per capita material footprints that are compatible with global sustainability is that the statistics for material extraction, material consumption, trade in goods and resources and development are all *aggregate* amounts for each country provided by international agencies.[22] We can see the disparities between large industrialised countries such as the US and many low-income societies in Africa. However, we have no detailed figures for different social classes or the disproportionate use of resources by, for example, businesses that are export orientated.

The United Nations Environment Programme International Resources Panel (UNEP) recommended in 2014 that the world aim for sustainability by reducing material extraction from 70 million to 50 million tons per annum, or a per capita material consumption rate of 6 to 8 tons by 2050.[23] In 2015, the National Commission on Sustainable Development in Finland adopted the UNEP 2050 target for per capita material footprints.[24] Other analysts argued for as little as 3 to 6 tons by 2050.[25] Whichever figure is aimed for, there exists no definitive figures for the carrying capacity of the earth. Instead, material footprints are based on averaging statistics that take a particular country's material extraction, material consumption and other indicators and then subdivide these by the size of population to arrive at per capita footprints. This is a very unsatisfactory methodology which covers up profound social and institutional inequalities in actual rates of per capita material consumption. Currently, affluent OECD countries have an average of 27 tons per capita material consumption compared to low-income countries with per capita consumption ranging from two to six tons. While these figures clearly tell us about the glaring inequalities between countries, they provide insufficient detail about how to remedy the inter-class inequalities within each country and between countries. For example, many businesses over-produce goods or extract more minerals than are actually used. There are also major differences between the material footprints of households in individual countries depending on income and wealth.

I strongly support the need for material consumption to be reduced by affluent sections of national populations. However, the struggle between 'democracy and sustainability' will be partly fought over claims and counter claims as to what constitutes an equitable future per capita level of material consumption. Social justice movements cannot afford to accept 'aggregate' material footprint statistics from agencies that prioritise 'green growth' within capitalist societies, whether UNEP, OECD, EUROSTAT or the World Bank, because the latter fail to breakdown the unequal class structure of existing forms of material consumption and production. We know that greenhouse gas emissions require material extraction, production and consumption to decline if we wish to avoid catastrophic climate breakdown. However, the larger issue of material footprints embraces much more than carbon footprints.

The political agendas and success of degrowth movements also depend on having more nuanced and detailed figures concerning material footprints if they are to persuade millions of affluent people to reduce their material consumption by up to 80 per cent of their current levels, a level of reduction that may be unnecessarily high if it can be shown how misleading a picture is created by averaging aggregate statistics. For instance, Jason Hickel points to the fact that Europe already spends 40% less per capita than the US and yet achieves better results on most social indicators.[26] One reason for this is that US expenditure on health is highly privatised and favours high tech, thus benefitting health care corporations and 'big pharma' at the expense of uninsured low and middle-income people. Similarly, people will justifiably object to having to make do on just 6 to 8 tons per capita material footprints while their 'sacrifice' is squandered by most businesses and institutions geared to unnecessary high production and consumption instead of improving the living conditions of the poorest people in the world.

Crucially, any reduction of material footprints will need to be semi-voluntary at the individual level and directed phased reduction at the macro-extraction and production levels. This is because no government currently has any intention of enforcing caps on material consumption at individual or household levels and must be politically strongly backed by electorates to reduce extraction and production in various industries. Even in the unlikely event that governments agree to global targets and caps, few national governments are likely to enforce such divisive measures without popular domestic support and no international organisation currently has the power to impose penalties on nation states that fail to adhere to international agreements. On this issue alone, we see how decisive the conflict is of 'democracy versus sustainability'.

Politically, it is also important to differentiate attempts to restrain population growth from calls to reduce the size of material footprints. Currently, political demands to curb both population growth and consumption growth are either conceived as violations of individual freedoms and democratic rights or else interpreted as class or social justice issues that necessitate the redistribution of wealth. It is impossible to reconcile *unlimited* individual freedoms with the need to prevent environmental catastrophe or end social inequality. Measures to halt the spread of Covid-19 have already shown that while the majority of people will voluntarily adhere to curbs on their freedom, the longer self-isolation is required, the larger dissenting behaviour grows and is met by force. To imagine that it is possible to construct comprehensive 'social states' based on sustainable production *without* major polarised political conflicts is wishful thinking.

The wide variation in how governments have responded to the worldwide crisis caused by the Covid-19 pandemic also highlights the deep political divisions over existing 'social states' in most OECD countries and the absence of equivalent social welfare in low and middle-income countries. More than a decade of austerity measures in Europe and North America have exposed the serious underfunding of health facilities and social security systems unable to cope with millions of people left unemployed and without income or killed due to lack of medical supplies and health workers. The variation in state provided benefits was even sharper in non-OECD countries ranging from very minimal income, medical and social support, to the impoverished conditions faced by hundreds of millions of people in Latin American, Asian and African countries with no welfare 'safety net'.[27] The rise of 'solidarity networks' providing support to suffering populations is a positive development, despite the inability of these non-state movements to adequately cope with the scale of the crisis.[28]

Advocates of degrowth such as Giorgos Kallis argue that a degrowth transition has to be democratic "otherwise a forced downscaling of consumption can easily drift into eco-authoritarianism."[29] While I agree, this begs the question of the narrow window of opportunity we have to prevent centurieslong climate breakdown, and whether environmental sustainability can be pursued if representative or participatory democracy continues to be supressed in many countries. Conversely, it is apparent that the future for equitable and sustainable per capita material footprints is far from guaranteed, especially if citizens in affluent democracies with large material footprints strongly oppose major reductions in their level of consumption.

While democracy is definitely preferable, it is not indispensable to sustainability. Technically, there is nothing to stop authoritarian governments from making emergency decrees on greenhouse gas emissions, adopting ecological modernisation of production or introducing degrowth via new compulsory regulations on levels of consumption. As long as these reforms do not jeopardise the power of the one-party state, or military and other forms of authoritarian rule, it is conceivable that some level of environmental sustainability as a goal could be supported by these regimes. Crucially, without this support, and in the absence of democracy, the planet will have little chance of reaching even dangerous targets of no more than 2° Celsius additional global warming.

This aside, authoritarian regimes are still dependent on international capitalist markets unless they opt for autarkic isolation. Competition between businesses and between capitalist countries is tied to capital investment, technological innovation and the struggle to grow or maintain market share. Labour-saving technology, enterprise cost-cutting through organisational efficiencies (meaning job cuts) and intensification of work practices all contradict goals of sustainability and the maintenance of social order unless, and this is a crucial caveat, labour shedding and exploitation are partly cushioned by an expansion of social welfare. With or without a 'democratic façade', what kind of social welfare is compatible with an authoritarian regime which itself is highly integrated into the international capitalist production and consumption system? Currently, no country in the world, with or without democratic institutions is rapidly implementing decarbonisation processes or creating environmentally sustainable production and consumption systems. Many countries *with* democratically elected governments still lack extensive, comprehensive social welfare services. However, *no* government *without* democracy (apart from Singapore) has even managed to implement the inadequate level of social welfare seen in various OECD countries. Notably, Singapore itself is dependent on a mass of poorly paid and housed immigrant labour that is excluded from its paternalistic welfare system.

THE 'GOOD LIFE' AND TRANSGRESSING PLANETARY BOUNDARIES

Recently, Daniel O'Neill and colleagues carried out a comparative survey of 150 nations to assess whether these countries met a range of social needs, such as education, income, nutrition, health, employment, life satisfaction and democratic equality without transgressing planetary boundaries including carbon emissions, material footprints, nitrogen, phosphorous and other biophysical indicators.[30] The academic survey not only lacked a clear politics and set of priorities but contained a number of problematic concepts including attributing goods consumed to a particular country rather than identifying where they were actually produced.[31] Overall, the findings were not very surprising. No country managed to satisfy social needs without transgressing per capita safe planetary boundaries. Conversely, all countries that stayed within the safe boundaries of biophysical indicators were also the same societies that failed to provide their populations with adequate social services or democratic and egalitarian social relations.

Despite the shortcomings in the comparative research findings, this survey of 'the good life within planetary boundaries' stands as a powerful and sober reminder to all who still adhere to the old paradigm 'capitalism versus democracy' as well as to those who wish to create an alternative post-capitalist society without adequately considering environmental factors. Any future notion of state planning (whatever the model) needs to specify how both social and environmental indicators can be organised to ensure that success in one area is not at the expense of the other. Developing more detailed regional and national criteria of social satisfaction and ecological sustainability is one of the vital tasks that needs to be fulfilled by political movements. This will involve painful choices that will test the capacity, awareness and resolve of future political actors to create alternative solutions to existing problems.

As for pro-market governments struggling to preserve the status quo while minimising the negative fallout from future crises, this will depend on how well they manage not just two old contradictory processes, namely, maintaining political legitimacy while ensuring the accumulation of capital, but two new additional interrelated processes which are:

- sustaining private accumulation and profitability on the one hand while trying to minimise environmental destruction on the other; and secondly,
- maintaining social order and adequate social safety nets in the midst of ecological threats yet ensuring that the latter do not negate profitable capital accumulation.

It will be extremely difficult to achieve one of these goals, let alone all four. We still don't know the scale of job shedding though automation and AI in the next decade or so, but we do know that technological innovation will create many casualties and seriously damage communities. Governments can minimise disruption, pain and political instability by funding costly and extensive social welfare programs that will probably undermine both profitability and the 'work ethic' tied to paid employment. Whatever the political solutions, the latter are extremely difficult to implement by any government that lacks political legitimacy, whether in representative democracies or one-party states. If so, it remains to be seen whether the commonly voiced issue of environmentally sustainable 'just transitions' can be resolved with or without democracy.

Politically, in contrast to movements 'from below', we have two quite different dilemmas confronting governments. Shortly, all governments will be required by domestic and international pressures to embark on deep emissions cuts and other policies that will cause more unemployment rather than more 'green jobs', *unless* 'green jobs' are created in those areas that increase the 'social state', like care work, building better public transport, retrofitting housing for those who cannot afford to do so, providing education and retraining for the unemployed and disadvantaged, improving public health through pollution reduction and so forth. These ecological modernisation options may be compatible with capitalist systems that are both democratic and authoritarian. The crucial question therefore remains: what kind of comprehensive social welfare services and environmentally sustainable economic policies are non-negotiable because they are *incompatible* with both the medium to long-term profitability and viability of capitalist systems as well as with the maintenance of safe biophysical planetary boundaries? In the next chapter I will discuss how the tensions between 'democracy and sustainability' manifest themselves in social welfare policies.

As to movements 'from below', sharp differences already exist between those Western environmentalists and ecological economists who stress sustainability and biodiversity and their equivalents in low-income countries who emphasise social well-being. For instance, Indian environmentalist, Sharachchandra Lele rejects the exclusive focus on sustainability if it means that social justice for hundreds of millions of impoverished villagers and urban residents comes second.[32] He favours combining social justice, biodiversity and sustainability. Although this is not new, as notions of 'environmentalism of the poor' have long been pursued by 'degrowthers' such as Joan Martinez-Alier[33] and eco-socialists, if not by those centre-Left advocates of 'green growth'. Ultimately, Lele comes down on the side of further democratisation and education rather than an explicit political strategy to combat inequality and unsustainability.[34] Thus, he and other advocates of well-being cling to a naïve faith in democratisation as the solution to the world's problems. In the meantime, local villagers, indigenous communities and poor urban dwellers in many countries have to battle against rapacious developers, violent landlords, businesses generating toxic industrial waste and fumes from mines and factories, to mention just a few of the struggles waged for environmental justice.

BETWEEN 'ECOLOGICAL LENINISM' AND 'ANTI-POLITICS'

What strategies are possible to bring about a post-carbon society that advances environmental and social justice? In the Introduction to this book I cited Marx's reference to those who 'timidly conjure up the spirits of the past to help them'.[35] A good example of this borrowing of past slogans, costumes and language' can be seen in 'unreconstructed' Swedish Leninist, Andreas Malm. He makes the valid observation that social democracy has no concept of catastrophe because it believes in incremental steps that are completely inappropriate in a 'situation of chronic emergency'. This leads Malm to declare that it is "incredibly difficult to see how anything other than state power could accomplish the transition required, given that it will be necessary to exert coercive authority against those who want to maintain the status quo."[36] While I agree with this prognosis, we part company over the meaning of 'coercive authority'. It is one thing to argue for the necessity of legislation that coerces businesses to decarbonise rather than letting them voluntarily do so at a snail's pace, and quite another thing to imagine that a Leninist party could achieve sweeping political economic transformation.

Malm regresses to political fantasy when he declares: "The whole strategic direction of Lenin after 1914 was to turn World War I into a fatal blow against capitalism. This is precisely the same strategic orientation we must embrace today – and this is what I mean by ecological Leninism. We must find a way of turning the environmental crisis into a crisis for fossil capital itself."[37] Malm conveniently overlooks the fact that Lenin's strategy of a 'fatal blow against capitalism' was an abysmal failure everywhere, even in Russia where the Czarist regime collapsed without Bolshevik involvement. Moreover, one cannot have 'ecological Leninism' without a vanguard Leninist party strategy and this, as I have argued in Chapter Twelve, is historically obsolete. If Malm is simply promoting the idea of concerted action to transform state policies in the direction of environmental sustainability, then there is no disagreement here. However, he is misguided if he thinks that 'ecological Leninism' will transform the 'crisis of fossil capital' into a socialist revolution. When not promoting his Leninist rhetoric, Malm has made many valid criticisms of the main Swedish parties and their environmental and social policies. Rather than 'ecological Leninism', he supported Corbyn's Labour agenda as far better than the centrist policies pursued by the Swedish Social Democrats and Greens.[38]

Like many other Marxist-Leninist radicals, Malm is caught between the old revolutionary framework and the realisation that this type of politics is utterly ineffective. What may sound clear and effective is in fact a longing for a less complex society than the one we currently inhabit. This nostalgia lingers on in other contexts. German Marxist Ingar Solty is typical of traditional revolutionary Leftists when in an answer to a question about contemporary class struggle states that "social revolution in advanced capitalist societies today depends more on 'wars of fixed positions' and less on 'wars of movement', more on transforming the capitalist state into a democratic state rather than storming the Winter Palace."[39] In other words, strip away the 'revolutionary rhetoric' and one finds that most Marxists across the world struggle for an environmentally sustainable socialist society in very similar fashion to non-Marxists, regardless of the names of the parties or movements they support. This struggle is waged through organised protests, mobilising unions or other social movements, campaigning electorally for Left or green parties and so forth. It is also paradoxical that most radical parties, like centre-Left parties and movements, are engaged not in revolutionary action but in the necessary defence of political and legal institutional processes of 'bourgeois democracy' against far-Right parties and movements who wish to suspend or tear these down.

On the other hand, it is equally necessary to dispel the illusions held by supporters of 'anti-politics' movements such as Extinction Rebellion (XR). On September 1, 2020, XR released a statement that declared:

> Just to be clear we are not a socialist movement. We do not trust any single ideology, we trust the people, chosen by sortition (like jury service) to find the best future for us all through a #CitizensAssembly A banner saying 'socialism or extinction' does not represent us.[40]

The notion that handfuls of selected people in 'Citizen's Assemblies' represent the views of the vast majority of 'the people' is no more credible than the claim by Leninists that the Party represents the views of the working class. While it is certainly possible for valuable ideas to emerge from Assemblies, the path to a post-carbon society is not possible without political organisations mobilising people to directly or indirectly change government policies through either elections or pressure on businesses and other institutions. In pursuing 'anti-politics', XR are doomed to a series of protests with little or no impact on governments in between elections. Whatever emerges from Citizen Assemblies can be quickly ignored (as Macron did in France) or would need to be adopted by parties in the political institutional process. Either way, 'anti-politics' is a dead end and only compounds despair and disillusionment when revealed as ineffective. Neither is it a case of 'socialism or extinction' as socialists such as Mark Montegriffo proclaim in opposition to XR.[41] Socialism is still vastly unpopular just like XR. To campaign on a platform of 'socialism or extinction' is to guarantee that little will be done to solve the climate emergency. The dilemma facing us all is that neither socialism nor forecasts of doomsday will mobilise sufficient numbers of people to make a difference.

Perhaps it is possible to build a non-Communist 'modern prince', a broad-based party (without all the old Left baggage) that is able to manoeuvre and advance a post-carbon transition to a safe climate. It will not be a 'fully sustainable' society, as this is an ongoing process that has to be continually identified and redefined by each generation. Nevertheless, it will have a range of socio-economic policies that directly speaks to current needs for greater equality and social justice. This is a promising start if it at least diverts us from the current disastrous political trajectory and helps build popular support for more substantial future changes. After all, parties will always be with us so long as there are state institutions that need to be controlled and made to serve social needs.

By contrast, most degrowth movements are anti-statist, quasi-anarchist or founded on self-management principles that are politically marginal and ineffective. The values and ideas of degrowth movements, XR and many other concerned groups need to be engaged with to help create new political organisations. We need degrowth objectives to be advanced by movements and parties that take contemporary state institutions seriously, not just as apparatuses to be opposed but as the basis of new political arrangements that can institutionalise and facilitate social justice and sustainability. I am therefore certainly not against having a strong political party/movement to simultaneously combat Right-wing policies and advance social justice and sustainability policies. However, if this party is neither an updated form of Leninism nor a fragile or incoherent coalition of movements such as a 'social bloc', it will need to mobilise and combine social and political constituencies by either detaching these from their commitment to existing parties and/or attract all those who are currently politically disengaged.

In the current interregnum of uncertain political choices and strategies, it is easy to change one's mind on the choice between developing strong parties or strong movements. Actually, as we know, few strong social change parties can be successful without strong social movements and grass roots action to back their agendas. There is a valid argument that all progressive social change first required mass mobilisation of social movements and that these should continue to bring about a new post-carbon social order rather than rely on cautious vote-orientated 'catch-all' parties. This strategic position is countered by those who argue that political energy must focus solely on decarbonisation policies in the short-term given that emissions reduction is an urgent priority and anti-capitalist struggles or degrowth are still too unpopular or unfamiliar. Then again, others advocate that all supporters of ecologically sustainable socio-economic policies should boycott all elections. Advocates of this 'anti-politics' claim that legitimacy needs to be completely withdrawn from the existing failed electoral and legislative system by mass electoral boycotting of all centre, Left and green parties for it to be thoroughly cleansed and democratised. In response, opponents of this 'anti-politics' strategy point out that this will only consolidate the power of the Right for years to come rather than leading to new political parties that replace mainstream centre-Left and green parties. At an international level, some environmentalists believe that it is necessary to obtain the support of authoritarian governments in powerful countries such as China in order to help enact international treaties. Hence, it is suggested that we should not alienate these governments by campaigning for human rights and democracy.

Posing such strategies and priorities is very divisive. It can, however, help sharpen the minds of social activists about which policies and strategies are best pursued and what are the current possibilities of forging a new kind of politics at local and international levels. On the other hand, some argue that both electoral politics and extra-parliamentary movements are already too fragmented and that specific campaigns, for instance, on human rights, for jobs and better working conditions or against racism, will go on regardless of climate emergency priorities decided upon by other movements. What is unclear is whether most countries are currently stuck in the era of disunited, 'post-strategic politics' that developed from the 1960s onwards and that it is every movement for itself rather than waging joint campaigns. However, one can certainly point to numerous protests and campaigns where a range of social movements have joined together. Besides, democratisation has been both the necessary basis of political action and also the process by which agreement over priorities have often been impossible to achieve.

We are no longer in a historical period where people will tolerate being told by a single individual what is the 'correct path' and 'what is to be done'. Our mistakes and successes are collective mistakes and successes. While we know that 'green growth' agendas will not address deep-seated forms of inequality, we also know that degrowth and eco-socialist movements are marginalised due to lack of political power or influence. In this situation, could the lack of adequate social welfare and jobs be combined with sustainability issues to forge a new political majority? This idea is hardly new but the policies to achieve this broad strategy have changed in recent years. In the next chapter I will discuss what an updated strategy of the 'social state' means and whether it is a viable way forward.

15. DECOMMODIFIED SOCIAL ALTERNATIVES TO WELFARE STATE CAPITALISM

THE CONFLICT BETWEEN 'DEMOCRACY AND SUSTAINABILITY' manifests itself in capitalist countries with representative democracies in the ongoing political struggles over whether a future political economy of 'democratic sustainability' is possible or not. In undemocratic countries, the issue of environmental sustainability is simultaneously a problem for governments of how to solve ecological problems without conceding domestic demands for democratic rights and also how to maintain international relations with countries that democratically implement new environmental protection legislation affecting trade and investment. A particular major problem for both democratic and authoritarian regimes is how to fund and provide alternative universal services and income without relying on the revenue flowing from environmentally unsustainable production and consumption. The question of properly funding an adequate 'social state' without transgressing the biophysical planetary boundaries required for sustainability is crucial here. As to advocates of social revolution, they continue to provide few specific indications of how a post-capitalist society would organise socio-economic practices without replicating the problems of former Communist countries or contemporary capitalist systems. And all this even before we get to the crucial problem of how a post-capitalist democracy could be made compatible with environmental sustainability.

Turning to the critics of capitalist production and consumption growth rates, for decades there has been an inadequate public discussion over how *not* to kill the capitalist goose (or economic system) that lays the golden eggs of taxation revenue *even before* the transition to an alternative post-capitalist economy is established. It is this controversial issue that takes us back to where this book began. In what follows, I propose to show why we need to move beyond both existing 'welfare states' and the narrow views of decommodification put forward by radical critics of 'welfare capitalism'. I will also examine various welfare systems from around the globe in low and middle-income countries that do not conform to the conventional picture of 'welfare states' in OECD countries. Finally, I will outline feasible sustainable alternatives to existing failed and inadequate capitalist welfare regimes.

WELFARE AND MARKETS – FROM 1795 TO CONTEMPORARY CONFLICTS

In Book One, I analysed the serious inadequacies and flaws in Karl Polanyi's conception of the conflict between 'capitalism and democracy'. Polanyi's thesis outlining the establishment of the capitalist market in the late eighteenth and early nineteenth centuries involved an account of the 1795 Poor Law in Speenhamland in County Berkshire. This Poor Law lasted until 1834 and provided poor relief to able-bodied men and not just to the infirm, aged and dependent. In the same year, François-Noël 'Gracchus' Babeuf and his fellow Jacobin conspirators in the Society of Equals met in Paris and went beyond Robespierre's policies in their plan for an insurrection to establish a quasi-socialist republic based on equality and happiness.[1] Despite widespread support across Paris, the revolt was crushed in 1796 and Babeuf and others were executed in 1797. The conflicting responses to poverty and inequality by the Poor Law and by the Society of Equals would go on to help shape social policy right up until the present day.

From Marx and Engels onwards, revolutionaries would praise Babeuf and company as early originators of communism who showed that poverty and inequality could not be eradicated until private wealth was redistributed. On the other hand, Speenhamland had a much more confused historical legacy. Conservative critics of the Poor Law such as Thomas Malthus and David Ricardo would attack it for fostering laziness, idleness and sexual promiscuity. Joseph Townsend and Malthus believed the provision of poor relief bread would enable populations to breed and outstrip food supply. Without hunger and work discipline or frugality, social discipline would break down, including children not waiting to get married in order to have sex. By contrast, Marx and Engels criticised Speenhamland for immiserating the life of workers as landowners paid workers less and relied on Poor Law to subsidise reduced wage levels. Instead of a minimum floor level of wages,

Speenhamland set a maximum that kept both workers and the unemployed suppressed. Polanyi also agreed that the Poor Law prevented the development of a capitalist market by not forcing the impoverished off the land to seek higher wages in the towns. But he added that the Anti-Combination laws prevented workers from organising to win better wages and conditions, thus ensuring misery.[2]

What is the relevance of Speenhamland and Babeuf's Society of Equals to social policy in the twenty-first century and the central issue of 'democracy versus sustainability'? Given that Babeuf's call for revolutionary insurrection is a tradition and strategy that has virtually disappeared in developed capitalist countries and almost disappeared in low and middle-income capitalist societies, we are left with new updated versions of Speenhamland – minus its historical social conditions and paternalism. These are now called universal basic income (UBI) and other such proposals. Polanyi used Speenhamland to criticise the advocates of self-regulated markets and defend the need for state intervention to help 'protect society' against the ravages of 'the market'. Yet, as Fred Block and Margaret Somers reveal, Polanyi's account (like Marx's and Engels) was based on flawed historical sources that did not incorporate the criticisms of other historians who advised him that Speenhamland was far from typical in England. Importantly, historians in recent decades have used additional sources to show that the Poor Law had actually aided rather than degraded those receiving poor relief.[3]

When President Richard Nixon's 1969 proposed version of basic income called the Family Assistance Plan was being drafted, both Nixon and his advisors were alerted to Polanyi's analysis of the Poor Law. The White House staff now read passages from *The Great Transformation* to see whether Nixon's proposed legislation would have the same so-called negative impact as Speenhamland. Despite taking into consideration Polanyi's critical analysis, Nixon pressed on with his legislation. It was ultimately defeated by Democrats in the Senate because, among other things, the proposed legislation offered extremely low assistance to families. A range of free marketeers and many conservatives were also opposed to Nixon's scheme for reasons that echoed Malthus and Townsend views plus a strong dose of American Right-wing racism.[4]

The move from Christian concepts of charity (the deserving and undeserving poor) to contemporary universal social rights has been a rocky road of progress and setbacks. During the 1940s, both during the war and the immediate post-1945 years, considerable progress was made in introducing a more extensive 'welfare state'. The Beveridge Report of 1942 was part of the theoretical ammunition that laid the basis for the Atlee Labour government's welfare and health reforms. Despite Beveridge influencing the Roosevelt administration, neither saw the creation of the welfare state in terms of universal human rights.[5] Roosevelt's 1944 State of the Union speech talked of the right of all to food, shelter, education and health service, but his New Deal policies opposed universal health care and the expansion of the welfare state (see Chapter Three). The United Nations 1948 Universal Declaration of Human Rights was an expression of world-wide demands for an end to inequality, oppression and poverty. For all its advances, it was, as Alastair Davidson describes in detail, a document that has been adopted in limited fashion because it left member nation states to enforce these rights. Hence nationalism has triumphed over universal rights in practice.[6] The dark history of the second half of the twentieth century and beginning of the twenty-first century attests to how widespread are the continued violent abuses of human rights.

British liberal sociologist T. H. Marshall expounded his theory of the connection between social rights and citizenship in 1949.[7] While his linking of the two remains important, Marshall's work was characterised by a number of glaring silences, a failure to include full social rights for women and an absence of any discussion of how citizenship in the UK could be compatible with the violation of the human rights of over eight hundred million subjects living under British dictatorial or paternal rule in the colonies of the British Empire.[8] In fact, seventy years after Marshall's lectures on social rights and citizenship, the vast majority of former British, French, Dutch, Belgian, Portuguese and American colonies in Africa, Asia, Latin America, the Caribbean and the Middle East either have no 'welfare state' worth its name, nor secure democratic social rights.

The glaring level of poverty, inequality and the all too widespread practice of political repression across the world of course makes the goal of 'democracy and sustainability' particularly difficult to achieve, let alone ensuring that the former is mutually compatible and viable with the latter. It is bad enough that a chasm exists between social welfare conditions for low and middle-income people within OECD countries, for example, the low expenditure and social protection in the US, Turkey, Chile, South Korea, Mexico or Greece compared with the more supportive income and social provisions in Sweden, France and Norway. This chasm widens dramatically when we consider the minimal or pre-welfare state conditions in more than 150 non-OECD countries. It is clear that the absence of adequate social welfare states constitutes a great barrier to achieving the goal of a sustainable democratic world. At present, however, the two parallel and dominant discourses on 'welfare states' and 'environment states' can appear decidedly parochial and myopic in their main focus on Europe and the way they ignore the global socio-economic chasm discussed above.

Polanyi also plays an indirect role in the continuation of this pervasive parochialism through his theoretical influence over one of the most widely used frameworks for understanding different 'welfare states' of the past thirty years, namely, Gøsta Esping-Andersen's *The Three Worlds of Welfare Capitalism*.[9] Ironically, Esping-Andersen's work was published in 1990 at the fall of Communism in East European countries, the expansion of capitalist market practices across the world and the rise of neoliberal restructuring of the 'three worlds of welfare capitalism'. Combining a mixture of neo-Marxist, social democratic and Polanyian insights, Esping-Andersen offered some very valuable accounts of three groups of countries: Anglo-American liberal capitalist countries (including the US, UK, Australia, Canada and New Zealand); the social democratic Scandinavian bloc; and the conservative corporatist countries such as Germany, Austria, France and Italy. Each of the liberal, social democratic and corporatist types of regimes had welfare delivery based on means tested or universal benefits or promoted religiously influenced welfare that upheld conservative concepts of the family.

Recall that both Marx and Polanyi argued that capitalism reduced labour power to a commodity, but that human labour was not like other commodities as it could not be detached from the worker, hence the need to have a certain level of *non-market* support conditions and social relations to ensure that workers could live and continue labouring. It was Claus Offe, and not Esping-Andersen, who originally developed the concept of 'decommodification' during the 1970s. According to Offe, workers in the private monopoly sector and competitive small business sector were commodified as they had their labour power bought and sold at prices determined by the level of political struggles or absence of trade unions in various countries. Closely related, workers in the public sector are remunerated according to political-administrative conditions *indirectly* determined by the market. However, the sector of 'residual labour power' is the extreme pole of decommodification. The 'residual labour' sector is made up of the unemployed, pensioners, college students, prisoners, drafted soldiers and all other categories of people outside the labour market who receive social benefits or payments that are politically determined and not mediated by markets. In short, all those people outside the labour market receive income that does not correspond to some relationship between the work performed and remuneration paid.[10]

What is the socio-political significance of the level of decommodification in a particular country? Influenced by Marx and Polanyi,[11] Offe argued that in early capitalist societies, welfare was mainly provided by families, charities, religious organisations and other non-state bodies. By the first half of the twentieth century, welfare was transformed into legal entitlements provided by states, thus ensuring that social benefits or non-commodified support systems became increasingly politicised. The extension of universal voting, parliamentary government and recognition of trade union interests has resulted, Offe claimed, in legal welfare entitlements becoming relatively 'rigid' or even irreversible.[12] This view from the 1970s turned out to be premature in the light of neoliberal assaults on welfare during the past thirty years (especially in the US). Offe also underestimated the market-mediation of welfare benefits by business groups and their political allies to ensure that decommodification was strictly controlled or reduced. Before publishing his classic on welfare capitalism in 1990, Esping-Andersen had already been influenced by Offe and James O'Connor and wrote for the neo-Marxist journal *Kapitalistate* that was published during the 1970s and early 1980s.[13] He took Offe's analysis of decommodification and developed it into a detailed study of the 'three worlds' of welfare capitalism. Accordingly:

> The variability of welfare-state evolution reflects competing responses to pressures for decommodification. To understand the concept, decommodification should not be confused with the complete eradication of labour as a commodity; it is not an issue of all or nothing. Rather, the concept refers to the degree to which individuals, or families, can uphold a socially acceptable standard of living independently of market participation.[14]

In Book Two, I argued that there is no uniform size of the 'social state' or level of social expenditure and environmentally sustainable policies as a percentage of GDP beyond which capitalist political economic orders are threatened and begin to decompose. What is tolerable and beneficial for businesses in Norway or France may be regarded as beyond the pale by capitalists and governments in the US, Japan or Australia. Why is this lack of a clear tipping point so important? Because any transition to an environmentally sustainable post-capitalist society would almost certainly involve a process of decommodification. Hence, any specific political economic 'just transition' will encounter quite distinct levels of hostility or toleration from

businesses and conservative political forces depending on a country's political history and the current balance of class forces in particular societies.

Indeed, it would be a big mistake to think that a nominal increase in
expenditure on health, housing, income support, social insurance protection
for the unemployed, child-care and aged-care or retirement pensions automatically leads to decommodification. Certainly, it is preferable to have a
society spend a larger proportion of GDP on social expenditure. Nevertheless, comparing nation states by their level of fiscal spending on welfare
services is a crude device that only tells us what these countries allocate
rather than the quality of particular services, and especially whether they
uphold market practices or undermine capitalist commodity relations. What
was perceived before the 1980s as a threat to capitalist relations, namely,
growing state social expenditure that loosened the dependence of most
people on private markets for daily care, sustenance and income, has been
largely halted or even significantly scaled back in some OECD countries.

Both Offe and Esping-Andersen had a narrow view of decommodification
because they wrote before the marketisation of social welfare became more
evident after the early 1980s (even though Esping-Andersen published his
book in 1990). Hence, they mainly viewed decommodification through the
prism of the labour market, namely, whether one had to sell one's labour
power to survive or was outside the labour market and on welfare benefits.
Importantly, they paid inadequate attention to the other aspect of decommodification, that is, whether health, social care, education, pensions and
other services were delivered as non-market, decommodified social relations
or transformed into profit-making commodified services. Today, many
former non-market public welfare services such as health, housing, transport,
aged-care, child-care and other services have either been commodified
through privatisation or the *de facto* privatisation of the latter via outsourcing
the delivery and provision of these services to private businesses. Families
and individuals have thus incurred higher costs and also continue to be
subjected to harsher profit-making market criteria.

Financial institutions and private providers of everything from job
retraining to medical care are also able to siphon off scarce public fiscal
resources in the form of contract fees per 'case load' and tax subsidies, all in
the name of 'market efficiency'. The outcome is usually inferior and less
secure services, such as reducing the number and quality of care providers
(often less costly casual employees or contract case workers, cleaners, private
prison guards and so forth) while increasing the number of patients, the aged
and others in need of care. Covid-19 revealed the disastrous death rates due

to lack of adequate public health system capacity in the US and especially the large outsourcing to private providers of services in countries such as Australia, the UK, France, the US and Sweden employing low-paid precarious labour in health systems and aged-care.[15] Retirement income or pensions are now divided between those with remaining large public contributory schemes but growing private pension systems (such as Germany, France, Norway, Italy), and a range of private pension systems (in Anglo-American countries, Switzerland, the Netherlands and elsewhere) which account for up to 42% of pension assets alongside public systems. For example, the 1981 privatised Chilean system is highly unpopular, fosters increased poverty due to years of poor market earnings plus ineligibility criteria, all compounded by the Covid-19 economic slump.

With over $USD45 trillion globally in private pension assets in 2019, pension funds now play an increasingly powerful role in equity markets.[16] Workers are thus becoming more dependent on fluctuating share market performance as well their pension fund's property, bond and infrastructure investments. Most new workers are no longer entitled to decommodified 'defined benefits' pensions upon retirement, as private and public pension fund benefits are often determined by market gains or losses.

In other words, decommodification entails far more than whether a person is reliant on the private capitalist labour market or not. Today, decommodification will only occur if the social relations between the providers of care and social income are not constrained by market disciplinary measures. We are now in the era of pseudo-care and time limits on social benefits that do not undermine market relations. Notable examples include the quick 'turnover' of patients and larger numbers of children to each carer in private child-care, or contract providers of dead-end job retraining schemes for the unemployed who are treated as little more than new commodities. Most contemporary private or public welfare services do not aim *primarily* to improve the welfare and wellbeing of the recipients, despite the good intentions and demanding work of many underpaid and overworked staff. If these services do not earn profit for the private contractors, then contracts are not renewed, and severely understaffed public services are required to come in to fill the gap by trying to provide care for those in need.

Consequently, the coming struggle in many countries will be over the extent to which vitally needed social welfare services free of private market criteria can be won by political movements. Creating a 'social space' for decommodification, despite opposition from businesses and conservative political forces is also highly relevant to the future character of either 'green growth' or sustainability as will shortly become clearer. In the meantime, if we are to understand the wider picture of 'democracy versus sustainability', we must recognise the following aspects of welfare state regimes. Initially, we must come to terms with why Esping-Andersen's framework is historically obsolete. Then we need to ask why the lack of adequate social welfare for the vast majority of the world's population prevents the realisation of democratic sustainability. Finally, our political responses need to be structured in ways relevant to the current new stage of capitalist development. This unfolding new stage of development means that the old social democratic policies of yesteryear as well as the prevailing mixture of neoliberal and paternalist authoritarian forms of enterprise-based welfare are grossly inadequate and unreliable. They both serve to fuel rather than solve the scale and character of the twin calamities of inequality and dangerous unsustainable growth.

OLD 'WORLDS' OF WELFARE AND NEW REGIONS OF NO WELFARE

Well before we entered a new period of capitalist development characterised by financial crisis, austerity measures, escalating environmental problems, a slowdown in world trade and the stalling of rapid industrialisation of low and middle-income countries, there were already a range of criticisms made of Esping-Andersen's 'three worlds' framework. Feminists argued that he had ignored the care work and domestic labour of women in households and the transformation of families and labour processes by focussing on male workers.[17] Others devoted articles and books to challenging his ideal types and how they ignored many countries, mismatched societies by including them in one or other of the 'three worlds' and used measures of decommodification that did not reveal the true nature or extent of how particular welfare systems actually worked.

In addition, some argued that welfare regimes did not correspond to the ideology of liberalism or social democracy as most countries had mixtures of different delivery systems depending on whether it was the health system, unemployment insurance or education. Although other critics pointed out that Esping-Anderson's model ignored Mediterranean countries and those in Eastern Europe or the 'productivist' Confucian welfare states such as Taiwan, Japan, Singapore or South Korea,[18] most of these criticisms were 'internal' debates within academic comparative social policy forums rather than concerned with the transition from capitalism to post-capitalism.[19]

Like the 'Varieties of Capitalism' school that was closely linked to welfare policy debates inaugurated by Esping-Andersen's work,[20] most discussions of social policy were geared to social democratic reform rather than the crucial issue of the connection between socio-economic growth and environmental sustainability. In short, they did not focus on how social welfare could be greatly improved without relying on a capitalist growth system that was environmentally unsustainable.

Crucially, it is not enough to point to a range of countries in the wider capitalist world which do not conform to the 'three worlds' framework. If most welfare analysts largely accept the present political economic framework as only amenable to small piece meal incremental reforms, this will leave major problems unresolved. Creating another ideal type or another list of countries that differ from Esping-Andersen's list is not what is needed to advance social change in the direction of decommodifying social relations.[21] Instead, we need to identify why the analyses like that of Esping-Andersen's and his earlier critics belong to a historical phase that is now largely irrelevant to people living under quite different regimes in the present-day world.

Even if we were to re-examine the original welfare regimes that Esping-Andersen and others analysed in the past three decades, many have witnessed dramatic changes. Since 1980s, the 'social democratic regimes' have watered down their former features following the election of Right-wing neoliberal governments.[22] Conservative countries have become less socially conservative due to feminist pressures to reject previous church-influenced family and gender welfare guidelines and also because businesses now employ more women. Meanwhile, the 'liberal' countries have become even more market-orientated, as they have eroded or outsourced welfare services established in the decades prior to the 1980s. Hence, thirty years later, the debates surrounding Esping-Andersen's 'three worlds' looks very dated. This is even more the case when it comes to the rise of China, India and other Asian-Pacific countries. The problem is that many of these 'emergent markets' have very poor, undeveloped welfare systems and yet they are being increasingly pressured to simultaneously decarbonise their societies and also take care of hundreds of millions of market casualties neglected by exploitative businesses.

Opposition to existing welfare capitalist regimes continues in socialist, green degrowth and other movements across the world which propose alternatives such as universal basic income schemes, the decentralisation of welfare to local non-bureaucratic community organisations and universal basic services schemes. Whether all, some or none of these proposals can be realised in coming years is not just a matter of the level of political mobilisation possible in particular countries. Political movements and policy makers need to recognise and account for the following political economic factors.

Firstly, why models of advanced welfare regimes such as those in Scandinavian countries or France (that were developed in earlier historical periods under more favourable conditions) are irrelevant to most low and middle-income countries. Secondly, what the differences between the way capitalist and Communist countries fund and establish eligibility criteria in their welfare regimes tell us about the massive financial and organisational challenges confronting advocates of alternative social states.

On the first point, Scandinavian countries have long offered more comprehensive social welfare to their tiny populations and have also been good international 'citizens' in contributing higher percentages of their GDP as foreign aid. However, they are small countries and carry little weight at a geopolitical level within the wider world. Characterised by high levels of unionisation of workers, social democratic parties that remain or were in office for long periods of time developed a highly skilled workforce, sophisticated manufacturing, large fossil fuel assets (Norway) and benefit from close proximity to Germany and the large EU market. These Scandinavian countries have forged favourable historical conditions that few other OECD countries, let alone most low and middle-income countries can replicate. Even the socio-economic disparities between other northern EU countries and poorer Balkan member countries such as Romania, Bulgaria, Croatia and Greece (leaving aside non-members Albania, Montenegro and Serbia) are wide and unbridgeable in the medium term unless there is radical change within the EU.

As the dynamo or lynch pin of the EU, Germany refuses to support an EU-wide 'social state' that transitions to far greater social equality. While other EU national governments also support Germany's conservative fiscal policies, the dominance of Right-wing domestic forces in Germany, France, the Netherlands, Italy and Austria means that the prospects for even a Green New Deal with a substantial increase in the 'social state', let alone radical alternatives to existing welfare policies, is less than fifty-fifty at best in the next decade. Formulated before the Covid-19 crisis, the official 2019 EU Green New Deal is a ten-year strategy that promises significant change but only commits less than a third of the funding needed. Environmental movements have heavily criticised this EU proposal for failing to target a large reduction in the material footprint of wealthy member states.[23] Not only are the figures very rubbery, but member countries are divided over emission targets and the modest jobs and social welfare programs proposed for the next ten years. We are unlikely to see the bridging of the wide gap in income, welfare services and neglected infrastructure within the EU, especially in Southern and Eastern Europe, unless there is a shift to Left/Green governments or the scale of recession/depression necessitates major policy changes. Once again, the only language conservative EU policy makers understand is the threat from 'the street' and/or the electoral success of anti-EU parties that could wipe away the seventy-five-year old European project.

While the residues of Esping-Andersen's 'three worlds' are still visible in less than half the member states of the EU, the future of Europe will require a further erosion of at least two of the 'three worlds' (following Brexit). Either the EU becomes even more marketised and the last vestiges of social democratic and corporatist welfare disappear, or the EU is democratised, and social and labour processes are made much more equal across the EU. If the EU as a 'social state' becomes the dominant operative model, then national criteria of welfare eligibility would need to be broken down as EU citizens and residents become entitled to social benefits, such as protective social insurance and other supranational services regardless of where they reside. This would mean a fundamental reorganisation of national, local and supranational welfare budgetary allocations with profound consequences on labour processes in terms of wages, social insurance contributions and the relation between state institutions and business sectors.

Such a 'social state' could not be introduced without a significant loss of private corporate and small and medium business power. It could also not be introduced without sidestepping the German Federal Constitutional Court's ruling in May 2020 that deemed the German Bundesbank may no longer participate in the European Central Bank's Public Sector Purchase Program. Without a future German government being able to legally manoeuvre ways to help fund the EU's socio-economic packages or the EU increasing its own borrowing and revenue raising methods such as new EU-wide taxes, there will be no major transformation of EU social programs.[24]

Outside the EU, there is no African country that has a comparable welfare state to those in Northern Europe. Some countries such as Ghana have the formal legislative commitment to providing health, education and other social welfare, but not the resources. In 2004, Lesotho introduced the old age pension for people 70 and over. However, with an average life expectancy of 44 (and still only 54 years in 2020) this reform is largely meaningless for most of its citizens. From Botswana to Uganda, Mozambique to Nigeria or Angola to Libya, African countries *exclude* far more of the total 1.2

billion people on the continent from social benefits than the minority who are able to access their woefully under-resourced social programmes. Add numerous civil wars, climate induced drought and a catalogue of debilitating diseases from HIV to malaria and tuberculosis, and there is no possibility of these low-income countries imitating European social welfare programs without massive foreign aid, cleansing corrupt governments and a cessation of civil wars.

On the second point, it is necessary to consider what capitalist and Communist funding of welfare tells us about future challenges. In order to evaluate whether a particular country has the capacity or political will to make the 'just transition' to an environmentally sustainable and adequate social welfare system, it is important to understand the connection between existing social welfare systems and the dominant political economic institutional practices within which they are embedded. One of the key differences in the quantity and quality of social welfare between different capitalist and Communist countries is to be found in the both the sources of revenue and whether their services and social insurance income are provided by central or sub-national governments or by state-owned or private enterprises. Within OECD countries, there are also significant differences between the proportion of total annual revenue collected coming from *direct* taxes on wages and company profits as opposed to *indirect* taxes, charges and regulatory fees such as consumption taxes, license fees, pay roll taxes and so forth. Also critical are the presence or absence of national compulsory contributory systems covering pensions, unemployment insurance or health care. Some countries have lower direct taxes but very high consumption taxes that are highly regressive as they fall most heavily on low and middle-income people. Any strategy to provide a universal basic income or a range of essential basic services must closely examine the political tolerance and economic capacity of sections of the population or diverse industries to support significantly increased revenue collection in the form of direct or indirect taxes.

By contrast, the old Communist system in the USSR had a welfare system that was heavily based on industrial enterprises and collective farms. The non-independent Soviet trade unions helped administer welfare provision alongside enterprise management. Workers and their families were provided with health services, pensions, holidays at communal resorts and other such social provisions. Standards of living were low due to low wages. But direct taxes were low, as also public transport fares, rent, utilities and other basic service charges. For those not connected to an enterprise, there was a minimal government pension which was not enough to survive on and gave rise to extensive poverty, including many beggars. The Soviet 'social wage' cost enterprises about 25% of their labour costs. In the decades before the collapse of the Soviet Union, the 'social wage' increased faster than the money wage. During the 1990s, labour costs increased to 50% as the collapse of the USSR and the transition to market capitalism put tremendous pressure on both old Soviet enterprises and millions of workers to survive. Growing food on small residential plots also constituted up to 50 per cent of the post-Soviet 'social wage' when wages fell, a devalued currency impoverished people, life expectancy declined, and social convulsion swept former Communist countries in the ten to twenty years after 1989 and 1991. Millions of people in the former USSR and Eastern European countries were made destitute when their enterprises collapsed and cost them not only their jobs but also their social welfare, accommodation and increased prices for essential utilities and services.

The lesson here is that any non-universal social welfare system based on a person's employment (or former employment) at an enterprise can turn into a disaster once the enterprise closes or is privatised. Apart from the more extensive provision of social welfare by enterprises in the former Soviet Union that one should *not* imitate, less comprehensive but specific employer-tied social benefits, such as key aspects of the US health system are also vehicles of inequality. Under this patchwork of benefits and entitlements, many workers may get health insurance from their employers (so long as they are employed), but it leaves millions of others with no protection or inadequate health coverage. Consequently, a social welfare system that is democratic and universal is preferable. The crucial problem is how to fund such a system and ensure that the revenue it needs does not come from environmentally unsustainable economic growth. More will be said on this shortly.

When we look at the possibilities of sustainable welfare systems in China and India that account for almost 40% of the world's population, the existence of enterprise-based welfare continues to deliver major inequalities. These two massive countries are completely different from Esping-Andersen's 'three worlds' of welfare capitalism. It is not just that the vast majority of India's population have no adequate universal welfare system. This is true of the US as well. However, the standard of living in India is far lower. Caught between relying on meagre family and communal support in thousands of poor villages, barely surviving on the streets or in the urban slums while working in the large informal sector, or fortunate enough to get a job in the formal private and public sector, India is a social *disorder* of daily degradation, deep layers of discrimination, violence and prejudice. The country somehow manages to survive despite widespread shocking poverty and hope-lessness for hundreds of millions of people.

Governments in Mexico, Brazil, Iran, Egypt, Tunisia and other countries have paid cash transfers or subsidies for fuel and energy rather than a universal basic income (UBI) to families, some in return for ensuring school attendance, immunisation against diseases and other requirements. Riots have ensued in Ecuador, Chile and other countries when these subsidies were removed or reduced. The Indian government's 2016-17 Economic Survey proposed a targeted UBI, to minimise existing misallocation of funds and corruption (about twenty per cent of eligible people fail to receive their tiny government support). However, this targeted UBI would have been a replacement for most food, fuel and other subsidies going to the poor rather than an additional and more generous payment.[25] If existing payments-in-kind have failed to reach millions due to corruption and administrative ineffi-ciencies, how will a UBI be paid if most Indians do not have a bank account? Moreover, this absolutely meagre income equivalent of just 90 British pounds, not a month but per year, to 75% of the poorest people (not even a universal income), would have cost about 5% of India's GDP if funded without cutting other goods and income subsidies. This is affordable but is no solution to a social system based on a range of systemic injustices and institutionalised discrimination.

CHINA'S FUTURE AND THE 'SOCIAL STATE'

If India is the world's 'largest democracy' in name rather than in practice, China, as Daniel Vukovich has argued, is *not* a society in transition towards a liberal market democracy.[26] This 'political orientalism' practised by Western liberals misrecognises the historical origins and character of Chinese Communist institutions and relations as 'illiberalism'. Instead, China needs to be understood within its own political cultural terms, as it never had a liberal system, even decades before the Communists came to power in 1949. China has global economic interests, but it has no desire or ability to repli-cate the history of Western imperialist military and colonial conquest. Richard Smith argues that while China is not a capitalist society like America,

> there's plenty of capitalism in China today: there's state capitalism, crony capitalism, gangster capitalism, normal capitalism – China's got

them all. China has more billionaires than the US; many state-owned industries produce extensively for market, and the majority of the workforce are self-employed or work for private companies. Even so, it's not a capitalist economy, at least not mainly a capitalist economy. It's best described as a hybrid bureaucratic collectivist-capitalist economy in which the bureaucratic collectivist state sector is over-whelmingly dominant. China's Communist Party rulers do not own their economy privately like capitalists. The state owns the bulk of the economy and CCP owns the state – collectively. The market does not organise most production in China.[27]

In this massive society where national planning prevails, the conse-quences of a 'hybrid bureaucratic collectivist-capitalist economy' are ecologi-cally disastrous. It is not just that China's industrial development has come at a shocking price of domestic environmental catastrophe, but that it is also 'cooking the planet' with its hyper development agenda driving dangerous emissions. Smith calls this system the 'engine of environmental collapse'. However, there are also obvious signs that China is moving away from just relying on earlier forms of dirty, hazardous production. The rapid growth of a 'cleaner' digital economy in financial, health, education and other services has driven urban employment[28] but also led to higher numbers of younger 'independent professionals' working with inadequate social protection.

Despite major socio-economic changes during the past forty years, both India and China still have hundreds of millions of extremely poor people, especially in rural areas. As the Hong Kong based *China Labour Bulletin* observes:

> The problems in China's social security system can be traced back to two key events: The break-up of the state-run economy, which had provided urban workers with an "iron rice bowl" (employment, hous-ing, healthcare and pension), and the introduction of the one-child policy in the 1980s, which meant that parents could no longer rely on a large extended family to look after them in their old age. In other words, as the economy developed and liberalised in the 1990s and 2000s, both the state and social structures that had supported workers in their old age, ill-health and during times of economic hard-ship gradually vanished, leaving a huge vacuum to fill.[29]

China's future ability to develop a comprehensive social welfare system is also closely tied to the central government's ability to transform the relationship between rural and urban socio-economic relations within the context of a 'mixed economy' of state-owned enterprises and an extensive private sector.

In 2020, it is clear that China has conspicuously failed to fill the vacuum left by the demise of the 'iron rice bowl'. As a so-called 'socialist society with Chinese characteristics', it forged the greatest industrial development in human history but still failed to create a universal social welfare system for its people. Instead, China has a range of state-provided and enterprise-provided social insurance, health and other services that are governed by employment, residency, age and other criteria. These diverse entitlement schemes have institutionalised widespread inequality as hundreds of millions of people continue to be caught between entitlements according to their status as permanent urban residents, transient migrant contract workers or small land-owning residents in rural communities. Like the internal passport system in the former USSR, China retains a version of this divisive system. Several key factors determine the deeply unequal conditions of either insecurity or well-being of the Chinese people.

Firstly, their residential registration status or *hukou* is all important as this determines whether urban residents receive social benefits and welfare from their employer. Rural migrant workers are excluded from these urban benefits even though they may be long-term residents and regularly employed. Instead, they have user rights over collectively owned land in their rural towns and villages. Hundreds of millions of migrant workers fear losing their entitlements to rural land without obtaining *hukou* status in cities. In response, the Communist Party decided in 2014 to increase urban residents from 54% to 60% of China's approximately 1,430 million people by 2020. Of these, 100 million more urban residents with urban *hukou* would be raised from 35% of the total working population to 45% thus shifting these people permanently to urban areas.[30]

Secondly, China has a number of social welfare funds that cover housing, pensions, health care and so forth. These are based on contributions made by workers, employers and central or provincial governments that entitle workers to services and income according to the years of contributions made and other eligibility criteria. What nominally looks good on paper in providing degrees of welfare is far from the grim reality experienced by tens of millions of people. This is due to many private employers fraudulently avoiding contributing their legal requirements, provincial governments deliberately or neglectfully failing to enforce legislation for years on end, hospitals woefully underfunded or corruptly selling services and medicines to those who can afford to pay, and numerous other such widespread erosions of a patchwork system that is inherently flawed.[31]

Thirdly, and closely tied to the first two points is the incompatible dynamics driving the public and private sectors that has produced conflict in urban and rural areas. Labour law analyst, Mary Gallagher, points out that:

> The two leading causes of social unrest in China are labour disputes and rural land disputes. These disputes are usually analysed and considered as discrete problems, each related to the respective dysfunctions of the urban workplace and rural local governments. However, the two are closely intertwined. The declining access to land security among rural residents drives the increasing demands and expectations of rural migrant workers. As access to land security decreases, demands for social security climb. Farmers pushed out of villages by land expropriation must seek out jobs and employment security in cities to replace what they have lost in their hometowns.[32]

Here we have the social security system of the most populous country in the world that directly pits the growth of its state planned capitalist economy against the security of its population and the environmental sustainability of the whole society. The more that workers lose their land and sustenance due to provincial governments failing to provide adequate social welfare and employment while permitting property developers (in conjunction with local officials) to seize land and transform ecological habitats into concrete towers, the more hundreds of millions seek employment in cities but are denied access to social benefits. Once in the cities, many of those with *hukou* status are robbed of their entitlements by private businesses which are increasingly geared to exploitative practices and the cutting of labour and social welfare costs. This is a dynamic that has explosive consequences for the whole world. Unless, both the Chinese central government and provincial governments can institute and enforce a non-corrupt nationwide universal social welfare system that provides workers and their families with adequate entitlements, the greater the danger of major socially and politically explosive disturbances.

The Chinese government now faces the need to break the cycle of decades of increased inequality due to private business growth fuelling a substantial proportion of the population left with inadequate social protection and facing looming environmental catastrophe. The government must be able to reorganise the funding of the universal social welfare system that directly challenges and replaces the existing system whereby enterprises provide most of the social welfare. We are not talking about radical degrowth here, because the Chinese regime still fervently believes in incessant growth and global free trade. The regime's planning models do have room to incorporate 'green growth'. Yet, this option is not sustainable for more than a decade or so once deeper emissions cuts and reductions in the material footprints of its substantial but minority middle-class of several hundred million necessitates de-escalating unsustainable consumerism. With or without democratisation, the government will be forced to expand state social welfare and increasingly subordinate private sector practices to greater regulation.

The more that Chinese businesses compete in international markets, especially in the high-tech capital-intensive sectors, the more they will shed labour or cut workers' conditions, thus exacerbating enormous existing social problems. Those who argue that there will be a shortage of workers because China's over 65 ageing population will more than double between 2020 and 2050 (from 12% to 26% of total population), are presenting a false picture. Either millions more will be impoverished in their old age or else the government will have to change the existing structure of the economy from one of industrial growth to a new expanded 'social state'. With an additional 150 to 200 million over 65s needing adequate health care, pensions and a range of services, the government will come under enormous pressure to institute a more universal care structure that does not depend on the failed system currently run by private businesses and state enterprises.

If, on the other hand, the state sector does not expand and the private sector grows at the expense of environmental sustainability and adequate funding of social welfare, the regime will be increasingly called upon to use force as social disturbances increase. The notion that authoritarian regimes do not have to worry about their legitimacy is delusionary as witnessed by the 2019-2020 protests in Hong Kong. Conversely, if by some unexpected development the Communist Party loses its power and democratic institutional processes emerge, it is most unlikely that these would be socialist-inclined if the pattern of post-1989 marketisation in Eastern Europe is repeated in China. We could thus see even greater levels of inequality and social problems common in other countries but magnified many times over in the absence of strong social democratic, green or eco-socialist parties.

China is heading for very major challenges regardless of whether it opts for a state-led social agenda or an increased private market trajectory. Nonetheless, it could short-circuit these problems by instigating a carefully planned state-led response to existing social welfare failings and environmental threats. If holding on to power and both 'nation building' and 'regional power building' without losing legitimacy is the primary motive of the ninety million-strong Communist Party, then for purely pragmatic reasons it could implement the following combination of policies that include: even more cleansing of corruption and abuses by officials; enforcing a comprehensive state-run universal welfare system by taking over all the private and other enterprise-based schemes that are highly unpopular because of their constant cheating and abuse of workers' entitlements; significantly improving social conditions in rural areas by providing adequate income and social support for the large but very poor rural population. Curbing forcible land appropriation for property development could effectively complement cleaning up the worst forms of rampant pollution and environmental destruction.

The Chinese government claimed that it would eliminate extreme poverty by 2020 and set about improving living conditions in rural areas. This is a positive development but is a long way from ending poverty given that rural income has been falling since 2014 and the 'poverty line' benchmarks are so low that hundreds of millions of people will still live in very poor conditions and have far less income and resources than their urban counterparts.[33] There are no minimum national wages in China. Instead, wages vary significantly from region to region and from sector to sector and are testimony to a very unequal society even before we consider the many wealthy business and property developers. For example, agricultural workers may earn approximately 36,000 Yuan annually which is half of what construction workers earn and far less than many employees in a range of other sectors earning between 80,000 and 148,000 Yuan annually. It has been claimed that labour's share of national income in 'socialist' China is not only lower than that going to labour in the UK, the US and Germany, but lower than labour's share in India and Brazil.[34] Leaving aside the difficulty of whether accurate comparative measurements for these countries could be collated, nevertheless, the dire state of exploitation of workers in China remains a key reason for providing comprehensive improvements in wages and social conditions.

A three-pronged strategy of anti-corruption, universal social welfare and improving ecological sustainability would thus enhance both the legitimacy of the regime and the well-being of its people even if full democratic reforms were not implemented. The major problem facing anti-corruption strategies is that they are only as effective as the degree of democratic freedoms given to citizens to first be able to expose corruption and abuse. Yet, democratisation may not achieve greater equality on its own if people interpret greater freedom as the right of individuals and businesses to increase their own wealth rather than using their new freedoms to pursue community well-being and curb ecological destruction. Without strong eco-socialist or degrowth values, 'democracy' can degenerate rapidly and be equated with simply more private enterprise and individualism as in former East European Communist countries. If this is the outcome, then we will not only see more conflict over 'democracy versus sustainability', but also a regressive shift to the full-scale open conflict of 'capitalism versus democracy' as has been the case for more than a century in Western countries.

The challenge of China solving its immense social welfare and environment problems has vital consequences for the entire world. Countries in Asia account for 60% of the global population (over 4.5 billion people) not counting 40 million people living east of the Ural Mountains in Russia. The 1.9 billion people living in countries outside China and India, from Indonesia to Pakistan or Bangladesh to Vietnam, are strategically part of the Asia-Pacific expansionary capitalist world that has shifted east from the Atlantic, Baltic and Mediterranean. Across the Pacific, several major Latin American countries have made their economies increasingly dependent on extraction industries and the export of resources and agriculture to Asian countries. Apart from Brazil, most other countries in Latin America such as Chile, Bolivia, Argentina, Columbia or Venezuela do not have large manufacturing export industries compared to Asian countries. They are also heavily reliant on the export of fossil fuel and will be hit hard in coming years once drastic cuts to carbon emissions become mandatory. With desperately needed land reform required in several countries, reactionary oligarchies and backward state governments presiding over corruption, clientelism, deep-seated inequality and pervasive violence never far from the surface, the prospects for establishing comprehensive social welfare systems in these Latin American countries are grim. Even more challenging is the fact that the dominant model of 'modernisation' favoured by pro-market policy makers – one that is based on industrial development geared to the export of manufacturing goods – itself will become environmentally unsustainable in coming decades.

It is true that there is a significant level of intra-trade between several Latin American countries, especially revolving around Brazil's economic growth. Yet, the more that Latin American commodity exports to Asia and North America become increasingly dependent on conventional industrial expansion and property development in these regions, the greater the social crisis will become. Hence, global trade will require major transformation and new forms of domestic employment to avoid catastrophic climate change. On current high emissions scenarios, with 3.2° Celsius warming occurring by 2070, a projected 3.5 billion people would experience a mean average temperature of higher than 29° Celsius, which is currently only found on 0.8% of the planet's surface, mostly in the Sahara.[35]

If it is bad enough that Asian-Pacific countries lack adequate social protection for their populations at the moment, what are the governments in these countries going to do in the next one to three decades to prevent global warming that will make large areas of their countries uninhabitable? Conventional 'business as usual' solutions advocated by corporations, international development agencies and governments to generate jobs, export income, foreign investment and tax revenue are already creating massive social and environmental problems. These disastrous strategies will be impossible to implement in future years at the same rate due to the need to adhere to a combination of political economic and environmental constraints. So far, the old struggles between 'capitalism and democracy' have not adequately addressed the crucial issues of sustainability. Instead, nearly all governments on the political spectrum in Asia and Latin America subscribe to the mantra of incessant industrial growth while sleepwalking toward disaster.

Few mainstream policy makers and political parties are doing the serious thinking about how to cope with the new capitalist developments that confront us all. Incrementalism remains the *modus operandi*. Unfortunately, the socio-economic and environmental problems that require urgent resolution are not themselves increasing incrementally, year by year. Instead, we are seeing massive disruptive crises, as in the case of the COVID 19 pandemic and other escalating threats, whether it be to secure employment, financial stability, a safe climate, social security or the capacity of cities and governments to even deliver on their very modest electoral manifestos. In 1973, James O'Connor analysed how the growth of the corporate sector increasingly created environmental damage and a surplus population of the unemployed alongside homelessness, mental illness and numerous other problems which were left for the state to 'clean up'. Fifty years later across the world, the surplus population and related social and environmental problems have grown significantly. O'Connor believed that a political alliance between public sector workers and their 'clients' (whether those on welfare, in care facilities and so forth) would develop to fight for a 'social-industrial state' as opposed to the US military-industrial complex.[36] His hopes were dashed by the Rightward shift a few years later that has gone in the opposite direction of cutting America's meagre welfare provisions and the capacity of governments to compensate for corporate vandalism. Today, we are at a juncture point. Throughout the world the old 'welfare state' band aids have become grossly deficient and unable to even paper over let alone cure the massive social and environmental problems we confront. Little wonder then that there has been a resurgence of radical proposals and utopian solutions.

POSSIBLE NEW FORMS OF DECOMMODIFIED SOCIAL WELFARE

I have tried to show that all those who apply variations of Esping-Andersen's model of the 'three worlds' of welfare capitalism are relying on a framework that no longer exists in its original form in OECD countries and is also not applicable to most other countries across the capitalist world. Instead, we have 'productivist' forms of enterprise-based welfare in industrial countries in Asia such as South Korea and formal but grossly underfunded mixtures of public and private welfare in African and Latin American countries that either exclude large numbers or provide derisory benefits. We also have the residues of earlier Soviet style welfare alongside new market schemes in former Communist countries in Eastern Europe and Central Asia. Whether in South or South East Asian countries, the Middle East and the Gulf states, there is no country in the world that currently has a system of welfare that is intentionally or unintentionally seriously eroding market social relations. There is not a country that provides a 'decommodified space' for people to become independent of the market for the duration of their lifecycle from birth to death. At best, various social welfare systems provide partial safety nets in the form of pensions, childcare, healthcare and other support at different stages of a person's life which is not equivalent to entirely freeing people from the constraints of market relations.

We therefore need to ask what an alternative system based on significantly decommodified capitalist social relations would look like? How could it be funded and developed, and would it be compatible with both democracy and environmental sustainability?

Currently, there are a few prominent preferred alternatives to existing welfare capitalist regimes championed by movements that are critical of capitalism. These include decentralised provision of social needs by largely self-sufficient local communities; universal basic income schemes; universal basic services proposals; and hybrid mixtures of the latter that embrace national and supranational entitlements and delivery systems. Depending on whether these are proposed for existing capitalist societies or as ultimate goals in a post-capitalist society, so the funding, organisation and delivery of these preferred options changes. For instance, most of the strategies for funding alternative schemes *within* capitalist societies include: proposals for new higher income and company taxes on businesses and wealthy individuals; closing tax havens, abolishing the numerous subsidies of fossil fuels and closing many tax loopholes and preferential treatment of businesses; imposing carbon taxes and wealth taxes at national and international levels; cutting military expenditure and redirecting it to social needs; taxing businesses for each new robot or AI machine deployed that causes job losses; and also imposing new financial criteria that price the real cost of natural resources and habitats thereby shifting production and consumption away from destructive practices.

What characterises these funding options is that most of them depend on a fundamental contradiction, namely, having to raise revenue from the continued growth of market commodities in order to expand a social system based on anti-capitalist decommodified social relations. Many analysts either hostile to or supportive of degrowth and eco-socialist social relations have already drawn attention to the inherent contradictions of relying on capitalist growth to fund degrowth or decommodified relations.[37] Two main problems are highlighted in these criticisms. If degrowth is successful in reducing production and consumption, this will result in lower taxation to fund alternative schemes unless taxation rates or levels of borrowing are increased. For example, degrowth at one to two percent reduction in GDP growth rates per annum could possibly result in economies being 10% to 20% smaller within ten years and as much as a 40% smaller economic revenue base in 20 years, unless non-material services replaced material production and consumption as a key source of revenue. Similarly, if political movements in particular countries are successful in legislating higher taxes and various measures such as closing tax avoidance loopholes, this could also be a disincentive to capitalist enterprises and produce capital flight and the closure of businesses.

As for post-capitalist societies, apart from debates on the merits or problems of central or decentralised planning, market socialism or self-sufficiency, little actually exists in terms of discussions of different revenue and funding models for the socialist or green post-work society. Such is the absence of detailed thinking about post-capitalist and post-Communist revenue and expenditure models, that it is entirely unclear whether these societies will still use money, whether individual income tax, consumption tax and other taxes will exist or not, what will be the responsibility of local, national or supranational institutions for the delivery and funding of a range of social services, and numerous other crucial aspects related to the organisation of daily life.

Given these dilemmas and lack of detail in alternative plans, it is necessary to indicate which current proposals should be abandoned or seriously questioned by social change activists because they have little chance of succeeding. I will then present the argument for which scheme has a better chance of success on its own or in combination with other policies.

SELF-SUFFICIENT 'LOCALISM': DEMOCRACY VERSUS EQUALITY

To begin, we need to abandon universal notions of social life based on small communities and production confined mainly to craft-based co-operatives. These are fine for a very limited number of people but would be inappropriate solutions for a world of at least nine billion people in coming years. Local provision should be encouraged wherever possible. However, any model that assumes that a local community can provide all of a person's or a household's needs is dangerously foolish. This is the productivist illusion that was originally developed by utopian socialists in the nineteenth century that was essentially based on agrarian or provincial self-sufficiency principles. It also partly emerged from socialist notions of worker's control or self-management that assumed that if only 'the factory' could be controlled by the working class then all other social relations in the community could equally be self-managed. While containing an element of truth, the self-managed factory or farm is historically inappropriate given the rise of service-sector economies and the emergence of complex social institutional structures that cannot be reduced to overcoming alienated production in a factory setting. Stripped of its democratic qualities, this model of worker's self-management was retained for propaganda purposes in the one-party Soviet model of enterprise-based welfare *without* workers' control. Moreover, these enterprises perpetrated inequality as they were neither self-sufficient nor capable of meeting workers' essential needs, for example, the USSR had to continually import grain to feed its population and basic consumer goods (not luxury goods) were in short supply.

Radicals are correct to say that workers in future workplaces, whether factories, offices, educational institutions, communication and cultural enterprises or community health and other social care providers, could either self-manage their organisations or at the very least dramatically increase their say in how these socio-economic and cultural institutions are run. But this democratisation of control would not be equivalent to determining the revenue and resource-base for the whole local community as the vast majority would still depend on varying levels of external resources to survive.

For a democratically run degrowth, anarchist or eco-socialist local community to operate quite differently to a Soviet factory, radicals would first of all need to define what is a 'local community'. The following questions would need to be posed and addressed. What is the approximate optimal size of such a community? Is it small enough to be a face-to-face 'community' or is 'local community' equivalent to a city or part of a city where most people will never come to know their fellow 'community' members? Size and scale are critical when it comes to the revenue and resources base of 'the community' and the capacity to organise and deliver a range of decommodified social services is entirely different for a very small town compared with a city with a population ranging from one million to thirty million people. Some 'communities' are clearly more 'local' than others. Most require complex levels of organisation, supply chains and revenue in order to deliver equality for all and access to democratic decision-making.

Just as we are well past the point of debating and thereby giving credibility to climate change deniers, it would be more productive if we moved beyond the wasteful energy of debating the possibility of a stateless or semi-stateless society. Not only is such a future a utopian fantasy, but a stateless society is a toxic political concept that distracts from and jeopardises the challenging task of attaining durable, decommodified and universal social relations and sustainable eco-systems at local, national and supranational levels. Anarchists have played an invaluable role in critiquing bureaucracies, deflating pompous authoritarian tendencies and reminding us that all people can make important decisions if given the opportunity. One can also understand the desire of many radicals to end repressive state apparatuses and replace bureaucratic institutions with self-managed social institutions. However, the latter goals are not feasible or sustainable in small or large 'local communities' without the co-operative involvement and support of new non-repressive state institutions. In fact, it is both ludicrous and highly dangerous to believe that the level and scale of inequality and threats to the earth's life support systems can be dealt with adequately without any state institutions to redistribute wealth and income, help coordinate complex social processes or institute necessary environmental protective measures.

We need restructured state institutions that facilitate decentralised forms of democratic participation rather than utopian anti-statist solutions. Social struggles by movements 'from below' can quite easily lead to political dead-ends or the usurpation of power by technocrats and authoritarians once the practical problems of managing society without state institutions results in crisis and disillusionment. Better for these grass roots movements to aim for control of restructured democratised state institutions than to subscribe to the political nonsense that one can create a new completely horizontal world without some degree of vertical co-ordination given our world of gross inequality. In this respect, advocates of horizontal stateless utopias appear like the flat earthers of today.

CAN UNIVERSAL BASIC INCOME DECOMMODIFY SOCIAL RELATIONS?

As I discussed in detail in *Fictions of Sustainability* (Chapter Six), the belief that existing welfare states can be replaced by an adequate universal basic income scheme (UBI) is the prevailing illusion widely held across the world. It is a seductive illusion because it directly taps into the prevailing ideology of individualism and desire for individual self-control. The temporary provision of income support for the massive numbers of unemployed caused by Covid-19 has produced a further outpouring of articles and commentary about the need for a UBI. We need, however, to clearly differentiate between the short-term emergency income support measures for the unemployed and most existing UBI proposals. None of the stimulus measures or temporary income support schemes in response to Covid-19 have been either universal or have provided permanent ongoing basic income. Instead, they have been given by governments to a varying percentage of unemployed workers (excluding many casual, immigrant and assorted categories of workers) or else provided to employers as subsidies so they can keep workers temporarily employed.

No country has the fiscal capacity to keep even these non-universal income support measures going for more than a couple of years at the most, without undermining the stability of capitalist societies. Even Left advocates of modern monetary theory (MMT) argue that governments can issue or print money without worrying about high debt levels *only* so long as printing money for massive stimulus measures or a UBI does not result in continually rising inflation. If every country in the world could simply print money to employ everybody or pay all people a decent UBI without having to worry about lack of tax revenue or a run on a devalued currency or lack of investment capital and so forth, then the magic pudding of endless money supply could take care of all of our worries. Unfortunately, even UBI schemes have to be financed in some way and this is true of both capitalist and future post-capitalist societies.

While it is within the financial capacity of many governments to provide a very austere UBI well below existing pensions or unemployment benefits, this would hardly decommodify market social relations as the UBI would be far too little to live on. Hence, most existing UBI proposals would still require people to find additional paid work or welfare services to supplement their income. The much-touted so-called Finnish UBI experiment of paying a few thousand long-term unemployed people 560 euros a month or 129 euros a week was hardly a success as it was based on a miserly income that was insufficient to live on without all other welfare state supplements. This experiment terminated in December 2018 and was not a UBI as it was means tested and designed for individuals between 25 and 58 to get people back into the paid workforce.[38]

Only an adequate UBI that would be at least equal to but preferably above the official poverty level in different countries would begin to erode decommodified capitalist relations. Still, when we add the cost of keeping existing social welfare services (health care, housing support, child-care, etc.) to a modest poverty level UBI, the total fiscal outlay would provide only minimal benefits for the very excessive costs of providing it to all people regardless of need. For example, a very austere UBI in America of US$10,000 per annum which is well below the US poverty line, would cost a prohibitive US$3 trillion annually or almost equal to the initial stimulus measure against Covid-19.[39] Despite this enormous annual cost, the vast majority of wage workers would have little incentive to stop working and try to live on the massively reduced income provided by a UBI.

Not only would a UBI be prohibitively expensive, it would also require additional tax revenue that would fall most heavily on workers rather than on businesses. Depending on the manner in which a UBI is financed, it is quite possible that it could be a regressive move if the tax burden fell heavily on low and middle-income people. In addition, let us imagine that a minimum of twenty to forty percent of workers (especially those in low-paid work) left their jobs to live on an adequate UBI, the capitalist class would bitterly oppose this even before the scheme got off the ground. Let us then assume that those capitalist opponents would not be able to prevent a UBI from being implemented. As most direct tax revenue and indirect taxes (such as consumption taxes) are collected from wage workers, a UBI would also create major political divisions within the working class between those receiving a UBI and all other wage and salary workers having to pay higher taxes and/or suffer cuts to their own welfare services as well as incur higher costs for living expenses caused by businesses passing on their increased taxes to pay for a UBI. And this would only be the beginning of likely political divisions. The more that workers deserted wage labour and opted for a UBI, the more that this transitional period of about ten to twenty years would leave public and private pension schemes funded by workers and employers' contributions in a critical predicament. These pension funds would either default, cut pension benefits or be unable to support all those millions of people about to retire within the coming decade, let alone the many millions of retirees already living on pensions that were much higher than the income provided by a meagre UBI.

Aside from schemes providing austere, tiny payments, to date we have not seen proposals for a UBI that are electorally and financially feasible. This is because it is impossible to meet the progressive utopian notions of a UBI without either dramatically undermining capitalist societies or creating divisions in precisely those working class and middle-class constituencies needed to win electoral majorities to implement UBI legislation. So far, there is no agreement amongst advocates of a UBI as to whether a UBI would only apply to citizens over a certain age (say 18 to 67, even though millions of people under the age of 18 work), whether people over 65 would receive it, whether one could continue to receive a pension, unemployment benefit or student allowance as well as a UBI, whether residents and not just citizens would also receive it, and whether those living within supranational entities such as the EU would get the same UBI. These eligibility criteria are all very divisive. Remember, we are not talking about a targeted basic income directed at people near or below the official poverty level. Rather, we are confronted by divisions over what 'universal' means and how universal are different notions of a universal basic income. Take for example, the Socialist/Podemos coalition government in Spain which introduced in May 2020 a basic income of 462 euros per month for individuals and up to a maximum of 1,015 euros for families to reach 850,000 homes or approximately 2.3 million people. While this is a very positive development to help combat extreme poverty amongst a section of the population, it is far from being a universal income scheme.

Although the ideals behind a UBI sound attractive in terms of ending bureaucratic policing of people on welfare, encouraging a whole range of people to take up voluntary community care activities and artistic and self-realisation pursuits, the irony is that this decommodification of social life would only be possible if large numbers of workers continued performing wage labour in order to deliver the tax revenue needed to fund a minority of the population on the UBI. Once more people crossed the viability threshold and received a UBI rather than engaged in wage labour, the scheme would progressively require exceptionally large increases in taxes or collapse.

Conversely, the positive images of a UBI have to be weighed up against its likely boost to market individualism. People on a UBI may choose to do co-operative social labour and other care work in their free time, but there is no guarantee that they will, given that a UBI is geared to sustaining so-called autonomous individuals. Instead, any introduction of a UBI within capitalist societies would need to function with all the hyper-individualism of existing cultural relations still intact. Transforming individuals who lack the cultural capital, motivation and political values so that they can engage in creative activity or anti-market socially co-operative community practices would be an overly optimistic and ambitious task. There is no clear indication that a state provided UBI (even if it were fiscally viable) would result in most people ceasing to do what they currently do in their fragmented and alien-ated individualistic lives. No wonder so many free marketeers also endorse a UBI and see this as a strategy to abolish a range of social welfare services without fearing that people will adopt co-operative socialist values and practices.

At the moment, most proposals for a UBI are linked to the call for Green New Deals, degrowth alternatives or technological, post-work utopian solutions to capitalism. Advocates of Green New Deals or degrowth societies may be opposed on the issue of economic growth, but they both succumb to unrealistic notions of how to fund an adequate UBI. As to those techno-utopian post-capitalist scenarios where either all people or the vast majority are on a UBI and robots perform necessary labour while tax revenue somehow magically flows to state coffers or to the self-managed local community, this rests on sheer fantasy. It is certainly possible to see a signifi-cant reduction in the paid working week and the increasing automation of production and administration to reduce unpleasant, hard, dirty, unsafe or boring labour. But whatever kind of taxes will be collected, these will be affected by environmental pressures that require reductions in material foot-prints. Not only will this mean fewer workers and businesses paying direct taxes, but also less consumption which will mean less consumption tax revenue.

In contrast to advocates of degrowth who place environmental sustainability at the centre of their alternative visions, the 'technological Prometheans' who promote 'fully automated luxury communism' reveal a complete ignorance of environmental constraints and barely even recognise the need to reduce material footprints. All is somehow overcome by 'zero marginal cost' goods, the colonisation of other planets, and the unleashing of fantastic technology that is created without a major depletion of resources and other such fictitious scenarios.[40]

All future societies will still require many workers in both familiar and new occupations to perform necessary labour. Societies could *never* become 'post-work' and function smoothly on a daily basis if essential services were only provided in a purely voluntary manner. Liberating labour time performing alienated labour is a vital and crucial objective for workers. However, let us not fall for the fairy tale that a UBI will be the magic bullet that cures all ills, provides enough for all to have a happy life, and best of all, we won't even have to worry about whether this wonderful scheme requires incessant economic growth to pay for it because it will be magically delivered universally across the world to nine billion people and yet be environmentally sustainable!

THE RADICAL IMPLICATIONS OF UNIVERSAL BASIC SERVICES

What kind of alternatives to existing capitalist welfare regimes could simultaneously undermine competitive individualism, reduce widespread inequality and poverty and lay the foundations of genuine decommodification? I believe that a universal basic services scheme (UBS) would help do precisely what a UBI is unable to do, but it could *not* achieve decommodification on its own. While still in a developmental stage, advocates of UBS believe that all should be eligible for any of the essential services necessary to achieve comparable standards of living to that enjoyed by their fellow citizens or residents. A UBS in its less radical form is supported by neo-Keynesian social democrats seeking an alternative to neoliberal austerity. It is also advocated by radical critics of capitalism who tie UBS to a broader anti-capitalist strategy.

The concept of universal basic services is relatively new and is a direct or indirect response to the popularity of UBI proposals.[41] Elements of UBS, however, have been advocated for many years. These include the demands for universal healthcare, education, childcare and other essential services. Feminists have long campaigned for the provision of public community services to alleviate the care burden carried by women performing unpaid domestic labour. Even social democrats such as Australian Labor Prime Minister, Gough Whitlam, won the 1972 election on a platform of extending essential services, including the provision of connected reticulated sewerage systems to all homes. This was laughed at by some but in fact is a necessary basic service to improve the health and well-being of not just people in OECD countries, but especially the health and well-being of hundreds of millions of poor people in low-income countries.

In contrast to the moderate version of UBS, there are compelling arguments for a radical agenda and conception of UBS. It is easy to gloss over the simple fact of how revolutionary it is to ensure that impoverished people across the world have an adequate diet, access to health cover, decent housing, education, public transport, connection to water, electricity and other essential utilities necessary for communication, whether telephone or internet. In recent years, various social movements and policy analysts have attempted to tackle a series of socio-economic and environmental problems by applying the concept of UBS, even though they often do not use this term to describe their goals and strategies. I will therefore outline what I perceive to be the key reasons why the development of a broad UBS strategy simultaneously offers the most viable 'just transition' to a decommodified, sustainable alternative to existing failed, inadequate or non-existing capitalist welfare regimes. The following key reasons for preferring a UBS include:

- It is immediately aimed at those most in need. In contrast to a universal income scheme that is indiscriminately aimed at all individuals regardless of income and wealth, a UBS would initially prioritise lifting the quality of life for the bottom 30% to 50% of low and middle-income people in OECD countries and 60% to 75% of people in low and middle-income countries. Far too many people suffer from curable diseases, die prematurely or are incapacitated for life due to inadequate health care, dental care and mental health care. Homelessness and sub-standard accommodation are widespread. Essential utilities such as electricity, running water, sewerage or safe urban living conditions free of violence, toxic pollution and industrial noise should be provided to all people as well as minimal levels of greenery and

recreational spaces. Contemporary education, employment and
social interaction requires access to telecommunication facilities
as well as a good free public transport system. While all people
would be eligible for services, preference would first be given to
those who could not afford privately-run services and had no
access to essential public services because none exist, or they are
in short supply or grossly underfunded and understaffed.

- It would cost less compared to the prohibitively expensive cost of
a minimal UBI. The provision of a range of universal services
would also cost less and be much more effective than a UBI in
combatting poverty and inequality. For example, instead of
spending $3 trillion per annum on a sub-poverty level UBI in the
US, the equivalent amount or even $2 trillion per year on basic
services would lead to dramatic improvements in the quality of
care services, housing and healthcare in a five to ten-year period.
Twenty to thirty trillion dollars of additional expenditure over a
decade would deliver a vastly improved 'social state' for tens of
millions of low and middle-income Americans. Similar levels of
expenditure as a proportion of GDP in dozens of countries would
also vastly improve the quality of life for countless millions of
people living without adequate basic services.

- It is more likely to promote social co-operation and solidarity.
Whereas a UBI provides no assurance that individuals will stop
living highly individualistic lives and indeed is based on a form of
individualism, a UBS could help develop deeper connections
between members of households and communities. The
improvement and creation of essential services would
simultaneously provide jobs in many care sectors, improve the
quality of life for the recipients, and undercut the market
provision of these services that millions of people currently can't
afford. By contrast, UBI schemes do not improve essential
services because they are geared to the provision of income at
such an austere sub-poverty level that millions would still not be
able to afford healthcare and other such basic services. A UBI
would in fact set back and undermine the establishment of good,
universally accessible public health and social care systems in the
many countries that currently lack these services. While a UBS
will not be cheap, it will not create major political divisions over
funding compared to the divisiveness of a UBI because it will

benefit many workers directly and indirectly. An improved social wage would also facilitate political coalitions between the recipients of essential services and those who pay the taxes for these services because many will simultaneously be taxpayers and beneficiaries of an improved social wage.

• It would greatly help improve the lives of women and men currently performing domestic labour. The claim by some feminists that a UBI or 'wages for housework' will improve the lives of most women is only partially true at best. 'Wages for housework' was originally not proposed as a realisable demand because its cost was prohibitive. Rather, the main purpose was to highlight women's inequality and the indispensable role played by women's unpaid domestic labour in caring for male workers as a cost-free subsidy for capitalists. Unless supplemented by an extensive social support system, 'wages for housework' would commodify care work (like sex work) and strip the many positive social aspects of domestic labour (including nurturing children and creating social bonds). Instead of a decommodified social system that would see domestic labour equally carried out by both men and women, a UBI or 'wages for housework' would do the opposite. Covid-19 has already shown that government income supplements for male workers in lockdown at home witnessed an increase in domestic violence and abuse, increased mental illness and so forth. The lesson here is that a UBI would not necessarily cause violence or mental illness but it would also do little to change the masculinist and depressed socio-cultural relations with or without a UBI. Any income-only alternative such as a UBI scheme would still leave women and men without desperately needed community infrastructure such as childcare, housing, healthcare and other social support services. By contrast, vital UBS provisions would help counter the isolation and overburdened carers otherwise left to cope alone at home with only a poverty level or sub-poverty level UBI. The illusion that such minimal UBI payments would give women independence and transform their lives without an extensive support network of basic services is one held mainly by those in the affluent middle-class who live comfortable lives and do not know what it is like to survive on inadequate welfare services or no welfare.

• It would help eliminate unemployment and underemployment. A

UBS scheme would have much greater impact if it were linked to a job guarantee program offering decent wages by governments to all who voluntarily desired to work. In contrast to those advocates who propose paying workers on job guarantee minimum wage rates, I believe that all prospective workers should be given the choice of either full-time or part-time work with prevailing minimum wage rates being only the minimum floor level. Instead, workers should be paid rates earned by workers with different skills, training or professional qualifications. A UBS scheme would complement a full employment society by providing a rising level and range of social wage services. If social goods and services remain privatised or outsourced to private contractors, full employment would not necessarily decommodify social relations. The higher percentage of the work age population employed in job guarantee programs, the higher the level of decommodification of labour from the market determined wage relation. If ten to twenty-five per cent of a country's labour force is initially freed from competitive labour market conditions, this could give all those employed in private sector businesses greater political bargaining strength. Stagnant wages and deteriorating work conditions over the past thirty years have been made possible in many countries by high unemployment and under-employment levels. Eliminating unemployment, under-employment and precarity through a job guarantee would thus restore the capacity of workers to face employers on a more equal footing. It is the newly employed job guarantee workers who will simultaneously help deliver and also benefit from the expanded UBS programmes at national, regional and local levels. They will, very importantly, help cover part of the cost of a job guarantee and UBS by earning wages and paying taxation revenue.

- It would facilitate the 'just transition' to an environmentally sustainable political economy. The crucial advantage of a properly implemented and wide-ranging UBS program is that it will not repeat the negative consequences of earlier labour market booms. One of the negative features of high employment is that it has usually fuelled unsustainable consumption. By contrast, a UBS will assist in the necessary reduction of material footprints in those countries where per capita consumption is already unsustainable. It will do this by shifting the present emphasis on mainly money

wages to a higher percentage of reward in the form of
comprehensive social wages, i.e., healthcare, housing, public
transport and a range of socially provided needs. In conjunction
with campaigns to reduce the length of the paid working week to
first 30 hours and later 25 and 20-hour full-time working weeks
over a transitional decade, the relationship between existing
consumption driven economies and unsustainability would be
repaired and rectified. Any transformation of households and local
neighbourhoods from purely sites of consumption to new sites of
alternative consumption and production (such as growing food
and providing shared services) would be made much easier if
people initially worked a reduced four-day and then a three-day
week. Currently, in OECD countries with more developed welfare
provisions, approximately 20% to 30% of household income
comes from state provided benefits. Lifting this to at least 50% of
household income over a transitional period would fundamentally
alter the balance between commodified wage labour and
decommodified social services. Also, most of these social wage
services would be less carbon embodied or requiring the same
level of material resources as existing major capitalist industries
such as private automobile production.

The old dilemma of how to fund degrowth and social welfare systems
that depend on the revenue derived from the continued growth of unsustainable commodity production is partially solved by developing a UBS. This
does not mean that a UBS scheme would become independent of capitalist
production. But it does mean that the growth of employment in the various
'social' sectors or the 'care economy' would simultaneously generate taxation
from employees, help change patterns of consumption and reliance on
private service providers. As discussed earlier, the proportion of durable
goods (such as cars or whitegoods), non-durable goods (food, fuel and clothing) and services (mainly private services such as health, IT communications,
insurance, personal care and tourism) has changed in OECD countries over
the past fifty years in the direction of more services and less durable goods
consumed annually. A UBS could certainly push this historical trend in the
direction of more publicly provided decommodified services, less imported
goods and boost other measures such as waste management and recycling of
production materials to help make individual per capita and national material, carbon, water and other footprints more ecologically sustainable.

A UBS requires interventionist states with enhanced capacities to help plan, co-ordinate, fund and implement the many facets of a UBS strategy. I am not talking about the old centralised and monolithic state apparatuses of yesteryear or today. Instead, there are many ideas being developed about how to introduce new conceptions of the relationship between UBS and what others call the 'foundational economy'. This group of theorists in Manchester, Barcelona, London and other cities start with the following premises:

Firstly, central governments should not abdicate responsibility and leave cities and regions suffering from decades of under-development to deal with inequality and lack of resources. However, because most central national governments lack the imagination and knowledge to deal with local and regional problems, it is necessary to reinvent, empower and develop the micro-level capacities of local and regional governments who are most familiar with their own needs in regard to employment, services, industries and ecology.[42]

Secondly, instead of beginning with abstract concepts of 'the market' or an 'undifferentiated capitalism', it is crucial to recognise that the basic materials of everyday life "are exceptionally diverse in their production cycles, their economic geographies, the complexity of their inputs, their spatial relations and reliance on land..."[43]

Thirdly, rather than focus on the tradeable and competitive parts of the production system as if they were the whole economy, the 'foundational economy' approach divides each local, regional and national economy into zones of which the tradeable and competitive market businesses are only one zone. The other zones consist of essential services in health, education, transport, housing, energy and so forth, the family or household core zone, and the occasionally used zone of activities such as holidays or haircuts.

While the Foundational Economy group are not all geared to radical post-capitalist change, they do overlap with advocates of UBS in emphasising the need to develop essential services and those zones of regional and local economies. These would help shift social and economic activity away from commercial tradeable commodities to decommodified services, employment and infrastructure that would reduce poverty and inequality in a manner that is compatible with environmental sustainability. Central or federal government funding would be necessary alongside national monetary, fiscal, energy, trade and communication policies, but these would depend on far greater local and regional input to help design and facilitate new socially needed services and infrastructure.

HOW A UBS COULD CHANGE 'DEMOCRACY AND SUSTAINABILITY'

We are now seeing the emergence of different hybrid versions of UBS which combine it with basic income for targeted low-income people rather than a universal income scheme. It is also proposed for different excluded groups such as First Nations peoples with different social needs and suffering greater discrimination than others. Each city, region or country has different levels of dilapidated, scarce or unavailable infrastructure and public resources – from parks and social housing to running water – and hence is in need of specifically formulated transitional strategies that could be provided initially through free goods and services or public sector and non-profit private providers such as cooperatives conforming to strict social guidelines. These new guidelines would be an alternative to many existing public-private enterprise contracts that are geared to profit-earning formulas that generate high returns on private capital investment rather than prioritising social needs.

The benefit of a broad UBS strategy is that it could provide target goals at local and national levels for the development of 'social wage' essentials for workers and families in conjunction with reducing per capita and national material footprints. Typical forms of mainstream welfare incrementalism offered by centre-Left parties during election campaigns usually aim to maximise electoral support instead of coherent planning that best resolves major social problems. By contrast, a UBS strategy could facilitate public participation in local, regional and national government annual, five and ten-year planning targets to maximise social services and shift employment towards core and foundational ecologically sustainable economic zones.

No environmentally sustainable economy is possible without a major cultural shift in both the attitude of citizens and the various socio-political movements that are often set in their ways. During the 1980s, for instance, the Greater London Council facilitated the involvement of ethnic groups, women, gays and lesbians, arts groups and those in need of basic services such as transport users. While a new progressive coalition was formed, the British Labour Party and trade union movement remained largely uninvolved and set in their ways.[44] This enabled the Thatcher government to more easily dissolve the GLC in 1986. Without the support of national political parties and union movements, local and regional governments and social movements in most countries are too weak on their own.

A broad UBS strategy has the potential to strengthen union movements through the job guarantee and full employment. But such an achievement could easily be undermined by the continuation of conservative trade union policies narrowly aimed at wage increases rather than the deliberate development of 'social wage' services. Whether unions or other civil society movements and organisations, it is very difficult to make the transition from the excluded position on 'the street' (protests and oppositional action) to the decision-making institutions and forums of power. Fear of being either incorporated or excluded necessitates a change of political consciousness and action. Few movements have made this transition in consciousness and practice and yet the democratisation of society depends on it.

Today, any 'just transition' to an ecologically sustainable society without a political revolution means that the existing trade union movements, mainstream electoral parties and social movements will almost certainly have to negotiate a set of major socio-economic and environmental problems that have no precedent in the past. Are they capable of representing disadvantaged groups? This depends on how vocal and active social movements are in pressuring reluctant mainstream parties or bypassing them with new political organisations of their own. No organisation or political movement will be able in the future to simply rest on conventional practices. It is not a question of 'if', but rather 'when' present-day parties and movements will be overwhelmed and overrun by the scale of problems and challenges for which most of them are currently unprepared. Politically and culturally, we are fast approaching a time when people will have to make a choice between suffering under mounting economic, social and environmental problems that cannot be resolved by conventional crisis-management techniques or adopting new socio-environmental solutions.

Developing a broad UBS program lends itself to unifying disparate social movements under a unified umbrella in each country or region. It simultaneously promises work, social care, renovating dilapidated urban environments or neglected urban and rural areas that lack basic infrastructure and services while ensuring that the focus is on providing the latter within sustainable biophysical boundaries. If developed coherently, it provides a sense of direction and an alternative macro-economic and political framework to counter the failed policies of present-day governments and business policy makers.

Whether a UBS strategy is adopted depends on the form new political movements will take, an unknown direction to be determined by people in each country. However, we do know that without a notion of how to plan the shift from commodified to decommodified social relations, all political practice will remain just oppositional and trapped within the parameters of existing capitalist political economies. There should, nonetheless, be no illusions about the likely reception given to a broad UBS strategy. A range of business groups, governments and sections of the electorate will bitterly resist such an alternative program. A significant minority of the electorate in countries with free elections or those workers in authoritarian countries will oppose an increase in the 'social wage' at the expense of higher money wages. Imbued with individualism and notions of the 'sovereign consumer', they will resist the need to reduce their material footprints and shift consumption from glittering objects to essential needs for all.

Although democratisation is essential for the long-term health and engagement of people in running their own institutions and workplaces, it is necessary to demystify 'democracy' as some kind of end goal or panacea that will solve all problems in favour of a sustainable egalitarian society. Many people on the Left believe that democracy is incompatible with capitalism. However, this is only true of more radical forms of democracy rather than what passes as 'democracy' in the present-day world. On the other hand, democracy may well prove to be incompatible with environmental sustainability if the content and meaning of democracy is interpreted as being equivalent to little more than individual choice, the right to enjoy one's liberty and civil rights at the expense of others, and the complete disregard of environments that many can neither immediately see nor experience. Even if suddenly capitalist societies miraculously transformed and capitalism ended, a constant tension in the foreseeable future will remain between the democratic desire of many people to maximise their rate of consumption and the need to keep material footprints below the threshold of unsustainability. This will also become the major problem in all those countries without any semblance of democracy.

The degree of conflict over private consumption at individual and household level and the collective consumption needs of communities is not something fixed or uniform in each society. Politics will not cease in some future utopia; it will simply change in content and form. How disputes are resolved at local, national and international levels will ensure that the politics embodied in 'democracy versus sustainability' will remain a central characteristic of both capitalist and post-capitalist societies.

I have therefore tried to highlight why the conflict between 'capitalism and democracy' and the parallel conflict over 'democracy and sustainability' will frame all so-called 'just transitions' from capitalism to post-capitalism either directly, or indirectly in those countries with authoritarian regimes. If political movements aiming to decommodify social relations do not first strive to assess the capacity to deliver their socio-economic goals within particular contexts, then political failure will be difficult to avoid. Opting for techno-fixes rather than necessary social changes will undoubtedly prove irresistible to some when faced with future extremely difficult challenges.

Overcoming deep inequality is impossible without also reducing the unsustainable material footprints of affluent populations across the world. Convincing people they will have a richer and happier 'inner world' despite forgoing parts of their 'outer' material possessions is much easier in theory than in practice. Either one believes in change through social protest and electoral politics or opts for revolutionary strategies. If electoral politics remains the dominant process of change then phased-in reductions of material footprints in OECD countries will only be feasible if governments can simultaneously promise job and income security alongside basic universal services. Without concrete policy strategies to deliver the latter in societies where wage and salaried employees are heavily divided along a series of socio-economic and cultural lines, all manifestoes about ending inequality and poverty will lack broad popular support and remain mere rhetorical gestures. Nonetheless, these painful choices will soon become unavoidable. It is better to be aware of deep and widespread economic and environmental pressures and plan for the future than be the victims of decisions made for us by others. Without a notion of what we are aiming for, politics is reduced to the daily scenario and ritual of ad hoc policies and counter responses. At least the goal of universal basic services alongside a job guarantee gives people an objective to aim for and an agenda that they can help create to meet their specific local and national social and environmental needs.

CONCLUSION

I HAVE ATTEMPTED to write this book so that it is both accessible and informative to different generations of readers with quite diverse social and political experiences. This approach was influenced by my own early formative political development being raised in a politically active family. My self-educated immigrant parents worked in factories in Melbourne and were 'true believers' in a future world of communist equality and social justice. They took me to Left protest marches and political gatherings in the late 1940s and early 1950s. I also started working full-time at the age of 14 in factories, offices and department stores for six years (while attending night school), so my embrace of radical politics in the 1960s was informed by working class life and not just student politics or detached abstract theory. Nonetheless, I was relatively ignorant of the political experiences and history of the generations that came before my own. This lack of political knowledge was also largely true of the generation of the 'long sixties'. The politics and history of the 1920s and 1930s was unfamiliar ancient history, just as today, the 1960s, 1970s and 1980s must equally appear to be ancient history to many young activists.

The key emphasis in this book has been on how to shape and transform the future rather than dwell on the past and 'what could have been'. My main reason for examining earlier political and socio-economic developments and struggles is to benefit contemporary social change advocates and activists by enabling them to recognise why the unfamiliar problems we face will require breaking with old stereotypes and narratives in order to develop a different type of politics and analytical framework. In trying to explain to a new generation how we have come to find ourselves in the current political conjuncture, it was necessary to re-read and re-educate myself and also to re-evaluate my own experiences, assumptions and conceptions of the world. This meant critically appraising long-held analyses of political economic and cultural practices and evaluating their relevance or obsolescence when confronting present-day environmental, cultural and technological developments. Many of these new challenges defy the explanatory capacity of old theories.

I therefore set out to attempt to explain the origins and changes to the dominant paradigm of 'capitalism versus democracy' during the period of the first half of the twentieth century that decisively helped shape the second half of the century right up to the 1980s and early 1990s when the current generation of 'millennials' were being born. The Second World War and Cold War may be kept alive for younger people by such things as movies, popular spy novels or games but it was the defeat of fascism and the transformation of capitalist societies in the decades after 1945 that also reshaped notions of democracy in both positive and negative ways. I argued in Book Two that it is particularly misleading for sections of the Left to characterise the three decades between 1945 and 1975 as a period of the 'democratic control of capitalism'. Constructing future alternatives to what is called 'the era of neoliberalism' that emerged after 1975 requires us to be free of the historical nostalgia for the period before the 1970s. It also necessitates rejecting the pessimism that arises from exaggerated accounts of de-democratisation and the so-called invincible nature of neoliberal states.

We are often unaware of earlier debates and struggles, particularly when we imagine that we are engaged in 'original' practices or insights only to later discover that we have merely reinvented the proverbial wheel. Take for example, the radical journal, *Jacobin,* that has just celebrated its tenth anniversary. Publisher Bhaskar Sunkara named it after the Black Jacobins in Haiti (initially led by the 'black Robespierre' Toussaint Louverture) who carried out a successful slave rebellion (1791 to 1804) and stood for a purer form of Jacobinism based on full independence from their French colonial masters. Sunkara aimed his controversial title at an American Left audience that opposed deep-seated racism and US imperialist policies. Nonetheless, the original French revolutionary Jacobins under leaders such as Maximilien Robespierre were also synonymous with a new nationalist centralised state, censorship and revolutionary terror as well as other policies that were hardly compatible with socialism. In 1918, Gramsci wrote that "Jacobinism was the substitution of one authoritarian regime for another," but as Alastair

Davidson noted, Gramsci claimed that "the Russian revolution could not be Jacobin because it was proletarian."[1] Gramsci's hopeful but naïve view was quickly invalidated.

As a journal, *Jacobin* is a welcome addition to what was a Left media lacking vitality. It usually contains many interesting and informative articles from across the world that help expand the political understanding of a very parochial and inward-looking American audience. On the other hand, it regurgitates old Communist and Trotskyist agitprop style socialist pieces on behalf of Left political candidates that could be straight from the 1920s, 1930s and 1940s. Reaching out to the world of Generations X, Y and Z (who are largely unfamiliar with old political debates between revolutionaries and reformists), most of the writers and editors of *Jacobin* thus remain firmly locked in the old paradigm of 'capitalism versus democracy'. While they occasionally cover environmental and other issues relating to the digital economy, these are nearly always discussed through the prism of traditional socialist politics as if all could be solved by the development of labour-orientated mass socialist parties like the Democratic Socialists of America (DSA). I do not wish to underestimate the major achievement of getting tens of thousands of Americans to join a party in a country where socialism remains a dirty word. Nevertheless, the argument of this book is that the ability of DSA or Left parties in other countries to grow depends in part on how successful they are in recognising and developing policies that are appropriate for current social and environmental crises. These crises are manifested in the conflict between 'democracy and sustainability' and not only in the traditional capital and labour issues of 'capitalism versus democracy'.

What seemed relatively clear-cut to Leftists before the 1940s, namely, capitalism and fascism on the one side and socialism and democracy on the other, has turned out to be much more complex. The broad Left had always been divided. From the late 1950s onwards, the long fragmentation of the Left into a multitude of positions was driven by a range of factors including greater awareness of Stalinist crimes and repression in China and other Communist countries as well as criticism of both social democratic 'welfare states' and Communist countries for their bureaucracy and cultural rigidity. When Khrushchev delivered his secret speech in 1956 denouncing Stalin's crimes and 'cult of personality', Slavoj Žižek comments with characteristic flair that:

> During the speech itself, a dozen or so delegates suffered nervous breakdowns and had to be carried out and given medical help; a few

days later, Boleslaw Bierut, the hard-line general secretary of the Polish Communist Party, died of a heart attack, and the model Stalinist writer Alexander Fadeyev shot himself. The point is not that they were 'honest communists' – most of them were brutal manipulators who harboured no subjective illusions about the nature of the Soviet regime. What broke down was their 'objective' illusion: the figure of the 'big Other' that had provided the background against which they were able to pursue their ruthless drive for power. The Other onto which they had transposed their belief, which as it were believed on their behalf, their subject-supposed-to-believe, disintegrated.[2]

The initial positive consequences of a Left simultaneously shocked and liberated from the shackles of Stalinist groupthink gradually descended into greater disunity and factional wars. Meanwhile, a new generation of social movement activists transformed cultural attitudes and raised awareness of the natural world, and of sexism and racism that were strikingly different to the authoritarian politics of the old Left. I tried to capture some of these difference in Book One and why the old theory of 'capitalism versus democracy' developed by Karl Polanyi and kept alive by his admirers is historically dated and fundamentally flawed as a way of understanding a profoundly altered contemporary world.

The revival of Marxism in the 1960s and 1970s, also had mixed consequences. The upsurge of neo-Marxist theory had a powerful impact on all sorts of criticisms of politics, economics and socio-cultural aspects of life in capitalist societies that continues to remain highly influential to the present-day. Nonetheless, a new generation of Marxists promoted a variety of crude and sophisticated versions of Marxism which in their own differing ways led to political failure.

First, the crude version. It was the repressive response of governments to the upsurge of radical protest movements in the 1960s that helped split the New Left in the US, West Germany, Italy, France and other countries where sections of the Left adopted a strategy of armed struggle rather than continue with conventional forms of non-violent protest. These small groups of armed radicals articulated half-baked critiques of capitalism which nonetheless contained elements of truth that tapped into the hopes and fears of a wider circle of Left sympathisers. They misread both the political atmosphere in OECD countries and struggles against 'imperialism in the Third World'. In their imagination they believed that revolutionary anti-imperialist struggle in the 'Third World' would soon trigger armed revolution in the West. The only problem was that the 'mass proletariat' were not eagerly waiting for the 'world-historical' revolutionaries in secret groupings to lead them in overthrowing capitalism; instead, they detested these new 'saviours' for bombing, killing and disrupting the social order. Jeremy Varon describes the delusions of the Weathermen and Baader-Meinhof group (RAF) which also applied to the Red Brigades in Italy in the 1970s.

> Both groups fell victim to equally flawed, contradictory assumptions, between which they oscillated. In one emphasis, defined by an exaggerated pessimism, they saw imperialism as a monolith. Its power to absorb, delude, and dispirit its subjects was so great that no sustained internal resistance was possible. ... In a second emphasis, driven by an exaggerated optimism, the Weathermen and the RAF saw imperialism as on the brink of collapse. Resistance was everywhere – in the Third World certainly, but also in the institutional fabric of their own societies: in the schools, the military, the factories, the bureaucracies, halfway houses, ghettos, and working- and middle-class homes. Their violence, in this model, needed only to light the spark to ignite mass discontent into revolutionary conflagration. Both views, despite their apparent polarity, had the same effect: to discourage the difficult work of addressing, through redoubled efforts to educate and organise ambivalent populations, possibilities that lay somewhere in between.[3]

One only has to read and listen to present-day activists combatting racism, neo-fascism and the socio-economic crisis caused by years of unemployment, cuts to social welfare and failure to act on the climate emergency to get a sense that an updated 'Weathermen' or RAF perspective must still resonate amongst a certain percentage of people. Like their predecessors, for the vast majority of contemporary radical activists the key debates remain whether to confront mainstream, conservative social democratic parties by setting up new radical parties, work at building coalitions and grass roots social movements or transform mainstream centre-left parties from within. However, if violence from neo-fascist nationalists escalates in contemporary America, Europe and most other capitalist societies, it won't be surprising to find that there will be small groups who believe that only militant armed action will protect Black Lives Matter protestors from being killed or prevent neo-fascist movements taking power. The same is true of many supporters of Extinction Rebellion who oscillate between an 'extreme pessimism' concerning the wilful failure of mainstream parties to implement drastic cuts to greenhouse gases, and an 'exaggerated optimism' that their desperate non-violent civil disobedience will trigger mass resistance. According to this view, either nature will take its revenge and civilisation collapses or XR activism will prevent climate catastrophe and help bring about the end of destructive capitalist civilisation.

Secondly, the sophisticated versions of Marxism took different forms from the 1970s onwards. One influential school of structural Marxism centred on theorists such as Louis Althusser mutated into an anti-Marxist post-structuralism, especially in France and Anglo-American countries led by the Foucauldians. Following the quelling of revolutionary optimism in post-1968 France and the discrediting of the Maoist Cultural Revolution and Solzhenitsyn's account of the Soviet 'gulag' in the mid-1970s, a profound de-radicalisation of intellectual life prevailed. Each generation confronts loss and disappointment in its own way. Observing this loss of hope, the late Marshall Berman argued in 1982 that,

> Foucault reserves his most savage contempt for people who imagine that it is possible for modern mankind to be free...there is no freedom in Foucault's world, because his language forms a seamless web, a cage far more airtight than anything Weber ever dreamed of, into which no life can break. The mystery is why so many of today's intellectuals seem to want to choke in there with him. The answer, I suspect, is that Foucault offers a generation of refugees from the 1960s a world-historical alibi for the sense of passivity and helpless-ness that gripped so many of us in the 1970s. There is no point in trying to resist the oppressions and injustices of modern life, since even our dreams of freedom only add more links to our chain; however, once we grasp the total futility of it all, at least we can relax.[4]

By contrast, some Maoists and Leninists like Žižek, Alain Badiou and various Trotskyist or other radical parties still try to maintain the relevance of Leninist or Maoist theory and practice. Sadly, despite their 'sophistication' this Marxism/Leninism as a form of political practice is as irrelevant to contemporary politics as the religious conflicts of the sixteenth century were to the Bolsheviks in 1917. Actually, the majority of contemporary advocates of social change neither adhered to a variety of Leninism nor subscribed to false hopes about anti-imperialist struggles. Instead, energy was poured into local and global environmental struggles, anti-war movements and combatting harsh neoliberal social policies.

Unfortunately, many of the now old, but former New Left offered little in the way of alternatives and instead devoted energy to analysing the defeats of the labour movement, the rise of globalisation and the seemingly impregnable domination of neoliberal regimes. This gave rise to both a pessimistic anti-capitalism and a new form of 'exaggerated optimism' in the form of 'Accelerationism' and visions of fully automated post-capitalism. André Gorz anticipated the 'anti-politics' of the 'Accelerationists'. In 1983, he summed up a generation of critiques of the welfare state and conventional Communist and social democratic politics in his analysis of 'paths to paradise' or the kind of social change that is possible after 'farewelling the working class' from the centre stage of anti-capitalist politics. He predicted that "when the Left, in Europe and America, can conceive of no solution to the crisis other than, state-managed capitalism, and still looks to Keynes for remedies which, already ineffective under Roosevelt, have become inapplicable, then it is clearly about to die from lack of imagination. There are times, when, because the social order is collapsing, realism consists not of trying to manage what exists, but of imagining, anticipating and initiating the potential transformations inscribed in present changes."[5]

Gorz was a political ecologist who is now claimed by both technological utopians and 'degrowthers'. Indeed, a new generation of radicals such as Mark Fisher, Nick Srnicek, Alex Williams, Helen Hester, Paul Mason, Aaron Bastani and the Promethean technological utopians writing in *Jacobin* initially went beyond Gorz.[6] They rejected conventional Left party politics and opted for utopian proposals such as demanding 'full unemployment' and a UBI to break the old sterile social democratic and labour movement agendas. I argued in *Fictions of Sustainability* and in this book that they all favoured an environmentally impossible automated 'post-capitalism'. Several soon switched to conventional politics by supporting Corbyn and Sanders after 'Accelerationism' had run out of political steam, but this 'path to paradise' now looks equally blocked or without clear direction.

Instead of post-work utopianism, the conventional remnants of the old New Left turned their attention to globalisation and the de-democratising power of the EU 'Hayekian state'. This also oscillated between 'extreme pessimism' and 'exaggerated optimism'. As I discussed in Book Two, many radical Leftists including Wolfgang Streeck and *New Left Review* editors knowingly or unknowingly pursued an updated version of Lenin's commitment to the right of small nations to secede from the USSR which Stalin in

1922 had attacked as 'national liberalism'. Whereas Stalin wanted a centralised USSR, Streeck and company aided and abetted 'national neoliberals' in their indirect support of Brexit under illusory names such as Lexit. Just as the Weathermen and Baader-Meinhof fantasised about igniting a revolution, the Lexiteers and other Eurosceptics split the Left into nationalists versus internationalists and assumed that Left 'national sovereignty' would be better than the EU 'Hayekian state'. Their 'exaggerated optimism' was shared by the hapless Eurosceptic Jeremy Corbyn who formally backed the Remain case but campaigned for it with little conviction.

Crucially, the UK like all countries in Europe, lacked a strong Left to make a Left nationalist programme a reality, especially in Tory 'little England'. Many neo-Marxists and post-Keynesians who advocated 'national sovereignty' ignored their own detailed analyses of how financialisation and multinational corporate interlocking supply chains had largely nullified any possibility of creating 'socialism in one country'. Their concept of 'capitalism versus democracy' especially gave indirect *de facto* support to racist policies against refugees and immigrants, even though most were anti-racist. They particularly misread the capacity of the Left to win on the nationalist political terrain that had been occupied for so long by the racist parties of the Right.

Apart from the genuine believers in Lexit, others conceivably had no illusions about the possibility of a successful Left government and instead played the 'long game'. If most European countries were hostile territory for the Left, better to break the EU status quo and first cause disruption in crisis-dominated post-Brexit UK before hopefully triggering similar anti-EU ructions in Italy and other Eurosceptic countries. Instead of Steve Bannon attempting to overthrow 'liberal elites' by energising the 'sliver' of the nationalist Right, it is possible that some cynical or strategic far Leftists imagined that breaking up the EU would ultimately lead to the break-up of Britain (including Scottish independence) and also create a more 'fluid situation' with open hostility in Europe between southern and northern and eastern and western countries freed from what they continue to see as the shackles of the EU. It is a dangerous 'game' that is yet to be played out in a world riven by economic and environmental crises and growing global regional polarisation. Crucially, this 'long game' strategy can only be played because national politics still remains central and claims about the EU 'Hayekian state' de-democratising member countries is an exaggerated prognosis that has largely benefited the neo-fascist Right and assorted neoliberal nationalists.

Equally importantly, I have endeavoured to show that the conflict between the nationalist and cosmopolitan Left within the Atlantic countries was the last gasp of a Left – whether Marxist or Keynesian social democratic – that only paid little more than lip service to environmental sustainability issues in the form of support for various proposals for 'green growth'. As currently constituted, the conflict of 'capitalism versus democracy' is between various centre-Right and centre-Left supporters of hybrid neoliberal policies on the one side and a range of radical anti-neoliberal Left, green and nationalist Right forces on the other. It is a conflict that will continue in modified form even though it is now being superseded and transformed by the urgent related conflict of 'democracy versus sustainability'.

The perennial question asked by those interested in social change concerns the issue of how to attract large numbers of people to build a mass movement. Objectively, empirical evidence shows that we live in capitalist societies which are dominated by the class that owns and controls the means of production and the lion share of private wealth. However, subjectively, apart from some countries such as the UK where conservative class distinctions are still very pronounced, most people across the world do not uphold a class view of the world (as opposed to subscribing to simple divisions between 'rich' and 'poor'). Instead, they often see themselves as either primarily individuals or members of traditional religious, communal, caste or kinship groups rather than as members of a particular class. Most countries during the past six decades have witnessed the progressive individuation of societies. Whether this individuation has replaced class or merely creates the impression of 'individual choice' while masking structural expressions of class culture or 'cultural capital',[7] has been the subject of intense debates in recent decades. In other words, are the ways that individuals are divided by their tastes in music, art, household furnishings or numerous other items of symbolic and material consumption due to their individual acquisition of different levels of education or 'cultural capital' rather than just their income and ownership of 'money capital'? Or are they heavily interconnected with online and offline marketing strategies that target different social classes, genders, income groupings and other demographic factors? The reality for the vast majority of populations across the world (apart from a small minority) is that social mobility is highly restricted and the ability to accumulate both 'cultural capital' and 'economic capital' is still largely determined by class location and deep class divisions.

In today's contemporary hyper-individualised consumer societies, it may be impossible to disentangle the intrinsic value of individual needs from the constructed desires heavily promoted by public relations industries and constantly being refined by algorithms and other forms digital tracking and marketing. It is no accident that socialist parties have generally declined in most countries over the past five decades and that even the recent boost of membership numbers of the Democratic Socialists of America or the British Labour Party are minuscule when placed against the size of the vast majority of 'non-joining' or uncommitted individuals in the overall population. The process of individuation is also evident in most low and middle-income countries where the dual impact of consumer marketisation and a secular individual rights culture is rapidly spreading but remains unable to triumph or make consistent headway against the strength of particular authoritarian and traditional forms of religious, communal or kinship structures that exist alongside or interrelate with capitalist market practices.

What is the relevance of the individuation process of many contemporary societies to the possibilities of transitioning to a post-capitalist society? If social change movements advocating socialism, degrowth or other such collective or co-operative agendas are to grow, then they have to be able to reverse or transform decades of socialisation of generations born since the 1950s who have mainly experienced a pervasive form of deep-seated competitive economic and cultural individualism that has extensively eroded but not completely replaced earlier forms of class solidarity. Large numbers of people regard socialist and degrowth movements as too alien and unattractive because they fear what they regard as socialist 'big government' regimentation and bureaucracy or imagine degrowth as the loss of all the material forms of urban comfort that only 'barefoot hippies' and vegans could enjoy. It does not necessarily matter to most people living their detached and apolitical private individual and family lifestyles that having a secure job, saving the environment or developing a richer 'inner life' are also individual and not just social goals.

Unfortunately, what counts for most people is whether achieving these alternative objectives will be too disruptive and personally costly in terms of jobs, income and material assets. I am fond of quoting Bertolt Brecht who recognised this problem in 1943. "History shows", he observed, "that peoples do not lightly undertake radical changes in the economic system. The people are not gamblers. They do not speculate. They hate and fear the disorder which accompanies social change. Only when the order under which they have lived turns to an indubitable and intolerable disorder do the people dare, and even then, nervously, uncertainly, again and again shrinking back in turn, to change the situation."[8]

Currently, despite mass unemployment, the climate emergency and other widespread failures and neglect, eco-socialist and degrowth ideals are unable to successfully compete in the short-term with people who are *not* gamblers but myopically prefer a consumer culture. A frugal, ethical life based on such things as generating biogas with biodegradable organic matter like food waste or making or recycling second-hand clothes may help make households more energy and resources independent for 'downsizing' and the necessary 'energy descent' required for sustainable consumption. But these practices will struggle to complete with the comforts and glamour of desirable fashionable goods unless there is a major environmental or economic crisis that ends current levels of material consumption.

Consumer capitalism produces its own perversions, anxiety and demands on individuals but nonetheless, revolves around the satisfaction of immediate desires. Unsurprisingly, both pro-market individuals immersed in an individualist culture and anti-market activists hoping to replace capitalism are attracted to unaffordable universal basic income schemes. It does not challenge individualism, keeps things largely as they are without having to do paid work (if the UBI is set at an adequate but fiscally unaffordable level) and does not require recipients to think about other neglected social needs. As long as the market 'delivers the goods' for most people, radical social change will be rejected. However, the problem facing most capitalist societies is that the deep structural crises which radicals prematurely identified several decades ago are only now beginning to register. These inbuilt constraints and dysfunctional socio-economic and environmental processes will undermine the ability of capitalist political economies to keep 'delivering the goods' without increasingly destroying the environment and jobs that people depend upon for their survival. This is what distinguishes the contradictions of political ecology from conventional technocratic notions of environmentalism.

For all my agreement with the need for 'planned degrowth' as an absolute necessity, I pointed out in Book Three that degrowth movements have yet to produce even rudimentary conceptions of how their objectives can be translated into identifiable institutional structures at national or supranational levels. There is a glaring failure by most advocates of degrowth to formulate clearly defined domestic institutional structures and a set of foreign policy principles and strategic responses to the dangerous state of international relations. Habermas's distinction between solidarity and law is pertinent here.

Even today, how much inequality the citizens of a wealthy country want to live with is still a question of solidarity and not of law. It is not the constitutional state that curbs the growing numbers of young people out of work, of the long-term unemployed and of people in precarious employment, of elderly people whose pension is barely enough for survival, or of impoverished single mothers who have to rely on what are in effect soup kitchens. Only the policy of a legislator who is responsive to the normative claims of a democratic civic community can transform the claims to solidarity of the marginalised or their advocates into social rights.[9]

To date, 'degrowthers' have been strong on putting forward normative claims regarding the 'good society' while weak or silent about how these would translate into legal rights and socio-economic legislation. There is very little or no discussion of whether political parties will exist, how power will be restructured and numerous other elementary aspects of contemporary life that will need to be replaced, modified or retained. Instead, as I have argued, most effort is currently devoted to decentralised local alternatives. In this respect, they conform to what Srnicek and Williams call 'folk politics'. I partly agree with Srnicek and Williams when they declare that "the most important division in today's Left is between those that hold to a folk politics of localism, direct action, and relentless horizontalism, and those that outline what must become called an accelerationist politics at ease with a modernity of abstraction, complexity, globality, and technology."[10] Where I would differ is that one may be comfortable with complexity and abstraction without promoting what is effectively an 'anti-politics' of fully automated and unsustainable visions of post-capitalism. Similarly, one can advocate greater local, decentralised socio-economic practices without subscribing to a utopian horizontalism that unrealistically rejects all vertical political-administrative institutions. While household and local community practices as modes of 'prefigurative' action are important, they are utterly marginalised in a world where key fiscal, social, military, trade and environmental decisions continue to be made at national and international levels.

Paradoxically, in many ways degrowth movements mirror the prevailing individualist mainstream culture with the exception that they reject material consumerism and believe in horizontal and autonomous small groups. Any attempt to develop more centralising or national political organisations have been strongly opposed by degrowth movements in France and other countries.[11] These movements share a detachment from conventional political

engagement, such as joining or forming parties that aim to transform legislative policies and state power. Supporters may attend protest marches in
support of action on the climate emergency and other issues but have little
or no political involvement in campaigning for a range of immediate socio-
economic policies. Instead, politics is conceived as radiating out from the
household and local neighbourhood community which still leave the key
political institutions and most forms of production, communication and
military apparatuses of capitalism barely touched. Importantly, to assume
that complex problems such as reducing national material footprints can be
left to poorly defined local communities is to guarantee failure even before
having the power to implement such strategies. Instead, there is a pervasive
unrealistic optimism shared by many degrowthers that is seemingly blind to
the obstacles confronting major transformative change. We still await the
necessary careful evaluation within each country of what can be locally
extracted or produced, what needs to be imported, which social groups or
sectors within different countries or particular neglected regions need more
rather than less material production and consumption to improve their lives,
which businesses and private forms of consumption have to be cut or scaled
back and at what annual or periodic rate of deceleration. All is currently so
vague or undeveloped that ordinary citizens have no real clue as to what each
will be expected to change in terms of consumption of durable and non-
durable goods and services, or what employment, income and the organisation of existing institutions will be possible if the goal of sustainable practices are to have a chance of being realised.

Moreover, without broad based political movements beyond the household and neighbourhood there will be no transition to a post-growth society.
The scale and complexity of 'planned degrowth' transcends decentralised and
fragmented households. A grass roots degrowth culture still needs to develop
organisations capable of formulating policies and implementing these at
national and local levels. Without these fundamental steps, degrowth movements risk remaining ineffective and unpersuasive at both the policy and
organisational level. In short, a detached 'anti-politics' in the guise of
autonomous horizontal groups is self-defeating in current social and institutional systems based on the accumulation and centralisation of power. At the
moment, those advocating various forms of Green New Deals have the
advantage of tying their socio-economic and environmental reforms to
readily identifiable structures and policies. Little such coherent outline of
alternative proposals is provided by degrowth movements. Rejecting involvement in national political organisations will not make the system collapse but

only confine degrowth advocates to a ghettoised subculture of communication with fellow 'degrowthers' while the political caravan moves on.

The political lesson of diverse political movements in the twentieth century is that none were successful until they either captured state power directly or managed to persuade one or more political parties to legislate social and political reforms. The same could be true of the twenty-first century where the clash between 'democracy and sustainability' will play out in social movement struggles that may ultimately lead to particular state policies of one sort or another. Hence, it is to be hoped that the next phase of the degrowth movement will be much better politically and economically grounded, and especially more critically aware of the need for new strategies to overcome hostile democratic social practices rather than just capitalist authoritarian political and economic obstacles. Let us not forget that in the US alone, over a half a million enthusiastic people left the cities in the late 1960s to form alternative communes. All failed within a short period of a few months to three years of being formed. Like earlier founders of alternative communes, we cannot rely on good intentions and radical values to be transmitted to people of the same generation, let alone from one generation to another if the socio-economic, legal and cultural institutional processes are either unclear or established on shaky, unviable foundations. Rather than be left with the unpalatable choice of either business as usual or a modified 'green growth' agenda, we need a different and more politically mature form of degrowth that directly engages with the mass of the population rather than promoting poorly grounded alternative visions.

BETWEEN DISASTER AND UTOPIA

We live in a new era where there is a fundamental disjuncture and disconnect between the policies pursued and the infrastructures being laid by governments and businesses on the one side and the hopes and political strategies advocated by a range of mainstream and radical critics of carbon capitalism on the other. Until recently, there was an optimism shared by business groups and neoliberal policy makers that a global market was not only being created but would ensure the future of capitalism. By the 1990s, many radical critics of capitalism also assumed that capitalist globalisation and the formation of a 'global ruling class' was the reality of political and economic power that had to be encountered and overcome in future struggles. Instead, we are currently witnessing the development of a deep-seated regionalism which is quite different to Polanyi's and Streeck's notion of regionalism. Military, security and energy 'grids' are being established that will shape the economic and socio-cultural pathways of all societies in the next ten to thirty years. The *real politik* and utopian approaches to the new regionalism take radically different forms.

Realists argue that regardless of whether Trump or Biden wins in November 2020, American policy makers will continue to pursue a policy of 'containment' in regard to China's industrial, technological and military power. This will ensure that new telecommunications and cyber security grids will develop along separate regional lines. Advanced military equipment and security and surveillance regimes are largely inseparable from one another. Depending on the regional power most countries will align with in coming years, so most of the industries operating with new digital technologies in particular countries will be increasingly affected by 'great power' military and high-tech hardware and software. The EU is also attempting to develop its own military force, an 'internet of things' and other innovative technology to give it more muscle in competition with the US and China. However, it is less able to gain independence from the US because of the reliance of the EU on US military protection and dependence on the American market for its exports and finance.

Closely tied to the shape of future digital products and industries are the divergent energy grids and logistical infrastructure facilities being built. China's Belt and Road connecting North and South Asia to Europe via Central Asia and the Middle East is now being resisted in Europe and elsewhere. Germany and Europe are almost locked in to the Russian-German giant gas pipeline and Japan, South Korea and other Asian countries are heavily dependent on Australia as the world's largest exporter of natural gas. The US and Canada are still too committed to new fossil fuel extraction projects to surrender these to rising renewable energy companies and a new decarbonised energy grid. The large political question relating to all these diverse infrastructure and energy grids is what happens to regional and individual national economies once these massive energy infrastructure projects and existing production facilities become 'stranded assets' by 2040 at the latest? In other words, we have the interrelated military, security and technological grids heavily reliant on either developing or sustaining for as long as possible fossil energy networks and supply lines that are environmentally unsustainable. What does this mean for opponents of capitalism?

Clearly, Marxist radicals or utopian advocates of degrowth have no power to prevent current military and technological developments. All the technological utopian proposals about peer-to-peer communication networks without either hierarchies or large rentier giants such as Google, Facebook and Amazon are unrealistic unless governments break-up these oligopolies. Decentralised energy generation run by local communities are also in a weak position given that corporations are currently consolidating their hold over large renewable energy grids. However, climate activists have growing power concerning the need to switch from fossil fuels to renewables mainly because of the ever-growing impact of climate breakdown and also because many businesses and governments are also worried about the near future. It is actually on the social and employment fronts that critics of capitalism have greater future leverage despite the current weaknesses of labour movements. This is because leading governments and business groups have few answers about how to sustain employment, income and consumption without increasingly moving towards heavily involved government socio-economic and environmental schemes whether they are called 'green new deals' or something else. It will be the coming struggles over providing sufficient employment and social services that will generate debate over what kind of policies and forms of consumption are sustainable or unsustainable. Recognising the regional diversity of different military, high-tech, energy and 'social state' developments and alternative possibilities is what will increasingly define political conflict now and in the future.

In my companion book *Fictions of Sustainability*, I analysed and critiqued the influential utopian ideas of both pro-market and anti-market policy makers and theorists. Those who wish to rescue and preserve capitalist economic growth from the constraints of nature continue to believe in the utopian notion of absolutely decoupling growth from the biophysical limits of the natural world. Similarly, radical post-capitalists subscribe to a range of technological utopian ideas that rest on fanciful notions of environmental abundance. In this book, *Capitalism Versus Democracy?* I have built on these arguments by focussing on two related themes: firstly, the emergence and transformation of the dominant paradigm 'capitalism versus democracy'; and secondly, why the future of both capitalist and post-capitalist societies will be driven by new tensions between 'democracy and sustainability' that the old conflicts over the democratic or authoritarian character of capitalism still fail to fully recognise, explain or resolve. There are, however, important theoretical links between the two paradigms.

The Hungarian revolutionary György Lukács interpreted Marx's critique of capitalism as signifying "above all the end of the domination of the economy over the totality of life."[12] This was in 1920, a decade before he had read Marx's 1844 newly discovered manuscripts on alienation in 1930. Echoes of Lukács' view were to be heard from his fellow Hungarian Karl Polanyi through to the neo-Marxist and socialist Left of previous decades right up until the contemporary degrowth movement of today. The desire to end all forms of alienation is readily visible in 'degrowthers' vision of an alternative society. While it is both highly desirable and possible to end the obsession with the growth of GDP and even the dominance of the economy over all aspects of life as ends in themselves, this goal is not in itself equivalent to ending both wage labour and the division of labour. Regardless of the continued conflict between 'democracy and sustainability', the notion of ending *all* alienation and fully reconciling 'humans' and 'nature' will forever be a romantic, utopian illusion. A substantial portion of alienated labour can certainly be overcome. The notion that all jobs and all forms of work will become pleasant, engaging and satisfying, however, remains unbelievable at this conjuncture.

If we are to avert possible disasters in the form of climate chaos, nuclear war or economic depressions, it also means that we should come to terms with utopianism. This book has critiqued the utopian ideas that merely distract energy from the difficult political tasks ahead. It is not utopian though to believe that capitalist regimes and social relations can be replaced with decommodified, caring and co-operative social relations and institutional practices. This ought certainly to be the goal of all who desire a more environmentally sustainable future. However, as many before me have pointed out, it is illusory to think that some future semi- or fully automated production system will have no division of labour. There will still be divisions between hundreds of occupations and practitioners of specialised forms of knowledge, unless we all return to the simplicity of the soil. Crafts may once again flourish but definitely not as the main providers of social needs for a global population of nine billion plus.

It was Nietzsche who believed in an *Übermensch* or human beings who could give meaning to their life on earth without the need for a God or an afterlife. Leaving Nietzsche's problematic politics aside, we need a radical conception of the relationship between democracy and sustainability that dispenses with mythical utopian or quasi-religious ideas such as achieving the end of all alienation, being completely at one with nature or constructing the fully embedded society. These are unattainable idealist diversions that only obscure and obstruct our ability to confront and deal with the complexity of socio-economic and political relations. Also, the early Hegelian-influenced Marx conceptualised all pre-socialist class-divided societies as the stage of 'pre-history' and that 'history' would only begin when the class-conscious proletariat took power and consciously made history rather than having it made 'behind their backs'. I have argued that the unfolding struggle of 'democracy versus sustainability' will be quite different to the utopian goals generated by 'capitalism versus democracy'. There will be no division between 'pre-history' and the 'historical dawn' of a sustainable just society. On the contrary, 'democracy versus sustainability' will continue as a permanent ongoing struggle. Sustainability and democracy are not end goals that once achieved remain perpetually in place. Instead, the political task of trying to minimise local or global *unsustainability* is an ongoing conflictual process as is the battle to win democratic power for populations suffering under varying levels of authoritarian rule.

Most contemporary radicals no longer believe, as did previous generations of socialists like Polanyi, that 'capitalism versus democracy' is a struggle which, despite major setbacks such as fascism, will nonetheless see socialism inevitably triumph. Instead, wherever and whenever democratic processes are established there is no guarantee that people will choose socialism or green, degrowth social values over capitalist market practices. At the moment, in most countries people are divided by various levels of awareness of the need to prevent climate breakdown but disagree over the measures required to create a safe climate. Similarly, 'sustainability' is a word that is widely invoked without any deep understanding or agreement as to the major policy changes needed to achieve this goal. If democracies become genuinely participatory, there will always be varying degrees of conflict and disagreement over how to reduce material footprints, maximise the protection of biodiversity and especially how to improve the lives of more than five billion people currently suffering from poverty, inequality and insecurity.

In recent decades, we have seen a range of prominent thinkers such as Jürgen Habermas, Anthony Giddens, Ulrich Beck and others highlight the complexity of 'modernity' and why the old belief in the overthrow of capitalism and the establishment of self-managed worker's control is no longer possible. The fulfilment of Enlightenment values now requires, they argue, a new self-reflexivity that simultaneously questions economic policy, science and other aspects of social life while recognising that highly complex urbanised societies based on elaborate technologies, specialised professional divisions of knowledge and multiple global interconnections cannot be reduced to the old socialist model of the proletariat controlling 'the factory'. Habermas claims that capitalism can no longer be replaced by revolution. It is therefore necessary to defend the 'life world' of social values, subjective experiences and relationships from being 'colonised' and destroyed by the 'social system' of market practices. The 'lure of technocracy' has to be kept at bay and defeated if deliberative democracy, rationality and equal, respectful relations between people are to prevail.

Although these theorists make powerful points that all of us cannot afford to ignore, they are also conservative when it comes to environmental issues and essentially fail to confront the reality of the increasing conflict of 'democracy versus sustainability'. Habermas, Giddens and Wolfgang Streeck may oppose one another in terms of their support or opposition to the democratisation of the EU, but they all champion a variety of ecological modernisation or 'green growth', either in market or non-market forms. This approach has merit in reducing greenhouse gas emissions but nevertheless takes the world in a direction of dangerous unsustainability. The goal of a social democratic 'social state' may be far better than current forms of neoliberal austerity and inequality. However, social democracy as conceived in both its reform orientated non-radical version and in its radical alternative form is environmentally unsustainable. Its goals can no longer be realised if confined to conflicts between labour and capital or disputes over how to restructure social and political administration without an adequate consideration of the ecological consequences of growing material footprints. Large material footprints are, as we have seen, incompatible with precarious biophysical processes and resources. Particular national or supranational forms of the 'social state' are no longer sustainable if they are based on revenue from existing forms of incessant growth in production and consumption in capitalist societies, no matter how self-reflexive, tolerant and modernised.

It is important to recognise that ecological sustainability can never be fully secured or compatible with democracy as long as each group of people in diverse locations or each new generation of people redefine their needs and make claims on natural resources that can neither be met nor successfully renewed. Similarly, advocates of social change are divided between those who have long recognised that political disputes will continue in post-capitalist societies and others who adhere to images of the 'alternative society' as a harmonious and cooperative social order, free from the irrationality and power relations typical of existing societies. Yet, as I have argued throughout this book, the tension between democratic practices and the need to ensure environmental sustainability will involve fluctuating political dynamics that will always be potentially antagonistic, characterised by competing notions of what is desirable and feasible for local communities as opposed to national and international constituencies.

Nevertheless, between disaster and utopia there is a great deal of political space for many radical goals to be adopted and promoted by social movements and parties. Each political group of activists must think of how their policies and social goals enhance either democracy or sustainability or possibly both. We cannot afford to succumb to 'exaggerated pessimism' or like Wolfgang Streeck, for example, wait for capitalism to slowly decompose like the human body or the old Roman Empire. Nor can we adopt a 'sophisticated' form of rational modernisation or 'civilised capitalism' that is propelled by market growth but is deeply incompatible with achieving greater global social justice based on more equal and sustainable material footprints. In 2009, Anthony Giddens criticised green activists and projected an optimistic scenario of 'green growth' based on techno-fixes such as 'clean coal' carbon capture, geo-engineering heat shields, nuclear power or Jeremy Rifkin's zero marginal growth and trillions of sensors providing decentralised renewable energy. Many of the latter are either dangerous or utopian.[13] It is striking that Giddens advocated many of the same techno-fixes that the Accelerationists and Promethean technological utopians supported, except that the latter linked these to the radical creation of a post-work, post-capitalism whereas Giddens, Beck, Habermas and other ecological modernisers favoured a more egalitarian, social democratic, 'civilised capitalism' as practical 'utopian realism'.

Sadly, but unsurprisingly, the optimistic belief of Giddens and other advocates of a mixture of capitalist markets and limited government planning (Lord Stern, Jeffrey Sachs and an army of well-intentioned ecological modernisers) have utterly failed to stop the rise in greenhouse emissions or help alleviate poverty, inequality and violent conflict. Instead, most governments and enterprises are conservative and reactive and avoid taking the lead on social and environmental issues. The political and economic system at national and international level has inbuilt institutional processes geared to frustrate, delay and avoid even minimal social change. Without fear of punishment in the form of losing office or losing business, political and business leaders prefer to do as little as possible and hope that only a minority will notice. As long as this charade continues and electorates fail to act and instead put their faith in 'good leaders', little will change and only deteriorate.

On the other hand, the possibility of revolution is equally unrealistic at present. Dozens of countries from India to Nigeria, Pakistan to Brazil, desperately need social and political revolutions to end the shocking levels of inequality and poverty, the rampant corruption and sheer degradation of environments and human life. However, these are unlikely to occur in the near future in countries that are divided by sectarian religious and communal hatreds presided over by narrow nationalists and outright repressive governments. Revolutionary movements currently lack domestic or international support for either peaceful or armed resistance. Importantly, few other societies wish to follow the 'cult of personality' of authoritarian so-called socialists such as Hugo Chávez and Nicolás Maduro despite the widespread squalid conditions of present-day life in their own countries. The era of 'Third World' revolutions triggering revolution in advanced capitalist countries died decades ago. Socialist revolutionaries will get no support from either Putin or Xi as they are more interested in developing capitalist markets than social equality and democracy.

As to OECD countries, it is not just a matter of protecting the 'lifeworld' from being colonised by the market 'social system'. This has already largely occurred in most advanced capitalist countries and is spreading across the globe. However, colonising 'consumer individualism' can be stopped and even reversed at individual and social levels. For this socio-political process to succeed, a growing number of people and political movements will first need to recognise that the goal of environmental sustainability requires adjusting and transforming both personal consumption and public policies so that they keep within the limits of the earth's biophysical carrying capacity. Such recognition is still confined to a minority in most countries. To reach majority public awareness will be an uphill political struggle that will require liberal social democrats, radical Marxists, greens and a range of other social and political movements and governments across the world to redefine their expectations and social goals. This will not begin to happen until parties and organisations across the political spectrum are pressured by mass movements to reduce or abandon their commitment to incessant material economic growth.

Without careful steering between disaster and utopia there will be no successful institutional and organisational transition from capitalism to post-carbon or post-capitalist sustainable democracies. Currently, we are subjected to the daily war of competing models, whether on forecasts of global warming, economic growth, natural resources, mental illness or levels of poverty. If only half of these projections prove to be correct, then we will require urgent preventive action. This will require a transition to societies based on entirely different socio-economic and ecological principles to those presently driving such potential disasters. These struggles will be protracted, highly conflictual and quite uneven depending on the character of political forces in each particular country. For some countries it will be violence and extensive loss of life. For others, transitions will be relatively peaceful.

Although the working class is hardly in a pre-revolutionary state of mind, we cannot rule out deepening crises and loss of confidence within middle classes that have been the bedrock of stability in many capitalist countries. Government crisis-management policies have failed to resolve debt, employment and other socio-economic problems to ensure that the children of the affluent professional middle-class have an upwardly mobile future. The combined effect of climate crisis, economic stagnation and 'no future' for both working-class and middle-class populations can erode confidence and even lead to collapse once triggered by unexpected events. Let us remember that the USSR was riddled with long-term crises but most of the Soviet population were still unable to imagine such a quick and sudden collapse. The collapse of capitalist societies is hardly desirable if chaos follows and there is no preparation for an alternative social system. Competitive consumer individualism and authoritarian practices need to be weakened and replaced with alternative conceptions of cooperative sustainable democratic institutions and social relations. Without these alternative imaginaries, protracted crises could well lead to 'democracy' in its consumer individualist form increasingly coming into conflict with many aspects of sustainability – a dangerous political scenario with dire consequences.

On the positive side, the climate crisis has awakened global populations to the fragility of familiar socio-economic processes and opened up questioning of the material processes of production and consumption well beyond the issue of decarbonisation. Hence, the potential future realisation of egalitarian, sustainable and culturally tolerant values will depend on a range of different but related political and cultural struggles. At the centre of these diverse struggles will be whether both democratic and authoritarian regimes based on selfish 'competitive consumer individualism' are undermined and seriously weakened. It is imperative that individual rights not be sacrificed but differentiated from the negative characteristics of consumer individualism. Political solidarity must be based on the recognition that individual rights and well-being are inseparable from social well-being. The struggles against unemployment, poverty and inadequate public services need to be linked to political campaigns centred on universal basic services. These essential services and associated public employment will require fundamental changes in the allocation of existing goods and services. They are critically needed in all countries and must be closely tied to transforming material footprints so that both key producer countries and dependent consumer societies head in the direction of greater environmental sustainability.

Crucially, this redirection of socio-economic resources is not solely aimed at the poor and the suffering. It is a strategy that culturally and socially enriches the lives of all people no matter how resistant many will be initially as they cling to dominant competitive materialistic values. A reorientation of research and development in science and technology away from many of their existing military and consumer market priorities will be needed if there is any chance of creating detailed sustainable alternative political economic strategies for each country, locality or region. While we cannot regress to an earlier phase of semi-closed local communities and reliance on simple craft production if social innovation and creativity are to prevail, we must reject the environmental dangers posed by Promethean technological utopians. There is no need to wait for futuristic techno-fixes such as 'zero marginal cost products' or environmentally unsustainable 'fully automated luxury communism'. We already have the technology, the ideas and the fiscal resources. The only thing lacking is the political will and sufficient popular support.

For planned degrowth to be successful and relevant to the vast majority of humanity, we have to both utilise and carefully scrutinise the complex array of technology and science, devise macro-economic public policies that maximise biodiversity while countering the destructive socio-economic policies of market capitalism. Greater social equality cannot be achieved by retreating to totally decentralised local communities at the expense of the vast number of people and regions that are resources and income poor. A future based on outward-orientated international cooperation and shared resources, a cosmopolitan embrace of diverse cultures rather than fear and racism is the way forward. Young people are currently exposed to global cultural activities and values as never before. We can build on these international links by enriching local life with a more diverse set of cultural exchanges and new social bonds rather than retreating to parochial semi-isolation and the 'steady state'. As the Chinese proverb on my desk calendar states: "Be not afraid of growing slowly, be afraid only of standing still."

It is an illusion to think that all hierarchical forms of administration can be abolished and yet have adequate forms of coordination to facilitate the production and distribution of food and resources, knowledge and culture or goods and services. If material footprints are to become fair and equal, then this can only be achieved by complex planning targets and international negotiations that are based on the recognition of local and regional needs. A sustainable democracy is not possible without a critical politics that challenges problematic accounts of the past and simplistic concepts of the way forward. Achieving ecological sustainability requires maximum citizen participation and is no less difficult or complex than achieving greater social justice and a successful democracy. Both processes rely on informed and knowledgeable publics. It is this vital condition, powerful social tool and political weapon that I hope this book has made a small contribution to strengthening and promoting.

NOTES AND REFERENCES

Introduction – Setting the Scene

1. See for example, Slavoj Žižek, *Pandemic! Covid-19 Shakes the World*, OR Books, London, 2020; Patrick Wintour, 'Coronavirus: who will be winners and losers in new world order?', *The Guardian*, April 11, 2020; Adam Tooze, 'Shockwave', *London Review of Books*, April 16, 2020.
2. John Bellamy Foster and Intan Suwandi, 'COVID-19 and Catastrophe Capitalism Commodity Chains and Ecological-Epidemiological-Economic Crises', *Monthly Review*, June 2020.
3. Dani Rodrik, 'Will Covid-19 Remake the World?', *Project Syndicate*, April 6, 2020.
4. Clancy Yeates, "Australia won't look the same': ANZ's Elliott warns coronavirus impact will be generational' *The Age*, April 4, 2020.
5. George Soros, 'Capitalism versus Democracy', *Project Syndicate*, 27 June 2000.
6. For a brief sample of the literature and diverse accounts of 'populism' see C. Mudde and C. Rovira Kaltwasser (eds), *Populism in Europe and the Americas: Threat or Corrective for Democracy?*, Cambridge University Press, Cambridge, 2012; S. Gherghina, S. Mişcoiu and S. Soare (eds.), *Contemporary Populism: A Controversial Concept and Its Diverse Forms*, Cambridge Scholars Publishing, Newcastle upon Tyne, 2013; B. Moffitt, *The global rise of populism: Performance, political style and representation,* Stanford University Press, Stanford, 2016; plus many articles by a range of authors in special editions of *Politics and Governance*, Vol. 5, no. 4, 2017; *Economy & Society*; vol.46, no.1, 2017; *Thesis Eleven*, vol.149, December 2018 and *Constellations*, vol.26, no.3, 2019.
7. An account of the exchange between Varoufakis and Schäuble is given by Yanis Varoufakis in his lecture 'Is Capitalism Devouring Democracy?', Cambridge Forum, Boston, 9th May 2018. Andy Storey, 'The Myths of Ordoliberalism', Working Paper 17-02, ERC Project 'European Unions', University College Dublin, 2017, observes that Schäuble had "the chutzpah to cite Eucken approvingly on the need for risk-takers to bear losses as well as to reap gains..." (p.14) Despite rejecting the needs of the Greek people, Schäuble ensured that little or no 'Ordoliberal discipline' was applied to German finance institutions when he bailed them out.
8. See Stephan Pühringer, 'Think Tank Networks of German Neoliberalism: Power Structures in Economics and Economic Policies in Postwar Germany' in Dieter Plehwe, Quinn Slobodian and Philip Mirowski (eds.) *Nine Lives of Neoliberalism*, Verso, London, 2020.
9. Quinn Slobodian, *Globalists: The End of Empire and the Birth of Neoliberalism*, Harvard University Press, Cambridge, 2018 and Thomas Biebricher, *The Political Theory of Neoliberalism*, Stanford University Press, Stanford, 2018, especially ch.7, 'Ideas, Uncertainty, and the Ordoliberalization of Europe'.
10. Interview with Yanis Varoufakis, "The European Union Is Determined to Continue Making the Same Errors It Made After 2008", *Jacobin*, April 8, 2020. Also see Yanis Varoufakis, 'Europe Is Unprepared for the COVID-19 Recession', *Project Syndicate*, March 18, 2020. As he put it, "The 2015 Eurogroup meetings offer listeners a front-row seat on the blood sport that is unaccountable power. It's all there: Crucial decisions flying in the face of science and simple mathematics. Bullying the weak until they surrender. Thinly disguised theft. Fake

news weaponized against those who dare to resist. And last, but not least, contempt for transparency and the other checks and balances essential in any democracy."

11. Karl Marx, On the Jewish Question (1843) reprinted in Loyd D. Easton and Kurt H. Guddat (eds), *Writings of the Young Marx on Philosophy and Society*, Anchor Books, New York, 1967.

12. See for example, Jason Brennan, *Against Democracy*, Princeton University Press, Princeton, 2016.

13. Thomas Piketty, 'Brahmin Left vs Merchant Right: Rising Inequality and the Changing Structure of Political Conflict (Evidence from France, Britain and the US, 1948-2017), *World Inequality Lab*, Paris, March 22, 2018 and edited version republished in Thomas Piketty, *Capital and Ideology*, trans. by Arthur Goldhammer, Harvard University Press, Cambridge, 2020, ch.15.

14. Gareth Dale, *Reconstructing Karl Polanyi: Excavation and Critique*, Pluto Press, London, 2016, pp.70-71.

15. Vladimir Lenin, *The State and Revolution*, translation published by Foreign Languages Publishing House, Moscow, 1952, p.22.

16. See Claus Offe, *Contradictions of the Welfare State*, edited and translated by John Keane, Hutchinson, London, 1984; James O'Connor, *The Fiscal Crisis of the State*, St. Martin's Press, New York, 1973 and Jürgen Habermas, *Legitimation Crisis*, trans. by Thomas McCarthy, Beacon Press, Boston, 1973.

17. Claus Offe, 'Competitive Party Democracy and the Keynesian Welfare State: Factors of Stability and Disorganization', *Policy Sciences*, Vol. 15, No. 3, 1983, pp. 225-246.

18. *Ibid*, p. 228.

19. Claus Offe, *Contradictions of the Welfare State*, p.153.

20. For a historical analysis of how neoliberal notions of human rights triumphed after the 1970s, see Jessica Whyte, *The Morals of the Market Human Rights and the Rise of Neoliberalism*, Verso, London, 2019. Whyte, however, is weak on the use of military intervention to enforce human rights.

21. Jürgen Habermas, *Philosophical Introductions Five Approaches to Communicative Reason*, translated by Ciaran Cronin, Polity, Cambridge, 2018, p.131.

22. Edmund S. Morgan, *Inventing the People: The Rise of Popular Sovereignty in England and America*, W.W. Norton, New York, 1988, pp.13-14.

23. Alexei Yurchak, *Everything Was Forever, Until It Was No More: The Last Soviet Generation*, Princeton University Press, Princeton, 2005.

24. In 2016, Adam Curtis, inspired by Yurchak, produced his BBC documentary *Hypernormalisation* about how contrived forms such as 'fake news' had become synonymous with a new socio-political condition across the world.

25. Partha Chatterjee, *I Am the People: Reflections on Popular Sovereignty Today*, Columbia University Press, New York, 2020, pp. 60-63.

26. *Ibid* p. xii.

27. Freud's starting point is similar to Marx's opening critique in the *Grundrisse* of the eighteenth-century political economists (the Robinsonades) who erroneously started from the premise of the utopian isolated individual following Daniel Defoe's *Robinson Crusoe*.

28. Eric Fromm, *The Dogma of Christ and other essays on religion, psychology and culture*, Routledge and Taylor & Francis E-library edition, London, 2004, p.3.

29. Daniel J. Levinson, Else Frenkel-Brunswik, Nevitt Sanford, and Theodor W. Adorno, *The Authoritarian Personality*, Harper, New York, 1950.

30. Pierre Rosanvallon, *Counter-Democracy: Politics in an Age of Distrust*, trans. by Arthur Goldhammer, Cambridge University Press, Cambridge, 2008. Also see John Keane, *The Life and Death of Democracy*, Simon & Schuster, London, 2009 who focuses on 'oversight' in the development of 'monitory democracy' globally through many types of civil society groups, agencies and institutional bodies.

31. Pierre Rosanvallon, *The Society of Equals*, translated by Arthur Goldhammer, Harvard University Press, Cambridge, 2013, p.1.

32. See Colin Crouch, *Post-Democracy*, Polity Press, Cambridge, 2004. Crouch has revised his notion of post-democracy in the light of major crises since 2008, see *Post-democracy after the Crises*, Polity Press, Cambridge, 2020.

33. John Keane, *The New Despotism,* Harvard University Press, Cambridge, 2020.

34. See Evgeny Morozov, *The Net Delusion: The Dark Side of Internet Freedom,* Allen lane, London, 2011 and Colin Crouch, *Post-Democracy*, Polity, Cambridge, 2004.

35. Paolo Gerbaudo, *The Digital Party: Political Organisation and Online Democracy*, Pluto Press, London, 2019. The Five Star Movement recently managed to reduce the number of sitting parliamentarians.

36. Stephen Rammler, 'I'd rather die in a democracy than live in a sustainable dictatorship', interview with Claudia Detsch, *International Politics and Society*, 30 May 2019.

37. Naomi Klein, *This Changes Everything: Capitalism vs. The Climate*, Simon & Schuster, New York, 2015.

38. See for example, Jason Hickel, 'Is it possible to achieve a good life for all within planetary boundaries?', *Third World Quarterly*, vol. 40, no.1, 2019, pp.18-35.

39. Iago Otero, et al., 'Biodiversity policy beyond economic growth', *The Conservation Letters,* Wiley Online, April 13, 2020.

40. Andrew McAfee, *More From Less: The Surprising Story of How We Learned to Prosper Using Fewer Resources – and What Happens Next*, Simon & Schuster, New York, 2019.

41. See Nafeez Ahmed, 'Green Economic Growth is an Article of 'Faith' Devoid of Scientific Evidence', *Resilience*, July 15, 2020.

42. Johan Rockström, et al. 'Planetary Boundaries: Exploring the Safe Operating Space for Humanity', *Ecology and Society*. Vol.14, no.2, article 32, 2009.

43. On the 'four cheaps' (labour power, food, energy and raw materials), see Jason W. Moore, 'World accumulation and planetary life, or, why capitalism will not survive until the 'last tree is cut", *IPPR Progressive Review*, vol 24, no.3, 2017, pp.176-202.

44. See Stuart Rosewarne, 'The Structural Transformation of Australian Agriculture: Globalisation, Corporatisation and the Devalorisation of Labour' *Journal of Australian Political Economy* No. 84, 2019, pp. 175-218.

45. For the most detailed examination of 179 reports that claimed decoupling, see T. Vadén, V. Lähde, A. Majava, P. Järvensivu, T. Toivanen, E. Hakala and J. T. Eronen, 'Decoupling for ecological sustainability: A categorisation and review of research literature', *Environmental Science and Policy*, 112, 2020, pp. 236-244.

46. See the latest detailed statistics on inequality analysed by a range of contributors such as Robert Wade, Jayati Ghosh, et al in The Inequality Crisis, *real-world economics review*, issue no.92, June 2020.

47. Jodi Dean interview with Tomislav Medak & Petar Jandrić, 'Embrace the Antagonism, Build the Party! The New

    Communist Horizon in and Against Communicative Capitalism', *Postdigital Science and Education*, published online 29 August 2018.

48. Guillaume Pitron, 'Dirty Rare Metals: Digging Deeper into the Energy Transition', *Isles of the Left*, March 22, 2019.

49. For major technological obstacles in the foreseeable future to replacing fossil fuel for airlines, see National Academies of Sciences, Engineering, and Medicine, *Commercial Aircraft Propulsion and Energy Systems Research: Reducing Global Carbon Emissions*, The National Academies Press, Washington, DC, 2016. For carbon emissions from aviation, see Mark Carter, *The Elephant in the Sky: The Hazards of Aviation Emissions and How We Can Avoid Them*, Melbourne, October 2018.

50. Aaron Bastani, *Fully Automated Luxury Communism A Manifesto*. Verso, London, 2019.

51. Joshua Clover, 'The Roundabout Riots', *Versobooks Blog*, 9th December 2018.

52. The resurgence of neo-fascism has also seen a revival of interest in Nietzsche which is different to the earlier interest in Nietzsche, Heidegger and Schmitt by post-Marxist French and Anglo-American theorists – see Ronald Beiner, *Dangerous Minds: Nietzsche,*

Heidegger, and the Return of the Far Right, University of Pennsylvania Press, Philadelphia, 2018.

53. See for example, Christian G. De Vito and Anne Gerritsen (eds.) *Micro-Spatial Histories of Global Labour*, Palgrave Macmillan, Cham, 2018.

54. George Monbiot, 'Neoliberalism: the deep story that lies beneath Donald Trump's triumph', *The Guardian*, 14 November 2016.

55. See, for example, Hayden White, 'The Question of Narrative in Contemporary Historical Theory', *History and Theory*, Vol. 23, No.1, 1984, pp.1-33; Carolyn J. Dean, 'Hayden White, Metahistory: The Historical Imagination in Nineteenth Century Europe', *The American Historical Review*, Vol.124, no.4, 2019, pp. 1337-1350; also see Alex Callinicos, *Theories and Narratives: Reflections on the Philosophy of History*, Polity Press, Cambridge, 1995.

56. Max Blumenthal, *The Management of Savagery: How America's National Security State Fuelled the Rise of Al Qaeda, ISIS, and Donald Trump*, Verso, London, 2019, p.10.

57. Charles L. Heatherly (ed.) *Mandate for leadership: policy management in a conservative administration*, Heritage Foundation, Washington, 1981.

58. *La condition postmoderne: rapport sur le savoir*, Minuit, Paris 1979, English translation by Geoffrey Bennington and Brian Massumi, University of Minnesota Press, Minneapolis, 1984.

59. See *Jean-Francis Lyotard: The Interviews and Debates* edited by Kiff Bamford, Bloomsbury, London, 2020.

60. Michel Foucault, 'What is Enlightenment?' (delivered as a lecture in May 1978) and reprinted in Paul Rabinow (ed.), *The Foucault Reader*, Pantheon Books, New York, 1984, p. 46.

61. Adrian May, *From Bataille to Badiou Lignes: The Preservation of Radical French Thought, 1987–2017*, Liverpool University Press, Liverpool, 2018, p.170.

62. Baudrillard quoted by May, *Ibid*, p.172.

63. *Ibid*, pp.172-73.

64. Angela Nagle, *Kill All Normies: Online Culture Wars From 4Chan and Tumblr to Trump and the Alt-Right*, Zero Books, Winchester and Washington, 2017, p.3.

65. See Samantha Bradshaw and Philip Howard, *Troops, Trolls and Troublemakers: A Global Inventory of Organised Social Media Manipulation*, Computational Propaganda Research Project, Oxford University, Working Paper no. 12, 2017.

66. See Bill Dunn, 'Against Neoliberalism as a Concept', *Capital & Class*, vol.41, no.3, 2017, pp.435-54.

67. German economist Alexander Rüstow coined the positive term of neoliberalism in 1938. Rüstow was active in post-1945 economic circles that included Friedrich von Hayek, but his ideas differed from Hayek's, see Oliver M. Hartwich, *Neoliberalism: The Genesis of a Political Swearword*, Centre for Independent Studies, St. Leonards, May 2009. For critical concepts of neoliberalism, see for example, Damien Cahill, Melinda Cooper, Martijn Konings and David Primrose (eds.) *The Sage Handbook of Neoliberalism*, Sage, London 2018; Simon Springer, Kean Birch and Julie MacLeavy (eds.) *The Handbook of Neoliberalism*, Routledge, New York, 2016 and Rajesh Venugopal, 'Neoliberalism as concept', *Economy and Society*, vol.44, no.2, 2015, pp.165-187.

68. See Eva Illouz, *The End of Love: A Sociology of Negative Relations*, Oxford University Press, New York, 2019.

69. William Davies, 'The New Neoliberalism', *New Left Review*, no.101, 2016, pp.121-134.

70. See my analysis in 'Beyond Labourism and Socialism: How the Australian Labor Party Developed the Model of New Labour', *New Left Review*, no.221, 1997, pp. 3-33.

71. Max Horkheimer, 'The Jews and Europe' *Zeitschrift für Sozialforschung*, December 1939, reprinted in Stephen Bronner and Douglas Kellner (eds) *Critical Theory and Society: A Reader*, Routledge, New York, 1989, p.78.

72. The closest experiences were in the sixteenth and seventeenth centuries known as the 'little ice age' when temperatures dropped by two degrees Celsius, - see Philipp Blom, *Nature's*

Mutiny: How the Little Ice Age of the Long Seventeenth Century Transformed the West and Shaped the Present, Liveright, New York, 2019.

73. Karl Marx, 'The Eighteenth Brumaire of Louis Bonaparte' (1852) reprinted in *Karl Marx The Political Writings, Volume II. Surveys from Exile*, Verso, London, 2019.

74. See Jens Beckert, *Imagined Futures Fictional Expectations and Capitalist Dynamics*, Harvard University Press, Cambridge, 2016 and Jens Beckert and Richard Bronk (eds.) *Uncertain Futures Imaginaries, Narratives, and Calculation in the Economy*, Oxford University Press, Oxford, 2018. Unfortunately, Beckert does not analyse radical post-capitalist imagined futures or how our conception of environmental crisis affects economic calculations and expectations.

75. Daniel Innerarity, *The Future and Its Enemies: In Defense of Political Hope*, Translated by Sandra Kingery, Stanford University Press, Stanford, 2012, p. 3.

76. *Ibid.*

77. Stevphen Shukaitis, David Graeber (eds) with Erika Biddle, *Constituent Imagination: Militant Investigations // Collective Theorization*, AK Press, Oakland, 2007, p.33.

1. Forget Polanyi!

1. Some mainstream analysts have recently turned to Lenin's account of imperialism in order to explain big-power rivalry between the US and China, see Jean Pisani-Ferry, 'Europe and the New Imperialism', *Project Syndicate*, 1 April 2019.

2. K. Polanyi, 'The Essence of Fascism' reprinted in Claus Thomasberger and Michele Cangiani (eds.) *Karl Polanyi Economy and Society: Selected Writings*, Polity Press, Cambridge, 2018, p.105.

3. Wolfgang Streeck, *Buying Time: The Delayed Crisis of Democratic Capitalism*, German edition 2013, translated by Patrick Camiller, Verso, London, 2014, p.173.

4. 'Fascism and Marxism' in Thomasberger and Cangiani (eds.), *op.cit.*, p.129.

5. Karl Polanyi, *The Great Transformation: The political and economic origins of our time*, (1944) Beacon Press, Boston, 2001.

6. See Gareth Dale, *Karl Polanyi: A Life on the Left*, Columbia University Press, New York, 2016 for a fine biographical analysis of his life and ideas.

7. Since 1988, the Karl Polanyi Institute at Concordia University in Montreal as well as a flourishing international academic industry of publications and conferences has dissected and documented the intricacies of Polanyi's life and work.

8. See for example, Joseph Stiglitz's Foreword to the 2001 edition of *The Great Transformation*, Beacon Press, Boston; Mariana Mazzucato, 'The Entrepreneurial State - Towards an Innovation and Investment-led Recovery in Europe', *Journal For a Progressive Economy*, 8 October 2016, p.14 and Dani Rodrik, *Has Globalization Gone Too Far?*, Institute for International Economics, Washington 1997.

9. See for example, P. Anderson, 'Jottings on the Conjuncture', *New Left Review*, November /December 2007. no. 48, pp.5-37; C. Crouch, 'Europe beyond neoliberalism', *Eurozine*, 16 April, 2019; N. Fraser, 'Marketization, social protection, emancipation: Toward a neo-Polanyian conception of capitalist crisis', in C. Calhoun and G. Derlugian (eds.), *Business as Usual: The Roots of the Global Financial Meltdown*, NYU Press, New York, 2011, pp. 137–158; J. Habermas, *The Post-National Constellation*, Polity, Cambridge 2001, ch.4; D. Harvey, *Spaces of Global Capitalism*, Verso, London, 2005; Thomas Piketty, 'Toward a Reconciliation between Economics and the Social Sciences, ch.22 in Heather Boushey, J. Bradford DeLong, Marshall Steinbaum (eds.) *After Piketty:The Agenda for Economics and Inequality*, Harvard University Press, Cambridge, 2017; and W. Streeck, *Buying Time: The Delayed Crisis of Democratic Capitalism* trans.by Patrick Camiller, Verso Books, London 2014.

10. N. Klein, *The Shock Doctrine*, Penguin, London, 2008. For a review of Klein's book *This Changes Everything: Capitalism vs the Climate*, Simon & Schuster, New York 2014 from a neo-

Polanyian perspective, see Paul Adler, 'The Environmental Crisis and Its Capitalist Roots: Reading Naomi Klein with Karl Polanyi', *Administrative Science Quarterly*, no.2, June 2015, pp.13-25.

11. See G. Monbiot,' Greece is the latest battleground in the financial elite's war on democracy' *The Guardian*, May 8, 2015.

12. John Gray, *False Dawn: The Delusions of Global Capitalism,* Granta London 1998, ch.1.

13. Heather Horn, 'Pope Francis's Theory of Economics', *The Atlantic,* 26 November 2013.

14. Kurt Huebner, 'Why Brussels Needs to Read Karl Polanyi', *Social Europe,* 28 November 2014.

15. Patrick Iber and Mike Konczal, 'Karl Polanyi for President', *Dissent Magazine*, May 23, 2016.

16. See Harrison Fluss and Landon Frim, 'Behemoth and Leviathan: The Fascist Bestiary of the Alt-Right', *Salvage*, no.5, 21 December 2017. Alain De Benoist and the Nouvelle Droit as well as Marine Le Pen's National Rally have long used Gramsci to develop a Right-wing 'counter hegemony' against 'liberal elites.

17. See Bertrand Renouvin's Blog, 'Marine Le Pen: La rentière du malheur Rechercher', 27 February 2012.

18. Nicolas Colin, 'Brexit: Doom, or Europe's Polanyi Moment?', *The Family Papers*, June 26, 2016, p.2.

19. Mariana Mazzucato, M. *The Entrepreneurial State Debunking Public vs. Private Sector Myths*, Anthem Books, London, 2013.

20. Colin*, op.cit*, p.6.

21. *Ibid* pp.19-20. Colin seems to ignore the fact that Mazzucato and Perez have worked together and that Mazzucato was an adviser to Corbyn.

22. Polanyi's later views aligned with the 'socialist humanism' of his friend the psychoanalytic theorist Eric Fromm and historian E. P. Thompson – see Gareth Dale, *Karl Polanyi: a life on the left*, ch.7 for an account of Polanyi's views in the late 1950s and early 1960s.

23. See Fred Block, 'Karl Polanyi and twenty-first century socialism', *Open Democracy*, 22 May 2016. Block has been a tireless promoter of Polanyi in recent decades and tends to present him as thinker who has a close affinity with contemporary social democracy.

24. *The Great Transformation: The political and economic origins of our time*, Beacon Press, Boston, 2001 edition, p.3.

25. Polanyi was also hampered by the extremely limited available historical and political sources on the grand topics he analysed. Today, with hindsight and infinitely more resources, we are better able to understand the world that Polanyi was not able to see as clearly, especially because he was also a participant in the unfolding crises of his day.

26. Robert Kuttner, 'Karl Polanyi Explains it all', *The American Prospect*, April 15, 2014.

27. Fred Block and Margaret R. Somers, *The Power of Market Fundamentalism Karl Polanyi's Critique*, Harvard University Press, Cambridge, 2014, p.218. For a growing range of contemporary publications that focus either positively or negatively on Karl Polanyi, see for example the bibliographies and references in Ayse Bugra and Kaan Agartan (eds.) *Reading Karl Polanyi for the Twenty-First Century Market Economy as Political Project*, Palgrave Macmillan, Basingstoke, 2007; Fred Block and Margaret Somers, *The Power of Market Fundamentalism: Karl Polanyi's Critique;* the three books on Polanyi by Gareth Dale, *Karl Polanyi The Limits to the Market*, Polity, Cambridge, 2010; *Karl Polanyi: a life on the left* (2016) *and Reconstructing Karl Polanyi:Excavation and Critique,* Pluto press, London, 2016; also see Chris Hann and Keith Hart (eds.) *Market and Society: The Great Transformation Today,* Cambridge University Press, Cambridge, 2009; and various contributors to the Special Issue, New Directions in Polanyian Scholarship, *Economy & Society*, Vol.43, no.4, 2014.

28. Martin Jay, 'Historical Explanation and the Event: Reflections on the Limits of Contextualization', *New Literary History*, vo.42, 2011, pp. p.559.

29. Block, Introduction to *The Great Transformation*, p.9.

30. Christopher Holmes, *Polanyi in Times of Populism*: *Vision and Contradiction in the History of Economic Ideas*, Routledge, London, 2018.

31. *Ibid*, p.9.
32. John Quiggin, *Zombie Economics: How Dead Ideas Still Walk Among Us,* Princeton University Press, Princeton, 2010, p.1. For an earlier and different take on Left and Right zombies, see my *Zombies, Lilliputians and Sadists: The Power of the Living Dead and the Future of Australia,* Curtin University Books and Freemantle Arts Centre Press, Freemantle, 2004.
33. Marx made a number of methodological critiques of those economists who ignored major historical differences and assumed that general categories such as 'rent' were equivalent in ancient, feudal and capitalist societies - see *Grundrisse, Foundations of the Critique of Political Economy (Rough Draft)* translated by Martin Nicolaus, Penguin Books and New Left Review, Harmondsworth, 1973, pp. 83-111.
34. Bortolotti and Siniscalco's data cited by Damien Cahill, *The End of Laissez-Faire? On the Durability of Embedded Neoliberalism,* Edward Elgar, Cheltenham, 2014, pp.15-16.
35. Thomas Piketty, *Capital in the Twenty-First Century* trans.by Arthur Goldhammer, Harvard University Press, Cambridge, 2014, p. 475.
36. See discussion in Chapter Six of why some Polanyians dispute this account of 'disembeddedness'.
37. *The Great Transformation*, p.3.
38. *Ibid*
39. *Ibid*, pp.237-38. Also see Samuel Knafo, *The Making of Modern Finance: Liberal Governance and the Gold Standard*, Routledge, New York, 2013, pp.30-32, for a critique of how Polanyi ignored those aspects of liberalism and the gold standard that did not fit his thesis.
40. *Ibid,* p.147.
41. *The Great Transformation*, p.3.
42. Shoshana Zuboff, *The Age of Surveillance Capitalism: The Fight for a Human Future at the New Frontier of Power*, PublicAffairs, New York, 2019, p.39.
43. *The Great Transformation*, p.4.
44. Karl Mannheim, *Man and Society In an Age of Reconstruction Studies in Modern Social Structure* (1935) trans. By Edward Shils, Routledge & Kegan Paul, London, 1940.
45. See Fred Block, 'Karl Polanyi and the writing of The Great Transformation', *Theory and Society*, vol. 32, no.3, 2003, pp. 275-306.
46. Ludwig von Mises, *Bureaucracy*, Yale University Press, New Haven, 1944.
47. J. A. Schumpeter, 'The March into Socialism', *The American Economic Review*, vol.40, no.2, 1950, pp. 446-456.
48. In recent years, only a small minority of the Left would see China and other Communist countries as 'socialist'. Some view them as 'market socialist' or capitalist. See for example, David Schweickart, 'China: Socialist or Capitalist?', *Perspectives on Global Development and Technology*, Vol.14, no. 1-2, 2015, pp.13-25. Schweickart does not see China as capitalist but is unconvincing in seeing it as a form of market socialism.
49. Vivian Gornick, 'What Endures of the Romance of American Communism', *The New York Review of Books,* April 3, 2020.
50. Despite criticisms of the USSR by his brother Michael who had direct experience of the Soviet regime, Karl Polanyi strongly rejected his brother's adverse judgements of the political economic system of the USSR. See Gareth Dale, *Karl Polanyi: a life on the left*, ch.4, for an account of the Polanyi brothers opposing reactions to their niece's imprisonment for 16 months on trumped up charges of not only being a Trotskyist conspirator but one who also smuggled swastikas into her ceramics! Dale argues that Karl Polanyi was typical of many British Christian socialists who strongly supported the USSR during the 1930s.
51. Gareth Dale, *Reconstructing Karl Polanyi Excavation and Critique*, Pluto Press, London, 2016, ch.4.
52. *The Great Transformation,* pp.255-6.
53. *Ibid.*
54. *Ibid*, p.255.
55. *Ibid*

56. For example, Robert Conquest, *Harvest of Sorrow Soviet Collectivization and the Terror-famine*, Oxford University Press, Oxford, 1986, estimated 14.5 million died from violence and famine, whereas R.W. Davies and Stephen Wheatcroft, *The Years of Hunger: Soviet Agriculture, 1931-33*, Palgrave, London 2009, using archival sources unavailable to Conquest, argue that 4.5 million died from the famine. They also see it as a shocking catastrophic loss of life but reject Ukrainian nationalist views that it was a targeted 'genocide' of Ukrainians as Stalin's policies were applied across the USSR with disastrous consequences for all Soviet people.

57. Mark Harrison, 'Soviet Agriculture and Industrialisation' in John A. Davis and Peter Mathias (eds.) *Agriculture and Economic Growth from the Eighteenth Century to the Present*, Oxford: Blackwell, 1996, pp. 192-208.

58. See for example, Andrea Graziosi, 'Stalin's Antiworker 'Workerism', 1924-31', *International Review of Social History*, vol.40, no.2, 1995, pp. 223-258, for an account of how Stalin extended Trotsky's earlier 1920-21 'militarisation of labour' into brutal work conditions from the late 1920s onwards.

59. Leon Trotsky, 'On the Future of Hitler's Armies' (August 1940) published on Trotsky Internet Archive, Marxists.org.

60. Polanyi wrote briefly about why socialism was necessary rather than any detailed outline of his socialist model. See for example, his 1922 article 'Socialist Accounting' translated and introduced by Ariane Fischer, David Woodruff, and Johanna Bockman and reprinted in *Theory and Society*, Vol.45, 2016, pp.385-427.

61. See K. Polanyi, 'Universal Capitalism or 'Regional Planning'' (1945) reprinted in Michele Cangiani and Claus Thomasberger (eds.) *Karl Polanyi, Economy and Society Selected Writings*, Polity, Cambridge, 2018, pp.232-236.

62. Leon Trotsky, *The Class Nature of the Soviet State*, October 1933, republished on Trotsky Internet Archive.

63. James Burnham *The Managerial Revolution: What is Happening in the World*, John Day, New York, 1941 and Bruno Rizzi, *The Bureaucratization of the World: the USSR: bureaucratic collectivism*, (1939) translated by Adam Westoby, Tavistock, London, 1985.

64. Polanyi, 'Why Make Russia Run Amok?' *Harper's Magazine*, March 1943, reprinted in Michele Cangiani and Claus Thomasberger (eds.) *Karl Polanyi, Economy and Society Selected Writings*, pp.215-225.

65. Polanyi, 'Universal Capitalism or 'Regional Planning'' (1945) in *Ibid*, p.235.

66. *Ibid*.

67. In 1945, Polanyi argued that "Marshal Tito's partisans bid fair to solve the problem of Balkan hatreds simply because they start from the assumption of a system no longer market-ridden and no longer managed by the middle class." p.236. in 'Universal Capitalism or 'Regional Planning'' (1945) reprinted in Michele Cangiani and Claus Thomasberger (eds.) *Karl Polanyi, Economy and Society Selected Writings*. Tito certainly drastically reduced the public display of nationalist and religious tensions but could not eliminate these deeply entrenched, non-economic prejudices.

68. *The Great Transformation*, p.248

69. *Ibid*, pp.30-31.

70. Eric Hobsbawm, *Age of Extremes: The Short Twentieth Century 1914-1991*, Abacus, London, 1994, p.497.

71. See my analysis in 'The Gulag Archipelago and The Left', *Theory and Society*, Vol.1 No.4, 1974, pp.477-495.

72. See David M. Kotz with Fred Weir, *Revolution from Above: The demise of the Soviet system*, Routledge, New York, 1997.

2. Fatalism, Economism and Naturalism

1. For example, see Bertrand de Jouvenel, *On Power*, trans. by J. F. Huntington, Viking, New York,1949.

2. Karl Popper, *The Open Society and its Enemies,* volumes one and two, Routledge & Kegan Paul, London, 1945.

3. Published by Regnery, Washington, 1991. Also see, Paul Gottfried, *Fascism: The Career of a Concept*, Northern Illinois Press, DeKalb, 2016, ch.4.

4. György Lukács, *The Destruction of Reason*, (1952) trans. by Peter Palmer, Merlin, London, 1980.

5. See 'Fascism and Marxism' (1934) and 'The Essence of Fascism' (1935) as well as 'The Fascist Virus' (1940) which was the prelude to *The Great Transformation,* all reprinted in Michele Cangiani and Claus Thomasberger (eds.) *Karl Polanyi, Economy and Society Selected Writings*.

6. See Herbert Marcuse's 1934 essay reprinted in *Negations: Essays in Critical Theory*, translated by Jeremy J. Shapiro, Beacon Press, Boston, 1969, pp. 3-42.

7. Marcuse, op.cit, p.5.

8. *The Great Transformation*, p.48.

9. *Ibid*, p. 171.

10. *Ibid*, p. 245.

11. See Tim Rogan, *The Moral Economists: R.H. Tawney, Karl Polanyi, E.P. Thompson, and the Critique of Capitalism*, Princeton University Press, Princeton, 2017 and Gareth Dale, *Karl Polanyi A Life on the Left*, ch. 4.

12. *The Great Transformation*, p.268.

13. See António Costa Pinto, 'Authoritarianism and Corporatism in Latin America The First wave', in António Costa Pinto and Federico Finchelstein (eds.) *Authoritarianism and Corporatism in Europe and Latin America Crossing Borders*, Routledge, New York, 2019.

14. Wilhelm Reich, *The Mass Psychology of Fascism,* trans. by Mary Boyd Higgins, Farrar, Straus Giroux, New York, 1970 and Lee Baxandall (ed.) *Wilhelm Reich Sex-Pol Essays, 1929-1934*, Vintage, New York, 1971.

15. See Martin Jay, *The Dialectical Imagination: A History of the Frankfurt School and the Institute of Social Research 1923-1950,* Heinemann, London, 1973, chs. 4-7.

16. See Roger Griffin, *Modernism and Fascism: The Sense of a Beginning Under Mussolini and Hitler,* Palgrave Macmillan, Basingstoke, 2007.

17. A. Gramsci, *Selections From the Prison Notebooks,* edited and translated by Q. Hoare and G. Nowell Smith, Lawrence & Wishart, London, 1971.

18. *The Great Transformation*, p.32.

19. *Ibid*, p.228.

20. See for example, Stanley G. Payne, *A History of Fascism 1914-45*, Routledge, London, 1995, for a great variety of academic mono-causal and multi-causal definitions that Payne argued were inadequate and could be disproved on specific or general grounds.

21. See David Renton, *Fascism Theory and Practice*, Pluto Press, London, 1999 which makes some good points in critiquing academic approaches to fascism but suffers from its narrow Trotskyist perspective.

22. *Ibid*, p.257.

23. Barrington Moore Jr., *Social Origins of Dictatorship and Democracy: Lord and Peasant in the Making of the Modern World*, Beacon Press, Boston, 1966.

24. Michael Mann, *Fascists*, Cambridge University Press, Cambridge, 2004.

25. Ishay Landa, *The Apprentice's Sorcerer: Liberal Tradition and Fascism,* Leiden, 2010, pp. 322-327. Landa argues that Mann's emphasis on the ability of liberal political institutions in Britain to withstand fascism is only partially valid given the conditions facing Britain were quite different to Germany's. He wonders how long liberalism would have survived in Britain if military defeat, loss of empire, major class conflict and mass socialist and fascist parties had

developed between 1918 and the 1930s as in Germany? And what of Britain's liberal traditions and political institutions during the 1930s permitting fascism to conquer Spain and invade Czechoslovakia?

26. *The Great Transformation*, p.246.
27. *Ibid*, pp.246-7.
28. Richard Sandbrook, 'Karl Polanyi and the Formation of this Generation's New Left', *IPPR Progressive Review*, 17 April,2018.
29. See Walter Goldfrank, 'Fascism and the Great Transformation' in Kari Levitt (ed.), *The Life and Work of Karl Polanyi: A Celebration*, Black Rose, Montreal, 1991, pp.87-92.
30. Vladimir Lenin, *The State and Revolution*, translation published by Foreign Languages Publishing House, Moscow, 1952, p.22.
31. *Ibid*, pp.15-16.
32. Polanyi, 'Fascism and Marxism' (1934) reprinted in Michele Cangiani and Claus Thomasberger (eds.) *Karl Polanyi, Economy and Society Selected Writings*, p.126.
33. 'The Essence of Fascism', in *Ibid*, p.111.
34. *The Great Transformation*, p.250.
35. *The Great Transformation*, p.247.
36. See Max M. Ward, *Thought Crime: Ideology and State Power in Interwar Japan*, Duke University Press, Durham, 2019.
37. See Tasuku Noguchi, 'Japanese Monopoly Capitalism and the State', *Kapitalistate*, no.1, 1973, pp.85-95.
38. See Helen Callaghan & Martin Höpner, 'Changing Ideas: Organised Capitalism and the German Left', *West European Politics*, vol.35, no.3, 2012, pp.551-573.
39. *The Great Transformation*, p.153.
40. *Ibid*, p.226.
41. *Ibid*.
42. *Ibid*, p.227.
43. See Jay Tate, 'National Varieties of Standardization' in Peter Hall and David Soskice (eds.) *Varieties of Capitalism: The Institutional Foundations of Comparative Advantage*, Oxford University Press, Oxford, 2001.
44. *Ibid*, pp.557-560.
45. See Claus Offe, *Disorganised Capitalism: Contemporary Transformations in Work and Politics*, MIT Press, Cambridge, 1985 and Scott Lash, and John Urry, *The End of Organised Capitalism*, University of Wisconsin Press, Madison, 1987.
46. Germa Bel, 'Against the mainstream: Nazi privatization in 1930s Germany', *The Economic History Review*, vol.63, no.1, 2010, pp.34-55.
47. Franz Neuman, *Behemoth: The Structure and Practice of National Socialism*, Oxford University Press, Oxford, 1942.
48. W. Goldfrank, *op.cit.*, pp.88-90.
49. *The Great Transformation*, p.245.
50. For a discussion of fascist forms of corporatism, see the various contributions in Antonio Costa Pinto (ed.) *Corporatism and Fascism: The Corporatist Wave in Europe*, Routledge, New York, 2017.
51. Oswald Mosley, *Fascism: 100 Questions Asked and Answered*, B.U.F. Publications, 1936, question number 35.

3. The New Deal's Controversial Legacy

1. Adam Tooze, *The Wages of Destruction: The Making and Breaking of the Nazi Economy*, Allen Lane, Penguin, London, 2006, p.21.
2. Franklin D. Roosevelt, Transcript of Campaign Address at Madison Square Garden, New York City. 'We Have Only Just Begun to Fight.' October 31, 1936.

3. See Ann Pettifor and Jeremy Smith (eds.) *Karl Polanyi Five Lectures on The Present Age of Transformation, Bennington College 1940*, reprinted by Prime, London, 2017. These lectures were characterised by a conventional orthodox democratic socialist class analysis and concept of feudal, bourgeois and socialist stages of history – an approach that Polanyi abandoned in *The Great Transformation* even though other themes in the lectures were retained and developed.

4. Thorstein Veblen, *The Theory of the Leisure Class* (1899), edited with an Introduction by Martha Banta, Oxford University Press, New York, 2007.

5. See Claus Offe, *Reflections on America: Tocqueville, Weber & Adorno in the United States*, translated by Patrick Camiller, Polity, Cambridge, 2005.

6. Werner Sombart, *Why is There no Socialism in the United States?*, edited and with an Introductory Essay by C.T. Husbands, M.E. Sharpe, White Plains,1976.

7. See Ben Zimmer, 'Did Stalin Really Coin 'American Exceptionalism'?', *Slate*, 27 September 2013.

8. *The Great Transformation*, p.257.

9. Rapid abandonment of the gold standard by many countries in 1929, hastened recovery compared with those countries that kept their currencies pegged to gold, see Michael Mann, *The Sources of Social Power: Global Empires and Revolution, 1890–1945*, volume 3, Cambridge University Press, Cambridge, 2012, ch.7. Also see Alan Nasser, *Overripe Economy: American Capitalism and the Crisis of Democracy*, Pluto Press, London, 2018, chs. 3 and 4.

10. See Adam Tooze, 'How to Mishandle a Crisis', *New Left Review*, no.92, March-April 2015, pp.135-143, for a discussion of various interpretations of the causes of the Great Depression (including Polanyi's) and the financial crisis of 2007-08; Pavlina R. Tacherneva, 'What Would Roosevelt Do?', *Project Syndicate*, March 20, 2020; Adam Tooze, 'Time to expose the reality of 'debt market discipline', *International Politics and Society Journal*, May, 25, 2020; Nouriel Roubini, The Coming Greater Depression of the 2020s', *Project Syndicate*, April 28, 2020.

11. Adam Tooze, *op cit.*, ch.5. Tooze cites a study commissioned by the Ford Motor Company comparing American standards of living with the standard of living in its fourteen European locations. The study was undertaken by the International Labour Office in Geneva and found a wide gap between even the lowest paid workers in Dearborn and those in Germany and other European countries.

12. See Kristin Ross, *Fast Cars, Clean Bodies: Decolonization and the Reordering of French Culture*, MIT Press, Cambridge, 1995.

13. All figures quoted are drawn from Robert J. Gordon, *The Rise and Fall of American Growth: The U.S. Standard of Living Since the Civil War*, Princeton University Press, Princeton, 2016, Part One and Alan Nasser, *Overripe Economy*, ch.3.

14. See Cotten Seiler, *Republic of Drivers: A Cultural History of Automobility in America*, University of Chicago Press, Chicago, 2008 for a detailed analysis of how car culture intersected with American notions of freedom and class relations, race and the position of women. For the opposite affect of how cars also led to the extension of police powers and restrictions on democratic freedom, see Sarah A. Seo, *Policing the Open Road: How Cars Transformed American Freedom*, Harvard University Press, Cambridge, 2019.

15. See David E. Noble, *America By Design: Science, Technology and the Rise of Corporate Capitalism*, Alfred Knopf, New York, 1977.

16. See Lizabeth Cohen, *Making a New Deal: Industrial Workers in Chicago, 1919-1939*, Cambridge University Press, Cambridge, (1990) second edition 2014, chs.6 and 7.

17. See Ahmed White, 'Memorial Day, 1937', *Jacobin*, 29 May 2017, for an account of the massacre of 10 of the 1500 striking steel workers and their supporters as well as the brutal injuries inflicted by police and the killing of a further six workers in support of the Republican Steel Corporation, Chicago in 1937.

18. The CIO changed its name in 1936 to Congress for Industrial Organization and broke away

from the AFL in 1938 as the Congress for Industrial Organizations representing workers in the US and Canada until it merged with the AFL in 1955 to become the AFL-CIO.

19. Mario Tronti, 'Workers and Capital', (1971) reprinted in *Telos*, no.14, Winter 1972, p.61.

20. Nelson Lichtenstein, *State of the Union: A Century of American Labor*, Princeton University Press, Princeton, 2002.

21. See Katherine Rye-Jewell, *Dollars for Dixie: Business and the Transformation of Conservatism in the Twentieth Century*, Cambridge University Press, Cambridge 2017 for an analysis of how the Southern States Industrial Council forged a coalition of businesses to fight the New Deal and how the South morphed from conservative Democrat to Republican strongholds.

22. *Ibid*, p.113.

23. Michel Aglietta, *A Theory of Capitalist Regulation the US Experience*, trans.by David Fernbach, Verso, London, 1979.

24. See Jean-Pierre Durand, *Creating the New Worker: Work, Consumption and Subordination*, Palgrave Macmillan, Cham, 2019, for a comparison of Gramsci's theses on the formation of the 'new worker' in the 1920s and 1930s and the passage from 'Fordism' to the 'new worker' of 'post-Fordism' and subsequent transformations in labour processes and everyday life in recent decades since the 1980s.

25. Kim Moody, *An Injury to All: The Decline of American Unionism*, Verso, London, 1988.

26. 'Union Members Summary', *US Bureau of Statistics*, January 22, 2020. Public sector workers had levels of 33.6% unionisation or more than five times the rate of private sector workers. While 14.6 million workers were unionised, this was a mere 10.3% of the total US worforce and a halving of union members in 1983 (20.1%).

27. See Alan Nasser, *Overripe Economy*, pp.114-120 and John Henry, 'Reflections on the New Deal: The Vested Interests, Limits to Reform, and the Meaning of Liberal Democracy', *Levy Economics Institute*, Bard College, Working Paper no.905, May 2018.

28. See my discussion of Hansen and the revival of fears about secular stagnation since 2007 in *Fictions of Sustainability*, ch.1.

29. Matt Bruenig, 'No, Finland Is Not a 'Capitalist Paradise'', *Jacobin*, December 9, 2019.

30. See Billy Fleming, 'Design and the Green New Deal', *Places Journal*, April 2019.

31. Ira Katznelson, *When Affirmative Action Was White: An Untold History of Racial Inequality in Twentieth-Century America*, W. W. Norton, New York, 2005, ch.2; also see Richard Iton, *Solidarity Blues: Race, Culture, and the American Left*, The University of North Carolina Press, Chapel Hill, 2000 for an analysis of racism in various unions and the general situation of non-whites during the New Deal.

32. Peter Beinart, 'Breaking Faith America's Empty Churches Problem', *The Atlantic*, April 2017.

33. See Steve Bruce, *Secularization: In Defence of an Unfashionable Theory*, Oxford University Press, Oxford, 2011, ch.8.

34. Arthur Goldberg, 'The Secularisation of America's Religious Colleges and Universities', *Public Discourse*, March 23, 2018.

35. Peter Beinart, op.cit.

36. Jefferson Cowie, *The Great Exception: The New Deal & the Limits of American Politics*, Princeton University Press, Princeton, 2016.

37. *Ibid*, p.22.

38. See Jason A. Josephson-Storm, *The Myth of Disenchantment Magic, Modernity, and the Birth of the Human Sciences*, University of Chicago Press, Chicago, 2017, ch.1.

39. Max Horkheimer and Theodore W. Adorno, *Dialectic of Enlightenment* (1944) Allen Lane, London, 1973.

40. See Franz Neumann, Behemoth, p.471 and also Jeffrey Herf, 'Engineers as ideologues' in *Reactionary Modernism: Technology, culture, and politics in Weimar and the Third Reich*, Cambridge University Press, Cambridge, 1984, ch.7.

41. See Herf, *Reactionary Modernism*.

42. K. Polanyi, 'Universal Capitalism or Regional Planning?' (1945) reprinted in Michele

Cangiani and Claus Thomasberger (eds.) *Karl Polanyi, Economy and Society Selected Writings*, p.232.

43. *Ibid.*
44. *Ibid.*
45. *Ibid* p.233.
46. *Ibid.*
47. *Ibid.*
48. See Gareth Dale, *Reconstructing Karl Polanyi Excavation and Critique*, Pluto Press, London, 2016, p.6.
49. *Ibid.*
50. Pierre Rosanvallon, *The Society of Equals*, trans. by Arthur Goldhammer, Harvard University Press, Cambridge, 2013, pp. 202-3.
51. See Gareth Dale, 'Social Democracy, Embeddedness and Decommodification: On the Conceptual Innovations and Intellectual Affiliations of Karl Polanyi', *New Political Economy*, Vol.15, no.3, 2010, pp.369-93.
52. The North Atlantic Treaty Organisation, Organisation of American States, Central Treaty Organization, Southeast Asian Treaty Organisation and the Australian, New Zealand, United States Security Treaty.
53. Orwell's article 'Not Counting Niggers' quoted in David Renton, *op.cit.*, p.86.
54. Wolfgang Streeck, 'The International State System after Neoliberalism: Europe between National Democracy and Supranational Centralization', *Crisis & Critique*, vol.7, no.1, 2020, pp. 215-34.
55. Peter Evans, 'Reconstructing Polanyi in the Late Neoliberal Era: A Critical but Optimistic Perspective', Paper prepared for Social Movement Seminar, Tokyo, July 20, 2014.
56. Gareth Dale, *Karl Polanyi A Life on the Left*, p.286.
57. *Ibid*, p.287.

4. From Windrip to Trump: The Evolution of 'American Fascism'

1. For a comparative analysis of changing perceptions of America, Italy and Germany in the 1930s compared with the period after 1945 – from socio-economic policies, architecture, mode of communication and so forth – see Wolfgang Schivelbusch, *Three New Deals: Reflections on Roosevelt's America, Mussolini's Italy and Hitler's Germany*, trans. by Jefferson Chase, Metropolitan Books New York, 2006.
2. Oswald Mosley, *op.cit.*, answer to question number 77.
3. In recent years, the American alt Right for quite different reasons to the old Left in the 1930s, namely, their campaign to combat the contemporary Left, have heavily promoted the view that Roosevelt and the New Deal were fascist – see e.g., Dinesh D'Souza, 'FDR and the Left's Romance with Fascism', *Breitbart.com.* 17 August 2017.
4. See Michael Donnelly, 'Wall Street's Failed 1934 Coup', *Counterpunch*, 2nd December 2011.
5. Ryan Alford, *Permanent State of Emergency: Unchecked Executive Power and the Demise of the Rule of Law*, McGill-Queen's University Press, Montreal, 2017.
6. See Martin Jay, *The Dialectical Imagination*, ch.7. Like many other analysts, Polanyi cited Catholic priest Father Charles Coughlin, a leading Right-wing anti-Semite, who alone had over thirty million listeners to his radio program in the 1930s.
7. See Joseph W. Bendersky, *The "Jewish Threat": Anti-Semitic Politics of the U.S. Army*, Basic Books, New York, 2000, for a historical survey of the policy impact of the anti-Semitism of senior military officers from 1900 until the 1970s.
8. Arno J. Mayer, *Plowshares into Swords From Zionism to Israel*, Verso, London, 2008, p. ix.
9. C. Wright Mills, *The Power Elite*, Oxford University Press, New York, 1956. During the late

1930s, Harold Lasswell developed the notion of a 'garrison state' which was a non-radical notion of a military-industrial society based on an amalgam of political regimes in Europe, Asia and North America. It was too generalised to be a sharp critique of American power relations – see H. Lasswell, 'The Garrison State', *American Journal of Sociology, Vol.46, no.4, 1941, pp.455-468*.

10. See Leo Lowenthal and Norbert Guterman, *Prophets of Deceit: A Study of the Techniques of the American Agitator* (1949) second edition, Pacific Books, Palo Alto, 1970. This was part of the Frankfurt School's large project on the study of authority.

11. See Douglas Kellner's Introduction to his edition of *Herbert Marcuse Technology, War and Fascism: Collected Papers of Herbert Marcuse, Volume One*, Routledge, London, 1998, pp.1-38. Also see Raffaele Laudani (ed.), *Franz Neumann, Herbert Marcuse and Otto Kirchheimer Secret Reports on Nazi Germany: The Frankfurt School Contribution to the War Effort*, Princeton University Press, Princeton, 2013.

12. Unpublished and originally sent to Max Horkheimer in 1947, now published in Douglas Kellner (ed.) *Herbert Marcuse Technology, War and Fascism*, pp.215-227.

13. Hannah Arendt, *The Origins of Totalitarianism*, Meridian Books, New York, second edition 1958. Russell Jacoby in *Social Amnesia: A Critique of Conformist Psychology From Adler to Laing*, Beacon Press, Boston, 1975, ch.1, describes *The Origins of Totalitarianism* as a 'basic Cold War text'. For Arendt's admiration of Luxemburg, especially the latter's strong anti-Leninism, see 'Rosa Luxemburg 1879-1919 a review of J. P. Nettl, Rosa Luxemburg' (1966) reprinted in *Men in Dark Times*, A Harvest Book, New York, 1968. In contrast to Arendt's academic analysis, Marcuse had been part of the Spartacist uprising in Berlin in 1919 led by Luxemburg and Karl Liebknecht before they were murdered, and the revolt crushed.

14. Herbert Marcuse, *One Dimensional Man*, Routledge, London, 1964 and 'USA: Questions of Organization and the Revolutionary Subject: A Conversation with Hans Magnus Enzensberger' (1970) in Douglas Kellner (ed.) *Herbert Marcuse The New left and the 1960s Collected Papers of Herbert Marcuse, Volume Three*, Routledge, London, 2005, p.138.

15. See Michael Joseph Roberto, *The Coming of the American Behemoth: The Origins of Fascism in the United States, 1920 – 1940*, Monthly Review Press, New York, 2018, for a survey of American Marxists in the 1930s such as Lewis Corey who viewed the New Deal as laying the foundations of fascism.

16. See Daniel Lazare, 'America the Undemocratic', *New Left Review*, Nov-Dec. 1998, pp.3-40.

17. Sheldon Wolin, *Democracy Incorporated: Managed Democracy and the Spectre of Inverted Totalitarianism*, Princeton University Press, Princeton, 2008, p.228.

18. David Frum, *Trumpocalypse Restoring American Democracy*, Harper, New York, 2020.

19. Anne Applebaum, *Twilight of Democracy: The Seductive Lure of Authoritarianism*, Doubleday, New York, 2020.

20. Bertram Gross, *Friendly Fascism: The New Face of Power in America*, South End Press, Boston, 1980.

21. Sheldon Wolin, *Democracy Incorporated, p.213*.

22. *Ibid*, p.239.

23. Hannah Arendt, *The Origins of Totalitarianism, p.138*.

24. Sheldon Wolin, *Democracy Incorporated, p.239*.

25. *Ibid.*

26. Charles Murray, *By the People: Rebuilding Liberty Without Permission*, Penguin Random House, New York, 2015.

27. Ian Millhiser, 'Jeb Bush's Favorite Author Rejects Democracy, Says the Hyper-Rich Should Seize Power', *ThinkProgress.org*, 26 May, 2015.

28. Published by Liveright/W.W. Norton, New York, 2020.

29. David Frum, *Trumpocalypse Restoring American Democracy*, ch.1.

30. Jason Stanley, *How Fascism Works: The Politics of Us and Them*, Random House, New York, 2018, pp.189-90.

31. Timothy Snyder, *On Tyranny Twenty Lessons from the Twentieth Century*, Tim Duggan Books,

New York, 2017; Madeleine Albright, *Fascism A Warning*, Penguin Random House, New York, 2018 and Steven Levitsky and Daniel Ziblatt, *How Democracies Die*, Crown Publishing, New York, 2018.

32. Carl Boggs, *Fascism Old and New: American Politics at the Crossroads*, Routledge, New York, 2018.

33. Christian Fuchs, *Digital Demagogue Authoritarian Capitalism in the Age of Trump and Twitter*, Pluto Press, London, 2018. Fuchs compares Trump's views and policies with classical definitions of fascism based on a single party-state, the use of terror, etc. provided by Franz Neumann and others. He also surveys the views of prominent Left critics such as Noam Chomsky, John Bellamy Foster, Cornel West and Slavoj Žižek on whether they think Trump is a fascist.

34. Henry A. Giroux, *America's Addiction to Terrorism*, Monthly Review Press, New York, 2016.

35. David Renton, *The New Authoritarians Convergence on the Right*, Pluto Press, London, 2019.

36. Shane Burley and Matthew N. Lyons, *Fascism Today: What It Is and How to End It*, AK Press, Chico, 2017.

37. See the various analyses of contributors in Roger Griffin, Werner Loh and Andreas Umland (eds.) *Fascism Past and Present, West and East: An International Debate on Concepts and Cases in the Comparative Study of the Extreme Right*, ibidem Verlag, Stuttgart, 2014. For a comparison of European and American Right-wing thinkers in Mark Sedgwick (ed.) *Key Thinkers of the Radical Right Behind the New Threat to Liberal Democracy*, Oxford University Press, New York, 2019.

38. Enzo Traverso, *The New Faces of Fascism: Populism and the Far Right*, trans. By David Broder, Verso, London, 2019.

39. See for example, Mike Wendling, *Alt-Right From 4chan to the White House*, Pluto Books, London, 2018, for an analysis of the alt-Right's anti-feminist 'manosphere' and other cultural approaches that differ from 1930s fascism; also see Julie Stephens, 'Mother Hate: The anti-maternal fantasies of the alt-Right', *Arena Magazine*, no.160, 2019, pp.36-39.

40. See for example, Daniel Penny, '#Milosexual and the Aesthetics of Fascism', *Boston Review*, 24 January 2017.

41. David Thorstad, 'Homosexuality and the American Left', *Journal of Homosexuality*, vol. 29, no.4, 1995, pp.319-350.

42. Wendy Brown, *In the Ruins of Neoliberalism: The Rise of Antidemocratic Politics in the West*, Columbia University Press, New York, 2019, p. 174.

43. *Ibid*, p.178.

44. *Ibid*, p. 180.

45. See Ashley Jardina, *White Identity Politics*, Cambridge University Press, Cambridge, 2019.

46. Niels Spierings, Marcel Lubbers & Andrej Zaslove, 'Sexually modern nativist voters': do they exist and do they vote for the populist radical right?', *Gender and Education*, vol.29, no.2, 2017, pp.216-237. For more recent analysis, also see Caroline Marie Lancaster, 'Why the radical right is no longer the exclusive domain of older, male voters', *Social Europe*, 26 September 2019.

47. See Arwa Mahdawi, 'The troubling ascent of the LGBT right wing', *The Guardian*, 26 October 2017.

48. Fedya Sayan-Cengiz and Caner Tekin, 'The 'gender turn' of the populist radical right', *Open Democracy*, December 16, 2019.

49. Julie Stephens, 'Mother Hate: The anti-maternal fantasies of the alt-Right'.

50. Enzo Traverso, *The New Faces of Fascism*, p.25.

51. Brad Evans and Julian Reid (eds.) *Deleuze & Fascism: Security: war: aesthetics*, Routledge, New York, 2013, pp.1-4.

52. Aurelien Mondon and Aaron Winter, *Reactionary Democracy How Racism and the Populist Far Right Became Mainstream*, Verso, London, 2020.

53. See for example, Robert Paxton, *The Anatomy of Fascism*, Vintage Books, New York, 2005.

54. Marilyn Ivy, 'Foreword: Fascism, Yet?' in Alan Tansman (ed.) *The Culture of Japanese Fascism*, Duke University Press, Durham, 2009, pp.vii -viii.
55. William I. Robinson, 'Can Twenty-First Century Fascism Resolve the Crisis of Global Capitalism?', *Union of Radical Political Economics*, April 28, 2019.
56. In contrast to Robinson, radical activists recognise the differences between 'the poor' and the 'working class' and the difficulty of building unified resistance movements, see Michael Truscello and Ajamu Nangwaya (eds.), *Why Don't the Poor Rise Up? Organizing the Twenty-First Century Resistance*, AK Press, Chico, 2017.
57. Prominent mainstream commentators such as Martin Wolf, 'Prepare for the 100-year war between the US and China', *Financial Times*, 5 June 2019, are also worried at not just the political economic consequences of American attempts to 'contain' China but about the racist tone of American attitudes to China.
58. Frederico Finchelstein and Jason Stanly, 'The Fascist Politics of the Pandemic', *Project Syndicate*, May 4, 2020.
59. Alexander Dugin, *Eurasion Mission: An Introduction to Neo-Eurasianism*, Arktos Media, Budapest, 2014.
60. Bernhard Forchtner (ed.) *The Far Right and the Environment: Politics, Discourse and Communication*, Routledge, New York, 2020.
61. See for example, Anand Toprani, *Oil and the Great Powers Britain and Germany, 1914-1945*, Oxford University Press, Oxford, 2019.
62. Reprinted in David Spratt and Ian Dunlop, *The Third Degree: Evidence and implications for Australia of existential climate-related security risk*', Breakthrough, July 2019.
63. See for example, John Bellamy Foster, Hannah Holleman and Brett Clark, 'Imperialism in the Anthropocene', *Monthly Review*, July 2019, for an analysis of how American administrations have devised strategies to maintain imperial power while failing to deal with the climate crisis.
64. Janet Biehl and Peter Staudenmaier, *Ecofascism: Lessons from the German Experience*, AK Press, Edinburgh, 1995, pp.48-58.

5. Flawed Notions of the 'Liberal State'

1. See Tom Nairn, 'The British Political Elite', *New Left Review*, no. 23, 1964, pp.19-25 and Perry Anderson, 'Origins of the Present Crisis', *New Left Review*, no.23, 1964, pp26-53.
2. K. Polanyi, 'The economy as an instituted Process', in K. Polanyi, C.M. Arensberg, and H.W. Pearson (eds.), *Trade and Market in the Early Empires: Economies in History and Theory*, Free Press, New York, 1957, pp. 243-70.
3. Karl Marx, *Capital A Critique of Political Economy, Volume One*, (1867) this edition translated by Ben Fowkes, Penguin Books and New Left Review, Harmondsworth, 1976, p.275.
4. For an analysis of the historical transformation of family life in different phases of capitalist development, see Wally Seccombe, *Weathering the Storm: Working-Class Families from the Industrial Revolution to the Fertility Decline*, Verso, London, 1993.
5. Nancy Fraser and Rahel Jaeggi, *Capitalism A Conversation in Critical Theory*, Edited by Brian Milstein, Polity, Cambridge, 2018.
6. *Ibid*, p.191.
7. *The Great Transformation*, p.242.
8. Max Weber, 'Politics as a Vocation' in *From Max Weber: Essays in Sociology*, edited and translated by Hans Gerth and C. Wright Mills, Oxford University Press, New York, 1958, p.78.
9. Even New Zealand, that was subjected to savage neoliberal policies in the 1980s and 1990s resulting in the fastest growth of inequality in the OECD, still collects approximately 30% of tax revenue as a percentage of GDP.
10. Goffman developed his 1957 work on the 'Characteristics of Total Institutions' in *Asylums: Essays on the Condition of the Social Situation of Mental Patients and Other Inmates*, Anchor Books,

New York, 1961. His analysis of mental asylums, prisons and other state institutions preceded the work of Foucault who also analysed these same institutions but deployed a different methodology.

11. Published by Basic Books, New York, 1977.

12. Jacques Donzelot, *The Policing of Families* trans. by Robert Hurley, Pantheon, New York, 1979.

13. Nancy Fraser, 'From Discipline to Flexibilization? Rereading Foucault in the Shadow of Globalization' *Constellations*, vol.10, no.2, 2003, pp.160-171, argues that Foucault was the great theorist of Fordist social regulation, writing at the zenith of the Keynesian welfare state, a phase that has been replaced by neoliberal globalisation. Her concept of 'Fordism' is rather loose as she sees it extending from the First World War to the fall of Communism, at least two to three decades before Keynesian policies and more than a decade after the rise of neoliberalism in the late 1970s. Thomas Lemke, 'Comment on Nancy Fraser: Rereading Foucault in the Shadow of Globalization', *Constellations*, vol.10, no.2, 2003, pp.172-79, partially agrees with Fraser but argues that Foucault was aware of the demise of Keynesianism and began developing his theory of the state or governmentality which remains politically relevant beyond 'Fordism'.

14. Kevin Mattson, 'An Oracle for Trump's America', *The Chronicle of Higher Education*, March 26, 2017. Also see my 1990s critique of the Right-wing populist turn of the former Left-wing journal *Telos* and their promotion of Lasch and other populist thinkers well before the Alt-Right became prominent - 'Confronting Neoliberal Regimes: The Post-Marxist Embrace of Populism and Realpolitik', *New Left Review*, no.226, 1997, pp.57-92.

15. See for example, the many different schools of neo-Marxist theories of the state in the eleven issues of the journal *Kapitalistate* between 1973 and 1983.

16. See Graham Burchell, 'Liberal Government and Techniques of the Self', *Economy and Society*, vol. 22, no.3, 1993, p. 276; and Nikolas Rose, 'The Death of the Social? Refiguring the Territory of Government', *Economy and Society*, vol. 25, no. 3, 1996, pp. 327-56.

17. Nikolas Rose, 'Governing "advanced" liberal democracies' in Andrew Barry, Thomas Osborne, Nikolas Rose (eds.) *Foucault and political reason: Liberalism, neo-liberalism and rationalities of government*, UCL Press, London, 1996, p.38.

18. See Jürgen Habermas, *The Philosophical Discourse on Modernity Twelve Lectures*, trans. by Frederick Lawrence, Polity Press, Cambridge, 1987, pp. 238-293; and Axel Honneth, *The Critique of Power Reflective Stages in a Critical Social Theory*, trans. by Kenneth Baynes, MIT Press, Cambridge, 1993, ch.4. Thomas Lemke, *Foucault's Analysis of Modern Governmentality A Critique of Political Reason*, translated by Erik Butler, Verso, London, 2019, acknowledges the criticisms made by Foucault's critics but makes an unconvincing case that there was another radical 'Foucault', despite not specifying what kind of society he preferred.

19. See Ian Hunter, Denise Meredith et al. *Accounting for the Humanities: the language of culture and the logic of government*, Institute of Cultural Studies, Griffith University, Brisbane, 1991.

20. For example, Michael Hardt and Antonio Negri, *Empire*, Harvard University Press, Cambridge, 2001, combine Foucault's bio-politics and Marxism to develop a decentred concept of capitalist globalisation that is highly problematic. Also see Bob Jessop, 'Constituting Another Foucault Effect: Foucault on States and Statecraft', in Ulrich Bröckling, Susanne Krasmann and Thomas Lemke (eds), *Governmentality Current Issues and Future Challenges*, Routledge, New York, 2011 and Pierre Dardot and Christian Laval, *Never-Ending Nightmare: The Neoliberal Assault on Democracy*, Translated by Gregory Elliott, Verso, London, 2013.

21. See my analysis and critique of governmentality in 'Confronting Neoliberal Regimes: The Post-Marxist Embrace of Populism and Realpolitik', *New Left Review*, no.226, 1997, pp.57-92.

22. See discussion by contributors in Daniel Zamora and Michael C. Behrent (eds.) *Foucault and Neoliberalism*, Polity Press, Cambridge, 2016. Also see Stephen W. Sawyer and Daniel Steinmetz-Jenkins (eds.) *Foucault, Neoliberalism, and Beyond*, Rowman & Littlefield, London, 2019.

23. See Mitchell Dean, 'Foucault, Ewald, Neoliberalism, and the Left' in Zamora and Behrent (eds.), ch.4.

24. For example, see John G. Glenn, *Foucault and Post-Financial Crises: Governmentality, Discipline and Resistance*, Palgrave Macmillan, Cham, 2019.

25. Foucault recognised this centralising power of capitalism in his discussion of Schumpeter's arguments as to why monopoly capitalism would lead to socialism, a concentration of power that alarmed both Schumpeter and Foucault - see Michel Foucault, *The Birth of Biopolitics, Lectures at the* Collège *de France, 1978-79* edited by Michel Senellart, translated by Graham Burchell, Palgrave Macmillan, New York, 2008, p.177.

26. Loïc Wacquant, *Punishing the Poor: The Neoliberal Government of Social Insecurity*, Duke University Press, Durham, 2009, p.308. Wacquant's and Bourdieu's work has been used by Javier Auyero, *Patients of the State: The Politics of Waiting in Argentina*, Duke University Press, Durham, 2012, to analyse how welfare offices regulate the poor.

27. *Ibid*, pp.2-3. Also see the various studies in Ruha Benjamin(ed.), *Captivating Technology: Race, Carceral Technoscience, and Liberatory Imagination in Everyday Life*, Duke University Press, Durham, 2019, that explore the application of new surveillance technologies against minority populations.

28. See Wendy Sawyer and Peter Wagner, 'Mass Incarceration: The Whole Pie in 2019', *Prison Policy Initiative Report*, March 2019, prisonpolicy.org. In recent years, between 10.6 and 11.4 million people per year have been churned through the jail and prison system with close to 540,000 incarcerated people not convicted or sentenced but are unable to afford bail money.

29. John Clegg and Adaner Usmani, 'The Economic Origins of Mass Incarceration', *Catalyst*, Vol. 3, Issue 3, 2019.

30. See Catherine Besteman and Hugh Gusterson (eds.) *Life by Algorithms: How Roboprocesses are Remaking Our World*, University of Chicago Press, Chicago, 2019.

31. See Foucault, 'On Popular Justice: A Discussion with Maoists' in Colin Gordon (ed.), *Power/Knowledge Selected Interviews and Other Writings 1972-1977*, Pantheon Books, New York, 1980; and James Miller, *The Passion of Michel Foucault*, Simon & Schuster, New York, 1993, pp.202-205.

32. The publication of Aleksander Solzhenitsyn's book *The Gulag Archipelago* in 1974 had a much bigger impact on the Left in France than in most other countries, mainly due to a reaction against the historical power of the Stalinist French Communist Party and the belated awareness of the naïve gullibility of so many prominent Maoist intellectuals, see Richard Wolin, *The Wind from the East: French Intellectuals, the Cultural Revolution, and the Legacy of the 1960s*, Princeton University Press, Princeton, 2012. Glucksman, for example, ended up supporting Sarkozy.

33. Foucault was criticised by the Left for rejecting Marxist politics and universal human rights, and by the Right for attacking imperialism and supporting uprisings against oppression such as the Iranian revolution in 1979 - see Michel Foucault and Farès Sassine 'There Can't Be Societies without Uprisings' (1979) reprinted in Laura Cremonesi, Orazio Irrera, Daniele Lorenzini and Martina Tazzioli (eds.), *Foucault and the Making of Subjects*, Rowman & Littlefield International, London, 2016.

34. Jessica Whyte, *The Morals of the Market Human Rights and the Rise of Neoliberalism*, Verso, London, 2019, ch.5.

35. Perry Anderson, *In the Tracks of Historical Materialism: The Wellek Library Lectures*, Verso, London, 1983, p.32. Anderson's account ignored the fact that Paris still had many radical thinkers and activists, but it was clear that he was upset that prominent French thinkers which *New Left Review* had introduced to English-speaking readers were no longer radical.

36. See the CIA's December 1985 report 'France: Defection of the Leftist Intellectuals', Office of European Analysis, Central Intelligence Agency, released to the public on 13 May 2011.

37. Foucault quoted by Colin Koopman, *How We Became Our Data: A Genealogy of the Informational Person*, University of Chicago Press, Chicago, 2019, p.180.

38. Nikolas Rose, *Our Psychiatric Future: The Politics of Mental Health*, Polity Press, Cambridge, 2019, particularly ch.3 'Is It All the Fault of Neoliberal Capitalism?'.

39. Quinn Slobodian, *Globalists: The End of Empire and the Birth of Neoliberalism*, Harvard University Press, Cambridge, 2018, p.85.

40. *Ibid.*

41. Whether Ordoliberalism is merely the ideology used to justify EU policies or Ordoliberalism has been implemented across the EU is the contentious issue. For two opposing views see Andy Storey, 'The Myths of Ordoliberalism', Working Paper 17-02, 2017, ERC Project 'European Unions', University College Dublin and Thomas Biebricher, *The Political Theory of Neoliberalism*, Stanford University Press, Stanford, 2018, ch.7.

42. See for example, Colin Koopman, *How We Became Our Data: A Genealogy of the Informational Person*, which is a study of data collection by American governments ranging from births, deaths and marriage to social security and other data and how this helped shape policies and social identities and racial divisions.

43. See Keith Gandal and Stephen Kotkin, 'Governing Life in the U.S.A. and the U.S.S.R', *History of the Present*, no.1, February 1985, pp. 4-14.

44. M. Foucault, *The Birth of Biopolitics, Lectures at the* Collège *de France, 1978-79*, p.94.

45. Thomas Lemke, *Foucault's Analysis of Modern Governmentality A Critique of Political Reason*, translated by Erik Butler, Verso, London, 2019, ch.9, endnote 5.

6. Abandoning Simplistic Concepts of Socio-Political Change

1. See *The Great Transformation*, Chapter Eleven.

2. See for example, Peter Evans, 'Is an Alternative Globalization Possible?', *Politics & Society*, Vol. 36, No. 2, June 2008, pp. 271-305; Ronaldo Munck, (2010): 'Globalization, Crisis and Social Transformation: A View from the South, *Globalizations*, Vol.7, no,1-2, 2010, pp.235-246; Christopher Holmes, 'Ignorance, denial, internalisation, and transcendence: a post-structural perspective on Polanyi's double movement', *Review of International Studies*, Vol.39, no.2, 2013, pp. 273-290; Gustavo Esteva, Salvatore Babones and Philipp Babcicky, *The Future of Development A Radical Manifesto*, Policy Press, Bristol, 2013, pp.97-100.

3. According to Timothy D. Clark, 'Reclaiming Karl Polanyi, Socialist Intellectual', *Studies in Political Economy*, Autumn 2014, p.64.

4. Embeddednes is much discussed in economic sociology. See for example, Mark Granovetter, 'Economic Action and Social Structure: The Problem of Embeddedness', *American Journal of Sociology*, Vol. 91, No. 3, 1985, pp. 481-510; various leading contributors such as Greta Krippner, et al, 'Symposium on Polanyi: a conversation on embeddedness', *Socio-Economic Review*, no.2, 2004, pp.109-135; Jens Beckert, *The Great Transformation of Embeddedness: Karl Polanyi and the New Economic Sociology*, MPIfG Discussion Paper 07/1, Max Planck Institute for the Study of Societies, Cologne, January 2007 and John Ruggie, 'International Regimes, Transactions and Change: Embedded Liberalism in the Postwar Economic Order', *International Organization*, vol.36, no.2,1982.

5. See Fred Block, 'Karl Polanyi and the writing of The Great Transformation', *Theory and Society*, vol. 32 no.3, 2003, pp. 275-306.

6. Gareth Dale, *Reconstructing Karl Polanyi: Excavation and Critique*, Pluto Press, London, 2016, Ch.1.

7. *The Great Transformation*, p.60.

8. *Ibid.*

9. Polanyi argued that the destruction of traditional institutions in colonial regions in order to set up a labour market had devastating 'disembedding' consequences. "Now, what the white man may still occasionally practice in remote regions today, namely, the smashing up of

social structures in order to extract the element of labor from them, was done in the eighteenth century to white populations by white men for similar purposes." *The Great Transformation*, pp.171-172.

10. Fred Block, Introduction to *The Great Transformation*, p. xxvi. Polanyi's daughter rejects Block's claim that 'disembeddedness' was not important, see Kari Polanyi-Levitt, (2006) 'Tracing Polanyi's institutional political economy to its central European source', in Kari Polanyi-Levitt and Kenneth McRobbie (eds.) *Karl Polanyi in Vienna: The Contemporary Significance of The Great Transformation*, Black Rose, Montreal, 2006.

11. *The Great Transformation*, p.171.

12. N. Fraser, 'Can society be commodities all the way down? Post-Polanyian reflections on capitalist crisis', *Economy and Society*, Volume 43, No. 4, 2014, p.547.

13. *Ibid* p.544.

14. See Marx and Engels, 'Communist Manifesto', in *Karl Marx and Frederick Engels, Selected Works, Volume 1, FLPH, Moscow, 1950, p.35.

15. Andreas Bernard, *The Triumph of Profiling: The Self in Digital Culture*, Translated by Valentine A. Pakis, Polity, Cambridge, 2019.

16. See e.g., the debate between Elizabeth Fox Genovese and Nikki Hart in N.R. Keddie (ed.), *Debating Gender, Debating Sexuality*, NYU Press, New York, 1996. Also see Julie Stephens, *Confronting Post Maternal Thinking: Feminism, Memory and Care*, Columbia University Press, New York, 2012.

17. See Sharon Zukin and Paul DiMaggio, 'Introduction' in P. DiMaggio and S. Zukin (eds.), *Structures of Capital: The Social Organization of the Economy*, Cambridge, Cambridge University Press, 1990, pp. 1-36.

18. Elmar Altvater and Birgit Mahnkopf, 'The world market unbound', *Review of International Political Economy* no.3, Autumn 1997, pp. 448-471. Altvater and Mahnkopf actually depended much more on Marx and contemporary political economy and sociology than on Polanyi.

19. See Bob Jessop, 'Knowledge as a Fictitious Commodity: Insights and Limits of a Polanyian Perspective', in Ayse Buğra and Kaan Ağartan (eds), *Reading Karl Polanyi for the Twenty-First Century: Market economy as a Political Project,* pp.115-134; and Michael Burawoy, 'Marxism after Polanyi', in M. Williams and V. Satgar (eds.) *Marxisms in the 21st Century*, Johannesburg, Wits University Press, 2013, p.50.

20. Shoshana Zuboff, *The Age of Surveillance Capitalism*, p.437.

21. Zuboff has proposed this in 'It's not that we've failed to rein in Facebook and Google. We've not even tried', *The Guardian*, 2 July 2019. For an analysis of why international flows of data require protection and regulation of citizens' rights beyond national laws, see the analyses of various authors in Didier Bigo, Engin Isin and Evelyn Ruppert (eds.) *Data Politics: Worlds, Subjects, Rights*, Routledge, New York, 2019.

22. *The Great Transformation*, p.226.

23. I have discussed the many socio-political problems associated with small, self-sufficient communities in *The Post Industrial Utopians*, Polity, Cambridge, 1987.

24. See for example, Thomas Barth, Georg Jochum, Beate Littig, 'Transformation of what? Or: The socio-ecological transformation of working society', *Institute for Advanced Studies*, Vienna, IHS Working Paper 1, February 2019.

25. *The Great Transformation*, p.76.

26. Gregory Baum, *Karl Polanyi on Ethics and Economics,* McGill-Queen's University Press, Montreal, 1996. Baum imputed to Polanyi a support for moderate rather than radical environmentalism – "He would urge that this mobilization not become ideological, that it not separate itself from existing institutions, that it try to stay close to the popular sector of society..." p.19.

27. See Ian Angus, *Facing the Anthropocene Fossil Capitalism and the Crisis of the Earth System,* Monthly Review Press, New York, 2016, p.42.

28. Diana Stuart, Ryan Gunderson & Brian Petersen, 'Climate Change and the Polanyian

Counter-movement: Carbon Markets or Degrowth?', *New Political Economy*, published online 21 December 2017, and in vol.24, no.1 2019, pp.89-102.

29. See for example the essays by Left social scientists in Ayse Buğra and Kaan Ağartan (eds), *Reading Karl Polanyi for the Twenty-First Century: Market economy as a Political Project*, Palgrave Macmillan, Basingstoke, 2007.

30. See W. Streeck, 'Taking Crisis Seriously: Capitalism on Its Way Out', *Stato e Mercato*, no.100, April 2014, pp.45-68 and 'How Will Capitalism End?', *New Left Review*, May/June 2014, no.87, pp. 35-64 and his collection of essays, *How Will Capitalism End?* Verso, London, 2016.

31. See ch.15.

32. Polanyi does mention that "even the climate of the country which might suffer from the denudation of forests, from erosions and dust bowls, all of which, ultimately, depend on the factor land, yet none of which respond to the supply-and-demand mechanism of the market." p.184. However, his focus is primarily on land and market rather than on nature in its non-agricultural or broader ecological sense.

33. Bill McKibben, *The End of Nature*, Random House, New York, 1989.

34. See Christer Agren, 'Clear the Air', *Journal For A Progressive Economy*, May 5, 2015, pp.37-39 and Julian Kirchherr, 'Europe's Airpocalypse', *Project Syndicate*, July 17, 2015; also see *World Health Organization*, News release, Geneva, 25 March 2014 for global deaths and Damien Carrington, 'Global pollution kills 9m a year and threatens survival of human societies', *The Guardian*, 20 October 2017.

35. James O'Connor, 'Capitalism, nature, socialism; a theoretical introduction', *Capitalism, Nature, Socialism*, vol.1, no.1, 1988, pp.11-38.

36. See for example, the debates between Marxists in Ernest Mandel and Alan Freeman (eds.) *Ricardo, Marx, Sraffa: The Langston Memorial Volume*, Verso, London, 1984.

37. David Harvey, *A Companion to Marx's Capital, The Complete Edition*, Verso, London, 2018, ch.10, vol.2, does not question Marx's definition of what is included in Department 1 and Department 2. He does draw attention to the fact that Marx's model of the crises stemming from the relations between the two Departments did not take into account the impact of anti-consumerism or what today is called degrowth or wellbeing. Also, Harvey argues that the reference to 'metabolic rift' in Volume One of *Capital* is nowhere evident in Volume Two, thereby indicating that Marx's model of capitalist accumulation did not integrate environmental factors into his theory of capitalist crisis.

38. Ernest Mandel, *Late Capitalism*, trans. by Joris de Bres, New Left Books, London, 1975, ch.9.

39. See Marx's 'Critique of the Gotha Programme (May 1875) reprinted in Karl Marx, *The Political Writings, 3 volumes*, Verso, London, 2019.

40. Kohei Saito, *Karl Marx's Eco-socialism: Capitalism, Nature, and the Unfinished Critique of Political Economy*, Monthly Review Press, New York, 2017. Also see Fred Magdoff and Chris Williams, *Creating an Ecological Society: Toward a Revolutionary Transformation*, Monthly Review Press, New York, 2017. One can make the same arguments about 'capitalism versus the biosphere' without trying to attribute everything back to Marx.

41. For example, John Bellamy Foster and Kohei Saito have engaged in scholastic debates over whether or not Marx was a Promethean advocate of new technological solutions or a fore-runner of contemporary eco-socialism – see their contributions in Marcello Musto (eds.) *Marx's Capital After 150 years Critique and Alternative to Capitalism*, Routledge, New York, 2019, chs. 9 and 10. On the other hand, Foster has made a valuable and more relevant inter-vention by critiquing Left hyper technological solutions put forward by socialists in *Jacobin* magazine no.26, 2017, see John Bellamy Foster, 'The Long Ecological Revolution', *Monthly Review*, November 2017. These criticisms, however, could have been made without refer-ence to Marx's ideas on technology and ecology.

42. The issue of 'scientific Marxism' has been debated for decades. See for example, Alvin Gouldner, *The Two Marxisms: Contradictions and Anomalies in the Development of Theory*, Macmillan, London, 1980.

43. See Will Steffen, Paul J. Crutzen and John R. McNeill, 'The Anthropocene: Are Humans Now Overwhelming the Great Forces of Nature?', *Ambio*, vol.38, no. 8. 2007, pp. 614-21. These authors do acknowledge that coal was produced before the 18th century. However, their concept of the 'Industrial Revolution' is bereft of any historical notion of what the capitalist mode of production is and how it developed. The same is true of Dipesh Chakrabarty, 'The Climate of History: Four Theses', *Critical Inquiry*, vol.35, Winter 2009, pp.197-222, who as a former historian of capitalist development in India, has even fewer excuses for his metaphysical discussion of 'humans as the overwhelming great forces of history'. Chakrabarty speculates about thousands of years of human history, but this history is overgeneralised 'human history' with fleeting connections to an overgeneralised ecology.

44. See Jason W. Moore, *Capitalism in the Web of Life: Ecology and the Accumulation of Capital*, Verso, London, 2015.

45. Ian Angus, 'Anthropocene or Capitalocene', *The Vancouver Ecosocialist Group.org*, 27 September 2016.

46. See Elmar Altvater, Eileen Crist, Donna Haraway, Daniel Hartley, Justin McBrien, Jason Moore, Christian Parenti, Justin McBrien, *Anthropocene or Capitalocene?: Nature, History, and the Crisis of Capitalism*, PM Books, Oakland 2016. If these concepts were not contentious enough, Donna Haraway throws the 'Chthulucene' (an interspecies future) into the mix. Also see Christophe Bonneuil and Jean-Baptiste Fressoz, *The Shock of the Anthropocene: the earth, history, and us*, translated by David Fernbach, Verso, London, 2016 and Clive Hamilton, *Defiant Earth: The Fate of humans in the Anthropocene*, Allen & Unwin, Sydney, 2017.

47. See for example, Jason W. Moore, *Capitalism in the Web of Life Ecology and the Accumulation of Capital*, Verso, London 2015 and John Bellamy Foster's response to Moore 'In Defense of Ecological Marxism', *Climate & Capitalism*, June 6, 2016.

48. Aaron Bastani, *Fully Automated Luxury Communism A Manifesto*, Verso, London, 2019. Also see my analysis of the various 'technological fantasists in the realm of scarcity', in *Fictions of Sustainability*, Ch.4.

49. See my critique of Long Wave theories in *Fictions of Sustainability, ch.1*.

50. Edward Webster, Rob Lambert, *Andries Bezuidenhout, Grounding Globalization: Labour in the Age of Insecurity*, Blackwell, Oxford, 2008, Ch.1.

51. Timothy Clark, *op.cit.* p. 76.

52. Michael Burawoy, 'From Polanyi to Pollyanna: The False Optimism of Global Labor Studies', *Global Labour Journal*, Vol. 1, Issue 2, 2010, pp.301-2.

53. Beverly Silver, *Forces of Labour: Workers Movements and Globalization Since 1870*, Cambridge University Press, Cambridge, 2003, p.20. Also see Michael Burawoy, 'For a Sociological Marxism: The Complementary Convergence of Antonio Gramsci and Karl Polanyi', *Politics and Society*, vol.31, no.2, 2003, pp. 193-261.

54. Globally, even pro-Polanyi researchers such as József Böröcz,'Global Inequality in Redistribution: For a World-Historical Sociology of (Not) Caring', *Intersections East European Journal of Society and Politics*, vol.2, no.2, 2016, pp.57-83, has concluded that the 'double movement' does not apply to the poorest, most discriminated against societies in the world.

55. Mark Blyth, *Great Transformations: Economic Ideas and Institutional Change in the Twentieth Century*, Cambridge University Press, New York, 2002, p.5.

56. See my analysis 'Beyond Labourism and Socialism: How the Australian Labor Party Developed the Model of New Labour', *New Left Review*, no.221, 1997, pp.3-33.

57. See Martin Höpner, Alexander Petring, Daniel Seikel, Benjamin Werner, *Liberalization Policy: An Empirical Analysis of Economic and Social Interventions in Western Democracies*, Wirtschafts und Sozialwissenschaftliches Institut, Dusseldorf, Discussion Paper no.192, 2014.

58. See Rawi Abdelal, 'Writing the rules of global finance: France, Europe, and capital liberalization', *Review of International Political Economy*, vol.13 no1, February 2006, pp. 1-27.

59. J. Habermas, *The Post-National Constellation*, MIT Press, Cambridge, 2001. Also see his interview with Stuart Jeffries, *Financial Times*, April 30, 2010 in which he states: "the current

phase of financial-market-driven globalisation should also be followed by a strengthening not only of the European Union but of the international community. Today, we need institutions capable of acting on a global scale."

60. Michael Brie, 'For an Alliance of Liberal Socialists and Libertarian Commonists: Nancy Fraser and Karl Polanyi—a Possible Dialogue' in Michael Brie (ed.), *Karl Polanyi in Dialogue: A Socialist Thinker for Our Times*, Black Rose Books, Montreal, 2017.

61. Nancy Fraser, 'A Triple Movement? Parsing the Politics of Crisis after Polanyi', *New Left Review*, 81, May-June, 2013 p.131.

62. *Ibid*, p.128.

63. Nancy Fraser and Rahel Jaeggi, *Capitalism A Conversation in Critical Theory*, Edited by Brian Milstein, Polity, Cambridge, 2018, p.203.

7. Perpetuating Myths about Democratic Control

1. See Donald Sassoon, *One Hundred Years of Socialism: The West European Left in the Twentieth Century*, Fontana Press, London, 1996. Ch.2.

2. Milovan Djilas, *The New Class: An Analysis of the Communist System*, Harcourt Brace Jovanovich, New York, 1957. Djilas was an 'insider' who used his experience to put forward critiques of the party apparatus broadly similar in tone to those articulated decades earlier by Trotsky who called the Soviet bureaucracy a 'caste' rather than a 'class'. The difference is that Djilas was lionised by Western conservatives and liberals during the Cold War whereas Trotsky remained a pariah.

3. Peter Hall, *Cities in Civilization: Culture, Innovation, and Urban Order*, Weidenfeld & Nicolson, London, 1998, p. 886.

4. C.V. Devan Nair, (ed.), *Socialism That Works: The Singapore Way*, Federal Press, Singapore, 1976), p. ix.

5. See John Kelly, *Contemporary Trotskyism: Parties, Sects and Social Movements in Britain*, Routledge, London, 2018.

6. Walter Baier, 'Considerations on the European Elections', *transform! European network for alternative thinking and political dialogue*, 26 July 2019.

7. For a sample of the many articles and books on Marxists disputes over the continued relevance or not of imperialism, See Murray Noonan, *Marxist Theories of Imperialism A History*, I. B. Tauris, New York, 2017 and John Bellamy Foster, 'Late Imperialism Fifty Years After Harry Magdoff's The Age of Imperialism', *Monthly Review*, July/August 2019, pp.1-19.

8. Samir Amin, *Capitalism in the Age of Globalization: The Management of Contemporary Society* (1997) Zed Books, London, 2014, pp. 4-5.

9. *Ibid* p. xxxiii.

10. See F. A. Hayek, *The Road to Serfdom*, Routledge, London, 1944.

11. See Paul Addison, 'Why Churchill Lost in 1945', *BBC History*, 17 February 2011.

12. Alec Nove, *The Economics of Feasible Socialism*, George Allen & Unwin, London, 1983 offers a very good and insightful overview of the debates on planning from a market socialist perspective. Perry Anderson, *In the Tracks of Historical Materialism*, pp. 99-104 praised Nove to the sky. I was more critical of the inherent problems of market socialism despite Nove's perceptive criticisms of my own position, some very fair, some unfair. Today, I no longer hold some of the arguments I made concerning 'productive and unproductive labour' and aspects of planning. Unfortunately, since 1985 there has been little advance in resolving the complexities of socialist planning. See the Nove/Frankel debate: Alec Nove 'Beyond the market? Comments on Boris Frankel', *Radical Philosophy* number 39, 1985, pp. 24-27; B. Frankel, `The Historical Obsolescence of Market Socialism', *Radical Philosophy*, No.39, 1985, pp. 28-33; A. Nove, 'A Reply to Boris Frankel's Reply, pp.34-35; Chris Arthur, 'Nove and Frankel on Unproductive Labour', pp.36-37; and B. Frankel, `A Reply to Alec Nove', *Radical Philosophy*, No.41, 1985, pp.47-48.

13. Leigh Phillips and Michal Rozworski, *The People's Republic of Walmart: How the World's Biggest Corporations are Laying the Foundation for Socialism*, Verso, London, 2019.

14. Herman Finer, *Road to Reaction*, Little, Brown, Boston, 1945, p.1.

15. F. A. Hayek, 'Letters to the Editor: The dangers to personal liberty', *The Times*, London, 11 July 1978.

16. Dani Rodrik, *The Globalisation Paradox: Democracy and the Future of the World Economy*, W. W. Norton and Company, New York, 2011, ch.9.

17. Gustavo Piga, 'Rodrik's trilemma is false: the euro trilemma is another one', www. gustavopiga.it, 8 October 2012. Also see Matjaz Nahtigal, 'EU Experimental Governance: Going Beyond Rodrik's Trilemma', *SSRN Electronic Journal*, January 2014.

18. See Jon Emont, 'The Growing Urban-Rural Divide Around the World', *The Atlantic*, January 4, 2017.

19. See Simon Griffiths, *Engaging Enemies Hayek and the Left*, Rowan & Littlefield, London, 2014.

20. Naomi Klein, 'It was the rise of the Davos class that sealed America's fate, *The Guardian*, 9 November 2016.

21. Michael Hardt and Antonio Negri, *Empire*, Harvard University Press, MA, 2000

22. Robert H. Wade, 'Rethinking the world economy as a two bloc hierarchy', *realworld economics review*, no.92, June 2020, pp. 4-21.

23. See for example, David Harvey, 'Realities on the Ground', *Review of African Political Economy* February 5, 2018, *http://roape.net*; John Smith, 'Imperialist Realities vs. the Myths of David Harvey', *http://roape.net,* March 19, 2018; Patrick Bond, 'Towards a Broader Theory of Imperialism', April 18, 2018, *http://roape.net*; and Walter Daum, 'Is Imperialism Still Imperialist? A Response to Patrick Bond', May 16, 2018*, http://roape.net.*

24. Anatol Lieven, 'The New Nationalism', *The National Interest*, July/August 2017.

25. See 'The New Left and its legacies Michael Rustin talks to Sally Davison and Jeremy Gilbert', *Soundings,* no.74, 2020, pp.136-163, an insider's account of how the Left perceived *New Left Review* from the 1960s to the present.

26. See Perry Anderson, 'After the Event', *New Left Review*, no.73, 2012, pp.49-61 and 'Why the System will still win', *Le Monde Diplomatique*, March 2017; Susan Watkins, 'Editorial: The Political State of The Union', *New Left Review*, no.90, Nov-Dec. 2014, pp.5-25 and Wolfgang Streeck, *Buying Time*, ch.3.

27. See Perry Anderson, 'The Europe to Come', *London Review of Books*, 25 January 1996; and Glyn Morgan, 'Hayek, Habermas and European Integration', *Critical Review*, nos.1-2, 2003, pp.1-22.

28. *Ibid* pp.97-112.

29. *Ibid*, pp.101-2.

30. For a selection of diverse views on Europe before and after the Maastricht Treaty, see Peter Gowan and Perry Anderson (eds.) *The Question of Europe*, Verso, London, 1997.

31. See Colin Crouch, *The Strange Non-death of Neoliberalism*, Polity, Cambridge, 2013.

32. Wolfgang Streeck, *Buying Time: The Delayed Crisis of Democratic Capitalism*, German edition 2013, translated by Patrick Camiller, Verso, London, 2014.

33. Thomas Piketty, 'Europe and the Class Divide' originally published in *Le Monde,* May 11, 2019, translated by David Fernbach and reprinted in *Verso Blog*, December 19, 2019.

34. W. Streeck, 'Heller, Schmitt and the Euro', *European Law Journal*, Vol. 21, No. 3, May 2015, p. 365.

35. See Neelam Srivastava, 'The Travels of the Organic Intellectual: The Black Colonized Intellectual in George Padmore and Frantz Fanon', in Neelam Srivastava and Baidik Bhattacharya (eds.) *The Postcolonial Gramsci*, Routedge, London, 2012, ch.3.

36. See for example, Juan Linz and Alfred Stepan, 'Toward Consolidated Democracies', *Journal of Democracy,* Vol.7, no.2, 1996, pp. 14-33; Philippe C. Schmitter and Terry Lynn Karl, 'What Democracy Is... and Is Not', *Journal of Democracy*, Vol. 2, No 3, 1991, pp. 75-88.

37. W. Streeck, *Buying Time,* ch.3.

38. W. Streeck, 'Globalization and the Transformation of the International State System',

Norbert Lechner Lecture, Diego Portales University, Santiago, Chile, November 14, 2018, p.4.

39. W. Streeck, 'Comment on Wolfgang Merkel, 'Is capitalism compatible with democracy?', *Zeitschrift für Vergleichende Politikwissenschaft*, 7 February 2015, p. 53.

40. Mike Davis, 'The Political Economy of Late-Imperial America', *New Left Review*, no.143, January-February 1984, p. 8.

41. *Buying Time*, pp.13-14. Franz Neumann objected strongly to Pollock's concept of 'state capitalism' but the latter was defended by Horkheimer and Adorno who proceeded to eliminate references to monopoly capitalism and other Marxist concepts in their published manuscript of *Dialectic of Enlightenment*, see Manfred Gangl, 'The Controversy over Friedrich Pollock's state capitalism', *History of the Human Sciences*, Vol. 29, no.2, 2016, pp. 23-41.

42. Ernest Mandel, *Late Capitalism* trans by Joris de Bres, NLB, London, 1975.

43. *Buying Time*, pp.18-19.

44. Michal Kalecki, 'Political Aspects of Full Employment', *Political Quarterly*, no.4, October 1943, pp.322-330. See my discussion in *Fictions of Sustainability*, pp.121-125 on why Kalecki's analysis needs to be modified when considering the divisions among businesses in regard to environment policies.

45. *Buying Time*, p.25.

46. *Ibid*, p.5.

47. *Ibid*, p.38 and Colin Crouch, 'Privatised Keynesianism: An Unacknowledged Policy Regime', *British Journal of Politics and International Relations*, Vol. 11, 2009, pp.382-399.

48. Armin Schäfer and Wolfgang Streeck, 'Introduction: Politics in the Age of Austerity' in Armin Schäfer and Wolfgang Streeck (eds.), *Politics in the Age of Austerity*, Polity, Cambridge, 2013, ch.1; and Streeck, *Buying Time*, pp.79-96.

49. Sandy Brian Hager, 'What Happened to the Bondholding Class? Public Debt, Power and the Top One Per Cent', *New Political Economy*, vol.19, no.2, 2014, p.176.

50. *Buying Time*, p.116.

51. See Streeck, 'The Crises of Democratic Capitalism' *New Left Review*, September-October 2011, pp.5-29

52. See Slavoj Žižek, *Living in the End Times,* Verso, London, 2010, p. xi.

53. W. Streeck, 'Taking Crisis Seriously: Capitalism on Its Way Out', *Stato e Mercato*, no.100, April 2014 p.45.

54. *Ibid* p.46.

55. See Streeck Interview with Ben Jackson, 'Capitalism, Neoliberalism and democracy', *Renewal*, no.3/4, 2014.

56. Baptiste Touverey, 'Capital's Revolt: Interview with Wolfgang Streeck', *Verso Blog*, 2 June 2017.

57. *Ibid* pp.60-68.

58. It is only belatedly that *New Left Review* 'discovered' environmental issues after decades of neglect. Yet, it has only published a mere handful of articles since 2018 on the critical relationship between environmental sustainability and political economy. Streeck briefly mentioned climate change and support for a Green New Deal very recently, see W. Streeck, 'Four Reasons the European Left Lost', *Jacobin*, May 30, 2019.

59. See discussion by Nikolas Abercrombie, Stephen Hill, Bryan S. Turner, *The Dominant Ideology Thesis,* George Allen & Unwin, London, 1980.

60. For the continued impact of the Taft-Hartley Act see Rich Yeleson, 'Fortress Unionism', *Democracy*, no.29 Summer 2013, pp.68-81.

61. See William Graf, 'Anti-Communism in the Federal Republic of Germany', *Socialist Register*, 1984, pp.164-212.

62. See Herbert Kitschelt and Wolfgang Streeck, 'From stability of stagnation: Germany at the beginning of the twenty-first century', *West European Politics*, vol.26, no.4, 2003, pp.1-34.

63. For an analysis of Ordoliberalism see Werner Bonefeld, *The Strong State and the Free Economy*, Rowman & Littlefield, New York, 2017, p.10.

64. See Quinn Slobodian, *Globalists*, pp. 190-93.

65. Jürgen Habermas, *Legitimation Crisis*, trans. By T. McCarthy, Beacon Press, Boston 1973.

66. James O'Connor, *The Fiscal Crisis of the State*, St. Martin's Press, New York, 1973

67. See W. Streeck, 'The Post-capitalist interregnum: The old system is dying, but a new social order cannot be born' *Juncture*, vol.23, no.2, 2016, pp. 68-77.

68. See Herbert Kitschelt and Wolfgang Streeck, *op.cit.* p.18.

8. Supranational Capitalism versus National Social Democracy

1. Torben Iversen and David Soskice, *Democracy and Prosperity Reinventing Capitalism through a Turbulent Century*, Princeton University Press, Princeton, 2019.

2. See Justine Nolan and Martijn Boersma, 'The long and winding road to respecting workers' rights in supply chains', *Social Europe*, 1 October 2019.

3. Iversen and Soskice, p.20. Olli Rehn, a neoliberal 'austerity hawk' quoted this passage from Iversen and Soskice's book approvingly – see Olli Rehn, 'Living with populism - reflections on the economy and democracy in Europe', Speech by Mr. Olli Rehn, Governor of the Bank of Finland, Waiting for Populism? Problems of Interpretation and Policy Issues: Four Lectures and a Conversation, Central Bank of Malta, Valletta, 9 May 2019, p.3.

4. See my analysis of the relation between developed and developing countries other than the 'middle income trap' in *Fictions of Sustainability*, Ch.2.

5. Kees van der Pijl, 'Democratic Capitalism in the Last Stages? Capital as Agency in Wolfgang Streeck's Analysis of the Crisis', Paper for the 5th EU experts' Discussion, Rosa Luxemburg Stiftung, Berlin, 11-13 December 2015. I also do not share both Streeck's and van der Pijl's use of 'Fordism' as a broad explanatory model of a 'stage' of capitalism.

6. See Simon Clarke, 'New Utopias for Old: Fordist dreams and Post-Fordist Fantasies', *Capital and Class*, 42, Winter 1990, pp.131-153.

7. *Ibid*, p.146.

8. Kees van der Pijl, *The Making of an Atlantic Ruling Class*, Verso, London, 1984, Ch.1

9. See discussion of the crisis of Fordism by Alain Lipietz, 'The National and the Regional: Their Autonomy Vis-a-Vis the Capitalist World Crisis' in Neil Brenner, Bob Jessop, Martin Jones, and Gordon MacLeod (eds.) *State/Space A Reader*, Blackwell, Oxford, 2003.

10. By the year 2000, 'neo-Fordism' and 'post-Fordism' was succeeded by 'financialisation' – a concept also partly developed by the Regulation School, see Robert Boyer, 'Is a Finance-led growth regime a viable alternative to Fordism? A Preliminary Analysis', *Economy and Society*, vol.29, no.1, 2000, pp.111-145.

11. See Philip Mader, Daniel Mertens and Natascha van der Zwan (eds.) *The Routledge International Handbook of Financialization*, Routledge, New York, 2020.

12. Michel Aglietta, 'Capitalism at the Turn of the Century: Regulation Theory and the Challenge of Social Change' *New Left Review*, no.232, November/December 1998, p. 56.

13. World Economic Forum and A.T. Kearney, *Readiness for the Future of Production Report 2018*, WEF, Geneva, 2018.

14. See Ashok Kumar, *Monopsony Capitalism Power and Production in the Twilight of the Sweatshop Age*, Cambridge University Press, Cambridge, 2020 and Phu Huynh, 'Developing Asia's garment and footwear industry: Recent employment and wage trends', *International Labour Organization Asia-Pacific Garment and Footwear Sector*, Research Note Issue 8, October 2017.

15. Stephen Roach, 'Global Growth – Still made in China', *Project Syndicate*, 29 August 2016

16. For figures of union strength in OECD countries see 'Employment Outlook, Trends in Trade Union Memberships', OECD, Paris, 1991. Ch.4.

17. Bob Jessop, 'The Organic Crisis of the British State: Putting Brexit in Its Place', *Globalizations*, Vol.14, no.1, 2017, pp.133-41.

18. Robert Boyer, 'French Statism at the Crossroads' in Colin Crouch and Wolfgang Streeck (eds.) *Political Economy of Modern Capitalism: Mapping Convergence and Diversity*, Sage, London, 1997. ch.4, p.79.

19. See my critique of Aglietta, Mandel and others in *Beyond the State? Dominant Theories and Socialist Strategies*, Macmillan Press, London, 1983, pp.35-44.

20. Aglietta, *op.cit.*, p. 57, f.12.

21. See Wolfgang Streeck and Anke Hassel, 'The crumbling pillars of social partnership', *West European Politics*, vol.26, no.4, 2003, p.104.

22. See W. Streeck, 'Heller, Schmitt and the Euro', *European Law Journal*, Vol. 21, No. 3, May 2015, pp. 361-370.

23. See Jörg Bibow, *How Germany's Anti-Keynesianism Has Brought Europe to Its Knees*, Levy Economics Institute, Working Paper no.886, March 2017.

24. See Thomas Biebricher, *The Political Theory of Neoliberalism*, Stanford University Press, Stanford, 2018, especially ch.7, 'Ideas, Uncertainty, and the Ordoliberalization of Europe'.

25. See my analysis in 'Beyond Labourism and Socialism: How the Australian Labor Party Developed the Model of 'New Labour', *New Left Review*, no.221, 1997, pp. 3-33.

26. See US Bureau of Labor Statistics, 'Union Members Summary', January 22, 2020.

27. See figures for union density in OECD release, 'The Future of Work', 2 May 2019.

28. Baptiste Touverey, 'After Capital's Revolt: an interview with Wolfgang Streeck', *Verso Blog*, 2 June 2017.

29. Dieter Grimm, *Sovereignty: The Origin and Future of a Political and Legal Concept*, translated by Belinda Cooper, Columbia University Press, New York, 2015, p.112.

30. F.A. Hayek, *Denationalisation of Money -The Argument Refined: An Analysis of the Theory and Practice of Concurrent Currencies*, Institute of Economic Affairs, Third Edition, London, 1990 (First Edition 1976).

31. *Ibid*, p.24. It is noteworthy that Milton Friedman, prominent anti-Keynesian and one of the 'fathers' of neoliberalism, was also a strong opponent of the Euro and, by extension, the 'Hayekian state', see Milton Friedman, 'The Euro: Monetary Unity to Political Disunity' (August 28, 1997) and republished in *Project Syndicate*, 27, June 2016.

32. See Grahame F. Thompson, 'Central Banks and Fin-tech Governance in a Global Context' Draft paper for Workshop on *'The Changing Technological Infrastructures of Global Finance'*, Queens University, Waterloo, Canada, May 30-31, 2017.

33. See Sinclair Davidson, Primavera De Filippi, and Jason Potts, 'Disrupting Governance: The New Institutional Economics of Distributed Ledger Technology', 2016, https://ssrn.com/abstract=2811995 and Brendan Markey-Towler, 'Anarchy, Blockchain and Utopia', ssrn.com/abstract = 3095343, 2 January 2018.

34. W. Streeck, 'The Rise of the European Consolidation State', MPIfG Discussion Paper 15/1, Max Planck Institute for the Study of Societies, Cologne, February 2015, p.23.

35. See Ministry for Finance, *The Budget Bill for 2016 – Investing in Sweden's future*, 21 September 2015, Stockholm.

36. See for example, Amanda Billner, 'Sweden's Budget Credibility at Risk', National Forecaster Warns, *Bloomberg Business*, December 22, 2015.

37. The danger of unelected power is well recognised by Paul Tucker, an ex-senior official of the Bank of England. See his analysis written from a liberal democratic perspective in *Unelected Power: The Quest for Legitimacy in Central Banking and the Regulatory State*, Princeton University Press, Princeton, 2018.

38. W. Streeck, 'Heller, Schmitt and the Euro', p.366.

39. Jean Pisani-Ferry, 'When Facts Change, Change the Pact', *Project Syndicate*, April 29, 2019.

40. Agnès Bénassy-Quéré et.al. 'Reconciling risk sharing with market discipline: A constructive approach to euro area reform', *Centre for Economic Policy Research*, *Policy Insight*, No.91, January 2018, pp.1-23.

41. *Ibid*, p.21.

42. See Andrew Watt, 'Welcome but inadequate: European measures to counter the corona crisis', *Social Europe*, March 20, 2020; Emmanuel Saez and Gabriel Zucman, 'This crisis calls for massive government intervention: here's how to do it', *The Guardian*, March 17, 2020; and Adam Tooze, 'Is the Coronavirus Crash Worse Than the 2008 Financial Crisis?', *Foreign Policy.com*, March 18, 2020.

43. See proposals in Andrew Watt, 'Europe needs a strong macroeconomic policy core – but not a Six or (Two) Pack', *Social Europe*, February 6, 2020.

44. See Wolfgang Streeck, 'Playing Catch Up', *London Review of Books*, May 4, 2017, pp. 26-28

45. Adam Tooze, *Crashed: How a Decade of Financial Crises Changed the World*, Viking, New York, 2018, p.93.

46. Wolfgang Streeck and Lea Elsässer, 'Monetary disunion: the domestic politics of euroland', *Journal of European Public Policy*, Sept. 2015, pp.1-24 and *Buying Time*, p.148.

47. Streeck, 'Scenario for a Wonderful Tomorrow', *London Review of Books'*, 31 March 2016.

48. Costas Lapavitsas interview with Michael Calderbank, 'Socialism starts at Home, *Red Pepper*, October 24, 2018.

49. See W. Streeck, 'The EU is a doomed empire', *Le Monde diplomatique*, May 19, 2019.

50. W. Streeck, 'German Hegemony: Unintended and Unwanted', http://wolfgangstreeck.com May 15, 2015.

51. *Ibid.*

52. Aljazeera, 'German ruling on bond purchases sparks worries over EU resilience', May 6, 2020 and Phillip Inman, 'Jolt to eurozone as German court warns against central bank stimulus', *The Guardian*, May 6, 2020.

53. John Weeks, 'German court decision ends treaty pretences', *Social Europe*, May 11, 2020.

54. See Anatole Kaletsky, 'Europe's Hamiltonian Moment', *Project Syndicate*, May 21, 2020.

55. See Katharina Pistor, 'Germany's Constitutional Court Goes Rogue', *Project Syndicate*, May 8, 2020.

56. Adam Tooze, 'Time to expose the reality of 'debt market discipline', *International Politics and Society Journal*, May 25, 2020.

57. 'The EU needs a stability and wellbeing pact, not more growth', Letter signed by 238 European academics, *The Guardian*, 16 September 2018.

58. See feminist critiques of Piketty such as Kathleen Geier et al, 'How Gender Changes Piketty's 'Capital in the Twenty-First Century', *The Nation*, August 6, 2014 and Diane Perrons, 'Gendering inequality: a note on Piketty's Capital in the Twenty-First Century, *British Journal of Sociology*, Volume 65 Issue 4, 2014, pp.667-677.

59. Thomas Piketty, *Capitalism and Ideology*, translated by Arthur Goldhammer, Harvard University Press, Cambridge, 2020.

60. W. Streeck, 'Piketty, the Global Tax on Capital, and the Fiscal Crisis of the State', wolfgangstreeck.com 2015.

61. Streeck, 'Comment on Wolfgang Merkel, "Is capitalism compatible with democracy?", p.60.

62. See Baptiste Touverey interview with Streeck, *Verso Blog*, 2 June, 2017.

63. Streeck, 'Small-State Nostalgia? The Currency Union, Germany, and Europe: A Reply to Jürgen Habermas', *Constellations*, Vol. 21, Issue 2, June 2014, p.219, German original published in *Blätter für deutsche und internationale Politik*, no.5, 2013, pp. 59-70.

64. W. Streeck, *How Will Capitalism End? Essays on A Failing System*, Verso, London, 2016, p. 229.

65. See W. Streeck, 'Taking Crisis Seriously: Capitalism on Its Way Out', *Stato e Mercato*, no.100, April 2014, pp.45-68 and *How Will Capitalism End?*

66. See Yanis Varoufakis, 'Egalitarianism's latest foe: a critical review of Thomas Piketty's Capital in the Twenty-First Century', *real-world economics review*, no.69, 2014, pp.18-35. It is unfair of Varoufakis to describe Piketty as a 'foe' of egalitarianism when the latter places overcoming inequality at the centre of his work. Also, if Piketty's proposal for wiping out much of Greece's debt had been adopted by the EU, Varoufakis may have still continued as Finance Minister in a more popular Syriza government.

67. Piketty, *Capital in the Twenty-First Century* p.481.

68. *Ibid*, ch.13.

69. OECD, *Revenue Statistics 2018*, OECD, Paris, 2018.

70. See IMF 2020 figures and table in Peter Bofinger, 'The 'frugal four' should save the European project', *Social Europe*, May 4, 2020.

71. See Robert Skidelsky, 'How Much Debt Is Too Much?', *Project Syndicate*, January 28, 2016. From a mainstream perspective, even the IMF does not believe that debt restricts growth over longer periods, see Andrea Pescatori, Damiano Sandri and John Simon, *Debt and Growth: Is There a Magic Threshold?* IMF Working Paper/ WP/14/34, International Monetary Fund, 2014; also see Adair Turner, *Between Debt and the Devil: Money, Credit, and Fixing Global Finance*, Princeton University Press, Princeton, 2015.

72. See Florian Fastenrath, Michael Schwan & Christine Trampusch, 'Where states and markets meet: the financialisation of sovereign debt management, *New Political Economy*, vol.22, no.3, 2017, pp. 273-293.

73. Geoff Dow, 'Wolfgang Streeck's conception of the crisis phase of democratic politics: A post-Keynesian critique', *Australian Journal of Political Science*, vol.51, no.2, 2016, pp.255-271.

74. T. Piketty, 'Germany has never repaid its debt. It has no right to lecture Greece.' Interview in *Die Zeit*, 8 July 2015. For a broader analysis linking Europe-wide solutions to debt with reform of EU structures and political, tax and social policies, see Piketty and 13 other French political economists, 'Our Manifesto for Europe', *The Guardian*, 2 May 2014 and Piketty, 'A New Deal for Europe', *New York Review of Books*, February 25, 2016.

75. There have been numerous suggested anti-austerity policies proposed within the framework of market economies. See for example, European Economists for an Alternative Economic Policy in Europe - EuroMemo Group, *What future for the European Union – Stagnation and polarisation or new foundations? www. euromemo.eu 2015.*

76. Figures produced by The Global Commission on the Economy and Climate, *Seizing the Global Opportunity: Partnerships for Better Growth and a Better Climate,* Washington DC, July 2015. Noam Chomsky and Robert Pollin with C. J. Polychroniou, *Global Crisis and the Green New Deal: The Political Economy of Saving the Planet*, Verso, London, 2020, Appendix, provide a more modest fiscal programme of $2.6 trillion by 2024.

77. William Mitchell and Thomas Fazi, *Reclaiming the State: A Progressive Vision of Sovereignty for a Post-Neoliberal World*, Pluto Press, London, 2017.

78. Bishop and Payne, *op.cit.*, p. 92.

79. See thefullbrexit.com with analyses provided by Lee Jones, Danny Nicol, Philip Cunliffe, Maurice Glasman, Philip Whyman, Costas Lapavistas, et al and supporters such as William Mitchell, Thomas Fazi, David Goodhardt, and dozens of others including supporters of Nigel Farage's Brexit Party such as James Heartfied and Peter Ramsay. Despite their discomfort, supporters of Lexit formed an informal united front with the political Right, a consequence of pursuing so-called self-proclaimed 'non-nationalist' policies.

80. John Bellamy Foster, 'The Rise of the Right, Interview with Farooque Chowdhury' *Monthly Review*, October 1 2019.

9. Cosmopolitans and Nationalists: A Divided Political Culture

1. Philip B Whyman, *The Left Case for Brexit: Active government for an independent UK*, Civitas, London, September 2018.

2. Paul Mason, 'Johnson's folie de grandeur', *Social Europe*, September 7, 2020.

3. See Heiner Flassbeck and Costas Lapavitsas, *Against the Troika: Crisis and Austerity in the Eurozone*, Verso, London, 2015 and W. Streeck, 'Why the Euro Divides Europe', *New Left Review*, no.95 Sept-Oct 2015, pp. 5-26. Streeck is also persuasive in his critique of Haber-

mas's concept of money which is reduced to a neutral technical instrument divorced from socio-economic relations, see pp.9-10.

4. See Wolfgang Streeck interview with Giuliano Battiston for *L'Espresso*, 7 July 2015 republished in *Verso Blog*, 29 July 2015. Streeck also talks about paying workers in combinations of national currencies and Euros, a solution that could be worse than the straight Euro if markets decide the national currency has little value. Also see Fritz W. Scharpf, 'The southern euro', *International Politics and Society*, 26 December 2017.

5. Martin Höpner, 'The German Undervaluation Regime under Bretton Woods: How Germany Became the Nightmare of the World Economy', MPIfG Discussion Paper 19/1, Max Planck Institute for the Study of Societies, Cologne, February 2019.

6. *Buying Time*, p.175.

7. Colin Crouch and Wolfgang Streeck (eds.) *Political Economy of Modern Capitalism: Mapping Convergence and Diversity*, Sage, London, 1997, Introduction, p.14.

8. *Ibid*, p.17.

9. Colin Crouch, *The Globalization Backlash*, Polity Press, Cambridge 2019.

10. Streeck, 'Small –State Nostalgia? The Currency Union, Germany, and Europe: A Reply to Jürgen Habermas', *Constellations*, Vol. 21, Issue 2, June 2014, p.218.

11. K. Polanyi, 'Universal Capitalism or Regional Planning?' (1945) reprinted in Michele Cangiani and Claus Thomasberger (eds.) *Karl Polanyi, Economy and Society Selected Writings*, Polity, Cambridge, 2018.

12. Wolfgang Streeck, 'The International State System after Neoliberalism: Europe between National Democracy and Supranational Centralization', *Crisis & Critique*, vol.7, no.1, 2020, pp. 215-34.

13. Perry Anderson, *American Foreign Policy and its Thinkers*, Verso, London, 2015.

14. Tariq Ali, 'We Need to Have a Clear Alternative' in Stijn De Cauwer (ed.), *Critical Theory at a Crossroads: Conversations on Resistance in Times of Crisis*, Columbia University Press, New York, 2018, p.109.

15. See various contributors to *The Brexit Crisis. A Verso Report*, Verso Books, London, July 2016.

16. See my critique of Labour's earlier 1970s and 1980s Alternative Economic Strategy in *Beyond the State? Dominant Theories and Socialist Strategies*, Macmillan, London, 1983. While the political economic strategy of the 1970s and 1980s was based on conditions that have significantly changed compared to those faced by Corbyn's Labour Party, many of the same viability problems confront Left nationalist strategies whether in the UK or elsewhere.

17. *Ibid*.

18. W. Streeck, 'Comment on Wolfgang Merkel, "Is capitalism compatible with democracy?", *Zeitschrift für Vergleichende Politikwissenschaft*, February 2015.

19. See Jürgen Habermas, 'Democracy or Capitalism? On the Abject Spectacle of a Capitalistic World Society fragmented along National Lines', reprinted in *The Lure of Technocracy*, translated by Ciaran Cronin, Polity, Cambridge, 2015, (German original published in *Blätter für deutsche und internationale Politik*, no.5, 2013, pp. 59-70) and Streeck's reply in same journal no.9, 2013, pp. 75-92, English translation reprinted in 2014 as 'Small-State Nostalgia? The Currency Union, Germany, and Europe: A Reply to Jürgen Habermas', *Constellations*, Vol. 21, Issue 2, June 2014, pp.213-221.

20. See e.g. Jürgen Habermas, 'The European Nation-State and the Pressures of Globalization', *New Left Review*, May-June 1999, pp.46-59 a critique of the EU and the need for democratisation and a European social state that indicates how close he was to NLR, Streeck and Scharpf in an earlier period; also see J. Habermas, 'Europe's Post-Democratic Era', *The Guardian*, November 11, 2011.

21. See for example, H. Eichel, J. Habermas, R. Koch, F. Merz, B. Zypries, 'We are deeply concerned about the future of Europe and Germany', *Handelsblatt Today*, 25 October 2018.

22. W. Streeck, 'Progressive Regression Metamorphoses of European Social Policy', *New Left Review*, July/August 2019, no.118, pp.117-139.

23. See Streeck, 'What about capitalism? Jürgen Habermas's project of a European democracy', *European Political Science*, vol.16, June 2017, pp.246-53.

24. See Fritz W. Scharpf, *Legitimacy Intermediation in the Multilevel European Polity and Its Collapse in the Euro Crisis*, MPIfG Discussion Paper 12/6 Max Planck Institute for the Study of Societies, Cologne October 2012; and Fritz W. Scharpf, *After the Crash: A Perspective on Multilevel European Democracy*, MPIfG Discussion Paper 14/21, Max Planck Institute for the Study of Societies, Cologne, December 2014.

25. Streeck, 'What about capitalism? Jürgen Habermas's project of a European democracy' p.250.

26. Jürgen Habermas, 'Democracy or Capitalism? On the Abject Spectacle of a Capitalistic World Society Fragmented Along National Lines' reprinted in J. Habermas, *The Lure of Technocracy*, p.98.

27. See *Ibid*.

28. For discussion of these manifestos and proposals see for example, the annual Euro-memorandum published by European Economists for an Alternative Economic Policy in Europe, www.euromemo.eu; Thomas Fazi, *The Battle for Europe*, Pluto Press, London 2014; Lorenz Del Savio and Matteo Mameli, 'Against the European Parliament', *Open Democracy*, 8 January 2015; Ulrike Guerot and Victoria Kupsch et al, 'Europe in the 21st century: a new version of Europe is available', www.european-republic.eu 9 June 2015; Protesilaos Stavrou, 'EU federalism and the German Question', *Open Democracy*, 14 October 2015; T. Fazi, 'A Critique Of Yanis Varoufakis' Democracy In Europe Movement (DiEM25)', *Social Europe*, 9 February, 2016 and Yannis Varoufakis's led Democracy in Europe movement 25, http://diem25.org; Colin Crouch, 'Europe beyond neoliberalism', *Eurozine*, 16 April, 2019; Michael D. Higgins, 'The future of Europe: rebalancing ecology, economics and ethics', *Social Europe*, 18 July, 2019.

29. See for example, Thomas Piketty, 'Our Manifesto to save Europe from itself", *The Guardian*, 10 December 2018. The 'Manifesto for the Democratisation of Europe' had already received support from over 117,000 signatories across Europe by early-2019.

30. Streeck, 'Comment on Wolfgang Merkel, "Is capitalism compatible with democracy?", *Zeitschrift für Vergleichende Politikwissenschaft*, February 2015.

31. See Tim Ross, 'Boris Johnson: The EU wants a superstate, just as Hitler did', *The Telegraph*, 15 May 2016.

32. See his discussion linking Hayek and Schmitt and the EU in 'Comment on Wolfgang Merkel'.

33. Karl Polanyi, 'Marxism Restated', *New Britain*, no.58, 1934, p.159.

34. See Joseph Schumpeter, *Capitalism, Socialism, and Democracy*, Harper & Row, New York, 1942, p.150.

35. Seymour Lipset, *Political Man: The Social Bases of Politics*, Doubleday, New York, 1960.

36. See Richard Florida, *The Rise of the Creative Class: and how it's transforming work, leisure, community and everyday life*, Basic Books, New York, 2000. There have been many critiques of Florida's thesis, but few arguments that intolerance and authoritarianism are incentives to a vibrant and creative society.

37. See e.g. Will Hutton, 'Litvinenko's murder shows why Putin's Russia will never prosper', *The Guardian*, 24 January 2016.

38. See Daron Acemoglu, Suresh Naidu, Pascual Restrepo, James A. Robinson, 'Democracy Does Cause Growth', *NBER Working Paper* No. 20004, March 2014.

39. Claus Offe, *Europe Entrapped*, Polity, Cambridge, 2014.

40. *Ibid*, pp.82-89.

41. *Ibid*, p.87.

42. W. Streeck, 'Caution: European Narrative. Handle with Care!' in Ash Amin and Philip Lewis (eds.) *European Union and Disunion: Reflections on European Identity*, The British Academy, London, May 2017, ch.2.

43. W. Streeck, 'The Rise of the European Consolidation State', MPIfG Discussion Paper 15/1, *Max Planck Institute for the Study of Societies*, Cologne, 2015, p.26.

44. For example, see Adam Tooze, *Crashed*, ch.4 for an analysis of the extensive scale of irresponsible European bank lending and the lack of adequate financial institutional controls in the EU.

45. See Yanis Varoufakis, *Adults in the Room My Battle With Europe's Deep Establishment*, Penguin Random House, London, 2017, Part One.

46. See *Pension Markets in Focus 2019*, OECD, Paris, 2019

47. W. Streeck 'Reflections on political scale', *Jurisprudence*, vol.10, no.1, 2019, pp.1-14.

48. *Ibid*, p.8.

49. David Goodhart, *The Road to Somewhere: The Populist Revolt and the Future of Politics*, C Hurst & Co, London, 2017.

50. Quoted by Harold James, 'Say More: Interview with Harold James', *Project Syndicate*, 22 October 2019.

51. According to Alexander Rüstow, nomadic people such as herdsmen were more aggressive and dominated agrarian communities but then ultimately sought to integrate with the superior values of settled societies. This is partly true but ignores the war-ridden history of agrarian societies that were the foundation of endless wars carried out by the knights and assorted lords and masters of the local peasants – see Alexander Rüstow, *Freedom and Domination: A Historical Critique of Civilization*, Abbreviated Translation by Salvator Attanasio, Edited and Introduced by Dankwart A. Rustow. Princeton University Press, Princeton, 1980.

52. Wendy Brown, *In the Ruins of Neoliberalism: The Rise of Antidemocratic Politics in the West*, Columbia University Press, New York, 2019, p. 186.

53. *Ibid*, p. 187.

54. *Ibid*, pp.187-88.

55. Jonathan Rutherford, 'The closing of the conservative mind: Towards a new left conservatism', *New Statesman*, 26 June 2019.

56. W. Streeck, 'Caution: European Narrative. Handle with Care!' in Ash Amin and Philip Lewis (eds.), *European Union and Disunion: Reflections on European Identity*, British Academy, London, May 2017, pp.14-22.

57. Stephen Pax Leonard, 'No Jihad Here' in *Travels in Cultural Nihilism: Some Essays*, Arktos, London, 2017.

58. W. Streeck, 'Inclusion and Secession: Questions on the Boundaries of Associative Democracy', *Politics & Society*, Vol.20, no.4, 1992, pp.513-20.

59. *Buying Time*, p.180.

60. W. Streeck, 'Collapsing Constructions: Reflections of British Exit', *Verso Blog*, 3 July 2016.

61. W. Streeck, 'Can there be peace in Europe?' Interview for *Liberal Culture*, January 12, 2016. Streeck is very sensitive to charges that he is a nationalist. I do not think that he is anti-Semitic in his use of *marktvolk*, but his distinction between 'nation state' and 'nation' is regularly overridden by his strong dislike of multiculturalism and cosmopolitan values and political goals that leads him to fall back on nationalist cultural values. See his angry response to Adam Tooze's perceptive review of '*How Will Capitalism End?*', *London Review of Books*, 5 January 2017 and Tooze's exchange with Streeck in the Letters page, *LRB* 19 January 2017.

62. W. Streeck, 'Out of the Euro', *Verso Blog*, 18, March 2015 (my emphasis).

63. See W. Streeck, 'Can there be peace in Europe?'; also see his critique of Merkel's policy on refugees, 'Scenario for a Wonderful Tomorrow', *London Review of Books*', 31 March 2016, and Postscript '*Exploding Europe: Germany, the Refugees and the British Vote to Leave*', Sheffield Political Economy Research Institute, Paper 31, August 2016. Yet, Streeck's analysis is notable for the absence of even a single sentence expressing any sympathy for the plight of refugees.

64. W. Streeck, 'Whose Side Are We On? Liberalism and Socialism Are Not the Same' in David

Coates (ed.), *Reflections on the Future of the Left*, Agenda Publishing, Newcastle upon Tyne, 2017, pp. 137-158.

65. W. Streeck, 'A renewed left as the imperative of political reason', *Defend Democracy Press*, 27 September 2018.

66. See W. Streeck, *Between Charity and Justice: Remarks on the Social Construction of Immigration Policy in Rich Democracies*, Danish Centre for Welfare Studies, University of Southern Denmark, Working Paper 2017-5, 2017.

67. See W. Streeck, 'Trump and the Trumpists', *Inference-Internal Review of Science*, vol.3, no.1, 2017.

68. W. Streeck, 'Reflections on the politics of scale', p.8.

69. *Ibid.*

70. See Replies to Streeck in *Inference-Internal Review of science*, vol.3, no.2, 2017 by Alana Lentin, Owen Goldin, Ben Tarnoff, Christopher Prendergast, Guenther Roth and Robert Horwitz who all point to major problems with Streeck's depiction of the American 'working class' that voted for Trump.

71. W. Streeck, 'Heller, Schmitt and the Euro', *European Law Journal*, Vol. 21, No. 3, May 2015, p.365.

72. Quinn Slobodian and William Callison, 'Pop-Up Populism The Failure of Left-Wing Nationalism in Germany', *Dissent*, Summer 2019, p.47.

73. Streeck and other Left nationalists have incurred criticisms from many on the Left, see Julian Göpffarth, 'Can left nationalism stop the rise of the far-right in Germany?', *Open Democracy*, 24 January 2019; Angela Mitropoulos, 'Wolfgang Streeck's 'neo-romantic' sociology', *OSF.io*, 28 March, 2019; Gareth Dale, 'Leaving the Fortresses: Between Class Internationalism and Nativist Social Democracy', *Viewpoint Magazine*, 30 November 2017.

74. Matthew Bishop and Anthony Payne, 'The left and the case for 'progressive reglobalisation'', *Renewal*, vol.27, no.3, p.85.

75. Donald Thoresen, 'Beyond Left & Right: Wolfgang Streeck's Buying Time: The Delayed Crisis of Democratic Capitalism', *Counter-Currents Publishing*, North American New Right, 2015.

76. *Buying Time*, p.189.

77. See for example, Clare Ellis, *The Blackening of Europe Vol.1 Ideologies & International Developments*, Arktos Press, 2020. Ellis undertakes a critique of Kant, the Frankfurt School, Habermas, liberal multiculturalists and others who wish to 'blacken Europe in a world where the white race comprise only 13% of the world's population.

78. See Alberto Spektorowski, 'Fascism and Post-National Europe: Drieu La Rochelle and Alain de Benoist' *Theory, Culture & Society*, vol.33, no.1, 2016. pp.115-138 and Tamir Bar-On, *Where Have All the Fascists Gone?* (*2007*) Routledge, New York, 2016.

79. See for example, Katja Kipping, 'If we want to change anything in Europe, we have to start in Berlin', *International Politics and Society Journal*, June 3, 2020.

80. W. Streeck, 'Die Zeitbombe ist der Zerfall Italiens Interview mit Thomas Thiel', *Frankfurter Algemeine Zeitung*, May 6, 2020.

81. Dewey quoted by Gerard de Vries, *Bruno Latour*, Polity, Cambridge, 2016, p. 200.

82. The Dynamics of Capitalism: Inquiries to Marx on the Occasion of His 200th Birthday, Conference jointly organized by the MPIfG and the Hamburg Institute for Social Research, Hamburg, May 3-5, 2018.

83. See for example, Victoria Fareld and Hannes Kuch (eds.) *From Marx to Hegel and Back: Capitalism, Critique, and Utopia*, Bloomsbury, London, 2020. This collection is typical of many other collections by 'critical theorists' who engage in textual analyses of Marx but say little or nothing about the relevance or irrelevance of his work to contemporary capitalist social relations and current environmental crises.

84. John Bellamy Foster and Brett Clark, *Capitalism and the Ecological Rift: The Robbery of Nature*, Monthly Review Press, New York, 2020.

85. Roberto Mangabeira Unger, *The Left Alternative*, Verso, London, 2009. It is incredible that

after years of protests by environmentalists and socialists, and in the year of the failed Copenhagen COP on the climate crisis, Unger could ignore ecological issues as part of a so-called 'Left alternative agenda'. In 2019, he published *The Knowledge Economy*, Verso, London, and discussed issues of scarcity without a single mention of environmental issues although he appears to support 'green growth', see OECD Secretary General's Advisory Group Report *Beyond Growth: Towards a New Economic Approach, OECD, Paris, September 17, 2019*. The Advisory Group comprises Andy Haldane, Michael Jacobs, Nora Lustig, Mariana Mazzucato, Robert Skidelsky, Dennis Snower and Roberto Unger. Their recommendations, despite the Report's title, are not to be confused with degrowth.

86. Joel Wainwright and Geoff Mann, *Climate Leviathan A Political Theory of Our Planetary Future*, Verso Books, London, 2018, p.25.

87. W. Streeck, *Re-Forming Capitalism: Institutional Change in the German Political Economy*, Oxford University Press, New York, 2009, states: "Basically what we did was introduce into historical institutionalism a model of *imperfect reproduction*, similar to received models of change in evolutionary biology." p. 238.

88. For example, since 2008, and well before proposals for Green New Deals, post-Keynesian Bill Mitchell, advocated a 'just transition' for coal mining regions to switch away from coal mining and embrace renewables, see Bill Mitchell et al, *A Just Transition to a Renewable Energy Economy in the Hunter Region*, Australia, Centre of Full Employment and Equity, University of Newcastle, Australia, June 2008. Like other post-Keynesians, Mitchell has long advocated a 'jobs guarantee' and other socio-economic policies to combat neoliberalism. However, all of these policies would comfortably fit into conventional pre-1970s social democratic, growth-driven frameworks rather than contemporary degrowth policies.

Introduction to Book Three

1. See Do-Wan Ku and Hyoung-Beom Yeo, 'Alternative Development: Beyond Ecological Communities and Associations' in Qingzhi Huan (ed.) *Eco-socialism as Politics: Rebuilding the Basis of Our Modern Civilisation*, Springer, London, 2010, Ch.11.

2. *Ibid*, pp.172-73.

3. Bengi Akbulut, Federico Demaria, Julien-François Gerber, Joan Martínez-Alier, 'Who promotes sustainability? Five theses on the relationships between the degrowth and the environmental justice movements', *Ecological Economics*, vol.165, November 2019.

4. Roldan Muradian, 'Frugality as a choice vs. frugality as a social condition. Is de-growth doomed to be a Eurocentric project?', *Ecological Economics*, 161, 2019, pp. 257-260.

5. Paul Ehrlich, *The Population Bomb*, Ballantine Books, New York, 1968.

6. Lyla Mehta, Amber Huffa, Jeremy Allouchea, 'The new politics and geographies of scarcity', *Geoforum*, vol.101, 2019, pp.222-230 and Ian Scoones, Rebecca Smalley, Ruth Hallc, Dzodzi Tsikatad, 'Narratives of scarcity: Framing the global land rush', *Geoforum*, vol.101, 2019, pp.231-41.

7. Murray Bookchin, *Post-Scarcity Anarchism* (1971) 2nd edition, Black Rose Books, Montreal, 1986, with a New Introduction in which Bookchin recognised much of the environmental damage caused by both corporate capitalism and Communist regimes. In fairness to Bookchin, he did not envisage affluent market consumerism for all when he talked about 'post-scarcity'.

8. Leigh Phillips, *Austerity Ecology & the Collapse-Porn Addicts: A Defence Of Growth, Progress, Industry and Stuff*, Zero Books, Alresford, 2015.

9. See for example, T. Parrique, J. Barth, F. Briens, C. Kerschner, A. Kraus-Polk, A. Kuokkanen and J. H. Spangenberg, *Decoupling Debunked: Evidence and Arguments against green growth as a sole strategy for sustainability*, European Environment Bureau, July 2019.

10. Conflicting Pathways to Post-Carbon Democracy

1. See Adrian E. Raftery et. al, 'Less than 2°C by 2100 unlikely', *Nature Climate Change*, 31 July 2017. The major problem with statistical projections is that they are devoid of politics and how actual policy developments can undermine future projections.
2. Jonathan Watts, 'Climate worst-case scenarios may not go far enough, cloud data shows', *The Guardian*, June 13, 2020.
3. Ross Gittins, 'How we caught the economic growth bug, but may shake it off', *Sydney Morning Herald*, January 4, 2020.
4. For a critique of 'green growth' see Jason Hickel & Giorgos Kallis, 'Is Green Growth Possible?', *New Political Economy*, vol.25, no.4, 2020, pp. 469-486.
5. For a global overview of all political economic, technological and social aspects of waste, see Kate O'Neill, *Waste*, Polity Press, Cambridge, 2019.
6. See Richard Smith, 'Elon Musk's electric planet-suicide vehicle: Automobiles, emissions and degrowth', *The Ecological Citizen*, vol.3, Suppl B, 2020, pp.47-53. Electric vehicles will be more material hungry than petrol-cars, have shorter lives like other battery-driven products such as mobile phones and create enormous waste-disposal problems.
7. Simone D'Alessandro, André Cieplinski, Tiziano Distefano and Kristofer Dittmer, 'Feasible alternatives to green growth', *Nature Sustainability*, Vol.3, April 2020, pp.329-335.
8. Daniel W. O'Neill, 'Beyond Green Growth', *Nature Sustainability*, Vol.3, April 2020, pp.260-61.
9. See the contributions by Neil Davidson, Heide Gerstenberger and Charles Post in the symposium on Davidson's book *How Revolutionary Were the Bourgeois Revolutions?* (2012) in *Historical Materialism,* Vol, 27, no.3, 2019.
10. For a survey and analysis of the competing accounts of the origins of capitalism see Ellen Meiksins Wood, *The Origin of Capitalism A Longer View*, Verso, London, 2002.
11. Jason A. Josephson-Storm, *The Myth of Disenchantment Magic, Modernity, and the Birth of the Human Sciences*, University of Chicago Press, Chicago, 2017, p.301.
12. E. P. Thompson, *The Making of the English Working Class*, Victor Gollancz, London, 1963.
13. *Ibid*, p.213.
14. See Perry Anderson, *Arguments Within English Marxism*, New Left Books, London, 1980, ch.2 and Tom Nairn, 'The English Working Class', *New Left Review*, no. 24, March-April 1964, pp. 43-57.
15. See W. Streeck, 'The Post-capitalist interregnum: The old system is dying, but a new social order cannot be born' *Juncture*, vol.23, no.2, 2016, pp. 68-77.
16. James C. Scott, *Seeing Like a State: How Certain Schemes to Improve the Human Condition Have Failed,* Yale University Press, New Haven, 1998, p.348.
17. Richard Smith, *China's Engine of Environmental Collapse*, Pluto Press, London, 2020, p.2.
18. See for example, Howard T. Odum and Elisabeth C. Odum, *A Prosperous Way Down: Principles and Policies*, The University Press of Colorado, Boulder, 2001.
19. Troy Vettese, 'Against steady-state economics', *The Ecological Citizen*, vol.3, Suppl B, 2020, pp.35-46.
20. Jay W. Forrester, *World Dynamics*, WrightAllen Press, Cambridge, 1971, developed the systems dynamic models used by the Club of Rome report *Limits to Growth* published in 1972. There are finite material natural limits to infinite growth but not strictly as conceived by Forrester who presented insightful but problematic analyses of capitalism and the interaction between political economy and ecosystems.
21. Herman Daly, 'From a Failed Growth Economy to a Steady-State Economy' *The Solutions Journal,* vol.1, no.2, 2010, pp.37-43.
22. Herman E. Daly, *Beyond Growth: The Economics of Sustainable Development*, Beacon Press, Boston, 1997. See Giorgos Kallis, *In Defense of Degrowth: Opinions and Minifestos*, edited by

Aaron Vansintjan, Open Common, 2017, pp.159-60 for a critique of Daly on immigration and the 'steady state'.

23. See Dan O'Neill, Rob Dietz, and Nigel Jones (eds.) *Enough is Enough Ideas for a Sustainable Economy in a World of Finite Resources The report of the Steady State Economy Conference*, Centre for the Advancement of the Steady State Economy and Economic Justice for All, Leeds, 2010.

24. See Nan Tian et al, 'Trends in World Military Expenditure, 2019', *Stockholm International Peace Research Institute (SIPRI)*, Solna, April 2020.

25. Ann Pettifor, *The Case for the Green New Deal*, Verso, London, 2019, ch.5.

26. Tim Jackson, Peter Victor and Ali Naqvi, *Towards a Stock-Flow Consistent Ecological Macroeconomics*, WWW for Europe, Working Paper no.114, March 2016.

27. Shulan Zhang, 'Conceptualising the Environmentalism in India: Between Social Justice and Deep Ecology', in Qingzhi Huan (ed.) *Eco-socialism as Politics: Rebuilding the Basis of Our Modern Civilisation,* ch.12.

28. Ted Trainer, 'On eco-villages and the transition', *The International Journal of Inclusive Democracy*, vol. 2, no.3, June 2006.

29. Vincent Liegey and Anitra Nelson, *Exploring Degrowth A Critical Guide,* Pluto Press, London, 2020, pp. 96-7.

30. David Holmgren, *Permaculture: Principles & Pathways Beyond Sustainability*, Holmgren Design Services, 2002.

31. On why the old thesis of 'peak oil' lacks credibility, see Antonia Juhasz, 'The End of Oil is Near', *Sierra Magazine*, September/October 2020. In *Fictions of Sustainability* (2018), I deliberatively avoided subscribing to the 'peak oil' thesis as it had long been clear that this thesis was based on a flawed methodology. The current oil glut might well decline in the next few years due to cuts in production, but this will not indicate that we are running out of oil.

32. Sam Alexander and Brendan Gleeson, 'Suburban Practices of Energy Descent', *American Journal of Economics and Sociology*, Vol. 79, No. 3 May 2020, p.919.

33. Serge Latouche, *Farewell to Growth* (2007) trans by David Macey, Polity Press, Cambridge, 2009.

34. For an analysis of post-industrial theories see my critique in *The Post-Industrial Utopians*, Polity Press, Cambridge, 1987.

35. Daniel Bell, *The Coming of Post-Industrial Society: A Venture in Social Forecasting*, Basic Books, New York, 1973.

36. Daniel Bell, *The Cultural Contradictions of Capitalism* (1976), second edition, Basic Books, New York 1978.

37. Ingolfur Blühdorn, 'The legitimation crisis of democracy: emancipatory politics, the environmental state and the glass ceiling to socio-ecological transformation', *Environmental Politics*, vol.29, no.1, 2020, pp. 38-57.

38. Christopher Lasch, *The Culture of Narcissism: American Life in An Age of Diminishing Expectations*, Warner Books, New York, 1979 and Richard Sennett, *The Fall of Public Man*, Cambridge University Press, Cambridge, 1977.

39. See Julie Walsh, *Narcissism and Its Discontents*, Palgrave Macmillan, Basingstoke, 2015 for an insightful critique of Lasch and Sennett.

40. Ulrich Beck and Elisabeth Beck-Gernsheim, *The Normal Chaos of Love* (1990), translated by Mark Ritter and Jane Wiebel, Polity Press, Cambridge, 1994; and Ulrich Beck and Elisabeth Beck-Gernsheim, *Individualization: Institutionalized Individualism and its Social and Political Consequences* (2001), translated by Patrick Camiller, Sage Publications, London, 2002.

41. Anthony Giddens, *The Transformation of Intimacy: Sexuality, Love and Eroticism in Modern Societies*, Polity Press, Cambridge, 1992, ch.10.

42. Zygmunt Bauman, *Liquid Modernity*, Polity, Cambridge, 2000 and 2012 edition.

43. Ulrich Beck, *Risk Society: Towards a New Modernity* (1986) translated by Mark Ritter, Sage, London, 1992.

44. See the position of Giddens and Beck in Jane Franklin (ed.), *The Politics of Risk Society*, Polity, Cambridge, 1998.

45. Christopher Lasch, *The True and Only Heaven Progress and its Critics*, W. W. Norton, New York 1991.

46. See Julie Stephens, *Confronting Postmaternal Thinking: Feminism, Memory and Care*, Columbia University Press, New York, 2012.

47. Christopher Lasch, *The Minimal Self: Psychic Survival in Troubled Times*, W. W. Norton, New York 1984, p.98.

48. Eva Illouz, *The End of Love: A Sociology of Negative Relations*, Oxford University Press, New York, 2019, p.22.

49. *Ibid.*

50. Ian Craib, *The Importance of Disappointment*, Routledge, London, 1994, p.161.

11. The Possible Emergence of New Social Change Agents

1. See Karl Marx, *Capital A Critique of Political Economy, Volume One*, translated by Ben Fowkes, Penguin and New Left Review, Harmondsworth, 1976, p.574.

2. Gilles Deleuze, *Negotiations 1972-1990*, translated by Martin Joughin, Columbia University Press, New York, 1995, p.20.

3. See Sabine Hake, *The Proletarian Dream: Socialism, Culture, and Emotion in Germany,1863–1933*, de Gruyter, Berlin, 2017, for a fine study of the gap between the power of symbolic and emotional hope vested in the 'proletarian dream' and the reality of the political weakness of revolutionaries.

4. See Sebastian Strunz, Melissa Marselle, Matthias Schröter, 'Leaving the "sustainability or collapse" narrative behind', *Sustainability Science*, vol.14, 2019, pp.1717-1728.

5. Rupert Read and Samuel Alexander, *This Civilisation is Finished Conversations on the end of Empire—and what lies beyond*, Simplicity Institute, Melbourne, 2019.

6. The Australia Institute, 'Polling – Response to the Climate Emergency', January 2020. The poll was conducted in November 2019 before the worst of the bush fires occurred in the following months.

7. 'Prediction by Extinction Rebellion's Roger Hallam that climate change will kill 6 billion people by 2100 is unsupported', *Climate Feedback*, August 22, 2019.

8. Quoted in David Spratt's and Alia Armistead's *Fatal Calculations How Economics Has Underestimated Climate Damage and Encouraged Inaction*, Breakthrough - National Centre for Climate Restoration Melbourne, April 2020.

9. See Andreas Malm, *Fossil Capital: The Rise of Steam Power and the Roots of Global Warming*, Verso Books, London, 2016., ch.1.

10. See varying figures in Australia Institute report using Potsdam Institute for Climate Impact Research figures cited by Peter Hannam, 'Emissions surging to high after fires', *The Age*, January 25, 2020 and *Trends in Global CO2 Emissions: 2016 Report*, PBL Netherlands Environmental Assessment Agency, The Hague, 2016.

11. See Daniel Moran, Keiichiro Kanemoto, et. al, 'Carbon Footprints of 13000 Cities', *Environmental Research Letters*, Volume 13, no.6, June 2018 for a discussion of the complexities associated with gathering data.

12. For an analysis of the difficulty of measuring carbon footprints, see Mike Berners-Lee, *How Bad Are Bananas? The Carbon Footprint of Everything*, Greystone Books, Vancouver, 2011.

13. Adam Tooze, 'How Britain beat Germany in the race for green Energy', *Prospect Magazine*, December 9, 2019.

14. Andreas Malm, *Op.cit.*.

15. Timothy Mitchell, *Carbon Democracy: Political Power in the Age of Oil*, Verso Books, London, 2011.

16. Andreas Malm, 'Long Waves of Fossil Development: Periodizing Energy and Capital', in

Brent Ryan Bellamy and Jeff Diamanti (eds.) *Materialism and the Critique of Energy*, MCM Publishing, Chicago, 2018, pp. 161-95.

17. See my arguments in *Fictions of Sustainability*, pp.24-26.

18. Andreas Malm, 'Long Waves of Fossil Development: Periodizing Energy and Capital', p.176.

19. Hartmut Rosa made these points in a lecture at the London School of Economics, January 12, 2017. Also see his book *Social Acceleration: A New Theory of Modernity*, trans.by Jonathon Trejo-Mathys, Columbia University Press, New York, 2013.

20. See Marc Levinson, *The Box: How the Shipping Container Made the World Smaller and the World Economy Bigger*, Princeton University Press, Princeton, 2006. The transformation of rail freight and shipping by containers began in the US in the 1960s before it moved to other countries. Although the teamsters became a powerful road-based union, they were not supportive of radical social reforms as earlier Left-wing rail and dock-worker unions across the world.

21. Alberto Posso (ed.) *Child Labor in the Developing World: Theory, Practice and Policy*, Palgrave Macmillan, Singapore, 2020.

22. See Antony Bryant, 'Liquid uncertainty, chaos and complexity: The gig economy and the open source movement', *Thesis Eleven*, vol.156, no.1, 2020, pp. 45-66.

23. In the EU the definition of 'worker' has been hotly contested. See Martin Risak and Thomas Dullinger, *The concept of 'worker' in EU law: Status quo and potential for change*, European Trade Union Institute, Report 140, Brussels, 2018.

24. Andre Gorz, 'Redefining Socialism' in *Capitalism, Socialism, Ecology*, trans. by Chris Turner, Verso, London, 1994, pp. 60-61.

25. Michal Kalecki, 'Political Aspects of Full Employment, *Political Quarterly*, no. 4, October 1943, pp. 322-330.

26. Simon Kuper, 'The Myth of Green Growth', *Financial Times*, October 24, 2019.

27. Nick O'Donovan, 'From Knowledge Economy to Automation Anxiety: A Growth Regime in Crisis?', *New Political Economy*, vol.25, no.2, 2020, pp. 248-26.

28. Karl Kautsky, *The Agrarian Question, Volumes One and Two*, translated by Pete Burgess with Introduction by Hamza Alavi and Teodor Shanin, Zwan Publications, London, 1988.

29. See Nadia El-Hage Scialabba, et. al, *Natural Capital Impacts in Agriculture*, Food and Agricultural Organization, Rome, June 2015.

30. IPCC, *Special Report on Climate Change, Desertification, Land Degradation, Sustainable Land Management, Food Security, and Greenhouse gas fluxes in Terrestrial Ecosystems*, WMO and UNEP, Geneva, August 7, 2019.

31. See George Monbiot, 'We can't keep eating as we are – why isn't the IPCC shouting this from the rooftops?', *The Guardian*, 9 August 2019.

32. See Michael Le Page, 'Going fully organic would increase farm emissions', *New Scientist*, 26 October 2019, p.9.

33. Graeme Lang, 'Urban energy futures: a comparative analysis', *European Journal of Futures Research*, vol. 6, article number 19, 2018 and Jason C. Bradford, 'The Future Is Rural: Societal Adaptation to Energy Descent', *American Journal of Economics and Sociology*, Vol. 79, No. 3 May 2020, pp. 753-98.

34. David Holmgren, *Retrosuburbia: The downshifter's guide to a resilient future*. Melliodora Publishing, Hepburn Springs, Australia, 2018.

35. Sam Alexander and Brendan Gleeson, 'Suburban Practices of Energy Descent', *American Journal of Economics and Sociology*, Vol. 79, No. 3 May 2020, pp.907-940.

36. See Ian Scoones, Marc Edelman, Saturnino M. Borras Jr., Ruth Hall, Wendy Wolford & Ben White, 'Emancipatory rural politics: confronting authoritarian populism', *The Journal of Peasant Studies*, vol.45, no.1, 2018, pp.1-20. Also, Julien-François Gerber, 'Degrowth and critical agrarian studies', *The Journal of Peasant Studies*, vol. 47, no.2, 2020, pp. 235-264.

37. See Salena Tramel, 'Global Peasant Movement Assesses and Responds to a Heated Political Moment', *HuffPost*, July 28, 2017.

38. Ian Angus, 'Ecosocialists and the Fight for Climate Justice' (2015) reprinted in I. Angus, *A*

Redder Shade of Green: *Intersections of Science and Socialism,* Monthly Review Press, New York, 2017, ch.12.

12. Political Organisational Challenges

1. Max Weber, 'Politics as a Vocation' in Hans Gerth and C. W. Mills (eds) *From Max Weber Essays in Sociology*, Oxford University Press, New York, 1946, p.128.
2. See Paulina Caroca Soto et al. 'The anatomy of the 2019 Chilean social unrest', *Chaos* 30, July 21, 2020.
3. For a discussion of Kirchheimer see André Krouwe, 'Otto Kirchheimer and the catch-all party', *West European Politics*, vol.26, no.2, 2003, pp. 23-40. Kirchheimer was concerned about the reduction of politics to the mere management of the state and the breakdown of links between parliamentary parties and diverse social groups.
4. See discussion by Mark Blyth and Richard Katz (2005) 'From Catch-all Politics to Cartelisation: The Political Economy of the Cartel Party', *West European Politics*, vol.28, no.1, 2005, pp.33-60.
5. Jürgen Habermas, *Structural Transformation of the Public Sphere An Inquiry into a Category of Bourgeois Society* (1962) translated by Thomas Burger with Frederick Lawrence, Polity Press, Cambridge, 1989.
6. In response to Habermas, see Alexander Kluge and Oskar Negt, *Public Sphere and Experience: Toward an Analysis of the Bourgeois and Proletarian Public Sphere* (1972) translated by Peter Labanyi, Jamie Owen Daniel, and Assenka Oksiloff in 1993 and reprinted with Foreword by Miriam Hansen, Verso, London, 2016. Also see critiques of Habermas's concept of the public sphere in Mike Hill and Warren Montag (eds.) *Masses, Classes, and the Public Sphere*, Verso, London, 2000.
7. György Lukács, *History and Class Consciousness: Studies in Marxist Dialectics*, Merlin, London, 1971, p. 330.
8. Antonio Gramsci, *Selections From the Prison Notebooks* edited and translated by Quintin Hoare and Geoffrey Nowell Smith, Lawrence & Wishart, London, 1971, pp.123-205.
9. Stuart Macintyre, *Little Moscows: Communism and Working-Class Militancy in Inter-War Britain*, Croom Helm, London,1980.
10. For a survey of just transition proposals see Damian White, 'Just Transitions/Design for Transitions: Preliminary Notes on a Design Politics for a Green New Deal', *Capitalism Nature Socialism*, vol.31, no.2, 2020, pp.20-39.
11. Democracy in Europe Movement 2025, *The Green New Deal for Europe: Blueprint for Europe's Just Transition*, 2nd edition December 2019, gndforeurope.com.
12. See for example, Thomas Wiedmann et al. 'Scientists' warning on affluence', *Nature Communications*, 2020, 11:3107 | https://doi.org/10.1038/s41467-020-16941-y
13. See the many articles over the past thirty years by *Arena* journal editors Geoff Sharp, John Hinkson, Alison Caddick and others.
14. Quoted by Peter Hallward in Preface to Philippe Le Goff and Peter Hallward (eds.) *The Blanqui Reader Political Writings, 1830-1880 Louis Auguste Blanqui,* translated by Philippe Le Goff, Peter Hallward and Mitchell Abidor, Verso, London, 2018.
15. See for example, Branko Milanovic, *Capitalism, Alone The Future of the System That Rules the World*, Harvard University Press, Cambridge, 2019; Dani Rodrik, 'New firms for a new era', *Social Europe*, February 19, 2020 and Paul Collier, *The Future of Capitalism: Facing the New Anxieties*, Allen Lane, London, 2018.
16. See Thomas Piketty, *Capital and Ideology,* trans. by Arthur Goldhammer, Harvard University Press, Cambridge, 2020, Chapter 17 and Conclusion on proposals for 'participatory socialism'.
17. *Ibid*, Conclusion, p. 1035.

18. For a withering critique of Piketty's *Capital and Ideology*, see Frédéric Lordon, 'Why are you acting the Marxist', reprinted in *Verso Blog*, 27April 2020.

19. Thomas Piketty, 'Capital and Ideology', Public lecture Podcast, London School of Economics, February 7, 2020.

20. See for example, Robin Blackburn, *Banking on Death or, Investing in Life: The History and Future of Pensions*, Verso, London, 2002.

21. Bertolt Brecht, *The Measures Taken and other Lehrstücke*, translated by Carl Mueller, Bloomsbury, London, 1977, p.29.

22. Oliver Simons, 'Theater of revolution and the law of genre – Bertolt Brecht's The Measures Taken (*Die Maßnahme*)', *Germanic Review*, vol. 84, no.4, 2009, pp. 327-352.

23. Nick Srnicek and Alex Williams, *Inventing the Future: Postcapitalism and a World Without Work, Revised and Updated Edition,* Verso, London, 2016, p.163.

24. *Ibid.*

25. Andrew Arato, 'Socialism and populism', *Constellations,* vol.26, no.3, 2019, pp. 464-74 and Jean Cohen, 'What's wrong with the normative theory (and the actual practice) of left populism', *Constellations*, vol.26, no.3, 2019, pp. 391-407.

26. Jean Cohen, *Ibid*, p.399.

27. See special issue on deliberative democracy in *Dædalus, the Journal of the American Academy of Arts & Sciences*, no.3, Summer 2017.

28. See Ernesto Laclau, *On Populist Reason*, Verso, London, 2005; Chantal Mouffe, *Agonistics Thinking the World Politically*, Verso, London 2013 and 'Interview with Chantal Mouffe on Left Populism', *Verso Blog*, 4 August 2017.

29. Chantal Mouffe, *For a Left Populism*, Verso, London, 2018.

30. Ecological blindness is a persistent and resilient affliction, see for example, Frank Ruda and Agon Hamza (eds.), *The Future of Europe*, Special Issue, *Crisis & Critique*, vol.7, no.1, 2020 in which a collection of Left radicals discuss the future of Europe with virtually no mention of environmental crises, let alone a detailed analysis of how this will require new political economic responses.

31. In *Fictions of Sustainability*, Chapter Five, I discussed the 'varieties of capitalism' theorists, such as Lucio Baccaro and Jonas Pontusson, who analyse the 'divers of growth' and 'social blocs' but completely ignore environmental issues.

32. Tim Jackson, *Prosperity Without Growth: Foundations for the Economy of Tomorrow*, Second Edition, Routledge, London, 2017.

33. See 2018 figures provided by World Bank in 'Household consumption, percent of GDP by country, around the world', *The Global Economy.com*.

34. Adair Turner, 'The Rich World Must Take Responsibility for Its Carbon Footprint', *Project Syndicate*, February 20, 2020.

35. See Mariana Mazzucato, *The Entrepreneurial State Debunking Public vs. Private Sector Myths*, Anthem Books, London, 2013; Michael Jacobs and Mariana Mazzucato (eds.) *Rethinking Capitalism: Economics and Policy for Sustainable and Inclusive Growth*, Blackwell, Oxford, 2016; Mariana Mazzucato, *Mission Oriented Research and Innovation in the European Union: a problem solving approach to fuel innovation-led growth*, EU Publications, February 2018 and Laurie Macfarlane and George Dibb, 'Delivering a mission-oriented industrial strategy', *IPPR Progressive Review*, Vol.26, no.1, 2019, pp.32-38.

36. John-Baptiste Oduor, 'Socialism or Democracy', *Verso Blog*, January 10, 2020.

37. Robert Michels, *Political Parties: A Sociological Study of the Oligarchical Tendencies of Modern Democracy (1911)* translated by Eden and Cedar Paul, The Free Press, New York, 1962. Michels used the German Social Democratic Party rather than Lenin's Bolsheviks as his case study.

38. Daniel Freund, 'How many lobbyists are there in Brussels?', *Transparency International EU*, 21 September 2016.

13. 'Our dreams don't fit into your ballot box'

1. Timothée Parrique, *The political economy of degrowth*. Economics and Finance. Université Clermont Auvergne; Stockholms universitet, 2019. English. NNT: 2019CLFAD003, Hal Id: tel-02499463.
2. *Ibid*, pp.315-18 and p.464.
3. See for example, Jason Hickel, The Imperative of Redistribution in an Age of Ecological Overshoot: Human Rights and Global Inequality', *Humanity: An International Journal of Human Rights, Humanitarianism, and Development*, Vol.10, No.3, Winter 2019, pp. 416-428.
4. Jeroen van den Bergh, 'Environment versus growth – A criticism of "degrowth" and a plea for "a-growth"', *Ecological Economics*, vol. 70, issue 5, 2011, pp. 881-890.
5. See Giorgos Kallis, 'In defence of degrowth', *Ecological Economics*, vol. 70, issue 5, 2011, pp. 873-880.
6. See Parrique, *op.cit.* Appendixes 1 to 6, pp.820-860 that cover invaluable suggestions for transforming existing societies.
7. See Samuel Alexander and Brendan Gleeson, *Degrowth in the Suburbs: A Radical Urban Imaginary*, Palgrave Macmillan, Singapore, 2019.
8. Slavoj Žižek. *A Left that Dares to Speak Its Name: Untimely Interventions*, Polity Press, Cambridge, 2020, p. 21.
9. Tim Jackson and Peter Victor, *LowGrow SFC: a stock-flow-consistent ecological macroeconomic model for Canada*, Centre for the Understanding of Sustainable Prosperity, University of Surrey, Working Paper No 16, 2019. Their modelling is in need of serious revision following increased debt caused by Covid-19.
10. See Sanna Ahvenharju, 'Potential for a radical policy-shift? The acceptability of strong sustainable consumption governance among elites', *Environmental Politics*, vol.29, no.1, 2020, pp.134-154.
11. Wally Seccombe, *Weathering the Storm: Working-Class Families From the Industrial Revolution to the Fertility Decline*, Verso, London, 1993.
12. Samuel Alexander and Brendan Gleeson, *Degrowth in the Suburbs A Radical Urban Imaginary*.
13. See the survey of various alternative schemes in Parrique, *op.cit.*, Ch.11.
14. Kristofer Dittmer, Alternatives to Money-As-Usual in Ecological Economics: A Study of Local Currencies and 100 Percent Reserve Banking, Ph.D thesis, Universitat Autònoma de Barcelona, September 2014.
15. See Mark Alizart, *Cryptocommunism*, trans. by Robin Mackay, Polity Press, Cambridge, 2020 (forthcoming).
16. See Julia Timpe, *Nazi-Organized Recreation and Entertainment in the Third Reich*, Palgrave Macmillan, London, 2017.
17. See Sabrina P. Ramet, *Alternatives to Democracy in Twentieth Century Europe: Collectivist Visions of Modernity*, Central European University Press, Budapest, 2019.
18. Samuel Alexander, *Art Against Empire: Towards an Aesthetics of Degrowth*, Simplicity Institute, Melbourne, 2017.
19. Herbert Marcuse, *The Aesthetic Dimension Toward a Critique of Marxist Aesthetics*, Beacon Press, Boston, 1978, p.53.
20. Herbert Marcuse, *Five Lectures: Psychoanalysis, Politcs, and Utopia*, translated by Jeremy J. Shapiro and Shierry M. Weber, Allen Lane, London, 1970, p.38.
21. See Robin Hahnel and Erik Olin Wright, *Alternatives to Capitalism: Proposals For a Democratic Economy*, New Left Project, 2014 in which Wright makes a number of criticisms of Parecon.
22. Leigh Phillips and Michal Rozworski, *The People's Republic of Walmart: How the World's Biggest Corporations Are Laying the Foundation for Socialism*, Verso, London, 2019.
23. Alec Nove, *The Economics of Feasible Socialism*, George Allen & Unwin, London 1983.
24. David Schweickart, *Economic Democracy*, Next System Project, 2015, the nextsystem.org.
25. Lennart Erixon *The Rehn-Meidner model in Sweden: its rise, challenges and survival*, Department

of Economics, Stockholm University, Stockholm, February, 2008 and Peter Gowan and Mio Tastas Viktorsson, 'Revisiting the Meidner Plan', *Jacobin*, 22 August 2017.

26. For a survey and discussion of 3-D printing and other new technologies see John Urry, *What is the Future?*, Polity Press, Cambridge, 2016.

27. Rohinton P. Medhora and Taylor Owen, 'A Post-Covid-19 Digital Bretton Woods', Project Syndicate, April 17, 2020.

28. See for example, Kate Raworth, *Doughnut Economics: Seven Ways to Think Like a 21st-Century Economist*, Penguin Random House, London, 2017.

29. See for example, Daniel Jeffries, 'Why Everyone missed the most Mind-Blowing Feature of Cryptocurrency', *Hackernoon*, 1 August 2017.

30. See Andreas Duit, Peter H. Feindt and James Meadowcroft, 'Greening Leviathan: the rise of the environmental state?', *Environmental Politics*, vol.25, no.1, 2016, pp.1-23 and in the same issue Ian Gough, 'Welfare states and environmental states: a comparative analysis', pp.24-47. Also see Dan Bailey, 'Re-thinking the Fiscal and Monetary Political Economy of the Green State', *New Political Economy*, vol.25, no.1, 2020, pp.5-17 and Robyn Eckersley, 'The Green State in Transition: Reply to Bailey, Barry and Craig', *New Political Economy*, vol.25, no.1, 2020, pp. 46-56.

31. Daniel Hausknost, 'The environmental state and the glass ceiling of transformation', *Environmental Politics*, vol.29, no.1, 2020, pp.17-37.

32. Amanda Machin, 'Democracy, disagreement, disruption: agonism and the environmental state', *Environmental Politics*, vol.29, no.1, 2020, pp.155-172.

33. Marit Hammond, 'Sustainability as a cultural transformation: the role of deliberative democracy', *Environmental Politics*, vol.29, no.1, 2020, pp.173-92.

34. Ingolfur Blühdorn, 'The legitimation crisis of democracy: emancipatory politics, the environmental state and the glass ceiling to socio-ecological transformation', *Environmental Politics*, vol.29, no.1, 2020, pp. 38-57.

35. See for example, Peter Hall and David Soskice, 'An Introduction to Varieties of Capitalism' in P. Hall and D. Soskice (eds.), *Varieties of Capitalism: The Institutional Foundations of Comparative Advantage*, Oxford University Press, Oxford, 2001, pp.1-68.

14. National and Local Democracy Versus Global Sustainability

1. IMF, 'World Economic Outlook Update, *International Monetary Fund*, Washington, January 20, 2020 and Stephen Roach, 'A Global Economy Without a Cushion', *Project Syndicate*, January 27, 2020.

2. Umberto Mario Sconfienza, 'The post-sustainability trilemma', *Journal of Environmental Policy & Planning*, vol.21 issue 6, 2019, pp.769-84.

3. Anu Bradford, *The Brussels Effect: How the European Union Rules the World*, Oxford University Press, New York, 2020.

4. See for example, Hans-Hermann Hoppe, *Democracy the God that Failed: The Economics and Politics of Monarchy, Democracy, and Natural Order*, Transaction Publishers, New Brunswick, 2001, ch.7.

5. Anne Hendrixson and Betsy Hartmann, 'Threats and burdens: Challenging scarcity-driven narratives of "overpopulation", *Geoforum*, vol.101, 2019, pp. 250-59.

6. Figures from UNHCR the UN Refugee Agency, 2020 April 2020. Also see Ibrahim Awad and Usha Natarajan, 'Migration Myths and the Global South', *The Cairo Review of Global Affairs*, Summer, 2018.

7. *Ibid.*

8. Arman Bidarbakhtnia, 'Measuring Sustainable Development Goals (SDGs): An Inclusive Approach', *Global Policy*, Vol.11, no.1, 2020, pp.56-67 and Saadiya Razzaq, Kashmala

Chaudhry et al, National Level Preparedness for Implementing the Health-related Sustainable Development Goals (SDGs) in Seven South Asian Countries: Afghanistan, Bangladesh, Bhutan, India, Pakistan, Nepal and Sri Lanka', *Global Policy*, vol.11, no.1, 2020, pp.191-201.

9. See Gustavo Esteva, Salvatore Babones and Philipp Babcicky, *The Future of Development A Radical Manifesto*, Policy Press, Bristol, 2013, ch.2.

10. See Jason Hickel, 'The contradiction of the sustainable development goals: Growth versus ecology on a finite planet', *Sustainable Development*, vol.27, no.5, 2019, pp.873-884 and Mary Menton, Carlos Larrea, Sara Latorre et al, 'Environmental justice and the SDGs: from synergies to gaps and contradictions', *Sustainability Science*, April 9, 2020

11. See Reda Cherif and Fuad Hasanov, *The Leap of the Tiger: How Malaysia Can Escape the Middle-income Trap*, Working Paper 15/131, IMF, Washington DC, 2015, p.2.

12. David Woodward, 'Incrementum ad Absurdum: Global Growth, Inequality and Poverty Eradication in a Carbon-Constrained World', *World Economic Review*, no.4, 2015, pp.43-62.

13. Global Financial Integrity, the Centre for Applied Research at Norwegian School of Economics, et al, *Financial Flows and Tax Havens: Combining to Limit the Lives of Billions of People*, Washington DC, 5 December 2016 and Jason Hickel, 'Aid in reverse: how poor countries develop rich countries', *The Guardian*, 28 March, 2017.

14. Gustavo Esteva, Salvatore Babones and Philipp Babcicky, *The Future of Development A Radical Manifesto*, pp.22-23.

15. *Ibid*, p.23.

16. *Ibid*, p.24.

17. See the debate on Europe's role in the world by Christoph M. Abels, Helmut K. Anheier, Iain Begg and Kevin Featherstone, 'Enhancing Europe's Global Power: A Scenario Exercise with Eight Proposals', *Global Policy*, Vol.11, no.1, 2020, pp.128-142 and the articles by Kishore Mahbubani, Marco Buti, Robert H. Wade and Yee-Kuang Heng as responses to Abels, et.al in same issue of *Global Policy*.

18. Sharon Burrow, 'A New Social Contract', *Social Europe*, June 24, 2020.

19. Stein Emil Vollset et al, 'Fertility, mortality, migration, and population scenarios for 195 countries and territories from 2017 to 2100: a forecasting analysis for the Global Burden of Disease Study', *The Lancet*, July 14, 2020.

20. Figures cited by Heinz Schandl, 'Contribution of the 3Rs to achieving the Sustainable Development Goals – Science and Policy for the 2030 Sustainable Development Agenda', Presentation at the Seventh Regional 3R Forum for Asia and the Pacific, Adelaide 2-4 November 2016.

21. See Monika Dittrich, Stefan Giljum, Stephan Lutter and Christine Polzin, *Green economies around the world: Implications of resource use for development and the environment*, Sustainable Europe Research Institute, Vienna, 2012.

22. See methodologies discussed in Stefan Giljum, Monika Dittrich, Mirko Lieber and Stephan Lutter, 'Global Patterns of Material Flows and their Socio-Economic and Environmental Implications: A MFA Study on All Countries World-Wide from 1980 to 2009', *Resources*, no. 3, 2014, pp.319-339.

23. UNEP, *Managing and conserving the natural resource base for sustained economic and social development. A reflection from the international resource panel on the establishment of sustainable development goals aimed at decoupling economic growth from escalating resource use and environmental degradation*, United Nations Environment Programme, Nairobi 2014.

24. Sanna Ahvenharju, 'Potential for a radical policy-shift? The acceptability of strong sustainable consumption governance among elites', *Environmental Politics*, vol. 29, no.1, 2020, p. 137.

25. Jason Hickel, 'The contradiction of the sustainable development goals: Growth versus ecology on a finite planet'

26. Jason Hickel, 'Degrowth: a theory of radical abundance', *real-world economic review*, issue no.87, 2019, pp. 54-68.

27. See the International Labor Office survey of initial emergency responses in both OECD and non-OECD countries in the Asia-Pacific region 'Social protection responses to the

Covid-19 crisis: Country responses in Asia and the Pacific', *International Labour Office*, March 25, 2020.

28. Marina Sitrin and Colectiva Sembrar (eds.) *Pandemic Solidarity Mutual Aid During the Covid-19 Crisis* Foreword by Rebecca Solnit, Pluto Press, London, 2020.

29. Giorgos Kallis, *Degrowth*, Agenda Publishing, Newcastle upon Tyne, 2018, p.119.

30. Daniel W. O'Neill, Andrew L. Fanning, William F. Lamb and Julia K. Steinberger, 'A good life for all within planetary boundaries', *Nature Sustainability*, Vol 1, February 2018, pp.88-95.

31. See evaluation from a degrowth perspective by Jason Hickel, 'Is it possible to achieve a good life for all within planetary boundaries?', *Third World Quarterly*, vol. 40, no.1, 2019, pp.18-35

32. Sharachchandra Lele et al. (eds.) *Rethinking Environmentalism: Linking Justice, Sustainability, and Diversity*, Strüngmann Forum Reports, vol. 23, 2018, MIT Press, Cambridge, 2018; and Sharachchandra Lele, 'Environment and Well-being *A Perspective from the Global South*', *New Left Review, 123,* May-June 2020, pp.41-63.

33. Joan Martínez-Alier, *The Environmentalism of the Poor A Study of Ecological Conflicts and Valuation*, Edward Elgar, Cheltenham, 2020.

34. *Ibid*, pp.62-3.

35. Karl Marx, 'The Eighteenth Brumaire of Louis Bonaparte' (1852) reprinted in *Karl Marx The Political Writings, Volume II. Surveys from Exile*, Verso, London, 2019.

36. Dominic Mealy, 'Interview with Andreas Malm: "To Halt Climate Change, We Need an Ecological Leninism"', *Jacobin*, June 19, 2020.

37. *Ibid.*

38. Andreas Malm, 'Deeper Into the Dark', *Jacobin*, September 14, 2018 and Jonathan Feldman, 'Is a Swedish Green Conversion Possible?': The Strengths and Limits to the Left's Response', *Stockholm Centre for International Social and Economic Reconstruction*, November 28, 2019, an account of Malm's debate with Green Party spokesperson and Vice Prime Minister Isabella Lövin.

39. Ingar Solty interviewed by Darko Vujica, 'German Deunification', *Monthly Review*, June 2020.

40. Extinction Rebellion UK @XRebellionUK, September 1, 2020 quoted by Mark Montegriffo, 'Yes, "Socialism or Extinction" Is Exactly the Choice We Face', *Jacobin*, September 4, 2020.

41. *Ibid.*

15. Decommodified Social Alternatives to Welfare State Capitalism

1. Alastair Davidson, *The Immutable Laws of Mankind: The Struggle For Universal Human Rights*, Springer, New York, 2012, ch.11.

2. See Fred Block and Margaret Somers, 'In the Shadow of Speenhamland: Social Policy and the Old Poor Law', *Politics & Society*, Vol. 31 No. 2, June 2003, pp. 283-323.

3. *Ibid*

4. See *Ibid*; Rutger Bregman, 'Nixon's Basic Income Plan', *Jacobin*, May 5, 2016 and Melinda Cooper, 'Neoliberalism's Family Values: Welfare, Human Capital, and Kinship' in Dieter Plehwe, Quinn Slobodian and Philip Mirowski (eds.) *Nine Lives of Neoliberalism*, Verso, London, 2020.

5. Samuel Moyn, *Not Enough: Human Rights in an Unequal World*, Harvard University Press, Cambridge, 2018, ch.3.

6. Alastair Davidson, *The Immutable Laws of Mankind: The Struggle For Universal Human Rights*, ch.12.

7. T. H. Marshall, *Citizenship and Social Class and other essays*, Cambridge University Press, Cambridge, 1950.

8. Samuel Moyn, *op.cit.* ch.2.

9. Gøsta Esping-Andersen, *The Three Worlds of Welfare Capitalism*, Princeton University Press, Princeton, 1990. See Interview with Esping Andersen by Maya Adereth, 'The Postindustrial Welfare State', *Phenomenal World,* May 14th, 2020 in which Esping-Andersen discusses Polanyi's influence on his work.

10. Claus Offe, 'Crisis of Crisis Management: Elements of a Political Crisis Theory', *International Journal of Politics*, Vol. 6, No. 3, Fall 1976, p.43.

11. Claus Offe, *Contradictions of the Welfare State*, edited and translated by John Keane, Hutchinson, London, 1984, pp.262-3.

12. Claus Offe, *Contradictions of the Welfare State*, p.264.

13. See Gøsta Esping-Andersen, Roger Friedland and Erik O. Wright, 'Modes of Class Struggle and the Capitalist State', *Kapitalistate Working Papers on the Capitalist State*, no. 4-5, 1976, pp.186-220.

14. Esping-Andersen, *The Three World's of Welfare Capitalism*, p.37.

15. Lisa Pelling, 'Sweden, the pandemic and precarious working conditions', *Social Europe,* June 10, 2020 and Evan Jones, 'COVID-19 Hits the French Health System', *Journal of Australian Political Economy* No. 85, 2020, pp. 94-100.

16. For country by country figures, see *Pension Markets in Focus 2019*, OECD, Paris, 2019.

17. See for example, Jane Lewis, 'Gender and the Development of Welfare Regimes', *Journal of European Social Policy*, vol.2, no.3, 1992, pp.159-173 and Clare Bambra, 'The worlds of welfare: Illusory and genderblind?, *Social Policy and Society*, vol.3, no.3, 2004, pp. 201-212. Esping-Andersen recognised his failure to discuss gender in his later works such as Esping-Andersen, *The Incomplete Revolution: Adapting to Women's New Roles*, Polity Press, Cambridge, 2009.

18. Roger Goodman and Ito Peng, 'The East Asian welfare states: Peripatetic learning, adaptive change, and nation-building', in G. Esping-Andersen (ed.), *Welfare states in transition: National adaptations in global economies*, Sage, London, 1996, pp.192-224.

19. Esping-Andersen acknowledged these other 'welfare regimes' in *Social Foundations of Post Industrial Economies*, Oxford University Press, Oxford, 1999.

20. See e.g. Waltraud Schelkle, 'Collapsing Worlds and Varieties of welfare capitalism: In search of a new political economy of welfare', *LSE Europe in Question Discussion Paper*, no.54, 2012.

21. See for example, the competing comparative analyses such as Stephan Leibfreid, 'Towards a European welfare state' in Z. Ferge and J. E. Kolberg (eds.) *Social Policy in a Changing Europe.* Campus-Verlag, Frankfurt, 1992, pp.245-79; Olli Kangas, 'The politics of social security: on regressions, qualitative comparisons and cluster analysis', in T. Janoski and A. Hicks (eds.) *The Comparative Political Economy of the Welfare State.* Cambridge University Press, Cambridge, 1994, pp.346-65; Walter Korpi and Joakim Palme, 'The paradox of redistribution and the strategy of equality: welfare state institutions, inequality and poverty in the Western countries', in *American Sociological Review*, vol.63, no.5, 1998, pp.662-87 and Ive Marx, Lina Salanauskaite and Gerlinde Verbist, 'The Paradox of Redistribution Revisited: And That It May Rest in Peace?', *Institute for the Study of Labour*, Bonn, May 2013.

22. For the impact of neo-liberal policies on Nordic countries see Jon Erik Dølvik, Tone Fløtten, Jon M. Hippe and Bård Jordfald, *The Nordic model towards 2030 A new chapter?* trans. by Walter Gibbs, Fafo, 2015; and Luis Buendía and Enrique Palazuelos 'Economic growth and welfare state: a case study of Sweden', *Cambridge Journal of Economics*, vol.38, 2014, pp.761-777.

23. See Friends of the Earth, 'EU Green Deal: fails to slam on the brakes', December 11, 2019 and 'Circular EconomyPlan: EU Commission 'burying its head in the sand', *Friends of the Earth*, March 11, 2020.

24. Antoine De Cabanes and Clément Fontan, 'Why Germany's Far Right Wants Judges to Rule Europe's Monetary Policy', *Jacobin*, May 24, 2020.

25. See Economic Survey, 2016-17, Government of India Ministry of Finance Department of Economic Affairs, Economic Division, January 2017, pp.173-195.
26. Daniel F. Vukovich, *Illiberal China: The Ideological Challenge of the People's Republic of China*, Palgrave Macmillan, Singapore, 2019, pp. 8-11.
27. Richard Smith, 'Why China Isn't Capitalist (Despite the Pink Ferraris) A Reply to Eli Friedman', *Spectre,* August 17, 2020.
28. Zhang Jun, 'China's Rapid Shift to a Digital Economy', *Project Syndicate*, September 7, 2020.
29. 'China's social security system', *China Labour Bulletin*, October 15, 2019.
30. See Mary Gallagher, *Authoritarian Legality in China: Law, Workers, and the State*, Cambridge University Press, Cambridge, 2017
31. See details of how workers are denied their entitlements and rights in 'China's social security system', *China Labour Bulletin*, October 15, 2019.
32. Mary Gallagher, *op.cit.*, p.9.
33. See 'China's countryside returning to poverty, finds report', *The Economic Times*, November 3, 2019.
34. Hao, Qi, 'Power relations and the labour share of income in China', *Cambridge Journal of Economics,* vol. 44, 2020, pp. 607-628.
35. There are numerous reports warning of environmental changes creating desertification, water shortages and uninhabitable areas of the world affecting Asian and Latin American countries. See for example, Chi Xu, Timothy A. Kohler, Timothy M. Lenton, Jens-Christian Svenning and Marten Scheffer, 'Future of the human climate niche', *Proceedings of the National Academy of Sciences of the United States of America (PNAS)*, May 4, 2020.
36. James O'Connor, *The Fiscal Crisis of the State*, St. Martin's Press, New York, 1973, ch.9.
37. See T. Parrique, *The Political Economy of Degrowth*, pp.430-32 for a survey of various criticisms of those who rely on growth to make possible the transition to degrowth.
38. Even this very limited scheme had mixed results, see Philippe van Parijs, 'Basic income: Finland's final verdict', *Social Europe*, May 7, 2020.
39. Figures quoted by Richard McGahey, 'Universal Basic Income and the Welfare State', October 2016, published in Jose Antonio Ocampo and Joseph Stiglitz (eds), *The Welfare State Revisited*, Columbia University Press, New York, 2018.
40. For my critique of the 'radical Prometheans' writing in *Jacobin Magazine*, and Jeremy Rifkin, Paul Mason, Nick Srnicek, Alex Williams, Aaron Bastani, the Xenofeminists and others, see *Fictions of Sustainability*, ch.4.
41. Institute for Global Prosperity (IGP), Social Prosperity for the Future: A Proposal for Universal Basic Services, UCL, London, 2017; Anna Coote, 'Building a new social commons', *New Economics Foundation*, 2017; Boris Frankel, *Fictions of Sustainability*, 2018, ch.6; Anna Coote, Pritika Kasliwal and Andrew Percy, *Universal Basic Services, Theory and Practice: A Literature Review*, London, UCL Institute for Global Prosperity, 2019; Ian Gough, 'Universal Basic Services: A Theoretical and Moral Framework', *The Political Quarterly*, vol.90, July-September, 2019, pp.534-42; Katharina Bohnenberger, 'Money, Vouchers, Public Infrastructures? A Framework for Sustainable Welfare Benefits', *Sustainability*, vol.12, no.2, 2020, pp.596-624.
42. Justin Bentham, Andrew Bowman, Marta de la Cuesta, Ewald Engelen, Ismail Ertürk, Peter Folkman, Julie Froud, Suhkdev Johal, John Law, Adam Leaver, Michael Moran, Karl Williams, *Manifesto For the Foundational Economy*. Centre for Research on Socio-Cultural Change, Manchester, CRESC Working Paper No. 131, 2013.
43. Stephen Hall and Alex Schafran, 'From foundational economics and the grounded city to foundational urban systems', *Foundational Economy*, Working Paper No.3, 2017, p. 8.
44. This is Bea Campbell and Martin Jacques argument cited by Pat Devine, *Democracy and Economic Planning: The Political Economy of a Self-governing Society*, Polity Press, Cambridge, 1988, p. 269.

Conclusion

1. Quoted by Alastair Davidson, 'Gramsci and Lenin 1917-1922' (1974) reprinted in Leo Panitch and Greg Albo (eds.) *Class, Party, Revolution, Socialist Register*, Haymarket books, Chicago, 2018.
2. Slavoj Žižek, 'Introduction' in *Lenin 2017 Remembering, Repeating, and Working Through V. I. Lenin*, edited by Žižek, Verso, London, 2017.
3. Jeremy Varon, *Bringing the War Home: The Weather Underground, the Red Army Faction, and Revolutionary Violence in the Sixties and Seventies*, University of California Press, Berkeley, 2004, p.10.
4. Marshall Berman, *All That is Solid Melts into Air: The Experience of Modernity* (1982) Penguin Books, London, 1988, pp.34-35.
5. André Gorz, *Paths to Paradise: On the Liberation From Work* (1983), translated by Malcom Imrie, Pluto Press, London, 1985, p. vii.
6. Mark Fisher, *Postcapitalist Desire: The Final Lectures* edited with Introduction by Matt Colquhoun, Repeater Books, London, 2020. Fisher discussed many of the Accelerationists in his 2016/2017 lecture course and also admitted to the students when questioned about aspects of a universal basic income that he knew nothing about economics (Lecture One November 7, 2016).
7. Pierre Bourdieu, *Distinction: A Social Critique of the Judgement of Taste (1979)* trans. by Richard Nice, Routledge & Kegan Paul, London, 1984.
8. Bertolt Brecht, 'The Other Germany' (1943) in *Gesammelte Werke, Vol. XX*, Suhrkamp Verlag, Frankfurt, 1967, pp.283-9.
9. Jürgen Habermas, *The Lure of Technocracy*, translated by Ciaran Cronin, Polity, Cambridge, 2015, p.25.
10. Nick Srnicek and Alex Williams, 'Accelerate: Manifesto for an Accelerationist Politics' in Robin Mackay and Armen Avanessian (eds.) *#ACCELERATE: The Accelerationist Reader*, Urbanomic Media, Falmouth, 2014. p.354.
11. See Vincent Liegey and Anitra Nelson, *Exploring Degrowth A Critical Guide*, Pluto Press, London, 2020.
12. György Lukács, 'The Old Culture and the New Culture' (1920) trans by Paul Breines in E. San Juan (ed.), *Marxism and Human Liberation: Essays on History, Culture and Revolution by Geörgy Lukács*, A Delta Book, New York, 1973, pp.5 and 12.
13. Anthony Giddens, *The Politics of Climate Change*, Polity Press, Cambridge, 2009.

INDEX